MW00736681

Of One Mind and Of One Government

Early American Places is a collaborative project of the
University of Georgia Press, New York University Press,
Northern Illinois University Press, and the University of
Nebraska Press. The series is supported by the Andrew
W. Mellon Foundation. For more information, please visit
www.earlyamericanplaces.org.

ADVISORY BOARD
Vincent Brown, *Duke University*
Andrew Cayton, *Miami University*
Cornelia Hughes Dayton, *University of Connecticut*
Nicole Eustace, *New York University*
Amy S. Greenberg, *Pennsylvania State University*
Ramón A. Gutiérrez, *University of Chicago*
Peter Charles Hoffer, *University of Georgia*
Karen Ordahl Kupperman, *New York University*
Joshua Piker, *College of William & Mary*
Mark M. Smith, *University of South Carolina*
Rosemarie Zagarri, *George Mason University*

New Visions in Native American and Indigenous Studies

Series Editors   Margaret D. Jacobs, Robert Miller

Of One Mind and Of One Government

The Rise and Fall of the Creek Nation in the Early Republic

KEVIN KOKOMOOR

Co-published by the University of Nebraska Press and the American Philosophical Society

© 2018 by the Board of Regents of the University of Nebraska

All rights reserved

Manufactured in the United States of America

Library of Congress Cataloging-in-Publication Data
Names: Kokomoor, Kevin, author.
Title: Of one mind and of one government:
the rise and fall of the Creek Nation in the early
republic / Kevin Kokomoor. Other titles: New
visions in Native American and indigenous studies.
Description: [Lincoln, Nebraska?]: Co-published
by the University of Nebraska Press and the
American Philosophical Society, [2018] |
Series: New visions in Native American
and indigenous studies | Includes
bibliographical references and index.
Identifiers: LCCN 2018028073
ISBN 9780803295872 (cloth: alk. paper)
ISBN 9781496212337 (epub)
ISBN 9781496212344 (mobi)
ISBN 9781496212351 (pdf)
Subjects: LCSH: Creek Indians—Politics and
government—18th century. | Creek Indians—
Politics and government—19th century. |
Creek Indians—Government relations.
Classification: LCC E99.C9 K75 2018 |
DDC 975.004/97385—dc23 LC record
available at https://lccn.loc.gov/2018028073

For my parents

Contents

PART 3. THE FATE OF THE CREEK NATION

Illustrations

Figures

Maps

Acknowledgments

You could say I started writing this book about a decade ago, more or less, when I first read a plaque on Seminole Indian Removal in a city park, in the middle of the night, in downtown Tampa. The journey from that night to this page has been a long one, full of twists and turns, and I have plenty of people to thank for the assistance and encouragement they've provided—some knowingly, some unknowingly—along the way.

I would first like to thank those whose generous financial support has made the journey possible. Dan and Sylvia Walbolt, who endowed the Walbolt Dissertation Fellowship at Florida State University, funded me for a semester while I began the research that forms the foundation of this book. In the summer of 2012 the American Philosophical Society funded me as a Research Fellow, and then so did the Manuscripts, Archives, and Rare Books Library at Emory University. Those two opportunities came at a critical time in my research, and I am thankful for both. Most recently, I had the pleasure of working in the William L. Clements Library at the University of Michigan as a Howard H. Peckham Fellow on Revolutionary America. That fellowship gave me the time and the means to wrap this project up in one of the best academic atmospheres I could have imagined. I am exceedingly indebted to the staff there, including Terese Austin and Cheney Schopieray, not only for their help guiding my research but for the time they set out, every day, just to chat. Without such examples of generous support this project would probably never have come to be.

Although it took years to go through all of it, the majority of the archival research for this project came in just a few places. I would like to thank the staff at the Georgia Department of Archives and History, Dean Debolt and his staff at the University Archives and West Florida History Center at the University of West Florida, and James Cusick and his staff at the P. K. Yonge Library of Florida History at the University of Florida. They all made me feel at home in their libraries for days and weeks at a time. I would like to thank John Cusick in particular, though, for giving me free range of the microfilm as well as the microfilm reader in his office, for sharing his mastery of the library's rich Spanish sources, and even for taking me to lunch. When you're inexperienced and overwhelmed, you don't forget help like that.

The writing that made this project, on the other hand, came in a ton of places. Trying to make ends meet as a historian has kept me on the move, from Florida and Vermont to Pennsylvania and Michigan, and now to South Carolina, and I brought this project along with me wherever I went. So thank you to all the library staffs out there for their support and assistance, including at the Universities of South Florida in Tampa and in St. Petersburg, the New College of Florida, and Temple University. And I certainly am grateful for the staff at the Kimbel Library at Coastal Carolina University, where I am currently, for keeping the doors open late and assisting me as I put the finishing touches on this project.

Brian Nance and Amanda Brian, and the rest of the History Department at Coastal Carolina University, have been incredibly supportive of me in the past few years. I also appreciate the friends and professional colleagues, several of whom I met while in graduate school, like Jon Grandage, Lauren Thompson, and Chris Gunn, who have kept me motivated over the years. Kim Wescott read an early version of this manuscript, and I am grateful for her input. Thank you, Robbie Ethridge and Steve Hahn, whose own work guided me through graduate school. They read the manuscript carefully on more than one occasion and gave me the criticism that was necessary to complete and polish something that was, at one point, pretty rough. And thank you also to Matthew Bokovoy and Heather Stauffer, and the rest of the staff at the University of Nebraska Press. Their dedication and support made the submission and revision process not only easy but downright enjoyable.

I am deeply thankful for, and deeply humbled by, those who have guided me and taught me from the very first days I decided to pursue a career as a historian. John Belohlavek at the University of South Florida, and Gary Mormino at USF St. Petersburg, first inspired me while I was working on my master's degree. At Florida State University I am grateful to Robinson Herrera, who pushed me to pursue my research and writing aggressively and seriously. Of course I am most indebted, by far, to Andrew Frank. For years now he has remained not only my mentor but my chief supporter, answering my many questions and giving me well-needed criticism. He has done much more than simply help me with this manuscript, and as much as he once pressed me to do, I doubt I will ever see myself as his equal. Lastly and most importantly, I would like to thank my family. This has been a long journey, with several ups and downs, and I mean both professionally and personally. There is simply no way I would be where I am now without the unwavering support of my mother and father, my brother and sister, and even my grandparents, even if some of them were not quite sure, at times, what I was thinking. Thanks for keeping the faith.

Yes, indeed, the writing of this book has been a journey. I can't wait for the next one.

OF ONE MIND AND
OF ONE GOVERNMENT

Prologue: A Crisis in Creek Country

On Christmas Day, 1773, a Creek war party descended on an isolated group of Georgia settlements on the northern frontier of the province, and they did so without much warning. First, they killed a Mr. White and his entire family, including his wife and his two children. Georgia governor James Wright was soon aware of the attack, but he hoped it "was rather an accidental thing," occasioned "by too much rashness on both sides." As Indian superintendent John Stuart lamented shortly after, however, that blow to the frontier "was soon followed by another." Another war party arrived at the farm of a Mr. Sherrall, who lived only miles away from White. By that time Sherrall was fortifying his home and was, according to reports, "determined to stand his ground." His farm, however, was attacked before he was able to make good on his resolve. Raiders surprised him, shooting him down as he built his stockade and killing his wife and one of his daughters as well. Two of his sons and two slaves made it to the house, where they fended off the rest of the attack and spread the alarm. While the rest of Sherrall's family and farm survived, the grim reality was that the raid killed seven. And when added to the White family, the body count was near a dozen. The attacks on the White and Sherrall farms, which put a "very gloomy aspect" on regional affairs, according to Stuart, did not come without a response. When Governor Wright dispatched a militia party and then two dozen mounted provincial rangers to hunt the perpetrators down, however, the party was ambushed and embarrassed. A handful of the rangers were killed and the remainder fled without as much as firing a single shot. The panic that ensued, Wright lamented, could "hardly be expressed." The militia deserted, backcountry settlers along the frontier abandoned their homes, and everyone crowded into Augusta for protection.[1]

The Christmas Day killings, although they were relatively isolated, were a direct response to a dispute over the "Ceded Lands," which was not so isolated.[2] It was a disagreement that had been smoldering between Creeks, Cherokees, and British merchants and their traders for years, and by 1773 it was clear that the anger of some Creek communities could no longer be contained.[3] The confrontation was rooted in events that began years earlier, in 1770, when a group of traders associated with merchants in Augusta came up with a scheme to discharge the Cherokee trading debts that were mounting on their ledgers. There was a stretch of land, between the Savannah and Broad rivers on the northern frontiers of the Georgia province, which was "of the richest and best quality" and could prove quite lucrative to the members of the British trading houses that owned the Cherokee debts. It was land that Cherokees claimed ownership of and, according to one trader, "in order to pay the debts they owe . . . have voluntarily offered to cede."[4] Soon the merchants, traders, and a group of Cherokee headmen, "deputised from every town in the nation," met to talk over the idea, which seemed at the time to suit everyone. The traders quickly turned to Stuart, who as Indian superintendent in the Southeast, would have quite a bit of say in the success of the deal. His assistance, they hoped, would soon add such a "valuable part to the province of Georgia."[5]

One clear problem with the plan was that, although Cherokee headmen seemed enthusiastic about the cession and might even have been the ones to suggest it, little of the land was actually theirs to give—at least not unilaterally. Creeks also asserted ownership of almost all of those lands. Chunks of it became theirs by right of conquest during their last war with the Cherokees, Creek community leaders asserted, while the rest of it had simply always been theirs.[6] While those claims would seem to pose pretty clear problems, to merchants in Augusta and even to some Cherokee headmen things were much hazier. While they admitted that some Creek communities might claim some of the land for some reason or another, the merchants and even some Georgia provincial authorities were sure that the Creek claim was only theoretical, much like the Cherokees' own claims. The lands were "not occupied by either of them, nor of any use to them as a hunting ground," particularly because they were so close to already established frontier settlements. As far as hunting land went that stretch was of little use to the supposed Creek owners, the British merchants were sure, and could be parted with easily on the right terms.[7]

Decades of previous dealings with Creeks over land cessions suggest that the merchants should have known better. Land was notoriously difficult to get from Creeks with legitimacy, as colonial officials like Stuart and Peter Chester, the governor of British West Florida, were almost at that very moment being made keenly aware. While the Augusta land deal was developing they were trying their luck with Creek headmen from the Upper Country for a separate and much smaller piece of land, just above Mobile and Pensacola. Emistisiguo, the most well-respected and influential headman present at the negotiations, and a political ally of Stuart's, knew the piece of land well. Even though he was on excellent terms with the British, he still resisted the deal sternly. Not only was he not interested, he likened past cessions to the building of a brick wall, one that was not to be torn down or moved. And when Stuart kept pressing him, he grew irritated: "I am still the same man I was and not like a child varying my opinion every instant. My sentiments still remain the same they were."[8] Emistisiguo was clear: Creek land was valuable and guarded closely, and headmen were not going to give it up easily. As strenuously as they negotiated for the land, Stuart and Chester were rebuffed again and again by an equally determined set of Creek headmen, suggesting that there was much less haziness in the Cherokee deal than the Augusta traders were suggesting. Gaining a much larger and richer swath of hunting lands from Creek communities—communities that gained nothing from the deal, no less—was not going to proceed nearly as easily as the traders presumed.

The Mobile deliberations revealed the largest hurdle that the architects of any land deal had to overcome. Creek Country was not a place where decisions could be made by one man, or even a sizable collection of them. Emistisiguo stated this plainly enough. When Stuart and Chester continued to push him to bargain for a piece of land that he was familiar with, and hunted on personally, he responded that in no way was it in his power to do such a thing: "My nation is numerous and every child in it has an equal property in the land with the first warrior. Making any alteration in the boundary line without the consent of the whole will be improper."[9] Chester, who was at the conference, complained that Emistisiguo was only being evasive. Yet his observations were essentially the same as Stuart's. Creek property "was vested in common among them," and they "were not authorized to make any grant without consulting their whole nation." Not only was Emistisiguo personally disinterested in the deal, in other words, he did not have the authority to make it in the first place.[10] His sentiments demonstrated a fundamental aspect of Creek government and politics that had remained consistent for generations: men like Emistisiguo were the leaders of individual communities in a sprawling and loosely knit region of politically autonomous communities. While they were influential, they were not necessarily authoritative.

While that concept might have been new to Chester, Stuart knew better. Making a legitimate treaty with Creeks for much of anything took a lot more work than what the Augusta merchants and traders were putting in to their own deal. In Pensacola a decade earlier, for instance, Stuart met with several headmen from the length of Creek Country. The agreement made there was merely a continuation of old boundary lines, trade arrangements, and other issues that were of a less than critical nature. Still, thirty-one chiefs made their mark on the document, including most of Creek Country's leading headmen. Before that, Stuart met with literally hundreds of headmen from the stretches of the region at Fort Picolata, on the St. Johns River in East Florida, in 1765. And that was after he toured much of Creek Country and the Florida peninsula personally. That conference established Georgia's colonial boundary—an important occasion that Stuart clearly took seriously.[11] His previous experiences had demonstrated what it took to make a council legitimate. That was nothing like the deliberations taking place in 1772 and 1773 for the Cherokee lands, so it was little wonder that the more Creek headmen caught wind of the bargain, the more anxious they became. As rumors slowly reached Emistisiguo that such a deal was moving forward, his words of warning grew loud: "I have heard a little of the Cherokee talks but they are only like puff of wind." The British had already promised that they would ask for no more land and that they would stop locals from claiming it, he reminded Stuart, and he was looking to them to keep their word.[12]

Later, when British commissary David Taitt visited Emistisiguo at the Hickory Ground, the Augusta traders had already sent the headman talks directly, assuring him that if he and others agreed to the deal they would promise them "a very good trade" at deeply discounted prices. This Emistisiguo also scorned. Their talks, he complained to Taitt, were "just like a man telling a fine storey to his Children to make them Merry at Night but in the Morning would be foregot." Emistisiguo's frustration was not exceptional. Even the mention of hearing a similar talk by the merchants to be read at Hookchoie, "demanding lands for the payment of their Debts," caused "a great murmuring" among several headmen. Importantly, reports of the deal also began to draw divisions between communities, some of whom appeared interested at least in hearing the talks while others, like Emistisiguo's, wanted nothing to do with it. The Mortar of Hookchoie arranged for a conference over the latest letters from the merchants, for instance, but when word spread through the Upper Country it only caused arguments. The Second Man of Little Tallassee could not convince the Tallassee King of Chavaucley, or the Half-Way House, "as he seemed doubtfull of some bad talks being amongst them."[13] Even talking about the cession was spreading irritation through Creek Country.

At first British authorities were also firmly against the arrangement, and no one more so than Stuart. The deal was irresponsible and sure to bring violence to the region, he correctly surmised. Not only was he irritated, he resented the traders who had usurped his authority by planning the deal in the first place.[14] As Emistisiguo's words of caution hinted, the idea of the cession was already causing agitation in Creek Country, and even though Stuart was doing everything he could to assure headmen that the government had no hand in the deal and would not allow it, "yet it serves to increase the general discontent."[15] Governor James Wright, on the other hand, was an enthusiastic proponent of the scheme, giving the traders the encouragement they needed to continue pushing it onward, and eventually around Stuart. First they met up with a group of Cherokee headmen "upon the frontiers and marked out the land they had accepted of contrary to my advice," Stuart fumed. Then they arranged a meeting with both Cherokee and Creek representatives, without his presence, which proved disastrous. The Cherokee deputation "supported what they had done with threats and in such high terms as shocked the pride of the latter," their Creek counterparts, who returned to their communities "much disgusted." Stuart was disgusted as well, complaining that while the traders dealt recklessly and with only their immediate advancement in mind, they were undermining his authority and the Creeks' trust, and they were endangering the stability of the entire region.[16] Unfortunately for Stuart, however, British legislators slowly came around to the cession, which a growing chorus of traders and merchants, along with Wright, readily supported. By 1772 British officials at the highest levels officially directed Stuart to hold a conference to that end.[17]

Although he made his unhappiness clear, by that point there was little Stuart could do. He directed David Taitt to Apalachicola in the

Lower Country, where the deputy agent held a council with several headmen from the region and heard what they thought of the deal. Escochobey, or the Young Lieutenant of Coweta, was deeply indebted to one of the trading firms and was a friend to powerful Georgia trader George Galphin. He might be amenable to the cession if his debts were forgiven and was willing to see some Cherokee representatives to negotiate with him. Salleche of Ooseoochee, a bit further south along the Chattahoochee River, was much more militantly opposed, and resistance was widespread in his neighborhood. Meanwhile others in the Upper Country, with Emistisiguo, continued to express their own displeasure. They were not so heavily indebted and only stood to lose valuable hunting lands.[18] Indeed, the more Taitt's expedition revealed Creek thoughts on the deal, the more dangerous it seemed. Economic and political interests split headmen apart from each other, even locally up and down the Chattahoochee River, while there was almost no sense of regional cohesiveness. Many Creeks were too attached to the land to agree to any cession no matter the terms. Others had debts, but not enough to make the deal worthwhile, while still others were not indebted at all. Only a small portion of Creek Country had anything to gain from the Cherokee land deal but plenty of them had lands to lose, making the cession a tough sell for Stuart and his subordinates.

Despite widespread resistance throughout Creek Country, Stuart had little choice but to support the deal, and in the spring of 1773 several Creek and Cherokee headmen met in Augusta to continue the negotiations. Thomas Gage would later write Stuart suggesting that, based on the clear irritation of many Creeks, Stuart's meeting would probably "not be a very friendly one."[19] Gage was right, as famed British naturalist William Bartram also came to realize. He wandered into Augusta at almost the same time as the councils, he witnessed them, and his observations demonstrated pretty plainly that Creeks were not happy with the situation, that they were not interested in the cession, and that violence was imminent if the sale moved forward without their consent. They "were unwilling to submit to so large a demand, and their conduct evidently betrayed a disposition to dispute the ground by force of arms," Bartram witnessed, "and they could not at first be brought to listen to reason and amicable terms." The Creek delegation demanded to know "on what foundation" the Georgians had built their claim to the land, and when the colonial representation responded that they had bought the lands "from their friends and brothers the Cherokees," many of the Creeks became enraged. "Nettled and incensed at this, a chief and warrior started up, and with an agitated and terrific countenance, frowning menaces and disdain," confronted and humiliated his Cherokee counterparts.

He and others then threatened to close the congress and return home—a move that would probably trigger violence—unless the Georgians "consented to annul the secret treaty with the Cherokees" and acknowledge "the exclusive right of Creeks to the land in question." Bartram did not detail precisely what happened next, but extravagant presents and "the cool and deliberate counsels of the ancient venerable chiefs" seemed to prove too powerful an enticement for many to resist; ultimately, the merchants declared the transaction complete. Bartram planned on moving through Creek Country after the close of the conference, but Stuart urged him not to, thinking it "not alltogether safe to go then into the Indian Countries." Cajoled and bribed, and now clearly bitter, the Creek headmen were returning to a region that would not be safe for British visitors. Bartram moved on nevertheless, traveling with a sizable group of surveyors and trustees appointed by Wright to mark out the new cession.[20]

In recalling the Augusta conference the traders, merchants, and even Wright seemed not to recall its confrontational nature, instead glossing over the simmering Creek resentment to declare that the cession went over smoothly and equitably for all parties involved. Accordingly, his surveyors made quick work setting out the new boundary line.[21] "I lately returned from a tour through a part of the ceded lands," Wright penned the Earl of Dartmouth, which were "in general very good and a fine healthy country." Within days of the news, in fact, applications for hundreds of thousands of the tract's almost two million acres of land were already on his desk.[22] Things looked bright for the Georgia province indeed. Creek hunters, on the other hand, did not walk away satisfied. At the same time Wright praised the conference, both he and Stuart were receiving alarming reports that many Creeks had "meditated something hostile against us," which they were to decide upon later in the summer. Stuart remained cautiously optimistic that it was not "the intention of the nation in general to break with us," but mounting evidence suggested that anger was widespread and that violence was a possibility.[23]

In the Upper Country, when confronted with more talks that suggested the land deal was moving through, Emistisiguo met with the Second Man of Little Tallassee to consider the options. An outsider overheard parts of their conversation, which were not at all conducive to peace. Emistisiguo at first angrily declared that he was for war, "that they were men and must show themselves so, if the white people wanted to take away their lands for the Augusta traders as it was a large body of land." After more discussions with the Second Man he foresaw that fighting would, in the end, have dire consequences for Creek Country, and he began to temper his anger. Yet he still did not see "how it could be avoided." Others would not be so moderate, he warned, and he would not be able to stop them. After hearing that, one of the outside guests charged Emistisiguo with complacency or even of inciting violence, which the headman flatly denied. There was simply only so much he could do. People were angry and he would not be able to control them. He would do what he could to divert his own angry young men, but "then if he met with them again they must take their chance."[24]

The conversation between Emistisiguo, the Second Man, and the unnamed visitors at Little Tallassee not only revealed simmering anger in the region but also reinforced how little authority Creek leaders wielded even in their own communities, let alone elsewhere. Months later, in the wake of the Christmas killings, the only thing headmen like Emistisiguo could do was swear they had played no role in the violence and condemn those who did. Very soon after the attack, for instance, James Wright received letters from headmen in both the Upper and Lower countries assuring him that they "had no concern in it or knew nothing about it" until weeks afterward.[25] Stuart, Wright, and Lieutenant Governor John Moultrie believed those reports, recognizing that "the nation in general," in Wright's words, "I am convinced beyond a doubt had no concern in it, nor did they know of it until after the murders were committed." Creek men and women were widespread in and around plantations in East Florida and nearby St. Augustine, Moultrie added, and several of them had come to him and were "much concerned at the mischief done."[26]

Very quickly, in fact, Georgia authorities honed in on those responsible, and what they found was at first encouraging. The attacks were not the act of even a handful of Creek communities. Instead, a few "runugate Indians" had long "frequented the ceded lands and with a view to prevent their being settled," and they were the ones who had perpetrated the attacks. James Wright pointed to "a few of those belonging to the Coweta Town," and reports from Taitt and another deputy, Alexander Cameron, came to the same conclusion. The town to which they referred was not the larger one on the Chattahoochee but a smaller outlying village referred to as the Standing Peach Tree, which was situated on the Okmulgee River about seventy miles away from the Georgia boundary. It was principally Cowetas who lived there, however, "and all Lower Creeks," Stuart was sure. After the killings the attackers returned triumphantly, displaying the scalps of some of their victims. Yet their display only spread disconcertion through the town and upset many of the headmen, suggesting that even among that small community the attacks were divisive.[27]

Unfortunately for Stuart and the Georgia authorities, knowing where the attacks originated did little to secure justice for the dead. The Christmas killings demonstrated within weeks how discordant Creek Country could become when pressed by the weight of a regional crisis, even if generated by the actions of a single community. When the Coweta warriors returned, for instance, not only did their actions disconcert others in their village, they clearly scared nearby headmen. Yet while many of them were quick to pen letters to Wright disavowing the murderers, they did little else.[28] Headmen could do as little to rectify the killings, their inaction proved, as they could to prevent them, helping turn a relatively isolated set of attacks into a regional crisis. The inability of Creek communities to fulfill their obligations, either through Native or European systems of justice, not only damaged Euro-Creek relations but strained intercommunity Creek relations as well, revealing the weak nature of the cultural glue that was supposed to keep Creek Country connected.

Georgians were certain to demand satisfaction for the murders. If they attempted to rectify the situation according to Creek customs, which called for eye-for-an-eye satisfaction, upwards of a dozen of the perpetrators or their family members would have to be killed, and there was simply no way that would be possible. Even though retributive justice—blood vengeance, in other words—was Creek law, it functioned better in theory than in practice. No Creek clan would consent to give up so many of its own to be killed, regardless of their guilt. Not even a more European interpretation of law, which only demanded the deaths of the warriors most involved in the killing, was acceptable. The kin of the perpetrating Cowetas would not allow satisfaction on even such a relatively limited scale, and no friendly headmen had the power to force a resolution. Even the most authoritative Creek chiefs wielded only a fraction of the power that the kin members of dead and even of the accused did when it came to making amends for crimes, particularly involving death.[29] In the case of the Christmas killings, the kin of the accused would be the ones to give up the murderers to be executed, and they refused to do so. Their relations and kinship connections were spread so far throughout the region that even the friendliest chiefs, British authorities lamented, "having no coercive power," could do nothing definitive without bringing waves of retributive violence back upon their own communities or even themselves. Cowetas were unwilling to participate in their own system of justice, and with Georgians seething for retribution, their inaction was placing even the friendliest headmen in a difficult situation. It just "may draw in and involve the whole nation in a general war," Stuart lamented, "though the outrages were begun by a few villains unknown to the nation."[30]

James Wright quickly called a conference in Savannah that he hoped would push things along, but only a handful of headmen made the journey.[31] Nevertheless he took that opportunity to lay out how he, Stuart, and other officials planned to break the impasse. They could call out military forces, he first warned: "We have soldiers enough, the Great King will send us as many as we want if there is occasion and we ask for them." But there was a better way, he continued, one that did not include the use of force. All trade into Creek Country would be cut off until the killers were brought to justice. The trade "must be stopped," Wright declared, "and no goods can be carried to your nation till satisfaction is given."[32] Unfortunately, it was practically only Captain Alleck from Cusseta, Emistisiguo from Little Tallassee, and another, St. Jago, who were on hand to hear the governor's talks. And while, from the top, British authorities were confident that such a demand would make quick work of the perpetrators, such was not the case. The headmen present needed little chiding; they were among Wright's and Stuart's most supportive and dependable allies in Creek Country. Nevertheless, St. Jago expected satisfaction would be given and said that he was determined "to live and die with the white people," while Captain Alleck lamented that so few "mad young men should have it in their power to involve the whole nation in a war with the white people." But the headmen, despite their optimistic words, could offer little by way of solution. They made no definitive promises, admitting in person what other headmen had already done on paper. Not only did they deny involvement, but they continued to deflect responsibility. They placed blame squarely on the Coweta town, suggesting as well that Cowetas were the ones who should pay. Cutting off every Creek's trade connections was not only unhelpful, it was unfair.[33]

Emistisiguo in particular was highly critical of the trade stoppage, not only placing his people apart from the offending town but placing them in a more privileged position than even his neighbors. A particular trader tied to the Coweta town had involved them in the killings, Emistisiguo explained, and had "shut up the path between us," referring to the trading path that passed from Augusta, through Coweta and Cusseta, to the Upper Country. Several communities in the Upper Country got their trade along that path, which made Coweta intransigence all the more bitter. While Emistisiguo took the opportunity to again criticize the reckless actions of the local Georgians, he also declared, somewhat defiantly, that the killings and the shuttered Georgia trade would not affect his community. He had his own trade paths, "friends in Pensacola and Mobile and would see them, and then he expected a trade from thence," even though Wright reminded him that the traders there were British citizens as well, and the trade moratorium would include Mobile and Pensacola. Nevertheless the chief's assertion that his talk was all his own, "and that nobody gave him directions what to say," only further demonstrated his intention to speak for his own community, not for all Creeks, or even his neighbors. Further south, in Florida, talks from Seminole communities were the same. The White King was "greatly surprised and afflicted on account of the bad disposition of the Nation; declairing they themselves were innocent, & knew nothing of any harm against the whites," while another headman warned Bartram that he could not be protected from "any hunting parties that frequently visit this part of the Florida from the Nation," who would surely also be very mad at the trade stoppage.[34]

Emistisiguo also tried with other headmen in both the Upper and Lower countries to right the situation themselves. He along with Coweta chiefs Escochobey and Sempoyaffie were all of the Panther clan. Many of the Christmas killing perpetrators were kinsmen, meaning that perhaps he could exert enough pressure on Panther kin in Coweta to force the situation from within. So he tried, but when he made his demand the families of the perpetrators responded that if the accused were killed, not only would they retaliate violently, they would do everything in their power to shut down the trade paths through their communities and make life in the Upper Country as miserable as they could. Suffice to say, Emistisiguo's attempt to exert clan pressure did little but raise tensions further. Soon he warned Sempoyaffie that the Coweta actions were going to cause a civil war. Cowetas "should not stop their trade," and they "must stand for themselves."[35] Despite those warnings, little happened. Cowetas refused to act, no one could apply enough pressure on them to force anything decisive, and, in the meantime, the entire region suffered.

Despite the negative impact that the trade embargo was having on regional politics, neither Wright, nor Stuart, nor Chester budged, forcing more attempts from headmen like Emistisiguo to find a solution. In May the Little Tallassee headman traveled through the Lower Country with David Taitt, trying to gather other headmen to meet both Stuart and Wright in Savannah. That attempt produced only mixed results at best; while the two could not convince many to follow them, they did leave "all the leading and sensible men" well inclined to punish at least "the chief promoters" involved in the killings, which was a step in the right direction.[36] Later, in Savannah, Emistisiguo and his small delegation negotiated possible terms of retribution with colonial officials. If at least four of the perpetrators involved were executed it would do the region tremendous good and would be the means of clearing up the trade blockage. That was something Emistisiguo and Captain Alleck left thinking they could accomplish.[37]

After Emistisiguo returned to Little Tallassee he wasted little time, calling a sizable council that brought in community leaders from across Creek Country. "The whole Creek confederacy were assembling at one of their principle towns to delebirate how to obtain peace & commerce again with the whites," Bartram reported. There Emistisiguo explained the demand, which did not seem extraordinary: the council was "determined to oblige the Cowetas who were the agressors to give up the Murderers or sacrifice the whole Nation." By Creek terms of retribution, three or four lives in exchange for over twice as many Georgia ones was a great deal. Instead, as soon as the headmen from the Lower Country arrived back into their own communities and word spread, "the delinquents immediately absconded and made off which shows they were apprehensive of danger."[38] A local gathering of Hitchitis, Apalachicolas, and Okmulgees met anyway and condemned three of the perpetrators in absentia. Notably absent from the meeting were Coweta headmen, however, who represented the communities where the perpetrators originated. While they remained not only disinterested in the deal but protective of the accused, enforcing the will of most Creeks remained impossible.

When Cusseta executioners traveled over the Chattahoochee River the accused fled. When the posse dispatched one of the men, Oktulkee, anyway, it enraged the man's kin, as well as Escochobey, illustrating the fatally problematic nature of Creek retributive traditions. Not only did the killing distance Cowetas from Stuart and Wright, and pull Escochobey closer to his former Spanish allies along the Gulf Coast, the slain man's relations threatened everyone along the trading paths and plotted to assassinate British agent Alexander Cameron in retaliation.[39] If three more Cowetas were killed it was clear that retaliatory attacks threatened to grip the Georgia backcountry and even the Lower Country in violence. With that one killing pulling in the Lower Country to the brink of chaos and with two more of the condemned on the run, headmen had accomplished almost nothing. The situation was only further complicated months later. Cusseta warriors managed to kill two other men, hoping to trade their lives for the lives of the two Cowetas they could not kill. It was an obvious attempt by Cusseta headmen to reconcile Creek ideas of blood vengeance with the European desire for justice in an attempt to make the situation right for all parties involved. Perhaps it also demonstrates the desperate measures some Creeks were being driven to because of the ongoing trade stoppage. The two had been accused of killing whites in West Florida years previous, but neither had been a part of the Christmas Day killings. In the end, the killings only further enraged Cowetas and alienated them from their more peaceful counterparts across the Chattahoochee River, while Stuart and Wright rejected them as unrelated to the original demand. To the chagrin of headmen in both the Upper and Lower countries, the British "agreed to insist on their giving the satisfaction which he had before demanded" and would continue to withhold trade until their original demands were met.[40]

By the fall of 1774 the killings remained unresolved, making the Earl of Dartmouth doubtful, "and much afraid, that they will not compleat the Satisfaction required of them." The three Cowetas remained the only ones killed, and only one of those was meaningful. In fact, in a letter from the Pumpkin King and Hitchitis, headmen made it clear they thought killing Oktulkee and the others had been more than sufficient and were not interested in executing anyone else, despite what Wright would say. When Wright and Stuart pushed, the Pumpkin King and the other Hitchiti and Chehaw warriors gave only mixed responses.[41] Meanwhile, letters from the Upper Country revealed a region deeply torn. One arrived via Oakfuskee hunters who were feeling the weight of the trade stoppage. They expressed their hope for peace as well as "declaring that they had no concern with the Cowetas, who had done the Mischief." They were suffering because of the stoppage and hoped to have their own trade restored, "repeating again, that they in the Upper Towns, who are for Peace, and desire to have a supply of goods, think it hard to suffer on account of the Cowetas, with whom they have nothing to do, and will have nothing to say."[42] Nothing new was being done about the murders, however, meaning the Oakfuskee words would likely fall on deaf ears.

The killings were, ultimately, never satisfied. Regular trade only returned to Creek Country because the colonial crisis brewing between British authorities and American colonists made the Christmas killings seem trivial in comparison, not because Creeks had solved anything among themselves. British fears of an open American insurrection were growing, and the Earl of Dartmouth, like other colonial officials, recognized that Creeks were much too important as allies to have their relationship compromised over a relatively small and isolated set of killings. With everything in Creek Country in the same place it had been six months previous, he pressed Wright and Stuart to find some sort of solution, and do it quickly. With that in mind, the two met several headmen in Savannah again in October 1774 to work out new terms for a settlement. Emistisiguo was present with a dozen leaders from the Upper Country. Tallachea of Okmulgee, the Pumpkin King of Ooseoochee, LeCoffe of Coweta, and five other headmen arrived from the Lower Country. There the headmen made several promises, including renewing their plan to kill the two remaining Cowetas. Over the course of weeks and months they made several meaningful gestures, including returning stolen cattle and horses, and even a dozen or so runaway slaves. Yet by the outbreak of the American Revolution, the two Cowetas were still alive. When word spread about the renewed death sentences the men again fled, and Coweta warriors renewed their threats against traders and travelers, causing one to flee for his life. The 1774 Savannah council, like the several that had come before it, accomplished little in the end.

Stuart reopened the Creek trade in 1774, but only because he was forced to by deteriorating American relations and by his superiors.[43] With revolutionary fervor spreading throughout the Southeast, British officials were forced more or less to forget about the killings, leaving them as a stain on the region that illustrated how problematic Creek legal traditions could be when put under outside pressure.[44] The killings remained unsettled, and no combination of threatening or cajoling from anyone produced any meaningful solution. Efforts at decisive action pushed Creek communities further apart such that by the fall of 1774 several of them were in direct confrontation with each other and violence was a real possibility. The Christmas killings and the diplomatic impasse the followed presaged the larger and more destructive confrontations that would sweep through Creek Country during the Revolution. If Creeks failed to find a solution to a relatively isolated attack on the Ceded Lands, how would they deal with the chaos of the Revolution?

1 /   Introduction

At the beginning of the nineteenth century a political Creek people could be found spread through present-day Georgia, Alabama, and the Florida panhandle. You could even say there was a Creek Nation. The Creek Nation consisted of dozens of communities, big and small, bound together by a centralized political entity referred to widely as the National Council, or sometimes as the Executive Council. It was a governing body that both created and enforced regional laws. At one of its meetings, late in 1802, a half dozen or so members of the council came together to flex their coercive muscle, responding to the continued and threatening presence of Anglo-American adventurer William Augustus Bowles. At a meeting in Tallassee they debated and enacted laws they hoped would quash Bowles and break up his banditti, dissuade other similarly nefarious characters from repeating his mistakes, and project stability throughout the region. They would drive out disreputable white men, mischief-makers, and others "of a light character" and would also clamp down on illegal trading. Generally, they declared, those and "other articles" were designed for "keeping peace with all white people around them" and "for all Indian Nations to be at peace with each other and to be of one mind and of one government." The contents of the meeting were sent down to Pallachockola and further into the Florida panhandle, a warning to the wayward communities at the edges of Creek Country that were threatening the stability of the region. The talks would be read aloud in a public meeting, "to bring them of the same way of thinking as the whole nation is, and to be of one talk."[1]

Only a generation earlier, at the time of the Ceded Lands crisis, the National Council did not exist. In fact, the political atmosphere in the region was entirely different. There was no Creek Nation, only Creek communities and the hunting lands they all claimed in common—there was simply what is referred to in this study as Creek Country. In Creek Country the same communities existed, of course, yet there was no centralized political authority that bound them together. Instead they were governed entirely by local leaders who neither exercised nor claimed to exercise any meaningful amount of coercive authority even within their own communities, let alone outside of them. Economics and politics were localized as well, while cultural traditions like kinship groups and blood vengeance guided law and order. Any decision of regional importance could only be made with a massive plurality of local voices, and that was a rarity. One headman could not agree to cede land that he hunted on, for instance, because he was not authorized "to make any grant" without the approval of every Creek in Creek Country.[2] While that might have been a bit of a stretch, the reality was that Creek Country was a very different place than the Creek Nation.

During the Ceded Lands crisis, years before the Revolutionary War came to Georgia, a small group of Cowetas raided settler farms on the edges of Creek Country, where it met an expanding Georgia backcountry. Although the Christmas Day killings were isolated, it was because of the politics of Creek Country that they became a regional crisis. Traditions of local governance ensured that headmen from outside of the responsible Coweta community not only would deny any responsibility for the attacks but would declare their inability to discipline their wayward neighbors, even though they claimed to be the same people. The kinship-based system of justice then failed to right the situation because the kin of the killers simply refused, for one reason or another, to deliver them up to be executed, as they were bound to do by their own legal traditions. Specific headmen, attempting to exert what influence they could via those same kinship networks, also failed to find any sort of resolution. British legislators, unwilling to invade Creek Country, shut down all trade into the region in an attempt to force a solution. Those actions, however, only generated angry and divisive responses. Not all Creeks were the same, as it turned out, at least as several headmen protested, so why was everyone being punished for the actions of a single community? One headman complained bitterly that so few "mad young men should have it in their power" to involve so many "in a war with the white people," while another declared that the offending towns alone should bear the burden of the trade stoppage and "stand for themselves."[3]

The political indecision inherent in Creek Country stands in stark contrast to the decisive political nature of the Creek Nation. The difference between the two, only a generation apart, is telling. Charting the transformation from the one to the other, from the diffuse nature of Creek Country to the ordered framework of the Creek Nation, is the primary purpose of this study. It was a swift and sometimes messy transformation; the Creek Nation only emerged after Creek Country was driven to crisis. More importantly, it was a political as well as a cultural transformation, and one for which Creeks were largely responsible.

As the nature of the Ceded Lands crisis originally revealed, it was the state of Georgia, at least at first, that constituted Creeks' principal threat. Georgia settlers, once throttled by conservative British colonial officials, were unleashed by a state government as openly contemptuous of Creek culture as they were covetous of Creek lands. Waves of settlers pushed up against Creek communities and their hunting lands, sparking confrontations that dragged Creek Country slowly but steadily into political chaos. At first particular headmen responded to that movement independently, as they had done for generations. But years of political and economic negotiations as well as overlapping outside alliances, all of which shifted over time and differed dramatically from one Creek town to the next, produced little but confusion and hostility. Neighboring headmen were soon at odds with and even violently opposed to each other, not to mention Georgia state officials or their Spanish counterparts. Almost every attempt made by local leaders to react to Georgia expansionism both during the Revolutionary War and in the years afterward only worsened things in Creek Country, producing a cacophony of Creek voices that proved tremendously destabilizing. By the 1790s the region was in crisis, and the Creek political confederacy that had existed in the Southeast for generations was collapsing.

Tying their political evolution directly to American expansionism complicates interpretations of Creeks' cultural development that have, for some time, focused on earlier periods—on the coalescent period that followed first contact with Europeans, and then vis-à-vis French, Spanish, and British colonial governments in the generations afterward. Studies of coalescence in early Native American communities, for instance, focus on a specific period stretching from European contact in the sixteenth century to the end of the Yamasee War in the eighteenth century. In the wake of contact with Europeans, the Mississippian societies that dominated the Southeast broke apart and dissolved, and their remnants coalesced into groups like Creeks. That period is usually described as closing with the end of the Yamasee War, around 1718. By that time Spanish and British colonies stabilized and the Southeast had been demographically and politically reordered, with Native groups like Creeks having replaced the Mississippian societies that preceded them almost completely.[4] That only ushered in another, equally formative period in Creek history. Several ambitious Creek leaders articulated a regional policy of neutrality they used to manipulate competing colonial powers and, by doing so, maintain collective, if not vaguely defined, ideas of identity and sovereignty.[5] Even after the end of the French and Indian War British colonial authorities largely replaced Spanish and French ones, but the British were still unable to dictate their policy to southeastern Natives, meaning the regional approach stayed basically the same.[6] This period, from coalescence to the American Revolution, bracketed the ethnogenesis of Creeks as a people.

Creeks are commonly portrayed as a profoundly loosely organized but also established Native group during that expansive period—they existed in the post–Revolutionary War years in ways almost identical to generations earlier. Only decades into the nineteenth century did that change, when the Atlantic economy, the American civilization policy, and then the Indian Removal Act eroded Creek sovereignty and eventually forced the Creek people from the Southeast.[7] That trajectory describes Creeks as a people driven by cultural traditions that functioned independently of the changing world around them, however, in a way that denies them the political creativity and nimbleness possessed by other emerging groups in the same period, like emerging Americans. Although buffeted by political and economic conditions that were outside of Creek communities' control, which were constantly changing, Creek cultural and political traditions somehow went unchanged. Outside troubles did not produce factionalism and discord. Instead, Creeks remained a people at the same time rigid and flexible; a nation but not really; a confederacy perhaps but also not really; sometimes large and sometimes small; and at times remarkably strong but at other times surprisingly weak.[8] Creek political history was, in short, a paradox.

By examining their reactions to the American Revolution and to American expansionism in the years afterward, it becomes increasingly clear that Creek political history was not a paradox and that the Creek people were a politically complicated and at times very troubled people, beset by factionalism, confusion, disagreement, and even violence. Not only did Creeks struggle with state and American authorities, they struggled fiercely among themselves. The Revolutionary era was a period of such tremendous violence and struggle, in fact, that the differences between the prewar years and the decades that followed should mark distinct phases in the development of a Creek identity. Where previous studies describe the pre-Revolutionary century as the seminal one in the creation of a Creek identity, this study suggests that the long Revolutionary era deserves a place of equal importance.

Consider that period, which stretched from the Revolutionary War through the turn of the nineteenth century, one of modernization—the modernization of Creek political and legal culture. Creek society could still be described as coalescent at the beginning of such a period. After 1800, however, it functioned in ways more consistent with a nation-state, not unlike the American one to its east. That modernization, defined loosely as the movement of a Creek society based on unwritten, noncoercive tradition to another based on a more coercive legal authority, is central to this study. Important in that development was the breakdown of cultural and political traditions that were not flexible enough to deal with a rapidly intensifying American expansionism. These traditions evolved over several generations prior to the Revolutionary era to address internal and external threats but failed under the pressure of postwar American expansionism in less than one generation. The community-level political leadership that had defined Creek politics for over a century pushed communities apart, while the cultural traditions designed to pull them back together failed to keep them together. Particular Creek communities had not yet drawn a clear picture of themselves as a single, unified people, and their political and cultural traditions reflected their previous, semi-autonomous approach to Euro-Americans as well as to other Native peoples.

Perhaps, ultimately, it was the relatively weak and competing European colonial presences that were vying for Creek alliances in the Southeast, and not the strength or malleability of a Creek identity, that allowed for the period of relative stability Creek people experienced for the generations prior to the Revolutionary War. What is clear is that while Creek communities functioned well enough together when threats were localized and when disagreements were minor, it would be the times of truly regional upheaval that would test their cohesiveness. Such was the case during the Ceded Lands crisis and would continue to be so as the Revolutionary War arrived in the Southeast. Americans, beginning in the state government of Georgia, represented such a regional threat.

And when state authorities approached Creek communities aggressively beginning early in the war they splintered regional Creek politics with surprising speed. Headmen approached the new threat—or perhaps the new opportunity—individually, as they had in the past. That approach to American expansionism produced discord, however, instead of unity, and the web of cultural traditions that was supposed to bind communities together as a people did not prove strong and flexible but weak and ineffectual.

Creek kinship networks, for instance, were supposed to be a sort of cultural glue that kept otherwise disparate peoples connected in webs of real and fictive relationships. That cohesive power was not strong enough to overcome the divisive impact of local political decisions, however, which scholars have suggested might have been more central to a Creek individual's identity than has previously been thought.[9] Nor did kin-based systems of justice and retribution, or local governance by persuasion, bring either the sense of reciprocity or the regional stability for which they were designed. Communities attempted to invoke those cultural traditions as a means to solve problems both within Creek communities and with Georgians, but more often they made headmen resentful of each other when the actions of some villages, which their neighbors did not agree with, placed numerous others in jeopardy. Both state and national authorities were usually further offended that Creek systems of justice were called upon to fix the situation at all. The thought of killing an entirely different, innocent Creek for the crimes of another, who could not be found or whose kin would not give him up without committing acts of retribution themselves, was absurdly offensive to Euro-Americans. Those traditions, while long-standing and perfectly acceptable in Creek Country, failed to satisfy Americans' demands for justice.

Just as the clan-based system of justice often failed to right a wrong, nearby leaders could do little to coerce wayward communities when such action was desperately needed. When Georgian or American authorities confronted headmen with complaints about killings or stolen property, there was little they admitted they could do. Their positions of authority were vested in the powers of influence and persuasion, not coercion. Nor did they wield or even claim to wield the slightest degree of authority outside their own communities. The inability of Creek headmen to accomplish anything by force was yet another example of Creek political traditions that caused more problems in the years after the Revolution than they solved. They generated controversy more often than they tempered it and failed to keep Creek communities from pulling away from each other when unity was badly needed. Instead, Creek Country became so turbulent and dysfunctional that, by the 1790s, a common Creek identity ceased to exist there at all.[10]

Order in a political community, according to one sociological definition, can be understood in terms of its opposite, anarchy: "Anarchy reigns when each group takes the law into its hands until checked by the momentarily superior force of an opponent."[11] Political dysfunction generated a regional chaos in Creek Country very close to that definition of anarchy. It was strong enough to guarantee either the dissolution of Creeks as a people in control of their own destiny or the drastic restructuring of their political and cultural systems in ways as stabilizing for themselves as they were acceptable to their new neighbors. In that way the evolution of the Creek Nation was not only a struggle against Georgians but also a struggle among several once politically autonomous communities to find a single, capable, political voice. And only when confronted by deeply dysfunctional intercommunity relations, the reality of violence with Georgians, and the threat of much more violence with Americans did that appear to happen. Encouraged by federal officials like Indian agents James Seagrove and Benjamin Hawkins, an emerging group of Creek leaders began embracing systemic political changes they hoped would not only bring unity to their internal politics but earn them the respect and even assistance of Americans, further guaranteeing their own peace and prosperity as a sovereign people. Stability and security were what an evolving core of Creek leaders searched for, and what outsiders were demanding, and to find stability Creeks began pursuing changes to traditional concepts of collectivity, government, and justice, all of which bent old Creek customs to the new political exigencies of American expansionism. By the first years of the nineteenth century they had begun doing those things, having constructed a political entity that was, for a time, capable of dealing diplomatically with outside sources of danger while also policing internal sources of division and instability.

More particularly, the several consolidating steps headmen took were in many ways consistent with the creation of a Creek nation-state. Entangled in the concept of the nation-state are two separate and equally complex sociological and political models, both of which have been interpreted variously and sometimes contentiously over time, including in Native America. Yet some of the basic premises of both nation and state formation are relatively established, and both can offer tremendous insight into the changes that remade Creek politics. Understood generally, the development of nationalism concerns the growth of a unique, collective, exclusive identity. One specific form, cultural nationalism, describes a people who develop among themselves a distinct identity based on their shared cultural values and are bound together often on territory they claim collectively as theirs. A slightly separate subdefinition, political nationalism, describes the projection of political solidarity and determination among such a group of people. Nationhood, by these definitions, describes a people who construct an exclusive identity around a shared cultural heritage and assert it politically, particularly vis-à-vis outsiders.[12] Although there are also differing and contending definitions of statehood, in a general way it represents the organized machinery of a nation's political system, including the centralization of authority, its administration, its jurisdiction, and, perhaps most importantly, the legitimate use of force or violence within its defined territorial bounds. The state is the institutional framework within the nation that enforces order. The nation-state as it is defined here, in sum, consists of a people recognizing their sovereignty based on their distinctiveness, within a demarcated territory, with legitimized, institutionalized forms of administration, governance, law, and violence.[13]

Charting a Creek political modernization process based on these concepts is significant because ethnohistorians and Native American scholars have reached mixed conclusions about the degree to which the processes of nation building and statehood reflected the experiences of Native peoples in early America, if they did at all. Most of the historical sociology concerning the processes of nation and statehood, after all, focuses on their origins in post-Enlightenment Europe. From there they spread around the globe during the eighteenth and nineteenth centuries— centuries of intense competition over resources and security—including to North America.[14] Anthropologists and historians of Native America alike have recognized and criticized these origins; they have challenged the referring to Native peoples as "nations," for example, as Eurocentric constructions and symbols of colonialism and discouraged comparing Native groups to European nations on such terms. The British were much more inclined to refer to Creeks as such than were Creek people themselves, one such argument goes, or their Native neighbors for that matter, because it was the British who sought to trade and deal legally with Natives in ways they were already familiar with—ways in which they already approached other Europeans. For many scholars this example of Anglo-Creek contact exemplifies the inaccuracies and generalizations produced by imposing foreign European or Euro-American political concepts onto Native America.[15]

While many of those criticisms certainly are valid, as the study of nationhood continues to evolve scholars of Native America have been more cautiously accepting of such definitions, citing naturalness and an almost universality to the idea of peoplehood. Native groups, after all, openly and regularly conceived of themselves as distinct peoples—situated territorially in defined areas—before and without the interposition of Europeans, and they were quick to label other neighboring Native peoples as distinct as well. Is that conceptualization of selfhood not consistent with Euro-American understandings of nationhood? It has further been suggested that such definitions, however problematic they might be, can still be used beneficially as a way to divest ourselves of an older and even worse "tribal" paradigm and better define the Native perspective in more dynamic and realistic ways. Nations were not and are not static entities—they were dynamic and pluralistic, they shifted, and they were contested at times—concepts that would seem to fit well, in fact, in Native America. Even a careful acceptance of nationhood as a means to historicize Native communities, in other words, has already shifted the study of early America.[16]

Evidence of development consistent with political nationalism on the other hand was far rarer, and statehood even more so. With the cultural and political traditions of most Native peoples based on plurality rather than cohesiveness, and consent rather than coercion, it is not surprising that a single Native voice is often hard to locate even in what looks like a single Native community, or that the machinery and force of the state would have little resonance among Native leadership. Indeed, while several Native peoples might have conceived of themselves in ways consistent with what we now consider nationhood, few times did Native people speak in a single, clear political voice, and examples of the centralized, coercive actions consistent with state structures were practically nonexistent.

Consider the Iroquois Great League of Peace and Power, guided by the Grand Council. Not only did the Grand Council exist to promote unity among the Five (and later, Six) Nations of the Iroquois, it played an important diplomatic function as well, negotiating with French, Dutch, English, and other Native outsiders from the seventeenth to the nineteenth century. That was the case late in the seventeenth century, when the gathering of Iroquois sachems helped construct the "Covenant Chain," a tradition of relationships between Iroquois communities and English colonial governments that stabilized relations between the two groups for decades. Smaller confederacies also functioned in the Great

Lakes region in the late eighteenth century, like the Illinois Confederacy, the Three Fires of the Chippewa, Ottawa, Potawatomi people, and the larger Algonquian Confederacy that squared off against American forces late in the eighteenth and into the early nineteenth century.[17] But these structures, while they demonstrated collectivity both within a single Native group and among several of them that could be seen as being consistent with nationhood, were not centralized or hierarchical in nature. Many of the Algonquin confederacies were short-term solutions to American expansionism that were overwhelmingly military and defensive in nature. They were not state bodies, nor were they designed to be; the same could be said about New England's Algonquin groups as well.[18] Neither was the Iroquois Grand Council a centralized government structure. It did not wield coercive force over particular communities or produce a unified foreign policy. It was a spiritual body as equally as a political one, which still functioned through discussion, exchange, and passivity.[19] Collectivity consistent with nationhood was not uncommon in early Native America, these confederacies demonstrate, but collectivity was certainly not the same as state formation.

The Comanche Empire, which commanded tremendous economic and political power in the Southwest, invites closer comparisons. Comanche raiders drew other Native groups, Spaniards, Mexicans, and even Americans into their sweeping geopolitical world, Comancheria, beginning shortly after contact with Europeans in the sixteenth century and lasting well into the nineteenth. Operating in a defined territory, maintaining control of resources and extracting resources from others, and using coercive power to maintain that control were Comanche actions that were at least loosely consistent with state formation.[20] One need look no further than to Cherokee Country in north Georgia, western South and North Carolina, and eastern Tennessee, however, to find a people who embraced something much more consistent with statehood. Not only did the Cherokee people create a strong foundation of nationalism based on a shared culture, vis-à-vis Euro-Americans, they built a clear state structure atop that foundation. The Cherokee Nation constructed executive, legislative, and judicial bodies modeled directly after the American government. Under these branches was a National Council, which raised administrative state bodies around a written constitution and written laws and provided the coercive authority to enforce those laws. Most important, perhaps, the National Council asserted Cherokee territorial and political sovereignty and defended it for years in the face of intense state- and then national-level expansionism.[21] Neither nation nor state formation was impossible in the early Southeast, the Cherokee experience demonstrates; the influence of Euro-American political culture in Cherokee Country was unmistakable.

While the experiences of the Cherokee people have been held up as the best and perhaps the only example of nation-state formation in all of pre-Removal Native America, their experiences and those of the Creek people are strikingly similar. Both Cherokees and Creeks could be described as coalescent through most of the eighteenth century. By the early nineteenth, however, both were producing a single, culturally distinct political voice that they used to counter state and federal officials. Both had defined their own territory and asserted their own sovereignty in terms Americans could understand, even though it irritated them. More than that, though, both developed specific institutions to secure peace and stability within their territory, as well as in the larger region, by creating laws and the means to enforce them. They built hierarchical governance structures, produced a land policy, and to a lesser extent even a fiscal policy. These institutions are consistent with state formation in even the most conventional Western European traditions. Creeks, like Cherokees, embodied a National Council. Members of the council claimed jurisdiction over all of Creek Country, and when they convened, members of the council met and created regional laws, meted out punishments, and in a few instances agreed to land cessions. They also commissioned coercive bodies capable of enforcing their decisions with violence. Both, in short, generated structures consistent in many ways with nation-states.

Why were the experiences of those two people so similar? Although they were not the same people, clearly, Creeks and Cherokees did share comparable community governance structures and kinship networks. They were also confronted by the same American expansionism, at about the same time and in roughly the same place, and so it is no mystery they responded in similar ways. But Cherokees struggled far more than Creeks in the years before that period. Several of their towns were destroyed by Euro-American armies in the French and Indian War in 1760–1761, then again during the American Revolution, and then again during the Articles of Confederation period.[22] Creeks endured none of those waves of destruction. They emerged from the Revolutionary War in a much better position to fend off American advances than their neighbors to the north, and perhaps most importantly, they were the controllers of a sprawling territory expanding state governments—led by the state of Georgia—grasped for first. They were among the first of the southern Native peoples later referred to as the "Five Civilized Tribes" to respond to American expansionism, which many did in similar ways, ways sometimes consistent with nation-state formation.[23]

That response was an era of Creek political modernization. Although eighteenth-century Native America was often a place where there could be nations without states, or even nationalism, in short, perhaps the central argument to this book is that in Creek Country that changed, and it changed rather quickly. And not only did it change quickly, it did so largely in response to American pressure. As demonstrated in both Creek and Cherokee Country, it is clear that Native people challenged their own political traditions by importing others that were obviously of European or Euro-American origin. This, however, should not be surprising—it is in the Southeast, in fact, where the penetration and impact of Euro-American cultural, economic, and social traditions into Native America can be seen clearest. As Claudio Saunt, Kathryn E. H. Braund, and Robbie Ethridge have shown, the Creek people were pulled into the Atlantic economy by the regional deerskin trade and transformed by it, and generally not in positive ways—ways that inevitably led to debt, dependency, and dispossession. Few aspects of Creek culture, including gender roles, planting and ranching practices, and property ownership, were unaffected by Euro-American values in the process.[24] Even more recently, Christina Snyder has demonstrated that neither were most of the Native groups in the Southeast immune to Euro-American ideas of race or the institution of racial slavery. By the nineteenth century many Creeks and Cherokees were embracing the plantation system in ways remarkably similar to those of their Euro-American counterparts in the South.[25] All of these developments were only intensified later in the nineteenth century, when American authorities instituted a more coordinated, systematic "plan of civilization," including the use of Christian missionaries as well as federal agents. The entire system was based on an assumption that Natives could be successfully purged of their own cultural and economic traditions and taught to embrace more civilized ones, and be transformed thereby into respectable Americans.[26] The Native people of the Southeast were in no way impervious to foreign cultural and economic ideals. Creek and Cherokee people in particular were exposed to outside Euro-American values for generations, and visible, even fundamental, changes in their cultures resulted. Political concepts that included more Euro-American definitions of political nationhood and state formation, this study suggests, were no different.

Nevertheless, whether they did so voluntarily or under pressure, what Creek headmen were attempting involved challenging several long-standing traditions, relegating others to less importance, and developing others in novel ways. Few Creek political, cultural, or economic traditions went entirely unchanged during the period, making this study a combination of traditional and nontraditional historical approaches. It obviously focuses on Creek culture and is largely a study of it, utilizing anthropological and historical sources both to draw a clearer picture of Creeks as a people and to better understand their cultural and political traditions.[27] But it does not claim to be excessively ethnohistorical either, by privileging cultural continuities over periods of intense and sometimes traumatic change, or by ignoring the important and sometimes disruptive influence of outsiders. Rather, both threads are present.

It is clear on the one hand, for instance, that the Creek people were affected by Euro-Americans in ways so unsettling as to cause real political chaos, and the development of the Creek nation-state was in many ways influenced by outside forces that Creeks could not control. This approach to Native political history paints Creeks as reactionary; as ethnohistorically problematic as that seems, it was at least partially the case. Inadvertently or not, because of the violence of the period or even merely the threat of it, American expansionism collapsed more than a century's worth of a Native people's political and diplomatic traditions. Creek communities were confronted and transformed by state-level expansionists, and only a decade or so later much of their traditional political identity had changed. Like the Atlantic trade economy and the plantation system, Euro-American political and legal traditions were not only foreign to Creeks but posed direct challenges to many of their established traditions. Many of those values were imposed upon Creek communities by Americans, particularly by the well-studied Benjamin Hawkins and his far less studied predecessor James Seagrove, which made the Creek experience troubling. Would a Creek nation-state project have taken form without the influence of such men? It might not have. Furthermore, the "modernization" of Creek politics in that context also has a disturbing progressive, almost stadial feel to it. A primitive, tradition-based society gave way to a more familiar, developed system of law based on accepted legal authority?[28] Primitive and reactionary are, at best, unflatteringly ethnocentric ways to describe Native governing traditions that seemed to be working just fine until Euro-Americans insisted that they actually were not. But Creek systems of tradition-based governance did in fact face collapse, and their collapse brought the Creek people face-to-face with the possibility of violent dispossession.

Ultimately, the modernization process that began in the 1790s was an effort made by Creeks not just to stabilize intercommunity relations but to make themselves respectable neighbors in the eyes of wary Americans, which was done by incorporating Euro-American political traditions. As problematic as this sounds, it does not come without a sense of irony—at the same time Creeks were grappling with ideas of security and stability, so were Americans. The exigencies of the Revolutionary era were pressuring American leaders to mold what was essentially a European modeled nation-state to their own needs. Even by the successful conclusion of the Revolutionary War, however, many Americans did not share a common religion or timeless cultural heritage, or even many times a common descent. Nationhood did not come easily to Americans, and a viable state came with even more difficulty, as demonstrated in the troubled years of the Articles of Confederation period and even in the first few years of Federalist government control.[29] Neither the processes of nation and state formation nor the pressures producing them were exclusive to Natives, these shared experiences demonstrate. They were Euro-American ones as well.

In addition, the stresses shaping Creek decisions represent only half of the story. As clear as it was that outside forces had an influence on Creek political decisions, it is equally clear that it was the Creek people who recognized and initiated the changes that needed to be made to their political traditions. Creeks were the ones who made those changes, and they made them largely on their own cultural and political terms. While the rule of law might have represented more of a Euro-American concept than a Creek one, to cite one example, Creek *micos* and *tustunnuggees* would be the ones both to create those laws and to enforce them, and they would do so along the lines of long-standing Creek governing traditions. A close investigation into the origins and function of the National Council, which dominates the second half of this study, demonstrates as much. The National Council, which produced an overarching system of administrative law, certainly made several nontraditional decisions of incredible importance to Creeks—whether to beat or kill people or to sell land, for instance. But then again the National Council was only an extension of the local councils that had existed in Creek Country for generations, and most of the time for most Creeks, what the National Council did mattered little; local concerns and local relationships would always remain central to Creek identity and Creek life. Yes, a regional

governing body emerged and individual men grew much more powerful, but their local counterparts did not disappear, and micos continued
to assert local authority through consent. Meanwhile, tobacco was still
smoked and the black drink was still drunk. Uncles still taught their
nephews how to hunt, community fields still produced community corn,
and kinship groups ensured that all Creeks were still bound to each
other in real and fictive relationships. The Creek nation-state project was
no engine of political and cultural destruction, forced upon the Creek
people from above, and generally speaking the lives of most Creeks carried on as they had for generations. The National Council changed none
of that, which underscores the shrewdness and ingenuity in the Creek
political modernization project. That the Creek people would take some
aspects of a foreign American legal and political culture (like administrative justice) and graft them to their own traditions (like town councils) to create something uniquely theirs demonstrated that while they
were not entirely free of American influence, neither were they entirely
at the mercy of it. To study Creeks' political collapse together with
their ensuing recovery, in short, presents an excellent ethnohistorical
opportunity—the opportunity to study a sophisticated and eminently
political people whose decisions were not the product of timeless tradition alone but of diplomacy and political necessity as well.[30]

While there was an undeniable degree of cultural creativity associated
with the Creek political modernization project, equally undeniable was
the importance of violence and conflict. The processes of Creek nation
and state formation—to whatever extent either might have materialized—
were at the same time defensive and offensive ones, necessary to deal with
powerful outside threats embodied by American expansionists as well as
the internal divisions those threats generated in Creek Country. They
were dramatic breaking-down and rebuilding processes that resulted
directly from violence and, perhaps even more importantly, the threat of
much more violence. In that way the evolution of Creek politics fits not
only into larger studies of nation and state formation but also into the
already familiar narratives of conflict and violence that inform the most
recent studies of early America, particularly those that have recast Native
interactions with Euro-Americans along the frontiers. Only recently, in
fact, have violence and confrontation been described for their ability
to shape the evolution of peoples' politics or even culture in formative
ways. That was certainly the case when studying the development of
Euro-American identity, particularly along the trans-Appalachian
backcountry, where settler-Native violence had a tremendous impact

on Euro-American culture.[31] The power of violence was manifest along the Creek-Georgia frontier, where conflict with Natives certainly had an impact on the Georgia state identity. It is equally critical, however, to a better understanding of Creeks as a people. In short it was settler, state, and then national pressures that explain why the Creek Nation developed as it did.[32] It was, perhaps above all else, the threat of violent dispossession of their lands that forced Creeks to embrace new traditions—traditions that were difficult to grasp at times. Violence and struggle are key to understanding the search for a stronger, more unified Creek voice.

Even labeling the region of interaction between Creeks and Americans the Creek-Georgia frontier, and to a lesser extent the Creek-Tennessee or Creek-Mississippi frontier, recognizes the important role of conflict in those areas. They were places of struggle, not understanding, and encounters there were generally unpleasant. American settlers seldom accepted Creeks, no matter the circumstance, and federal authorities only did so when it was absolutely necessary to avert bloodshed. And even when Creeks wrestled with the idea of a centralized political system, they did so as the means to confront and repulse state and then federal attempts to appropriate their territory, either by trickery or by force. Indeed, the Creek-Georgia frontier reflects a region of cultural and physical interaction that produced far more instances of violent confrontation than ones of shared cultural experiences. It was a place where people saw the other not only as different but as inherently dangerous.[33] The Creek nation-state, although clearly modeled after Euro-American ones, was also an attempt to fight fire with fire.

This last suggestion is no better illustrated than with the disappointment and the eventual breakdown of the National Council, a process that began shortly after it generated some of the most stable years experienced in the region in decades. Not all was lost, in the end—a Creek nation-state endured until removal and, indeed, afterward.[34] Nevertheless, within a decade or so of the National Council claiming ascendancy in Creek Country, it was already struggling for legitimacy. By 1813 it was consumed in a civil war, the Red Stick War, which was a devastating period of inter-Creek conflict that ended in the death or displacement of thousands of Creeks, the loss of much of Creek Country to Americans, and finally the Removal era.

Most surprising about that breakdown was that, only two years before the Red Stick uprising began, it by no means seemed inevitable. To the contrary, Creek solidarity appeared rather strong early in the nineteenth century. But it was also definitely under assault. The Tallassee

King, speaking at the head of the National Council in 1811, issued a strong talk against American territorial expansion that demonstrated the threats Creeks faced. Having in his hands a request direct from the Madison administration to have an imposing public road built through his neighborhood, the Tallassee King produced a clear answer: "You ask for a path and I say no." He had taken time to look over the proposal carefully, he made clear, as had many others; "my chiefs and warriors have examined it," and "they tell you I must not allow it and must say no."[35] The Tallassee King, representing a Creek people struggling with a growing and ever-more aggressive American government, spoke with confidence, as though his answer indeed reflected the will of the Creek people. He would need that unity: confronting him were federal authorities that were stronger and bolder than the ones his predecessors faced, and they were far less interested in the Creek nation-state than their predecessors had been. William Eustis, James Madison's secretary of war, embodied the threat. The American government's proposal for the road was "founded in reason and justice," he replied, and the answer provided by the Tallassee King appeared to him "unreasonable" and was "by no means satisfactory."[36] American expansionists, as Secretary Eustis's answer suggests, were not simply challenging the National Council by 1811; they were preparing to ignore it altogether. The determination of the Jefferson and Madison administrations to build that road against the wishes of the National Council, or to insist on territorial access into Creek Country in the myriad other ways they did, not only undermined the legitimacy of the council but chipped away at Creek sovereignty until, by 1813, until it was more of a fiction than a fact.

Furthermore, even though the Tallassee King's talk sounded as though he was confident in what he thought was best for the Creek people, he was soon removed from his speakership position by a rival faction of neighboring headmen and replaced by a leader much more sympathetic to American needs. That sort of political infighting revealed how badly Creek political collectivity was suffering under the weight of American expansionism. Not only were American authorities no longer respectful of Creek sovereignty, their demands for territorial access produced regional sources of disagreement that the National Council could not mitigate. The council was conceived to deal with just those kinds of threats, but it was becoming increasingly clear to many Creeks that it could not. Disagreements over the position the council should take on such issues generated anti-state forces that began to pull it apart, eventually producing an insurgency in 1813 that was determined to destroy it and reverse the changes it had made to Creek political and legal traditions. The Red Stick insurgency represented communities sold short time and again by the National Council, a political body that could not protect Creek communities from continued American trespasses, that made promises with Americans on behalf of all Creeks that it could not guarantee, and that enforced its decisions using coercive measures that fell disproportionately on them. By the uprising Americans no longer respected the National Council, and the council no longer appeared to represent all Creeks.

Because the Creek nation-state faced such an insurgency, does that mean it was altogether a failure or, worse, that it never existed to begin with? Benjamin Hawkins certainly did not think that it never existed, which was something he made clear almost to the day he died. "The Government of the Creeks is not an ephemeral one," he declared in 1815. Not only did the National Council function for a decade previous to the Red Stick War it endured it, as Hawkins implied, and would rebuild in the years afterward in an almost remarkable way. But more importantly, as a force impacting the day-to-day lives of countless Creeks, it functioned for over a decade reasonably well as it was designed. It mitigated causes of conflict with Georgia settlers, like horse theft and assault, helped regulate interactions between Creeks and Georgians when they were most dangerous, and made the Creek people sufferable, if still unwelcomed, neighbors to Americans. The National Council was originally conceived to do those things, and the relatively peaceful years it provided across the turn of the nineteenth century would suggest not only that a Creek state did exist but that it was far from the abject failure it has since been labeled.

That in no way, of course, implies that the Creek state-building project was perfect, and it was far from perfect. The council certainly enriched particular headmen, who were keen to use their power for their own political and financial gain. Although there were several examples of that, and of other sources of internal struggle within the Creek Nation, they do not mean it was a failure. First, state structures have long been criticized as carefully constructed and often brutal mechanisms of power consolidation, economic exploitation, and social control, but that made them no less real.[37] And second, no nation—Native, European, or otherwise—has been defined in such unconditional terms as absolute acceptance or absolute contrivance. Nations grow and shrink and rise and fall, and far from monolithic and static entities, they are diverse, shifting, and often contested ones. Their people reconsider themselves, the threats facing them change, and their institutions evolve as a result. Scholarship on both nation and state formation clearly demonstrates, in fact, that both processes, even though they were designed to bring people together, also at times left people out. And as one scholar of the Shawnee has suggested, nowhere is this more relevant than in Native America. Any nation "evolves constantly, as various local, kin, or class-based groups negotiate and argue about the proper order, membership, and future of society."[38] Just because the National Council generated inequality or graft, or because it did not work for everyone, or because not every Creek completely trusted it does not make the Creek Nation fictional—it makes it even more real.

This is only further suggested by again turning to the American experiment, just to the north and during roughly the same period. Under the Articles of Confederation, which governed the country from the end of the Revolution to the ratification of the Constitution, a federal government existed that had the ability to do almost nothing. It could not effectively tax its citizenry or pay its war debts, leading in one instance to a popular uprising in the backcountry of Massachusetts referred to as Shay's Rebellion.[39] It could do even less to support and protect its backcountry settlers, particularly from Natives. Without the protection of an army of the United States or money to support effective militias, settlers in modern-day Indiana and Ohio suffered tremendously. Along the border of modern-day Tennessee and North Carolina settlers fared no better, where the same inadequacies led to the creation of the short-lived breakaway State of Franklin, which languished just beyond the northern limits of Creek Country for years before collapsing.[40] And in an episode central to this study, not only could the federal government not adequately throttle an overaggressive state of Georgia when it dealt with Creeks unilaterally in the 1780s, it could not support the state militarily when the Creek people responded by burning much of the Georgia backcountry to the ground. And just like they could not successfully negotiate with the Spanish for access to the Mississippi River, neither could federal authorities negotiate with Spanish officials to halt their military support of the Creek people. In these instances and in several others the government of the United States was either unresponsive or incompetent enough to generate popular protests, insurgencies, rogue states, and a not-inconsiderable amount of bloodshed. America could, for those reasons, be considered a failed state, yet it clearly was not. For all of its obvious flaws, foreign nations and the majority of its citizenry still recognized the existence of the United States, and the federal government would evolve over time to better reflect and support its citizenry. The Creek National Council suffered and grew similarly. Although it too had obvious flaws, Americans dealt with it for almost two decades as if it existed, and the majority of Creeks acted like it was a real thing for much longer.

That is not to suggest that the Creek people did not also end up west of the Mississippi River, and they certainly did not end up there by their own choosing. Since the National Council could not stop the American government from redefining and eventually rejecting Creek sovereignty, or stop the passage of the Indian Removal Act of 1830, or successfully resist removal, did that mean it was again a failure? That is a more complicated question. What the Creek National Council could do tolerably well was stabilize the Creek-Georgia frontier. What it could not do, however, was safeguard Creek sovereignty by halting American expansionism. The National Council could make Creeks decent neighbors, in other words, but it could not make Americans respect them as such. The Red Stick War might have dragged the Creek people into the Removal era, but looking back, ultimately, it would be hard to explain how even the most decisive Creek victory in the war would have changed the future. With the election of Andrew Jackson as president and the subsequent rise of American "Jacksonian" Democracy, there was no length any of the Southeast's Native peoples could go as good neighbors—or as farmers, ranchers, slaveholding plantation owners, or anything else, for that matter—that would have kept a more powerful American people from their lands. Creeks underwent a truly revolutionary experiment in political modernization, this study ultimately contends, but only as a means to ensure their permanence on ancestral lands. They not only used the National Council to make themselves good neighbors, they depended upon it as their best means for territorial security, and in that sense the Creek nation-state was an obvious failure. For decades the Creek nation-state existed and gave the Creek people a reasonable level of security and stability, but it did not last forever.

PART 1

The End of Creek Country

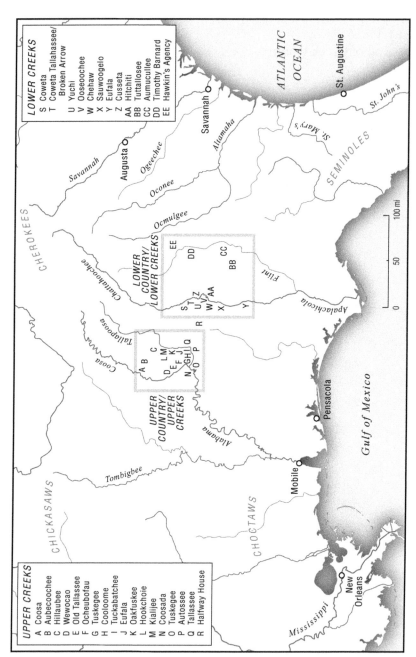

MAP 1. Creek Country and the Southeast. Map by Erin Greb Cartography.

UPPER CREEKS

A Coosa
B Aubecoochee
C Hillaubee
D Wewocao
E Old Tallassee
F Ocheubofau
G Tuskegee
H Cooloome
I Tuckabatchee
J Eufala
K Oakfuskee
L Hookchoie
M Kialijee
N Coosada
O Tuskegee
P Autossee
Q Tallassee
R Halfway House

LOWER CREEKS

S   Coweta
T   Coweta Tallahassee/
    Broken Arrow
U   Yuchi
V   Ooseoochee
W   Chehaw
X   Sauwoogelo
Y   Eufala
Z   Cusseta
AA Hitchiti
BB Tuttallosee
CC Aumucullee
DD Timothy Barnard
EE Hawkin's Agency

2 / Creek Partisans Emerge during the American Revolution

We are now just like a parcel of carpenters set to work to build a house without one single tool.
—George Galphin, October 26, 1776

In the Ceded Lands crisis the actions of a single Creek community brought confusion and animosity to Creek Country, calling into question for the first time in a long time the cohesiveness of Creek politics. Only years later the Revolutionary War engulfed the Southeast, threatening to magnify all of those divisive tendencies and, if not treaded carefully by community leaders, generate intercommunity violence. The struggle would test a Creek political structure that had existed for generations, and the results were troublesome. Strong British trade arrangements and the continued movement of settlers—now led by state-level expansionists—onto the Ceded Lands pushed several communities away from the American cause, while those with the closest political and familial ties to the traders that would become American partisans remained loyal to them. As the war intensified, those relationships revealed a Creek Country where local decisions and cultural traditions generated divisiveness among neighboring communities that slowly grew more confrontational. Traditions of retributive justice enflamed tensions with Georgians, and when headmen leaned on kinship connections, it did little good. Scores of communities with competing trade agreements, political friends, and clan connections all ensured that when British and American officials forced them to declare their loyalties and act on them, Creeks would not produce a single political voice. Even Cusseta and Coweta relationships were strained by the struggle, pulling apart two communities that shared some of the strongest cultural connections in all of Creek Country. As that situation in the Lower Country demonstrated, deep divisions over how to commit to the Revolutionary War emerged among even the closest of Creek communities. Those divisions revealed how disruptive outside political and economic forces could be in Creek Country and, ultimately, how shallow Creek solidarity could be when stressed.

Although British authorities turned their attention elsewhere, the Ceded Lands remained a contested and violent place. Georgians still considered them theirs and, albeit at a much slower rate, continued to settle them. Doing so was bound to incite more Creek violence, yet very few Georgia authorities were interested in returning so much as an acre of the lands— much of which had already been surveyed, parceled out, and sold, under both British and local supervision.[1] That land was now Wilkes County, and state authorities would make no efforts at conciliating Creeks on the matter. In Philadelphia, however, members of the newly formed Continental Congress had a more circumspect approach to Creek-American relations, which was not altogether different from that of their British counterparts. If any number of Creek communities ever united against Georgians, not only would the promising American state be over before it began, the whole Southeast would be in jeopardy. That possibility made keeping Creek headmen friendly, or at least neutral, a necessity of national importance. When reports surfaced in 1775 that a group of traders with loyalist persuasions were already pressuring headmen to sever their American ties, it seemed to many in the Congress that those fears were being realized.[2] Although the approach was certain to generate friction with local Georgia authorities, Congress appointed commissioners they hoped would mitigate local disputes and nudge Creek communities closer to the American cause. George Galphin and Robert Rae, among a number of other traders, were directed to do that, and instructed above all else to "preserve peace and friendship with the Indians and to prevent their taking part in the present commotions." Congressmen recognized that Creek involvement in the war threatened tremendous bloodshed and even the failure of their cause, and they were prepared to offer Creek leaders liberal terms "for their good office." They understood that traders were the best means to make Creek cooperation a reality.[3]

Congress's dependence on traders was no coincidence, and both Galphin and Rae were obvious choices as commissioners. For decades men in their position illustrated how trade had served as a pillar of Creek-European relations and, in its wider context, the economic force that drove diplomacy in the Southeast.[4] Generally speaking men and women in Creek communities, like elsewhere in the Native Southeast, only traded with friends and those they trusted. That drove young and entrepreneurial traders to form close bonds with the communities they represented for their British merchants, bonds that required an awareness and acceptance of Native cultural and political traditions. Many prospective traders were connected intimately with Creek women, for instance, while others ended up intermarrying with them and raising Creek children. Although those sorts of relationships created the deepest political connections and the strongest social bonds, which carried the weight of clan identity and kinship ties, they did not necessarily have to be the case. Creek headmen also integrated young, brash, and potentially exploitative European trading men directly into their communities simply as a better way to keep a watchful eye on them. Whatever their route into Creek Country, by the Revolutionary War a large number of European men were deeply imbedded in the political, social, and cultural life of practically every Creek town. Many of them earned the trust of the people there, serving as loyal friends and political allies to their community's leading men.[5] As the Revolution intensified, it was clear they would play important roles in the direction their communities would take.

Few men shared the experiences and connections of George Galphin and Robert Rae. Galphin, the "merchant prince of the Georgia forest," was a particularly potent American asset. An intrepid and ruthless trader who dominated much of the deerskin trade in Creek Country after 1763, he maintained a sizable plantation across the Savannah River from Augusta, which he named Silver Bluff. By the Revolution it was described as a sprawling place, complete with a two-story brick house and a hundred or more slaves, with visitors passing through constantly. Galphin married at least one Coweta woman and perhaps several others, and had many children of mixed ancestry. Because of those kinship ties, which were in addition to his long list of trade connections, Galphin wielded tremendous influence throughout the Lower Country. He built a powerful trading connection between Coweta and Augusta, and because of his kin ties his authority there was unrivaled. Both his trading operations and his relations stretched across the Chattahoochee into Cusseta, and his words would carry weight there as well.[6] Then there were his sons, like George and John Galphin, who with his various other hirelings exerted their own influence. Even nephew David Holmes was a powerful force in Coweta and impressed Escochobey, one of the leading chiefs there, early in the war.[7]

Robert Rae, and to a lesser extent his brother James, were Galphin's counterparts in the Upper Country. Although less is known about the Rae brothers than Galphin, Robert did have a close association with Oakfuskee, where he lived, and counted the Handsome Fellow, one of its most prominent chiefs, among his closest friends. He also reportedly had trading posts spread through the Lower Country as well, with one in the Chehaw towns along the Chattahoochee River.[8] Rae's Euro-American and Creek connections, along with Galphin's, had long made the men politically powerful, and as commissioners they would be the primary means of keeping Creek communities deaf to British talks. Together, though, the men's authority also represented the overlapping, complicated, and potentially disruptive nature of the Creek trade. While scores of smaller traders, factors, or their agents were affiliated to Galphin or the Raes, many others were not. In the heart of the Upper Country, for instance, British agent David Taitt recorded two traders operating in Tuckabatchee, one in Kialijee, one in Hookchoie, and two in Autossee.[9] Further up the river, a small town outside of Oakfuskee had an independent trader, as did Hillaubee. Hillaubee also had a Native factor associated with another separate trading operation, as did Tuskegee. And at the northern edges of Creek Country, there was a trader at Natchez, one at Tallasseehatchee, two at Wewocao, and one at Wetunkey. Things were much the same further to the south. There were fewer towns along the Chattahoochee, but the numbers of traders still guaranteed that, at the very least, even the smallest community had one. There were at minimum two traders and two Indian factors in the Coweta towns and two more across the river at Cusseta.[10] Further to the south, two traders and three Indian factors operated out of Hitchiti, two in Yuchi, one in Pallachockola, and one in Lower Eufala, near or over the Florida border.[11]

Many of those unnamed traders or Indian factors operated independently, having been fitted out with goods by merchants on credit in Augusta, Charleston, Pensacola, or another trading town. Others had more direct ties to merchants like Galphin and Rae, or Lachlan McGillivray. These included James Germany, Thomas Grierson, James McQueen, and Timothy Barnard, among many others.[12] James Germany, for example, resided in Cooloome, while a Mr. Vanden Velden at Little Tallassee served as a clerk for a Mr. McKay, a merchant in Augusta. McKay had a small trading house there and also evidently lived there from time to time. McKay also had hirelings at Autossee, and Velden, whom Taitt described as a "cracked brain dutchman," was known to travel into the Lower Country as well.[13] In the Lower Country, Robert Tool and James McQueen were agents of Galphin's and operated out of Coweta. Further to the south, James Burgess traded out of Yuchi and had strong connections in the nearby Hitchiti, Chehaw, and Broken Arrow communities. And then there was Barnard, who would play a commanding role along the frontier for more than a generation. He also had a Yuchi wife and raised several children. Nearby was the Rae store in Chehaw, and when Taitt passed through the town, both Barnard and Rae were there.[14]

Creek Country was, in short, a place overrun by merchants, traders, clerks, Indian factors, hirelings, and so on, many of whom competed with each other and all of whom had their own agendas. Many of the traders, and certainly their hirelings, had few political allegiances, and British legislators frequently questioned their moral uprightness. Other wayward traders, like James Leslie in Aubecoochee, Richard Bailey in Autossee, and John Pigg in Cooloome, were no more than shameless opportunists, with no loyalties at all. Even under the best of circumstances, several traders or hirelings operated in a community where one decently supplied and trustworthy man would suffice. That indeed was the case in Hocktawella, where headmen complained that there were three trading outfits in a town of only seventy or so hunters. The whole region, it seemed, was connected in overlapping and unregulated webs of competing merchants from different towns, shady business practices, crippling debts, trickery, theft, and of course plenty of blame, all of which created real problems for men like David Taitt, who struggled for control.[15] And all of that was before the war, when the traders were just worried about money. The multitude of independent men, operating on the leadership of particular communities, had the potential for much more damage as the atmosphere grew more politically tense. Galphin and Rae had already demonstrated the ways they were prepared to wield their own personal authority, threatening to call in their debts and shut off trade to whatever communities opposed the Ceded Lands deal.[16] As one man described decades later, "In the Revolution there never was a Tallassee or a [Natchez] known to take up arms against the colonies; that was the influence of McQueen and Dick Moniac," both local traders.[17] Because of long-standing economic and familial traditions, Creek Country was full of independent traders, each of whom with his own economic and political ambitions—none more so than Rae and Galphin—and each one capable of politicizing Creek communities as the Revolutionary War crept closer to the region.

While potential American partisans had a strong presence in Creek Country, agents of the British government certainly did as well, adding another layer to the Creek political morass. Colonial authorities recognized the havoc traders could spread in the region, and both John Stuart and David Taitt had worked hard to control them. They were well aware of the possible consequences if those same men began to advocate for the American cause, and when that appeared to be the case they quickly stepped up their efforts to counter the dangerous rebel talk. Stuart, long a witness to Galphin's scheming and manipulative ways, needed little warning.[18] Having recently fled Georgia for this life, neither did Stuart need to be warned of the violent tendencies of Americans. Chased by angry patriots out of South Carolina and all the way to West Florida, he made his headquarters in the shadow of the British garrison at Pensacola.[19]

The Americans were right in wanting Stuart dead or alive. He might not have had the strong kin connections of a man like Galphin, but few in the Southeast were as well versed as Stuart was in Native politics. He had long acted as the Crown's Indian superintendent in the Southeast, a position he had held since the end of the French and Indian War. Previously, he had served as a colonel in the British army in North America and was one of the few officers well respected enough by the Cherokees to survive the siege on Fort Loudoun during the Anglo-Cherokee War. Plenty of experience in the Native Southeast had given Stuart a knowledge of both Creeks and Cherokees that was unparalleled, and he was quick to build upon that knowledge as superintendent. Fellow agent Alexander Cameron was confident that he was "more beloved" by the southern Indians "than any other man."[20] Stuart began conversing with Emistisiguo, for instance, as soon as he took his post in the region. His authority continued to grow with the help of Emistisiguo's influence, and although aged, Emistisiguo was important enough to the Upper Country to have Governor Wright once describe him as "a man of by far the greatest consequence, weight and influence of any in the Creek Country." By the Revolution each man's rise in authority had come with the assistance of the other, and the two were close political allies and even close friends.[21]

Stuart's political authority was bound only to increase after he was forced to West Florida. There his proximity to a number of towns in the Lower Country, nearby on the Flint, Chattahoochee, or Apalachicola Rivers, allowed for regular visits that only strengthened his connections as the war progressed. By his death in 1779 he was one of the most well-respected men in all of the Southeast and a steadfast British asset. But he was not the only one. Perhaps just as important, Stuart spread handpicked agents and commissaries throughout the Southeast who reported directly to him. Many of these men developed familial connections in their respective posts so that by the Revolution they enjoyed many of the same local social and political relationships as did their American counterparts. By the early 1770s, for instance, there were agents in Cherokee and Chickasaw towns, at least two in Creek Country, and occasionally one or two further south in East Florida.[22] The most important two were John McIntosh and David Taitt, both of whom Stuart positioned in Creek Country and both of whom had long histories of their own in the region. Not as much is known about McIntosh as Taitt, although the former and his brother, Roderick, shared a Scottish lineage that dated back to the founding of Georgia, and John reportedly "was the ancestor of both red and white men." He was a Chickasaw agent before Stuart sent him into Creek Country, and his strong advocacy of strict colonial control over the deerskin trade and against traders had, at times, made him deeply unpopular locally. After his appointment, however, McIntosh made his headquarters in Chehaw, and many Flint River and Hitchiti headmen quickly took a liking to him.[23]

As for Taitt, Stuart appointed him a commissary in 1772 and sent him to Little Tallassee, where he also became a friend to Emistisiguo. Yet Taitt's connections went well beyond Emistisiguo's own influence. Also a Scottish immigrant, he had served as a surveyor in West Florida as early as 1764. More importantly, however, by his appointment in Creek Country he had a Creek wife and a child, and a claim to nearly five thousand acres of land along the northern border of West Florida, making him tied to the region as deeply socially and politically as any trader. Taitt was also a strong proponent of imperial control in the Southeast, and very quickly after his appointment he gained a reputation as a bitter opponent of traders like Galphin and Rae, whose machinations, he complained, had a destabilizing impact on the region. This was clear when he struggled against Galphin, Rae, and their agents during the Ceded Lands debacle, and although ultimately unsuccessful, he gained enormous respect from Creek headmen for defending Creek sovereignty in the face of the increasingly aggressive traders.[24]

The sweeping tour of Creek Country he made at Stuart's behest in 1772 only further deepened Taitt's influence in the region. For months he dined, danced, smoked tobacco, and shared many a black drink in what seemed like every town in Creek Country, and he sat in councils with various influential headmen as a welcomed representative of Stuart and of colonial authority. This was particularly so in the Upper Country, where he conversed both in private and in council with headmen in both Tallassee communities, the Hickory Ground, Tuckabatchee, Cooloome, Muclassee, Hookchoie, and Hillaubee, where he was received and treated with tremendous respect. Even at the northern limits of the Upper Country he found friends at Natchez and Aubecoochee. He was "very kindley received by the head men" of Natchez, who "told me to look on myself as being amongst my friends and not to be afraid of anything, for their fire was the same as Charlestown fire and they never had spilt the blood of any white man."[25]

Because of their strong political and personal connections, both McIntosh and Taitt made the British position in Creek Country as strong as that of their American counterparts. Lastly, there was Patrick Tonyn, the governor of East Florida. From his station in St. Augustine he conversed frequently with the Creek communities at the extreme south of Creek Country, around the confluence of the Flint and Chattahoochee rivers, further south along the Apalachicola River, and into north-central Florida. He enjoyed a particularly warm relationship with the Cowkeeper of the Seminoles, who were only a few days' ride from the city gates. The two conversed frequently, and Cowkeeper and various other leading Seminoles were regulars in the town and at the garrison.[26]

Colonial officials like Stuart, McIntosh, Taitt, and Tonyn, positioned to counter influential and meddlesome trading men like Galphin and Rae, and then scores of traders or hirelings doing their own thing, made Creek Country a very politically messy place. Traders were the source of overlapping economic agreements, political alliances, and personal relationships, all of which underscored the importance of the community in Creek Country. They also, however, had a destabilizing tendency among neighboring communities. Networks of competing, localized alliances did not serve to unite individual communities into something larger as the Revolutionary War intensified. Instead, they tugged communities in different directions, revealing how the autonomous nature of Creek politics at times made for deeply fragmented Creek politics. Emistisiguo, for instance, would remain perhaps the firmest British ally in the Upper Country throughout the war, the product of his long and close relationship with Stuart. Taitt also enjoyed a good relationship with him, as well as with the Beaver Tooth King of nearby Tuckabatchee. On the other hand, the Handsome Fellow and then the White Lieutenant of Oakfuskee would keep strong American ties because of the Rae brothers, while the brothers' and Galphin's trading ties to Tallassees were strong as well. This essentially tore the Upper Country in half as one community clung to British alliances while, close by, another embraced Americans.

In the Lower Country things were potentially even more complicated. Galphin was an inexorable force based out of Coweta because of his connections, but between Stuart, McIntosh, and Tonyn, British colonial officials had a strong presence in nearby Chehaw, Hitchiti, and Seminole communities. In 1775, for instance, Galphin approached the Cusseta King and claimed that he had replaced Stuart as superintendent in the Southeast. This was too bold a move even for Galphin, and the allegations were met with apprehension and denial; Stuart's ties were simply too strong in Cusseta to be severed so quickly.[27] Even some of Galphin's closest allies were unprepared to simply drop all communications with Stuart, while others friendlier to McIntosh quickly rebuffed the advance. The nuances and complexities of pre-Revolutionary Creek politics all but ensured that when forced to choose whether to assist the American or British war effort, Creeks would not do so in a single voice.

That multiplicity of voices was a defining quality of Creek political, cultural, and economic systems, shaped by European interaction for generations previous to the Revolutionary era. The arrival and presence of Europeans was, in fact, a seminal moment in the ethnogenesis of Creeks as a people. Previous to a sustained European contact, in the fifteenth century, the Southeast was dominated not by decentralized and politically autonomous communities but by sprawling and densely populated Mississippian chiefdoms. Each chiefdom represented a ranked society, where elites maintained power through religious ideologies, clan structures, control over prestige items, diplomacy, and warfare. They were distinguished foremost physically by the existence of massive mound structures but were also tied together culturally, politically, and economically into what historians and anthropologists consider the southeastern ceremonial complex. In the decades after contact, however, the chiefdoms were subjected to relentless waves of disease and an intense commercial slave-raiding culture supported by Europeans, all of which drove most of those societies to collapse. Ultimately the destruction of the chiefdoms gave rise to the formation of recombinant, coalescent societies, which included Creeks and Choctaws to the west, Cherokees to the northeast, and many others in the Southeast, like Chickasaws, Catawbas, and Tuscaroras. The social, religious, and economic structures of coalescent societies reflected the flexible, fluid, and inclusive qualities that were needed to incorporate many different people that shared sometimes tenuous religious, cultural, social, physical, or even linguistic similarities.[28]

Creek communities embodied the autonomy of coalescence. Entire groups of emigrants, including Hitchitis, Yuchis, Shawnees, Natchez, and Alabamas, had a presence in Creek Country, yet they spoke different languages and retained stubbornly distinct identities.[29] They functioned in loosely defined political and organizational systems; otherwise, they were communities that were in fact very different, and they acted differently. Several overlapping cultural traditions formed a sort of cultural glue that mitigated the many disparities that had the potential to put neighbors at odds with each other. Clans, for instance, represented family groups that stretched back to the creation of the Native world. Members of a single clan, like the Wind or Panther clan, stretched from the Upper to the Lower Country and could be found in almost every community. That meant that no matter where a Creek man or woman was, he or she could always find family, whether real or fictive. Kinship groups frequently lived together in a community but members married into different clans, creating webs of real and imagined relations that spanned Creek Country and connected people who otherwise might have little in common.[30] More examples of common Creek cultural traditions included white versus red moieties, the Green Corn or Busk ceremony, and reciprocal relationships like gift giving and blood vengeance. These were culturally driven traditions, representing inclusive forces that drew people together when, politically and economically, they frequently acted independently of each other.[31]

Political and economic autonomy, tempered by inclusive cultural forces, was an acceptable and even advantageous diplomatic alchemy that, whether intended or not, benefited Creeks tremendously for much of the eighteenth century. Community leaders and others claiming intercommunity authority, including notable Creek men like Brims, Malatche, and the Mortar, enjoyed the ability to manipulate Spanish, French, and British colonial forces, many times simultaneously, to gain what they wanted. Colonial forces competed with each other for Creek allies, and community leaders were only too happy to engage them, many times on their own terms. Community leaders sometimes did so while proclaiming a sense of commonality, but sometimes did not; regardless, they were able to negotiate favorably with their European counterparts because the latter groups were too weak to exert their own will in the region.[32] Not until the emergence of state-level expansionists during the Revolutionary War did that regional calculus see fundamental change.

With the French option gone and the Spanish option along the Gulf Coast severely limited, all Creeks now faced the same mounting pressure from Americans and local Georgians on the one hand and British authorities on the other, and as the Revolutionary struggle intensified the stakes grew as well. Each community continued to respond differently, as they had for generations, yet in the context of a much larger and clearer struggle, the choice was more binary than Creeks would have appreciated, and cultural traditions had a hard time slowing the centrifugal force created by the decisions of local headmen. In short, Creeks relied on cultural traditions of inclusion and cohesion to mitigate political differences, but in the stress of the Revolution, communities increasingly struggled to find commonality when political and economic forces began pulling them apart.

At first that effect was slight; early in the struggle neither British nor American agents asked their Creek allies to do anything more than stay out of what was essentially a political dispute.[33] The two began to intensify their rhetoric as the political dispute increasingly became a military one, and it was clear that sooner or later, everyone in Creek Country would have to choose sides. Stuart explained the importance of Creek involvement to his superior, Thomas Gage, warning him that the importance of "the friendship of the Indian Nations in this district will be great." He had to "strengthen the hands of all my officers" in order to counter "the emissaries of the malcontents," who by this point included Galphin, Rae, and most of their subordinates.[34] In an attempt to do that, Taitt spoke to groups of Yuchis, Lower Eufalas, Cussetas, and Apalachicolas at an Apalachicola village deep in the Lower Country, urging them not to heed any rebel talks. He did so at the behest of Stuart, who ordered him to "frustrate the machinations" of Galphin and anyone else the Americans intended to send. Stuart likewise wrote chiefs of the Cowetas, Abihkas, and Alabamas directly, in missives that coursed their way through both the Upper and Lower countries.[35]

Despite the early British attempts to discredit him, Galphin proved an able adversary, and he quickly made gains for the Americans. He delivered powerful talks that wound through the Upper Country at the same time a talk came from Wright and Stuart, and they immediately produced a fissure between communities. A British faction emerged, no doubt led by Little Tallassees and perhaps Tuckabatchees, who exerted "all there interest to bringe the rest of the nation to there way of thinking." They were unable to bring around several pro-American neighbors, however, who stubbornly insisted on hearing the American talks—a group almost certainly led by

Oakfuskees.[36] Galphin's talks were well received in the Lower Country as well, which was not surprising. A group of headmen, mostly Cowetas, were expected at his home at Silver Bluff by the end of October 1775, and Galphin vowed that he would "forfit [his] living" to keep them happy and, above all else, peaceable. Later he reported confidently that his interest in the Lower Country "was so great, that it was not in the power of any man to set them upon us if I opposed it." Sempoyaffie of the Cowetas, for example, refused to see Taitt when he requested his presence, while the Ooseoochee Mico seemed uneasy around him. "There seems a coolness among the headmen to me not usual among them," Taitt complained. Perhaps the Americans had already turned them, he worried. In the wake of Galphin's talks that seemed to be the case, and Sempoyaffie, Blue Salt of Cusseta, the Pumpkin King of Hitchiti, and even a Chehaw headman decided on a more neutral stance, which came to the dismay of both Stuart and Taitt, who had worked hard to win them over. Rae worked similarly in the Upper Country, creating intrigue there was well. He, along with Joseph Cornells of Tuckabatchee, traveled to Abihka with trade gifts while Taitt arrived at Tuckabatchee almost simultaneously. Indeed, while the Mad Dog of Tuckabatchee quickly declared himself a firm British partisan his community was in reality split, and both British and American agents were aggressively courting nearby headmen, setting the stage for further confrontation.[37]

Calls for direct participation in the war intensified when Stuart and Tonyn convened a meeting with several warriors and headmen from the Lower Country on the St. John's River in East Florida. In a ceremony marked with pomp and celebration, including the Eagle Tail dance, the superintendent and governor met several influential headmen, including the Long Warrior of the Seminoles, the Pumpkin King, and Kalique, the Chehaw Mico. "Set aside with detestation the mischievous machinations of the vile associated rebel committees," Tonyn pressed.[38] Kalique responded favorably; although a number of them had already received several American talks, he assured both Stuart and Tonyn, they had dismissed them and would continue to do so. It was reported, in fact, that because of the talk from Taitt, many of the surrounding communities had publicly vowed to listen to no one other than Stuart and to carry any unauthorized agents away in irons.[39] One headman, "one of the principal chief men of the Creek Nation," Tonyn was pleased to announce, confirmed that "all the red people were now the King's People, the same as the people of England," and were ready to assist them in any way they could.[40]

Despite the relative success of the St. John's council from a British perspective, the Lower Country was still very much divided. Although the Pumpkin King of Hitchiti, the Chehaw Mico, and several Seminole chiefs were present and very receptive to British overtures, representatives from Cusseta and Coweta towns, the largest and arguably the most powerful along the Chattahoochee, were conspicuously absent. Galphin, of course, was the reason for that absence. His influence in both communities was undeniable, and headmen in Cusseta never wavered in support of the American cause because of it. The situation in Coweta towns was apparently a bit more complicated, and several headmen still managed to assure Taitt that they would not allow American talks or even traders to enter the region by way of their trading paths. If anyone did, they would seize them.[41] That promise, while cautious, is intriguing. Galphin had direct ties to Coweta towns and controlled many of the traders operating there. Yet Coweta leader Escochobey, or the Young Lieutenant, was known to keep outside options open, including Spanish ones. He conversed with Spanish visitors along the Gulf Coast frequently and had visited Cuba personally. Although he surely shared ties with the Americans, he also had friends elsewhere. Also intriguing were the kin connections he shared with Emistisiguo in Little Tallassee. At certain times during the Ceded Lands crisis, Emistisiguo attempted to exert his authority in the region through that avenue, and he would continue to do so over the course of the Revolution. Then there were stronger, more traditional Creek cultural influences. Coweta communities traditionally led nearby neighbors in times of war. They were considered red towns—rather than white, peaceful towns—according to a Creek cultural classification referred to as a moiety. The leadership position of their headmen as war leaders would naturally have made Cowetas more responsive to the Revolution's calls for violence. For several reasons, then, including the willingness to juggle competing colonial powers, reliance on cultural traditions, and family ties, Coweta emerged as a battleground in the Lower Country, just as Tuckabatchee was growing more contested further to the north.

In an increasingly discordant environment Galphin exerted all the authority he could in order to rally communities to the American cause. To do that, he knew that a steady supply of trade goods was necessary. At first the Continental Congress, in a strange and unhelpful move, objected. Instead of financing a strong trade Congress banned it altogether, thinking such a move would somehow influence headmen's allegiances positively, or at least would keep arms and ammunition out of volatile communities. That was not a particularly shrewd calculation, as Galphin quickly made known. "We are now just like a parcel of carpenters set to work to build a house without one single tool," he would later write.[42] Such a decision would drive even the friendliest headmen to the British, he warned. Trade was what "keeps them in our interest," and without it, "they have great encouragement to go to the Floridas." Galphin was confident he could secure the allegiance of most of the Lower Country, but only if he had the support of the Congress. He might even be able to turn headmen further to the north to a more neutral position, so that even they would "do us no hurt." But if the Congress continued to alienate friendly communities, even unknowingly, by denying them trade, the consequences would be disastrous. Creek warriors would turn to Stuart at Pensacola, "& then we may expect an Indian war." When no more than forty straggling Creeks—a war party or two—could empty the frontier and make Georgia settlers flee, he wondered aloud, think "what must the whole nation do." His appeals evidently worked; soon he arrived in the Lower Country, presumably at Coweta, with wagonloads of goods as well as more supportive talks from the rebel Americans.[43]

Galphin's early victory in the Continental Congress brought him immediate returns. His talks were widely circulated, and despite the resolution of some headmen to reject them, including from Hitchitis and Chehaws, others grew more receptive. His invitation to meet at a conference in Augusta, for instance, was favorably received by a surprising number of communities. Taitt immediately left his post in the Upper Country, where the towns were disposed "to a man" toward the British, and traveled south to Chehaw to try his hand again at frustrating the American designs. There, with two other headmen, he assisted McIntosh in delivering a strong talk, hoping to drive Galphin out and reverse his fortunes. The effort was only a partial success, and a large contingency of Cowetas, as well as a few Cusseta headmen and even some Hitchitis, failed to give positive assurances that they would not travel to meet the Americans at Augusta. Taitt admitted to Tonyn that he had sent others, including Seminoles, down to St. Augustine, just so they would not be "drawn down to Augusta," where they might be turned "by some of the Rebel Agents."[44]

Galphin's talks, once absorbed, proved deeply divisive, demonstrating the power of traders and their influence on local politics. One warrior— perhaps a Coweta or a Chehaw—tried to assure Taitt that most communities in the Lower Country did not take the Americans' talks seriously and were only planning to go to Augusta out of curiosity.

Some headmen might even be able to relate the happenings back to the British when they returned. These assurances did little to assuage Stuart's apprehensions; he promptly dispatched a posse of friendly Yuchis out after a group of headmen that began the journey. Not even the intervention of neighboring headmen could dissuade the Cowetas and Cussetas from pursuing their own path, however, and they could not be turned back. They pushed on to Augusta "in spite of every argument" Taitt made to dissuade them—a victory for the Americans and a frustrating setback for Stuart.[45] Furthermore, Georgia officials did not disappoint Galphin and made the most of the visit, pressing the headmen aggressively to have Stuart and his emissaries expelled from their neighborhoods. There had been "nothing but disturbance" ever since they arrived, went one talk.[46] Although the Georgia letters still ostensibly stressed neutrality, the effect they had on Creek Country was terribly disruptive. By the time the Cussetas returned home, for instance, they constituted a powerful pro-American force in the Lower Country that could not be bargained with by McIntosh or Stuart, and they would not consent to fight at any price.

Meanwhile, the Handsome Fellow of Oakfuskee, the Beaver Tooth King of Tuckabatchee, and the Chavaucley Warrior of the Half-Way House were at Augusta as well, belying Taitt's assertions that the Upper Country was pro-British "to a man." Worse yet for Taitt, when the headmen returned from Augusta their accounts of the talks threw the region "into great confusion." And into both the Upper and Lower countries spread follow-up invitations, this time inviting headmen to Savannah. Those talks made it all the way south to Yuchi towns, which in the past had been some of the staunchest pro-British communities in the region. There traders John Miller and Timothy Barnard, once American allies but now apparently sympathetic to the British, came across them and passed them along to Taitt and McIntosh. Quickly Taitt recruited East Florida ranger Thomas Brown and the two met with a group of Chehaws, hoping to prevent others in the neighborhood from agreeing to the trip. Despite their best efforts, however, the Blue Salt of Cusseta took a sizable group of about sixty Cusseta and Coweta headmen and warriors to the Georgia coast. Taitt immediately ordered a group of friendly Upper Creeks under Emistisiguo to cut them off at the Oconee River but, in another twist, the Handsome Fellow from Oakfuskee promptly appeared and convened a conference over the Augusta talks. This well-executed stall tactic worked, preventing a large portion of Emistisiguo's men from proceeding and allowing the Cusseta and Coweta groups to make their way east.[47]

There were now American talks in the Lower Country as strong as the ones Stuart and Tonyn had given in East Florida, and competing ones in the Upper Country were creating friction there as well. Individual communities were absorbing Revolutionary rhetoric differently, and by 1776 the lines were growing clear. In the Upper Country, Emistisiguo and the Little Tallassees constituted the region's pro-British stronghold. Nearby, however, Oakfuskees, Big Tallassees, and Chavaucleys, or the Half-Way House communities, were staunch American partisans. Then there were Tuckabatchees, who were clearly split. Much of the remainder of the Upper Country, including Abihkas, Hookchoies, Cooloomees, and Hillaubees, favored British talks above American ones because of the strong British presence there. British officials early began to entice Creeks to raid the frontiers, and according to one report in October, a party of East Florida Rangers, operating under Brown's leadership, passed through the region recruiting warriors. He reportedly raised close to two hundred volunteers from across the Upper Country "to come out with them against the frontiers," which supports the assertion that most communities, aside from Oakfuskees, Tuckabatchees, Chavaucleys, and Big Tallassees, were leaning toward the British.[48]

When Brown tried recruiting in the Lower Country, on the other hand, he was disappointed to find American support there much stronger. Headmen declared that "they could not think of going against their friends," who had "given them such good talk[s]." Furthermore, they warned, if he continued to drum up support for raiding then they would retaliate on settlers in British West Florida "and give them war upon every quarter."[49] The Lower Country was a contested and downright unfriendly place, Brown soon realized. Smaller communities on the lower Chattahoochee, including Hitchitis, Ooseoochees, and Chehaws, were strongly associated with McIntosh and Pensacola. The Fat King of Cusseta, as well as the Blue Salt and Sempoyaffie of Coweta, however, were strong American partisans, while Escochobey embraced American, British, and even Spanish talks at times.[50] Further to the southeast, British support grew stronger as communities grew nearer to St. Augustine. Headmen including the Oconee King, who held "great influence among the wild people [Seminoles]," the Mikasuki King, and the Cowkeeper all embraced Tonyn.[51]

Galphin proved that he was a tremendous American asset, and his successes teasing headmen to Augusta and Savannah were impressive. Unfortunately for him and for the larger American effort, however, local Georgians undid much of his hard work.[52] Galphin's efforts at Augusta were entirely undone, for instance, because locals were either unable or unwilling to give satisfaction for various Creeks they had lately killed along the frontier. These were demands made by friendly communities in Creek Country who had hunters insulted, attacked, or killed, and if their demands were not satisfied, Americans stood to lose them as allies. That was clear by the earliest years of the war. In 1776 Coweta headmen still chafed at the killing of one of their own, before the war, while the Tallassee King talked of "taking a party against the settlements of Georgia," supposedly to avenge the death of his wife and child at the hands of a rebel scouting party. A better example, perhaps, was the Chavaucley Warrior's demands. He also had lost kin and expected to get justice from Americans, one way or another. "You must give satisfaction for my relation, whom some of your People have killed," he warned, "or blood will be spill'd." If the murderer was executed things would "be straight as formerly," but the odds of that happening were slim. Galphin promised him it would be done and had a few headmen stay behind in Georgia to witness the supposed hanging. Instead, however, state authorities hung a separate murderer in an attempt to trick the Chavaucley Warrior, who was not duped. These and other diplomatic blunders were only a handful of the many insults Creeks endured at the hands of local Georgia settlers and state authorities, making their withdrawal from the American camp no surprise. Along with the Chavaucley Warrior, for instance, the Coweta chief Sempoyaffie began conversing with Stuart much more frequently, which was a significant reversal indeed. Numbers of Coweta warriors, once strong American allies, were now preparing to raid the Georgia frontiers, and not even Galphin's relations could make amends for the Georgians' treachery.[53] The strength of kin associations and the importance of blood vengeance were strong cultural forces in the region, working in this instance in 1776 to undermine Galphin's political victories.

As Coweta attitudes changed in favor of the British, it turns out they would have devastating implications. As Galphin's nephew and his representative in Coweta, David Holmes was an important American agent, brokering trade goods to several towns in the Lower Country from Savannah and Charlestown. He was instrumental in securing many Coweta and Cusseta towns to the American interest as late as 1776. Yet it appears he switched sides sometime in early 1777 and afterward was trading British supplies out of Pensacola. At first Tonyn distrusted Holmes and was convinced he was a spy who was still delivering Galphin's talks. This was a sentiment that Stuart seemed to share as well.[54] By 1778, however, Stuart had changed his mind and now considered Holmes a British asset. The trader had "a great deal of influence among the Indians" and personally offered his assistance in guiding a group from the Lower Country to the British at St. Marks, and then on to St. Augustine, when Tonyn called on them to help in the defense of the province. With him was fellow trader Timothy Barnard, who had also been in the employ of Galphin. Now, however, he was directing Creeks and Seminoles against Georgians as well. In the fall of 1778, the two arrived in St. Augustine with upwards of fifty warriors from various towns in the Lower Country and along the Florida border.[55]

Very few things could have caused such an abrupt defection of such serious consequence. There had been difficulties getting American goods in the past, surely, but Holmes was a well-connected trader and he had a commission from Congress. And all of that was in addition to his kin ties in the Lower Country, which were deep. The logistical issues he faced could not have been nearly dire enough to cause his withdrawal from the American cause, which brought with it the loss of so many Cowetas. His reversal, instead, was almost certainly a product of the local political situation among the Coweta towns in which he worked. Traders in his position, with close social and even familial ties to a community, abided by the decisions of its headmen; their allegiances flowed with the local political currents. To a man like Holmes concerns for financial stability, not to mention safety, hinged on his political decisions.[56] Although not directly, then, by affronting the Cowetas at Augusta Georgians had driven Holmes out of the American camp and into the outstretched arms of the British. Not only did Americans lose several powerful Coweta headmen, Georgians lost strong trading and diplomatic allies as well, which would reverberate throughout the Lower Country. Coweta war parties alone would have a devastating impact on Georgia's farms over the next few years, making the letdown at Augusta a true diplomatic catastrophe.[57]

Deteriorating relations between Creeks and Georgia state actors also routinely discredited American efforts to keep Creek communities neutral. It was an impossible task trying to convince headmen that Americans were friends of Creeks and attentive to their desires when state officials continued to make it clear they absolutely were not. Settlers constantly trespassed on Creek hunting lands, they attacked and killed Creek hunters at will, and instead of apologizing state legislators threatened invasion in response to Creek retaliation. All of that of course was in addition to the ongoing Ceded Lands debacle, which remained a tremendous source of Creek animosity. Stuart had known the struggle well; he had labored previously to get Creeks to forgive similar transgressions and to have headmen "look upon the English in a respectable and friendly light," but his efforts were "too often interrupted by little accidents chiefly from the behaviour of our frontier people."[58] Both Emistisiguo and Sempoyaffie had dealt with trespassers personally, and the former headman had complained in 1770 that it was no wonder "if red men forget talks if white people do so; for the talk was that white people should not hunt in their lands which were now full of them."[59] Years later, in 1774, little had changed. The "incessant requisitions for land affords matter of discontent and jealousy to all the Indian tribes," Stuart worried, "and that they cannot see our advances into the heart of their most valuable hunting grounds with pleasure."[60] By that time, at least, headmen were beginning to understand the distinction between men like Stuart and backcountry settlers. Angry Creeks were not interested in killing Englishmen, agent Alexander Cameron explained, but did not hesitate to attack "Virginians"—a term Creeks widely used to describe any backcountry settlers—who stole their horses and "settle upon their land."[61]

It was not long after that Stuart and other British authorities were freed of their obligation to keep locals and Creek hunters from each other's throats, and instead could now use headmen's anger at unscrupulous settlers to their benefit. Georgians wanted Creek lands and they could not be trusted, Stuart and his officers often warned headmen—warnings that were not lies. While British officials pushed for moderation Georgia surveyors and land speculators, backed by their local legislators, paused for no one, not even their own congressional representatives. With Revolutionary violence increasing and the neutrality of Creeks evermore critical, men like Galphin, American general Robert Howe, and Continental representative Henry Laurens, among others, viewed the Ceded Lands in particular as counterproductive to American interests and a potentially fatal move for Georgians locally. A single state's claims—dubious claims at best—were going to incite a general war with Creeks, they feared, to say nothing of undoing Galphin's delicate and expensive peace overtures. But no strong American authority capable of countering locals stepped into the vacuum created by Stuart's departure, and no authority existed under the Articles of Confederation either to generate a meaningful Native policy or to control state governments. In the absence of that power, confrontation along the Creek-Georgia frontier escalated quickly.

At times the actions of locals could be confounding, particularly to men like Galphin, whose mandate was to conciliate and even recruit Native communities to the American cause. By their own admission settlers and speculators were antagonizing even the most peaceful Creek communities, hoping to use conflict to seize even more land than they already claimed. "The people upon the ceded land have killed another *Creek*," Galphin complained in late 1776, "and say they will kill them wherever they meet them." Because of those attacks, his work had just about ground to a halt by the fall of 1776. He could find neither a Georgia courier willing to carry his talks west to Creek towns nor a Creek one willing to travel east. Evidently, both cared too deeply for their lives to risk journeying into such unwelcoming territory. Galphin, however, was quick to point the finger east. Georgians were openly threatening to invade Creek Country and kill whatever Creek they could lay their hands on. He had for a time kept a handful of trustworthy young Creek men at Silver Bluff as messengers, but ultimately he was forced to send them home because "some of the people upon the ceded land said they would come down and kill them." It was a hard task indeed, he complained, "to keep the *Creeks* our friends when both our enemies and the people that should be our friends want us to be at war with them." The situation in the region was so tense that Galphin requested even the friendliest headmen not cross the Oconee, under any circumstances, until he could make sure they would be safe.[62]

Talks from Georgia about invading Creek Country only increased through 1776, further revealing how difficult Galphin's task was, negotiating for peace against the wishes of his own citizens. It was a ridiculous and dangerous position that he, along with other American authorities like General Howe, repeatedly disparaged. Such "zealots" for a Creek war, Howe lamented, did not understand what it would do to them. The backcountry would be utterly destroyed and Creeks would raid all the way to Savannah. Only an army of regular forces would be able to push them back, and South Carolinians and Virginians would probably watch their overly aggressive counterparts to the south burn rather than agree to such an undertaking. What, he asked, "in the name of Heaven is to become of you [Georgia] should you be hurried into this measure? The answer to this question is dreadful to think of." Instead, he pressed wholeheartedly to have "spirited and highly penal" acts put into law threatening "individuals who by wanton injuries were endeavouring to involve [Georgia] in a war that would probably end in the utter ruin of it."[63] Howe, along with Galphin and Laurens, lobbied with increasing vigor to cut off Georgia surveyors and sooth angry Creek headmen, but it was clear they represented the minority.[64]

Despite their best efforts, escalating violence over the Ceded Lands and Georgians' unwillingness to give up on their claims was one of the major reasons Creeks turned away from the American war effort in 1776 and 1777. Georgian and Continental officer Lachlan McIntosh angrily lectured a group of headmen that Stuart and "other bad men" had convinced them to steal, to "set our houses on fire, and do every thing in their power to make us angry."[65] McIntosh's aggressive tone did little to soothe agitated Creek headmen, however, who responded with angry words of their own and a commitment to more violence. Exchanges like those, Galphin repeatedly protested, were doing more damage than Stuart's talks ever could. After a particularly devastating set of Creek raids in October 1777, for instance, he explained that "all Stuarts goods should not have sent them upon us if we had not killed there people," referring to an attack by local Georgians on Creeks on the Ceded Lands earlier that year.[66] In the spring of 1778 he raised similar complaints. With more Georgia surveyors about, he had resorted to trickery to keep Creeks from the Upper Country from massacring them. When a group of warriors confronted him about seeing the unmistakable marks of recent surveys on their lands, Galphin assured them that it was really a ruse by Stuart, who was creating fake surveying lines "all bout in there land to make them believe it was us that was running out there land." That excuse seemed to be holding warriors off for the time being but Galphin knew it was a lie, and he took pains to warn Henry Laurens that if the headmen ever got to the truth—that it was indeed the work of Georgia surveyors and that he could not stop them—it "wood not be in our power to keep them long in our interest."[67]

Galphin, forced by deteriorating relations along the frontier and having recently been resupplied by both Americans and the French, made renewed attempts to court Creeks to the American position. He penned another round of invitations in the spring of 1777 that promised strong talks and plenty of trade gifts, and he managed to bring another group of headmen to Silver Bluff, led by a sizable contingency of Cusseta headmen. There, with the American and French goods stacked high and with the boldest pro-American promises yet, he once again made strong gains. His successes proved that offers of trade stability and political neutrality were what many Creek communities still wanted to hear. American talks were listened to "by many of the Lower Creeks and they began to form a party and to debauch the minds of many," Stuart lamented, threatening again to throw the allegiances of a number of communities back into question.[68]

Again, however, Galphin's considerable gains were undone when groups of Georgia militiamen brazenly descended on Lower Creek towns, threatening the very Cussetas being entertained at Silver Bluff. The militiamen should have focused their attention not on the closest Creeks to them, which in their case happened to be the friendliest, but those further down the Chattahoochee, where communities were much more unfriendly to the American cause. There a group of Chehaws heard of the attack on their Cusseta neighbors, and they immediately determined "to strike a blow" in order to "fix the balancing resolutions of their countrymen," even if they still clung to American talks. Chehaw war parties promptly marched into Georgia and routed a group of mounted militia. As they returned a sizable British pack train lumbered down the trading path carrying "a plentiful supply of goods." The culmination of those events—another attack by unscrupulous Georgia forces on friendly Creek communities, successful raids by British partisans, and the fulfilling of British trade promises—combined almost at once to discredit Galphin's talks and keep more communities from taking the American talks seriously.[69]

Despite the setback, the latest turn of events did not dash American hopes altogether, and Creek Country remained deeply divided. Stuart still feared that the Americans' continued presence was enough "to give much plague and trouble to my officers" and foment what seemed to be a simmering distrust of every non-Creek in the region.[70] In fact, only two months after his last attempt was undone by the Georgia militiamen, the aging but persistent Galphin prepared for a third conference. He held nothing back in his latest attempt, coordinating with all the traders under his influence and stockpiling as much trade material in his warehouses as he could. And he succeeded yet again, bringing headmen from both the Upper and Lower countries to Silver Bluff. His successes there eclipsed all previous attempts, but they also generated the deepest divisions that Creek Country had perhaps ever seen.

Reports of the upcoming conference spread through Creek Country in April and May 1777. While Sempoyaffie of the Cowetas and Emistisiguo were reported to be "staunch in their promises" as steadfast supporters of the British, they seemed to be the only ones, and several curious headmen from both the Upper and Lower countries traveled to see what Galphin had for them this time. In addition to a number of Cussetas, the Chehaw Warrior and the Pumpkin King of Hitchiti came as well, representing a powerful bloc in the Lower Country that had been strongly British in the past. The Handsome Fellow of Oakfuskee and the Old Tallassee King were present from the Upper Country, which was less surprising. Taitt, who was then in Little Tallassee, attempted to speak directly with the Handsome Fellow in the hopes of persuading him not go, and he sent Sempoyaffie and two others to persuade the Old Tallassee King similarly. All of these attempts failed, however, and Taitt was "really at a loss what to do or advise the Indians to do for the best." There was nothing the rebels would not do "to gain them to their side." John McIntosh also tried to convince groups of headmen not to attend, but he was only able to prevent a handful from departing, and even then "by a great deal of trouble." Cussetas in particular were not to be dissuaded. McIntosh sent out a mixed posse from the Lower Country to "prevent them going down," but they would not be stopped.[71] Instead, the rift between Cusseta and Coweta widened. While Cussetas traveled west Coweta headmen rallied behind the British, even requesting the construction of a British fort in their neighborhood from which to counter the American talks. An onlooker at Pensacola fretted about the situation, noting that the Creeks were "much divided, so that it is not certain what part they may take as Golphin by promises and his interest keeps up a party in that nation."[72]

According to American reports, upwards of five hundred Creeks were on hand at Silver Bluff to hear Galphin's talk. While that was almost certainly an exaggerated American figure, even a fraction of the number would have been an impressive showing, considering the continued danger posed by nearby Georgians. If the reports were true, there were plenty of headmen present to ensure that the talks, if they were good, would be widely circulated. And they were apparently very good. With renewed and downright surprising vigor Galphin redoubled his assurances that the Americans were winning the war, adding that they were now allies with both the French and the Spanish and that everyone would soon be united against the British. From there the talks grew more aggressive. Galphin and other commissioners demanded that the chiefs "drive all the beloved men"—meaning British partisans and commissioners—out of Creek Country. The talks were strong indeed and evidently well received; many of the headmen "went back well pleased."[73]

As headmen returned home the true weight of Galphin's recent success came into focus. Groups of Cussetas and Yuchis, closest to Silver Bluff, were the first to return home. When they did the situation in that region deteriorated rapidly. Tonyn received ominous reports from

Philatouchi and his nephew Perryman of Hitchiti that not only were Tallassees, Oakfuskees, and Cussetas militarizing, even a handful of Cowetas expressed interest in the American talks. After enjoying "amazing quantities of rum" at Silver Bluff, according to another report, the Cussetas promised that when they returned home they would call councils to deliberate on and spread the American talks. The Cusseta King in particular promised "to get all the different towns" in the Lower Country to join the American cause. Also among them was Hopoithle Mico, who was the Old Tallassee King's son and who also went by the name of the Tallassee King. He was also a headman of the Half-Way House and an emerging leader in the Upper Country, and he promised to act likewise in his neighborhood. Few could deny, in fact, that Galphin's latest effort brought Americans spectacular returns. In Savannah, Governor Wright worriedly reported that about one hundred Upper Country Creeks alone had "entered into a kind of treaty with the rebels," while Taitt and Stuart struggled unsuccessfully to play the talks down.[74]

The success of the American talks produced more confrontation among neighbors than most Creeks had probably ever seen. American and British lines were shifting rapidly, and headmen were beginning to oppose each other with more aggressive words. With the Handsome Fellow now as strong a Georgia partisan as ever, he and Emistisiguo were now inveterate enemies, and they openly talked of assassinating each other. In the Lower Country, Cussetas threatened not simply to expel McIntosh but to kill and scalp him; those were strong words from Cussetas, suggesting that they were beginning to abandon their neutral stance for one more militantly American. Both McIntosh and Taitt did what they could to downplay the threats, remaining confident they could still count many Creeks among their friends. The Handsome Fellow and the Cusseta King alone were firmly attached to Galphin, they were sure, "whose influence in the creek nation is very small" and who had "no power out of their own villages." Taitt, in fact, was convinced that all of the Coweta towns could be depended upon and that they, with the Ooseoochee, Broken Arrow, and Hitchiti towns, were "eager to go against" the Georgia settlements. Nevertheless, even he had to admit that the situation in the Lower Country clearly had taken a turn for the worse.[75]

More aggressive American talks soon followed. The British all told lies "in order to get you Innocent Men to fight Battles," Galphin charged, "which they dare not shew [show] their faces in. . . . You must be sure ['tis] no regard they have for you." In a word, he and other Americans concluded, "I see no method for you to save your Country from ruin, than to *Kill* those men, who the King sends amongst you, to make you War against your Brothers." So much for the American calls for neutrality, Galphin's most recent talks demonstrated. More surprising, perhaps, was the degree to which once neutral Creeks embraced the new more violent message. A group of headmen, led mostly by Oakfuskees, responded not with words of caution but by assuring Galphin that if Stuart or any other British agents sent warriors out to the frontiers to attack Georgians, they would retaliate by sending war parties to kill British settlers in St. Augustine and Pensacola.[76] Meanwhile in the Lower Country the situation had deteriorated to the point where both McIntosh and Taitt now feared for their safety. The latter penned Tonyn directly from Chehaw, warning that things were "both very dangerous, and disagreeable here at present."[77]

On the heels of Galphin's talks, a group of Oakfuskees and Cussetas accepted another American invitation to visit Georgia and Charleston, late in the fall of 1777. There they toured the coastal forts and were treated to a military parade, all of which they found encouraging. The elderly Handsome Fellow died on the road back to Oakfuskee, but a group of Cussetas and Hookchoies traveling with him were determined to spread the American message and made extravagant claims in his name. Upon returning to their villages they went so far as to promise the assassination of any British traders they could find.[78] They convened a number of times, where their "poison spread to many more and further than was expected," in the words of a now very worried John Stuart. Threats turned to actions when a group of Cusseta warriors appeared at McIntosh's post at Chehaw with a view to murder him. He found shelter with a number of Coweta and Chehaw friends who had "refused to listen to the rebels" and who "guarded his house for several days and nights." Finally they convinced him to flee to Pensacola, and a group of warriors personally escorted him there. Taitt, at Little Tallassee, was similarly threatened, along with his assistant and his interpreters. Galphin had put bounties on their heads, and a group of Oakfuskees were determined to collect—they wanted his scalp as well as Emistisiguo's. Only the young Alexander McGillivray, whom Stuart had recently made a deputy agent, averted bloodshed by physically moving between the two parties and pushing the Oakfuskees away. Stuart, hearing of these threats, quickly ordered all of his agents out of Creek Country—a move that only further emboldened the pro-American parties. The Tallassee King, representing Half-Way House and Tallassee communities, sent belts out to the

Cherokees and Choctaws celebrating the removal of the British from Creek Country and urging unity in the American cause.[79]

At that point Americans viewed Galphin's latest efforts as a decisive stroke. General Robert Howe penned George Washington that because of Galphin's "unwearied" exertions, Creeks seemed "at present to promise peace."[80] They "have at last declared in our favor," one man exclaimed. Galphin himself was sure that he had "spared no pains nor left no stones unturned" in June 1778, while months later he remained convinced by talks from the Handsome Fellow and the Tallassee King, and even from Fine Bones of the Cowetas, that although "no stone has been left unturned" by the British, he had "got the better of them." There was "not a white man from pensacolo or Augustin" in Creek Country, and now only Americans were trading there.[81] The reports must have given Galphin great pleasure. When Taitt, McIntosh, and the other British commissioners left, it was reported, the British agents warned headmen that "they should receive no more goods from Pensacola." Creeks wanted no more goods, the headmen replied, and "they had goods enough in Charles Town." Both Taitt and McIntosh had been "compelled to fly to Pensacola," and groups of warriors were out "to take the scalps of the commissaries and friends of government." This was in addition to "a very considerable reward for the scalp of any beloved man," like the strongly pro-British chief Emistisiguo.[82] The turn of events seemed, by 1778, to be complete.

But Galphin's successes, however impressive they were, were nowhere near complete. Although his talks had militarized a number of communities and precipitated the retreat of British commissioners, they had not won over all of Creek Country. Several headmen still had strong British ties, and they responded to aggressive American overtures with moves of their own. Groups of Cowetas under Sempoyaffie were as militantly anti-Georgian as they had ever been. They, together with the Mad Dog of Tuckabatchee and a gang of Hookchoies with whom Sempoyaffie shared kinship connections, headed off together to raid into Georgia as a direct response to Galphin's actions.[83] Emistisiguo, at the head of "ten towns," declared that they had "no hand in the disorders committed by the Oakfuskees" and were even preparing to "harass the rebels immediately on their return home." Others, mostly Cowetas, enraged by the "late behavior" of the Oakfuskees and Cussetas, fell upon the northern frontiers of Georgia with terrifying effect. More Hookchoies, with Kialijees and Alabamas, were soon moving east for the same purpose.[84]

A British partisan group not only remained but was active. Together, the raiders from the corners of Creek Country harassed whatever Georgia groups they could find, while Escochobey traveled from Coweta to see Taitt and offer him his assistance.[85] For his part Stuart answered Galphin's bounties with bounties of his own, including one on Galphin, dead or alive. There was also a bounty on the newly arrived American deputies, including Daniel McMurphy, who was at that time stationed at Oakfuskee. A war party quickly came for him and he barely escaped with his life. A group of Oakfuskees hid and protected him in a way not unlike the rescue British partisans performed on Taitt only months previous. Meanwhile, groups of British Rangers under Thomas Brown's direction, working with more friendly Creeks from Coweta and the Lower Country, set out to burn Galphin's property and store, and then to "ravage the frontier." They accomplished much of that, murdering "severall of our people," according to one Georgian. They also ambushed and mistakenly killed an acquaintance of Galphin's only miles from his home, thinking it was Galphin.[86] As those strings of threats and retaliatory raids throughout 1777 and 1778 demonstrated, plenty of British partisans remained in Creek Country, and they had no plans to stand aside as American talks rippled through the region. Little Tallassee, Tuckabatchee, Hookchoie, and Coweta headmen were radicalizing as they countered the movements of their pro-Georgia neighbors. Galphin's life was in danger as were all Americans in the region. Coweta and Cusseta towns were on the brink of civil war in the Lower Country, while Oakfuskees, Tuckabatchees, Big and Little Tallassees, and Chavaucleys were at each other's throats to the north. While Galphin had motivated a number of headmen to declare for the American cause, by doing so he had badly fractured Creek politics.

Americans added to the intensifying intercommunity conflict in Creek Country because they could not sustain the diplomatic victory Galphin had so recently achieved. National authorities could not control backcountry settlers and they failed, in the end, to offer the quality and flow of trading goods Galphin had promised. The American mission along the Creek-Georgia frontier collapsed much quicker than it had taken Galphin to build it, so that by the end of 1778 the vast majority of Creeks had again repostured and were again British partisans. Georgia settlers, as they had been in the past, were one of the primary reasons for that reversal. This time their careless attacks on Creeks did irreversible damage. "When every thing promised fair for peace," American John Lewis Gervais complained, "a few Georgia people have put us on the eve of war." After a Creek war party killed a militia officer on the Ceded Lands, another militia detachment retaliated by seizing ten uninvolved Creek deputies being treated by Galphin personally, on behalf of the Continental Congress, and imprisoning them in Augusta. The seizures were a "great insult" and an embarrassment to all Americans, Gervais complained. The headmen, who for all intents and purposes had been kidnapped, were technically ambassadors under the protection of the Congress, and they were seized from under the direct care of a Continental Commissioner of Indian Affairs.[87] Horrified by the reports and their implications, General Howe immediately issued a warrant for the arrest of the officers responsible. When the group, led by Captain John Dooley, refused to turn themselves in, Continental officer Samuel Elbert threatened to burn down the house they were holed up in and drag them all away in chains.[88]

It is not clear whether the men were ever arrested. They probably were not, but by that point their fate was almost irrelevant. Many in Creek Country were fuming after the seizure of so many headmen, who after all had been invited to Georgia, and several communities began to turn their backs on the American war effort.[89] Locals were unhinging "all we are doing," an elderly and despondent Galphin lamented. State authorities had also just apparently recommended surveying the Ceded Lands, and even the friendliest headmen were coming around to the realization that when British commissioners had warned them of the Americans' disreputable intentions, they were right. And those warnings in 1778 remained as accurate as ever. More Georgia authorities than ever were pushing for a Creek war, and reports suggested that they were going so far as personally threatening to kill Galphin for acting as an advocate of peace and neutrality.[90] That sort of madness was not lost on Savannah merchant Joseph Clay, who complained on multiple occasions that it was all he and others could do to keep the Georgia assembly from declaring war on Creeks, while at the very same time "these people as a Nation were giving us the most convincing proofs of their pacific disposition towards us." Some Georgians were going so far as tricking members of the state assembly into thinking that they could raise fifteen companies of militia and that the Continental Congress would pay for them. Of course there was no chance of that happening, as General Howe had made clear in the past, and it was obvious that plunder and enrichment were the true motives at work. If such nefarious characters got their way, it was obvious to Clay that "we must have been broke up as a state at once."[91] It was locals and local authorities, Galphin again warned Laurens, and not the

British, who were doing the most to destroy Creek-American relations, and if backcountry surveyors and settlers did not cease soon, "it will not be in my power to keep peace long." Although he had managed to that point to stem the bloodshed, Galphin was becoming convinced that he was fighting a losing battle against his own people, and it would not be long before they "would drive me and the Indians both to the Devil."[92]

Creek communities were also confronted by the logistical shortcomings of the American trade. American pack trains were irregular and Congress struggled to provide the goods that communities wanted. The complete loss of British support, followed by the inability of Americans to make up for it, added to the injury of local Georgians. Within months those letdowns put Creek headmen in a difficult and ultimately repentant situation. Soon they were asking to bring British commissioners back into their communities and promising to push the American replacements out.[93] Even the most recalcitrant headmen— Oakfuskees in particular—began to send representatives to Pensacola, offering apologies to Stuart for the actions of their young men. Stuart, along with Tonyn and other British commanders, moved quickly to capitalize on those reversals. They took an aggressive stance against the Americans, which was something they had struggled to do in the past. Although supportive, their talks were much sterner than before, making clear that they meant to use the Creek reversal to force as many headmen as they could away from Galphin and the Americans. In the Lower Country, Tonyn sent instructions "to upbraid those with ingratitude to His Majesty" and required a number of headmen to travel to St. Augustine personally before things could be made right.[94]

There, surrounded by friendly chiefs and warriors, and with strong words, Tonyn made groups of Cussetas, Cowetas, and others "promise to relinquish their engagements with Galphin," who was a lying, treacherous man.[95] Stuart acted likewise, stepping up his own efforts to solidify the British influence in Creek Country in the spring of 1778.[96] Although he was hesitant to use overly confrontational speech, he hosted groups of Oakfuskees, Tallassees, Cussetas, Hitchitis, and Apalachicolas at a conference in Pensacola, where he spoke in no uncertain terms to "remove any misunderstanding on account of their former behavior." He demanded that the headmen drop all contact with any rebels, "place their whole dependence upon supplies" from him and his agents, and not oppose any groups that offered to assist British troops militarily.[97] At the same time Coweta war parties, whose aggressive assaults on the frontiers were disrupting the Americans' abilities to distribute what little trade materials they had, continued undoing Galphin's promises and helped convince even the most disaffected headmen that the British were the safer choice.[98]

In March 1778, these demands destroyed whatever notion of Creek neutrality remained in the region. Several communities from the Lower Country were applying to have McIntosh returned "in the most pressing manner," while several from the Upper Country traveled south to Pensacola and insisted to Stuart "upon conducting Mr. Taitt . . . back to his station."[99] By late spring it was confirmed that both were back at their posts. McIntosh found the Hitchiti, Chehaw, and Flint River Indian towns overwhelmingly friendly, and even some Cussetas were coming around. Taitt, back in Little Tallassee, found a similar disposition with Tallapoosas, presumably in addition to groups of Abihkas, Hookchoies, and Tuckabatchees. Only Oakfuskees, Big Tallassees, and some Cussetas, representing the most vehemently pro-American towns, resisted the British resurgence.[100] After only a few months, in short, the reversal of Galphin's fortunes was complete. Stuart declared that his adherents had "now dwindled to about 30 or 40 desperados; all the rest of the nation have taken an active part, and their having fallen upon the frontiers of Georgia and Carolina."[101] Galphin of course struggled desperately to reverse this tragic change of events, but he did so largely without success outside of Oakfuskee. His labors had "been immense," Georgia governor John Houstoun lamented, "but I fear Stuart's presents have got the better of them."[102] He had "strained every nerve and exhausted every resource to supply them with goods to secure their friendship, in vain," complained Rawlins Lowndes.[103] Many local Georgia authorities began to change their tone as well. No longer did they relish the idea of a preemptive strike into Creek Country, and increasingly did they worry about the possibility of finding Creek raiders at their door.[104]

Although relations now generally favored the British, years of intensifying political jockeying had taken its toll on the region, revealing divisions that would not be mended easily. Tensions remained high between Cussetas and Cowetas, with the former continuing to warn that if any more Coweta warriors went out against American settlements, they would raid British ones around Pensacola in retaliation. Galphin reiterated those warnings. There were still plenty of American partisans, he insisted—enough to make Stuart hesitant to "give out any bad talks against us" in consequence of their threats.[105] The pro-American threats were not idle, either. After a raid in the late summer of 1778 Galphin was assured by friendly headmen—although he did not elaborate on which ones specifically—that they would make reprisal raids in Pensacola and Mobile.[106] Although most Creek headmen had turned their backs on the Americans, the region was still wracked by factionalism and alienated community leaders. The Cusseta towns' stubborn pro-American stance, in fact, prompted some of the region's most open confrontations yet. When McIntosh was preparing to leave with a group of warriors to raid the Georgia frontiers, parties of Cussetas with American emissaries did everything in their power to deter them. They went so far as to contemplate another attempt on McIntosh's life. But, for the second time, "he had timely notice and was guarded by a strong party of his friends the whole night" until he could make his getaway with a Chehaw war party.[107]

Perhaps the most important moment in the regional Creek power struggle came at the end of the war. While Americans were never able to reverse their failures in Creek Country, the larger war effort collapsed around the British after they invaded the South in 1778 and 1779. British armies from New York and St. Augustine made tremendous gains in Georgia and South Carolina only to lose them shortly after.[108] That invasion touched off a dramatic and almost desperate surge in violence across the backcountry, a surge in which countless Creek warriors participated. Communities surely must have looked on with tremendous anxiety, then, as the British offensive unraveled in front of their eyes. First, the Americans' Spanish allies proved anxious to avenge their losses in the French and Indian War and initiated a campaign to take back Louisiana and the Floridas.[109] An immense Spanish fleet, under the aggressive leadership of Louisiana governor José de Gálvez, began the reconquest of West Florida in 1780 when he captured posts on the Mississippi and at Baton Rouge. Next to fall were Fort Charlotte and Mobile, reducing Great Britain's hold on West Florida to Pensacola. Gálvez began his siege of Pensacola in May 1781 and forced British general Archibald Campbell to capitulate shortly after.[110] The loss of Pensacola was a severe blow to the British-Creek relationship. Both headmen and British agents had made clear in the past that St. Augustine was too arduous a journey to make under any other than the direst of circumstances. This was particularly so from the Upper Country. Taitt, at Little Tallassee, was more than five hundred miles away, and in order to get to the gates of St. Augustine he had to trudge through "a wild uncultivated country destitute of every necessity." In 1779, when Tonyn sent him a letter requesting his immediate assistance, it took Taitt almost a month and a half to reach him.[111] Yet with the loss of Pensacola, the Indian superintendency was transferred to St. Augustine, meaning that many Creeks in the Upper Country were that much farther away from their allies.

The pace of that collapse quickened when British armies began their evacuation of the South. Eventually Charleston, Savannah, and Augusta were abandoned by the British and retaken by American forces. While all equally represented the collapse of the British southern strategy, the loss of Augusta was a particularly difficult blow to pro-British allies in Creek Country; by abandoning that town the British handed back one of the Southeast's key trading posts. Although most Creek communities still supported the British, it was probably clear to them by that point that they were on the losing side.[112] By the fall of 1782 all of Georgia was under American control, and so with no other British option than St. Augustine, Creeks from both the Upper and Lower countries descended to Thomas Brown, who had been appointed superintendent after Stuart's death. Yet with neither money nor goods there was nothing he could offer, and he sent them home.[113]

Perhaps the final blow came with the death of Emistisiguo, the pillar of pro-British support in the Upper Country. When he received reports of increasing Spanish and American attacks late in 1782, the elderly chief led a force of his warriors in a last-ditch effort to prevent the American forces' retaking Savannah and eventually found himself squared off against Continental general Anthony Wayne.[114] Although the Creek warriors caught the American force by surprise and temporarily overwhelmed them, Wayne rallied his men to turn the battle. All the while, Emistisiguo fought fearlessly. Having just been bayoneted he still managed to shoot the horse from under Wayne, "encouraging his warriors all the while." He almost got to the general but was struck again by an American cavalryman and killed. He fought gallantly, Wayne and others would recall, with the former describing the slain chief as "our great enemy, and principle warrior of the Creek Nation." Yet when he fell, the largest British contingent in the Upper Country collapsed.[115] Indeed, Emistisiguo's death in 1782 marked the end of most Creeks' resistance to Georgians. By that time, Creek communities were split among themselves and, facing the defeat of their allies, in turmoil. That most Creeks ultimately became British partisans was all the more troubling. Although Stuart and his agents succeeded in rallying most of Creek Country into the British cause, within a few short years he was dead and the British were defeated, leaving Creeks to deal with Georgians more or less alone. That guaranteed that one of the major causes of Creek discord—conflict with an aggressive and expanding Georgia—would only intensify in the postwar years.

3 /   Georgia Treaties and Creek Partisans

They attempted to avail themselves of our supposed distressed situation.
Their talks to us breathed nothing but vengeance.
—Alexander McGillivray, September 5, 1785

The end of the Revolutionary War did not meliorate the factionalism and distrust that had been building during the struggle, either between Creek communities and Georgia authorities or among Creeks themselves. Instead, confrontational exchanges between Creeks and the expanding state of Georgia intensified rapidly, while questions about how to approach state authorities further divided Creek communities into clear and distinct partisan groups as headmen positioned themselves in the postwar period.[1] Diplomatic quarrels began almost immediately after the fighting ended, and they pitted Georgia legislators who struggled to legitimize their victory against a complicated and often discordant mix of Creek headmen. The disastrous treaties of Augusta (1783), Galphinton (1785), and Shoulderbone (1786) punctuated the period.

Some headmen—mostly from Cusseta, Big Tallassee, the Half-Way House, and Oakfuskee—had long been American partisans and welcomed talks from their American friends. Others, from Coweta, Chehaw, and Tuckabatchee, quickly replaced British allies with Spanish ones and rejected Augusta lawmakers with as much militancy as ever. At the same time the Fat King of Cusseta and Tallassee King of the Half-Way House were meeting with Georgia authorities in Augusta, for instance, another group led by Creek and former British agent Alexander McGillivray was meeting with Spanish governors in Pensacola and St. Augustine, cementing their position as inveterate anti-American partisans. Bitter disagreements between those groups came to dominate the postwar period, continuing to demonstrate that the autonomous

Creek approach to diplomacy was an increasingly untenable one—the growing threat represented by Georgia was not producing a common Creek political response, and the result was undermining regional stability. Creeks were not yet thinking of themselves as sharing even the most basic common political objective: their mutual survival, vis-à-vis American expansionists. Instead, a reliance on the older "play-off" approach to diplomacy revealed communities with competing interests that edged Creek Country ever closer to political turmoil. Georgians, in short, increasingly called for the conquest of Creek Country, while Creeks increasingly responded by calling each other traitors.

As British support disintegrated before their eyes in the early 1780s Creek communities were forced to wind down their own participation in the Revolution, and many headmen responded by listening to American peace talks. Yet relatively few words from the state of Georgia were wasted on reconciliation. Many more were spent explaining how Americans had won an epic struggle, where patriot forces had battled and defeated Creeks as completely as they had the British. In one of the first of many talks, for instance, Georgia governor John Martin warned in 1782 that further resistance by Creek warriors was useless. If the Creeks finally rejected McIntosh, Brown, and the other "Tories & King's people among you," both Georgians and their friends the Spaniards would be happy to reestablish friendly relations.[2] Defeat and tragedy, however, doomed those who continued their hostile ways. Emistisiguo, Martin reminded the chiefs, for the sake of a few trifling English presents, "did wantonly fall upon our warriors in the night in hopes of cutting them off, a people that never wanted to injure you but always sought your friendship." Brushing of course past the innumerable murders and outrages committed by state militias against Creeks on the Ceded Lands and elsewhere, which had had long informed Emistisiguo's actions, Martin skipped to the end. Georgians had prevailed, and the deceitful actions of the slain chief had left Creek women widowed and their children fatherless. Their blood was "upon their own heads."[3]

These cautionary words set the tone for more worrisome talks that flowed regularly from Augusta into Creek Country in the immediate postwar years. The Georgia state response in that way was only reflective of the larger trend in the diplomatic exchange that dominated the post-Revolutionary frontier. Whether in New York, Pennsylvania, Virginia, or the Carolinas, Americans spoke as the victors when addressing their Native American neighbors, the vanquished.[4] That was of course a poorly oversimplified approach to the complex situation in much of Native America that produced only further confrontation, and the situation along the Creek-Georgia frontier was no different. The region had proved highly contested during the war, where many headmen counted Americans among their closest allies. For headmen in Big Tallassee, Oakfuskee, and Cusseta, news of the American victory came with a tremendous sense of relief, not dread. Yet Georgians, it was clear, did not see things the same way, and legislators in Augusta approached all of Creek Country in the same aggressive manner. "Have we not told you the truth?" Martin later boasted in a letter penned to the Tallassee King, of all people. "Did we not say that we should drive the red coats from off our land, which we have done?"[5] It never crossed Martin's mind that he was addressing one of the single most supportive headmen in all of Creek Country. Now, the governor wrote, the state of Georgia was going to make peace on its terms, with a people who had challenged Americans and had lost. State authorities would match whatever Creeks preferred, "the sword, or olive branch."[6]

Despite that deeply troubling first round of peace overtures many Creek communities embraced the American victory, and several headmen expected to be treated like the steadfast allies they had been. In September 1782 a contingency of these leaders went to Augusta to congratulate the Georgians and begin the process of rebuilding. Chiefs and warriors traveled east from Oakfuskee, Tallassee, and even Tuckabatchee in the Upper Country, and from Cusseta in the Lower Country, with upwards of two hundred men. Along with Tuckabatchees there were a handful of Cowetas as well as Hycutt of the Hitchitis, representing communities who took part in some of the war's most vicious raiding. There was at least the possibility that, if approached carefully, some of the more dangerous communities in Creek Country could be reconciled to the American cause. In fact, when Americans began requesting the return of goods and property taken in raids over the course of the war many headmen seemed willing to oblige. There were soon reports that the Tallassee King was gathering up all the "Negroes Horses and Cattle" from the Upper Country to bring with him to Augusta, which the Fat King of Cusseta was also doing.[7]

The Tallassee King and the Fat King took leading roles in these opening negotiations. In the first year or so of the peace, the two chiefs represented Creek communities that had supported Georgians most stubbornly, even under clear threat to their lives, and they looked forward to working with state officials to secure a long-standing peace. The

Tallassee King was Georgia's "firm & fast friend," James Rae wrote, and had "ever ben our principle support."[8] The immediate postwar leadership of Oakfuskee headmen was similar. These were the men who stayed the most loyal to Georgians even when British victory seemed imminent. It was no surprise, then, that they embraced the opportunity to renew a formal and lasting peace with the Americans.[9] Their comforting words led several Georgians to declare that the "Head Men of the Nation in general" were "intirely devouted to deliver up the Prisoners and Negroes," and more groups on their way to Augusta were eager to "renue the chean of friendship."[10]

Coincidentally, most of the Creeks making those decisions were also leading headmen in towns with strong cultural ties to peace and negotiation. As Coweta's active wartime leadership role had already hinted, the distinction between a town that led in times of war and one that led in times of peace may have played a powerful role in the Tallassee King's and Fat King's actions. While murky and not completely understood by either contemporaries or modern scholars, moieties might help provide some explanation as to why those two men in particular were so persistently peaceful with Georgians, even when their state counterparts made it so difficult to do so. Red and white symbolism could be seen to the north, in Cherokee Country, as well as to the south, in early Florida Seminole settlements, suggesting that its role in regional politics was more than theory.[11] The splitting of towns into white and red—peace and war—was an important cultural thread in the Southeast that, like kinship, was thought to distribute authority among communities and was further evidence of the importance of reciprocal and complementary relationships in the larger Native Southeast.

According to these traditions the color white signified the old, established, stable, and peaceable, and leaders from white communities traditionally held political sway during times of peace. The color red, on the other hand, signified disorder, instability, war, and conflict, and leading men from red towns directed wartime decision making.[12] Coweta, during the Revolution, might have emerged as a community of particular importance because of its classification as a red town, which might also explain why Cowetas were quick to retaliate against Georgians and raid the frontiers. Headmen in white towns, however, as members of safe and civil places were supposed to have authority in situations exactly like the one that existed at the end of the Revolutionary War, when negotiation was critical. That in turn might explain why the Tallassee King and the Fat King appeared so prominently in postwar discussions with

Georgians. Although dual organization offered another possible layer of cultural cohesiveness, like kinship, it also had the potential to generate discord because of the ways it complicated local decision-making processes. The Cusseta-Coweta dynamic, for example, was particularly strong in the Lower Country, and the establishment of Cussetas as white and of Cowetas as red can be traced all the way to certain creation and migration stories, which describe the original settling of those two communities on the Chattahoochee.[13] Yet the Revolution demonstrated that the red-white dichotomy did little to bring the two closer together.

Once American and British authorities forced Creeks to choose sides, moiety structures provided another source of confrontation between Cowetas and Cussetas, not a source of understanding; one community was bound to lead in the fighting while the other seemed equally bound to keep it from breaking out. It is clear that whatever balance the moiety structure was designed to create in the everyday lives of Creeks, when superimposed onto local political and economic relationships during a time of tremendous regional struggle, the tradition proved unhelpful at best. Ultimately, by the end of the war it had contributed to an environment where Cussetas openly threatened retaliation against Cowetas and others when their raids upset neutrality, which did actually happen. And all of Creek Country was potentially divided in such a way. According to one anthropologist, Oakfuskees, Tallassees, Half-Way House communities, Abihkas, Hookchoies, Wewocaos, and others in the Upper Country were white towns while Tuckabatchees, Kialijees, Autossees, Hillaubees, Alabamas, and others were red. In the Lower Country, Cussetas, Hitchitis, Yuchis, and Apalachicolas were white, while Cowetas, Chehaws, Ooseoochees, and Eufalas were red.[14] Webs of dual organization, in other words, might have been one of the inclusive traditions that had defined Creek Country by the Revolutionary War. When widespread fighting came to the region, however, it had more potential to frustrate attempts by community leaders to produce a regional political response than to provide regional harmony.

It would be difficult to place the importance of something like a town's red or white classification—if such a distinction even existed in practice at all—above more tangible connections like trading or family relationships. Cussetas benefited from close trading connections with Galphin, as did Oakfuskees from Rae, and so on. Galphin also had family in Creek Country along with scores of other traders, and then so did men like Taitt. These must be considered the primary reasons why Oakfuskee and Cusseta remained such firm American allies, while others were such enthusiastic British partisans.[15] Yet those ties do not explain Creek decision making fully, and cultural traditions like moieties might help explain why that was the case. Why did Cowetas do so much damage to the Georgia backcountry when Galphin had so many connections there? Why did Chehaws constitute such a powerful British pillar of support in the Lower Country when Rae had a major trading operation there? And then there were communities about which less is known, like Hitchiti and Apalachicola in the south and Abihka and Hillaubee in the north. Hitchiti warriors took part in some of the most devastating raids against the Georgia backcountry, but headmen like Hycutt were also regulars in Georgia state conferences. Sometimes-vague cultural traditions, like moieties, might explain that complexity but only in conjunction with the clearer trade and familial ties. The actions of the Tallassee King and the Fat King are suggestive of such complicated political and cultural realities. Headmen from a handful of communities that were at the same time sympathetic to Georgians and peace-oriented were also the few to listen to the earliest Georgia state talks, and they were among the majority of those that appeared at the state's earliest treaty councils.

As for the Tallassee King and the Fat King particularly, both their trading ties and traditional leadership roles must be considered when trying to explain why they were so quick to make peace with Georgia authorities. The actions of the two also provide continued evidence that whatever was meant to provide stability in Creek Country in theory only produced more trouble in reality. Despite ample evidence of widespread dissent, the Tallassee King and the Fat King both clearly saw themselves as leaders in post-Revolutionary Creek Country, and they acted as such. The reasons why they eschewed confrontation during the war, or acceded to the desires of Georgia authorities afterward, might have been complex. The reaction to their decisions in Creek Country, however, was not. Rather than generate stability, their decisive actions generated waves of intense anger and partisanship that made a mockery of their perceived authority as well as the idea of a unified Creek people.

Both the Tallassee King and the Fat King, for instance, were guaranteeing to Georgia authorities the return of slaves, horses, and other property seized in raids in which their own people had taken no part. Their words carried little weight outside of their own communities, and there was little hope they would be able to make good on their earliest promises. Headmen friendly to the Georgia position were definitely the minority in Creek Country, where more communities at the very least were reluctant to talk to state authorities so openly.[16] The provocative talks coming from Augusta might influence the few friendly headmen already dedicated to peace, but they would do little to win over anyone else. To the contrary, by that time several communities had already embraced the arrival of Spanish governors in Florida, and many remained as radical in their rejection of Georgians as they had ever been. From Tuckabatchee, for instance, one of the Rae brothers complained that when he gave talks obliging headmen to come to Savannah the Mad Dog, who wielded incredible influence there and had been no friend to Americans in the past, arrived with Spanish talks that seemed much more popular. While some groups were meeting with Rae and the Georgians, "the encouragement given them by the Spaniards & Brittish" were preventing many more doing so.[17] And while the Tallassee King and Fat King promised to gather up stolen property, most of it was being spirited south and sold in Spanish Pensacola, where a black market for horses, cattle, and slaves was booming.[18] Georgia peace overtures would do little to stem that market or prompt men like the Mad Dog to embrace their new American neighbors.

Several communities made their displeasure with the war's outcome known in no uncertain terms. Headmen from Coweta and others along the Flint River in southern Creek Country protested desperately after being notified of the British evacuation of Florida. Okaigigie spoke on behalf of the Flint River Creeks, and Fine Bones spoke for the Cowetas, as well as on behalf of a number of his kin in the Upper Country. They reminded the British that countless Creeks not only had been loyal partners in the war but had lost men of their own. "The King and his warriors have told us they would never forsake us. Is the Great King conquered?" Okaigigie asked. "Or does he mean to abandon us? Or does he intend to sell his friends as slaves, or only to give our lands to his and our enemies?" When the Cowkeeper—Tonyn's strongest ally in Florida—heard the news, he was enraged. Seminole warriors arrived in St. Augustine to "swear vengeance against the King that gave away their country," claiming that they would kill any Spaniard that would try to take possession.[19] As those responses suggested, there were more headmen determined to resist the end of the war than accept Georgians' one-sided peace terms.

As for the many other communities that were still somewhere in the middle—not rejecting Georgians entirely but still deeply distrustful of them—they were forced one way or another in the fall of 1783. By that time state officials were pressing for a formal treaty to solidify their war victories and convened a treaty council in Augusta.[20] There Edward

Telfair and Elijah Clarke, among other state-appointed commissioners, met with the Tallassee King, the Fat King, and the Cusseta King. It was a far smaller cross section of headmen even than had assembled twenty years earlier, when the contentious Ceded Lands were at stake. What was clearly nowhere near a legitimate representation of Creek Country troubled state officials little, however, and the conference moved forward quickly.[21] After renewing their earlier requests for the return of property, to which the headmen responded favorably, the commissioners moved on to more important business. They found it necessary to "have a piece of land, from the Indians as far as the Oconey's, this being a natural boundary."[22] By the end of the negotiations the state commissioners claimed to have secured it, gaining a cession of land that extended from the Savannah River to the Oconee River and then the Altamaha, and from there to the coast.[23]

The Treaty of Augusta represented Georgians' first attempt to extend their boundary in the post-Revolutionary years. The conference was concluded quickly and quietly, and from the commissioners' accounts, without a hitch. The ink had barely dried on it when settlers began flooding west, across the Ogeechee River and onto Creek lands. Georgia was "settling again very fast," and "especially the backcountry," according to Joseph Clay.[24] Within days of the signing, in fact, Elijah Clarke was confident that "numbers of inhabitance will be out from other states in order to settle the land between this and the spring of the year."[25] Surveyors were appointed to "circumscribe the Indian Hunting Grounds," and a state act was passed creating two new counties by March 1784.[26] There were "a thousand men with their families" ready to settle by September.[27] The boundary was delineated by the Oconee River and by marked trees, and within years reports of speculation were already widespread.[28]

Despite positive reports in Georgia and the rapid pace of settlement, the reality was that only a handful of American partisans from a few communities were present to negotiate the Treaty of Augusta. There is little evidence to suggest that the majority of Creeks even knew it was happening at all.[29] As could be expected, when they learned not only that there had indeed been a treaty but that because of it some of their most prized hunting lands between the Oconee and Ogeechee rivers now allegedly belonged to the state of Georgia, they did not react well. When the Tallassee King returned to the Upper Country he was immediately dressed down at Tuckabatchee by over thirty headmen, who demanded he "give an account of his negotiations" and, specifically, why he thought he and the Fat King had the right to grant "so large a tract of Country, the property of the Creek Nations in Common."[30] When pressed he backtracked, explaining that once at Augusta he and the rest of the entourage were threatened, even with death. "The Georgians finding they could not prevail with the Chiefs, they had recourse to threats," Alexander McGillivray later explained. Over several days the besieged delegation held out, according to this narrative, until finally they "were threatend with Instant death if they did not comply." Under those circumstances, to spare their lives and those of their compatriots, the two did what they had to do. And so they consented to a cession "which they knew the Nation woud not Confirm."[31] That explanation seemed to keep the mob from killing the Tallassee King immediately, but the confrontation at Tuckabatchee was a clear sign that red-white moieties did not trump local decision making or that one or two headmen could even dream about doing what they had done at Augusta. A massive plurality would still be needed to produce a decision as weighty as the sale of so much land, and there had been no such plurality at Augusta.

But the situation was evidently more complicated. Conflicting accounts suggest that the treaty might not have been as coerced as McGillivray's retelling of it suggests, that the Tallassee King may have been exaggerating events in order to save his own skin, and that a rift between American and Spanish partisan groups was already developing. Perhaps the men were not necessarily unaware of what they were doing. Perhaps they were not forced to sign the document under the threat of death, and perhaps they were not even altogether unhappy with it afterward.[32] The developing crisis also demonstrated the tangled claims of specific communities to landownership that made dealing in land so difficult in Creek Country. As Peter Chester and John Stuart lamented a decade earlier when dealing with Emistisiguo, it was notoriously difficult to get a legitimate cession of Creek land. As Emistisiguo declared, everyone in Creek Country had a right to the lands, and so everyone in Creek Country essentially had to agree to dispose of it. Stuart was irritated by such difficulties while Chester simply did not believe that land could be so communally owned. It is possible that Emistisiguo also had a more local reason to resist the deal: he was not interested in disposing of the lands above Mobile because those were the lands he and his community hunted on personally. It is also possible that Cusseta and Little Tallassee headmen had a similar take on land stewardship—one that blended both regional and community ownership of resources.

It is difficult, but not impossible, to draw from contemporary accounts a general idea of regional land claims in Creek Country. Creek hunting lands stretched from modern-day Alabama to the west, to Tennessee to the north, to central Florida to the east. All Creek communities claimed either ownership of those lands or hunting rights on them through several avenues. They might have asserted such claims through military victory, as was the case with once Choctaw or Cherokee lands on the western and northern borders of Creek Country, respectively. Upper Creeks like Emistisiguo claimed the Tensaw lands above Mobile because they took it from Choctaws, which Creeks were known to quarrel with regularly. Creeks as a whole could also claim the right to access lands based on incorporation or alliance with outside or refugee groups, like Shawnees, Alabamas, or Natchez, who themselves had asserted ownership of the lands in the past.[33] But then there were more detailed claims, which suggest that particular communities might have asserted more control over one stretch of land than others—another marker of the region's sometimes fierce political autonomy.

Those at the northern reaches of Creek Country, for instance, regularly hunted into modern-day Alabama and into Choctaw or Chickasaw Country to the west and northwest, or to the Cumberland River in Tennessee to the north.[34] Other communities in the Upper Country, including Tallapoosas and Tallassees, regularly hunted further south around the Tensaw, Mobile, and Pensacola.[35] Things were just as complex to the east. According to talks from Chehaws they, and probably the others that joined in with them, including Okmulgees, Ooseoochees, and Hitchitis, hunted regularly on the Altamaha, which lay southeast of the junction of the Oconee and Okmulgee. Many of those same communities probably followed Chehaws, Eufalas, and Yuchis as they moved south and southeast into central Florida to hunt, along with Mikasukis and Seminoles.[36] Those groups, with Cowetas, Yuchis, and most other communities on the Flint and Chattahoochee rivers, found the lands in southern Georgia and northern Florida, including the Okefenokee Swamp, particularly inviting. Yuchis were reported to "generally hunt down the Oakmulgee and Alatamaha," while a Chehaw explained that he not only had "hunted many years" in the swamp and on the St. Mary's River but "used to go towards St. Augustine" on hunts and sometimes even further. It was also clear that Cussetas and others from the Lower Country regularly ranged the Oconee headwaters to the northeast and even toward the Cumberland River as well. That was made abundantly clear in the 1790s because Georgia settlers were in the nasty habit of shooting them there, along the

Apalache and Little rivers. That might have been because Cussetas were the only Creek hunters that dared venture anywhere close to Georgia settlements, but then again perhaps it hinted at Cussetas' primary stake in those hunting lands—the ones they began to cede to Georgians starting with the Treaty of Augusta.[37]

As the relations of individual communities suggests, many hunters looked east for their deerskins. That made the Ogeechee, Okmulgee, Oconee, and Altamaha River basins some of the most prized and productive hunting grounds in Creek Country, and during the winter season they were filled with young men from across the region.[38] Hunters ranged along the length of that frontier, which was now also the border with the Georgia and, to a lesser extent, South Carolina, traveling further and further as deer became rarer. The specific descriptions given by some community hunters do, however, suggest that they could have claimed certain lands as reserved more for themselves than others. Both Cussetas and Tallassees regularly hunted on the Oconee lands, in the Okefenokee swamp, and to the east, above the St. Mary's and below the Altamaha River, which were the exact lands they claimed the authority to dispense to Georgians at Augusta. Tallassees in particular were known to range deep into the Okefenokee. One Chehaw hunter, talking about his own hunting exploits in the swamp, added that "some of the Tallassee people had been in much farther than he had."[39] Specific community claims are rare indeed, and relatively little is known about the particulars of regional versus local land claims. Yet the actions of both the Fat King and Tallassee King, in the context of their hunting patterns, are enough perhaps to suggest that they thought the lands they hunted on were theirs enough to sell, at least if the price was right.[40] An American official thought so even years after, explaining that "as the Creeks have no written laws or customs, it was to be supposed the people of Georgia would in reason view that purchase as good which they were to make from the people who were in the indisputed possession and use— the case of your Lower Towns."[41]

If the evidence for claims by specific communities to land is vague, much clearer are the various accounts of the treaty proceedings at Augusta. They tell a surprising tale, painting a much rosier picture than the chiefs later related to McGillivray and others. Both the Fat King and the Tallassee King, as well as their entourages, were showered with an array of trade gifts in "consequence of their fidelity and Attachment to their white brethren during the late War, and for their acquiesance and support in the late acquired Cession."[42] According to the Fat King, the commissioners had not threatened them with instant death but had "requested land of us as far as the Oconee," to which he and the other headmen voluntarily agreed. In return, they expected "to have had plenty of goods," which it seems they got.[43] Georgia authorities recorded starkly different accounts of the treaty than the chiefs, when pressed by their fellow headmen, retold upon their return. John Habersham of Georgia's Executive Council would later recall to the chiefs "what passed at the treaty last year" at Augusta, and "all the good talks between you and our Great men." The groups "agreed to open the path again, and to keep it white and straight," and to "take each other by the hand as friends and brothers." Timothy Barnard—first an American commissioner, then maybe a British spy, and now assisting the state of Georgia—was even more candid. He reminded a group of headmen from the two communities that the land cession was "to make us retaliation for the damage you did us which was not a little."[44] Barnard reported several months later that they seemed "disposed for peace." They had dropped "all bad talks about the land," and "the generality of them seem inclinable that the white people should settle it." Of course Georgians were pleased with this, as it testified to the legitimacy of their dealings. "We are glad you invite us to settle the Oconee lands—this our people intend doing—immediately," one response went.[45]

The most telling information came from the headmen themselves. The treaty came up in their conversations several times and with very little ambiguity. Speaking with Barnard in 1784, for instance, the Cusseta King confirmed rather straightforwardly that he and his fellow headmen "gave up their lands last fall as far as the Oconee Rivers" at Augusta. And later, the Tallassee King "seemed fully to acknowledge the cession of the Oconee to the white people, and said he hoped the people who settled there would be good to the Indians when they happened to come and see them."[46] Spanish officials in Florida, surprised and dismayed by the treaty, also confronted the Cusseta King, and the story was the same. When asked why his people preferred Americans at Augusta over Spaniards at Pensacola, the Cusseta King replied that his people "were always friends with the Americans, and so were their fathers." And when asked if the Spanish could depend on the Cussetas for military support, the chief "answered no—that the Indians were friends to the Americans and would hold out their hands to both." That was a sentiment shared by the Tallassee King. Oakfuskees, Tallassees, Half-Way Houses, and Cussetas, in addition to Chickasaws and Choctaws, were all friendly, he declared. The Fat King and the Chickasaws were "one fire," and the Tallassee King and Oakfuskees "are as brothers."[47]

The likelihood of the Creek delegation having their lives threatened at Augusta, that sort of confidence suggests, was slim. Rather, the Fat King, the Cusseta King, the Tallassee King, and to a lesser extent Oakfuskees appeared to be acting after the Revolution in a manner remarkably consistent with their efforts during the war. Nevertheless, the Augusta delegation's confidence in their political authority was clearly misplaced. Cussetas' assurances that others in the Lower Country would stand behind them was particularly dangerous. Even if Cussetas enjoyed the strongest claim to local control of the land, they were badly mistaken to think they could parlay that into the authority for a sweeping land deal that would inevitably take land away from Coweta or Hitchiti hunters as well. As the Cusseta King was also forced later to admit in the Upper Country, Hillaubee and Aubecoochee were definitely going to be problematic, while the Tallassee King soon hedged on his earlier assumptions of solidarity. "One half the Nation looked one way & the other half looked the other."[48] When thirty headmen accosted him in Tuckabatchee—far more than were at Augusta—it was proof enough that the treaty would not be accepted in Creek Country as smoothly as the Tallassee King and his allies had promised.

Facing waves of dissent that quickly began to radiate from all corners of Creek Country, state authorities remained firm at first. The treaty was legitimately made, they contended, and it most certainly was legally binding.[49] It was too late to complain, Timothy Barnard made clear in the summer of 1784, and legislators would "not put a stop to its being settled as it is gone too far and the people has all marked oute there fields already and will not be stoped from settling." State authorities were not interested at all in giving up any of their newly acquired lands and made clear that resistance to the treaty was useless.[50] That position slowly became more untenable, however, as word of the treaty spread throughout Creek Country, and Tallassees and Cussetas were pushed further into the minority. Not only did Creeks overwhelmingly reject the treaty and disclaim the authority of the delegation that made it, the so-called council at Augusta convinced many once hesitant headmen of the direction they needed to take, and it was not toward the Americans.

It was during the fallout from Augusta that Alexander McGillivray emerged as a leading voice of anti-Georgia discontent. His ability to harness and project communities' anger generated the most powerful and cohesive Creek voice that Georgians would be forced to deal with since the beginning of the Revolution. Already by April 1783, when he first heard word of the approaching Augusta conference, he was confident that "all the district are determined in opposition to the Rebels intended demands," and "the Lower Creeks I am sure will do the same and this of course will be a cause of contention between the states and us." Yet he was confident that Georgia was too weak to enforce its will. He and other headmen had already "taken the necessary measures to spoil their talks" and neither Georgia nor North Carolina "in their present situation" could "oblige us to a compliance." It was with his assistance, indeed, that a growing but still diverse chorus of angry headmen was able to mount a threat to Augusta that state authorities could not overcome. Practically the whole region was "on the point of rushing to war," McGillivray declared in June 1784, seething for retribution.[51] These warnings, the first of many, proved potent. Georgia authorities toned down their rhetoric almost immediately, and more importantly, they appeared to slow settlers' movement west.[52] State legislators soon invited another group of headmen to Galphinton, on the Oconee River, where they hoped to clear up any confusion and to legitimize their recent gains.[53]

While McGillivray's ability to project a unified Creek response was powerful, behind this temporary victory for most of Creek Country there was plenty of damage that had already been done. Anger about the treaty rippled through the region, compounding much of the distrust between headmen that had been lingering after the war. The decisions of the Fat King and the Tallassee King quickly crumbled any vestige of legitimacy they claimed outside of their own communities, and they were already being threatened personally.[54] But the treaty also prompted communities to seek support elsewhere, and again, with McGillivray's help, they found it in the Spanish authorities that were returning to the Floridas. Vincente Manuel de Zéspedes y Velasco was one of the nearby Spanish governors to respond almost immediately. He replaced Tonyn as governor of East Florida and made his residence in St. Augustine. As governor of West Florida, Arturo O'Neill de Tyrone acted likewise in Pensacola. Lastly, Esteban Rodríguez Miró assumed the governorship of New Orleans. Along with their superiors in Cuba and Spain, these newly arrived authorities made it clear that they would be willing and enthusiastic allies to the Creek people.

The Spanish claimed authority over much of the same land that Creeks did, after all, from the Ogeechee River into modern-day Tennessee to the north, and all the way to the Mississippi River to the west. Their most pressing concern was controlling access to the Mississippi, which they rightly understood was the key to the interior of America. And to help them control the westward movement of their American neighbors, they quickly turned to Native groups like Creeks.[55] As Arturo O'Neill explained, they would prove immensely useful "as a vanguard for the protection of the Mississippi and these other dominions of our king, which the insatiable and turbulent ambition of the Americans menaces."[56] While Spaniards and Creeks were interested in stopping the flow of Georgians west for different reasons, they certainly shared a common immediate goal in keeping them as far east as possible. That was the basis for a mutually beneficial and rather remarkable relationship that began to develop between the two groups very quickly after the close of the war. Spanish governors gained a buffer against Americans' attempts to develop along the Mississippi, while Creek headmen got a strong European power capable of providing the guns and other material aid they would need to keep their hunting lands free of settlement. To what extent either group considered the lands west of the Ogeechee as actually theirs mattered little at the time—whether they were under Creek control or Spanish title, they were absolutely not American.

Spaniards correctly recognized that trade remained the key to keeping Natives strong political allies.[57] They acted quickly to ensure that there were no delays in the regular availability of the trade goods that had been so important for the British during the war. To do that, Spanish authorities turned to the British trading firm Panton, Leslie and Company. It was the most significant trading operation in the Southeast by the end of the Revolution, and it certainly had the deepest connections in Creek country. However, with the British removing from the region, the future of the company was uncertain. Although Spanish governors deeply distrusted the merchants' loyalties and always kept a watchful eye on them, they were ultimately forced by the exigencies of Creek friendship to accommodate them. Not only did they allow Panton and Leslie to remain in business, they issued them what was effectively a state-supported monopoly on the Creek trade.[58] Spanish governors sympathetic to Creeks were now directly connected to the important trading centers at St. Augustine, Pensacola, Mobile, and New Orleans, where both royal Spanish warehouses and commercial ones were now open to Creek headmen.[59] The transition was surprisingly smooth, tying the administration of gifts, supplies, and even guns in Creek Country directly to Spanish governors and their aggressive anti-expansionist policies.

All of the Gulf Coast governors welcomed and embraced McGillivray as their best means to connect to Creek communities. Spaniards depended upon headmen as well as men with mixed ancestry, or "creoles living in the nation," in the words of O'Neill, because they usually already had strong trade ties and were easier to communicate with than other headmen. Most also happened to be "strongly opposed to the name of Americans" and would eagerly help the Spaniards resist them.[60] Alexander McGillivray certainly was that kind of man. Born of mixed Creek and European ancestry, he was educated by his father, Lachlan, and had worked under British merchants. He had strong trading connections because of his father, which is perhaps why John Stuart authorized the young McGillivray to act as one of his agents when he returned to Creek Country during the Revolution.[61] He did not waste any time, however, reaching out to the Spanish when it was clear the British were ultimately going to evacuate the region. Even while Tonyn was still in East Florida, in fact, McGillivray approached all three Spanish governors and impressed them with his strong and defiant anti-American rhetoric.[62] As a "free Nation," he argued to O'Neill, Creeks had the right to choose their friends and allies, and as long as the Spanish were responsive to Creek desires, their future together looked bright.[63] Creeks were going to retain their land, McGillivray declared to Zéspedes, and if Georgia picked a fight, Creek warriors were ready to "all take up the hatchet" and carry the fight to the state. McGillivray's confidence and enthusiasm impressed the governor, who was convinced that he would be "an individual of consideration among the Creek Indians." Miró, who at Orleans was the most powerful governor in the region, was likewise influenced, appointing him senior commissioner in Creek Country.[64]

McGillivray's position made him a critical link between Spanish armories and Creek communities, and it quickly made him an influential man. With that authority and surrounded by headmen desperate for the means to resist expansionist Georgians, McGillivray was soon the spokesman for a vibrant Spanish partisan group of Creeks that stretched throughout the region. Indeed, as Georgians grew more aggressive after Augusta, and as stronger, more supportive talks came from the Spanish governors, McGillivray grew stronger as well. Nevertheless, the Spanish turned out to be much more skillful Native diplomats than were their American neighbors. While Georgia state authorities preferred to deal with as few headmen as possible, Spanish authorities developed as many relationships as they could throughout Creek Country. McGillivray was a noteworthy example of building relationships with particular men, but he was not the only one to receive goods or talks directly from Spanish authorities. While he and Alexander Cornells, the son of British interpreter and trader Joseph Cornells, were in Pensacola late in

1783, for instance, several other headmen from the Lower Country were meeting with Zéspedes in St. Augustine.[65] The governor entertained them personally, providing assurances that the king of Spain desired to keep Creeks under his protection, and he promised that their lands and their trade would be secure from the American threat. If Creeks needed anything, they could find it at St. Augustine.[66] Zéspedes frequently spoke with Creek headmen directly, in fact—something his British predecessor was noted for doing. It was something both O'Neill and Miró did as well. The Spanish return to the Southeast certainly privileged McGillivray, but he was not the only one.

Spanish administrators offered clear evidence of their willingness to conclude the widest-ranging treaties possible when they invited headmen to their councils. In an approach that differed from Augusta in striking ways, Spaniards encouraged large turnouts at their treaty conferences in 1784 in hopes of gaining broad acceptance of their alliances. At Pensacola and Mobile, groups of Creeks, Choctaws, and Chickasaws were invited to look upon the Spanish "as their friends and Brothers."[67] At the council at Pensacola, in 1784, which was attended mostly by Creeks and Seminoles, the turnout was enormous. The treaty made there was subsequently well received in Creek Country, and afterward Zéspedes, O'Neill, and Miró worked diligently to sustain the alliance. They regularly explained that they had assisted the Americans during the Revolution, as had the French, "which was the reason they conquered the English." They no longer considered Americans friends, however, because "they were mad people, and were always encroaching on the Indians land." Word of such talks and promises made their way to Americans, of course, who cautiously reported that Creek warriors could go to the Spanish "and get supplied with arms and ammunition and big guns whenever they wanted them."[68]

Not everyone, however, flocked to Pensacola. Conspicuous in their absence from these councils were prominent pro-American community leaders, most notably Oakfuskee, Tallassee, Half-Way House, and Cusseta headmen. That was no surprise, of course, because what Spaniards and Creeks agreed to at Pensacola openly rejected what Georgia state authorities claimed to have accomplished at Augusta. The two treaties, which stood in direct contradiction to each other, split Creek Country essentially into two partisan groups, just as the Revolution had done a decade earlier. Nevertheless, the Spanish agreements brought stability to many Creek communities, where they were celebrated as the means to keep Georgia expansionists at bay.[69] And the Spaniards, to their credit, lived up to their promises. By the spring of 1785 O'Neill and Miró provided their first shipments of arms and ammunition in the Lower Country, something that must also have brought a collective sigh of relief.

McGillivray was happier when a Panton and Leslie packtrain arrived in the Upper Country loaded down with goods. That, he declared, would "enable the nation to make a powerfull stand against the Americans encroaching" so far from their "real boundary."[70] Having positioned himself firmly between Creek communities and the Spaniards, he benefited tremendously from the flow of trade goods, and his voice quickly became one of the most powerful in the region. And McGillivray did not waste that voice; he seldom restrained himself when speaking either to Georgians or about them. They showed "a great inclination to persist" in seizing Creek lands, he wrote. Those were the actions, he later admitted in a letter to O'Neill, that would "probably at one time or another create a War."[71] Georgia authorities meant to carve up Creek Country and sit down on Creek lands "as if they were their own." Preaching "flattering appellations of friends and brothers," they were "stripping us of our natural rights."[72] McGillivray, like his Spanish allies, did not hesitate to drum up Creek support by advocating violent opposition to the state of Georgia—talk that made them all very popular.

State authorities in Georgia were in a very different place. While Creek headmen and Spanish governors were growing more confident in their situation, backcountry settlers and their state legislators were squabbling with Congress over how aggressively to approach Creek Country. State officials, taken aback by the angry reaction to Augusta, soon drew up plans for their proposed follow-up conference at Galphinton. Witnessing the fallout from Augusta and the development of a serious Spanish problem along the Gulf Coast, congressmen in Philadelphia were much more circumspect. Once again they pressed their state counterparts for moderation and appointed a set of commissioners to attend Galphinton and oversee the negotiations. That feeble first attempt by the federal government to intervene in Creek-Georgia affairs, however, was only one of the issues that made the Treaty of Galphinton more controversial than its predecessor. By the time the conference approached, for instance, most Creek headmen knew better than to actually attend. Cognizant of Georgians' approach to Augusta few jumped the opportunity to meet again, regardless of whether representatives of the United States in Congress would be present. Most communities in the Lower Country, with the exception of Cusseta, were by 1785 firm Spanish allies, and in a rare talk on the subject, a group of Coweta chiefs declared to Georgia governor Samuel Elbert that while state authorities had "frequent meetings and talks" with a handful of Creek towns—presumably much friendlier ones like Cussetas—these were the first talks Cowetas had sent them since the Revolution. Before that time, the headmen continued, Georgians made few demands. Now they were making significant encroachments on their hunting lands, and if they continued to do so, peace "can not be long."[73]

The cautionary talk from Coweta was not an exceptional one. As McGillivray wrote to Andrew Pickens, one of the congressional commissioners, Georgians were almost universally despised in Creek Country because of their own actions. "They attempted to avail themselves of our supposed distressed situation," he wrote, and "their talks to us breathed nothing but vengeance."[74] While hearing such angry warnings from McGillivray was not exceptional, getting them directly from Coweta communities was; a growing number of Creek community leaders understood what state authorities wanted from them, and they were not at all interested. There was little hope, in short, of seeing them at Galphinton. McGillivray, for his part, briefly considered attending the conference to give that sentiment more weight—to counter Georgian designs to fix the treaty, in his words, "where they please to our injury."[75] "Sensible to their insidious views," however, he advised most headmen not to get involved at all, and as the time for the treaty arrived his approach matched the larger Creek one. There were "not twenty Indians in the whole that went to Ogeechee," he later reported to Miró and O'Neill, and even then the few who showed were "not of any consequence." He did not show, and few others did.[76]

With a complicated mixture of Georgian and American commissioners on one side of the council ground and a clearly inadequate Creek representation on the other, it is no surprise that Galphinton did not go over well. When the congressional commissioners arrived they were appalled at what they found. The delegation, which included future Indian agent Benjamin Hawkins, was first annoyed by the paltry Creek presence. Soon, however, they found more to complain about in their state-appointed counterparts. Suspicions had been circulating that Georgia authorities had sped up the conference timetable, hoping they could get most of their cajoling in before their federal brethren even arrived. If congressional authorities helped moderate a deal that ended up nullifying Georgia's claims to so much as a fraction of the lands the state claimed after Augusta, after all, it would be a deal few Georgians would be interested in.[77] To Hawkins and the others that was only speculative; the actions of the state commissioners, however, certainly did not generate a positive atmosphere of camaraderie and mutual respect between the two groups, and suspicions quickly mounted. Soon after Hawkins and the rest of the delegation made camp it became clear to them that the Georgia commission was doing everything short of actually kidnapping them to keep them from meeting with any Creeks at all. Arguing over "the wrong measures the [Georgians] were pursuing," Hawkins and the others departed in disgust to try their hand with the Cherokee.[78] That departure did little to derail the conference, however, freeing up state authorities essentially to repeat their approach at Augusta. The only Creeks that mattered were the ones who were there, and so again, the same familiar faces that Georgians recognized from Tallassee, Half-Way House, and Cusseta—the ones who ignored McGillivray's warnings and traveled to be their friends—were the only ones present.[79] To the vexation of the thousands of Creeks not represented at Galphinton, and perhaps the United States Congress as well, Georgians soon claimed to have concluded another successful treaty with the Creek people, and one that included the cession of even more land than before.[80]

The Tallassee King, Fat King, and Cusseta King comprised the lion's share of the Creek representation at Galphinton, just as they had at Augusta. What resulted was also similar, including in the way Georgia authorities as well as Creeks responded to it. First, there was the glowing state response. Timothy Barnard, one of the Georgia commissioners, contended that the Cusseta chief was "the most principal one in the nation to act in that matter," again suggesting that all parties involved, including the Cussetas, understood what they were doing.[81] The Fat King was joined by the Tallassee King in clearing up any confusion that might have remained, declaring that "the Nation has laeft the wholle to them to act, in part of the Nation," and were interested in settling "every piont of the lien and bouendarey, of land, and all other matters relating to thaer nation."[82] Not only did they confirm their actions at Augusta, this new delegation proceeded to gift Georgians an even larger tract of land than before, including a particularly profitable piece that stretched south from the Altamaha to the St. Mary's River. Barnard was one of the only state authorities, in fact, to voice any words of caution. Almost alone, it appears, he recognized that such a small Creek delegation would be as problematic as before—insufficient, he worried, "to settle matters about the land."[83] Few others shared in his pause, though, and state authorities instead moved swiftly to embrace the updated treaty and the enlarged cession. "I observe from the last treaty the Creeks have ceded some land from the fork of the Oconee & Oakmulgee to the head of St. Mary's River," one anxious planter quickly reported of the additional land, in particular, and "this I suppose will be laid out in a county."[84]

Just as similar as the Galphinton experience was to Augusta, so was the Creek response. Timothy Barnard was right to worry. The vast majority of headmen, none more so than McGillivray, were soon convinced that nothing short of violence would put a stop to Georgian expansionism. Augusta and Galphinton clearly did not represent Creek Country, McGillivray warned James Habersham, as "no acts of a few or part can or does bend the whole."[85] It was "a rule of law," he continued to Zéspedes, that no decision by such a small representation of headmen could "make any cession or grant of land in prejudice of the rights of the nation."[86] Little had changed from the Emistisiguo's days a generation earlier. Regardless of any individual claims to hunting lands, cultural traditions governing landownership were as strong as they had ever been, regardless of how Cusseta or Tallassee headmen rationalized their decisions at Augusta or Galphinton.

Congress also recognized that Galphinton was a disaster and that violence was imminent, and they quietly but quickly dispatched another complement of commissioners to soothe Creek anger, seek common ground, and, they hoped, avert bloodshed.[87] That proved timely; in the meantime Creek communities chose to demonstrate their resolve for the first time by force. "I have repeatedly warned them of the ill consequences of such measures," McGillivray complained to Governor O'Neill, "& the dangers it might bring upon them," but state authorities "do not listen to it & still persist in their encroachments." The time for a diplomatic solution had passed, he concluded.[88] Almost immediately after word of Galphinton coursed its way through the region, headmen were making plans to strike at the illegal settlements Georgians had already constructed. McGillivray had previously discussed such plans to the Hallowing King, explaining to the Coweta headman that the governor of Georgia "had heard our talks about our lands," but no one seemed to be listening and instead "still encroach." Creeks would have to "stir ourselves in the matter, & drive off from the okonee all encroachers, for if we sit still & only complain, our grievances will never be remedied, nor listened to."[89]

Months later, in March 1786, a war council met at Tuckabatchee to debate such a plan publicly, and headmen from almost every community in Creek Country were present. The council was the largest regional meeting that had taken place in Creek Country for some time, evidence that the Georgia menace had produced a real crisis. For days chiefs and warriors deliberated their next move, and ultimately they resolved to strike a coordinated blow. "Under such circumstances," McGillivray declared afterward, "we cannot be quiet spectators."[90] The situation "becoming more critical," he explained to Zéspedes, Creek Country would "now take up arms in our hands to oppose the Americans." After a near-unanimous decision in council, headmen from various communities ordered their warriors to "traverse all that part of the country in dispute & whenever they found any American settlers to drive them off & to destroy all the buildings."[91] It being "full time to execute the intended business," McGillivray declared to O'Neill and others, ten broken days were sent across Creek Country to prepare for the strike. One bundle of sticks was delivered to each participating community; each day after receiving the bundle, one stick was pulled out, broken, and discarded. After all of the broken days were consumed, the attack would begin.[92]

Warriors from Little Tallassee, Tuckabatchee, and Hillaubee from the Upper Country, along with more from Coweta, Hitchiti, and Ooseoochee from the Lower Country, all made coordinated plans to strike.[93] Now, McGillivray pressed the governors, the Spanish needed to keep their end of the bargain. Creek attempts to solve the problem diplomatically had proved "fruitless and without effect," and Georgia expansionists were now threatening both Creek and Spanish interests. Augusta and Galphinton were both clearly illegal, even to Congress, yet just as clear was the Georgia determination to stick with them.[94] Fighting was "absolutely a case of the last necessity," McGillivray explained to O'Neill, and now Creek warriors needed the arms and ammunition he and the other governors had promised. O'Neill passed these requests along the line to Zéspedes as well as the Spanish minister in Philadelphia, Don Diego de Gardoqui, who seemed to agree. Soon powder and ammunition were being distributed from royal warehouses in New Orleans.[95]

While Galphinton unified many Creeks in the realization that violence was the only thing capable of stopping Georgia expansionism, the well-established enclaves of pro-American support rushed to reaffirm their support of the Georgians. Creek resolve was by no means total. By harkening back directly to the Revolutionary War, headmen from Cusseta, Half-Way House, and Big Tallassee, among others, reminded Georgians anew that they "never took the English talks but stuck to the Virginia people." These headmen, including of course the Fat King and the Cusseta King, promised state authorities that they were as firm American allies as they had ever been. They went so far as to promise satisfaction for any deaths that Georgians might suffer at the hands of their own neighbors.[96] While aggressive, those assurances influenced little. Across the Chattahoochee, Cowetas were vocal advocates of violence, while state officials were fearful that Chehaws were soon to move on their southern frontier as well.[97] Broken Arrows, Ooseoochees, and Hitchitis would be likely to follow, proving that the Lower Country was much more violent than Cussetas suggested. To the north, the Half-Way House and Big Tallassees remained strong American partisans while little was heard of Oakfuskee. They almost certainly refused to take part in the raiding, yet they and their allies were also outnumbered. Little Tallassees had agreed to the raiding, and Tuckabatchees and Hillaubees were already on their way south to meet with Spanish agents and gather ammunition. Once they had it, they "were to turn out to kill burn and destroy," and their involvement would surely bring Abihkas, Hookchoies, and Cooloomees to the frontier as well.[98] While the persistence of some Cussetas and Big Tallassees demonstrated that Creek Country was not unanimously supportive of violence, it certainly seemed to be moving in that direction.

Word of the Creek preparations swept across the American backcountry, spreading fear as far north as the Cumberland River and Kentucky settlements.[99] Even though Georgia authorities prepared for violence, they remained convinced of their legal right to the land in question and welcomed the chance to gain by force what they had failed to gain by treaty. Although an earlier voice of caution, Timothy Barnard was now "sorry to hear the Indians our friend take the Spandards bad talks which will prove as much to their ruin as the Inglish talks did and is not gone and left you to be poor." Spaniards would "serve you the same and only wants to set you at war and git you all killed," he warned.[100] A few state authorities even responded to the threat of Creek raids by calling for a first strike, a move reminiscent of Georgia threats during the Revolutionary War.[101] Underneath that aggressive talk, however, was a state just as woefully unprepared to deal with Creek raiding as before. Indeed, when congressionally appointed Indian superintendent James White recognized the excellent position McGillivray and the Spaniards enjoyed, and how weakly Americans would be able to oppose them, he was exactly right.[102]

Creeks proved that point soon enough. In April 1786 the sticks ran out, and headmen kept to the plans they made at Tuckabatchee. Soon warriors were along the length of the Georgia frontier, but they focused on the highly exposed Wilkes County (which was the product of the Ceded Lands) and then Washington, Greene, and Franklin counties, which comprised much of the recently claimed land.[103] Soon reports were widespread that families were being "drove off from there small farmes" in large numbers.[104] To the north, the militia of Franklin County was expected to "get weaker every day some moving and others talking of moving," while to the south, one particular alarm "broke all inhabitance south of ogechee."[105] Eufalas, Yuchis, and Chehaws from the Lower Country were active by May, while parties led by Tuckabatchees were converging more or less on Washington County, with directions to drive away all the cattle and horses and to "kill all the people they could find." The county was doomed, many feared, and soon Burke County, further to the east, was on the verge of breaking as well.[106] "I expect every day to here more people being killed by them," one Georgian disparaged. Within a month of the offensive that gloomy outlook had been proven accurate; war parties had already killed several settlers and state officials were struggling to maintain a defensive posture. By the dead of summer a party of one hundred Hillaubee and Kialijee warriors added to the mayhem. Perhaps those were the warriors one report described in August: "several parties of Creek Indians" had "marched to the frontier settlements and committed murders and depredations," causing "much alarm and distress."[107] By the fall the western parts of the state were wholly at the mercy of Creek warriors and could turn nowhere for support.

Meanwhile, Tallassee and Cusseta chiefs had already taken pains at the outset of the offensive to remind the Georgians that they had always been friends and were determined to stay that way. After hearing of the first rounds of attacks in May, Cussetas complained that "mad people from the Upper Creeks," led by McGillivray, attacked settlements "unknown to us your friends." And, facing widespread participation by war parties from the Lower Country, Cusseta headmen declared that they at least "are still your friends."[108] Barnard also claimed to hear of rising animosity toward the raiders, and particularly toward McGillivray for his role in coordinating the attacks. There were numbers of communities in both the Upper and Lower countries that were actually inclined to peace, he charged, and even those groups that were raiding were being manipulated by the Spanish. Many, he wrote, "I hear seems to be offended with Mr. McGillivray for what he has done which I imagin was intirely by instructions of the Spanards."[109] While there certainly were groups of headmen incensed by the raids, Barnard's assertions seem overblown, which the Tuckabatchee conference had proven. McGillivray certainly was working with Spanish governors, but the decision to strike made at Tuckabatchee was done by the votes of dozens of headmen, of various rank, and not on either McGillivray's or Spanish orders. Although the raiding did reveal the hardening of American and Spanish lines in the region it was also a successful show of Creek cohesion during a time of regional crisis.

Most importantly, perhaps, the offensive had just the effect Creeks hoped: an immediate softening of the Georgia tone. Although they complained bitterly of Creek atrocities, state officials did begin to back away from the frontier counties. If permanent, that retreat would most likely have brought an end to the struggle. Even the most unfriendly headmen could be open to a peace if state authorities renounced the treaties of Augusta and Galphinton and moved off the debated hunting lands. Raiding began to taper off immediately, for instance, when word spread about the possibility of a new conference with state officials.[110] One talk from Chehaw, Okmulgee, Ooseoochee, and Hitchiti headmen, representing the bulk of the Lower Country save Cussetas, insisted that the voice of their "old and young warriors" was to stay neutral for the time, and they were "inclinable to go to their hunting grounds in peace."[111] The raids produced a unity that was a specifically focused response to a regional crisis, the talk revealed. They had already made their point, spreading panic along the frontier, burning settlers from their homes, and forcing Georgia legislators to the bargaining table.[112] Governor Edward Telfair appeared amenable, hurriedly promising McGillivray that "no further encroachments will be suffered" until the groups met, assuring him at the same time that if he and the other Creek headmen had a sincere wish to make things right, "he never had a more favorable opportunity."[113]

McGillivray assured Georgians that "it intirely rests with yourselves Whether we War or not." Although Georgians appeared humbled, and the Creek position strong, Creek terms were stiff. Only a complete removal of Georgian settlements from the disputed hunting grounds between the Ogeechee and Oconee rivers would bring a lasting solution. The theft of the lands was the "greatest harm that could be done us," McGillivray explained, and was "the principal Ground for quarrel & differences." There could be no peace while they remained in dispute; only when Georgians relinquished everything they gained at Galphinton could they again "become Steady & firm friends."[114] Faced with that ultimatum, of course, the reformed Georgian position proved remarkably short-lived. Despite being once humbled, both settlers and their local representatives proved stubbornly resistant to such a reversal of their fortunes. State legislators did of course face a serious practical dilemma with such a proposal, even if they had no ideological opposition to it. Much of the land under dispute had already been surveyed, sold, and even settled, and the sales had provided Georgia with perhaps the only reliable source of state income it had seen since long before the Revolution. There would be no reasonable way to reverse the course the state government had already charted, no matter how questionable it was.

There was little worry of having to face that conundrum, certainly, because state authorities also found the Creek ultimatum ideologically repulsive. Georgians had fought the American Revolution against the Creek people almost as equally as the British; their people had suffered tremendously, but they had won, and they deserved the Treaties of Augusta and Galphinton. The lands Georgians gained in those treaties belonged to them, not Creeks; state forces had bled for them, they gained them legitimately, and there was no way they were giving them back because Creeks had now burned their frontier farms for a second time. Rather than begin a dialogue with the Spanish partisan base, then, state authorities attempted yet again to have the cessions legitimized. Based on Barnard's and the Cussetas' intelligence, and not McGillivray's, state lawmakers declared that the recent unfortunate raids were actually localized and isolated attacks, and not a coordinated response to the treaties, and that the land dispute could still be resolved to their benefit. In fact, they argued, there was actually widespread acceptance of the treaties in Creek Country, and scores of friendly community leaders were being held under the heel of Spaniards, McGillivray, and perhaps a small group of renegade headmen. That was the position that guided state officials through what became a steadily intensifying set of confrontations with Creek communities—a path that ultimately led to much more bloodshed.

First, authorities appointed Daniel McMurphy state agent to the Creeks and empowered him to travel into Creek Country and rally support for the state. McMurphy, who once worked under George Galphin and was no stranger to the region, was soon on his way into the Lower Country. Despite his arriving at a time when raids were still ongoing, he struck an aggressive line, demanding satisfaction for all the settlers who had lately been killed as well as for their destroyed farms, and he called a general council to press his position.[115] The agent began his adventure among the same friendly cast of headmen whom Georgians had depended on in the past, and so it was not altogether bizarre, then, that he was not

immediately killed. Indeed, although his words were by no means conciliatory, he did not fail to drum up at least some support. When local
headmen were informed he was en route, in fact, they promised that they
would "give him all the satisfaction he may think reasonable."[116] Both the
Fat King and Tallassee King then reaffirmed their loyalty at the ensuing
conference, held at Cusseta, and the American must have been thrilled
with his accomplishments thus far.[117]

McMurphy gained more favorable intelligence from James McQueen,
a long-time trader in the Lower Country who had been associated with
both the Galphin and Rae trading operations. His American loyalties
clearly had not changed much, and he began telling McMurphy more
of what the American agent wanted to hear. McGillivray had sworn to
sweep the Georgians off of the debated lands if it meant the ruin of the
whole nation, for instance. McQueen, however, "said that McGilvery was
much mistaken, for he could never get the whole nation to take his talks."
Furthermore, after everyone heard McMurphy's talks, he promised,
McGillivray "would not be so well" received as he had been.[118] Soon the
agent was pleased to report that "more than three parts out of four of the
lower Creeks are for peace and say that if the upper Creeks are for war
they must fight themselves."[119]

Based on assurances from Cussetas that Lower Country headmen
"would not agree to any talk, but peace," McMurphy left to try his hand
in the Upper Country. On his way there he visited the second pillar of
American support, the Tallassee King, at the Half-Way House, at the
same time McGillivray and the Mad Dog were away visiting Pensacola.
Taking advantage of that situation, the Tallassee King's conversations
with McMurphy demonstrate how contentious the atmosphere in Creek
Country had become, even in the midst of Creeks' military successes.
According to McMurphy's accounts, the headman clearly and repeatedly confirmed what most other Creek headmen had flatly denied. He
and his allies did indeed have the authority to give up the Oconee lands,
which was done "to cover the blood that they had spilt when they took
the English lying talks, and the whole nation sent him to make peace."[120]
For the second time McMurphy found clear evidence of support for the
Georgia position, as well as a rejection of the radical pro-Spanish partisans. So far, McMurphy's trip had done quite a bit to legitimize the state.
American support in Creek Country, he was sure, was a powerful force
working in Georgia's interests.

There certainly were communities of American support in both the
Lower and Upper countries that entertained McMurphy, but speaking

as he was from his bases in Cusseta and then the Half-Way House McMurphy was badly mistaken to assume that those sentiments were widespread. The Fat King and the Tallassee King clearly did not have the pulse of most Creeks, and in the end their words of encouragement almost got the American killed. Having heard nothing but positive reassurances, McMurphy ventured further into the Upper Country, and there his prospects quickly dimmed. The Tallassee King and the White Lieutenant of Oakfuskee attempted to call another council in the hopes of hearing more American talks, first at Big Tallassee and then at Oakfuskee. Both efforts were frustrated by McGillivray and the Mad Dog, who had just returned from West Florida. The two sent runners in every direction requesting headmen to ignore the summons, which it appears they did.[121] According to trader and interpreter James Durouzeaux, McGillivray would surely "stop the Upper towns if any of them is inclined to attend."[122] These reports portrayed not only a strong unity in the region but an ongoing power struggle, pitting Georgia allies in the Half-Way House, Big Tallassee, and Oakfuskee against Spanish partisans in Tuckabatchee, Little Tallassee, and further to the north. As McMurphy moved further away from the Half-Way House and Big Tallassee and into that more volatile region, his message was sure to attract a much more mixed audience.

The more McMurphy attempted to project state authority, in fact, the deeper his talks buried him. Now firmly in the Upper Country he began to notice that most Creeks produced Spanish documents and trading papers, and not American ones, which he made a point of contention. He began declaring that they were illegal, and he attempted to seize them and enforce Georgia trade licenses. When he confronted offenders, however, they simply ignored him.[123] And when he demanded satisfaction for slain Georgians, as he had done in Cusseta and Big Tallassee, he was laughed at, scorned, and even threatened. Several headmen then informed him that they had Spanish talks from Pensacola telling them that "they weren't to listen to any Americans." Furthermore, they declared openly, when they renewed their efforts to drive the Georgians back across the Oconee, the Spanish would continue to stand behind them.[124] Despite being ineffective and in growing jeopardy, McMurphy remained confident that he would be able to clarify all of these matters to the Georgians' advantage. While his position grew dodgier almost by the day he continued to request a conference from which to press state demands. McGillivray finally obliged him, but in an almost humorous twist he made plans to have it held at Tuckabatchee, rather than at Tallassee. Tuckabatchee was as inhospitable a place for a Georgian as existed anywhere in Creek Country, and McMurphy would find an untimely death there before he found any friends of Galphinton. Soon there were reports that he gave up—even that he fled—bringing the latest state attempt at legitimizing the two treaties to an abrupt and embarrassing end.[125]

Before he left, however, McMurphy spent just enough time with McGillivray and other headmen in the Upper Country to understand just how polarized the region had become. When he asked why neither the Tallassee King nor the Cusseta headmen were present, the agent got quite an answer. "We believe they are ashamed of their bad conduct, respecting the Lands," McGillivray declared, "& of which they have been often told of."[126] Georgians were not the only ones disinterested in compromise, the exchange clarified—neither were most Creek headmen, and it was a lesson that almost cost McMurphy his life. Galphinton had solidified Georgian and Spanish factions in Creek Country, leaving little place for common ground. While McMurphy's visit no doubt left many Creeks as mad at state authorities as ever, his mission to legitimize the Georgian position also worsened the tension building between communities in the Upper Country, while state support to the south was limited almost entirely to Cusseta. Further compounding matters, while Spanish governors had already been providing weapons and ammunition to all but a handful of Creek communities for some time, McMurphy's visit prompted them to intensify their efforts. Headmen were soon returning from the Gulf Coast with shot and gunpowder practically by the wagonload, and "from these circumstances," a worried Timothy Barnard reported, "we may expect nothing but a war." Spaniards were promising warriors "all the assistance they can give them," which was evidently no exaggeration. Arturo O'Neill was particularly aggressive, not only increasing the flow of weapons and ammunition from Pensacola but suggesting Spanish authorities counter American agents by increasing their own official presence in Creek Country.[127]

With partisan groups deeply entrenched and with little hope for a peaceful acceptance of Galphinton, Georgia legislators prepared for a third treaty conference, to convene at a landing on the Oconee River referred to as Shoulderbone. Coming on the heels of an impressive show of Creek power, and in the face of an aggressive Spanish position along the Gulf Coast, the council at Shoulderbone represented, on the one hand, the possibility of a genuine and meaningful dialogue with Creek headmen, who were clearly more powerful than state authorities had previously assumed. Perhaps a compromise, under the right circumstances, might even have been possible. Unfortunately for their constituents, state legislators chose a very different approach; from its very conception, indeed, Shoulderbone was planned as an exercise in intimidation. If everything went according to state plans drawn for the upcoming conference, the Creek commissioners would be militarily outgunned, diplomatically overwhelmed, and, Georgians hoped, humiliated. A handful of commissioners would demand the acceptance of the terms of the Treaty of Galphinton while a sizable state army lingered menacingly in the wings. The commissioners would then, in addition, demand life-for-life satisfaction for killed settlers, the return of stolen property and reparations for raids, and hostages of Creek headmen to ensure that the terms of the agreement would be complied with promptly. And if their Creek counterparts in any way refused to do those things, the commissioners would threaten to retire and empower the military men with them to invade Creek Country and retaliate by force. Such an overwhelming show of power was guaranteed to cow the renegade headmen into complete submission, gaining the state the unconditional victory that had eluded them for so long.[128]

In the face of terrific Creek resistance such a combative approach to a treaty conference seems bizarre almost to the point of being unbelievable. It probably would be unbelievable had the commissioners not left such detailed accounts of their proceedings or had Creeks not retaliated so mercilessly afterward. It was clear by the design of Shoulderbone, however, that state legislators looked upon themselves as being victimized by Creeks in the failures of their past treaty attempts, and they approached the council accordingly. It appears they also believed McMurphy's reports from the region without qualification. Only a handful of headmen, directed by McGillivray and the Spaniards, were holding many more friendly communities hostage, and Shoulderbone provided the opportunity to overpower the hostage takers and crush the radicals. Considering McMurphy barely escaped Creek Country with his life that assertion seems unlikely, but state authorities were nonetheless convinced. And perhaps they even believed that this latest diplomatic approach was indeed what was in the best interests of their citizens. Whatever their rationale, the treaty commissioners were resolved. They complained of their previous attempts to "cultivate" friendship, to "treat on principles of amity," and to "evince a pacific disposition." For their earnest and heartfelt efforts at Galphinton Creek warriors attacked Georgians practically out of nowhere, killing innocent state citizens and burning their property.[129] Both Augusta and Galphinton were legitimately made and even benevolent, the commissioners concluded, and if Creeks pushed Georgia into enforcing the terms of those agreements with violence and intimidation, then so be it. That sort of posture was remarkable in itself, yet of all the puzzling arrangements made by state authorities, the most bizarre was by far their explicit instructions to the commissioners *not* to encourage a large attendance of Creek headmen. The treaty would be "more for their advantage than our own," Governor Telfair explained, and so a large contingent of Creeks would not be necessary.[130]

It will forever remain a mystery whether state authorities actually considered Shoulderbone a legitimate attempt to secure a peace or whether they were simply using the meeting as a justification for invasion. By constructing the conference in such a confrontational way, however, Georgians obviously were not prepared to initiate any acts of conciliation. "Open your ears wide, and hear the wrongs we have suffered," the commissioners began, which set the tone for their upcoming talks quite nicely. Creeks were responsible for scores of murders and robberies that Georgia's innocent, peace-loving settlers had suffered, "without the smallest provocation," and in violation of the several solemn treaties headmen had made with state authorities in good faith. Satisfaction had to be made for such betrayals, and liberally. If the raiding had gone on any longer, the commissioners warned, Creek towns "would have been on fire, and your people killed, or driven into the Wilderness." To prove that their threats carried weight, the commissioners kept to their plans. They paraded what they reported later was upwards of fifteen hundred militiamen, armed to the teeth, around the conference grounds.[131]

With their soldiers lingering, the commissioners commenced insulting the chiefs repeatedly, then proceeded to read aloud various threatening and remonstrative letters penned by McGillivray. It was "owing to what this man has said," they warned, that the conference was the way it was. This was an essential component of the commission's larger approach. If they could scare enough headmen away from McGillivray, victory could be had. They tried to do that, demanding the headmen kill McGillivray, along with various other voices of radical Creek resistance. Georgians would have no qualms burning Creek villages down if they did not get the satisfaction they were demanding, they then repeated. Continuing, they added to the list of those who needed to die. Satisfaction ought to be life for a life, they charged—which was of course Creek custom, not American law—for all of the murders Creek warriors had committed after Galphinton. Because of the success of the Creek raiding, that was not necessarily a small number.[132] "Every one in the parties concerned" in the raiding deserved to die, but the commissioners declared that the execution of six would be sufficient. It was a downright magnanimous gesture—a sign of their goodwill, the commissioners declared. Furthermore, however, five headmen had to give themselves up as prisoners, a bond of sorts to guarantee that the treaty stipulations would for once be complied with in a timely fashion.[133]

The state's approach to Shoulderbone was a bold one indeed. Years later, even Georgian Joseph Clay would write about the proceedings with shame.[134] By far the most bewildering aspect of the whole ordeal was that, and for the third time, across from the commissioners sat only their friends. The vast majority of Creek leadership, with McGillivray at their lead, had no intention of being found anywhere near Shoulderbone.[135] So for the third time it was mostly only a half dozen or so Cusseta, Half-Way House, Tallassee, and maybe Oakfuskee headmen who were present, not so much to negotiate as to bear witness to the blistering verbal assault that the state representatives produced. The headmen could only look at each other in amazement and disbelief as Georgians performed their act—reading aloud their complaints, parading around in arms, threatening war, and demanding prisoners. And they certainly did not need to sermonize against McGillivray, whom the headmen in front of them already despised and had disavowed on several occasions. "The Chief Person who has been against you is Alexander McGillevray," both the Tallassee King and Fat King assured them. They even threatened to kill him, which must have pleased the commissioners. They would "give him an opportunity of going away quietly. But we must remove him. If he chuses to live with the Spaniards he may go to them, or else he must also be killed." His talks as "the voice of the Nation are not so. They are of his own making, and to suit his private purposes, and make our Nation poor."[136] These were not lackeys of McGillivray, and neither were they allies to the Spanish, the headmen tried to reassure their Georgia friends. But at Shoulderbone none of that mattered. The commissioners did not budge, not even in their resolve to keep hostages as a guarantee that the "stipulations in the treaty are completed." Both the Fat King and Tallassee King were soon in shackles, along with almost everyone else at the conference. Only one was allowed to leave, a messenger to pass along the state's demands.[137]

Beyond what must have been the extreme sense of resentment and humiliation felt by all of the headmen in attendance, the state's approach proved particularly hard on the Tallassee King. He had lost kin to Georgia militiamen in the very recent past, after the Treaty of Galphinton, when his people had done nothing to deserve it.[138] He traveled to the conference hoping for so much as to receive satisfaction for his slain relations. Instead the commissioners were demanding the lives of more of his people, who, the Tallassee King sourly remarked, were their friends. Worse yet, he was now a prisoner. Georgians were "trying to make a war against them," he complained.[139] That and other complaints notwithstanding, however, the commissioners quickly declared the conference a success, having concluded it in the "usual form, conduct and manner of treaties with Indians."[140] By keeping the Creek headmen hostage state authorities hoped "that the friends of these Chieftans will consent to any sort of conditions just to gain their liberty." They demanded a council with other headmen, including the Mad Dog of Tuckabatchee, if the hostages were to be released.[141] That, of course, was not going to happen. Most other headmen in Creek Country, it soon became clear, didn't care if they ever saw either the Fat King or Tallassee King again. As Cussetas themselves explained, "The people you have there is of your friends and not of those who are against you," and seizing them was "only distressing your friends and detaining them will be no restraint on the bad inclind people of the upper towns who do not wish them ever to return." Furthermore, if any of these friendly men ended up hurt or dead at the hands of the commissioners it would destroy any relationship state officials still had with the few headmen willing to talk to them, and "therefore can answer no good purpose to keep them." It could only be attended "with very bad consequences."[142]

The Cusseta headmen were also correct in suggesting that most other Creeks probably would not mind if they disappeared for good. At the same time the Fat King, Tallassee King, and their allies were pleading with state authorities at Shoulderbone, trying to distance themselves from McGillivray and his allies, McGillivray was outwardly calling them traitors. They, with "a few others that have been long in the American interest," were actively working against all other Creek people, he complained to Zéspedes. It was a shame that Creek customs did not permit dealing with them "by giving them the usual punishment," by which he probably meant death. They had traveled to meet the Americans "against the wills of the Nation." Now they were humiliated and made prisoners, and they deserved all of their misfortune. And if Georgians hoped to use them as hostages to their advantage, they would be sorely disappointed. By their "bad conduct" these chiefs forfeited "every pretension to consideration." Their detention was "of no concern," and their Georgia friends were "welcome to keep them as long as they chuse."[143]

Shoulderbone, in short, revealed a Creek Country torn but also on the verge of all-out war. The headmen seized at this latest so-called treaty conference were the same ones who supported their American allies during the Revolution, and in the postwar years they remained stubbornly sympathetic to their state neighbors even in the face of repeated, and now withering, insults. With most of its leadership held as hostages in the wake of this latest outrage, however, the ranks of this pro-Georgia partisan group were not particularly well positioned for success. The Spanish partisans, on the other hand, certainly were, and violence in the wake of Shoulderbone was all but guaranteed.

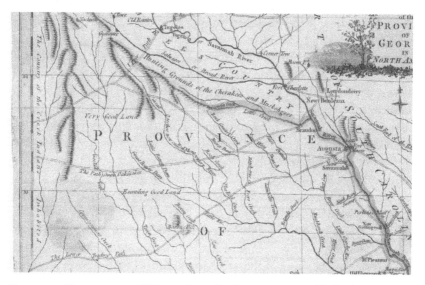

FIGURE 1. Georgia, 1779. This portion of a Georgia map published in 1779 accurately depicts the contradictory claims to some of the Ceded Lands, located on the headwaters of the Ogeechee River and below the Broad River. Despite heavy raiding by Creeks in the Revolutionary War, Georgia authorities organized the land as Wilkes County, and it was raided heavily again during the Oconee War. Note the location of several Creek trading paths, as well as notations for "very good land," "exceeding good land," and, most importantly, "Hunting Grounds of the Cherakees and Muskohgees." Courtesy of the Hargrett Library, University of Georgia.

FIGURE 2. Wilkes County Headright Survey, 1783. This head-right survey, filed in 1783, contained over 2,000 acres of land on the headwaters of the Ogeechee River, in newly established Wilkes County. Note how a Creek "War Path," perhaps the Oakfuskee trading path, passes through the middle of the land claim, crossing over the south fork of the Ogeechee River. Courtesy of Georgia Archives, RG 3-3-26, wlks0754.

FIGURE 3. Wilkes County Headright Survey, 1784. This headright survey, filed in 1784, contained 250 acres of land in Wilkes County and encompassed a stretch of the south fork of the Little River. Note the two roads that pass through the claim, one labeled "Great Road from Washington Town to the head of Sherrals Creek." That road appears to be Georgia-44, placing this land claim just east of Union Point, Georgia, and on the western edge of the Ceded Lands that Creeks would have been raiding in the 1780s. Courtesy of Georgia Archives, RG 3-3-26, wlks0232.

4 /   Partisan Creeks at War

But there was a third party, (the Georgians) they said, which evidently meant injustice and oppression.
        —James White, May 24, 1787

Violence engulfed the Creek-Georgia frontier not long after Shoulderbone. In a particularly dark period in the history of the state of Georgia, which many later referred to as the Oconee War, Creeks burned scores of settlers from their homes, crippled the state government, and ultimately forced a federal intervention.[1] From the fallout of the third state treaty effort to Alexander McGillivray and his associates signing the Treaty of New York in 1790, the wide-ranging participation of warriors from across Creek Country demonstrated the power and possibility of a very desperate, very mad Creek people. There was little even the staunchest state partisans were willing to say or do to stop their neighbors from laying waste to the Georgia backcountry. Many of them, who not only were present at Shoulderbone but were taken hostage there, were too angered and stunned by those proceedings to make sense of anything. What resulted was a powerful moment in Creek politics driven by crisis, when Creek communities rallied from across the region to do forcibly what they had failed to do peaceably.

The extremism represented by Georgia expansionism aligned almost all of Creek Country during the Oconee War against a common enemy, which displayed on the one hand the flexibility of Creek notions of governance and war making. During such a time of crisis, even men without strong traditional ties to leadership, like Alexander McGillivray, could wield tremendous authority. On the other hand, solidarity during the Oconee War was deceptive in its suggestion of a longer-term sense of

Creek cohesiveness. Although the war demonstrated the ways Creek Country could project what appeared to be a united voice, it was misleading. Even when faced by external crisis several partisan groups soon emerged that, only a few years later, pulled the region back apart, revealing how the Oconee War was more the product of a matched response by multitudes of independently acting communities than the will of a truly unified Creek people.

Shortly after the end of the Revolution, for instance, there was a Spanish partisan base and a smaller Georgia one. By the outbreak of the Oconee War, the Spanish base was much larger and stronger, while its Georgia counterpart had faded almost into obscurity. Over the course of the war, however, the Spanish partisan group began to fragment while a new, American counterpart group emerged, influenced by new federal legislators with more moderate goals for peace that had broad appeal, even to McGillivray. The arrival of William Augustus Bowles created yet another source of political gravity, which also had consequences as the Oconee War progressed. The emergence of those competing factions challenge the idea of Creek cohesiveness even at a time when Creek communities appeared as coordinated as they perhaps had ever been. Such a powerful moment in Creek politics proved in the end fleeting—its roots were in extremism and crisis, not in Creek traditions of unity, and the crisis did not last forever.

Despite the relatively few Creek headmen at Shoulderbone—and the fact that only one of them was actually allowed to immediately leave Shoulderbone—the proceedings spread through Creek Country like wildfire. Alarming as they might have been, though, the reports only confirmed what McGillivray and several other headmen had long charged. Shoulderbone, like the treaties that preceded it, was never a sincere attempt at diplomacy. Had any chiefs or warriors of real importance actually attended it, Georgia authorities probably would have had them clapped in chains, like the others, if not executed outright. Cowetas in particular seethed for revenge.[2] Enraged by the seizure of their neighbors, they declared that if Georgians continued to act so belligerently they would "swell the list of your killed tenfold." It was better "to die like men Seeking revenge than at home like dogs."[3] Embarrassed by the actions of commissioners he approached as allies, not even the Tallassee King could hold his tongue. He "thundered out a furious talk & frightened the Georgians from their purpose of keeping them." Although his outburst got the Tallassee King released, authorities held on to the rest of their hostages—mostly Cussetas—which remained the source of almost feverish anger in the Lower Country. And as for the Tallassee King, no longer would he be as spirited a Georgia partisan as before. Returning home from one bad situation only to face a worse one, he arrived to face widespread ridicule in the Upper Country. The commissioners' aggression had taken its toll on even the friendliest of headmen, and it was unclear how they would act as the rest of the region came to grips with Shoulderbone.[4]

His wisdom and his diplomatic skill having been proven yet again, on the other hand, McGillivray emerged during the Oconee War in an exceptionally strong position. A constant and forceful critic of Georgia authorities for years by that point, his words carried more weight than ever. He wasted little time, intensifying his rhetoric as communities speedily prepared to renew their attacks. He was "determined the Oconee land shall not be settled if he can help it," Timothy Barnard reported, and there was no doubt most Creek communities were of a similar mind.[5] McGillivray's continued rise was understandable because of the crisis Creeks faced, but it was also a rather unique one—not reflective of his traditional cultural foundation in Creek Country but instead his extraordinary political acumen. It was well known and often remarked upon contemporarily, for instance, that McGillivray enjoyed more the life of a wealthy southerner than of a traditional Creek leader. From his extensive and fenced properties, his scores of slaves, and his home and library to his dress and speech, and even his religious beliefs, McGillivray could at times appear out of place in Creek Country.[6] That is not to say that he was somehow less Creek than his neighbors. He was the son of a Creek woman, and because Creek identity flowed matrilineally, Alexander's own identity was a product of his mother's Creek heritage, not his father's European one. He may or may not have considered himself Scottish because his father was, but in Creek Country that was of secondary importance. What was certain was that because his mother was a member of the influential Wind clan, so was he. Despite his at times European look, Alexander McGillivray was as much a Creek as any other Creek; that he was also a man of mixed ancestry meant little.[7]

While his Creek heritage was unquestionable, McGillivray did not have a particularly strong traditional claim to leadership authority. Along a Creek-Georgia border defined for years by confrontation and crisis, however, that did not seem to matter. Although only a few men could claim to be a traditional *mico*, many could be leaders, even headmen. Alexander McGillivray was one of those men; he was not a Creek chief even though contemporaries frequently referred to him as such. Instead he was an *isti atcagagi thlucco*, or a "Great Beloved Man," which was someone in great demand during the immediate postwar years. Historically, a beloved man functioned as an advisor or a spokesman in Creek councils, and there could be several of them in a single village. Usually one attained such a title through years of experience, but a beloved man was always chosen for his sound guidance and good advice.[8] Anthropologist Frank Speck described a Tuskegee beloved man only a bit differently, "as a man who amassed property or raised himself in public esteem by other means." He was someone, in other words, who was influential, even though he carried no civil or military title.[9] As a successful man with physical and cultural ties to Creek Country, strong economic ties to the Spanish and British, and nothing but the right advice when it came to the state of Georgia, McGillivray had all the qualities that would have made him a Beloved Man of the first rate. When groups of men were leaving the Lower Country to raid into Georgia, for instance, they found his input important. And when they heard that American commissioners were seeking peace, they "sent runners every were to stop and turn back all parties they could come up with, until we could hear from Mr. McGillivray, and have his advice on the matter."[10] The crisis that Georgians were quickly creating was the perfect—perhaps the only—means for Alexander McGillivray to gain the level of regional importance that he enjoyed after the conclusion of Shoulderbone.

Nevertheless, McGillivray's name did not contain *mico*, which meant that he did not carry the title of a community chief. His by-now inveterate foes the Tallassee King and Fat King, on the other hand, did carry those titles, reflecting much stronger traditional claims to authority based in Creek culture. Translated roughly as "king" or "chief," mico was a title that represented the highest civil position of leadership in a Creek community. That meant that the Tallassee King, or Hopoithle Mico, and the Fat King, or Eneah Mico, were both highly respected men. A mico's title was also complicated, and his power far from infallible, as the two headmen's troubled position after Shoulderbone also revealed. A mico was not necessarily a community's sole leader, for instance, and there could be several in a large town. Eneah Mico, Cusseta Mico, Fushatchee Mico, Tussekiah Mico, and Owlelo Mico, among others, all came from Cusseta and were all regarded as influential men. Furthermore, there was little unconditional or coercive authority attached to their position. As William Bartram remarked, a Creek mico "has not the least shadow of exclusive executive power." Their role as director of their community's politics was based on persuasion, consent, and above all else respect, and they seldom acted unilaterally. Still, such a man advanced to the highest position of community leadership because he was a shrewd and trusted leader who was revered immensely. As Bartram further explained, he was "universally acknowledged to be the greatest person among them, and he is loved, esteemed and reverenced." While on a surveying expedition in 1773 Bartram made note of the chief who led the Creek party accompanying the surveyors. After waking up for another day on the trail the mico smoked tobacco ceremonially and thundered out a talk outlining the group's movements: "He rises, his left hand bearing on his Gun, his Right armed with his Tomahoc their ensign of Authority, with a Heroick air & action, a loud & determined Voice speacks, than marches a head with his party."[11] A mico was a powerful headman of both words and actions, and when he marched, people followed him.

It was clear not only that McGillivray was not a man among that leadership class but that he held no civic title in Creek Country at all. His name did not contain mico, nor did it include *haujo, fixico, mathla, tustunnuggee,* or any other traditional marker of authority, experience, or even boldness.[12] He absolutely was not a warrior, his contemporaries were quick to note. Among his numerous shortcomings, one Spaniard explained in 1792, McGillivray "never carried on warfare at the head of his warriors."[13] Despite those shortcomings, his nontraditional claim to authority was not totally without precedent. As scholars of Creeks and Creek culture have already suggested, during times of crisis micos were not always the ones to lead. While one of a community's leading warriors, or tustunnuggees, might be the most obvious second choice, because leadership flowed from trust and consent it could perhaps be anyone who had the answers to the dangerous questions the community faced. During a time of true political or diplomatic upheaval, Creek leadership traditions could be remarkably flexible, making an untested man like McGillivray influential even though he benefited from little of the experience of a mico or a tustunnuggee. Leadership by consent, a foundation of Creek politics, theoretically allowed for any strong force to lead in a time of crisis.[14] As Shoulderbone demonstrated more clearly than ever, Georgians were generating such a crisis in Creek Country. McGillivray probably would have made few decisions of importance outside the confines of his plantation at Little Tallassee had the threat of Georgia expansionism not posed such a pressing threat to all Creeks. After Shoulderbone, however, McGillivray certainly was in a position to lead.

The stubbornness displayed by the remaining Georgia partisans demonstrated at the same time the limits of McGillivray's influence, even when it was at its highest level. Many headmen were certainly only listening to the young man because they had no other option. Even then they did so with marked suspicion, and at times they objected to his leadership more outwardly.[15] Long-standing disagreements between McGillivray and both the Fat King and Tallassee King illustrate the tension he created in even the most trying times.[16] They persistently countered his efforts in the face of repeated insults and at times to the bewilderment of their neighbors.[17] McGillivray grew much sharper and condescending in his criticism of their decisions after Galphinton, and he practically rejoiced in their seizure at Shoulderbone. The Tallassee King, by lashing out at the Georgians, "for once in his life time behaved like a man." However traitorous their complicity at Shoulderbone probably seemed, such abuse must have felt particularly insulting to men who considered themselves important civic leaders, and who certainly were not of a "second rank," as McGillivray would later describe them.[18] Several times both chiefs made it clear that they were in no way beholden to an upstart like the young and inexperienced McGillivray, whom they considered a "boy and an usurper."[19] That friction draws out the polarizing effects of the post-Revolutionary period on Creek politics. Conflicting ideas of leadership, even during such a time of crisis, was emerging as another tradition that generated disagreement and bitterness, and not necessarily understanding.

Despite their grievances the leaders of the Georgia partisans played a losing role in the post-Shoulderbone crisis. Anger at Georgians was raw, and no second Tuckabatchee conference was necessary to help communities plan their next move. Creeks "unanimously agreed to strike," with the exception, of course, of a small group of Cusseta, Tallassee, and Half-Way House communities, who although dumbfounded and no doubt outraged, were not yet ready to partake in the violence. Although they promised "not to have any hand in the matter," their words of neutrality were far less supportive than state authorities would have liked, demonstrating the true cost of the Shoulderbone fiasco.[20] While they would not participate in the impending war, neither would these once-strong American allies do much to stop it. Meanwhile, calls for war intensified further once word of the treaty made it to the Gulf Coast. McGillivray quickly passed accounts of the treaty on to his Spanish partners, making sure they knew at the same time that hundreds, even thousands, of warriors were now counting on them for support. As they had before, the governors responded supportively and even enthusiastically, praising the chiefs' resolve and assuring them that whatever assistance they needed, they would have it. The headmen had acted "not only legally but meritoriously," Zéspedes assured McGillivray, and could now "take up arms and by force of arms shall compel their neighbors to be just." Spanish authorities not only supported the Creek position, they relished the opportunity to give Americans a strong check on their westward ambitions, and they saw an opportunity in the Creek offensive to do so without open confrontation on their part.[21] They would not be the ones to lecture McGillivray or any other headman on moderation. Instead European rifles, powder, balls, and even war paint flowed from Spanish garrisons on the Gulf of Mexico and into Creek Country, where war parties were preparing to put them to good use.[22]

The availability of Spanish aid directly enriched Alexander McGillivray because of his role as a Spanish commissioner. He counseled Spaniards as to which headmen were friendly and which were more suspicious, and by doing so he influenced the flow of goods into many communities. "Several gangs of Indians" were down in Pensacola retrieving ammunition, Timothy Barnard observed, but "none are to get any but those that are recommended by Mr. McGillivray."[23] On the one hand there is little evidence to suggest that his political power extended beyond his abilities to make recommendations based on his grasp of regional politics. By doing that, however, he was an active and important asset, assisting Spanish governors as they established a strong, militant, anti-Georgian coalition. McGillivray's authority continued to strengthen as more Creeks struggled to understand the actions of their state counterparts to the east.

In addition, just as they had done in the summer of 1786, Spanish authorities also provided arms and ammunition directly to individual headmen, underscoring their policy of maintaining excellent community-level Creek relations as well as properly contextualizing McGillivray's own authority. The Hallowing King of Coweta and the Second Man of Ooseoochee both returned from Pensacola in August with their horses loaded down with powder and ammunition, for instance, and there was no mention of McGillivray.[24] Two months later groups of Oakfuskees— usually strong American partisans—appeared in Pensacola as well, where they also received a healthy supply of ammunition. Groups from the Lower Country routinely visited Zéspedes for the same purpose, and throughout 1786 and 1787 thousands of pounds of supplies made their way into Creek Country from St. Augustine.[25] By early spring of 1787

Timothy Barnard declared that it was "beyond a doubt" that Spaniards "have promised the Indians all the assistance they may Stand in need of to oppose us," and travelers noticed that "there was a Quantity of powder, and Bullets, Reposited in Every Town."[26] Spaniards were as comfortable working directly with the Creek people as they were with McGillivray, and they did so frequently. While McGillivray might have claimed control over a sprawling Creek Country, Spanish weapons shipments reveal a more complicated situation.

The rapid militarization of Creek Country was not lost on worried American onlookers, and state authorities were not altogether unaware of the impending violence either. Legislators recognized that "a renewal of hostilities may be every day expected," and they hurried to shore up their defenses.[27] At the same time they remained confident of their position and their strength, and familiar declarations were renewed. Not only would the treaty prevail, but Georgians would crush the Creek threat. "We are determined not to give them the satisfaction they require," Governor George Mathews declared, "and I flatter my self we have made such arrangements as will make them repent of their proceedings." Militiamen rejoiced "at the thought of having it in their power to chastise that Nation for all their past and present injuries." Unfortunately for Mathews and countless settlers along the backcountry, the defensive situation in Georgia was perhaps even worse than during the Revolution, meaning there was little force behind that rhetoric. This was made apparent in April 1787 when the first waves of warriors reached the frontier. By August war parties were reported along practically the entire frontier from the Cumberland settlements in modern-day Tennessee to the St. Mary's River, the boundary with Spanish Florida.[28]

The Creek offensive, much larger than a year or so earlier, quickly forced Georgia authorities to come to grips with the state's many weaknesses. Warriors swept across the frontier and militias struggled to repulse even the smallest war party. As early as June, in fact, Creeks had allegedly attacked twenty-five settler families without losing a single man themselves.[29] Short on guns, shorter on fighting men, and shortest on money, authorities at first turned to neighboring states for support. Governor Mathews, like other state authorities, regularly made appeals to neighboring states, to non-state entities like the Franklinites, and even with neighboring Native people. He struggled to supply the frontiers with men and provisions, even resorting to bounties of Indian land as future payment. None of these plans, however, ever came to fruition. Little regional aid would make it to the Georgia backcountry, and nothing even remotely resembling any army ever came close to making good on Mathews's own threats.[30] While Georgians pleaded for aid, war parties from the furthest stretches of Creek Country were crossing the Oconee River to the north and the Altamaha River to the south, penetrating all the way to the Ogeechee River and even in some cases beyond. Georgia militia units were hurriedly ordered out to "prevent the savages from making inroads" into some of the richest areas of the state, but they proved capable of doing little.[31] Soon, Governor Mathews somberly reported to the Georgia House of Assembly, the frontiers were under constant attack and militia units were failing to provide even the most basic degree of protection. The state was more or less bankrupt and what troops had been raised were going unpaid and even unfed.[32] This was only months after Shoulderbone. By that point, according to one report, thirty-one settlers were dead, twenty were wounded, and another handful had been taken prisoner.[33]

Mathews soon appealed directly to Congress, declaring that the frontiers had been "the scene of blood and ravages." That became obvious shortly after when Creek war parties put the torch to almost the entire town of Greenesborough. It had been laid out squarely on the Ceded Lands—then Wilkes County—and was one of the state's promising frontier settlements and a representation of the Georgia people's triumphs over their Creek neighbors. It was a particularly ironic loss, then, when Creeks burned the courthouse and "a number of other houses in different parts of the country."[34] Soon, according to outsider onlookers, there was "doubtless reason to fear" that even Savannah was under threat, and settlers were "so greatly alarmed" that they were fortifying the profitable seacoast town.[35] Meanwhile groups of Creeks from the Upper Country ravaged farms along the length of the frontier all the way to the Cumberland settlements in modern-day Tennessee. In one attack a group of Coosadas ambushed and killed American agent William Davenport, horrifying local authorities and forcing an early press for peace by settlers there.[36]

Signal victories like the burning of Greenesborough punctuated a Creek undertaking that was as straightforward as it was ruthless. War parties were there to remove Georgians, by sheer force, from their hunting grounds or, as Daniel McMurphy put it, "to burn and plunder every house on the other side of Oconey river as far as Ogechee."[37] Sometimes the raids were marked by visible acts of extreme violence. One man was found "barbarously killed," scalped, stripped naked, and skewered to the ground with a bayonet. More frequent, though, was the destruction of property, and in almost every one of the scores of depredation claims settlers filed in the years following the attacks, the first enumeration was usually for a burned house.[38] As one man explained, they "burnt my dwilling house, with two & a half wagon loads of corn, brook up my potato house & turned in a number of hogs to destroy what remaind."[39] John Armor in Greene County lost "one large shingled house with a quantity of household furnature and fore other hourses" that were "all burnt and distroyed by the Creek Indians," while Jacob Helveston lost his house, kitchen, another outbuilding, his garden, and all his fencing, which his son later despaired was his "total ruin."[40] The loss of property and the threat of continued attacks produced few options for those in the isolated and vulnerable outlying settlements that speckled the debated lands. Settlers could either give up on their farms and retreat toward the safety of Augusta or Savannah, or even the Sea Islands, losing all they had, or they could perhaps perish.[41]

By the fall of 1787 dozens of settlers were dead and scores more were homeless, an entire town had been burned, and an Indian agent had been killed. It was only a matter of time before the violence of the Oconee War drew the eye of the United States Congress. Even as delegates were mulling over changes to the Articles of Confederation, in fact, the Congress delegated James White to lead a regional peace effort south, and he arrived in Creek Country shortly after the raiding began. He was treated well by state authorities, who reported that he was "the means of settling all differences," marking just how swiftly the Creek offensive had softened a once-belligerent Georgia tone.[42] Moving into Creek Country, however, White would have to face a fierce Spanish partisan base in the midst of an ongoing embarrassment of the state of Georgia. Affairs certainly were not tilted in the American's favor as he began negotiating with McGillivray, and there was little McGillivray was willing to offer White by way of compromise. Although the two conversed cordially, that soon became clear as White laid out the Congress's vague and unhelpful position. He did not consider himself authorized to give Creeks the kind of satisfaction they required—Americans would not repudiate the state treaties—and to McGillivray's disgust he seemed unaware that the treaties were the cause of Creek anger to begin with. "He might as well have not come into our nation," McGillivray complained after the meeting, which in the end did nothing to stem the violence.[43]

While it was a clear political failure, White's visit was not altogether worthless. He was party to plenty of discussions—some surprising— that help flesh out not only a politically complicated Creek Country but a politically complicated McGillivray. Writing to Secretary of War Henry Knox he made it clear that Georgians still constituted for Creeks a strong unifying force. Along with Spaniards and Americans, he wrote the secretary, "there was a third party, (the Georgians) they said, which evidently meant injustice and oppression."[44] Nevertheless, not all was what it seemed. The Lower Country was tense, as perhaps could be expected because the threat of dispossession was clearer there. As White arrived in the region an important regional council was about to meet, either at Cusseta or Ooseoochee, where local headmen were to deliberate on the state of the offensive. McGillivray invited White to attend, so he could "learn their sentiments."[45] White did attend and was pleased with the sizable turnout. There he saw "so many of our particular friends assembled," including the "principle chiefs of the lower towns," in addition to the Tallassee King and McGillivray. Barnard and one of the Galphin brothers were also in attendance. White soon had the opportunity to deliver talks he had prepared on behalf of Congress, pressing for a peaceful solution to the Georgia crisis.[46] He was troubled to find, however, that headmen's responses categorically and angrily rejected the previous Georgia treaties, which was the case even from the very chiefs who had, in the past, endorsed them. The Tallassee King, when he spoke, officially repudiated the treaties, explaining that while he approached the Georgians as friends and expected to be treated as such, "the white people, their long knives in their hands, insisted on his making a cession of land, which he had no right to do."[47] That might not have been his personal view, of course—there is plenty of evidence to suggest he and the Fat King were under considerable duress during the conference. According to other reports both men were then censured ferociously for their actions during the previous state treaty councils. It was apparently quite a spectacle and was done right in front of an incredulous White. They sat "immobile like sentenced criminals" while White repeatedly pressured them to speak in defense of their actions.[48] Whether or not they wanted to was irrelevant; in the presence of their neighbors the two were unwilling to endorse any of the state treaties, suggesting that either by choice or by coercion, they were backing away from their Georgia friends.

It was then that the more aggressive headmen, representing several unhappy communities in the Lower Country, moved on to make the most of White's presence. The Hallowing King of Coweta quickly took the lead during the talks and "seemed principally to undertake to speak for the Indians in general." The Hallowing King was a preeminent war leader from a red town, not to mention a community that had done tremendous damage to the Georgia backcountry in the past; his leadership role in the council was further evidence that White would probably not hear much talk of conciliation. Creek lands were their life and their blood, the Hallowing King explained. "If we part with them, we part with our blood. We must fight for them." It was clear from the Hallowing King's aggressive response that Cowetas would not be assenting to anything White had in mind.[49] And it was not just about land. The Hallowing King reminded White of the seizure of the Cussetas at Shoulderbone, which, although perhaps well deserved, was still a source of tremendous resentment. Held at bay for the moment, Coweta warriors had already done extensive damage along the frontiers in the previous few months, and they seethed to retaliate further.[50]

Cusseta prisoners remained in state hands, and one of the younger men had "in his impatience of confinement, put himself to death." His apparent suicide was yet another source of anger that also had the potential to set into motion more retaliatory attacks by vengeful kin members. In short, if the Cussetas who remained were not soon returned, Creeks would finish what they had started, and the Hallowing King promised White that his warriors would take double the amount of prisoners the Georgians held from him.[51] In a surprising break from years of strongly pro-Georgia support, the Fat King and other Cussetas, who met Timothy Barnard at the Buzzard Roost around the same time, personally promised him likewise. If their headmen were not returned they would take them by force, and they would not be held accountable for the consequences.[52] And as for the land, White was soon convinced that Creek resolve was total; there were no compromises to be made: "When they were desired to declare if nothing would do but relinquishing the lands on the Oconee, they answered, that, or war."[53]

What White encountered in open discussion with Creek headmen was a region that seemed more united than it had ever been, and all because of the state of Georgia. Even the most consistent state allies, the Tallassee King and Fat King, had very little positive to say. What White heard when he spent some private time with Alexander McGillivray, on the other hand, was entirely different. Before he left White got the chance to sit down with McGillivray and converse with him confidentially, and it was clear from what he later reported that there was more opportunism and personal interest involved in McGillivray's actions than most Creeks probably recognized. Despite his having grown in influence in Creek Country as a voice of Spanish partisanship and extremism, McGillivray openly hinted that his position was open to change. He would give it all up, he declared, if Creeks could gain a more stable relationship with the American government and if he gained more complete control over the Creek trade.

A relationship with the American government, White later reported, was apparently what McGillivray secretly coveted. If Congress created a new American state on the East Coast, south of the Altamaha River, McGillivray would be "the first to take the oath of allegiance thereto." Not only would he do that, he would help Americans secure the Creek lands that the Oconee War was, at that very instant, being fought over. These were McGillivray's first hints that he was not nearly as invested in a Spanish vision for the Southeast as it seemed. More damning, perhaps, he was not as invested in Creek lands, or even Creek sovereignty, either. He was more concerned about his own economic stability and maintaining his authority via trade, and he apparently had already been questioning the Spaniards' ability to guarantee those things. Trading duties were too expensive at Pensacola, a surprised White conjectured, and if McGillivray could have those duties lowered by trading through a new American state, then he had no problem being American.[54] White passed a report of his conversation along to the Congress, providing some of the first evidence of McGillivray's flexible commitment to the Creek cause.

On his way out White made other interesting observations about how the war was affecting Creek politics. According to reports he gave to state authorities, headmen in the Upper Country seemed less emotional about the Oconee lands and less invested in the raiding than their eastern neighbors in the Lower Country, and there was no doubt that they "may be reconciled to the boundary as wished." Even though Creek Country was largely unified, fault lines still remained. Perhaps that was a division American authorities could, in the future, exploit. Further to the south, however, militancy gripped the Lower Country. There, White admitted to Henry Knox, the tenor "seemed not so well known till I went out." After the council, however, he understood the situation well, and the situation was not good. The Tallassee King and the Fat King might have agreed to the cession, but no one else in the region had. Headmen like the Hallowing King protested angrily "against what they termed the Georgian encroachments, which they declared they would repel by force." By that point even Cusseta headmen were in doubt. The very Indians "said to have made the grants," White explained, "were the first to accuse the State of having extorted land from them under pretence of cessions." He gave an even gloomier report to Georgia's Legislative Council when he traveled to Augusta. They should probably prepare for more violence, he admitted, also pointing out that "his personal safety was assured to be in danger, should he threaten the nation with the force of the Union."[55] White did manage to get a verbal promise of truce until he could meet with Congress, but that did little to ease tensions in the region. Raiding soon picked up again, Georgians continued reporting deaths, and soon Secretary Knox was constructing an aggressive plan of defense.[56]

While that was ongoing an attack by a group of state militia against Cussetas offered further proof that if Cussetas and other similar partisans did eventually abandon their American allies, it was only because of the continuous and increasingly outrageous actions by settlers and their local representatives. Shortly after White's visit a group of Hookchoies raided settlements along the northern frontiers of Georgia.[57] Another similar raid from the Upper Country into Greene County ended with the killing of two farmers in addition to the theft of a slave and a dozen or so horses. A militia unit claiming to be tracking those raiders instead ran across a group of friendly Cusseta hunters and promptly killed a dozen of them.[58] Of course those were not the same warriors who had perpetrated the attacks—they were not even from the same region. The hunters had just made camp and were busy eating dinner when the militia unit rode up on them and shot them down by surprise.[59] The Fat King and the Hallowing King immediately demanded satisfaction, but state authorities instead rationalized the militia action by making it clear that their men did not distinguish between friendly and unfriendly Creeks. As soon as the militiamen learned about the attacks on the settlers they crossed the Oconee and attacked. "It was impossible then to distinguish whether you were our friends or enemies." Rather than apologize, authorities issued a stern warning. "Remember the caution we now give you," they declared. "Should any acts of hostilities be in future committed" against Georgians, it would be impossible to "prevent our warriors from doing themselves justice." Ultimately, state authorities directed the Cussetas to take revenge on the Creeks that were the reason behind the wrongful attack rather than retaliating on the Americans. "In doing this, we shall be fully convinced of your brotherly love and friendship towards us."[60]

The massacre of the hunters—and perhaps more importantly the state's response to it—was a turning point in Cusseta. That people who claimed to be friends could act so callously was an insult to Cusseta headmen even worse than Shoulderbone had been and was destroying what weak relationship still existed between state authorities and the communities that remained at least somewhat neutral. Even by the terms of Shoulderbone, the Fat King countered, no one was to take "hasty revenges" in the event of an attack. Yet after being attacked Georgians did not "wait but for a little while & look around" to find "from whence the blow came," and instead fell upon the first Indians they could find. In this case, it was "your real friends who were daily among your houses & whose persons you well knew & Some that were taken declared themselves & Town to you, which you disregarded." They also resented the Georgians' unapologetic lumping together of all Creeks; Cussetas and other allies surely had been drawing differences. "You ought not to think of making us accountable for any measures of the Upper towns," he declared to Mathews. It was obvious that his hunters had not taken part in any of the raiding, and it was "in Vain that you call us friends & brothers & not Consider & treat us as Such." Ultimately the chiefs demanded satisfaction, declaring that only then the "tears of the relations of the dead will be dried up & our hearts be not continue hot against you."[61]

Barnard relayed these demands to Mathews, who responded furiously, further undermining Cusseta-Georgia relations.[62] The attack, and worse yet the unwillingness of state authorities to prosecute the offenders or even apologize for the attack, only added outrage to the injury already done at Shoulderbone and continued to push even the friendliest Creeks away from Georgians and toward violence. Even they, Timothy Barnard was now convinced, "say that they See a war is determined against them." He was particularly despondent because he had struggled mightily to keep towns in the Lower Country like Cowetas peaceable and "could have done it if this affair had not hapned."[63] It was a complaint remarkably reminiscent of Galphin's, a decade earlier, and the outlook was similarly grim. There were still groups of Tallassee and Half-Way House hunters out along the frontier as well who were friendly with the Cussetas, and there was no knowing how they were bound to respond. All Barnard could do now was urge Governor Mathews to prepare for the worst: "for all the inhabitants from the mouth of alatamaha up to be in as good a posture of defence as possible, as no one can tell where they may make there first attempt."[64]

This latest outrage quickly made a charade of White's peace initiative, and Creek war parties renewed their inroads into Georgia through the fall of 1787 and into 1788. In the spring of 1788 Anthony Wayne, trying to establish a rice plantation, complained that the war had "nearly desolated the whole of the frontier country and all the sea coast from Florida to *Sunbury*," and even within twenty miles of Savannah, and "from present appearances it will not terminate even there."[65] Such an attack on the friendliest Creeks, ambushed while hunting on their own lands, whittled away at whatever Georgia partisanship was remaining in Creek Country. With the Spanish partisan base surging, on the other hand, McGillivray's outlook was positively rosy. "We may reasonably conclude that the American lads have been pretty well drubbd," he congratulated O'Neill in November 1787. With a number of Cowetas and even a few Cussetas still unaccounted for, there was little doubt they would complete "the Just retaliation upon the Georgians." McGillivray pondered whether the fighting would need to continue through the winter. With Cussetas now mulling over the possibility of attacking the frontier out of sheer retribution, communities in Creek Country were speaking more in concert—whether they meant to or not—than perhaps they ever had been.[66]

McGillivray's boldness was not necessarily unwarranted. By 1788 Creeks were spreading real devastation into the state of Georgia, and not just along the backcountry. Along the coast "all the houses about Brunswick & South of the Alatamaha" had been burned while to the north, war parties were reportedly "victorious in every quarter" and had driven the bulk of the Cumberland settlers north over the Ohio River. The "State of Georgia now lays at our mercy," McGillivray declared, Creek warriors having "given the Georgians repeated defeats." Not a single building was standing "on the Contested lands," he charged.[67] Accounts from Georgia, albeit described in a different language, supported McGillivray's claims. A "great number" of settlers had lately "been killed & cruelly mangled, their houses burnt & stock drove away with every other depredation that cruelty could suggest."[68] Even in well-developed Chatham County, the seat of which was Savannah, the "Indians alarm" had thrown the people into a "distressing situation." The country was "very unsafe," crops were going to ruin, and the residents were desperately requesting a fortification and men for their protection. As late as October 1788 state militia general James Jackson complained that he had "continuously received dispatches from one quarter or other" describing some sort of Indian depredation.[69]

Creek war parties, in fact, were soon to be the victims of their own success—their offensive was so staggering that by the fall of 1788 the Spanish governors were starting to grow anxious. Spanish territorial goals in the Southeast focused on stemming American expansion west, which was something their Creek allies were clearly accomplishing. They were accomplishing it so swiftly, however, that a confrontation with the new federal government was becoming a possibility, and that began to worry regional Spanish officials. With the state of Georgia's westward movements effectively blunted they began to pursue a more moderate diplomatic approach to the region. That reassessment, however prudent it might have been, set into motion a shift in Creek politics that not only destabilized the Spanish base but led to the development of other partisan groups that began to erode whatever semblance of Creek solidarity that might have emerged during the Oconee War. In many ways, flagging shipments of ammunition late in 1788 did as much to curb the Creek offensive as did Georgians' suffering. But they did much more, complicating the relationship between Spaniards and Creek communities as well as between Spaniards and McGillivray, and even eventually introducing William Augustus Bowles to Florida. Even if they only recommended restraint, the actions of the Spanish still demonstrated how it was the crisis of Georgia expansionism, and not a deeper sense of political cohesiveness, that underpinned the Creek offensive; as soon as the crisis began to fade, so did Creek unity.

At almost the same time the Oconee War was reaching its crescendo representatives in Philadelphia were considering a new, stronger government framework—the Constitution—from which Georgia would most certainly benefit. Suffering badly from the inadequacies of the current Congress, many outsiders rightly understood, state legislators would quickly embrace a stronger federal government, if only for the sake of self-preservation, that otherwise would diminish state-level democracy.[70] For Spaniards that was worrisome. A stronger and more active federal government created a regional political dynamic that was more complicated and dangerous than what existed during the Confederation period—something that was lost neither on O'Neill nor on Miró. Arturo O'Neill was already looking for ways to draw the fighting down by the first months of the Oconee offensive, an approach Miró slowly began to match in 1788. The latter governor never doubted that the Spanish government would continue assisting Creeks as long as they were acting defensively and protecting Spanish interests and Spanish soil. But as the Creek offensive stretched further into Georgia, and even to the coast in some cases, he too began to think about the larger picture.[71]

Neither governor wanted to compromise Spanish neutrality by sparking a large-scale Indian war that would spread beyond Creeks and

Georgians, a worry they increasingly relayed to their superiors. Those superiors included Bernardo de Gálvez, the viceroy of New Spain, who suggested to Miró that while local governors should continue distributing arms and ammunition, they should begin doing so as clandestinely as possible. Although the Spanish were bound by treaty to support Creeks they needed to take care not to jeopardize Spanish-American diplomacy by making their support of the violence too overt.[72] Soon Miró was asking just how much he should give and what exactly he should promise, later penning that it would "not be inconvenient" to see the Creeks and Georgians reconciled. He was even advising Creeks against further attacks.[73] O'Neill did not act quite as cautiously, but he did resolve to send supplies into Creek Country with much more secrecy.[74] Bernardo de Gálvez in Mexico, and then officials in Spain, approved of the judicious approach.[75] While neither O'Neill nor Miró stopped providing Creeks with aid, they did realize that they were walking a fine line.

Spanish diplomats had their reasons for pushing Creeks toward moderation, just as they had their reasons for pushing them to violence. The situation was far less complicated in Creek Country, however, where the governors' newfound circumspection stood to reverse a hard-fought and very successful offensive. That quickly began to generate doubt. Just when Creek warriors were positioned to deal Georgians the decisive blow, McGillivray complained, they were not getting the support they needed.[76] Things came to a head in June when he confronted Miró directly. If the Spanish were interested in peace to the point of sacrificing Creek sovereignty, McGillivray charged, "we shall consider ourselves a ruined nation." Even as congressional commissioners were pressing for peace— and perhaps complaining to Diego de Gardoqui in Philadelphia—state authorities continued to attack peaceful hunting parties at will and steal Creek property. While Spaniards saw peace with the federal government as a favorable conclusion to the regional crisis, Creeks were much more skeptical. As far as they saw it, nothing short of the complete humiliation of Georgians would produce real change.[77] Creek concerns still focused on the state of Georgia, which Spaniards now unfortunately seemed to be looking beyond.[78]

There was clear reason for McGillivray in particular to criticize the new Spanish diplomacy. His control over the flow of goods and weapons from the Spanish was his source of authority in Creek Country, and it stood to suffer tremendously if Spaniards began to back away from the region. His earlier political successes, this period of trial reveals, were tied to a situation he neither created nor truly controlled. The governors' growing conservatism also helps explain McGillivray's conversations with James White as well as other Americans, like Andrew Pickens, earlier in 1785. He only applied to Spaniards "for our preservation, and from real necessity," he confided in Pickens, but Creeks "sincerely wish to have it in our power to be on the same footing with the States as before the late unhappy war." With the close of the war "we expected that the new Government would soon have taken some steps to make up the differences that subsisted between them and the Indians during the war, and to have taken them into protection, and confirm to them their hunting grounds." His conversations with White took place years later, but the two sounded awfully similar.[79] Perhaps, they suggest, McGillivray could be the voice of a strong Spanish partisan base, or he could be the voice of strong American one, whichever he thought would serve both the Creek people and himself best.

Unfortunately for McGillivray his political flexibility soon influenced the creation of another partisan group led by William Augustus Bowles, who came to Florida in 1788 more or less on his invitation and who ultimately orchestrated his political destruction.[80] Bowles's adventure in Creek Country, indeed, began straightforwardly enough: faced with the prospect of losing Spanish support, McGillivray panicked. He made plans for aid direct from British merchants in the Bahamas, whom he evidently still had connections with, and Bowles soon arrived with a ship full of goods. That decision naturally raised the ire of McGillivray's Spanish allies, as well his friends in the Panton and Leslie trading company. While Creeks still favored the Spanish, McGillivray tried to explain to Miró, the recent Spanish change was worrisome. Situated as he was, he certainly would welcome any help he could get.[81] That immediately damaged his relationship with several Spanish governors in a way that proved difficult to fix. According to Timothy Barnard, it at least partly "broke of the great friendship" between him and O'Neill. It had even angered Panton, with whom he shared a long and close friendship.[82] While McGillivray continued to reassure the Spanish of the innocence of his intentions, both O'Neill and Miró, who had been trusting and supportive allies in the past, surely must have viewed the arrival in the Gulf of a British vessel packed with weapons with a pointed sense of betrayal.[83] Eventually cooler heads prevailed and the Spanish governors were directed to step up their support if it meant keeping McGillivray loyal.[84] The two allies, however, never looked at each other quite the same way again. "I am positively harassed and wearied out by the restless life I am obliged to leave," McGillivray soon complained to Panton, "& the part I have to act with our New allies whose conduct appears so contradictory and suspicious." The foundation of the Spanish partisan base, it seemed, was starting to give way.[85] And however genuine he considered it, McGillivray's latest maneuver bore out ever more clearly the length to which his personal interests shaped his decisions.

Meanwhile, two years of relentless raiding along the backcountry had taken its toll on the state of Georgia. Over one hundred settlers had been killed or badly wounded. Another one hundred slaves had been taken or killed, close to one hundred farms had been completely destroyed, and thousands of cattle, horses, and pigs were either killed or pilfered.[86] Much of Georgia's recently gained Oconee lands were burned or barren, state authorities were powerless to stop the violence, and settlers were disheartened. Even the most aggressive legislators in Augusta were now receptive to federal initiatives for peace, when only years earlier they had mocked them. Although White's mission to Creek Country accomplished little in 1787, by that time delegates from a number of states had begun deliberating the future of the Articles of Confederation, which soon shifted to crafting and debating the Constitution. The state of Georgia was certain to benefit from the protection of a stronger federal government, as everyone there knew. Fighting along the Creek-Georgia frontier continued through the Constitutional Convention, after it adjourned, as Georgia legislators debated ratifying the Constitution, and after it was approved overwhelmingly early in 1788. Almost immediately Governor George Handley pressed Congress for federal intervention.[87] Soon, with peace a possibility, local authorities agreed without hesitation to a set of congressional mediators. Despite the reality that those commissioners probably did not have local settlers' best interests in mind, state authorities were no doubt relieved to see them appear in April 1788, and Handley hoped they would "induce the Indians to suspend hostilities on our defenceless citizens."[88]

Andrew Pickens and George Mathews were the commissioners appointed by Congress, and their mission represented at least the third serious attempt by the federal government to negotiate an end to the Oconee War. They forwarded an invitation to McGillivray before their arrival, and in the meantime they also penned several open letters to Creek Country, pressing headmen to halt their raids at least until they had the chance to meet. While most chiefs were apt to "be in readiness to make a campaign this spring" if the peace was not successful, according to McGillivray, in the end they agreed to recall their war parties.[89] State authorities heeded a similar request. Local militias were ordered to act only on the defensive and not to molest any Creeks while the peace conference approached.[90] That meant that finally, in the summer of 1788, raiding began to slow significantly. Richard Winn had by that time replaced James White as Congress's superintendent for Indian affairs, and while the commissioners prepared to meet with McGillivray he attempted to prime the discussions by sending an envoy, referred to only as a Mr. Whitfield, into Creek Country. Little is known about Whitfield, although he was described as "a respectable character," who had formerly been a trader in the region. Even less is known about his visit. Creek headmen, including McGillivray, were "highly pleased" with his talks, however, and expressed their interest to meet with the commissioners.[91] Even though almost nothing is known about it, in other words, this most recent American mission was already more successful than any of the state or federal efforts that had preceded it.

While Whitfield's talks were circulated and received widely in Creek Country, later events proved his approach exceptional. When they arrived, the federal commission made clear they were interested in talking with McGillivray and McGillivray alone, revealing how complete they figured his authority in the region truly was. Much of their confidence in his influence was derived, of course, from his control over the flow of information leaving Creek Country. As one of the handful of Creeks who could read or write, almost every piece of correspondence that came from the region was in McGillivray's handwriting, and naturally, in his many letters, he took time to craft a particular image for himself. It is not altogether unsurprising that Americans considered McGillivray as authoritative as he told them he was. His later troubles made clear his political power did not warrant such respect, but nevertheless at the time American authorities clearly thought it did. When they began talking regularly about the proposed peace talks in 1788, he was always going to play a central part in them. While a Creek Nation did not exist at that point, it did not stop McGillivray from claiming to lead it, and it did not stop American authorities from believing that he did.

Faith in McGillivray came from strange places. George Galphin Jr., the son of the Revolutionary George Galphin Sr., declared that there was "no measure to be fallen upon . . . without his voice." Even if groups of Creeks agreed to treat without him, any deal made "could not be a general one," and "therefore it would only be leaving matters in the same disagreeable situation that they are now in."[92] That was a surprising generalization, coming as it was from a man who, although he was a strong American partisan, had grown up around Creeks and who no doubt understood the cultural complexities involved in Creek leadership. Less strange was Henry Knox's confidence, coming as it was from someone who knew literally nothing about Creek culture. McGillivray possessed "great abilities" and an "unlimited influence over the Creek Nation." Besides "the Chiefs of the respective towns, the Creeks appear, at present, to be much under the influence and direction" of him, Knox was sure.[93] Even Whitfield returned from Creek Country in 1788 with the same conviction. McGillivray was "their head man," he told Winn, and if Americans were to expect peace, "it must be on his terms."[94] As he had already made known confidentially to American authorities, McGillivray's position was not nearly as demanding as that of countless other Creeks in the region, angry with the state of Georgia and flush with victory. American authorities had absolute confidence that McGillivray could overcome that opposition, even if a man like George Galphin Jr. should have known better.

None of the American commissioners even seemed to understand the Creek demands when they arrived in Creek Country, let alone accept them as the basis of a new federal compact. George Mathews, of all people, was one of them. It was under his watch as the governor of Georgia that some of the worst state outrages were committed on Creeks, and it was also under his watch when Creek raids were at their most terrifying; Creek negotiators obviously would get little by way of understanding from him. Naturally, exchanges between the two groups went nowhere. Headmen demanded the absolute repudiation of all past state treaties and a return to a pre-Revolutionary boundary, which was essentially the Ogeechee River, while the commissioners repeatedly and angrily countered that they were not authorized to do anything of the sort. There was no way Congress would even bring it up for debate and frankly, it was insulting. "At the same time we must observe," the commissioners chided McGillivray, "that that honorable body will not lose sight of doing equal justice to that State of Georgia." Creeks had already done incredible damage over "what you call the disputed lands," which, the commissioners reiterated, Georgians also claimed and which were "confirmed by three different treaties, signed by your head-men and warriors."[95] Whatever optimism McGillivray or any other Creeks had going into these negotiations, they got nothing from their congressional counterparts, and they left angry.

The two parties managed to agree on a truce until they could meet again, at the Rock Landing on the Oconee River, but that was almost the only thing they could agree on. The talks were nothing short of a complete failure and did little but produce a fresh air of crisis. Georgians were again arming and meant to "make another trial to accomplish by force," McGillivray complained, "what can't be obtained by peaceable means." To this, of course, headmen answered that they would respond in kind.[96] And McGillivray, for his role in putting a pen to Creek thoughts, endured withering criticism from his onetime admirers among the Americans. "The insolence of the Indian half-breed," one of President Washington's acquaintances complained, "ought to be checked." With more threatening news coming from Georgia and with no more word about the proposed peace conference coming from Americans, many Creeks made plans to renew their attacks. Eventually another round of conciliatory talks by the American commissioners did come, but not before McGillivray and headmen "of the whole Upper and Lower Creeks" held another war council in the Lower Country. There they reopened hostilities and began preparing to fan back across the frontier.[97] George Galphin, arriving at Cusseta in May, was unsettled by that news. Upwards of three thousand warriors, from the extremes of the Upper Country "down as far as the Seminoles," were already fitted for war "and intended to have drove Ogechee from the mouth to the head, which I fear they would have effected, after viewing the frontiers in such an unprepared state, and the Indians going on at such a surprise." This was definitely the case in Coweta, where "the whole body of warriors were in arms" and were "ready to turn out."[98] McGillivray evidently had gone into detail with them about his exchanges with the American commissioners, explaining that the chances of them getting their lands back peacefully were slim. Spanish officials, having agreed that the last American effort was nothing more than a charade, had given their blessing to the new offensive. They were providing, according to Galphin, fifteen hundred rifles and plenty of ammunition. That, McGillivray relayed from O'Neill, "was what they had orders to do by orders from the King." That was good news to the vast majority of Creek headmen; according to Galphin, they were "much exalted, and, I believe, would have turned out to a man, except the Cussetahs, who seemed much against it."[99]

Yet again Cussetas remained American allies and they, along with Timothy Barnard and the Galphin brothers, did all they could to slow the renewed offensive. Having actually attended the recent conference, Barnard was first to act. He was "trying all he could to put a stop to their rash proceedings," promising that peace would be made on any condition if headmen would agree to hold off on the assault even temporarily. Not only did his pleas fail, his life was directly threatened "and every exertion possible made use of, to prevent his going off, or sending down news to Georgia of what was going forward." With the situation out of his control Barnard turned to the Galphin brothers. John Galphin focused on Coweta, "having a good deal of influence . . . through our connection there" and cognizant at the same time that it was "the most strenuous for mischief." Later he reported traveling into the Upper Country as well. Meanwhile his brother, George, did what he could from Cusseta. Together the two Galphins demonstrated the continued power of both kin and trade relations—most communities agreed to hold the bulk of their warriors back, at least until they heard word from McGillivray. As George explained, "I was told, by many of the Indians, that, if any one else had come at such a time but myself, they never should have returned back."[100] The influence of the Galphin family, it seemed, was as strong as it had ever been. Even with their efforts, though, peace was not assured. Several of the war parties could not be intercepted in time, which meant that the spring of 1789 was punctuated by several raids and acts of violence perpetrated by both Georgians and Creeks.[101] A group of headmen from the Lower Country, most likely Coweta, hoped "there will be no blood spilt" but blamed Americans for not receiving peace talks in time, and vowed that their people were not going to be held accountable for what might happen.[102] Despite those worrying declarations the interposition of the Cussetas, Barnard, and the Galphins was still very meaningful. An American partisan group, it appeared, was beginning to emerge. It was a small but growing group that looked toward Congress and the new federal government for a regional solution to the Oconee War crisis.

Despite his frustration with the commissioners McGillivray also looked to the federal government, demonstrating how his political views continued to shift in favor of compromise. The renewed calls for violence from Creek communities disappointed him, but so did the American Congress, which did not seem genuinely interested in peace. Even though headmen were deeply hesitant, McGillivray remained cautiously optimistic that at the Rock Landing conference Congress would "set every thing to rights between us on the most equitable footing, so that we may become real friends to each other, settling on the same land, and having but one interest."[103] He was not simply buttering up the American commissioners; it was clear that the American government represented McGillivray's best hope for a long-term solution. For their part, Americans were more convinced of McGillivray's perceived authority than ever, even as they criticized him personally for his role in the failure of the recent negotiations. Only a few years earlier it had been possible to get headmen to a conference without him, Timothy Barnard explained, which was occasionally done "before when his superiority was not near as great over the nation as it is now." Now "the Indians has put the whole and sole power into Mr. [McGillivray's] hands, to treat or not to treat, war or peace." The Pickens and Mathews delegation was a disaster, yet Americans used it as proof that they needed to win over McGillivray, more than any other Creek headman or collection of headmen, if a deal was to be made. Both George Washington and Henry Knox certainly did that when making arrangements for Rock Landing. Washington requested personal friend and accomplished diplomat David Humphreys to aid in the negotiations, hoping to have him available to counter McGillivray directly. Humphreys was clearly of the same mind; he was quick to assure the president that McGillivray was "desirous of Peace—and his word is a law to the Creeks."[104] To American authorities McGillivray was the key to the conference's success, and they spared no expense as they prepared to deal with him.

As the three commissioners—Humphreys, Benjamin Lincoln, and Cyrus Griffin—approached Rock Landing and got settled, they reported a positive reception. Creeks expressed "in general terms their desire for peace, to smoke the pipe of friendship as a token of it, and to brush our faces with the white wing of reconciliation in sign of their sincere intention to wipe away all past grievances." Considerable talk, "expressive of a real desire to establish a permanent peace upon equitable terms, took place."[105] While all of this was quite positive, a strong Creek showing did not necessarily promise Americans success. The Hallowing King of Coweta was present and welcomed the commissioners, for instance, clearly figuring to play a prominent role in the negotiations. He represented a strong pro-Spanish, anti-Georgian partisan base in the Lower Country that had been terribly insulted by state authorities in the past and that also had done tremendous damage to the frontier as a result. He certainly did not come to Rock Landing with compromise on his mind. He had stood firm against state expansionism in the past, which was a position that probably would not change at Rock Landing. That was not good news for the American commissioners. Worse yet, over one thousand headmen were also present, as large a representation of Creek Country as had probably ever been assembled in one place.[106] Such a complete show of Creek political solidarity could only be explained as a show of defiance, not compromise, and the chance of them all consenting to the land deal Americans had in mind was, at best, impossible. The conference at Rock Landing, in short, was destined to fail.

On the other hand there was McGillivray. As the conference approached he again revealed, this time to friend William Panton, his growing willingness to strike a deal. With Spanish support flagging he explained that it had always been his true desire to bring the Americans "to terms and if they don't even Say as much as I want yet it may be in my power at a Conference to obtain some solid advantage for our Nation (in case I find myself obliged to admit of their holding that side of the [Oconee] river) by way of Equivalent." He ultimately believed the Creek and American differences would, in the end, have to be "determined in that way," meaning some sort of compromise. Creeks' Spanish allies were letting them down, and their actions "scarcely [leave] us hopes of being able to enforce our demands." Such a straightforward admission— that he would accept a compromise with Americans that would confirm at least some of the land cessions to Georgia—scared even Panton, who blamed McGillivray's attitude on "low spirits" and fatigue. His friend pressed McGillivray not to abandon the Spanish or give up on the lands east of the Oconee, warning him that nothing positive would result from so large a concession, and he was soon asking Miró for help.[107] While McGillivray it seemed was warming up to the idea of a compromise agreement, few others were—not the majority of other Creek headmen, his Spanish allies, or even his closest friends.

Those warnings did not appear to dissuade McGillivray from engaging with the Americans in ways that continued to demonstrate his willingness to bargain. As the commissioners approached he asked them for a private conversation, "previous to the opening treaty," and had several conversations with them, both at the Creek camp and theirs, over the course of two days.[108] What they spoke about is not clear, but if the talks were supposed to build the commissioners' hopes, they only made for a more dramatic letdown. Soon the private talks gave way to the much larger, more formal conference, and if the American commissioners came to Rock Landing thinking that McGillivray was the man they would have to convince in order to get what they wanted, they soon had the rug pulled from under them. At this conference it was his position as a beloved man, and not a mico or any other sort of community leader, that was clarified. With scores of Creek headmen determined to partake in the talks there would be few opportunities for McGillivray to converse privately with Humphreys, as he had done with White years earlier, or even for him to engage the Americans directly. Even if he had been able to deal, the compromise he would have brokered—something that would give up some Creek lands for an

American alliance and economic relationship—would not sit well with a much larger and more militant Creek delegation flush with victory over Georgians, distrustful of Americans, and friendly with Spaniards. While he almost certainly would play a leading role in the negotiations, McGillivray would not have the decision-making authority either he or his American counterparts assumed.

With opening ceremonies and good-natured gestures behind them the Americans laid out their first proposals, and as could be expected, the atmosphere soon grew tense. Among the American terms, of course, was a boundary from the Oconee River south to the Altamaha River, and then all the way south to the Spanish boundary on the St. Mary's River. The federal terms, in short, were the same as the state terms, as defined not even by the Treaty of Augusta but by Galphinton and the universally despised Shoulderbone. The commissioners also insisted on moving Creeks under the political and economic protection of the United States, a provision that would have eviscerated the Spanish Treaty of Pensacola. Not surprisingly, the Creek delegation found this first proposal almost entirely unacceptable and no doubt alarming.[109] Nevertheless, McGillivray and the sizable group of headmen with him took the terms to their camps on the west side of the Oconee, across the river from where the Americans were staying, and they spent the whole night debating them. When they returned the next morning they delivered their counterdemands, which in sum were an almost complete rejection of the American proposal. Humphreys crossed the river shortly after in an effort to negotiate and was received "with more etiquette," he later recalled, "than ever I had before witnessed."[110] That, however, would be about the last positive thing he would have to say about the proceedings. He focused his energy on McGillivray, naturally, and his professional and aggressive negotiating style grew tiresome and then insulting. Humphreys "shifted his ground, modes of attack in various shapes. The arts of flattery, ambition and intimidation were exhausted in vain. I at last told him by G—— I would not have such a treaty cram'd down my throat," McGillivray would later explain.[111] Having exhausted his welcome Humphreys eventually returned to the American camp, after which the headmen again deliberated all night. Ultimately, their response the next day was the same. They simply would not accept the commissioners' insistence on the Oconee lands.[112]

McGillivray and Humphreys were being upstaged at the conference and now were on antagonistic terms with each other, but they continued acting as though they were the solution to what was quickly becoming another diplomatic failure. McGillivray, seemingly unwilling to accept the decision of the rest of the Creek delegation, promised the commissioners that he would travel to their camp and "have a full and free conference" with them "upon the subject of the negotiations." But soon the commissioners learned that, instead, he and the whole of the Creek delegation had simply left. It was a move that angered the American delegation, perhaps justly, who had camped at Rock Landing for quite some time just to have their counterparts up and leave after barely one exchange of negotiations.[113] Two of the commissioners chased the Creek party down on horseback and tried desperately at least to get McGillivray to return, but there was little he admitted he could do. The headmen with him were not interested in further negotiations if they were going to be based on the Americans' terms. Since "a restitution" of territorial hunting grounds "was not to be the basis of a treaty of peace between us," they had decided it was time to return home.[114] Even if McGillivray was interested in making a deal he was clearly not in control of the situation and could not prevent their removal from Rock Landing. Although for days the commissioners had been referring to McGillivray as the "chief of the Creek nation," all he could do was retire with the rest of the delegation as the Treaty of Rock Landing fell apart.[115]

Almost all of that complexity was lost on American authorities. The treaty was disastrous, the region again threatened violence, and Georgia was again in crisis. Despite the fact that hundreds of headmen had taken part in the negotiations, Americans quickly pinned the failure of Rock Landing squarely on McGillivray, just as they had in the past.[116] He "had a great deal to say for his going away as he did," according to an exasperated Pickens, "but nothing in my opinion sufficient to justify his conduct." In fact, while almost nothing was said either about the Hallowing King or any other headmen for that matter, criticism of McGillivray was relentless.[117] The failure of the treaty also weighed heavily on McGillivray, who clearly sounded distraught when he returned home. "I arrived three days ago from the Oconee, sick, disgusted & fatigued to death," he wrote his friend William Panton. "From this beginning you will imagine that matters did not go on to my mind."[118] Again McGillivray's correspondence suggests that he had high hopes for creating a long-term peace with the American government, and he was as upset at the failure of the negotiations as were his American counterparts. As Humphreys's stubborn maneuvering proved, there was "naturally . . . no change of heart by the new American government." Unfortunately the commissioners had backed the state position, without wavering, and now things were again at a crisis.[119]

The outcome of Rock Landing was not nearly as significant a loss to most Creeks. Unlike McGillivray they saw in its collapse only a continuation of their Oconee War gains. Once again they remained resolute and refused to legitimize the previous Georgia treaties. To McGillivray, however, the hope of a peace brokered with the Americans was giving way to the looming prospect of a much larger war with the American government he feared Creeks would have little chance of winning.[120] It also dashed his personal hopes for a much stronger trade relationship than he presently enjoyed with his Spanish allies. With the Spanish trade questionable and with Bowles now lurking in Florida, he no doubt feared his control over the flow of goods was slipping; an American treaty probably would have helped reverse this trend. There was already evidence that headmen were irritated because the supplies he recently had promised them had not shown.[121] As the relationship between the Spaniards and Creek communities faltered, McGillivray suffered disproportionately, and he had just failed in his attempt to recruit new, stronger American allies.

Tormented by the fallout from the treaty, McGillivray sped up his retreat from the radical, militant position that had made him so powerful during the Oconee War. This became clear when he accepted a much quieter invitation to travel to New York and continue working on a treaty directly with the Washington administration, including with Secretary Knox himself.[122] McGillivray and about thirty other Creek headmen arrived in New York City in the summer of 1790 and began meeting with members of the administration almost immediately. The delegation dined in New York and conversed with Knox personally, and McGillivray stayed at the secretary's residence. In a move that underscored the dramatic transition McGillivray had made away from his position as a powerful pro-Spanish and radical anti-American partisan, the Tallassee King made the journey as well. No longer were the two inveterate enemies, evidently—the allure of an American peace proved quite enticing. And the Tallassee King was not just in New York for show; he spent time with Knox as well, and their conversations were among the most intense. Knox questioned him about the proceedings at both Galphinton and Shoulderbone, and the Tallassee King again declared he had no right to dispose of the land in the way state authorities claimed. When Knox asked him about whether he agreed to cede a particular tract of land south of the Altamaha River, which Georgians had already begun settling as the "Tallassee County," the Tallassee King said he had never consented to such a deal. Not only had he not consented, in fact, but when he learned that such a provision had been added to the treaty, he tried to snatch it out of the hands of the state commissioners and destroy it. The commissioners, however, prevented him from doing so. He also described the presence of the state militia troops at Shoulderbone, threatening to "invade the Creek Country," demanding lives and hostages, and also demanding the assassination of McGillivray and others.[123] The conversation certainly did not reflect well on the state of Georgia.

Not surprisingly, Knox also shared longer, more private and candid conversations with McGillivray. The two discussed all three of the previous state treaties and the circumstances around them, along with the 1784 Spanish Treaty of Pensacola. They both agreed that the earlier Georgia treaties were fraudulent but also that Rock Landing had been an insulting embarrassment, and soon they had inked a new agreement that included various open and secret terms. While McGillivray quietly gained a rank and salary in the American military, as well as the prospect of a protected American trade, outwardly he agreed to cede the majority of the Oconee lands to Georgia on behalf of the entire Creek Nation. And with that agreement, he and his entourage were soon on their way back south.[124] It was, upon inspection, quite a bargain. Although it certainly benefited McGillivray personally, it also gave security to Creek communities and provided for a prospect that had eluded both Creeks and Georgians now for more than a decade: long-term peace. All remaining lands would be protected against encroachment by the federal government in perpetuity.[125] McGillivray clearly saw it as an excellent deal, as did his American counterparts. For the latter group, in fact, New York was a landmark first for the new federal government. Not only was it the first treaty made with a foreign power to be ratified by the Senate, but in it Knox and Washington successfully exerted federal control over state interests—a constitutional power that had yet gone untested. "The interests of the United States and the Creeks henceforward are proposed to be the same," Knox triumphantly penned a military commander in Georgia. He enclosed in that letter twenty copies of the treaty, most likely to have distributed to state officials and Creek headmen. For his part McGillivray was so pleased by the treaty that, after landing back in St. Mary's, he actually apologized to a local settler who had been attacked in the years previous. McGillivray lamented that the man "had been broke up by their people—that they were very sorry for it"—and told the man he was welcome to return to the site of his old home and rebuild. It was quite the difference only a few months had made.[126]

While state authorities were sure to hate such a compromise, they had little choice in the matter. New York invalidated the several state treaties, which Creeks decried as coerced and fraudulent, and promised to protect the majority of Creek hunting lands from future aggression. Although that certainly was an accomplishment, the treaty also ceded thousands of acres of Creek hunting lands to Georgia, something that was certain to draw the ire of many Creek headmen. More importantly, perhaps, it was concluded at a time when Creek politics were shifting out of the unity of military force by necessity and back into the more familiar, but now larger and more complicated, realm of individual interests and political partisanship. Partisans who accepted the moderate approach of the new American government existed now, and Alexander McGillivray—as an American brigadier general no less—was their new mouthpiece. Yet Spanish partisans were not gone. Led by men like the Mad Dog of Tuckabatchee and the Hallowing King of Coweta they remained widespread in both the Upper Country and Lower Country. Anglo-American adventurer William Augustus Bowles was also now in Florida agitating against Euro-American influence in Creek and Seminole affairs. The immediate crisis of Georgia expansionism seemed to be ending, in short, but it remained to be seen how Creeks would respond and if the idea of Creek solidarity would endure. At the very moment McGillivray's voice declared success on behalf of all Creeks, there was already evidence to suggest that other strong voices were emerging.

FIGURE 4. Washington Peace Medal, 1789. Several of these peace medals, which were minted in 1789, were presented to the Creek delegation that visited New York for the treaty in 1790. Courtesy of the Alabama Department of Archives and History.

FIGURES 5 and 6. The Tallassee King, 1790, and the White Bird-Tail King, 1790. These pencil drawings were two of several that John Trumbull made of the Creek delegation that visited New York for the treaty in 1790. The first headman, the Tallassee Mico, was a steadfast American partisan during the American Revolution and shortly after but turned against Americans in the 1790s to embrace William Augustus Bowles and the Spanish. He died as a Red Stick insurgent. The second man, the White Bird-Tail King, would remain one of the American government's chief supporters in the 1790s, even after he was attacked by Georgia militiamen in 1793 and wounded so badly he was not expected to live. Yale University Art Gallery. Gov. Bd. Accepted October 1, 1947.

5 / Creek Country Faces Collapse

This country is in as convulsed a state as possible.
—James Holmes, April 20, 1793

The Oconee War demonstrated the unifying power of state aggression on Creek communities, but what Creeks gained in that time of crisis they quickly lost in what became a much larger crisis in the wake of the Treaty of New York in 1790. Although the treaty was designed to bring Creeks stability, it did the opposite; while Georgia expansionism slowly forced Creeks to construct a common voice, a single compromise attempt to make peace collapsed that voice with stunning speed. The region fractured as community leaders retreated from each other and political differences resurfaced that had evidently only temporarily been overcome during the Oconee War. The partisan groups that were slowly emerging by the end of the struggle hardened as Creek communities struggled to deal with the treaty. As community headmen reached out for competing sources of outside support they orchestrated the final collapse of an old political Creek order. Not only would the "play-off" system not survive this period of American expansionism and the intra-Creek factionalism it produced, but it would draw Creek Country closer to ruin than it had ever been.

Alexander McGillivray set the reversal in motion when he signed his name to the Treaty of New York. His attempt to translate wartime gains into what he saw as a reasonable compromise was simply unacceptable to other Creek community leaders, and local voices of radicalism quickly drowned out his voice of compromise.[1] While American talks largely supported peace and stability, the ranks of Bowles partisans, encouraged by his calls to reject the peace, swelled. Newly arrived Louisiana governor Francisco Luis Héctor, the baron de Carondelet, did not fail to drum up violent rejection of American authorities either. Groups of Shawnees soon appeared, having been victorious in their own confrontations with Americans to the north, and they developed upon their strong and historic kin connections in Creek Country. Together those talks contributed to a set of raids on the St. Mary's River and nearby—the Trader's Hill killings—that shattered the fragile Creek unity of the Oconee War period and ushered in the deepest, most divisive period of political crisis that Creeks had ever faced.

The treaty signed in New York was a tremendous American diplomatic and constitutional achievement, and the Washington administration hailed it as such. While it did not legitimize the state of Georgia's claims to the important strip of land below the Altamaha River that had already been organized as a new county—Tallassee—it did retain for Georgia a title to all the lands between the Ogeechee and Oconee rivers.[2] Creek warriors burned many of the settler homes from those lands between 1786 and 1788, and then a comprehensive Creek delegation simply walked away from the Rock Landing conference in 1789 when American commissioners even brought the lands up for debate. Those experiences in the not-so-distant past suggest that most Creeks probably would have wanted a better deal than they got in New York. And they probably would have fought for such a deal had they been in New York, but most were not. Instead, only McGillivray and a handful of other American-sympathetic headmen, including the Tallassee King, were on hand to meet federal authorities and to state Creek claims. It was a far cry from the scores of Creek leaders who had been at Rock Landing, but then again that was why Rock Landing failed. The situation in the American capital was different. There McGillivray was finally able to negotiate in good faith in a setting he was comfortable with, which he did, and with the very highest members of the Washington administration. He had always been willing to give up the Oconee lands, his trip to New York proved, as long as he got what he wanted from the American government and if the rest of Creek Country got at least a modest relief from the state of Georgia.

At thirty men, however, the delegation that made the journey with McGillivray to New York did not constitute anything approaching a legitimate representation of Creek interests. Two-thirds of the delegation that met with Knox and Washington, "liberally sprinkled," in the words of one historian, with McGillivray's kinsmen, were from the Upper Country. According to one man who met him on the road outside Baltimore, he was also traveling with three actual direct relatives, two of whom were in their teens. That further decreased the number of Creeks in McGillivray's entourage that had any justifiable claim to the kind of authority that would be needed on such a trip. And according to one copy of the Treaty of New York, three Cussetas, four Cowetas, and one Broken Arrow headman signed the document. Less than ten signatures came from the entirety of the Lower Country, in short, and at least half of those came from communities that were already on good terms with Americans. That contrasted with sixteen other signatures, representing Tallassee, Half-Way House, Tuckabatchee, Natchez, Coosada, Alabama, and Oakchai communities. Among the "Great Medal Chiefs" that were to be paid one hundred dollars annually for their acquiescence, the Tallassee King and an Oakfuskee headman were listed. A Tuckabatchee headman was listed as well, but it was not the Mad Dog of Tuckabatchee, who might not have agreed to the deal and therefore might not have warranted a "Great Medal Chief" distinction.[3]

Even more telling, not everyone that traveled to New York ended up signing the treaty. Thirty headmen made the trip to negotiate, but only twenty-four signed their names to the finished document. One of them did not even return south with the delegation, staying instead with a British agent to confer about Bowles and the British government's proposed support of the Creek people. In general, then, it is pretty clear that the Treaty of New York threatened to constitute a nonstarter among the majority of Creek people. At worst, McGillivray's delegation was simply pretense. At best, there was scant representation from the more volatile communities in the Lower Country that had the most to lose from the deal, and even of those that did attend not everyone was convinced that the deal was what was best for all Creeks.[4] If the delegation was indeed a sham, then it demonstrates the surprising depth of McGillivray's self-interest. If it was not, and he was acting in good faith, then it was because he and the headmen with him simply envisioned a more stable Creek Country that did not necessarily have to include the Oconee lands. Ironically, however, even the best-case scenario put McGillivray and his allies in a position very similar to what the Tallassee King and Fat King faced only years previous. Neither of those men fared particularly well when they attempted to cede the Oconee lands to the state of Georgia for what they saw as a more stable future. McGillivray, who had been an outspoken and even violent critic of those actions, turned around only years later to attempt almost the same deal. With Creek Country already struggling with renewed factionalism, there was no reason to suspect that McGillivray's effort would be any more acceptable than the ones that preceded it.

The vision for Creek Country that McGillivray shared with many of his associates at New York reflected the evolving place of Natives in the post-Revolutionary Southeast. It involved a philosophy on property ownership and land usage that was beginning to take hold in parts of Creek Country, and it had long informed McGillivray's life in ways that had already distanced him at times from many of his fellow Creeks. He, with a select few others, mostly in his immediate neighborhood, were already coming around to the idea of owning land privately and ranching and planting certain crops for profit. He was a part of the "New Order of Things," as one historian explained it—Creeks who were planters, traders, businessmen, and slaveholders, as well as Creek—and he saw little problem gaining money and security for what he increasingly considered unusable land. The Oconee lands were already too overhunted to depend on for the deerskin trade, but Americans were willing to pay handsomely for them. The future of the Creek people was not in the fur trade but in cash crops, or ranching, and with the federal government guaranteeing the remainder of Creek lands there would be plenty of territory left to make Creek people a self-sustaining and even wealthy one if New York was negotiated smartly. To McGillivray, a slightly smaller Creek Country was worth the package that American authorities were offering: a recognition of territorial sovereignty, security against the state of Georgia, a stable trade, farming technology, and plenty of cash.[5]

The problem with McGillivray's vision for Creek Country was that few others in Creek Country actually shared it. While there certainly were a few people who thought like McGillivray, they constituted a mere handful—he was two decades ahead of the times at least. Even his neighbors in the Upper Country were torn. After the entourage returned from New York, for instance, the Mad Dog held a council at Tuckabatchee, where McGillivray spoke about the results. "Some seem pleased," a witness wrote, while others threw "their tobacco into the fire, in disgust."[6] Few in Creek Country would deny that the deer population was flagging and that hunters were struggling with their trade debts. Regardless, not only did the Oconee lands remain the primary source of livelihood for numerous communities in both the Upper and Lower countries, they had also been a source of community identity for generations.[7] After

New York, however, headmen like the Hallowing King could only react with anger and disbelief as a handful of headmen representing localized interests in communities hundreds of miles to the west dispensed with them without consultation. The Oconee lands were again the source of resentment and violence, but in the wake of New York the threat was originating from within Creek Country.

This was the beginning of a response to the Treaty of New York that represented a particularly powerful moment in Creek politics by ushering in a new, albeit short and much more self-destructive, period of "play-off" diplomacy in the Southeast. It was system informed by a previous, and rather successful, era of Creek diplomacy that many in 1790 would still remember. As recent as a generation earlier, three European colonial forces vied for Creek support in the Southeast, and Creek factions responded by forcing them to compete for trade connections and even military alliances. The Spanish were first in the region in the sixteenth and seventeenth centuries and approached Creek Country from the Gulf Coast. The French were soon to follow from the Gulf Coast as well from the Mississippi River to the west, and even from among Creek communities, at Fort Toulouse at the confluence of the Coosa and Tallapoosa rivers. Meanwhile the British approached from South Carolina and Georgia to the east. The situation after the Treaty of New York, half a century later, was in one sense familiar—multiple parties still vied for Creek relationships. The French were long gone, but the Spanish remained. The British were also present, but not really. William Augustus Bowles said he spoke for the king of England, but he had almost no actual British support and was in fact not British. His promises were almost completely worthless, but Creeks could not have known that at the time. Georgia state authorities were around, but they clearly had little to offer. The addition to the regional calculus was the new American federal government. It was a steadily growing force and a formidable one—more so than the others—in a way similar to how British authorities functioned in the first play-off system. Nevertheless, it was still in no position to dictate much to the Creek people, making it again familiar. Interested in stability but also supportive of their expansionist state counterparts, federal legislators were already struggling with confederated Native Algonquin, Shawnee, and Illinois groups in the "old northwest"—modern-day Indiana, Illinois, and Ohio. The disastrous defeat of American forces attempting to quell Native resistance there in 1790 and 1791 embarrassed the Washington administration and forced it to approach the larger Native groups in the Southeast with more circumspection. Among those groups was a Creek population that had, for a time, embraced a common cause. More important to a man like Secretary of War Henry Knox, Creek warriors had already humbled the state of Georgia militarily, and had done so with flair.[8] But Creek solidarity was no longer strong, and as communities pulled back away from each other in the wake of New York, they set the conditions for a new play-off system to emerge.

While a few of the players at least appeared to be the same as before, the self-destructive nature of this new political atmosphere differentiated it from earlier eras because the stakes for Creeks were much higher and the political maneuvering much more desperate than before. The threat to Creek lands and Creek identity was tremendous, and at this particular moment weapons and ammunition were as important as any other trade goods. If Creek communities could not find outside sources of assistance that would help them continue to resist American expansionists the Creek people stood to lose land, and a lot of it. "If we part with them, we part with our blood," the Hallowing King of Coweta had put it only three years earlier.[9] This was the engine that drove the new play-off system, producing different voices within Creek Country only months after the conclusion of the Treaty of New York. As Creek communities turned to whatever means available to them to reject the treaty and prevent the loss of their lands, they opened Creek Country up to powerful forces of internal political factionalism as well as outside forces of manipulation, all of which had a swift and destructive impact on Creek cohesiveness.

The first of those voices came from the multitude of Creeks that began to turn their backs on McGillivray. His influence in the region began to erode almost immediately as communities rejected his attempt at compromise and looked elsewhere for anti-American support.[10] Within only months of the treaty, in fact, the Lower Country was no longer a place he felt safe, let alone welcome. A group of Americans, passing through Coweta on their way to the Upper Country, were fired on several times at random and found many of the residents "surly, morose and much displeased." The Cowetas appeared "very much dissatisfied" with the treaty and also with McGillivray, and they were making their disapproval known publicly. "Paying very little respect to his authority," they declared "that Congress might do what they pleased with the Treaty, for that they intended to do as they pleased with it." All of this was declared "in great contempt," and when the time came for the travelers to return home, McGillivray strongly recommended they take a different route.[11]

William Augustus Bowles was quick to capitalize on that anger, particularly in the Lower Country. He had already been in the region for some time promoting a British protectionist stance against both Spanish and Georgia officials, but his time had amounted to little. Whether he did so with any actual British backing or not, Bowles quickly expanded his radical overtures to include condemnation of the New York treaty, agents of the American government generally, McGillivray particularly, and even his neighbors in the Upper Country. They all, Bowles charged, were now working equally to dispossess communities in the Lower Country of hunting land. Reports circulated late in 1791 that he was already making promises of British military aid and was planning to resist the running of the new boundary line with violence if necessary. A few months later he made good on his threats against the Spanish traders he criticized so publicly for exploiting Creek hunters. With help from a number of warriors from the Lower Country and in Florida he attacked and looted the Panton, Leslie and Company warehouse at Apalache and even made menacing advances toward the nearby Spanish position at St. Marks (San Marcos de Apalache).[12] He was not a man of idle threats, Bowles proved, and his words of resistance quickly found enthusiastic followers in the Lower Country.

Growing support for Bowles revealed the dangerous nature of the political maneuverability Creek communities were attempting to revive. William Augustus Bowles was evoking a long tradition of British relations in the Southeast that was welcomed by many Creeks and actually remembered by several of them. Yet Bowles had almost nothing to offer the Creek people. His long-term vision for an independent Creek political entity was complete fantasy, and it did not take long for authorities in England to disavow him completely. He might have been able to arrange the arrival of a shipload or two of trade goods from Bahamian traders who were clearly just using him to compete with the Panton firm, but that would do little to give Creek people the security they were looking for. He could provide neither the aid nor the leadership that would be necessary for the Creek people to reverse the course they had made with Americans and chart a new one, independent of the federal government. Nevertheless, his voice was strong and his promises sounded very good to panicked Creek community leaders, an increasing number of whom turned to him and away from Alexander McGillivray.

The rapid development of this new anti–New York partisan group represented a particularly dangerous challenge to Americans who, pleased with the treaty, were quick to begin enforcing its terms. By the spring and summer of 1791 several companies of federal troops were dispatched to a new garrison at Rock Landing, which marked the American side of the new Creek boundary. There they were preparing to assist contractors, along with Creek and Georgia assistants, as they surveyed the northern limits of a new boundary line.[13] An officer was also en route with the government's first annuity payments to the Creek people, the first salary payment to McGillivray, and several individual payments to specific Creek headmen, including the Oakfuskee and Tuckabatchee headmen, the Tallassee King, and Cusseta, Coweta, and Mikasuki chiefs.[14] Despite reports of resistance to the treaty and of widespread anger at McGillivray, Knox remained confident in his newfound ally. McGillivray earned a commission as a brigadier general in the American army in one of the treaty's secret articles and was to operate with that title as the government's chief advocate of American interests in Creek Country. Knox even issued him a military liaison, explaining to the soldier that McGillivray was "the soul of the Creek nation, and that, by cultivating his esteem, you will succeed with the rest."[15]

Unfortunately for Knox, his confidence in McGillivray was badly, almost humorously, misplaced. The decaying situation in the Lower Country was already revealing how little authority the young man actually possessed in any regional sense. And slowly but surely, the only thing McGillivray could prove to his allies was how utterly unequipped he was for the difficult tasks that lay ahead. He demonstrated a decided refusal to confront Bowles, for instance, even when pressed to do so from those who were by that point his multiple bosses. Knox, Panton, recently arrived Florida governor Juan Nepomuceno Quesada, and of course Esteban Miró all demanded he confront the unwanted visitor, yet he did nothing.[16] He continued to do nothing after he learned that Bowles was traveling up to the powerful Coweta towns. If he succeeded in council there the results would certainly not be good, from either an American or a Spanish perspective.[17] That was clear to both Knox and Miró—both of whom were technically McGillivray's superiors at that point—and they both ordered him to make Bowles disappear. Rather than confront Bowles while he was still a relative political outsider, however, it was McGillivray that disappeared. In the meantime, Bowles solidified his position in the Lower Country. Both Hitchiti chiefs Perryman and Philatouchie declared their determination to aid him and "all his designs however base & injurious they may prove to their country in the end." McGillivray's only threats, it turned out, were the ones he could make in pen. Although he did plenty of that, he also admitted that his letters were not having the desired effect. Bowles's influence was growing in a way he was having a hard time countering. He was "making a great noise" among Chehaws, "& has perfectly confused & distracted the foolish & inconsiderate part of the Indians thereabout."[18] Though he insulted Bowles and belittled his growing base of support, it soon became obvious that McGillivray was not the one to do anything about it.[19] "Disturbances have lately been excited among the Creeks," Henry Knox feared, with Bowles having "set himself up in opposition to McGillivray." Either "McGillivray or Bowles must fall."[20]

Bowles's influence, and McGillivray's inability to counter it, was notable also for its ability to undermine a Spanish partisan base that had been dangerously strong since the end of the Revolution. Bowles had long advocated against both the Spanish government and the affiliated Panton, Leslie and Company trading house. But it was only in the wake of New York that communities began to respond. William Panton, for one, complained that Cowetas and Ooseoochees were the ones who sacked his trading post, while the Little Prince of Broken Arrow arrived at the ruins of the store just in time to bid Panton's trading partner, Robert Leslie, a sarcastic farewell as the ruined merchant surveyed the damage. Those three towns, in addition to Hitchitis and Chehaws, proved instantly receptive to Bowles's talks at the expense of allies who had not only been supportive of them in the past but instrumental in the defense of their lands. Not only was that cruel to the two traders, obviously, but it ostracized nearby Cusseta, Buzzard Roost, and Yuchi communities, who had come around to the Spanish as allies and who remained faithful to them in the wake of Apalache. Using nothing but vague and ultimately erroneous promises of future British assistance, in short, Bowles had split the Lower Country more or less in half only a few years after the region displayed almost total cohesion against the Georgia frontier. And the split, according to Panton, was visible. A group of headmen, led by Cussetas, realized what the others had done to the trading store when they returned from their winter hunts and "turned out a large body to proceed to Appalachy to revenge the insult and to punish Bowles."[21]

This mounting dissention was felt heaviest by McGillivray, who began to air his frustration in plainer terms. Bowles was driving Creek Country to ruin, he lamented to his friend William Panton, and he was not planning on sticking around to watch that all unfold. The last ten years he was "absolutely worn down," he complained. Unable to grasp his position in the larger scheme of things, McGillivray felt particularly betrayed by the actions of headmen in the Lower Country. By rejecting his compromise and turning instead to Bowles they were "wholly insensible of the destruction from which they have been saved by their friends."[22] He elaborated on the complaint at a meeting at the Half-Way House, where he made his disappointment known publicly. They, his fellow Creeks, "had thrown his talks aside . . . they had shamed him in his own country and made him out a liar before the white people." Undoing all of his hard work they instead embraced the talks of Bowles, a stranger and no friend to the Creek people. And now, he declared, he was through. Creeks would have to find someone else to read and write for them, or negotiate with the Americans, because he was leaving. They were all doomed, their land would soon belong to Georgia settlers, and he would have nothing more to do with them.[23] If that warning was meant to bluff the rival headmen, then they called it; by early 1792 McGillivray indeed had moved his property and slaves from his sprawling property in the Upper Country further south, to the area around Pensacola, perhaps for protection.[24] Even William Panton and Robert Leslie were shaken, wondering in a more critical tone why McGillivray had left rather than rise to the occasion. Leslie had gone so far as to explain exactly where Bowles was living, hoping to push McGillivray to confront, and (he hoped) kill, the interloper. Instead, Perryman of Hitchiti, among others, declared "in the most pointed terms that Mr. McGillivray had been obliged to flee the Nation to save his head."[25] Although he was still a Creek mediator as far as American and Spanish authorities were concerned, his removal from the heart of Creek Country revealed that, to a growing number of Creeks, his leadership was no longer welcome.

McGillivray's most supportive American allies soon began worrying as well. Knox questioned him about the reasons he fled "at this critical period." The secretary understood, perhaps, that the "disturbances excited by Bowles' appearance, and the countenance given him by a great part of the Lower towns," were dangerous. But that was when he needed to exert his authority the most. "Whatever may have been the reason for your journey," Knox pressed, "it would appear that Bowles has availed himself of it, describing it as a flight." To a lot of worried authorities, including Secretary Knox, that appeared to be the case. He was clearly alarmed by the development, even if he still believed McGillivray could control it. He was so alarmed, in fact, that he appointed James Seagrove as a temporary agent in the Southeast to begin assisting McGillivray, beginning Seagrove's own long tenure in the region. He also added two more companies of infantry to the garrison at Rock Landing.[26]

Although Knox was ostensibly continuing to support McGillivray, his faith certainly was shaken. He warned McGillivray of that directly, reminding him that American authorities in the region were ready and waiting to implement the treaty, and they were all waiting on him. McGillivray needed to fulfill his obligations to the Americans and see that the treaty was legitimized in Creek Country in the ways he guaranteed he was capable of at New York. The treaty was "sacred, and must be complied with, in all its parts." Soldiers and surveyors were waiting at Rock Landing to begin the work, and they had been there for months. The line was supposed to be completed by October 1791, Knox reminded McGillivray, and it was now February 1792. "Your reputation," he warned, "and all dependent thereon, will be blasted forever, if the line be not run as soon as the disturbances are quiet." Knox's tone was stern, but in his private correspondences with Seagrove the secretary voiced even more serious doubt. In February 1792, at least he still believed that the young man had a role to play in the region. By October, however, Knox was beginning to admit to Seagrove that he might have made a mistake placing as much confidence in McGillivray as he had. By that time Seagrove had already lost all faith.[27]

McGillivray's decline was not quite as simple as these criticisms suggest. It was not that he had been a tremendously authoritative figure before Bowles arrived, that he had lost all nerve in the face of his nemesis, and that he had now been overcome. Bowles, in other words, was not the cause of McGillivray's political decline. Whether he ever understood as much or not it was McGillivray, thinking he was a man influential enough to broker the Treaty of New York on his own terms and make it binding on all of Creek Country, who was the source of his own demise. As many local headmen were making clear by rejecting New York and turning their back on him, they were not pawns in a diplomatic game that was out of their control. They were not beholden to McGillivray, or to Bowles, for that matter. Local headmen were the ones who charted the course for their communities, and they made the decisions as to whom they would trust. To many of them McGillivray had been a dependable anti-expansionist voice in the past and a facilitator for armed resistance when it was needed. By evolving politically into a man of compromise he no longer offered those things, and the Treaty of New York simply was not the course many headmen saw as best for their communities. Perhaps Bowles, some of them even dared to hope, might offer something better.

Federal authorities, coming to realize as much, ultimately turned their back on McGillivray as well. Instead Knox turned to Seagrove, asking him to step up his efforts and develop what relationships he could with the few friendly headmen that remained in Creek Country. He even began to suggest placing more agents, under Seagrove, directly in Creek communities.[28] This was, above else, a move of sheer necessity. Not only was McGillivray unable to implement the Treaty of New York, his inaction was making it look like a joke. More capable and dedicated agents of the federal government were badly needed—men in the region building relationships from within Creek Country and mediating differences with locals directly. It was "by residents in the nation," Knox believed, "that the influence of the United States is to be silently and permanently established."[29] Seagrove would replace McGillivray as the federal government's connection to Creek Country, Knox had decided. And why not? A complete stranger could do no more damage than his predecessor, a man once described as the soul of the Creek People, had already done.

Nevertheless, Seagrove had quite the task before him. No outsider had attempted to gain influence in Creek Country since John Stuart, more than a generation earlier. Seagrove had no known Creek identity or kin, he had no familial trading connections, and it is unknown whether he was even from the Southeast; as such a political and cultural foreigner it was unclear exactly how he would succeed in such an important position of influence. Quickly, though, Seagrove proved more than capable. He went to work penning letters of introduction, and it did not take long for him to open dialogues with headmen from across Creek Country. By the spring of 1792 he had helped strengthen an American partisan core that stretched from Oakfuskee to Cusseta, representing several communities that at least did not openly hate what the Treaty of New York represented.[30] Although having such friendly headmen anywhere in Creek Country was a great start, Seagrove's successes in the Lower Country were critical. With McGillivray's influence there practically nonexistent, and with Bowles's talks coursing through several communities, the situation was worsening with each passing day. Seagrove correctly understood that if he could project a positive and trustworthy image of the federal government there, he could do tremendous good. His relationship with Cussetas was strong, but developing friends in the rest of the region was no easy task. To do that he first proposed a meeting with several headmen from the Lower Country at his station, which he made the federal garrison at Rock Landing. There, with a healthy supply of trade goods, he hoped to rally friendly headmen around the Treaty of New York and get them to exert their collective pressure on the more wayward communities in the region.[31]

Seagrove also initiated several conciliatory acts in person. When reports circulated that hunting parties were harassing Georgians, for instance, he toured down the Oconee and Altamaha rivers, speaking with hunters everywhere he found them. He made another such trip with Henry Gaither later that year, riding from Rock Landing to Fort Telfair on the Altamaha River, finding "all things peaceable and in good order." Whenever he found families or hunters he supplied them with food, and on one occasion he took eight Creeks with him "into the settlements," in an effort to soothe tensions with local Georgians and find common ground. He also made sure that when communities in the region were in need, he would be the first to assist them, letting them know of course that he was doing so on behalf of the U.S. government. That was the case in the fall of 1792, when several communities along the Chattahoochee River suffered crop failures and it was obvious they would have a tough time getting through the winter. He requested Knox purchase provisions and have them shipped south for him to distribute, and over ten thousand bushels of corn soon arrived.[32]

Seagrove was quick to initiate direct contact with Creek communities, but rarely did he cross the Oconee River into Creek Country, and he never made it very deep. With men like Timothy Barnard and John Kinnard in the south perhaps he did not feel it was necessary. It was much more difficult getting talks further to the west, but then again, those communities were some of the friendliest to American interests. Headmen in the Upper Country were, indeed, many of the first to respond to his letters, and soon they were his most vocal supporters. They included the White Lieutenant of Oakfuskee and the Mad Dog and Alexander Cornells of Tuckabatchee. Despite their questionable actions in the past—particularly from the Mad Dog, who had been both a British and Spanish partisan—those men had also been some of McGillivray's strongest allies. They all had been at least somewhat supportive of the New York treaty because McGillivray had been as well, and they were also among those receiving annuity payments from the government for helping to have it implemented.[33] If those men warmed up to Seagrove, as it appeared they were, the American position in the Upper Country looked promising.

By developing headmen in both the Upper and Lower countries Seagrove certainly was making concrete gains for the American government, but he still by no means was making the Treaty of New York popular. For the several influential Creek friends he was actually winning, and however altruistic his goal for regional stability was, Seagrove could not overcome the reality that the Treaty of New York had not been made with a respectable representation of Creek Country and that there were far more community leaders in the region who did not agree with its terms than there were ones who did. That made for a tricky geopolitical challenge indeed. Americans were not interested in giving up on the treaty, which Washington and Knox brokered personally, which had been confirmed by the Senate, and which had set an important precedent that validated the very authority of the new federal government. On the other hand, however, the Treaty of New York had no chance of acceptance by the majority of the people in Creek Country, making Seagrove's mission to use it as a means to generate stability in the region basically impossible. Although he was cultivating relationships with a handful of headmen in Creek Country, James Seagrove was not bringing the entire region around to the American position—he was merely contributing to the new play-off atmosphere by representing a plausible alternative to some Creek communities while, at the same time, hardening a position that many more communities were absolutely determined to counter.

The situation in the volatile Lower Country had at least the potential to improve for Americans after local Spanish authorities cut Bowles's tenure there short in the spring of 1792. After sacking the Apalache store, threatening the nearby Spanish garrison, and thoroughly disgracing their man Alexander McGillivray in the process, both Miró and O'Neill decided they had had enough. Spanish agents lured him onboard a navy vessel posing as a trade ship, clapped him in chains, and shipped him off for interrogation at New Orleans. Soon enough he was on his way to the Philippines and far, far away from relieved Spanish authorities.[34] Perhaps buoyed by his capture, McGillivray conspicuously reappeared about that same time at his home at Little Tallassee.[35] He quickly attempted to make a mockery of Bowles's popularity as well as revive his own, and did so by belittling many of the young men of the Lower Country as aggressively as he attacked Bowles himself. They were practically raised during the political jockeying and violence of the Revolution, he explained, and were "so accustomed to War & depredation that a regular life is disagreeable to them." They were clearly not as sophisticated as he—they were not interested in planting, ranching, or otherwise enjoying a more cultivated existence, like he and his neighbors had done for some time. Such young men "eagerly listen to & follow any one that holds out the temptation of plunder to them."[36] And as for Bowles, he assured Seagrove that he had dispatched the Mad Dog and a set of Coweta and Cusseta warriors to either capture or kill him, and a "considerable party accordingly set out for that purpose," but the Spanish seized him before his own posse arrived.[37] While he ridiculed the growing number of communities antagonistic to his vision for Creek Country, however, McGillivray was ignoring the severity of his predicament—Creeks were not only rejecting the New York treaty, they were rejecting him.

As for Bowles, the Spaniards' decisiveness after Apalache was impressive, but unfortunately seizing the adventurer did nothing to stop the centrifugal impact he had on the Lower Country. While he was technically their prisoner and definitely had been a nuisance, Spanish authorities were not entirely convinced that he ought to be locked up forever. Facing a resurgent American government, they actually seriously considered cultivating him as an asset, as they had McGillivray in the past. McGillivray had shed his Spanish partisanship long ago, Spanish officials feared, and perhaps Bowles might serve as a suitable replacement. To keep that avenue open they allowed him to continue penning letters back to his subordinates, like George Wellbank, who did not fail to circulate them and preach "every thing he can in Bowles' favor." To merchant Robert Leslie that was as terrible an idea as leaving Bowles where he had been, "blowing up the Indians with the hopes of vast supplies of Goods from Nassau & keeping up an inveterate Spite against the Spaniards for having stolen away their *beloved man their father.*" While those reports did not shine a particularly favorable light on the Spanish, his letters were doing a great job of stirring the Lower Country up against the Americans, and the governors could at least be pleased with that. Even though he was half a world away and would not return for almost a decade, packets of his inflammatory letters circulated through the Lower Country with regularity, and they continued doing terrific damage in the region.[38]

The complicated Spanish-Bowles situation was a demonstration not only of outside forces acting on Creeks but of the continued willingness of Creek communities to turn to those outsiders in an effort to stave off American expansionism. From one perspective Creeks were clearly being used by outside political forces, which is not a flattering assertion of Creek agency. Not only was Bowles manipulating Creeks for ends he could not possibly succeed in gaining, but Spaniards were now manipulating Bowles, as well as Creeks, in support of their own reinvigorated anti-American agenda. At the same time, however, Creek communities were enabling those outsiders by continuing to fall back on an approach to play-off diplomacy that had worked before. In the face of American expansionists, community leaders were willing to turn to whoever would assist them, and they were finding support now from multiple outsiders. From all appearances, for example, many Creeks were keen on William Augustus Bowles even though they had little to say about his own geopolitical vision for the Southeast. They had much more to say, however, about his aggressive anti-American talks, as well as the shiploads of goods he was promising. Robert Leslie was right to complain that as long as those promises were being read to Creek communities, there would be plenty of people eager to listen. He was also right to conclude that, in the end, those promises would prove ruinous.

By May 1792 an increasing number of towns in the Lower Country were more firm Bowles partisans than ever, a striking development considering Bowles was literally on the other side of the planet. A British flag was flying in Ooseoochee, and Wellbank was actually living in Coweta. Bowles had "a large majority of the Nation in his favour," according to one informant, and "all the Indians except two towns" were opposed to New York. And as for McGillivray, he had "given up all pretentions of commanding the Nation."[39] That was all very bad news for Americans indeed, but Seagrove gave a similar assessment: "Although Bowles is removed, such is the baneful effect of what he has done, that the strength of his party (even at this moment) in the Creek nation, is such, that we find General McGillivray compelled to submit to their will."[40] While Seagrove did not report to Knox that the allegiances of headmen in the Lower Country communities were totally lost, the situation was definitely distressing. Having met with Cussetas and Cowetas at Rock Landing and worked hard to win the latter communities over, Seagrove learned with dismay that Bowles "had been allowed to make so many friends to his cause in the Creek nation, that his influence would counteract any thing attempted in the towns." The confusion he caused "had not subsisted," and "further interference in the Creek councils had arisen." The Cussetas and Cowetas had to struggle even to physically get to Seagrove, James Durouzeaux wrote from Coweta, because they had been "confused in separate parties, by that Bowles," and they had been at "a loss to determine on any thing, by reason of the villains of Bowles' party."[41] As if on cue, McGillivray again bemoaned his situation. Creeks were "altogether regardless of his advice," he "was determined to quit them," and again he threatened to move his belongings into Spanish West Florida or Louisiana.[42] While Cussetas could still be depended on in May 1792, he complained, they were practically the only ones left in the Lower Country that were not hanging on Bowles's every word. Because of his promises, "a majority of the towns would agree to cede no more than the east side of Oconee, and now they are told to give none at all." If Americans continued to press for the implementation of the Treaty of New York, he feared, it would lead to "a diabolical war."[43]

Even with Bowles long gone McGillivray could do little to reverse that trend, leading Americans to criticize him more vocally. "I pray you, as early as possible," Knox pressed him, "to unravel this mystery, and inform me precisely of the nature and extent of this interference."[44] Seagrove, meanwhile, hated him. He had requested McGillivray come to Rock Landing when he was meeting with the headmen there earlier in 1792, an invitation McGillivray at first accepted.[45] But newly arrived Spanish governor of New Orleans Francisco Luis Héctor, the baron de Carondelet, quickly ordered him to desist. When he left the Upper Country with a group of headmen to meet with Seagrove anyway, groups of Creeks from both the Upper and Lower countries confronted him and refused to let him pass.[46] The Mad Dog of Tuckabatchee, a man who had been friendly to McGillivray in the past and who had also been talking to Seagrove, appeared with a Kialijee headman and the Tallassee King and they confronted the travelers, telling McGillivray that "he must not meet the Virginians" and that they had received talks from Bowles. The party never made it to Seagrove, who cut off all correspondence with McGillivray as a result and began insulting him more directly.[47] McGillivray, both Knox and Seagrove were now sure, was no friend of Americans. If there were any Creek headmen left in the region accommodating of the Treaty of New York, it was now up to Seagrove to support and assist them. But with even staunch American partisan the Tallassee King now disrupting federal efforts in favor of listening to Bowles's talks, Seagrove's task was becoming more impossible by the day.

The Baron de Carondelet further complicated the regional calculus, almost the day he arrived, by generating yet another strong, manipulative voice in the region. Miró, while he certainly had a hand in arming Creek warriors during the Oconee War, had also been a steady voice for temperance. It was under his watch, along with fellow governor Arturo O'Neill, that the official Spanish position in the Creek-Georgia struggle began to shift from war to conciliation. Not only was he one of McGillivray's chief supporters, he also at least did not hate the idea of the Treaty of New York, which he personally considered politically shrewd. That prompted many Creeks, including McGillivray, to look elsewhere for continued support, setting off the partisan chain reaction that left Creek Country in the confused state the Baron now entered. And that, he quickly declared, would not do. To counter the American menace he "began a series of vigorous efforts," according to one report, "to weld the southern tribes into an effective unit to halt American expansion."[48] And Carondelet had no problem saying that himself. He could not "look without concern on the repeated encroachments of the Americans, who successively become masters and possess themselves of the Lands belonging to the Indian Nations his allies." As an aggressive protector of Spain's claims to the Mississippi, Carondelet vowed to frustrate any American attempt to usurp those claims, including by opposing the Treaty of New York with violence, if necessary: he would "destroy the treaty between the Creeks and the Americans." And if Americans complained, he would make it clear that the king would not fail to protect the Creeks "when, as on this occasion, they are not the aggressors."[49]

The Baron de Carondelet reshaped the Spanish Gulf Coast into a key player in the new Creek play-off system almost overnight. If the Creek people were looking for assistance in the form of arms, ammunition, or strong anti-American and strong anti-Bowles talks, they would not fail to find any of those things now at any regional Spanish post. Unlike his predecessors, Carondelet also considered McGillivray more of an obstacle than an asset, and he wasted little time dealing with him as such. He was convinced of McGillivray's "slight in the worth of the Nation," and should Creeks go to war with the Americans, he would "retire from that Nation, abandoning them completely." He had already proven that much. Carondelet, it turned out, was a man who minced few words. McGillivray's fear of Bowles was "unequivocal," and he had "been proscribed by the last council of the chiefs of the Nation and is not allowed to return."[50] Very quickly, in fact, Carondelet made moves to directly undermine what little influence over the Spanish partisans McGillivray had left. Soon a man by the name of Don Pedro Oliver had arrived in Creek Country, seemingly poised to do just that. Carondelet appointed Oliver official agent to the Creeks, a position that directly usurped McGillivray's ability to control the flow of Spanish goods from the Gulf Coast. A captain in the Spanish army who wore "the uniform of the regiment of Louisiana," Oliver was charged with "promot[ing] & support[ing] the credit & authority" of the Spanish government, which was a nice way of saying he was McGillivray's replacement. He was "a man of great energy, prudence, and skill," Carondelet wrote, "and consequently will be able to discredit" his predecessor McGillivray and counter his questionable character.[51]

As a counterpoint to Seagrove, Oliver represented a bold Spanish addition to the new geopolitical play-off diplomacy that did not have the stabilizing effect most Creeks probably hoped for. Oliver was soon moving through both the Upper and Lower countries delivering strong talks direct from Carondelet, pressing everyone everywhere to reject New York and reject it openly, and offering more aid and weaponry from Spanish stores. Early in the summer of 1792 he was pushing through the Lower Country and had arrived in Coweta, requesting a council there before anyone left to meet with Seagrove at Rock Landing. There his talks were welcomed, Oliver soon reported, even by Cussetas, who "were satisfied with what I told them, particularly with not yielding to the cession of their land as proposed to the Americans." He also took McGillivray to task, explaining to the Cussetas how he had duped them, inducing them to sell the land by "assuring them that he received a great amount of gold and silver for it."[52] When Oliver continued to the north McGillivray complained at first, resisting the appointment of "a resident King's commissary before the Nation," particularly in his neighborhood, and delaying as much as he could having the Spaniard introduced to nearby headmen. But there was little he could do. Soon Oliver was living at one of his plantation houses and rewarding local headmen "and warriors who demonstrate their loyalty towards us" by distributing goods from Pensacola directly, which is to say without advice from McGillivray.[53]

The effect of the Spanish policies was quick, particularly on McGillivray. The flow of both weapons and trade goods increased precipitously without so much as a word from him, and that seemed just fine to many Creek headmen, who began requesting more Spanish agents.[54] As early as May 1792, in fact, McGillivray thought he might actually be reversing his decline in the Lower Country when, "to my surprise, some Indians, from Orleans, have given and spread reports that have made matters worse than ever." Oliver had declared that he had orders to prevent the boundary line from being run and to stop Creeks from "doing any other business" with Americans. "This last stroke," McGillivray groaned, "is too much: the Indians, at least a good many, are as mad as ever." Americans were still planning to mark out the new boundary line, but McGillivray advised them to postpone it, hoping "to avoid disputes and its horrid consequences."[55] Without asking for his counsel, or even advising him of his decisions, Spanish officials illustrated how out of favor McGillivray had become among the first allies he had ever made in the postwar years.

Before long Carondelet was speaking directly with William Panton and was even distributing supplies and talks to headmen personally.[56] Eventually he confronted McGillivray directly, warning him that he stood to lose his commission as a Spanish agent if he did not work immediately to repudiate New York. He also hinted that if he would not support the Spanish position, then perhaps Bowles would. That was something Spanish authorities had debated in the past, so it was no surprise that Carondelet would hold it over McGillivray's head, whether he was serious about the threat or not. Despite how much of an irritation he had been to Spanish governance in Florida, at least Bowles had already demonstrated that he was willing to "throw every obstacle in the way of the conclusion of the treaty, as he did the preceding year, and would procure us undoubtedly the most intimate connection with the creeks," and that was certainly more than Carondelet could say about McGillivray. On the other hand, Carondelet also promised McGillivray that his salary would see quite a significant increase if he gave up his American commission and threw his full support behind the Spanish.[57] Those threats clearly moved McGillivray, who was soon on his way to New Orleans to speak to the governor directly, and by July 1792 the two had come to an agreement. McGillivray formally renounced his American commission and renewed his position as a Spanish agent.[58]

The agreement made in July might have cooled Carondelet's temper, but it did nothing to reverse McGillivray's decline. He now no longer embraced his own compromise treaty. His Creek kin had largely abandoned him, Americans were working around him, and his new position as a Spanish partisan was a mockery. Although he was again a Spanish commissary, he was not the primary one, as he had been in the past, and soon he was only one of several. Indeed, nothing in the previous two years had brought a greater sense of stability to the region, which is what he had hoped would be his legacy when he spoke with Knox in New York.[59] Most Creek communities were still searching for an aggressive anti-expansion voice in the region, which is precisely what the new Spanish leadership was providing them. That left McGillivray, by late summer of 1792, wondering what sort of role he had to play in Creek Country at all. Again he moved his property out of Creek Country, now to land closer to New Orleans. It was even reported that he planned to burn his plantation at Little Tallassee but was persuaded to give it to Oliver, which he did. Although he was still technically a Spanish agent for the Creeks, more than ever it appeared he would be acting in that capacity from outside of Creek Country, not from within it.[60] While there were one or two friendly headmen who yearned for his return, they were the minority. Instead, "the truth is, he is ashamed to meet many of the Chiefs," James Seagrove explained, "who, he knows, would upbraid him for his conduct, and at the same time fears offending his Spanish friends." "Unfortunate man!" he later wrote. "I really pity him."[61] Seagrove must have been pleased when McGillivray fell ill outside of Pensacola less than six months later and was soon dead. While this came to the great discomfort of Panton and a small handful of other friends, very few others took pain in the once beloved man's passing.[62] By the time of his death, however, that was no longer McGillivray's title. By attempting to transcend his position as a beloved man he ultimately became an unwelcome man in the very place he was born. And Creek Country continued to divide into factions as he faded into obscurity.

McGillivray's decline and death marked the end of an intriguing era in Creek political history that saw his name thrown around quite a bit, but it did little to alter the trajectory of the new Creek play-off system. In the late summer and fall of 1792 Creek communities from both the Upper and Lower countries were listening to competing talks from Bowles and from the Spanish, while James Seagrove and the Americans continued to look optimistically—and in vain—toward the day they might finally at least get a boundary line marked out. Bowles's supporters held sway in the south, popular in every community except Cusseta. Spanish talks, which likewise called for the rejection of the Americans, were also popular. Cussetas remained overwhelmingly friendly to Seagrove, as was the Hallowing King of the Cowetas, and he represented a powerful ally. Around the federal post at Rock Landing, which was in the vicinity of the Cusseta and Buzzard Roost villages, there were around one hundred Creeks early in the summer, "all of whom seem perfectly disposed for peace," including several chiefs.[63] Even McGillivray had admitted as much. Cussetas, "at the head of those who are in the interest of the United States, are considerable," and "overbalance the other," by which he probably meant the nearby Coweta villages, who were more prone to violence. Yet he also admitted that they "have not firmness to oppose, with vigor, the other chiefs."[64] While the Hallowing King maintained a friendly correspondence with Seagrove, that in no way meant that even most Cowetas were friendly. Others, drummed up by the nearby presence of Wellbank, were itching to move against the backcountry. That, unfortunately, was the relatively stable portion of the Lower Country. Outside manipulation in communities further to the south, along the Chattahoochee River and then along the Flint and Apalachicola rivers, was much stronger, and it had taken its toll. According to a report from Timothy Barnard, Yuchis seemed fairly dependable, but others in the region, particularly Chehaws and Hitchitis, were more militant, and "that villain Bowles has put such notions in their heads that the devil seems to be in them ever since."[65] If they were to embrace violence, then other communities in the region, like Ooseoochees and Broken Arrows, would be happy to follow.

Further to the northwest, Seagrove had more friends. Support of the New York treaty still existed in the Half-Way House and Oakfuskee, and among at least some headmen from Tuckabatchee. Spanish operatives were also active in the Upper Country by that time, however, and Spanish talks radiated from McGillivray's plantation in Little Tallassee at an even brisker pace after his death. According to an exasperated Seagrove, Oliver "threw off *all mask*" in the summer of 1792 "by calling meetings in the towns, directing what the Indians should, and should not do." He "positively tells the Indians not to have any thing to do with the Americans" and had even traveled to the limits of the Upper Country, presumably among the Hillaubees, Kialijees, Aubecoochee, and Natchez, pressing warriors to go "against our people on the western waters," meaning the Cumberland settlements in present-day Tennessee.[66] That gave Seagrove serious reason to worry. Headmen that far to the north had traditionally been strong American allies, even in the era of the most aggressive Georgia state treaties. But with a slow march of settlers west into their traditional hunting grounds ongoing, and with strong Spanish words of resistance circulating, those communities appeared to be taking pause. If the reports were true, and they were now welcoming Spanish agents, it did not bode well at all for the American cause.

By the fall of 1792 it was violence, and not détente, that defined the play-off system that had taken root in the region. Every talk coming from a nearby Spaniard of any authority was calling practically for all-out war along the length of the American frontier, and "their influence," one worried Georgian reported, was "so great at this moment, that I don't believe, any thing short of the interposition of Government can check it."[67] Carondelet was doing "everything possible to hinder" the Treaty of New York, as he himself explained to his superiors, including supporting another general assault on the frontier. He promised to supply the Creeks with "ample & sufficient supplys of arms & ammunition, not only to defend their country, but even to regain their encroached lands, should the Americans refuse willingly & peaceably to retire in the time pointed out, or in case of the Creek Nation being unjustly attacked by any people whatever unprovoked."[68] Manuel Gayoso de Lemos, the Spanish commander at Natchez, curtly explained to Georgia governor Edward Telfair that the Spanish means to gaining Creek friendship and attachment was to "make them happy in the way that their situation requires," while elsewhere he "expressed his sorrow that any of the Indians made treaties with the United States" and that Americans "only deceive the Indians with the appearance of friendship" until they could steal their land. The debated lands belonged to the Creeks, de Lemos continued, "and they must have them; the king has so ordered." He would provide arms and ammunition as well, "and that if they could not themselves regain their lands, he would assist them with men." Likewise in Pensacola, Arturo O'Neill had recently talked to a number of Creek headmen, most likely from the Upper Country, about the Oconee lands. "He had ordered them to go and demand it, and if the whites would not go off civilly, to fall on them and cut them off."[69]

The summer and fall of 1792 represented an unprecedented expansion of Spanish influence into Creek politics, one that exceeded even that of the years after the close of the Revolution. Despite the assertiveness in their talks, however, Spaniards were not forcing anything on Creek headmen; at the core of each one of their talks was support for Creek sovereignty, Creek land rights, and a fair trade. That so many Creek communities were appreciating the Spanish resurgence reflected the deep resentment many of them had toward the Treaty of New York and American authorities. Seagrove certainly was making friends in Creek Country, but the success of the Spanish talks also demonstrated that many Creeks were much more interested in a treaty that secured them their Oconee hunting lands than one that took them away. By the turn of 1793, that was making American authorities look like fools for believing that the Treaty of New York was still viable, let alone popular. One skeptic did "not doubt that Mr. Seagrove had sanguine hopes" that the majority of the Creeks were peaceful, "for I know those kind of people are capable of deceiving any stranger, be their abilities as they may." He had a darker outlook on things: "I cannot suppose the Creeks will ever behave as friends." That was the way Governor William Blount of the Southwest Territory saw things, explaining that "young warriors, with a few of the Chiefs," went to Pensacola to "receive arms and ammunition," while others went to Rock Landing to meet Seagrove to "give good talks, and obtain all the presents they could, until the nation was quite ready for war."[70]

The same could be said of Bowles's talks, which were proving particularly powerful in Creek Country's southern communities. His talks also supported Creek sovereignty, land, and trade, and did so at the expense of both the Spanish and the Americans, yet it was the latter group that was clearly going to suffer the most from them. Timothy

Barnard certainly felt the impact, admitting that there were few friendly places in the Lower Country left for an American partisan. At least some headmen "from almost every town in the Lower Creeks, except the Cussetuhs," had joined him, and "it has put the friends of the United States in this quarter to a great deal of trouble." John Kinnard "and his people," deep in the Lower Country, "have left no stone unturned" in support of the New York treaty, and now his life was in danger. And as for Barnard, "I have myself done every thing in my power to convince the Indians that Bowles is leading them on to their ruin, which he has heard, and threatens my life."[71] Regardless of whether Creek deception was as deep-seated or as systematic as Blount suggested, or whether the threat on American partisans' lives was real, the impact of the play-off system was becoming obvious, and it was making for a very unstable region. Entire swaths of the Lower Country were firm Bowles partisans and in all of Creek Country his talks had "occasioned great feuds," while the Spanish menace to the north was intensifying with each passing day.[72] "The confusion excited by Bowles had not subsided," Seagrove regretted, and with the growing Spanish menace, "it was probable this combination of events" would at the very least keep the New York treaty from going into effect if it did not generate widespread violence.[73]

None of the talks were even remotely mutually inclusive, which highlights the chaotic and potentially disastrous impact the new play-off approach to diplomacy was having in Creek Country. While Bowles's and Spanish talks both called for the rejection of Americans, for instance, Bowles also outwardly called for the expulsion of the Spanish as well. Meanwhile Spaniards considered Bowles a regional threat and instead stressed the creation of a pan-Indian political coalition—a vision of Carondelet's that, like Bowles's efforts, had no foundation in reality. Specific communities in Creek Country were listening to the several overlapping talks intently but seemed to care little for the strategy behind them. The play-off system in Creek Country was no more than a reciprocal system of manipulation, this turbulent period was proving. Several Creek communities looked to Europeans and the Euro-American Bowles for the means to resist American expansionism, while those outsiders looked to Creeks for the means to accomplish their own regional objectives. None of that boded well for regional stability, which continued to deteriorate under the weight of the several mutually exclusive and heavily partisan talks.

The last group of partisans was the one Seagrove was desperately trying to rally around a foundering American message. Nonetheless, in July he was surprised at Rock Landing by hundreds of supporters, proving that the Treaty of New York was not dead quite yet. The group of mostly Cussetas and Cowetas promised to bring "the disaffected leaders" to Seagrove in another few months and "have all matters happily settled," but only in a few months. It was impossible, they admitted, "for any business being done in the nation, in the present state of confusion." Seagrove happily agreed, everyone left pleased, and the headmen were evidently "now working on the disaffected," he penned Knox, "and have already changed several." The White Lieutenant of Oakfuskee and Hopoie Mico of the Hickory Ground added their voices to the Cusseta King, the Cusseta Warrior, and the Hallowing King in penning him words of encouragement in August, and when November came around, the meeting turned out to be a big hit. Over one thousand "men, women, and children" of the Lower Country met him again at Rock Landing, where they were "to confirm the treaty which had been made with them at New York," a meeting that went over apparently very well.[74]

Other actors in the Lower Country shared Seagrove's convictions. John Kinnard continued doing everything he could among the Chehaws and their neighbors, which must have been a struggle.[75] When Seagrove asked nearby headmen to meet him on the St. Mary's River, Kinnard and John Galphin reported that "some busy person is still trying to stop the Cusetahs, and towns round them, from coming," but they were doing everything they could to make sure the headmen made it. Kinnard's influence impressed Seagrove, who was sure to thank him for his dedication to the American cause. Kinnard's tireless efforts to keep the communities in his neighborhood out of the grip of Spanish talks were "a convincing proof of your good understanding and friendship for your country," and his steadfast dedication to peace had even caught the attention of President Washington. More was needed, however, at such a critical period. So while he praised Kinnard, Seagrove also dispatched Barnard to "give him all the assistance in your power, and which your Great Father, General Washington, expects of you as his friend good friend in the Creek Land."[76]

American partisans remained much more common to the north. The White King from Eufala, high in the Upper Country, opened a friendly correspondence with Seagrove, for instance, inquiring on behalf of his communities and "several others" how they should respond to the Spanish talks circulating in their neighborhood, "which distracts them very much." New correspondence like the White King's was a welcome addition to the close personal relationships Seagrove already enjoyed with several headmen in the region, a few of which are worth noting. Penning the White Lieutenant in October 1792, for instance, Seagrove not only introduced himself but congratulated the Oakfuskee headman on keeping his neighborhood peaceful. "Although I never have had the pleasure of seeing you," he wrote, "yet I am well acquainted with your respectable character and good conduct in all matters between your country and mine."[77] Later, after another council at Rock Landing fell through, Seagrove promised him that there was "not a chief in the Creek nation I have a greater regard for, than yourself," and presented him with a gift of silverware.[78]

Seagrove's tireless correspondence in the late summer and fall of 1792 revealed that sizable groups of American partisans did indeed exist, but the larger Creek political landscape also revealed how dispersed those communities were in a sprawling region of discontent. With Bowles's talks drawing large crowds in the Lower Country and with Spanish agents passing through the larger Southeast at will, American supporters were by far the smallest of several partisan groups in a region where the Treaty of New York was still wildly unpopular. To that mix was added perhaps the most incendiary of all groups: the Shawnee emissaries who arrived from the north late in the summer of 1792. The Shawnee were a particularly dangerous influence because groups of them had migrated into Creek Country at various points in the seventeenth and early eighteenth centuries, creating social and political relationships that guaranteed the travelers' words would bear considerable weight.[79] Like the prophets that would visit Creek Country two decades later, these Shawnee visitors immediately began spreading reports of war with Americans further to the north, and they pressed for unified action.[80] The Shawnee travelers, part of a confederation of Natives that was flush with victory against two separate American armies in as many years, quickly moved south spreading the good news. That was bad news to Knox who, fearing the consequences, moved quickly to cut them off. He was preparing Seagrove as early as February 1792. "The entire defeat of our troops the last year, will render the hostile Indians intolerably audacious," he wrote. They certainly would send emissaries south, "and unless powerfully counteracted, it is but too probable they will obtain assistance."[81] Soon a Shawnee delegation was indeed on its way; they passed first into Cherokee Country, where headmen did not fail to spread their cheerful accounts of victory against the American expansionists. Seagrove drew an aggressive line, pressing Alexander Cornells in Tuckabatchee not to let them pass and instead to see them "severely punished for daring to come among you." That proved optimistic. In short time Shawnee talks were coursing through the extremes of the Upper Country. They pushed Cherokees and Creeks to assault Americans in the Cumberland settlements, which soon appeared to be happening.[82]

There was little American authorities could say or do to halt the talks as they slowly crept south. Seagrove pleaded with anyone who would listen, giving Barnard a packet of letters destined for the White Lieutenant, Fine Bones of the Cowetas, and John Kinnard, among others.[83] He directed Barnard to "peruse, deliver, and explain" the talks, "as well as enforce the objects of those talks home to those people, by all the address in your power." Those letters, penned in February 1793, were already too late. According to William Panton, "a deputation from the northern Indians had arrived at the Coweta Town, with a war Belt, the signal for a general reunion against the Americans." And, just as Knox had feared, they reported "having had an engagement with the American Army" and had crushed the expansionists.[84] Worse yet, Spaniards soon reported them along the Gulf Coast, where they met with Arturo O'Neill. Never one to pass up an opportunity to undermine his American neighbors, O'Neill promptly gave them gifts and sent them back north through Creek Country with an official interpreter at their side. Without much delay they arrived at Savannah Town, a small community of Shawnee in Creek Country. From that neighborhood, surrounded by kin, there was little doubt their talks would spread.[85]

The impact was felt along the frontier almost immediately. As early as the fall of 1792 Creek war parties were already beginning to move north. Among the first were Kialijees, Abihkas, Tuckabatchees, and others from the Upper Country, which was particularly troublesome because they undermined the communities nearby that were most supportive of Americans and of the Treaty of New York. Soon there were reports that scores of them were combining with groups of Cherokees to attack American settlers in the Cumberland settlements and nearby.[86] The Shawnee talks were uniting nearby Creeks and Cherokees against a common American enemy, while at the same time Spaniards were encouraging pan-Indian action and were supportive of every violent effort against the frontiers imaginable, and they were providing ample supplies from Pensacola and Mobile for that express purpose. By October 1792 the mixed Creek and Cherokee war parties had already devastated several farms. They burned one with nineteen settlers in it, according to several reports, and only four managed to escape.[87] "The root of the evil," Blount complained to Knox, "is the numerous and insolent Creeks, and it is they who encourage and lead forward the too willing young Cherokees to murder and rob."[88] While anti-American expansionist talks had been around for years, by the turn of 1793 they appeared to be getting their first violent returns.

Within months it was clear those first raids would not be isolated incidents. Governor Blount complained that Oakchais were among the raiders responsible for several Cumberland attacks, while another man, a James Ore, witnessed Kialijees bringing prisoners in from their own raids. While at Kialijee, Ore also "saw one party, consisting of five, and was informed there were several other parties on their way to Cumberland" expressly to raid, and "he also saw several large and new encampments, which had signs of war about them, and appeared as though the parties were going out on some war design."[89] With both Spanish and Shawnee forces acting in concert on the communities furthest to the north, it was not surprising that they were among the first to turn to violence. Yet in another raid that stretched well into modern-day Tennessee, warriors from Broken Arrow and Coweta, two communities deep in the Lower Country, were also implicated. In fact, as an informant remembered, "the chief who commanded the Creeks" at one of the attacks "was *Talotickee* of the Broken Arrow, a great friend of Bowles." While he was apparently a Bowles partisan he was clearly a Spanish one as well, having "blacked himself, and raised the war-whoop at Pensacola, and declared himself for war against the United States."[90] In fact, during one attack to the north groups of Cowetas and Broken Arrows openly boasted that they were doing "all they could to provoke the United States to war with them; that they killed and scalped men, women, and children."[91] Meanwhile Carondelet offered more words of extremism and outlined plans to distribute two hundred rifles and ammunition throughout the Lower Country, "that is to say the Cowetas and Cussitaws and especially those nearest Georgia," expecting widespread fighting there.[92]

While Henry Knox remained confident that those reports represented the extent of the damage, that did not seem to be the case. Intensifying violence was bringing larger numbers of raiders out of communities that had been strong American partisans.[93] Tuckabatchee warrior David Cornells—kin to the influential American ally Alexander Cornells—was confronted by Seagrove with settlers' scalps actually in his hand. The young warrior was clearly remorseful, insisting that Oliver and O'Neill pushed him and his people to commit the murders.[94] Nevertheless, Cornells's confusion had resulted in the death of a number of settlers, marking the growing participation of even the friendliest American partisans. A traveler in West Florida, meeting with Carondelet and O'Neill, reported more of the same. He claimed to have seen upwards of three hundred Creeks, "in different parties," on the trading path to Pensacola, "who said they were going for their ammunition and guns, and that on their return, they would go to war against Cumberland." That information, as well as talks from O'Neill and Gayoso de Lemos at Natchez, revealed that Eufalas, Little Eufalas, Hookchoies, the White Ground, the Hickory Ground, Oakfuskees, and Tuskegees, representing a sizable chunk of the Upper Country, all "were for war."[95] The militarization of many of those towns—particularly Oakfuskee, once a bastion of American support—was only more bad news to Americans.

American, Spanish, and Bowles's accounts all implicated many of the same communities in the raiding, including some surprising ones. At the same time the Mad Dog of Tuckabatchee or the White Lieutenant of Oakfuskee was chatting with Seagrove, for instance, Shawnees were nearby and Spanish authorities were reporting Tuckabatchee and Oakfuskee warriors collecting guns in West Florida and attacking American settlers in the Cumberland settlements. Either some of those accounts were wrong or communities like Oakfuskee or Tuckabatchee were proving to be complex and conflicted places, prone to political turmoil in ways reminiscent of the American Revolution. Coweta certainly had been a place of divided loyalties before, and that appeared to be the case now as well. The new play-off diplomacy was reproducing the same undercurrents of community individualism and discord that made the Revolutionary War so dangerous. In the hopes of reversing that distressing trend James Seagrove made another strong effort early in 1793 to find consensus among his friends. As usual he found encouragement in the Upper Country, even though the situation there was far less stable than it had been. When pressed at least to have the Shawnee dealt with, headmen "were of the same opinion respecting the Americans as they were and not to be deluded with the Shawanese talks."[96] Despite those reports, Seagrove also redoubled his efforts with Alexander Cornells of Tuckabatchee and the White Lieutenant of Oakfuskee, reminding them again to stay vigilant. "Those fellows that are among you, giving out bad talks from the Northern Indians," he wrote Cornells, "ought to be taken up, and sent prisoners to me, unless your people chose to punish them."[97] His tone to the White Lieutenant was similar. The Shawnee were like "a man a drowning, who will take hold of any bush, or even his brother, or best friend, and drown them to save himself. Open your eyes, my friends, and do not be made fools of those bad people."[98]

With several headmen replying positively, Seagrove remained hopeful that the Shawnee might be driven from the region before too much more damage was done. Instead, the regional situation continued to deteriorate. Shawnee talks were soon circulating south into the Lower Country, which had the potential to create real danger for Americans. Seagrove leaned on every ally he had in the region to cut the visitors off before they even arrived, offering Cusseta and Coweta men a horseload of goods for each Shawnee they could bring to him.[99] They were "your great enemies," Seagrove warned Fine Bones of Coweta, "and will ruin you if you are so unwise as to listen to their talks." Leave them to deal with the consequences of their own actions to the north, he implored the headmen, and do not get involved.[100] While Cussetas were sure to turn the visitors away, across the Chattahoochee Cowetas had been much more welcoming of British and Spanish talks in the past, and it was uncertain how they would react to the Shawnee councils. On "any account, as you value your happiness," Seagrove warned them, do not listen to the visitors "but drive them from your land."[101] In the end neither his most generous enticements nor his sternest warnings succeeded. Soon the Shawnee had arrived in Coweta, and rather than being seized they were given an audience in council.[102]

With Shawnee visitors solidifying their presence in Coweta squares, compounding the Spanish and Bowles talks in the region, Americans had just about run out of allies willing to stand up for the Treaty of New York. Along with Kinnard, Seagrove pressed James Holmes, another trader in the region, urging him to do absolutely whatever it took to either drive the Shawnee out or have them seized.[103] Then he turned again to Timothy Barnard, who also lived in the neighborhood, pressing him to at least attend the local councils, and to call ones of his own, in the hopes of countering the Shawnee talks and prevent Creeks "being led into a scrape by them for this purpose." Some of the "young disorderly" men in his neighborhood, he feared, were already stirred up, and "it behooves us to use our influence to prevent them." Nevertheless by March 1793 the Shawnee had made it even further south, to Broken Arrow, deep in the heart of the Lower Country, and they continued to give out scathing anti-American talks.[104] Broken Arrows had already been implicated in regional raiding, making the presence of the Shawnee there the most dangerous development yet. Barnard did what he could, calling a meeting at Cusseta. There he met with Kinnard and the Hitchitis from his neighborhood, as well as Cowetas, Cussetas, Broken Arrows, and Ooseoochees. The Mad Dog of Tuckabatchee and the White

Lieutenant arrived with Oakfuskee headmen as well, all in support of the Americans. Barnard belted out an aggressive talk, struggling to get assurances that the Shawnee would be turned away. They were, he warned, "only endeavoring to bring you into the same predicament into which they themselves are involved."[105]

Not only did Barnard fail to have the Shawnee kicked out, during his stay at Cusseta he was privy to plenty of local complaints that shed light on the lure of the northerners' talks. Of course land was an issue, but Barnard soon discovered it was not the only one. Georgians were abusing Creek lands, for instance, which was a growing irritation. Settlers were running their cattle into Creek Country and others were crossing over the rivers to hunt "with fire, and all day with rifles," and with "great gangs of dogs," destroying the little game that remained. This, Barnard admitted, "the Indians say they cannot put up with." The few headmen who had not yet completely repudiated the New York treaty were quickly becoming convinced that, even if a boundary line was run, it would do little to curb the lawless actions of local Georgians, whom state officials were not even pretending to control. Barnard found many of these complaints only too true, and found it equally amazing that Georgians could be "so foolhardy, till matters are settled, which ever will be the case while the people on the frontier go so head-strong to work." They gave dangerous credibility to Bowles, the Spanish, and the Shawnee, all of whose talks included the same warnings: nothing would satisfy Americans, who would never quit with their encroachments. Had it not been for the avaricious nature of local settlers, Barnard lamented, the Shawnee would not be having the effect they did, "as it was a good subject for the Shawanese to work on, telling them it was the way the white people served them to the northward." His conference came to an abrupt end when a group of Cowetas, unhappy with his strong American stance and defensive answers, declared they were going off to capture more cattle and "kill some of the inhabitants." Soon groups from several towns left to join in, despite both Barnard's and Kinnard's attempts to stop them. While the headmen who attended from the Upper Country—Oakfuskees and Tuckabatchees at least—continued to promise Barnard that they would do what they could, it was clear that neither they nor he would be able to do much.[106]

The early months of 1793 witnessed a steady increase in violence as these talks began to affect more Creek communities. Georgia settlements were "generally brooke from Greensborough up to Franklin," except for "those in Forts & some few are now a building."[107] Both Creeks and settlers, Governor Edward Telfair admitted, "render the situation of many innocent defenceless families on the frontiers, critical and dangerous."[108] Less than a month later, the situation worsened dramatically when a single string of attacks demonstrated just how torn the region had become. Several communities in the Lower Country, including Chehaws, Broken Arrows, Ooseoochees, Hitchitis, and even Cowetas, raided a trading store along the St. Mary's River and then plundered several settler families along the southern frontier in quick succession. The particularly brutal raids touched off waves of fear and panic, and then revenge attacks between state forces and Creek communities, which reverberated throughout the region. Not only did they crush any hope of keeping the Treaty of New York legitimate, Creek cohesiveness evaporated almost entirely in their wake, and threats of reprisals left the whole region on the brink of war.

In March 1793 Robert Brown and Daniel Moffitt were visiting James Allen, who lived on the St. Mary's River, when they were confronted by three young Creek warriors painted for war and "bent on doing mischief on this frontier." War was all over, the warriors declared, while several more were bent to "do mischief on the Oconee." They announced that they had already killed one settler family and were planning on more. After meeting up with John Galphin, who happened to be nearby, all four Americans inquired further. Galphin, with a long history in the region, tried to start a conversation with the warriors and learn their intentions. He was rebuffed, however, and in a surprising fashion the warriors declared that they "would not know him, saying he was dressed as a white man, and that the red people were all at war with the whites." Galphin made his way to the warriors' camp anyway. All of the Americans ended up in a larger group of ten armed Creeks on their way to a store further down the river, known as Trader's Hill, which was owned by Robert Seagrove, James Seagrove's brother. At the store they found John Flemming, a clerk, who invited everyone in for a drink. While one or two of the Creek men haggled with Flemming over selling some skins, possibly as a diversion, another stepped through the door and shot Moffitt at point-blank range, killing him instantly. Galphin ran outside to try to diffuse the situation and to chase down the murderer. Brown fled into the woods and witnessed the rest of the warriors rush into the store, execute Flemming, and badly beat a woman who also happened to be nearby. The gang then pilfered the store and fled.[109]

Around the same time or shortly thereafter, a sizable group of Creeks attacked plantations along the southern frontier of Georgia. Glynn

County residents were "robbed and plundered very considerably" by groups of warriors who were clearly "in a state of actual hostility . . . committing daily the most horrid robberies."[110] According to another report they "drove off all the horses cattle & hogs" along the Altamaha and "plundered some houses & took some Negroes threatening the Inhabitants." Georgian militia commander James Jackson heard reports of these attacks but at first did not believe them. As another resident soon reported, however, Glynn residents were "in every instance driven from their homes, their property in cattle & horses in a general way taken from them carried off by the Indians."[111] Similar accounts confirmed that raiding seemed widespread in the area and that numerous farmers along the Satilla and St. Mary's River were "murdered & plundered." Barnard noted that a group of warriors arrived "with four or five scalps from that quarter, and a great deal of plunder." John Forrester, living on the Spanish side of the St. Mary's, reported that all of the nearby trading houses had been sacked as well.[112]

Seagrove, hearing word of the attacks, hurried out to his brother's store and arrived there the next morning. Not only were Flemming and Moffitt dead but the war party had made off with thousands of dollars in trade goods. He soon came across the murdered settler family and buried them as well. In the wake of such an unprovoked attack Seagrove sent word to Major Henry Gaither, who commanded all of the federal troops in the area, and recommended he put his forces on alert. Seagrove could not believe, however, "that the Chiefs of the Creek nation are acquainted with this party being out."[113] He rightly suspected that the majority of the raiding originated far down in the Lower Country, where communities had been stirred up the most in the recent months. Nevertheless, he wasted no time penning blistering open letters to Creek Country. He even went so far as to order any remaining Indians in the area shot on sight. It was not important where the warriors originated, he charged; the actions of the previous six months implicated all Creeks, he warned, and if they did not want their country laid waste, everyone needed to take swift action, beginning with having the killers turned over immediately and having all of the pilfered property surrendered. Gaither was soon to elaborate, demanding not only the murderers "but the whole party concerned in the mischief," presumably meaning the raiding as well.[114] The Trader's Hill attack, it seemed, was quickly evolving into a regional crisis.

In hindsight, with so many Creeks angry for so many different reasons, and then tugged toward confrontation by scores of competing talks, violence was probably inevitable. Timothy Barnard had done everything in his power to keep them peaceable, he soon lamented, but the commotion and confusion of the previous few years had "put some of the Indians, I believe, nearly out of their heads."[115] Chehaw warriors stepped forward to claim responsibility for some of the raids, for instance, but claimed they had only done so after they had heard word from the Shawnee that war had already been declared and that attacks were already ongoing. Only then had they rushed off and "done mischief." Ooseoochees soon admitted likewise. "We had no intent to do any such thing of ourselves, but thought that the rest were bent upon the same." Other warriors arrived at the St. Mary's trading store and, seeing the dead, became certain of what they had heard. Only then did they descend on nearby plantations. Hoping to make the situation right they quickly brought to Seagrove "a great deal of property, such as horses, cattle, and negroes," explaining that "as we find that it is not a war, we don't think they belong to us."[116]

At least those admissions confirmed what Seagrove had hoped— that although devastating the raids were still isolated. But then again, that only prompted him to make more pointed, aggressive demands. Not only did Americans require the return of the stolen property, they required the lives of the perpetrators as well.[117] And that sort of demand, as it had already been proven several times in the past, was only going to go unmet. The offending communities would not satisfy such a demand and neighboring headmen could not enforce it outside of their own communities. Timothy Barnard expressed such fears almost immediately. Chehaw chiefs denied killing anyone, and they were not convinced that they should turn over warriors, perhaps to be tried in Georgia but certainly to be killed, simply because they misunderstood a situation and stole some horses. That was a widespread and frankly understandable position. Chehaws, Okmulgees, and Hitchitis "were in a restless situation," according to one trader, "and there was no probability of their demand of Mr Seagrove being complied with." His talks "were too hard."[118] Throughout the Lower Country, indeed, headmen were "much divided on account of the demand." Ultimately the most volatile and critical communities reacted to Seagrove's ultimatum essentially by digging in, which did nothing but worsen an already dangerous situation.[119]

Headmen from the Upper Country only further exacerbated the situation by falling back on familiar, localized political traditions. Instead of projecting a strong voice they quickly broke off all relations with their neighbors to the south. Several of them, including the Mad

Dog, the White Lieutenant, and Alexander Cornells, were outwardly declaring that they had nothing to do with anything that was taking place in the Lower Country. Being thus cut off, chiefs and warriors in several Lower Country towns must have felt increasingly isolated and resentful, and their actions reflected their animosity. Soon several important and very necessary people found themselves threatened. "For my own part," Timothy Barnard wrote, "as I know their disposition so well, I look upon myself in imminent danger." Both he and Kinnard were in quite the predicament, considering "how ticklish a foundation a white man's life stands, at this juncture, so near those villains." The two were in actual fear for their lives, according to Barnard, expressly because they were seen by those in the Lower Country as "instruments of setting the other towns against them," and it was well known by the militant towns that "the mouths of the heads of the Chiefs of the nation are open against them."[120] Even a well-respected leader like Alexander Cornells admitted that, while traveling through Lower Country after the attacks, "those mad people offerd to take my life." He did little to ease the tension, of course, when he declared that he looked upon himself as "one of General Washington Sons and mene to stand by him as long as I live."[121]

From the Lower Country, Cussetas were among the only to extend their support to Seagrove.[122] They were also among the first to pen both Gaither and Seagrove, ensuring them that they wished to remain friendly. Cussetas were "still as firm friends as ever," Barnard echoed, and they would do everything in their power to get satisfaction. Cowetas, on the other hand, were much more dangerous, and it was not known how militant they remained.[123] Despite calming talks from friendly headmen, the situation in the Upper Country was also complicated. The Tallassee King and some Cooloomes were undeniably out for war, with Alexander Cornells adding that they were like "mad people . . . running crazy." This was troublesome, even to Cornells. The Tallassee King had, for going on a decade, been such a dependable American ally that he had been ridiculed as a pawn of the state of Georgia: "He was the first man that gave the land away to the white people, and now, is the first that proposes doing mischief." Cornells placed the blame for this new development squarely on the Shawnee. Perhaps they had made more of an impression in the Upper Country then headmen there were willing to admit. Tallassee and Cooloome warriors were supposedly the only ones in the Upper Country to have "taken their talks," although plenty more warriors had done damage along the Cumberland River. Still, Seagrove's most dependable allies were there, and Cornells pleaded to Seagrove not to blame all of the Upper Country, "for we still stand to your talk, and mean to do so."[124]

The Trader's Hill attacks exposed a Creek Country that was practically in shambles. "This country is in as convulsed a state as possible," a clearly distraught trader wrote. Attacks on the Cumberland settlements were ongoing, and the Tallassee King, Cooloomes, and gangs of Half-Way House, Tallassees, and Tusehatchees continued to prey on the northern frontiers of Georgia.[125] Their actions were drawing the words of friendly chiefs like Cornells and the White Lieutenant into doubt while, farther to the south, there was very little faith that any communities would choose peace over war. At the extreme south of Creek Country, groups of Yuchis, Chehaws, Broken Arrows, and Ooseoochees had raided from the rich plantation region along the Altamaha River all the way to the Cumberland settlements.[126] Cussetas continued to declare their friendship but the tension between their communities and their neighbors across the Chattahoochee was as dangerous as it had been since the Revolution. While Cusseta communities were clearly struggling with the ramifications of the recent attacks, Cowetas were not. Although they had not participated in the Trader's Hill attack directly Coweta warriors had raided heavily in the aftermath, and they were not particularly sorry for what they had done. It was widely feared that if they rejected Seagrove's ultimatum, which was guaranteed, then nearby Chehaws, Broken Arrows, and others on the Chattahoochee would act similarly. If that was the case, then nowhere in Georgia would be safe. Worse yet, a number of reports suggested that Cowetas were actively trying to drag their neighbors across the river into war. According to Barnard, Coweta warriors were raiding in a way that they knew would bring Georgians to retaliate on Cussetas. Georgians had done that sort of thing in the past, and if it happened now the fallout would be catastrophic. Barnard pushed Gaither to make sure that Georgians did not rush to violence. Cussetas also did what they could directly, even though it brought them into more direct confrontation with their neighbors. When a group of Cowetas came in with scalps taken from the frontier it infuriated nearby Cusseta headmen, who made their anger known in strong terms. Yet there was little they could do; groups of Cowetas upwards of one hundred were out, and they were bound to do damage.[127]

With matters largely in the hands of conflicted Creek headmen, and completely out of his, all Seagrove could do was condemn the guilty and hope for the best. It was clear the Shawnee and Spanish talks were the principal cause of the violence, and Seagrove wasted no time lashing out at all the outside forces that he considered responsible.[128] Yet Creeks would ultimately have to bear the burden of his demands, and in the fallout from Trader's Hill it seemed difficult to imagine how that would happen. As news of more small attacks trickled in, the guilty parties grew more hesitant to return stolen goods or even give up the worst of the offenders.[129]

The Trader's Hill killings represented the culmination of years of disruption caused almost entirely by the failed Treaty of New York. Alexander McGillivray's attempt at a compromise agreement with Americans in New York turned out to be a nightmare that he did not even live to see play out. Rather than accept the compromise headmen looked elsewhere for support, and by doing so they did much more than simply destroy McGillivray—they initiated what was essentially a second regional southeastern play-off system. Creek communities turned to political outsiders, like Spanish authorities and William Augustus Bowles, as well as their Shawnee neighbors to the north. Internal political factionalism and external manipulation ensued, and unfortunately for the Creek people the Trader's Hill crisis resulted. While they attempted to manipulate outsiders to gain stability, by 1793 Creeks found their communities in chaos and threatened with war. Whatever sense of unity communities had shared during the Oconee War was gone. Instead, Creek Country was in crisis.

PART 2

Building a Creek Nation

6 / A Stronger Nationhood

Kinnard, I hear, means to stand his ground, and all the Cussetahs.
—Timothy Barnard, April 9, 1793

By 1793 Creek responses to the Treaty of New York left the region as crippled by factionalism and as politically dysfunctional as it had ever been. The Trader's Hill killings punctuated the retreat of many communities from the relative unity of the Oconee War period to an indecisive one of competing partisan interests, which now threatened direct confrontation with Americans. While the attacks ushered into Creek Country a true internal political crisis, it was a crisis that proved in the end necessary. It set into motion the systemic changes that laid the foundation for what would become the Creek Nation. In the wake of the attacks, American partisan headmen began that process by combining and unifying what had been to that point many disparate Creek voices. Their first efforts were largely rhetorical, but by speaking in nontraditional and increasingly authoritative ways—by invoking the idea of a collective Creek political identity—they were nonetheless transformative. They represented an emerging sense of nationalism, one that had never existed in Creek Country before.

The American partisan group that crystallized during the period was a cosmopolitan collection, composed of traders and men of mixed ancestry as well as leaders with deep traditional ties to Creek authority. American officials warned that only swift and decisive action would keep all of Creek Country from the wrath of both angry settlers and the federal government. An emerging Creek leadership group responded by creating a common Creek cause—they took responsibility for the actions of the offending towns and made promises for satisfaction that would bear on communities far away from their own. Some Creeks had spoken in a regional voice in the past, but never before had they projected a sense of solidarity during such a time of partisanship and upheaval. Even though changes in the tone of Creek leaders did not in most cases bring decisive results, it was the creation of a new Creek voice, consistent with Euro-American notions of cultural and political nationalism, that was notable during this critical period. Actions would eventually follow strong words, but for the moment the willingness of Creeks to produce strong words in a single, cohesive, political voice was important enough. That collectivity, although it developed slowly and unevenly, would be the foundation for the more systemic changes that would, eventually, remake the political landscape of Creek Country.

Seagrove turned out to be an excellent choice as an Indian agent. His steadying presence in Creek Country was a testament to his commitment to building personal relationships with leading Creek men as the best means to stabilize the Creek-Georgia frontier. As the American government's primary voice in Creek Country it was his responsibility to support headmen as well as persuade them to uphold their obligations. Seagrove was proud of his efforts by early 1793, even though the region was clearly torn, and he met praise from his superiors.[1] His positivity evaporated quickly, however, after Trader's Hill. When first confronted with reports of the murders and the subsequent raids, he simply refused to believe them. Yes, the region was torn, but he failed to understand how Creeks would commit such a widespread and devastating breach of the peace. Only after traveling south from Rock Landing and surveying the damage personally did he begin to address the developing crisis.[2]

Seagrove's tone certainly was stern, and many communities, particularly in the Lower Country, seemed hopelessly torn by his demands for satisfaction. He reacted to the killings aggressively—perhaps too aggressively—yet he did not turn his back on the headmen he had grown close to over the course of the previous few years. Many communities chafed under the pressure of Seagrove's ultimatum but others responded supportively, and they took several steps to demonstrate their willingness to work with him and other Americans to make the situation right. Although gaining American support had been unimportant and even offensive to many communities before Trader's Hill, Creek Country was now in chaos, and the prospect of a war with the American government was real. Seagrove's warnings, along with the ominous movement of Georgian militia forces along the border, provided the catalyst many headmen needed to act in nontraditional ways, particularly when the traditional approach to a regional dispute would have been for them to deflect responsibility. The first headmen to do so formed a core leadership group that responded collectively during a time of true regional upheaval, generating the first responses in Creek Country that were consistent with contemporary notions of nationalism.

Talks and symbols of peace arrived to Seagrove not long after the initial reports of the attacks. Cussetas, of course, were quickest to declare their continued friendship and support. Sending Seagrove a "beloved wing," the Cusseta King and Fushatchee Mico, also known as the White Bird-Tail King, hoped that he would be convinced of continued Cusseta determination. "I wish for peace, and always did," the White Bird-Tail King declared.[3] Around the same time a peace belt arrived from the Upper Country that reportedly represented several communities there, although Seagrove did not name exactly which ones.[4] Individual headmen from the neighborhood soon followed up with their own correspondence, including from Alexander Cornells, Charles Weatherford, the White Lieutenant, and the Mad Dog. They all confirmed that the raiding had not been done on behalf of their communities, or by large numbers of Creeks in general for that matter, but by only a few renegade groups. More important, their letters made some of the first intriguing statements to come from men who were, to that point, only individual community leaders, and leaders who had not partaken in any of the violence, nonetheless. Alexander Cornells had "done all that lies in my power; it is impossible to do more than I have done." He also declared that "if every man would exert himself as well as the Mad Dog, and the head-men of the Upper towns, and Mr. Weatherford, we should have an everlasting peace with our brothers of the United States." The Mad Dog explained that there were "many bad talks in the nation," but he personally assured Seagrove and Georgia authorities that he and his friends were "using every endeavor to make them better." And Charles Weatherford was "doing all he can for the good of the United States."[5]

That first battery of talks constituted an initial attempt to come to grips with the crisis and panic that the Trader's Hill killings had created for everyone in Creek Country, not just the guilty in the Lower Country. It also represented several men, many of whom had little in common with each other, who felt they had an equal stake in the stability of all of Creek Country. While many of them were well-respected and influential figures, not all were. They also hailed from different physical and cultural corners of Creek Country: a few were men of mixed European and Creek ancestry, like McGillivray, but many were not. While several came from the Upper Country, some from further to the southeast were just as influential. Some were headmen, even chiefs, while others were traders with deep ties to the region, and a few were of a much more dubious character. Nevertheless, when men like Charles Weatherford, the White Lieutenant, and John Kinnard began working with Seagrove more closely after Trader's Hill, they increasingly declared they were doing it on behalf of all Creeks, not just those in their own communities. They began to conceive of each other not just as neighbors who shared many of the same cultural values and social connections but as fellow members of a common cultural identity and a common Creek political voice. By speaking in that way, Creeks began to evoke a cultural and a political nationhood in a critical step that would form the foundation for future political development.

Iroquois, Algonquian, Illinoisan, and other large Native groups might have previously conceived of themselves in ways consistent with nationhood, but their collective histories also made it easier for them to do so. They shared languages, migration legends, ceremonial traditions, and folklore, providing a strong foundation for collectivity when necessary. That was less the case in the Southeast, however, where politically and culturally flexible groups like Creeks still reflected the traumatic coalescent period of the seventeenth and early eighteenth centuries. Different Creek communities not only spoke different languages but came from different places and had different creation stories that explained their existence in terms of moving from their original homes to the places where they now resided.[6] Those sorts of differences were perhaps what J. Leitch Wright Jr. meant when he suggested in the first sentences of his own study of the Creek people that his was a story of an Indian people that were not a people "and of Indian nations—the Creeks and Seminoles—that were not nations." The better alternative was to refer to individual Creek people the way they often referred to themselves, by linguistic group or community identity. The former category included Muscogee, Yuchi, Hitchiti, Koasati, Alabama, Shawnee, and Natchez, among others—unique and often mutually unintelligible languages that were all spoken in different parts of Creek Country. A Coweta man in the Lower Country who spoke Muscogee, in other words, would have needed a translator to do anything meaningful in either Hitchiti or Yuchi communities, even though they were only miles away and were considered just as Creek.[7]

Likewise, in Creek Country as well as further to the north in Cherokee Country or west, in Choctaw Country, people were also much more likely to describe themselves according to their community of residence rather than as part of a larger "tribe," or "nation," even though they were described as such by outsiders working with a specific, obviously Eurocentric, conceptualization of political nationalism. More often than Creek men and women would have referred to themselves by language, indeed, they would have referred to themselves as Coweta, Tallassee, or Oakfuskee, while a British or American official simply would have called them Creek.[8] Community identity in the coalescent societies of the Southeast was, for generations prior to the Revolutionary era, a person's primary identity, and that certainly was the case in Creek Country.

The Creek people in particular demonstrate how even though Native groups might have considered themselves distinct in ways consistent with peoplehood, seldom did they project it in a distinctly political fashion, and more particularly, in a fashion with which Euro-Americans would have been familiar. As was possible elsewhere in the world, in short, the Native Southeast was a place of nations without nationalism. As Steven Hahn has best articulated, Creeks might have embraced a common image of themselves as a territorially bound people by the middle of the eighteenth century, and had done so based on the inclusivity of close and constant social interaction, traditions like the Busk ceremony, shared linguistics, and of course kinship relationships. Nevertheless, finding a moment during those years when Creeks dealt with Europeans as a single collective legal entity is still elusive. The Creek Nation might have been more than "inchoate, subject to fission, even a figment of the collective British imagination," according to Hahn, but it was still notoriously difficult to define exactly. Indigenous and political nationhood were different, Hahn's study of the period still demonstrates.[9] This is an important distinction, one that grew clearer by the turn of the nineteenth century. Particular groups of Europeans or Euro-Americans would not have simply considered themselves distinct because of their language or shared culture—their conceptualization had a distinct political component to it. "The growth of nationalism," according to one preeminent sociopolitical scholar, "is the process of integration of the masses of the people into a common political form."[10] This definition, of course, was culled from European experiences, not Native ones, yet it was the one imposed upon the Creek people by Henry Knox and James Seagrove, at first, and would be the same one Benjamin Hawkins would pursue even more forcefully in the years that followed. Developing a political voice was an important component of nationhood according to Euro-Americans; Creeks, whose political flexibility had been seen as an asset for generations, lacked such a voice.

Returning to an earlier era in Creek history—the original play-off years in the mid-eighteenth century—demonstrates as much, having provided Creeks the possibility for effective moments of collectivity while remaining politically flexible. A long list of Creek leaders that included Chigelly, Brims, Malatche, the Mortar, the Gun Merchant, the Acorn Whistler, the Handsome Fellow, and the Wolf, were all able to unite smaller groups of Creek communities when common intercommunity interests were at stake.[11] Yet the flexibility and multiplicity of the alliances those leaders produced also suggest that Creek politics were fundamentally different in the first half of the eighteenth century than at the end of it. Even to suggest that under the best of circumstances Creek confederacies could shift significantly over time depending on the diplomatic winds presupposes that the image of political solidarity produced by them was not particularly strong. More importantly, manipulating Spanish and British regional politics for the purposes of trade in the mid-eighteenth century turned out not to be the same as struggling with Telfair, Carondelet, Bowles, and Seagrove over the very survival of Creek territory decades later. The threat represented by American expansionism was different, which infighting during the Revolutionary War, the rise of partisan groups during the Oconee War in the 1780s, and then the political chaos that followed the Treaty of New York all demonstrated as they slowly dragged Creek Country to political crisis. In other words, it was not simply that the cultural, religious, and ceremonial ties that were supposed to be strong enough to bind Creeks together as a people during such periods of upheaval failed. When those traditions were stripped away, there was very little left of a Creek people. The unwritten traditions that defined Creek cultural and political collectivity were never tested like they were in response to the expanding state of Georgia, and when they were tested they gave way, revealing the degree to which Creek solidarity during the earlier periods of neutrality were something more often explained by outsiders than understood by Creeks themselves.

The crisis period after the Trader's Hill attacks did not just collapse what remained of the old play-off and confederacy mentality, it generated a crisis strong enough to usher in a new period of truer European-style nationhood, forcing headmen to self-identify not only culturally and socially but politically as a single Creek people. Creeks were, perhaps, the first southeastern Native people to be pushed from a coalescent to a post-coalescent state in such a way. But they would not be the only ones; years later Cherokees could undergo the same process. Facing aggressive state authorities in Tennessee, an unhelpful federal agent in

Return Meigs, and the very real threat of removal west of the Mississippi, Cherokees responded in the first and second decades of the nineteenth century in ways remarkably similar to the ways Creeks responded late in the eighteenth century. "It has now been a long time that we have been much confused and divided in our opinions," the members of one Cherokee Council wrote in 1809, "but now we have settled our affairs to the satisfaction of both parties and become as one. You will now hear from us not from the lower towns nor the upper towns but from the whole Cherokee Nation."[12]

As the crisis period affecting Creek politics and the same struggles facing the Cherokee people later both suggest, the growth of Creek political nationalism was not a peaceful or voluntary development. As much as a Creek leadership group began to assert it, this aspect of Creek modernism was clearly driven by intensifying outside pressure—a pressure that their previous political systems could not alleviate. By the fallout from Trader's Hill it was clear that Americans certainly were expecting collectivity from the Creek people in ways consistent with political nationalism, if they were not demanding it at knifepoint. Even the headmen furthest away from the communities that committed the recent attacks were still Creeks, Americans insisted. Tuckabatchees were just as responsible for the killings as if they were Broken Arrows or Chehaws themselves, and they needed just as badly to make things right. These were the first of many similar demands made of all Creeks, setting into motion an interposition of Euro-American political theory onto Creek Country. If Creek communities considered themselves all the masters of a common territory, then they needed to act like it politically by maintaining safe and peaceful borders along the edges of that territory. Americans, in sum, demanded "good neighborhood." Creeks needed to provide American settlers justice for the murders and the raids, and just as important, they needed to make sure nothing else of the kind happened again. If the Creek people could not provide for their neighbors even that most basic level of regional stability, then they could not expect to remain at peace with them.[13] Seagrove's earliest letters to Creeks after Trader's Hill reflected that precise line of thinking, which it appears several headmen understood. Political solidarity was essential to the acceptance and very survival of Creek sovereignty.

The first responses to those demands came from the Upper Country. The region was split during the Revolution, and Oliver's residency at McGillivray's old plantation in the heart of the region had a terribly destabilizing impact on its politics. Many headmen there were also some of Creek Country's most vocal American allies, however, and after Sea-grove's appointment they developed into the base of American partisan-ship in Creek Country. Their support of his demands for the lives of the raiders and for the return of stolen property after Trader's Hill was par-ticularly revealing because they had played little or no role in the attacks, and only a few of their communities had even been implicated in the Cumberland raids. Most of the militancy in Creek Country originated far from them, low on the Chattahoochee River, yet the Mad Dog, the White Lieutenant, and Alexander Cornells did not necessarily deflect responsibility, which was all Emistisiguo could muster after the Ceded Lands attacks a generation earlier.

Relatively little is known about many of those men, but after the Treaty of New York, when Americans reached out for allies, they emerged as supportive figures. Even before Trader's Hill, in fact, Charles Weatherford and the White Lieutenant quickly stepped forward after McGillivray's death to assure state authorities that Creeks were still at peace with America and declared that they "wish to remain so."[14] They were, perhaps, the only Creeks friendly enough with McGillivray at the time of his death to make such a statement. Maybe not so friendly with McGillivray but sympathetic with his views of Americans were others, like the Mad Dog and Alexander Cornells. They all gained authority as Creek leaders because of their support of the federal government and their willingness to enforce acceptance of federal measures. All of these men hailed from different corners of Creek Country, making their collective action reflective of the sort of cultural and political nationalism that began taking root in the region.

Charles Weatherford represented one end of the cultural spectrum in Creek Country—a man not altogether dissimilar from Alexander McGillivray. He was described as "an enterprising Scotch pedlar and a passionate lover of horse-racing, who entered the nation from Geor-gia and speedily amassed a considerable fortune" in slaves and horses. Almost nothing is known about his mother, Mary, a woman reportedly of mixed Indian ancestry, or his father, Martin. Whether of mixed ances-try himself or not, Scotch or English, he came of age along the Creek-Georgia frontier. He grew up in Augusta and lived across the Savannah River from Galphin's Silver Bluff. He reportedly had a "good English education" and "great shrewdness." He married one of the daughters of Sehoy Marchand, who was also Alexander McGillivray's mother, mak-ing McGillivray his brother-in-law. He also probably bore the closest resemblance to McGillivray in his acceptance of Euro-American notions

of domesticity, private property, and wealth; he "acquired great popularity in the nation" because of his marriage into the Wind clan "and took
an active part in the political dealings with the Spanish and American
authorities." Later in life he lived on the Alabama River just below the
junction of the Coosa and Tallapoosa, near McGillivray's plantation, and
there he built a "good dwelling-house and store" and reportedly also had
a horse-racing track nearby.[15]

Weatherford was active along the frontier in the 1780s, with one
account placing him as a packhorse guide along the trading paths from
Pensacola into Creek Country as late as 1786, most likely for the Panton
and Leslie trading firm. As both a trader and relation to McGillivray he
also participated in some of the most intimate Creek political deliberations, a position of influence that suggested he also might have been a
beloved man, similarly integrated and trusted in the inner workings of
Creek society and politics.[16] As similar as he was to McGillivray, however, Weatherford would not count his brother-in-law among his personal friends by the troubling years of the 1780s. As a trader he owed
money to the Panton and Leslie firm, and ultimately McGillivray had
a hand in seeing him imprisoned in Pensacola for those debts. Being
thus insulted Weatherford turned informant. O'Neill used him as a spy
in 1788, explaining that "resenting past insults," he had "promised to
inform me secretly what is going on now."[17] Weatherford never forgot that
Spaniards were also the ones that threw him in jail, however, and he soon
turned on O'Neill as well. In 1792 he began giving Seagrove information
about Spanish movements in Creek Country. This included information
on Don Pedro Oliver, his residence in Tallassee, and his mission to incite
Creek violence, which Seagrove passed along to Washington.[18] In time
Weatherford became one of Seagrove's closest confidants in the Upper
Country, conversing with him regularly on the politics of the region. He
was clearly a Creek political actor and a developing American partisan
by that point, and federal agents like Seagrove placed tremendous trust
in him.

Oche Haujo, also known as Alexander Cornells, lived in Tuckabatchee.
He was the son of Englishman George Cornells and a Creek woman of
unknown origin. While Tuckabatchees had been strong British partisans during the war, and then Spanish ones afterward, Cornells slowly
transitioned into an American partisan during the 1780s. When Creeks
were searching for a suitable replacement after McGillivray's death, John
Kinnard thought he "was clever and able" enough to do the job. Like
most other headmen in the region, however, he was illiterate. Not nearly

as educated or politically savvy as McGillivray, there was little hope he would assume such a position of authority through the same avenues. Yet he also was a man square at the heart of the Creek and Euro-American crossroads—one of the best examples perhaps of the Creek cultural ability to absorb people of complicated backgrounds. A man of mixed heritage himself, he married one of the daughters of powerful Tuckabatchee headman the Mad Dog, which gave him particularly strong political and kin connections in the region. By all accounts, however, Cornells developed a Euro-American "model of the patriarchal, nuclear family."[19] He was man between worlds indeed, and it was a position in which he thrived.

As the years passed, Cornells moved into more influential leadership positions because of his unwavering support of the American government. Later in the 1790s he was one of Benjamin Hawkins's interpreters and assistants, and although Hawkins took issue at times with Cornells's drinking habits, otherwise he was a "half breed" of "a strong mind, and fulfills the duties enjoined on him by his appointment, with zeal and fidelity." According to Hawkins, in fact, by the turn of the century Cornells had cobbled together a very respectable life. He had a farm "well fenced and cultivated with the plough" and nine slaves "under good government." In 1801 his holdings were considerably larger. He had a flock of sheep and land with excellent fences, a large garden, a peach orchard, and fields of cotton, rye, and oats. He was "very attentive to all improvements suggested to him." There were still hints, however, that Cornells cherished his Creek identity as equally as his more cultivated, southern one. Aside from his illiteracy and continued reliance on the Creek language, Cornells also still evidently dressed like a Creek, all of which Hawkins lamented.[20]

Both Cornells and Weatherford represented the men in Creek Country with the most mixed ancestry. They had deep Creek cultural ties, yet they also embraced Euro-American concepts like private property and personal wealth. They were both politically active in their communities, and by Trader's Hill they were trusted American allies. With one foot in a Euro-American world their support of the federal government is not particularly surprising, but the two men characterized only a portion of the emerging Upper Creek power structure. Representing headmen of very different means and traditions was Efau Haujo, or the Mad Dog. Americans in 1789 explained him as being "next in authority" in the Creek Country, behind only the White Lieutenant of Oakfuskee.[21] By several accounts the Mad Dog's claim to authority could not possibly have been more different than Cornells's or Weatherford's. A "sometime militant with a strong traditional claim to Creek leadership," the Mad Dog was a recognized nativist and at times a shaman, a priest, or a conjurer—a man who wielded strong cosmological powers. When David Taitt toured the Upper Country in 1773 he passed through Tuckabatchee and found the Mad Dog "very bussie preparing Physick and Causing the people to dance every night on purpose to bring back to life their fire Maker," a Creek warrior who had lately been killed in a battle with the Choctaw. The *haujo* in the Mad Dog's title could be translated to mean something like reckless or crazy, as well as mad, and it commonly signified a man who fought ferociously and without regard for himself. According to one contemporary account the Mad Dog was that sort of man, who "maintains and exercises great influence in the nation; particularly in military affairs."[22] His adherence to traditional notions of blood vengeance was rock steady, further anchoring his authority in Creek culture. When one of his relations was killed by Georgians in 1792, for instance, he made it a point to take satisfaction personally and could not be dissuaded. James Durouzeaux tried his hardest to turn him back, but the Mad Dog's determination to avenge the slaying of a kin member was far too resolute. He would return, he told Durouzeaux, as soon as the business was done.[23]

Although his name did not contain "mico," that seemed to matter little. The Mad Dog's control over cosmological authority and his leadership in battle were two traditional markers of authority in Creek Country that were very strong, making the Mad Dog a clear regional leader. As early as 1786 he was being referred to as one of the leading headmen in the Upper Country; McGillivray recognized as much. He referred to him as "the Famous Mad Dog" and later explained that during a war council "the great chief called the Mad Dog" presided over the proceedings. The Mad Dog's traditional ties to Creek leadership were so strong, in fact, that McGillivray had relied on him when dealing with headmen more critical of his own claims to authority. After McGillivray's death, the Mad Dog retained that position of leadership and respect, and his regional influence only continued to grow.[24]

The Mad Dog had little reason to pursue centralized control as a means to accrue personal wealth, and he made very few attempts to do so. Well aged by the end of the Revolution, he derived much of his influence in the 1770s and 1780s because of his previous leadership successes, both in politics and in battle. Even late in life he had few of the trappings of civilized society. When he died he did so with some cattle and a few slaves that were legally his, but that was about all he shared with Cornells, who also lived in Tuckabatchee. Many years later, in fact, Benjamin Hawkins explained that while the Mad Dog had a handful of slaves and some stock, they were "of little use to him." The traditional Creek culture of gift-giving and exchange, which Hawkins loathed as uncultivated and lazy, certainly had not been lost on the elderly chief. Years of friendship with French and British traders were "so riveted" in him that he claimed that the property he had accumulated was simply "tribute due him, and one that never must be dispensed with." Despite his criticisms, Hawkins still recognized that the Mad Dog was "one of the great medal chiefs, the speaker for the nation at the national council. He is one of the best informed men of the land, and faithful to his national engagements."[25]

The Mad Dog wavered somewhat in his support of the Americans. He had been a staunch British ally during the Revolution and personally picked up ammunition and powder from Spanish governors during the Oconee War. Somewhere between the end of that crisis and 1790, however, possibly because of McGillivray's influence, he began to turn more toward the Americans. He was present to sign the Treaty of New York and remained a strong American partisan during the chaotic years afterward. When he arrived back home from the treaty signing, the Mad Dog was the one to call a council at Tuckabatchee to discuss the terms. Soon after, as the political cohesiveness on the Upper Country began to unravel, he demonstrated a willingness to depart from some traditional avenues of leadership and use coercive talks both within his communities and outside of them in an effort to stem the spread of radical anti-American talks. He was described by a Cherokee as "a good man" who, when confronted by the Spanish and Shawnee talks, "sent me in a good talk to keep peace if possible, as he wants to do, and not to give ear nor to take no notice of the Northward Indian's talk." Several headmen in the Lower Country, the Cherokee continued, were "glad of the Spaniard's talk, and the Northwards, and killed some people," and they would have done much worse except that "the Mad Dog interposed, and I hope he has put a stop to it."[26] The Mad Dog's revered status as a Tuckabatchee headman gave him tremendous influence in the Upper Country, but it would be his increasing attempts to wield authority outside of his community of influence that marked his investment in a new Creek political order.

The most revered voice in the Upper Country most likely belonged to Tuskena Atca of Oakfuskee, also known as the White Lieutenant.[27] Little is known about his earlier years, but one historian has suggested that he might have been the same man as a Billy Germany, who in 1759 was the twenty-two-year-old "half breed, Head Warriour Creek of Ockfusky." If that was the case then his father would have been James Germany, a trader who lived and traded in Oakfuskee as well as Cooloome from the 1740s well into the 1770s. James Germany married the Handsome Fellow's sister, who was the daughter of the Red Coat King, a powerful Oakfuskee mico. As the Handsome Fellow's nephew, the White Lieutenant would have succeeded him as a leading Oakfuskee headman after his death, which happened late in the Revolution.[28] Traditional Creek lineages did not get much more impressive than that. The White Lieutenant's kinship not only would have given him an incontrovertible claim to leadership and authority in Oakfuskee but would have set him up with perhaps the strongest traditional claim to authority among any of the headmen in the Upper Country that would become American supporters. During the Revolutionary War the Handsome Fellow was a close friend of the Rae brothers and one of the Americans' most outspoken supporters. Oakfuskees were strong American partisans—militant at times—and despite the chaos of the Oconee War and reports of Oakfuskees receiving weapons from the Spanish, the White Lieutenant remained a steadfast American ally. In 1789 he was described as having "the ascendancy" in the Upper Country, and he was "considered, in some respects," to be McGillivray's rival.[29]

The White Lieutenant, like the Mad Dog, was also a political ally of McGillivray's, propping up the young beloved man in a Creek Country where he lacked cultural connections of his own. As Barnard would later write, "in Mr. McGillivray's life time," it was through the White Lieutenant's influence "that he swayed the best part of the Upper Creeks." When American Caleb Swan passed through Creek Country after the Treaty of New York he described the White Lieutenant as a man of mixed ancestry but also "the great *War Mico* of the whole district of Oakfuskies," who exercised "sole influence over 1,000 gun men." At the same time, Swan noted that his appearance and countenance "savors more of civilization than any other Indian that I have seen."[30] Though he was a head warrior he also was a man of mixed ancestry who evidently looked like it to Swan, even though he was not nearly as cultivated a man as McGillivray or Cornells. Hawkins passed through Oakfuskee years later, in 1796, and missed the White Lieutenant because he was out hunting with the rest of the Oakfuskee men. That disappointed Hawkins; the White Lieutenant, it seemed, was not nearly as invested in ranching or farming as others in the neighborhood were. Neither did Oakfuskee impress Hawkins. The

women there were "not so well provided in their houses" as the Cherokees to the north, nor did they "have as many poultry, hogs or cattle."[31]
Although Tuskena Atca was a man of mixed ancestry he did not act like
it, as far as Hawkins was concerned at least. His traditional claim to leadership, in other words, was as strong as any headman's.

Like the Mad Dog, the White Lieutenant also grew in influence
among American partisans around the time of McGillivray's decline.
He was among the first headmen to begin conversing with the newly
arrived Seagrove. Perhaps building on the strong trading ties his uncle
had built, and his own strong American relationship now with Seagrove,
the White Lieutenant was soon the strongest American partisan in all of
Creek Country. He was also one of the first to begin outwardly projecting
authority beyond his Oakfuskee community and did not hesitate to
envision a more centralized Creek authority—one in which he would be
involved. "Don't think that I take upon me to write for all the nations,"
he penned Seagrove in 1792, "but, this is the mouth of their greatest part
of the head-men, and I look on myself as good as any, and request you to
keep your people in peace, and we shall do the same." He assured the agent
of "our friendly disposition towards our brothers and friends, the white
people of Georgia." The "greatest part" of Creek Country, he continued,
was still supportive of the New York treaty, and there was still a chance
that "we shall drink out of the same waters," meaning the Oconee River,
which he declared would, eventually, be the new boundary.[32] Later, when
Seagrove made plans for another meeting at Rock Landing, he informed
the White Lieutenant of it first, requesting that he "make this known
in all the Upper towns, and that you will take measures to bring the
number of chiefs required down with you."[33] As a man of mixed heritage
who had strong trading and familial ties, along with strong leadership
skills, the White Lieutenant was a powerful and well-connected leader
in the Upper Country who would not hesitate to extend his influence in
a time of crisis. Seagrove certainly understood that, and his relationship
with the White Lieutenant would be the foundation atop which a strong
Creek-American relationship would develop.

Far less is written, and far less is known, about leading men in the
Lower Country. That Cussetas would prove staunch American supporters, on the one hand, was not surprising. They had long been the most
dependable American partisans in the Lower Country. They had strong
trading relationships with Americans during the Revolution and they
remained friendly throughout the 1780s even in the face of increasingly brazen state actions. With powerful traders in their neighborhood,

including the likes of George Galphin and Timothy Barnard, neither the British nor the Spanish had much success recruiting Cusseta headmen to violence. That was clear to Benjamin Hawkins as well, who recognized that they "associate, more than any other Indians, with their white neighbors," although at the time he saw it more as a hindrance than an asset. There is enough evidence, however, to piece together the lives of a few leading headmen there. The Fushatchee Mico, or the White Bird-Tail King, became a prominent Cusseta chief in the years after the Revolution. His name contained mico, meaning that he held the strongest claim to civilian authority among his peers. He was with McGillivray at New York and signed the treaty there; as a local civil leader he probably had as much authority as anyone else in New York to sign the document, which he continued to defend even as it grew dangerously unpopular. And although little else is known about him, he mostly likely was not a man of mixed ancestry. Benjamin Hawkins generally had good things to say about him, although he was disappointed in 1799 that "he had no firmness enough, till this year, to break through the old habits of the Indians," referring to his unwillingness to farm with the aid of a plow.[34] Although he was a strong American supporter, he was above all else a traditional Creek community leader.

Also in the neighborhood of Cusseta was the Tussekiah Mico. Although he was another strong local chief who carried the mico title, in the late 1790s Hawkins had better things to say of him than his neighbors, having seen him absorb more American ideas of civilization than many others. The agent visited him when he first arrived in Creek Country and commented on how upstanding and cultivated the chief was—he was perhaps the most respectable in the region. He fenced his property and had some cattle and hogs, and he and "his wife and children all have the air and manners of well bred people." The Tussekiah Mico typified the Cusseta approach to Americans. As he proudly explained, the chief had "always had an attachment to the white people," which his father had taught him, and "on his death had enjoined it on him to hold all white people by the hand." Near him was the Efau Tustunnuggee, or the Dog Warrior, who as a leading warrior would become the voice of the Creek Nation's laws.[35] Less is known about the Eneah Mico, or the Fat King, who was perhaps the most controversial headman in the Lower Country. He certainly was a central Cusseta figure because of his long-standing American ties—relationships that generated tremendous tension during the American Revolution. Another mico, he was "a very principal man" in the Lower Country and was "the most principal one in the nation to act" on matters of land in 1785, according to Timothy Barnard.[36] Eneah Mico remained a vigilant informant and an unwavering American supporter when Spaniards, Bowles, and even Shawnee chiefs were making the region a dangerous and unpredictable place. By the Trader's Hill attacks groups of Cussetas, under his leadership, constituted perhaps the only pro-American group in the region, openly confronting their powerful Coweta neighbors as well as the more militant communities further south along the Chattahoochee River. In the wake of the attacks the Fat King continued to be one of Seagrove's most important allies, and Cussetas generally exercised a calming and then gradually coercive influence when the situation in the Lower Country demanded it.

Unfortunately, even less is known about other Cusseta or Coweta headmen, like Tuskenehau Chapco and Yaholo Mico. The latter, Yaholo Mico, also known as the Hallowing King, was described by Caleb Swan as one of the most influential chiefs in the region, "either in peace or war."[37] Like most other Cussetas and Cowetas mentioned during the period, the Hallowing King was probably not a man of mixed ancestry. And while his title as a mico gave him a strong claim to civil leadership, Coweta was a strong red town known to raid ruthlessly—raids in which the Hallowing King participated. Perhaps their classification as a war town also explains why Cowetas, although they had strong American trade connections, also became strong British and Spanish partisans in the face of repeated state insults and took a leading role in both the Revolutionary and Oconee wars. Nevertheless, the Hallowing King was in New York to sign the treaty in 1790 and Seagrove depended upon him for years afterward. The Lower Country was a complex place, Coweta and Cusseta proved, but there were plenty of traditional Creek leaders there upon whom Americans could depend.

While there were few Creek leaders of mixed ancestry in the south, there were several traders and other men of mixed ancestry who were politically active in the region, and they exerted an increasingly powerful influence in the years after Trader's Hill. Many of the traders who had been the cause of so much confusion and factionalism during the Revolutionary War remained in the Lower Country; they continued to affect how individual communities approached outside groups like the Spanish during the Oconee crisis, and they continued to have a say in community politics after the Treaty of New York.[38] Yet rather than tease Creek Country apart, as they had done in the past, many of those same men became important American assets. Timothy Barnard was a particularly powerful pro-American force. He was the son of a British colonel stationed in North Carolina and then Savannah before the Revolution, and he became an established trader in the Lower Country. Years later, when Hawkins passed through the region Barnard was there with him, along with a few of his several children. He had a plantation in the Lower Country on the Flint River that grew over the years, with a "dweling house, mostly the labour of his own hands," as Hawkins described it in 1797, including some peach trees and a few slaves, and was developing a dairy operation as well. Hawkins lauded him as a steadfast American ally: "The white and red men are much indebted to his constant, persevering and honest exertions to do just to all applications," Hawkins wrote; "it sometimes falls to the lot of one man, though apparently in the humble walks of life, to render most effectual service to his fellow creatures, than thousands of neighbors." Hawkins was clearly impressed with Barnard's service to America to that point. Most important, perhaps, Barnard had a wife from the Lower Country and, according to one account, "died a member of the tribe, leaving a large estate." When meeting with Hawkins, three of his boys were around, all of whom were referred to by their Creek names, which Hawkins spelled Homanhidge, Falpe, and Yuccohpee. His wife, in other words, definitely had a say over how their boys would be raised, which was a strong marker of Creek culture in the Barnard household. Although his father was British, and there were reports during the Revolution that he traded for the British as well, Barnard was applauded as a steadfast American partisan afterward and was enormously influential as a trade commissioner for the state of Georgia.[39]

These kinship and trading relationships made Barnard one of the most powerful and influential pro-Georgia men in all of Creek Country. During one set of negotiations in 1789, in fact, John Galphin seemed irritated that Georgia authorities considered Barnard as influential as he and his brother were. The governor was evidently "not more acquainted with business of this country, than to think that Mr. Barnard's influence could be of any service to that country," Galphin complained. While he did not doubt that Barnard was a friend to Georgians and an asset in Creek Country, "I must take the liberty to acquaint you that Mr. Barnard cannot do any thing here more than a trader, nor is in his power." Americans would get the best information, John assured one of the commissioners—and presumably the best service—from him and his brother George.[40] As irritated as the brothers seemed, as long as Cussetas continued to support Americans after New York and had a political role to play in the region, Barnard would remain important as well. Seagrove depended on him heavily in 1792 and 1793, and he struggled desperately to keep the Lower Country peaceful when he found himself in an increasingly hostile place, couched as he was among volatile groups of Yuchis, Chehaws, and Hitchitis. Hawkins would make Barnard one of his assistants years later, and it is no surprise that he was soon his most important and trusted one.[41]

Despite the Galphin brothers' criticism of him, Barnard had the same kinds of connection as they did. They were the sons of George Galphin Sr. and a Coweta woman and grew up along the Creek-Georgia frontier. They were influential men during the Revolution and critical American partisans during the 1780s who used their strong ties, both in Coweta and Cusseta, to avert bloodshed after the 1789 failure at Rock Landing. Barnard even suggested using John against McGillivray during the Oconee War when it was certain the latter was backing the Spanish. He could, with "any sharp person to back him . . . do a great deal towards settling matters in the Nation in a very short time, if he was properly encouraged, as he is an Indian as well as McGill[i]vray and can attack him with his own weapons." Georgia legislators soon appointed him a commissioner, along with Barnard.[42] Yet John Galphin was also more opportunistic than Barnard, and some of his dealings in Creek Country had a more disreputable air to them. It was clear by 1793 that Seagrove, with others, did not entirely trust him, and there were plenty of people who thought both he and George were double-dealing with the Spanish. Seagrove informed Barnard of "the rascally part" John had been acting just before the Trader's Hill killings, pressing him "to prevent his lies taking bad effect in the nation."[43] By John's accounts he and George had done what they could to diffuse the situation at the trading house, but others were not convinced. In the wake of the attacks both brothers, along with fellow trader John Burgess, were targeted directly for their alleged participation. Both the White Bird-Tail King and Cusseta King heaped blamed on John in particular, claiming that he in fact had instigated everything, and they promised Seagrove that he would be turned over to American authorities.[44] Despite their sometimes questionable motives, however, both brothers had long worked in the favor of the state of Georgia and then the Americans. While they certainly may have been a meddlesome duo, their influence was also proven, and Seagrove and then Hawkins continued to turn to them regularly for support.[45]

Even further to the south was John Kinnard, also commonly referred to as Jack, who by Trader's Hill was also one of Seagrove's more dependable assets in the Lower Country. His plantation, located between

Chehaw, Yuchi, and Hitchiti, and "on the borders of the lower Creeks and Seminoles," put Kinnard square in the middle of the most militant region in all of Creek Country. According to one American, the Seminoles in north Florida were also "said to be principally" under his influence.[46] His own history, however, is shrouded in intrigue. American agent Caleb Swan described him as a "Scotch half-breed" and a "rich half-breed chief," but little is known about whether he was actually a man of mixed Creek ancestry or not. He was wholly illiterate but according to Swan was a "noted trader, farmer, and herdsman" who had two wives, forty slaves, over a thousand head of cattle and horses, and a sizable amount of cash in Spanish currency.

How he came to own all that property, according to several accounts, was sketchy at best. He was described as little more than a war profiteer and a professional thief who made his living "entirely by plunder and freebooting." Swan bought horses off of a group of his slaves, for instance, when they crossed paths. The slaves were driving them to St. Augustine to be sold, which meant they were almost certainly stolen. The plantation, the slaves, and the trade in stolen property all painted Kinnard in an unflattering light, but no one could say he was either financially unsuccessful or politically weak. However nefarious his exploits they "raised him to the dignity of a chief, and enabled him to go largely into trade," and he was "of so much consequence, in his own country, as to threaten the Spaniards into compliance with almost any thing he demands."[47] More ironic yet, although a good portion of his property was probably once Georgia settler property, his wealth and influence were impressive enough to garner him respect even among American officials. Bowles and the Spaniards focused much of their efforts on the towns in his neighborhood—disruptive voices Kinnard was soon countering to the Americans' advantage. In 1792 he was "very active indeed." He "publicly opposes his people having any thing to do with the Spaniards."[48] Both Seagrove and Barnard leaned on him extensively as a voice of moderation when there were few others. Seagrove in particular had enough faith in him in October 1792 to propose making him one of his subagents, "placing him at the head of the lower creeks."[49]

James Durouzeaux and John Burgess emerged as American partisans as well, although almost nothing is known about them. Most of the time Durouzeaux could be found in Coweta, where he interpreted both American and Spanish talks for headmen in the region. That made his allegiances questionable, not unlike Kinnard and the Galphins. While he was clearly also working for the Spanish, for instance, he and John

Galphin penned Georgia authorities in 1787, hoping they would "consider us as friends, as you are sensible we are your friends." They harkened back to the Revolution, "when the English offered us great presents to go and kill you, we told them we would not; that you were our friends and brothers; we were born in one land, and we were your friends and brothers, and will be to the last day."[50] John Burgess was in a similar position. He had an extensive trading history, like Barnard and Kinnard, which stretched back before the Revolution, and made his home outside of a small Seminole town in north Florida. Because that region remained one of the most vulnerable to outside talks, Seagrove and later Hawkins depended on him as a messenger, interpreter, and stabilizing American presence there even though it was obvious they did not entirely trust him.[51]

After the Oconee War, Rock Landing, and then the Treaty of New York, people friendly to American interests were a rarity in Creek Country. Faced with waves of violence and threats of retaliation in the wake of Trader's Hill, Seagrove turned to all of them almost simultaneously. He wrote to gauge headmen's response to the killings, and he reached out to traders for intelligence, asking everyone to extend what stabilizing influence they could over their respective communities. But he also made demands, pressing for the immediate seizure of the perpetrators and the return of what was stolen, almost all of whom and all of which were in the Lower Country. In an approach that Benjamin Hawkins would later perfect, Seagrove did not focus his charges only on the offending communities or ask that neighbors exert what authority they could manage to right the situation. He made demands of good neighborhood that included all Creeks and backed them up with clear warnings about the cost of failure. "If you have a wish that your land should not be deluged with blood, and that you should possess the same, and live in it in peace," he declared in open letters, then something substantial needed to be done, and done quickly. "The outrage is so enormous and unprovoked, as not to admit delay on your parts. Vengeance will be showered on your nation, if justice is not immediately done." Thus Seagrove's gauntlet was laid down before over twenty headmen, and the agent directed his talks to be read aloud wherever possible.[52] He made it a point not to separate the guilty from the innocent, as many headmen were attempting to do; justice had to come from all in Creek Country, he warned, or all of Creek Country would suffer American vengeance.

Nearby Cussetas and even some Cowetas were among the first to send supportive talks in the immediate days after the attacks, but in the wake of Seagrove's ultimatums they did not exactly jump at the opportunity to take responsibility for their neighbors to the south or to take nontraditional steps to enforce regional order. Cussetas had already declared before the attacks, in fact, that in the case of bloodshed they would disavow the communities that perpetrated the killings. Headmen declared adamantly that "if it should be so that any of the other parts of the nation should stand out and make a war with the United States, that they will single themselves off from those that want war, and let them abide by the consequences of it."[53] While those declarations were meant to assure American authorities of their continued support, the Cusseta declaration represented a classic community-level Creek response that emphasized political distinctiveness and exclusivity. That approach was unhelpful when Emistisiguo advocated it during the Ceded Lands crisis in 1773, and it was just as unhelpful twenty years later. Yet it was the Cusseta response, and coming from the most supportive allies in the Lower Country it left Americans profoundly disappointed. Cussetas were "determined to stay, to separate themselves off from those that are determined for war," according to John Kinnard, and would not confront them.[54]

Without strong guidance the situation in the Lower Country deteriorated. While a "majority of the head-men are for peace," another reported, "and seem determined, at all hazards, to give satisfaction," other accounts revealed that many still clung to the older, less helpful political approach of simply ostracizing the guilty. The raiding had created fissures even in the offending towns. "So far from being the voice of the whole nation," Barnard explained, "since those villainous murderers arrived at their own towns," probably Chehaw or Broken Arrow, "they have been bullied and despised by all that were in the town."[55] Chehaw, and to a lesser extent the nearby neighborhoods of Broken Arrow and Ooseoochee, was emerging as the center of the discontented. "I am in dread of no danger from any part of the nation but the Chehaws below me," Barnard declared late in March. If that was the case the region could be stabilized relatively quickly if communities would act, even if only to prevent the raiding from continuing to escalate. Barnard had just been down that way and had spoken to the "head king of the town" for hours. Yet "he since hearing a flying report, that the Cowetas were gone out to do mischief, and some of the other towns had joined them, without waiting to hear the truth, set off with ten or twelve fellows to do mischief low down on the frontier." If Barnard or any Cusseta or Coweta coalition could put a stop to such rash decisions it could diffuse the entire crisis. But Barnard could not, and neither could Kinnard. Barnard received word in fact from Kinnard that if he had anything to send in to the region "to leave it to him, as he knew it would endanger my life to interfere too much in that business, as I was a white man, which I was daily informed of by Indians and white people from the Chehaws."[56] The situation was now so alarming that even a man with strong Cusseta ties like Barnard was unsafe.

Thankfully for Seagrove, John Kinnard emerged during that critical juncture as a force to be reckoned with. He, Barnard confided in Seagrove early after the killings, "I hear, means to stand his ground, and all the Cussetahs." Working on seemingly reluctant Cussetas, he and they together exerted the first real pressure to originate from within Creek Country that would bear on the offending communities. That included facing headmen from the offending towns directly; he was "doing all he can to urge them to give satisfaction."[57] He "has not ceased, since we went from this, in riding himself, and sending talks, to all the towns, in our favor." As soon as he heard word of the attacks he "sent to the chiefs of the towns whose people committed the violence" and "talked very severely to them." He warned them that "unless they gave immediate satisfaction for the murders and robberies," they "had nothing to expect but war and total ruin to their country." Because the attackers originated so far to the south of Creek Country he initially also blamed Burgess and confronted him as well. If Burgess "did not immediately have the goods collected, and sent back," Kinnard threatened he would "come and take all his property, and his life," blaming him in the Trader's Hill death of Flemming in particular. By the early summer of 1793, a very dangerous time to be a government man, Kinnard still had "the United States standard flying in his yard," and if any "American parties came, he would receive them with it."[58] Kinnard quickly make a name for himself as one of the most active American voices in the Lower Country, even among the most hostile communities, and it was because of him that Cussetas finally began to act as well.

These first efforts were overshadowed by the actions of leaders in the Upper Country, who were more receptive to speaking in a common Creek voice. A few communities there had raided, particularly Tallassees, but more headmen appeared friendly, and they too took pains to urge Seagrove not to blame those from their neighborhood. Alexander Cornells was stunned by the killings but even more by rumors of involvement by the Tallassee King and Cooloome warriors: "We cannot help it, therefore I hope you will not blame the Upper towns for it, for we still stand to your talk, and mean to do so."[59] But, unlike their counterparts in the Lower Country, they were also the first to threaten retaliation against the perpetrators, regardless of where they were. While Cornells maintained that the majority of Creek Country was peaceful, he also supported getting satisfaction for Americans by force if necessary, a proposition others around him shared. Within days of the attacks headmen from the region were meeting, some with the assistance of Barnard, and they pushed for swift action. At one council consisting of the Mad Dog, the White Lieutenant, and Cornells, which Barnard also attended, the headmen mulled over the possibility of chastising the Chehaw perpetrators directly, and Barnard got the headmen to issue "a very severe talk on that head," which they quickly sent south. More importantly, perhaps, the White Lieutenant, another headman by the name of the Mamouth (most likely from Kialijee), and "some more of the headmen" were on their way south directly to "stop them from doing any mischief to the inhabitants." That same group successfully pressured groups of Cowetas "to lie still" when they were itching to head out in their own war parties. That was an impressive feat in itself—keeping war parties at bay when their potential to extend violence along the frontier was tremendous and when their own neighbors, Cussetas, seemed unwilling to take a stand against them. But this group of Upper Country headmen went further yet, with Weatherford and Cornells declaring to Barnard that if asked, they would "soon run off the Spanish commissary, as, while they are there, there will be no good talks from them towards us."[60] Cornells would "impress every thing on the minds of the heads of the nation" to have their plans set in motion, Barnard confided to Georgia governor James Jackson.[61]

The progressively firmer steps taken by a select and shrinking group of headmen in the wake of Trader's Hill, despite the political and physical distances that separated them from the communities at the heart of the raiding, were important ones. They marked the beginning of a transitional period in Creek politics. The results of the earliest councils in the Upper Country were clear, even if they did not bring a swift end to the crisis. Headmen there would exert what influence they could, in a voice that transcended their own communities, to solve a regional Creek problem. The same group continued to act into the summer, when they traveled south to confer with Cusseta headmen in the hopes of crafting an even larger, unified response. Cornells and the Mad Dog were present, and the White Lieutenant and Charles Weatherford seemed to be as well. The latter two, along with the White Bird-Tail King of Cusseta, reaffirmed that they were "highly desirous for peace." Barnard was again present, as were several Cusseta headmen, illustrating what seemed to be a strengthening of their tone.[62]

Before too long, the headmen had guaranteed in these conferences, satisfaction would be taken. During the first council, in fact, a gang of Cowetas arrived carrying scalps that they declared they had taken from the northern frontiers—the result of past raids that could not be stopped. This enraged the Cusseta hosts, who thundered out threats and "were for making examples of those that did the mischief, immediately." It was only because several other Coweta war parties were still out, they later explained, that they held off doing so.[63] When more groups of raiders from the Half-Way House and Tallassee left for the northern frontiers in a separate war party, led by a now firmly renegade Tallassee King, it provoked similar outrage. Barnard dispatched groups of warriors to turn the men back, which they did. "They mean to spite the whole nation," Cornells angrily penned Seagrove, "if they can, by spoiling what talks we have had with you." He and the Mad Dog were particularly irritated at how completely the Half-Way House and Tallassees had been warped by the talks of both the Shawnee and another character, a "villain Grearson," and were determined that if there was any truth to the charges against him, it "shall cost him his life." Soon the headmen, this time supported more openly by Cussetas, backed up those threats with a new pledge, this time targeting the outlaw trader, Cowetas, and all the northern raiders.[64] A voice promising action now included headmen in both the Upper and Lower countries; both groups were willing to exert authority farther from their homes.

The decisive thinking made at these councils and following ones began to make for a trend. Again a growing group of headmen promised to right the crisis by bringing everyone they knew to bear on the offenders. Headmen continued to look for culprits and attempt judgments. This time it was George Galphin and another trader, whom the Cussetas claimed were directly involved in the raiding, who were to be seized and probably killed. In addition "the red men that were with Galphin," including two Chehaws, were also to be surrendered or executed, and the White King of Eufala was delegated to do the business. Although Cussetas were central to the council it was the delegation from the Upper Country, authoritative both in the deliberations and in the choosing of the executioner, which appeared ascendant. Cornells requested that Seagrove give them time to set their plans in motion, but he reiterated that "it is the wish of the Upper towns to do it" and that it would serve as "a warning to the young people; then they will mind what their head-men say to them, and not before." The Mad Dog continued, promising to Seagrove that if the towns from the Lower Country had "done mischief," then he would get satisfaction for it, "for we Upper towns all agree to it at our meeting."[65] They were, Barnard penned Seagrove, "for peace, and seem determined, at all hazards, to give satisfaction for the murder committed at St. Mary's."[66] Barnard was convinced that, "before many days," he would "hear of some of the offenders losing their lives, at least as many as were murdered on the St. Mary's."[67]

These several conferences connected in new and intriguing ways what had been in the past remarkably disparate political places in Creek Country during times of crisis. Of course headmen from all corners of Creek Country had met before, and worked together before, but what was happening in 1793 seemed different. Cussetas speaking for their neighbors in Coweta or Chehaw was not particularly remarkable when it came to trading with Euro-Americans. Threatening their neighbors over localized raids, on the other hand, was more remarkable. Even more remarkable was the willingness of Oakfuskees and Tuckabatchees to do so as well. Perhaps all Creeks shared responsibility for the actions of a few of them, these first overtures suggested, and together Creeks would see justice served. Such talks were, in short, suggestive of a visibly stronger sense of Creek political nationalism.

Creek headmen, however, soon found making good on their first promises altogether a different matter. Although the recent councils were an unprecedented step in the direction of a unified Creek political voice, their less-than-impressive results clarified to both the Creek and American leadership that the voice was more symbolic than functional. Although Timothy Barnard was confident that a few Creeks might die as a result of the important Cusseta conference, "as to their giving up the whole of the offenders to be punished, I fear that is totally out of their power."[68] The Big Warrior of Cusseta, who would rise in influence as a voice of centralized authority only years later, came to a similar conclusion. He agreed with the decisions made at the council, but Creek cultural traditions still governed justice as far as he was concerned, and even though Creeks talked about taking nontraditional actions, they were as yet untested. The Big Warrior promised to keep those around him from heading out to do more damage, but he could do little else. Creeks simply did not have laws "to restrain their people from doing mischief," and neither was it in their power "to command each other to take up arms to suppress such conduct."[69] There was little precedent in Creek culture for what Americans demanded, so these early efforts met with only mixed results. Although Creeks were talking in nontraditional ways, they were not yet ready to act in nontraditional ways.

Fulfilling the decisions made at the councils was particularly difficult in Cusseta. While that was ironic because the boldest statements had been made in the summer of 1793 at the Cusseta council, after all, the coercive action called for there would burden Cussetas more than any other group, as would any possible retaliation. Barnard asked Kinnard and the Cusseta King if Cussetas would be able to bring their own warriors to march against their neighbors along the Flint and Chattahoochee. Four or five towns' worth of warriors could take satisfaction themselves, he suggested, and the matter would be settled. The Cusseta King was not convinced, however, and Barnard lamented that he, among others, "said it was not in their power."[70] Although Cussetas were a people driven by their own cultural traditions to keep the peace, and even though it was their neighborhood that needed policing, they were still unprepared to use violence to keep that peace, at least in such a nontraditional way. Killing a trader and a few obvious Creek murderers was one thing, but raiding their neighbors, executing a dozen of them, and seizing their property was entirely different. As the Cusseta King, the Mad Dog, the White Lieutenant, and Kinnard assured Seagrove, Creeks were "determined to give satisfaction," but the raids had extended beyond their ability to make right so easily. "After there were so many of your people killed, it was out of our power to do any more with them." Handfuls of Cowetas and Tallassees, along with the Broken Arrows, Hitchitis, Yuchis, Ooseoochees, and Chehaws, had been "thrown off by the nation," and they were all huddling together in Chehaw. Americans responded to those admissions as expected—with disappointment. While the Creek talks were encouraging, they had accomplished little. "I have talked until I am tired," Kinnard despaired, and "likewise the Cussetah King, and the rest of our head-men, but to no purpose."[71] Seagrove reported similarly. The "intentions of the well-disposed," unfortunately, could not counterweigh the "bad men of a few towns." They had, to that point, "disregarded all advice, and denied all authority of the nation," and "are now become a riotous, murdering banditti."[72] While there were handfuls of friendly chiefs who seemed genuinely cooperative, Creek traditions would not yet allow them to do what was being demanded of them. By the early months of 1794 it was obvious that a group of Creek leaders was beginning at least to form a unified Creek voice, but it was equally clear that they would be unable to make good on the promising talks they had produced from Cusseta.[73]

With the heads of the friendly towns pressing to get satisfaction, but unable to do so, the Creek-Georgia frontier continued to grow tense. It was during that most recent council that the headmen first suggested a direct, outside military intervention. Seagrove did not agree with the idea, but even though he did so angrily he admitted that such a move might be necessary. "Know then," he charged, "who are our friends," that he had done all he could peacefully, "and here finishes all further application, until the *sword* hath brought bad men to a sense of their duty."[74] Seven out of eight Creeks were friendly, Creeks were quick to tell him, and even in the Lower Country there was little debate on the subject of an outside intervention, as long as none of the friendly towns were attacked.[75] Both Barnard and Kinnard soon advocated for the strike as well, to "give them one drubbing, and burn their towns, and drive what property they have out of the land." Without such a step they doubted any satisfaction would ever be had.[76] Seagrove was apprehensive that Georgians would take advantage of the call for military action, but Creek headmen responded to the idea supportively, even from Cusseta. What was needed was "for a sufficient number of horsemen to come up, and cross above the Cowetas, and to burn, kill, and destroy, all they can find in them four towns," and they "were sure to meet with no opposition from any of the other towns."[77] Georgia authorities were only so happy to oblige, of course, and quickly made plans for such an invasion.[78] Both Kinnard and the Big Warrior went so far as to recommend to Georgia military officials the best route to the towns that needed to be burned.[79] Such an army would find little opposition in the majority of Creek Country, where headmen friendly to Americans would "sit still, and view with pleasure the chastisement those villains may receive."[80] Headmen were not willing to cross traditional avenues of justice within Creek Country and pursue coercive action themselves, but they were willing to let Americans do it for them.

Headmen were so adamant that Seagrove began to come around to the plan himself. Unfortunately he had a hard time selling it to his superiors. Neither Henry Knox nor President Washington saw such a move as worth the cost of the regional problems it would cause and made clear military power needed to be avoided at all costs. Instead they renewed their hopes that together Seagrove and the friendly headmen allied with him could negotiate some sort of resolution to the crisis, a decision that prompted a softening of Seagrove's tone. Pressured by Knox, he stepped back from some of his harsher original demands, urging headmen to give him something he could at least use to begin a dialogue. Surrender at least one or two of the worst, guiltiest of the raiders, he suggested, and things could be made right. Ultimately, it was this change in position that led to Seagrove's journey into the heart of Creek Country.

Holding council was an integral part of Euro-American-Creek diplomacy that was steeped in tradition and ceremony, and Seagrove was the only Euro-American counterpart who had not done so from within Creek Country. Shortly before the Revolution, both John Stuart and his agent David Taitt made sweeping, months-long journeys through Creek Country. They sat in numerous councils and hothouses, smoked the chiefs' tobacco, and drank their fair share of the ceremonial black drink. Even Tonyn, meeting with groups of Seminoles and Creeks on the St. John's River, was present for a long and ceremonial meeting marked with elaborate eagle dances and other traditional symbols of diplomacy. Headmen like the White Lieutenant, Alexander Cornells, and certainly the Mad Dog would have been present at those meetings, and later they would have pointed to them during times of crisis as markers of trust and goodwill. Such meetings were critical to regional politics, Creeks had long declared, and the British rightly understood that they had to play along, even if they did not necessarily understand why.

Headmen looked to Seagrove to continue that tradition, which he was not particularly keen to do. To be fair to Seagrove the Creek-Georgia frontier was as unstable and frankly violent a place in 1793 as it had ever been, and an officer of the American government would have been foolish to suppose he could travel to several communities—particularly in the Lower Country—with any hope of coming back alive. Instead both Barnard and Kinnard, who resided in the region and had strong kinship ties to Creek communities, acted as Seagrove's proxies, and for Seagrove that seemed to work well enough. They were regulars in community councils and delivered his talks while he hovered much closer to the federal garrisons at the edge of Creek Country, like at Rock Landing or Fort Fidius on the Oconee, or at Coleraine on the St. Mary's River. And before that, obviously, the American government had McGillivray. Soon, however, McGillivray was gone, and with Oliver, Bowles, and then Wellbank actually living in Creek communities it was clear Americans would need to step up their own diplomatic effort, and not on their terms. Although there was no doubt it would be a perilous journey, after the Treaty of New York American allies in Creek Country were ever more convinced that Seagrove's presence would be the best—if not only—means of affecting permanent change.[81] If he could make it to Cusseta, Tuckabatchee, or Oakfuskee, it was almost universally seen as the means to seal long-term stability.

Such a journey would have done tremendous good after New York, but it was a necessity after the Trader's Hill killings, when communities were balking at Seagrove's heavy-handed demands. Timothy Barnard pressed him multiple times to make the journey, which even Knox was soon convinced would have to happen for the agent to succeed in his position.[82] "It is conceived that a residence within the nation is the only solid principle of conciliation," he wrote Seagrove after the attacks, pressing him, as soon as it was safe, to "repair to the upper as well as lower Creeks."[83] Most importantly, however, it was the headmen he claimed to be his friends who clamored loudest for such a visit. Americans were asking a lot of these leaders, who a year previous had only been community men, and several of them began to declare outwardly that nothing of importance could be done without such a show of good faith. The Mad Dog hoped that he "may be here speedily," which was something Cornells soon echoed.[84] The White Lieutenant's own request was particularly personal. "My unknown friend," he began, "I have very long had a particular desire to see you." Come forward, he continued, "and don't be daunted; now is the time you can be of service to us, and your country as we are determined to take your talks, and stand by you to the last moment." Their eager desire "for your immediate arrival in the nation will serve to convince you that they were fully satisfied of your good intentions towards them," Barnard elaborated.[85] By the summer of 1793, in fact, it was clear that if the Creek leadership was going to solve the Trader's Hill crisis, Seagrove would have to be there with them to do it.

Such a journey could also do much more. Not only would Seagrove's presence build trust with the friendly Creeks who were attempting to build a unified voice, it had the potential to pacify the more belligerent towns that had expressed little faith in American talks. Shortly after Trader's Hill, for instance, groups of Cowetas were growing restless, but Barnard, along with the White Lieutenant and the Mad Dog, assured Coweta headmen that Seagrove would "remove every reasonable obstacle that proved injurious to the peace of their nation." Barnard was similarly convinced that Seagrove's presence in a community like Coweta would do tremendous good. Later that summer, with the situation having further deteriorated, headmen began to demand the visit.[86] John Galphin penned one such letter from angry Coweta headmen direct to Georgia general Jared Irwin in August. The headmen first condemned state officials, whose desire for Creek lands, they charged, knew no limits. No boundaries "established by nature or by compact have stayed the ambitious or satisfied your people." Creeks would "adhere to a line fairly agreed on, but such agreement must be by the legislative body of the nation and not a clandestine bargain"—referring to the Treaty of New York—"with a few chiefs that have no manner of right to dispose of any lands." Next it was Seagrove's turn. He "called himself Agent, appointed by Congress," yet the only counseling he did with Creeks was from Georgia. "Why did he not come into the nation," they asked, "where matters might be long settled and we might have been in peace and friendship." Instead he was relying on Timothy Barnard, who "cannot, nor any other trader dare give out any talks in our council, or should it be supposed that we should put any confidence in such men."[87] Although it demonstrated the limitations of a man in Barnard's position, the stiff Coweta criticism was also Seagrove's most direct invitation to Creek Country yet.

Although they waited for Seagrove, the Creek leadership group also renewed their efforts in the summer of 1793 to pacify the wayward from within. In another strong showing of political solidarity that now included more of the Lower Country, a handful of Cussetas and Cowetas traveled north to sit in council at Tuckabatchee. Altogether eight headmen from the Lower Country were present, along with two dozen from the Upper Country. Although that did not make the Tuckabatchee council particularly large by treaty standards, the men present were continuing an important development. They were all that would be needed to get things done in Creek Country, they hoped. Voices from the Upper Country were again ascendant, yet everyone concluded "by the voice of the whole of the Upper Creeks and likewise the Cussetahs," to "take every step in their power to continue at peace with the United States," which meant to "give immediate satisfaction for the murders and hostilities on the inhabitants of Georgia."[88] Their words gave Barnard confidence that they were serious "and bent to do what they can to settle matters."[89]

The White Lieutenant, like Weatherford and the Mad Dog, promised Seagrove that the Tuckabatchee council carried weight, and the headmen there meant to stand by their decisions. First, the council resolved to gather Broken Arrows, Ooseoochees, Chehaws, and particularly Cowetas together and threaten them in the strongest possible terms not only to desist from any future hostilities but to return all stolen property. To do that, headmen from the Upper Country more than ever seemed "resolved that if they still continue obstinate to show what they can do by force." They also agreed on a swift retaliation to make good on the murders the warriors had committed, and this time Cussetas were dispatched "to do the business of killing five of the murderers," which they determined were Cowetas, Ooseoochees, and Chehaws.[90] As resolutions from the Tuckabatchee conference grew bolder, and the words of men like the Mad Dog and the White Lieutenant more authoritative, it appeared at the very least that a common Creek voice was continuing to emerge, dedicated to maintaining regional peace.

Not only were these Creek leaders proposing plans to prevent further misunderstandings, they were using the threat of violence to support them. For the second time, however, the first part of that approach was more successful than the second. This was the beginning of a frustrating trend for Americans. Their attempts to pacify the towns eager to raid were impressive, and the number of raids did in fact drop. Their more decisive decisions, on the other hand, like having people killed or property seized, were what the headmen continued to struggle with. A small group of Cowetas was not convinced of the plan, and with the help of Durouzeaux they "sent out talks that caused a disappointment in the business," which included having the stolen property seized. That put a halt to a separate group of Cowetas, who along with Cussetas had already gathered a good deal of property, including numerous horses. Cusseta warriors also had been out "to make a beginning on the murderers," when that goal too was frustrated. When the condemned realized they were to be killed, naturally they ran. Rather than kill their kin, the White Lieutenant waited to see if the offenders could be hunted down, which put a pause on the most significant decisions made at Tuckabatchee.[91]

This first exchange was one of many that left Americans scratching their heads. On the one hand, what was decided upon at Tuckabatchee ultimately did not come to pass, which made it a disappointment as far as Seagrove was concerned. Yet the meeting at Tuckabatchee was still encouraging, considering what Creek Country had looked like for the previous three years. The White Lieutenant's resolve was also positive, as were the actions of the Cusseta headmen and those of at least some of their Coweta counterparts. A surprisingly small group of headmen was actually beginning to debate kin-based revenge and the idea of exercising coercive control over all Creek communities. Not only was there plenty to make Seagrove hopeful, but Creek Country was beginning to look different. While their efforts at coercion were at best only partially successful, the resolve shown by the headmen at Tuckabatchee and afterward continued to look more familiar to Americans. The signs were positive; a small selection of Creek headmen were pulling all Creek communities together into a single political voice and were "determined to compel the whole creek nation" not only to surrender goods and lives but "to take one peace talk."[92]

Alexander Cornells's nephew David was chosen to deliver written accounts of Tuckabatchee to Seagrove and to confer with him over the proceedings personally. He was also directed to make the most of his journey through the Lower Country. On his way east he stopped at Cusseta to rally support in the neighborhood. There he met with both Cusseta and Coweta headmen and oversaw the appointing of men to "goe on the business of killing some of the murderers." Leaving, he reported that the Cowetas "consented to stick to the talks agreed on" at Tuckabatchee, which was good news indeed. Local headmen appeared willing to support the talks, empowering what was beginning to look like a Creek National Council. For the young Cornells, a future in that council looked bright indeed. Although young and brash and guilty of killing at least a few Georgian settlers himself, David was also described as a powerful and well-liked warrior, and an up-and-coming headman in the region. Barnard understood his potential, urging Seagrove and warning him at the same time to "use this young man well on my account & for the good of every friend to our country." He was "a bold resolute young man & of great sway."[93]

Tragically, David Cornells never made it to Seagrove. After visiting Cusseta he departed for Coleraine, the American fortification on the St. Mary's River where Seagrove spent much of his time. That took him through an unfriendly Georgia backcountry, however, and he was bushwhacked within miles of the post after local militiamen were tipped off to his approach. At full gallop the militia party rode up on him and a young boy riding with him, shooting him off his horse while he was holding his hat in his hand and screaming that he was a friend and an American ally. The posse then took its time, dismounting and surrounding Cornells to execute him as he lay wounded in the road. It was a killing that horrified Seagrove and several other government officials almost beyond words. Indeed, with his murder, Barnard lamented, "I fear the prospect of a peace is at an end."[94] The young man's killing, done in such a heinous way and at such a moment of hope, generated a fresh air of crisis that Barnard was sure would turn violent. Surprisingly it did not; instead it provided the means for a compromise between American and Creek parties that not only cemented Seagrove's authority in the region but further honed a Creek leadership group's unified political voice.

When he caught word of David's murder Seagrove retreated from the aggressive approach he had taken after Trader's Hill almost instantaneously. In a stark reversal of position he was now the one pleading with Creek headmen, begging them not to let anything rash take place until he had a chance to make things right. "I have only to say, my friend," he penned Alexander Cornells, "for you and the other relations and friends of the deceased," that full satisfaction would be made. He hoped that he, "the Mad Dog, White Lieutenant, your uncle Joseph Cornell, and all others concerned, [would] not . . . alter their good opinion of us, on account of this accident, or . . . take any hasty measures in consequence, as it is my determination to satisfy you fully on this business."[95] Headmen did hold off, which was a difficult-enough show of moderation considering how well-liked and deeply connected Cornells was in the Upper Country. More important, though, the killing forced Seagrove to admit that he needed to get into Creek Country as soon as possible. Very quickly he sent the White Lieutenant tentative plans to do so, asking him to have "as many of my friends as see fit" on hand to meet him at the Okmulgee River as the means to guide him into the region. He would head first to Cusseta, then to Tuckabatchee. Alexander Cornells, the Mad Dog, and Charles Weatherford were soon informed as well.[96] He was particularly candid with Cornells, declaring that if he could spirit him safely to Tuckabatchee, or another town of similar importance, "I doubt not, we can settle all affairs on a firm footing."[97]

For Seagrove's conciliatory journey to succeed he had to overcome the damage done and distrust generated over the previous few years, all of which was considerable. Simmering unhappiness in Creek Country about the Treaty of New York, scheming Spaniards and circulating Bowles talks, murdered Creek hunters and traders, and now a murdered young Creek leader had both Creeks and Georgians demanding satisfaction from each other in waves of insults that rippled across the frontier. Creeks might be talking in a common voice but their actions were far from decisive, and Georgia state officials would never give up one of their own to suffer for the death of a Creek. Cornells's death certainly marked a nadir of sorts along the Creek-Georgia frontier. Yet however tragic it was, the crisis offered Seagrove a unique opportunity to deal with the most contentious of the demands facing Creeks at least: justice for the Trader's Hill dead. Before Cornells's death Seagrove had largely been dictating the terms of peace, which Creeks were largely unable to fulfill. After David's killing, however, Creeks were on a much more level footing. Headmen, led no doubt by the powerful Alexander Cornells, were certain to demand satisfaction for the assassination of a powerful man, not to mention the young boy who was killed with him, who was also kin. That provided

Seagrove the opportunity essentially to trade lives.[98] "The plan I have all along proposed since this affair took place," he explained to Knox, "was by way of discount." Captain Flemming, who was killed at Trader's Hill, "was a valuable man," valuable enough perhaps to trade for Cornells. The other man killed at the store, Moffitt, would have his life traded for the boy, who was Cornells's cousin.[99] The deal might be a long shot but it was worth the attempt, and it might go a long way in smoothing over tensions on both sides of the frontier. With plans for a compromise in his hands, Seagrove continued organizing a trip that promised to reinvigorate the American partisan base and support the developing Creek nationalism.

Timothy Barnard, who was already preparing for Seagrove's arrival, had encouraging words. He reported from the Flint River that local communities seemed "more inclinable for peace than they have been this summer past," which was as surprising as it was positive. Not only did Cowetas and Ooseoochees promise not to commit any hostilities, there were even reports that they, along with the Chehaws, were actually anxious to see Seagrove. Repeated threats by Cusseta and Upper Country headmen seemed to be wearing on them; perhaps they hoped that Seagrove's visit might smooth things out with their neighbors and even prevent a few of them from being killed. Barnard also traveled through Cusseta and spoke with the Warrior King, who was "very attentive in striving to reconcile matters" and was doing an excellent job. Barnard sent him north to the White Lieutenant to get things prepared for Seagrove's arrival there, and he also gave a favorable outlook of the Upper Country. There was "a greater prospect" of peace there than "has been for some time past."[100]

As the time approached for Seagrove to set off in the fall of 1793, the atmosphere continued to improve. Along with the Warrior King of Cusseta, the White Lieutenant, and "several more of the heads" of Creek Country, by the end of October there were reports that upwards of one hundred Creeks would be waiting for him on the Okmulgee River. Creek Country was for peace, Seagrove declared to Knox, "and would conclude it with me, could I be amongst them."[101] That finally happened early in November when Seagrove, escorted by a handful of militiamen on federal service and led personally by Colonel Henry Gaither, reached the shores of the Okmulgee. There he met one hundred thirty chiefs and warriors, all of whom greeted him enthusiastically. Trading the militia for the Creek entourage Seagrove continued west and, moving slowly, arrived at Cusseta a week later. There he arrived to the sound of salutes and drums in a procession not seen probably in decades, and he was "received in great form by all the chiefs and people of the town, in the public square, as the Agent of the United States." Runners fanned out to the Lower Country to publicize his arrival and to announce plans for a general conference in Tuckabatchee. After a short stay he and an entourage of Cusseta chiefs began moving in that direction, "it being the place fixed on to settle the business of the nation." In another week they had arrived.[102]

Once at Tuckabatchee Seagrove "proceeded to business," kicking off one of the largest councils probably ever to be assembled there. Although "standing on dangerous ground, and surrounded by numerous enemies, both red and white," including Oliver, Seagrove would later declare proudly that he did his duty. Speaking "in plain and decided terms," he laid out past transgressions, demanded justice for the injuries done, and spoke hopefully for the future. For two days councils deliberated, and when headmen finally produced a unified talk, it was a strong and encouraging one. It was "unanimously determined on, that all acts of hostilities or depredations should, from that moment, cease between the United States and the Creek nations." Headmen from across Creek Country again agreed, this time in Seagrove's presence, to return as many prisoners and slaves, and as much livestock and other property, as possible. From what they also determined to do, it seems as though Seagrove's life-for-life trade went over well. Headmen agreed to execute "two or more of the principals" in the Trader's Hill killings rather than the handful Seagrove had demanded previously. And for his part, Seagrove solemnly promised to do everything in his power to "bring to punishment the murderer or murderers" of Cornells. He relayed that directly to Knox, hoping as secretary of war he could perhaps force state authorities to do something about "the perpetrators of that horrid deed."[103] Realistically, neither of those things would probably happen. There was absolutely no chance Georgia state authorities would try militiamen for the murder of Creeks, and there was little chance any Creeks would die either. Seagrove's agreement, amounting to a life-for-life forgiveness, was the best pragmatic solution available to both Americans and Creeks, and based on the reports from Tuckabatchee, it was a success.

Seagrove's visit extended for quite a while after the close of the conference. Although he stayed to polish the details of the agreement, he spent much more time building his relationships with the White Lieutenant, the Mad Dog, and even the Hallowing King of Coweta, who also stayed with him.[104] The White Lieutenant, by that point, was as close a friend any American would have in Creek Country. At one point during the council, for instance, the Tallassee King arrived, and he was clearly there to cause trouble. Having evidently been turned by the Spanish and Shawnee talks into an inveterate American enemy, he had "meditated my destruction," Seagrove would later explain. Assassins came for him one night and Seagrove only escaped because of the White Lieutenant's intervention. After having handfuls of his people killed and taken prisoner by Georgians, and "his son and three of his family killed by the Cumberland people, yet this was the man to step forward to save my life." It was a moment of bravery and friendship that Seagrove would not soon forget. Altogether, the chief was "a virtuous, good man, and his friendship to our country is not equaled by any in this land." Again, Seagrove concluded, "I shall not lose sight of such a friend to my country."[105]

When Seagrove finally left, months later, he was escorted back east by the Big King of the Cussetas and forty other chiefs and warriors, representatives of a Creek Country more unified than it had been in quite some time. But they did not stop to deliver Seagrove to safety, and instead the whole group continued to pay the state of Georgia a formal, almost state-like visit. Seagrove had forwarded accounts of the conference to legislators in Augusta, expecting and even threatening them to abide by its terms.[106] Soon, the White Bird-Tail King and the Big King of Cusseta, the Tuckabatchee King, a head warrior of the Big Tallassees, and several others, "all influential men," traveled with Seagrove to the state capital, determined to "brighten the chain of friendship with the Governor." They did not go representing their individual communities but all Creeks, punctuating the transformation in Creek politics that had been creeping through the region in the wake of Trader's Hill. In Augusta the headmen met George Mathews, who had recently succeeded firebrand Edward Telfair as governor, further brightening the prospects for peace. He "received the Indians chiefs with kindness; and I believe was fully satisfied, from what they informed him, of their ardent wish to live in peace with this country."[107]

As a delegation met with lawmakers in Augusta, other Creek leaders did what they could to implement the Tuckabatchee accord. Cusseta and Coweta headmen promised the Mad Dog, Alexander Cornells, and others further to the north that they would continue returning to Georgia property held by Yuchis and Ooseoochees, further to the south. The Big King and Dog Warrior from Cusseta were already moving south, and "if they will not give them up we are determined to take them & send them to their owners." According to the Cusseta King, both the Mad Dog and Cornells had already visited those towns personally. In a surprising show of authority, Cussetas and Cowetas turned around to press the same demands on the Upper Country. They singled out Aubecoochees; they "& other towns on that river for they are so far off that they think themselves out of danger but that is not the case with us." They requested that an Oakfuskee headman deliver strongly worded talks in that direction and get all prisoners and stolen property returned as soon as possible. "Let no time be lost for it requires the exertion of all good men to prevent trouble from coming on their Nation," they declared.[108] If leaders from the north were making demands, then Cowetas and Cussetas could as well.

Seagrove's visit to Creek Country, it appeared, exceeded all expectations. Although Creeks' success in enforcing their earliest demands— either from Cusseta or from Tuckabatchee—was limited, the sense of political collectivity achieved by the end of Seagrove's visit nonetheless punctuated a powerful transitional moment in Creek politics. The evolving leadership group had turned a corner in 1794, working to legitimize a very nascent sense of political nationalism that was just beginning to pull the region closer together. The Tuckabatchee conference and the follow-up Augusta visit promised both to sweep aside the violence that had plagued the frontier for the previous decade and to lay down the foundation for a more stable future—one based on a vision of Creek Country that downplayed local politics in favor of a unified Creek voice.

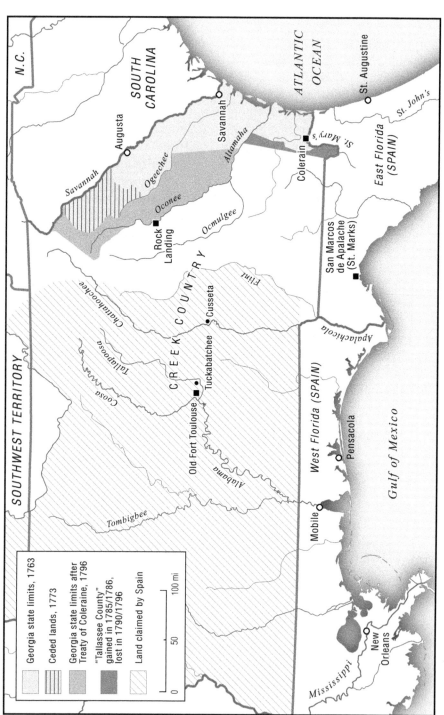

MAP 2. The Creek-Georgia Frontier to 1796. Map by Erin Greb Cartography.

7 / The Ascendancy of the National Council

The guilty must be punished, that honest men may not be afraid to show their faces.
—Benjamin Hawkins, July 13, 1797

From the Tuckabatchee conference in 1794 through the turn of the century a growing and evolving Creek leadership group developed upon a nascent regional sense of collective Creek identity, consistent with nationalism, and began enforcing regional laws. Early efforts to find a common voice immediately after the Trader's Hill crisis were important, but they were also largely rhetorical, and at best only partially successful. After the Tuckabatchee council in 1794 and particularly after the Treaty of Coleraine in 1796, however, headmen began making more material changes to Creek political traditions. Many of those changes were in response to new sources of confrontation with local Georgians, which continued to pressure headmen to alter traditional interpretations of governance and justice in order to maintain regional stability. Creeks responded by adopting several institutions consistent with an administrative state. They created laws to punish horse thieves and other mischief-makers, and did so in ways that directly challenged generations of Creek traditions.

Many of the changes to Creek governing traditions were a result of the creation of the National Council, a centralized body that consolidated jurisdiction in the hands of a new administrative and coercive entity. By creating such a governing body Creeks took political control away from local leaders and kinship groups and placed it in a single, central authority. They assigned new responsibilities for headmen and warriors, lessening community and clan influence over law. The council met regularly, debating policies, creating laws, and meting out punishments, all in a single Creek voice. By doing so, Creeks blended their traditional concepts of justice and governance with Euro-American ones consistent with state formation, all in an effort to mitigate the day-to-day sources of violence between Creeks and American settlers. What they achieved, in the end, was a uniquely Creek administrative entity that many hoped would make the Creek-Georgia frontier a safer place, and make Creeks good neighbors as far as Americans were concerned. By the turn of the century it was beginning to take shape.

With a Creek leadership group working with Seagrove and tempering the frontier, federal authorities looked to a more permanent solution to the Creek-Georgia situation. They returned to the Treaty of New York.[1] The time for having it legitimated certainly was right. Spanish diplomats were more concerned with European affairs than American ones, and American commissioners were already negotiating in Spain for access to the Mississippi River. The success of those negotiations soon made their way across the Atlantic, forcing Carondelet and the other Spanish governors to soften what had been a very aggressive tone. Soon American and Spanish diplomats concluded the Treaty of San Lorenzo, also known as Pinckney's Treaty. In it Spaniards relinquished their claim to the southern part of modern-day interior Georgia, which at the time meant resigning most of Creek Country outside of Florida to American influence.[2]

While the Treaty of New York was a landmark achievement for the federal government at the time, it had also certainly been a failure. Alexander McGillivray, its chief architect, died in disgrace, and its terms were being ignored equally by Creeks and Georgia state authorities, both of whom hated it equally. Nevertheless, both the George Washington and the John Adams administrations, led by Secretaries of War Timothy Pickering and James McHenry, still believed that the treaty was their best way forward. It was still a decent compromise, and Seagrove's peace initiatives had provided the best opportunity yet to get it legitimated. To do that, Seagrove and his superiors suggested a treaty be held at Coleraine in June 1796 in the hopes of reconciling everyone's disagreements.[3]

Seagrove enjoyed tremendous respect in Creek Country after Tuckabatchee, and inviting headmen to meet with American authorities was not a difficult task. In a break from previous treaty attempts, including at New York, he rightly understood that getting a comprehensive representation of Creek Country at Coleraine was crucial to its success, and he spared no effort bringing as many headmen as possible to the treaty site.[4] Secretary of War James McHenry appointed Benjamin Hawkins, George Clymer, and Andrew Pickens as commissioners to represent the American government, and the trio was soon on its way to the federal garrison at Coleraine. James Hendricks, James Jackson, and James Simms were appointed by the Georgia legislature to attend as well.[5] Only after repeated promises that the Creek delegation would be protected from locals (which created quite a response from the Georgian commissioners) did Creek representatives begin to arrive in early June.[6] Negotiations began two weeks later, and in addition to the six commissioners, Seagrove was present as Superintendent of Indian Affairs for the United States, and Colonel Gaither and the officers of the garrison at Coleraine sat in as witnesses. Across from the council square sat twenty-two "kings," seventy-five principal chiefs, and one hundred fifty warriors, with the White Bird-Tail King of Cusseta as the appointed chief speaker.[7]

The enormous Creek delegation, composing headmen from every significant community in Creek Country, was an indication that Creek political power was nowhere near being consolidated into the hands of a few regional leaders. Such a turnout would still be necessary to see that the Treaty of New York got reauthorized—something neither McGillivray nor Knox had considered particularly important in the past. But it was also evidence that much of Creek Country was at least now on the same page politically, and familiar voices were strong. And when the council began familiar headmen, including the White Bird-Tail King and the Hallowing King, led it with resolution, leaving little doubt that Creek collectivity was strong. Creek speakers did not hesitate to confront and even belittle the state commission during the negotiations, showing a confidence that was surprisingly aggressive at times. When the Georgia negotiators began to dwell on the legitimacy of their older state treaties, members of the Creek delegation began interrupting and even mocking them.[8] The state delegation was clearly still committed to the three treaties even though no one else was. Even the federal commissioners admitted they were at best illegitimate and at worst fraudulent, and at any rate had not been taken seriously.[9] The headmen rebuffed Georgians' claims to land, particularly when Hawkins clarified the American position to their advantage. "The people of Georgia cannot take your lands from you," he assured them in open discussion. "They are guaranteed to you by the treaty of New York." Georgians were only there to buy land, he insisted, and not to take it, and if Creeks were willing to sell them some, "they will bargain you for it." The delegation, led again by the White Bird-Tail King, made quick work of that proposal. They had already decided on the land issue several times before and nothing had changed. "If Georgia has any other business to introduce, let them mention it." Otherwise, "if we were to talk again, it would only be the same thing over again," and "any proposition on the subject of land, will meet the same answer." It was time to move on, he concluded.[10]

The Creek delegation grew bolder yet, making claims of their own that the New York treaty had been concluded unfairly and that McGillivray had duped them. While Hawkins was supportive when the Creek delegation challenged the state commission he soon clarified his position on New York, standing firmly against these new allegations. He was authorized only to legitimize the Treaty of New York, not to renegotiate it. Although headmen argued aggressively to have the boundary line altered to gain back more hunting grounds, Hawkins refused. Although those exchanges threatened to become disruptive, in the end the delegation, persuaded by Alexander Cornells, relented. Soon waves of headmen made their mark on the treaty, totaling well over one hundred. Representation from the Lower Country was particularly striking, with Broken Arrows, Hitchitis, Yuchis, Ooseoochees, Okmulgees, Lower Eufalas, and Chehaws signing the treaty in addition to dozens of Cussetas and Cowetas.[11] A new boundary line, moving west and northwest along the Altamaha and Oconee rivers, would separate Creek Country from Georgia. Important provisions would "show the watchfulness of the Government of the United States, to protect the red people in their rights." A federal trading house would guarantee Creek hunters fair prices for their skins, and installations manned by federal troops, posted along the Creek side of the Oconee River, would safeguard their territorial rights.[12] Although Coleraine did not achieve for Creeks everything they had probably hoped for they accepted it, and the feeling was that it would be implemented.

Benjamin Hawkins, who acquitted himself professionally at Coleraine, soon replaced James Seagrove as federal agent for the entire Southeast. By late 1796 he was already traveling through the region and, for the most part, Creek communities welcomed him. Most of them certainly looked at Coleraine as a compact that continued Seagrove's work, benefiting them with long-term security and a bulwark against local aggression. Peace, Hawkins later acknowledged, "can readily be accounted for arising out of the confidence they have in the justice of the U.S."[13] "We have had serious apprehensions for our safety," the Tussekiah Mico of Cusseta explained to him, but now, "I rely entirely on the assurances given by you, that we may remain at home, and be under the protection of the United States."[14] The chief's level of trust was not unordinary. "As soon as I can converse with them," Hawkins had written earlier, "they execute any order I give them with eagerness."[15] Soon he lauded the Creek-American friendship, whether from the Upper or Lower Country, as "almost universal."[16]

There was plenty in that first tour to make Hawkins pleased, but as a whole the Creek-Georgia frontier remained an extremely unstable and potentially violent place. Peace was a recent development and tremendous resentment still existed along the length of the backcountry. The threat of reciprocal violence loomed constant, threatening at any moment to upset the fragile calm that Coleraine had so recently established.[17] Settlers pushed west immediately after word of the treaty, and they populated the frontier at a brisk rate. Despite a theoretical hardening of boundaries and trade regulations and the establishment of new federal army posts, the new border in reality was almost useless. To the north the boundary coursed along small creeks and was observable by marked, burned, or felled trees. That stopped no one. Even further south the Oconee River, thought to be an obvious natural boundary, turned out to be quite crossable; both Creek hunters and Georgia settlers passed over it to hunt, range stock, and trade, and they did so it seemed with regularity. Almost all of this, unregulated, was illegal to begin with as far as American authorities were concerned. Understanding that the free intercourse of Natives and locals meant trouble more often than not, federal legislators passed regulations in 1790, 1793, and 1796 that were designed to control all manner of interaction between the groups, if not forbid it altogether.[18] Yet the borders were extensive and federal authorities few, making the intercourse laws almost impossible to enforce. With farms edging ever closer to Creek hunting grounds and cattle found further onto them, thefts, raids, and even an occasional murder marred the peace.

Beginning with Knox's assumptions and at least on paper, the treaty system and the intercourse laws accepted a modicum of Creek sovereignty. All of that had been developed at the Treaty of New York and it seemed legitimated at Coleraine.[19] But that only generated new legal issues and jurisdictional paradox. By the terms of New York and Coleraine, for instance, Creeks did not entirely control their own territory. They were bound to deliver up perpetrators of crimes against Creeks to state or federal jurisdiction in order to be tried as if they had committed the same crime within the United States. But the very foundation of Creek sovereignty meant that, theoretically, crimes committed on settlers by Creeks existed out of state jurisdiction, falling instead under the purview of federal agents. Indeed, by separate articles of the same treaties Creeks were also free to deal with squatters and other lawbreakers as they saw fit.

What did those sorts of inconsistencies mean for the region? The regulations directing Seagrove, Gaither, and then Hawkins were vague, if there were any at all. How would American—let alone Georgia— authorities hold Creek hunters liable for the crimes they committed? How would they deal with Georgians' demands for justice or their claims for recompense? Of course Hawkins could demand that a stolen horse be returned or a Creek murderer delivered up to face justice in a state court, but what happened when Creeks either refused to do so, or admitted that they could not, or, worse yet, had the kin of the perpetrator killed according to Creek custom? And what would be done about burned or destroyed property, or horses that could not be returned, or anything else lost to a Georgia citizen that could not or would not be restored? Locals had two options: complain to Hawkins or use force. Federal authorities were not interested in the use of force and states, confined by the constitution, could not act militarily against a people recognized by the federal government as sovereign, at least not except in the most extreme of circumstances. Benjamin Hawkins, in short, became a very important man.

These questions of course addressed only half of the sources of friction and violence that plagued Creek-Georgia relations. How would Georgians be held accountable for violent acts committed against Creeks, who now existed beyond their jurisdiction? There was little doubt that Georgia citizens were the source of tremendous violence in the region, but the American legal system was not designed to deal with sovereign neighbors who were, as far as the courts were concerned, noncitizens. How would a trial for theft or murder even function if noncitizen Creek accusers could not testify against a Georgia citizen accused of the crime? These questions, unfortunately, would go largely unanswered, which all but guaranteed that Creeks would respond violently, sooner or later, when they saw that the legal system Hawkins insisted they borrow from their neighbors never worked for them. But then again, that was not Hawkins's problem. His mandate was to whip into shape his "red charges," and he began by demanding that the Creek leadership work internally to provide the state of Georgia justice, when it was required, on terms Georgians could understand.

There was already limited evidence to suggest that headmen were beginning to do that, particularly after Tuckabatchee. Both Alexander

Cornells and the Mad Dog promised Barnard in the wake of the conference that he "may be certain no time will be lost in collecting the Prisoners agreeable to our resolution at the meeting."[20] The Mad Dog personally oversaw much of that process, assuring Governor George Mathews that he was "very intent on performing his promises." When he later arrived at Cusseta he collected headmen together and declared that they had a month to do what they could. He expected heavy resistance, particularly in Chehaw, yet he declared that if they did not give up the property fairly, "they shall by foul." Groups of Cussetas were reportedly ready to make good on that threat and seize the slaves held there by force, but the Mad Dog requested they not act until he returned. To Barnard this manifested that "the heads of the nation will, and are determined to do something more than has ever been done yet, to try to save their land."[21] That was comforting to newly appointed secretary of war Timothy Pickering. The Creek leadership was "determined to try their strength in the nation, to crush the plunderers and murderers, and to return the property from this country."[22]

Headmen also acted in a more resolute fashion against the wayward among them. The actions of the Tallassee King, for example, remained an issue. He had raided considerably since Trader's Hill, threatened Seagrove's life at Tuckabatchee, and continued to cause trouble even as the majority of Creeks began warming up to their American neighbors. Shortly after the conference he was still "determined for war," and many of his men "meant to make a stroke somewhere on the frontier." Quickest to react were Cussetas, who moved immediately to cut him off; they succeeded, turning the war party back before they had done damage. Later the Cusseta King and the Big Warrior of Cusseta, along with the Hallowing King of Coweta, were all on their way to north to "persuade the Tallassees to desist from their hostile intentions," and both Alexander Cornells and the Mad Dog assured Barnard that they would succeed as well.[23] In the months after Tuckabatchee it was clear that the emerging Creek leadership group, which pretty evenly represented both the Upper and Lower countries, was committed to fulfilling its promises. In those several instances, at least when it came to acting preventively, they were succeeding, keeping wayward Creeks from committing any more acts of violence.

Moments like those must have pleased Hawkins. What headmen had a more difficult time doing, however, was atoning for the offenses that had placed their communities in jeopardy in the first place. Some of those offenses were more prevalent than others, but the most pervasive by far was horse theft. It had long been an issue in the region, but during the tumultuous years of the early 1790s it had been pushed aside by more immediate troubles. After Coleraine, however, theft slowly reemerged as an issue, and at the rate Georgians complained of it, it was apparently a serious one. Creek hunters were constantly stealing settlers' horses. Georgia state authorities in turn counted up their lost property with impressive fastidiousness and turned to demand satisfaction from federal representatives.[24] As agents of the federal government assumed more control over the day-to-day affairs of the Creek-Georgia frontier, those accounts grew long, emerging as a problem Creek headmen would have to address; Creeks could not continue to accumulate such charges against Georgians without cost.

Years before Hawkins even arrived in Creek Country, in fact, American representatives were already warning Creek headmen that their actions would have consequences, even though it was unclear what those would be. Shortly after a young Creek man was killed by a settler in retaliation for a theft, for example, Henry Knox wrote McGillivray directly and rationalized the killing by explaining that "an act so atrocious merits high and prompt punishment, when committed by one white upon another." The Creek who was killed, therefore, "must be considered as bringing his own punishment upon himself." It was "of the utmost consequence," Knox declared, "that so nefarious a practice should be discountenanced by all the well-disposed part of the Creeks."[25] In the years that followed, however, claims continued to mount. Late in 1795 horses were going missing from farms on the St. Mary's River even in the shadow of the garrison at Coleraine, and even from the soldiers themselves.[26] The situation, by then, was out of control.

Seagrove tried to address the issue but had little success. He made his disappointment known when warriors brought stolen horses into Coweta, and although the headmen clearly disapproved, they were not doing anything about it. He expected that the young men would make foolish moves, Seagrove complained, but he also expected that the Coweta chiefs would have turned the pilfered property over immediately and would "have punished the thieves agreeable to your own laws." Yet the headmen were doing nothing, leading Seagrove to declare that if they did not bring a halt to the thefts, there would be a day of reckoning. "If you suffer a set of villains among you to steal horses," he warned, "and other property from this country, and will not exert yourselves in making severe examples, you cannot long expect to live in peace." State authorities surely would not sit idly by and "patiently suffer your people to rob them." Again he invoked good neighborhood, warning "as a friend, to put a stop to such doings, or you will bring ruin on your land." If they could not ensure stability then all Creeks would suffer, and he would be able to do little in their defense. "I have so often told you of these things, that I fear from your neglect of my advice, that you are not sensible of the dangerous ground you stand on; and that you will sit still, and allow the vitious men among you to go on from one bad act to another, until they bring the resentment, not only of the people of Georgia, but of the Government of the United States on you."[27] Headmen had stepped up after the Trader's Hill crisis to rein in the unruliest of their young men and stabilize the region. They needed to continue to do so, Seagrove warned, or peace would not last long.

The problem with horse theft was its complexity. Much of the problem, in fact, originated with unscrupulous traders. A young Creek man in the Lower Country had to look no further than Kinnard to see that much. Many traders, Hawkins complained, "were more depraved than the savages," had "all their vices without one of their virtues," and had "reduced the stealing of horses to a system." They encouraged Creek hunters to bring them horses regardless of how they came about them and quickly bought them up or exchanged them for trade goods. Just as quickly they swept the horses out of the region and south into Spanish Florida, as Kinnard had been seen doing, or north toward the Cumberland, or simply far enough away to ensure that a potential buyer either did not recognize the property or did not care, and then resold them at a handsome profit. And the profit could be quite handsome indeed, for all parties involved. A stolen horse could fetch a struggling Creek hunter the worth of dozens of deerskins. That was the equivalent of potentially months away from home at a time when deer were making themselves increasingly scarce. To a growing number of desperately indebted hunters, even the theft of a low-quality horse, taken directly off a settler's farm, was increasingly worth the risk. It was an evil rooted so deeply that Hawkins, shortly after his arrival in the region, admitted that he was unsure how he would be able to put an end to it.[28]

Regardless of how easily any number of traders could be tried and convicted in American courts for clear violations of the intercourse acts, it was usually Creeks doing the robbing, and it was almost always Georgians who were getting robbed. The complexities of the black market meant little to state authorities, who would do little to convict citizens of swindling savages. Evidently, they also meant little to Hawkins. Almost as soon as he and his assistants replaced Seagrove Hawkins picked up where his predecessor left off, warning headmen that if they did not put a stop to the practice it would bear disastrous consequences for all Creeks. That extended to Richard Thomas, one of Hawkins's aides, who preceded him into the Lower Country and was immediately distressed by claims for stolen horses. He had some of his own disappear as well. Faced with reports of theft that seemed to arrive constantly, Thomas began to word his caution to nearby communities in more aggressive terms. A group of hunters from the Lower Country had just stolen four horses from Georgia settlements in 1796, for example, and by the time Thomas caught wind of it they were already long gone. When he heard that more Cowetas were out "looking for a few more," he warned their headmen not to be surprised when a mounted militia unit from Georgia "should pay them a visit."[29] Thomas, like others, knew that a long list of stolen horses was being collected and that Creeks would have to pay somehow—in money, land, or blood.[30]

Facing such early waves of criticism, headmen were quick to assure their federal friends that the situation was in fact under control, and if anyone returned from their winter hunts with horses—when a theft was most likely to occur—they could "rely on their efforts to restore them immediately."[31] And there were scattered cases where they succeeded, particularly from Cussetas. They brought in stolen horses most frequently and could be depended on to hunt them down and take them from just about anyone. In April 1797 they delivered up to American authorities a group of eighteen that had recently been taken from the Cumberland, far to the north. Catching them as they were being secreted south, probably to Spanish Florida, that seizure had Timothy Barnard confident, a bit overconfident perhaps, that Cussetas could get "every Georgia horse delivered up in four or five days."[32] Barnard himself collected up when he could. The Little Prince of Broken Arrow, along with the Hallowing King and Tuskenhau Chapco of Coweta, returned a few but with "great difficulty & some expense." Later, when a group of Yuchis were out to steal more, it was the Cusseta King who "promised to take the horses away if they should bring any in." And when Ooseoochees stole five horses, Coweta warriors seized them and delivered them back to Georgians. Yet later that year it was Hopoie Haujo of Ooseoochee who, Barnard explained, "has always been a persevearing man to collect property" belonging to Georgians.[33] The same communities that were the first to steal under some circumstances, it seemed, could also be the first to return the same kinds of property. Horse theft was indeed complicated, and only a regional approach would succeed in bringing it to a halt.

There is some indication that headmen were adopting an authoritative approach to theft, as they had toward preventing violence, even before the outside pressure by men like Seagrove or Hawkins became uncomfortable. In 1792 Kinnard assured Americans that his friends in the southern part of the Lower Country, even in the Chehaw towns, were not horse thieves, "nor will they suffer them to do it," suggesting that they too might make an example of the thieves in a way that would please Americans.[34] Years later a group of Coweta headmen, concerned about the involvement of their hunters in horse theft, "agreed that they should all of them be answerable for the conduct of their young men." That certainly continued after Hawkins's arrival. A handful of headmen from Coweta and neighboring communities addressed the new agent early in 1797 on the matter, declaring to him that "probably some of their young men" would bring in horses when they returned from their winter hunts but that they would do what they could to "restore them immediately." They had already returned six stolen horses, five of which Hawkins was able to return to their owners, "which has given entire satisfaction." In turn headmen increased their pressure on the wayward in their communities. Confronting one older man whom Benjamin Hawkins described as a "remarkable horse thief," an emissary from several Coweta chiefs chided and then threatened the man, while the Dog Warrior of Cusseta assisted in the return of the horses.[35] More regional action was taken later at a council in Tuckabatchee, where headmen "gave out strong talks to their young people, advising them to refrain from stealing and deliver up what horses they have lately brought in." Soon, Richard Thomas reported, groups from the Lower Country had delivered up a few and were trying to get the rest, and if Georgians did not harass any Creeks during the hunting season, "I am in hopes that horse stealing will cease." Not long after two more horses take from the Cumberland River area further to the north were returned as well.[36]

None of this was enough for Hawkins, though, who was quick to demand more substantive action, and the post-Coleraine peace provided him the opportunity to insist on change in an aggressive tone. The Creek leadership had to hold their hunters and their young men more accountable on a more organized and regional scale, and they needed to control them more vigorously in a preventive way. He "applied very gravely" to a group of chiefs from the Lower Country, for instance, "to inform me who governed in their land, they or their boys, that I might know where to address myself for a violation of a treaty." The situation in and around Coweta, he later complained to Alexander Cornells, was intolerable.

Complaints from settlers were flooding in, Creeks had no way to pay for the charges they were incurring, and "the whole nation ought to be under serious apprehensions for their future tranquility unless a stop can be put to such abominable proceedings on the part of their young men."[37]

No one understood and demanded the importance of good neighborhood, it turned out, more than Hawkins. Take more decisive action, he pressed the Dog Warrior, to "do more than they have hitherto done" and "prove to our white brethren that the promise of the Creeks may be relied on."[38] The inability to do that, he complained, was becoming insufferable. Headmen had promised repeatedly to provide Georgians not only with justice but with security along their border, and they were failing to deliver on the latter promise it seemed with each passing day. Headmen were quicker to blame white traders than their hunters and were slow to take a stand against either the thieves or the conditions that made theft easy. Indeed, although there were several instances in which headmen responded favorably, their efforts did little to solve the problem in any systemic way. And as much as the headmen's complaints about traders were correct, Georgia authorities were positively deaf to them. State officials summoned militia forces to attack Creeks, not patrol for illegal traders, and none of that boded well for regional stability. Even in 1798 the residents of Camden County, low on the frontier, felt themselves sufficiently "alarmed by the continual thefts committed among us by the Indians" to renew their requests for a militia station on the Satilla River.[39] A peaceful solution to horse theft was clearly not going to come from that side of the border, meaning Creeks would have to do everything and do it quickly if the Creek-Georgia frontier was not going descend once more to a place of retaliatory violence.

This was a heavy burden for Creeks to bear, but bear it they would. American authorities like Hawkins were not just ignoring half the problem, turning a blind eye to the almost organized crime–like disrespect for federal law that was being flaunted by state citizens. They charged that Creeks' inability to unilaterally solve all aspects of horse theft was symptomatic of an alien and deeply dysfunctional Creek culture of justice and governance that had to be torn down and rebuilt. Community leaders and kinship groups maintained jurisdiction over crimes, a foundation of Creek legal culture that Americans found tremendously irritating. Worse yet, Creek justice was meted out many times in retributive, kin-directed attacks that seemed far too arbitrary and frankly repulsive to Americans. The evolving Creek leadership core had made enticing promises to move away from those traditions and in the direction of a more authoritarian voice after Trader's Hill, but little of that was being felt along the frontier. Hawkins's charges were, despite his own shortsightedness, still at least partially accurate. Horse theft underscored headmen's inability to properly control their people in the eyes of their neighbors.

Accusations of murder brought similar criticism, and they demonstrated almost simultaneously how impossible American justice was for the Creek people to achieve, as well as how revolting Americans considered Creek justice. Cussetas and Cowetas, closest to the Georgia border and the communities most often in contact with state settlers, were often the ones to bear the responsibility of both Creek and state crimes. Within months of the conclusion of Coleraine, for example, a group of Creeks, and probably Cowetas, killed a man on the Oconee River in retaliation for the murder of two Cussetas by settlers more than three years previous. Cussetas had kept their neighbors at bay for years and turned back at least one previous party that was bent on taking satisfaction. Nevertheless, Cowetas were quite determined to apply that pillar of Creek justice, it appeared, and could not be put off forever. After Cusseta headmen interposed again the killers waited until nightfall and "kept no path till they got too far to be followed." Having thus evaded their neighbors, the Cowetas achieved their murderous objective. Even though the Cusseta headmen condemned the killing, "much disturbed at what has been done," they could not, in the end, prevent the kin of the slain from taking their revenge.[40] With American justice denied Creeks responded according to their own laws—one episode of many, unfortunately, that made both Americans and Creeks look bad.

As was the case with horse theft, there were a few isolated instances in the years before Coleraine when headmen considered satisfying Americans by challenging those traditions.[41] More often than not, though, Georgia settlers were the ones initiating violence by attacking Creek hunters, and their crimes regularly went ignored by state authorities, let alone unpunished. Georgia settlers were far from innocent, and Creek headmen were quick to protest that if their people were to deal with crime like Americans, then Americans had to lead by example. When attacks from the Upper Country during the Oconee War initiated a heavy-handed Georgia response that killed twelve Cusseta hunters, the headmen angrily responded by highlighting their willingness to respect American forms of justice—a willingness that did not appear reciprocal. "You always promised that the innocent should not suffer for the guilty," the Cussetas complained. That the innocent should not suffer for the guilty was a distinctly American approach to justice, not a Creek one, but the headmen were willing to entertain that approach if it kept the frontier peaceful, and they expected that Georgians would act sensibly as well. Others were responsible for the killings, and state authorities needed to respond in a measured way so, in the words of the Cussetas, their friends would not "kill us for what other bad people did."[42]

Years later, after Trader's Hill, the White Lieutenant found himself in a similar position. After one killing he also asserted that his people would be willing to deal with murderers in accordance with American law, but the headman reminded Seagrove that American justice had, to that point, been a one-way street. When settlers killed a Cusseta and wounded another, his people made it a point not to pursue retributive justice and gave state authorities plenty of time to sort things out. Satisfaction, however, "never was given by your people, nor taken by ours, till twelve moons after the crime was committed." A war party ended up dealing with the issue themselves, the White Lieutenant admitted, but only because state authorities had refused to do so. While the White Lieutenant regretted the slaying he, like Cussetas before him, also suggested that if Americans practiced what they preached, the incident could have been avoided. Instead of killing kin members, which headmen had done in the past, the White Lieutenant and his friends renewed their insistence to pursue Seagrove's American approach to justice. He understood "by your laws that the innocent cannot suffer for the guilty; therefore, as eldest brother, hope you will not so much unman yourselves, as to deviate from your own laws, and copy ours."[43]

Benjamin Harrison's actions demonstrated rather clearly how much those complaints were lost on American authorities, who refused to hold their citizens accountable for even the most heinous attacks on the Creek people. In 1797 a group of Yuchis attacked a settler family on the Oconee and brutally killed them, burning their house down and destroying their property. The attack was not random, even though the victims were. The killings were, instead, a calculated response to the massacre of roughly a dozen Yuchis perpetrated by notorious Creek-hating settler Benjamin Harrison on his farm on the Flint River, years earlier. Yuchi bodies were floating in the river for days.[44] Americans, led by both Seagrove and Hawkins, had attempted to temper the enraged kin of the deceased and they promised to have justice done on several occasions. By the summer of 1797, however, too many of the deceased's relations decided that they had waited long enough.[45] The killings were, in short, as straightforward and frankly predictable an act of retributive justice as would ever come from Creek Country, and the Yuchis made their actions known publicly. Nevertheless, the killings were terribly destabilizing, both in Creek Country and along the frontier. Several headmen in the Lower Country, led no doubt by the pacifistic Cussetas, attempted to dissuade the warriors from the deed or at least slow them down, and after the killings several of them promised Hawkins that they would have the murderers put to death. Yet they could do neither of those things. Not only could they not stop the attack, but afterward several headmen met at Coweta—a meeting Hawkins attended—where they tried to formulate a plan to gain satisfaction. Yuchis would have none of it. Not only would they not consent to any sort of satisfaction, they were "determined to act on the defensive if the Creeks should insist on their giving satisfaction." To them the killing of the settler family was perfectly justified and, considering how many Yuchis had been slaughtered by Harrison, an inadequate retaliation at that. They had no intention even of apologizing, let alone submitting themselves to be killed. If the Creek headmen meeting at Coweta would see justice done to the family of the slain, to Georgia authorities, or to Hawkins, they would have to take it by force against the Yuchis, and that was not something they were prepared to do.[46]

To Americans, however, the situation was the most insufferable example yet of everything that was wrong with Creek justice, and they demanded that something decisive had to be done to put an end to such arbitrary violence. It was far too soon after making peace at Coleraine to "have had our sensibility roused by so unjustifiable an outrage against any of my fellow citizens in Georgia," Hawkins complained, regardless of what had happened in the past.[47] The first attempts made by the Creek leadership to find an acceptable regional solution only demonstrated how alien Hawkins's demands were and how strongly bound even the most supportive headmen still considered themselves to older traditions of governance that they probably saw as more efficient than the traditions of their neighbors. In the case of the Yuchi killings, headmen suggested that they could kill the Indian who led the raid "and one of the women," presumably of the killers' kin group, which was perfectly acceptable according to Creek traditions of blood vengeance. In the meantime they appointed Tustunnuggee Emautlau of Tuckabatchee to hunt the primary Yuchi murderer down and dispatch him, which would have been a tremendous achievement had he succeeded. Instead, the Yuchi fled to friendly groups of Savannahs, or Shawnees in the north of

Creek Country, and Tustunnuggee Emautlau returned empty-handed.[48] Meanwhile the headmen's alternate plan, the arbitrary killing of a Creek woman, was obviously not anything Hawkins would accept, and so the headmen pressed on, trying to get a death that would defuse the situation. Ultimately that meant that the Yuchi killings went unresolved, demonstrating both sides of a tricky diplomatic situation. Yuchis were right not to put their faith in the American justice system. Harrison, it seems, was never even arrested. But the impasse provided another opportunity for settlers to complain and for legislators to press Hawkins for satisfaction. Regardless of Harrison's crimes, according to American legal customs Creeks were still in the wrong, and the charges against them were mounting.

The years after Coleraine, filled as they were with a steady stream of thefts and attacks and then punctuated by a handful of very high-profile killings, predictably put more pressure on Creeks than on their Georgia neighbors. Agents to Creek Country like Hawkins were not concerned with the actions of Georgia state citizens, who were not their responsibility. And ultimately, their criticisms generated an atmosphere of tension dire enough to force Creek communities not only to conceive of government differently but to begin acting differently. The threats from regional authorities, for instance, were relentless, both warning that Creeks could not go on indiscriminately murdering American citizens without consequence and continuing to demand good neighborhood. It was time "for the chiefs to seriously think on the situation of their nation," Thomas charged, "and to recollect the long account which was against them at Colerain."[49] After the retaliatory attack by the Cowetas in 1796, Timothy Barnard lamented that Creeks, "by such rash steps as those and by not fulfilling their promises to the officers of the U. States," would "gain the displeasure of the President," and if that happened, their "residence in this land will be but short." And after the Yuchi affair in 1797, Hawkins continued with more of the same. "It must not be concealed from them that they are in a delicate situation," he wrote. "The disposition of our government is friendly to them to a very high degree, they must show by their acts they are deserving of our friendly attention." Locals were infuriated by the killings and they were only being kept from exacting their revenge by federal troops.[50] To American agents, whether Georgians were culpable was irrelevant, and whether the killings were legitimized by Creek culture was infinitely more irrelevant: "The people who do such wicked things must be punished to prevent the whole nation from being charged with countenancing such doings." The family of the slain cried out for American, not Creek, justice, that "no innocent man must suffer say they;" the guilty must be punished, "that honest men may not be afraid to show their faces."[51]

Although Creeks would ultimately be the ones to change their political and cultural landscape, the train of insults and charges leveled by Hawkins, Barnard, and others demonstrated that they also did so under extreme outside pressure. Of course the American legal system championed by Hawkins and Thomas was systematically denying even the most basic level of justice to Creeks while, at the same time, its agents were demanding Creeks embrace that very same legal model. And that must have both perplexed and angered Creeks, who saw their own system of justice working just fine. Neither the Coweta nor the Yuchi attacks were exactly universally condemned in Creek Country; many headmen probably knew that they would never get justice from their Georgia neighbors, no matter how loudly they complained. But the arbitrary killing of an innocent settler would do little to conciliate anyone, Hawkins was quick to counter. Not only were those traditions wholly contrary to traditions of American justice, they were doing nothing to keep the region stable, convincing him that they had no future there. He was unyielding in his criticism of Creek revenge culture and of Creek governance in general, insisting time and again that regardless of the insults done them, Creeks had to project stability and justice to Americans, which they were failing to do in even the most basic ways. Hawkins, it turns out, was far less circumspect in his demands than was his predecessor, particularly when it came to good neighborhood. By the terms of Coleraine, now, Creeks were required to control the people in the sovereign territory they claimed as theirs and in a way their American neighbors could at least accept would keep them from getting robbed or killed. As Creeks responded to those demands, they began a process consistent in many ways with state formation and did so because they were forced to.

Hawkins insisted that Creeks pursue the administrative state structures consistent with—or at least recognizable as—contemporary Euro-American ones. The process of state formation that they initiated was a dramatic one. State formation, whether successful or not, reflected unique struggles, which differed from region to region and from people to people, and such was the case in Creek Country. Creek headmen were not terribly concerned with supplying a stable workforce, standardizing sanitation or education, or reinforcing racial or gender roles, which might have been important state functions in a more industrialized or urban population with more European traditions. Creeks were, on the other hand, like Americans, very interested in legitimacy and regional stability, and the easiest way forward was reforming the ambiguous and seemingly arbitrary structures of law and governance that had, to that point, been the pillars of Creek society. Rather than rely on leadership by consent, kinship groups, or retaliatory vengeance, Creek headmen needed to lead clearly, decisively, and, if necessary, violently. They alone would wield the power to make war and peace and to deal politically and diplomatically with their neighbors. But most importantly, they would be the keepers of law and order. Times of peace, Hawkins declared, should be kept peaceful through careful governance, and "the Chiefs would take measures to govern their nation; and to punish an unruly individual, who should violate a solemn treaty."[52] As he summed up later, "any man who acts contrary thereto must be taught to know he do's wrong." As Hawkins implied to Alexander Cornells, such authority was critical. When "the hatchet is buried," headmen needed "to punish any unruly individual who will lift it up against the voice of the nation." By doing that, it was hoped, the Creek people could be brought around to becoming tolerable neighbors. Such a step "appears to me indispensable," Hawkins earlier concluded to Secretary McHenry, "to enable the nation to fulfil its engagements with us."[53]

Just as Creeks responded to the Trader's Hill crisis in ways uniquely consistent with nationalism, Creek leaders began responding to Hawkins in several ways uniquely consistent with statehood. The pressure to do so was ethnocentric and at times extreme, perhaps, but it was pressure nonetheless, and it would be a stretch of the imagination to assume that Creeks would attempt to alter their political structures in such fundamental ways had it not been for Hawkins's withering criticism. But the charges for good neighborhood were real and so were the threats; the reality, indeed, was that after the Treaty of Coleraine, the conditions were right for a man like Hawkins to influence Creek politics in transformative ways. American power was growing, which gave Hawkins's voice authority, as problematic as his message may have been. Meanwhile Creek Country was, in the years after Coleraine, a well-defined place geographically that was understood by Americans— albeit hesitantly at times—to be sovereign. A collective Creek identity consistent with nationhood was maturing, and a leadership group was emerging that was projecting a unified political voice. That development, coming as it was in an atmosphere of increasing American demands, created the conditions both necessary and possible for a Creek nation-building project to enter a new phase.

As much as raiding and murdering were the sources of friction along the border, stemming the day-to-day problem of theft was what headmen, along with Hawkins, considered most important at that moment. Regulations designed to combat the scourge of theft were among the first changes to governing culture that headmen began to consider seriously. And even though they were not the most transformative, they were noteworthy nonetheless. The complicated web of horse thieves and traders was "the source of so much evil in this land," Hawkins feared, that either heavily regulating the legal horse market or shutting it down completely was the only solution.[54] Late in 1797 headmen from the Upper Country, working with Hawkins's suggestions, attempted the former. They worked to stem theft by better regulating all horse transactions—to control the interactions between Creek hunters and both settlers and traders in their everyday activities. This was precisely why the trade and intercourse laws were written, of course, but with state and federal authorities unwilling to enforce their own law, Creeks were forced to attempt the same approach. According to the proposed plan, Creek buyers had to obtain licenses or certificates for each horse they bought, sold, or traded, no matter how they came upon them. Each license had to be verified by some combination of regional authority figures on both sides of the frontier, including trustworthy headmen, Hawkins or some other state or federal authority, and the trader or seller. What they proposed represented a certification, as accurately as was possible, that the ownership of the horse was transferred consensually and legally. Such a certificate or license essentially had to stay with the horse, constituting an ownership history that would make the illegal transfer of one much more difficult. When headmen from the Upper Country proposed something along these lines Hawkins offered a more detailed plan, which they quickly embraced. For his part, not only did Hawkins pass his plans along to his assistants, including Barnard and Thomas, he involved the War Department's agent with the Cherokees, David Henley, and U.S. factor Edward Price at Coleraine as well. He also employed assistants along the northern frontiers and in the Cumberland region specifically to further thwart any illegal transactions. He even alerted Spanish authorities.[55] The regulations would forever be fatally flawed as long as they offered no remedy for the other half of the theft problem: Georgia state citizens. Nevertheless, the eager adoption of the plan by Creek community leaders was still good news; the Creek people were at least willing to try new things, even if their state counterparts were not.

An almost simultaneous and more significant decision provided the means for the more direct, day-to-day policing of Creek hunters. It enjoined upon community leaders—chiefs and warriors—the oversight of each of their young men during the hunting season. The winter and early spring months, when Creek men were scattered along the frontier and largely unaccounted for, were when most of the raids and thefts took place.[56] In December 1797, for instance, when the hunting season was in full effect, Hawkins estimated that upwards of one thousand hunters were along the frontiers. Many of them would be coming close to the Georgia boundary if not encountering Georgia settlers directly, and most of them would not have produced the amount of deerskins they would need to satisfy their creditors. These were the conditions that turned hunters into horse thieves.

Having trustworthy headmen around hunters at that critical period not only reduced the likelihood of an incident but made available men in authoritative positions who could address incidents quickly should they arise. To make that possible Hawkins suggested appointing "prudent chiefs" who would be "answerable for the conduct of the hunters."[57] The decision was an interesting elaboration on Creek governing traditions, making it a movement in the direction of an administrative state that did not necessarily represent a direct challenge to Creek culture. It did not force headmen to act too far outside of their traditional communities or positions of influence, in other words. To the contrary, it was a position leading warriors were already familiar with. It did, however, require them to assume much more responsibility over their young men. It also placed more coercive power in their hands, in order to compel those around them to act responsibly, and made them directly answerable for the actions of others. No longer would local headmen govern their townspeople by persuasion alone, this sort of change suggested. When their hunters were out for the winter it was the responsibility of the local leaders to control them and, if they slipped up, to hold them accountable.

By licensing horse deals and overseeing hunters, headmen were elaborating on long-standing cultural traditions of local jurisdiction and governance to control the day-to-day actions of their hunters in ways that focused on the prevention of future crime. These efforts demonstrated how the Creek state-building project did not necessarily have to rewrite Creek governance traditions altogether—many times they only modified them. These early steps, however, were also only the beginning. To American authorities no community-level, kin-directed, revenge-based, and ultimately arbitrary system of justice would make Creeks good neighbors. Creeks needed a strong, centralized, and coercive governing body that wielded jurisdictional authority over its entire people, which is what law looked like in the burgeoning states. For something similar the Creek people would need a codified and institutionalized rule of law, with specific punishments for specific crimes, and which only duly authorized agents of the Creek Nation could administer. The Creek people might have been toying with new structures of governance, but Americans wanted much more. They wanted a state structure that much more closely resembled their own.

Such a political transformation was guaranteed to bring deep-seated and conflict-ridden changes to Creek Country. What Americans wanted threatened to overturn generations of local jurisdiction of law and governance by consent, defy the authority of clans, and even upset the equilibrium in the Creek cosmos that was kept in careful balance by acts of retributive justice, to name only a few examples. Those would not be easy changes.[58] Nevertheless there is, again, some evidence that Creek leaders might already have been thinking in that direction, at least in the wake of Trader's Hill.[59] By 1797, with violence intensifying and with Hawkins demanding change practically at the top of his lungs, the pressure was evidently enough to force headmen into action. The maintenance of borders and the rule of law would not only mitigate sources of tension along the Creek-Georgia frontier, Americans like Hawkins believed, but would bring the Creek people into political modernity. The engine of that modernization would be the National Council, the political structure of the administrative Creek state.

Such a suggestion is certainly contentious; the Creek National Council has generated very little debate, and not much of that debate has focused on its successes. A larger and perhaps more successful administrative structure developed later, in Cherokee Country, in the nineteenth century. Benjamin Hawkins, once the Indian agent for Cherokees as well as Creeks, attempted to institute many of the same changes in both regions, such as setting up a centralized political structure and removing clan control over justice. Yet when his title was redefined as agent only to Creek Country, after 1797, the earliest Cherokee national councils as well as the laws they made quickly faded into obscurity. Only years later did the Cherokee National Council and National Committee emerge as effective political bodies, which not only reduced factionalism within a once fiercely independent people but claimed to control Cherokee lands, their systems of law and order, finances, and even education and literacy.[60]

On the other hand there was the Creek National Council. Although it developed a decade earlier it is far less understood, apart at least from charges that it neither claimed to do all of the same things as its

Cherokee counterpart nor was nearly as successful. According to some scholars it never really existed at all. To others it was little more than the short-lived and failed pipe dream of Hawkins—a plan to force a Euro-American system of justice onto uninterested Creek communities, aside from perhaps a few corrupt Creek leaders of mixed ancestry who represented the second coming of Alexander McGillivray. Not only did Hawkins originate much of the council, as opposed to the Creek people, he also imposed much of it on them. "The Indians of the Creek agency," Hawkins himself once explained to Congress, "have been prevailed on, by the agent, to conform, in a considerable degree, to his ideas on the subject."[61] And, predictably, his ideas did not work. In the end no Euro-American alternatives replaced or even challenged the traditions of retribution or reciprocity that continued to order Creek law. If a national body did appear at all it did so much later, during the removal period of the early nineteenth century, and even then, it could do nothing to halt the actual removal of the Creek people west.[62]

A closer inspection of both the form and function of the National Council, however, based on what both Creeks and Americans wanted from it, complicates that interpretation. The National Council was certainly influenced by Hawkins, but it was not nearly such a source of cultural destruction, conceived by an outsider to force American civilization down the throats of unwitting or unwilling Creeks. And it certainly was not nonexistent. In a most basic sense, in fact, the National Council existed not only because Creeks said and acted like it existed but because it was an actual physical entity, composed of Creeks, which did indeed meet regularly. But more important, Creek politics in the years following the Treaty of Coleraine were very different than Creek politics during and shortly after the Revolutionary War, and it was the existence and functioning of the National Council that was the source of that change. Not only was real progress made in laying the foundation of a National Council, in short, but as the primary administrative tool of control in the Creek Nation, there is plenty of evidence to suggest that it succeeded reasonably well as it was designed—it made Creeks decent neighbors. Although what Americans got from the National Council was not nearly perfect, it certainly did provide Georgians with the stability they were demanding.

Not enough extant information exists to define precisely what the National Council was during much of its existence—sometimes it was referred to as the Executive Council, for instance—and it is not always clear how many people constituted it, what its exact structure was, and so forth. That may make drawing a picture of the council difficult but far from impossible. Consider the ways the National Council fit into accepted definitions of an administrative state structure. As the means to impact the day-to-day lives of Creeks, the National Council would have claimed jurisdiction over Creek politics, its legal authority, and the usage of violence; all political decisions, all acts of control, and, ultimately, all legitimate acts of violence in Creek Country flowed from it.[63] Those aspects of the council certainly represented challenges to fundamental Creek cultural and political traditions. Yet the National Council was also a democratic structure that derived its authority from the Creek people. Although it met regularly it was not necessarily an open forum and at times could be extremely contentious, but it still had deep ties to the egalitarian council customs that stretched back well into the eighteenth century. Indeed, although the National Council was novel because of its more centralized and coercive approach to authority, which was adversative to Creek political culture, much of it would have been surprisingly familiar. By combining the form and function of smaller local and regional councils into one single national entity, with Hawkins's prodding of course, a nascent Creek leadership movement slowly evolved into the Creek National Council by developing upon many long-standing traditions while at the same time attempting to alter or even dismantle others.

Ultimately the development of the National Council was feasible because, through it, Creeks were able to mold the more foreign and controversial aspects of American justice to the more understood and acceptable avenues of Creek government. At the center of Creek politics had always been oratory and debate in the town's square ground. For as long as Europeans visited Creek Country they witnessed and recorded accounts of Creek councils and remarked on how integral a part those debates were in both local and regional politics. The presence of a specifically defined council ground, in fact, was a defining aspect of a Creek community. It marked the difference between a politically independent community, known as a *talwa*, and a community that was dependent on another, known as a *talofa*. A talwa had its own council ground, or square ground, making it a self-regulating political entity where headmen could deliberate among themselves or host outsiders for debate. A talofa did not have its own square ground, making it a political extension of a nearby talwa. For that reason council grounds were widespread throughout Creek Country in the eighteenth century, as well as into Florida.[64]

While there are only a few accounts of the National Council, there are several extant descriptions of square grounds and the proceedings of councils held on those grounds. They all suggest that councils throughout Creek Country were remarkably consistent not only from one community to the next but over time as well.[65] During McGillivray's life, a council at Coweta took place in an open, square area at the center of that principal town. Four sets of three cabins, with each set of cabins walled on three sides, were situated on each of the council square's four sides, with the open face of each of the cabins facing the center. Twelve cabins in total faced the center of the council area in a way that left openings at the corners through which people entered the square. David Taitt, traveling throughout Creek Country twenty years earlier, described the Tuckabatchee grounds similarly. There the square was formed by four large buildings, each open in front facing the grounds but split into three separate rooms with two rows of cane mats for seating.[66] That would be the same square ground Seagrove visited in 1794.

When American Caleb Swan visited a square ground in 1791 he included more detail on the particulars of the grounds and their surroundings, taking note of the places where the ceremonial black drink and "war physic" were prepared. He also described how clan emblems painted on a plank over the top of a cabin denoted where headmen sat, as well as the "heterogeneous collection of emblems and trophies of peace and war" that were suspended in each cabin. Those included deeply traditional tokens of peace, like eagle feathers and swan wings. There were plenty of symbols reflecting war as well, including scalping knives, war clubs, and even scalps. Square grounds in prominent red, or war towns, "which have always been governed by warriors," were termed "painted squares" and were literally painted red. Some of the council grounds were even covered, although he did not list which ones.[67] As the National Council took shape, much larger councils were held at Tuckabatchee, Coweta, and the Hickory Ground, but the layout of the ceremonial grounds stayed very much the same. When the council moved from Tuckabatchee to the Hickory Ground in the early nineteenth century, for instance, it was a meeting of staggering size, but the layout was identical to that of Coweta and Tuckabatchee. According to a Spanish visitor, the grounds had four oblong buildings in a square, with each building oriented toward "the cardinal points of the compass." They created the same square structure with the same corner entrances. Even the seating arrangements were the same. Each of the buildings had cane mats on the floor where chiefs and counselors sat "according to rank."[68]

Councils, when convened, reflected the noncoercive nature of Creek politics that irritated Americans so tremendously. By the time it was convened, a regional council would have been packed with scores of headmen—micos and their advisors and assistants, along with warriors of all ranks, then religious leaders and other ceremonial guides, all of whom had traditional seats. Several peace and purification rituals opened the deliberations, including smoking tobacco and drinking the black drink. Only then would leaders begin to debate the issues at hand. Once that began, debaters worked to reach consensus, not force decisive positions. They operated by oratory and persuasion, not by coercion, and decisions were made by conciliating political differences and finding common ground. In fact, as one anthropologist described, a "good man was a man who avoided conflict with his fellows." Although debates could at times get quite heated and confrontational, harmony was valued above all else; usually the councils avoided disagreement, contention, and disrespect. According to an onlooker at a Coweta council in the 1750s, the orator "persuades his audience into a belief of all that he says, by his eloquence, and the excellence of his discourse." The assembly was stoic; "you hear no prattling, no indecency, no ill-timed applause and no immoderate laughter there." Because of their plural nature the debates usually did not result in rash or overtly strong decisions, and once adjourned, community leaders never considered their decisions to be binding on the entire region.[69] To Americans that structure only proved that chiefs were evasive and stubborn and that the governing body was impotent.[70] Yet councils formed the foundation of a Creek political structure that reflected an inclusive, noncoercive leadership style. Though the form of those debates would stay largely the same into the nineteenth century, they would take on new meaning as headmen began enforcing their decisions with more rigidity under the auspices of the National Council.

Some aspects of the National Council stayed rooted in tradition, but others more directly altered long-standing political customs. Many early accounts of square grounds and councils, for instance, and even Swan's description in 1791, recognized the centrality of clans. Kinship groups sat in designated cabins, usually with clan symbols drawn on them, and only then were subdivided according to rank. The presence and location of clans within square grounds ranged widely from town to town, reflecting each town's clan composition. During the National Council era, however, there was much less mention of particular clans within the grounds or within the debate. Because the council took on a more regional and one could almost say secular function, delegates were civil authorities—micos or tustunnuggees—and only then perhaps members of particular kinship groups. From several accounts of National Council proceedings, the authority of clans had clearly been subordinated to community representation. Similarly, moieties seemed not to determine the position of a council. Although most councils were held at Tuckabatchee or the Hickory Ground, they were also held at Little Tallassee and Coweta. Those locations were not chosen because the region was either at war or peace but because they were the current communities of residence of the Speaker of the National Council. In those two cases, square grounds became the center of the Creek Nation rather arbitrarily, or at least not according to long-standing Creek customs of kinship domination or peace versus wartime diplomacy. The importance of the red-white divisions, along with the role of clans in the assembly, seemed to decline as the National Council replaced regional ones.

The meeting of the National Council, which was supposed to represent a more predictable government operation, was also scheduled more recurrently than its more local predecessors. Soon after Hawkins's arrival the body met every year at least once, usually in the spring, and it brought headmen together from the reaches of Creek Country.[71] Community-level conferences on the other hand were held more often, and were impromptu, as for instance when a specific situation necessitated deliberation. For that same reason regional councils were rarer, and headmen could choose not to attend if they had no important stake in the proceedings. Throughout Georgia's colonial history, for instance, several councils operated exclusively in either the Upper or Lower Country and did not garner significant turnout from across the region.[72] Importantly, those councils continued to meet just as regularly after the National Council was functioning. That perhaps is another reason many Creeks found such a structure promising; although much of it was novel, the National Council only built a new level of regional administration atop already familiar local councils. It did not replace them, in other words, it only added to them. Hawkins and his aides certainly saw it that way. They relied on local councils regularly, calling together communities to deal with particular situations when they did not require the voice of all Creeks. For instance, in 1797, he spent "some times at the Coweta, Tallahassee and Cussetuh squares," debating specific issues that pertained only to them. At another Coweta conference, twelve towns were involved. His aide Richard Thomas was known to call conferences as well, in both the Upper and Lower countries.[73]

Several other aspects of the National Council reflected political Creek customs that did not seem to lose any importance. The black drink, a ceremonial tea that served critical purifying and clarifying functions before important councils, continued during the National Council era. Familiar symbols of peace, including the usage of white objects instead of red, were also common. Ceremonial opening displays like the eagle dance continued as well.[74] Both the arriving headmen and Hawkins provided food and other necessaries in accordance with older traditions because, like the older councils, once the National Council began there were few breaks, and depending on what was being debated, the meeting could go on for days.[75] Indeed, the National Council represented a state structure that clearly elaborated on preexisting Creek political traditions more often than it dismantled them. Participation in the National Council meetings did begin to shrink, however, as a smaller group of headmen increasingly claimed more authority in Creek Country. Usually no more than a half dozen representatives from each community were present at councils through the turn of the century, including micos, head warriors, and assistants, although sometimes that number was smaller, and representatives were not restricted by number. That turnout still made for a sizable council, meaning that National Council meetings would be much more than the whim of one or two headmen Hawkins had in his pocket. Still, they were smaller delegations than in the past, and they came at a time when the decisions they made in debate at the council carried more weight than before.

Hawkins, as the representative of the federal government, played an active role in the debates. He either sat on the council directly or stayed nearby at a specially prepared place where he could provide input if necessary. He was also usually the one to open the Council, beginning deliberations by reporting on the state of Creek Country, suggesting ideas and making claims for Georgians or the federal government. Even though it was often critical of Creeks, his input was still oratorical, carrying on Creek traditions of discussion and persuasion in the same manner as any other speaker. After such an opening the council appointed a Speaker and proceeded to deliberate on propositions that both they and Hawkins proposed, discussing and debating them night and day, and finally voting on whether or not to adopt each one. It is not entirely clear whether unanimity of votes was required, which would have reflected a close adherence to the conciliating and persuasive design of older council traditions. It probably was not. Nevertheless, ultimately votes were taken, agreements were pronounced, the council adjourned, and accounts were disseminated throughout the region.[76]

Hawkins's role in the National Council was at the same time a traditional marker of Creek diplomacy and an important development in council traditions that gave the idea of the larger Creek state meaning. As much as it was a vehicle of daily control the National Council also generated regional stability by mitigating disputes between Creeks and their American and European neighbors. While this was a diplomatic aspect of Native American councils that was common not only in Creek Country but elsewhere, the increased responsibility of an outsider like Hawkins was also an important elaboration. The presence of a man like Hawkins, whose oratories factored prominently in council debates, was a significant departure from previous Creek council traditions, when outsiders without kinship ties or other strong relationships generally were not welcome. Outsiders who had business with the Creek people, however, slowly grew more visible in National Councils. They included local traders and representatives of Panton and Leslie, for instance, who gave speeches and made requests of their own. The Creek council was evolving from a private affair, meant to resolve local disputes, into a more open regional forum, structured to solve problems with neighbors and outsiders as well as dictate internal Creek politics. Conceived to modernize Creek politics, it was a product of both traditional Creek governing traditions and the political exigencies of the period.

While very little is known about its exact composition, Hawkins's notes on the 1798 council were lengthy. If the councils stayed consistent over time, which it appears they did, then his participation in 1798 provides excellent insight into how it functioned. On the opening day of the council, which lasted four days, representatives of twenty-nine of the most sizable communities in Creek Country were present. Only four were missing, making it truly national in scope. The Mad Dog of Tuckabatchee, a chief of immense traditional authority in Creek Country, a long-time American ally, and a central figure in the evolving Creek leadership, was chosen to be the first Speaker of the Creek National Council and therefore the Creek Nation. After what was apparently a quick address by Hawkins the Mad Dog was the first to speak, declaring that the continuous oratorical form of the National Council would follow in the form of previous ones and that "we will then go on until we have accomplished the business we have met on." He made some opening remarks, listed many of his own complaints and concerns, and the council adjourned for the day.

The next day the Hallowing King was first to speak. He grasped a string of beads in one hand, further connecting this new council to generations of previous ones, explaining that it was usual to reference belts of beads "when we speak of peace." The one he currently possessed was appropriate—it was the one "we use on such great and important occasions." That tradition "was handed down to us by our forefathers. They are all dead and gone and we, their descendants, are following their ways." The National Council, the Hallowing King was making clear, was the continuation of a political process steeped in traditions that went back generations. Even his talk, recounting the history, tradition, and importance of such proceedings, was established custom. Years later, in 1802, the council began with an even more elaborate show. American commissioners entered the square at Tuckabatchee and were seated, followed then by their Creek counterparts. All of the delegates from both the Upper and Lower countries met "at some distance from them" and entered the square in one body, "two men in front dancing the Eagle tail dance, to the music accompanied by the voices of all the men and women," and the commissioners were "touched by the wings in the hands of the dancers." That opening ceremony was not unlike what Patrick Tonyn and John Stuart witnessed at the Cowford in East Florida decades earlier. Next a white staff, representing peace, was placed behind one of the American attendees. Nearby was a pit, dug specifically for the occasion. Soon a Creek delegation brought in a bow and arrow painted red, symbolizing war. They "showed them to the commissioners, broke them, put them into the pit, covered them with each, and that with white deerskins, spread the skins on a log and they sat down."[77] These elaborate ceremonies, representing peace and friendship, continued to frame councils as they had for generations.

After those opening gestures, however, there was usually little time wasted getting to the heart of Creek and American complaints. Such was the case in 1798, when Hawkins opened with Georgians' complaints for lost or destroyed property, with the theft of slaves and horses being the most pressing issues. On that very public occasion his language was as stern as it had ever been privately. The theft of horses to Georgians was like the theft of land to Creeks, he declared, and "in short, they might expect that this evil, unless checked would bring ruin to their land." The headmen immediately began debating his talks, and both the Mad Dog and Alexander Cornells "made two long and animate speaches to their own people." The oratory of those two, but particularly of Cornells, was telling. It took a man of immense respect to lead council talks in such a way, and although Cornells was a man of mixed ancestry, a man of considerable property, and by that point also on the payroll of the American government, it was evident he was also a man of authority in Creek Country. His and the Mad Dog's talks encouraged the rest of the council members to restrain their hunters from committing thefts, but the two headmen were quick also to counter that it was, in fact, the white traders in their communities who were to blame for almost everything Hawkins was complaining of. As they had done earlier, at Coleraine, headmen at the National Council were clearly confident and comfortable enough to speak their minds. And speak their minds they did.

The traders, their talks went on, must not "encourage mischief in our land," "circulate falsehoods," or "disobey our law." The two then singled out several traders, most of whom were present, and accused them directly. One of the traders denied the charges "and a warm altercation ensued." Several more of the traders "entered into the conversation," until finally Hawkins ended a debate that looked to be getting quite passionate. He used the heat of the moment—a moment uncommon in previous Creek councils—to explain the important function that was being exercised there. The council was "to examine into the affairs of the nation, and assist by their councils to restore peace at home and abroad." The group then adjourned for the morning, giving people time to cool off. The traders' aggressive position during the council—indeed, their presence there at all—was evidence of the politically and diplomatically constructive atmosphere Hawkins was suggesting.[78] Outsiders like Richard Bailey, one of the traders singled out for bad conduct and the one who defended himself aggressively, would never have been allowed into a council decades earlier. Had he found himself in one and spoke out in such a spirited way he probably would have been killed. The National Council, however, was a place for everyone involved in the welfare of Creek Country, including outsiders.

That tense interaction did not end the debate on the traders. Over the course of the council the headmen returned to them several times, determined to throttle what they saw as a dishonest and harmful influence on their hunters. They were "liars and meddlers and rogues" who disturbed "the peace of our land by their false and foolish stories which make our young men uneasy." That was not a line of debate Hawkins solicited or even suggested. Writing Edward Price late in the council, in fact, he explained that "there was not room for me to interpose one word, so determined were they to drive them out, and there was not one voice in their favour."[79] The traders again dominated the proceedings on the second day, and the headmen decided that a handful of them needed to go. Indeed, one of the first decisions made by the National Council was to expel untrustworthy traders. After a twenty-four-day period, they decided, "they are to commit their journey of banishment." Hawkins assisted the headmen as they penned letters to five of them, in Autossee, Tuckabatchee Tallassee, and elsewhere. Less than a month later Hawkins was sure that the number would only grow.[80]

If one of the primary functions of the National Council, as a state structure, was to keep Creek Country stable by preventing crime, then headmen used the council in 1798 to remedy what they saw as a tremendous source of instability. They made it clear that traders of disrepute were the cause of a lot of their troubles, and they probably were, as far as horse theft was concerned. But several days of debate did too little to address what Hawkins was more concerned with, however, so he again brought up the theft of horses and slaves that had already taken place, adding demands for satisfaction for several murders committed by unnamed Creeks from the Upper Country, by Cowetas, and by Seminoles. These demands revealed a much more unpopular and contentious issue. Their decision to punish nefarious characters in the region might stem future thefts or raids, but what about the ones that had already taken place? Several headmen accepted culpability for what clearly were crimes, but they were still unclear as to how they would respond. After Hawkins's address the Coweta Warrior spoke, outlining plans to deliver the proceedings of the council through Creek Country and also to press for the satisfying of some of those demands. For many of the Creeks in the council, that seemed to be enough. The Hallowing King declared proudly that after days in debate "we are now unanimous in what is proper to be done for the good of our nation," and he promised, after he returned to the Lower Country, "to do all I can to cause justice to be done to the white people." With these promises being made, the first National Council adjourned.[81]

Although Hawkins's journal covered only a fraction of the proceedings, it was clear from his reports that over the course of four days the National Council debated several issues, from horse theft to traders, and even to the blacksmiths among their communities. Despite their inability to fully satisfy Hawkins on all of his wishes, they approved a number of the changes that Americans had been suggesting for some time, and Hawkins was quick to express his pleasure with the proceedings.[82] And the results were indeed encouraging. Creek leaders, claiming to bear responsibility for all of Creek Country, were wielding the power of what could only be called a Creek state. Most of their successes came accordingly, in the preventive actions they either passed for the first time or renewed. Aside from banishing several traders, they promised again to collect and return as much stolen property as they could, which Hawkins matched by institutionalizing a reward for returning slaves and horses, the success of which he later explained "was equal to my aspiration as an experiment." The council also enlarged on previous arrangements with Hawkins to prevent minor crimes during the hunting season, renewing their plan to empower local headmen as the arbiters of local disputes, the preventers of crimes, and the correctors of them. That meant that each community's young men left for their winter hunting grounds again with "suitable persons appointed to accompany them and watch over their conduct" in an effort to keep them "well disposed toward their neighbours." Hunters were also directed to apply to either Hawkins or a federal officer on the boundary for a permit in order to pass into the white settlements, "naming the Indians & his business."[83]

These laws, designed to keep account of hunters and prevent attacks on settlers, were clear efforts on the part of the evolving Creek leadership to stem several causes of friction between their communities and Georgia settlers. And as Hawkins admitted, there was a cautious sense of optimism along the frontier that those measures might actually have an impact on the region—much more than could be said about the trade and intercourse acts. The administrative structure that Creek leaders were building by the council meeting in 1798 was a real thing, in other words, and it was something both Creeks and Americans believed could work. What was more questionable, however, was the extent to which the strongest claims made by Georgians would be honored—justice for crimes long committed—and as long as those debts went unpaid, Americans would never truly be content.

At least Creeks demonstrated a willingness to continue moving in that direction, even if slowly. Soon the National Council was debating measures to give teeth to their legislative actions—to begin altering how crime and punishment were dealt with in Creek Country. Some of their decisions were clear enough: they sentenced three young men to death, for instance, for particularly intense raids against Georgia settlers. They also resolved to have stolen property seized by force and designed a punishment structure to combat theft by whipping perpetrators that was surprisingly corporal in nature.[84] All of these were important steps made by the National Council that began to remove jurisdiction over crime and punishment from local community leaders and kin members and place it in their hands. These were unparalleled steps; the National Council, by taking such actions, was mounting the most direct challenges yet to the ideas of local governance, kinship guidance, and reciprocity that traditionally ordered Creek justice. By formalizing acts of crime, codifying punishments, and depersonalizing the violence associated with it, the administrative functions of the Creek state could be legitimized.[85]

Both the execution and whipping decisions, for instance, removed discretion from the hands of kin members almost entirely and placed it in the hands of authorized agents of the National Council. No longer would kin be able to negotiate the terms of retribution when their relations were charged with a crime. Neither would they have the right to seek their own avenues of retributive justice outside of the council without being guilty of wrongdoing themselves. That was true unequivocally in cases of capital punishment, but it was also applicable in cases of more petty crimes, like theft. According to older Creek traditions of justice, for example, when a theft or attack took place, it had been the responsibility of members of the perpetrator's clan to make the situation right. If a kin member stole or even killed, the clan would attempt first to reimburse the victim, somehow, for the value of the lost property or the lost life.[86] The 1798 whipping law directly challenged that pillar of Creek justice while also fundamentally altering the role of community leaders. Community leaders were now required to oversee an institutionalized system of corporal punishment where they used to seek mediation, eroding their power of persuasion and replacing it with coercive, disciplinary authority.

While the function of the National Council in the late 1790s was a clear adaptation of old Creek traditions, what was produced at the first two meetings was much more revolutionary. A decision about how to deal with horse theft might have been reached in a largely traditional way, but the laws created at the council carried a much more coercive weight, which was to be enforced more regionally, than previous laws. While much of the physical structure of the councils stayed the same, in short, each one of them constituted a larger cultural step away from the Creek Country of a generation earlier. This trend continued when the National Council assigned new coercive roles to warriors in 1798. With the council attempting a turn toward corporal, rather than kin-based, punishment, Creek leaders re-tasked warriors into an authoritative body that would carry out the more controversial consequences of their decisions. In time warriors would represent the only legitimate source of violence, enforcing the laws and jurisdiction of the National Council and representing the police power of an administrative Creek state. This evolving role for Creek warriors, like the makeup of the National Council itself, represented how both tradition and innovation informed the emerging Creek state. Specifically tasked warriors—"law menders" as they were later described—would have defined sets of duties and responsibilities that were not subject to the control of community leaders but instead to the National Council.[87]

This aspect of Creek political modernization was perhaps the one most consistent with state formation in a contemporary Euro-American sense, but it was also certainly reflective of the unique struggles faced by the Creek people. Community leaders, forced into questioning their political traditions because of a regional situation they had trouble controlling, looked to the National Council for security, stability, and, in the words of outsiders, good neighborhood. Meanwhile Americans looked to the nation and the state for those same reasons, but they also looked to manage economic industrialization in the Northeast, racial slavery in the South, and settler expansion in the West. These things did not concern Creeks and were not addressed in the first National Councils, or ever. Creeks were undertaking their own political journey on their own terms. And they would not be alone; Cherokees would begin the same process only a few years later, instituting "lighthourse" patrols "to suppress horse stealing and robbery of other property."[88]

The evolving roles for warriors as the enforcers of the new Creek state were also anchored in long-standing Creek political traditions. For generations warriors, or tustunnuggees, were an integral part of a community's political structure. Leading tustunnuggees were more like war chiefs than just warriors, and a counterpoint to a mico; they were community headmen who derived influence and authority from their leadership in war rather than in peace. A community could have several tustunnuggees, like micos, and they were also men of immense authority. They represented and exercised "the dignity of the mico," and their power was "entirely independent of the mico," according to one contemporary, which was particularly true in times of conflict. They taught the young men of their clan and community war-making traditions and, when the situation necessitated it, led war parties. That balancing of peace and wartime powers with their mico counterparts was another example of the equilibrium that directed much of the Creek world, a duality that reflected the reciprocal nature of Creek culture.[89]

Tustunnuggees also had a role to play in the everyday affairs of a community, carrying out the will of a mico or his council when the situation called for decisiveness rather than persuasion. They were also usually the ones to oversee justice when it was demanded. The Tustunnuggee

Emautlau of Tuckabatchee, for instance, was "a brave and determined man," Hawkins explained, "who had often signalized himself" when the situation "required a bold and decisive line of action." He was the one who had tried to apprehend the Yuchi killers, and even though he was unsuccessful, he clearly made an impression on Hawkins.[90] In another instance, which took place before headmen developed a whipping system for horse thieves, Hawkins learned that a young Cusseta hunter allegedly found two horses while hunting on the Oconee River. The Cusseta Mico sent men to retrieve the horses, which were clearly stolen, but also sent out the town's "head warrior" to "whip the lad for bringing them off."[91] While tustunnuggees were an embodiment of cosmological balance in the Creek cultural world, their day-to-day leadership in the maintenance of order and the adjudication of conflict had already made them central to community function in ways strikingly consistent with administrative state actors elsewhere.[92] If anyone would have a role in meting out violence in the new Creek state, tustunnuggees seemed like the clear choice—warriors like the Tustunnuggee Emautlau were already doing so, functioning as community police figures.

During the 1798 National Council and shortly after headmen were beginning to define those parameters more clearly. Warriors had been instrumental in approving the whipping law and would continue to be, Hawkins explained to Georgia governor James Jackson, and likewise would be the ones "to seize upon all property stolen from their neighbors and to restore it."[93] New roles for Creek warriors provide the clearest evidence yet that Creeks were creating a political body designed to stabilize the region by focusing on the day-to-day actions of hunters and young men, but they were doing so by blending new, controversial concepts of justice with more familiar and acceptable traditions, and all in response to their particular needs.[94] Several other mentions of the whipping laws hint at just how coercive—and at times how contested— that new police power was. After the Mad Dog adjourned the council in 1798, he and a handful of other chiefs including the Cusseta Warrior, Cusseta King, and Hallowing King left to "address our talk to all our towns" southward. When they did, they took sets of sticks with them. When they were cut "and put into the hands of the warriors," he explained, they "will exert themselves."[95] While he did not explain their meaning in more detail, others did: the warriors chosen to execute the council's laws would be using those sticks when carrying out whipping sentences. Shortly after the 1798 council, for instance, the Dog Warrior described how he and others had just used some of them to beat several horse thieves. They were, his description suggests, a disciplinary tool that physically symbolized the jurisdiction and authority of the Creek state. Groups of sticks were distributed throughout the region by members of the National Council, and reliance on them was almost certainly meant to indicate that the warriors inflicting the beatings were not doing so on their own, or by the decision of a specific kin group, but rather by the order of the National Council and therefore by the will of all Creek people.

As headmen spread the sticks throughout Creek Country and increasingly used them, they demonstrated a growing commitment to state authority. "Now I will try the experiment," the Mad Dog had declared to Hawkins at the conclusion of the National Council. It was for the good of Creek Country, he had decided, "and I think it will succeed." And it was clear where he thought the sticks would do the most good. Along with the Hallowing King, the Cusseta King, and the Cusseta Warrior, the Mad Dog was quick to return south, as they all had promised. With sticks in their hands, looking to impose the decisions of the National Council on the most volatile communities in the Lower Country, the headmen were confident. Soon they were in the neighborhood of Broken Arrow and Ooseoochee, where Hawkins admitted "lies the bulk of the complaints I have against the nation." Yet there the new coercive laws "had been approved of" and the sticks delivered, and warriors had convened "for the purpose of taking measures to carry them into effect, that the execution of all the Laws depended on them, and they were determined to fulfill all the promises made me by the National Council." The Tussekiah Mico declared it was time their wayward people acted like men: "The talk has been made and it has gone thro' our land that horse thieves should be beat; if beating will not tame them, something else must be done; it will not do for us to lose our land for a few mad men."[96] A more decisive role would be played by the Mad Warrior, also of Cusseta, yet he was resolute as well. The sticks were "now in the hands of the warriors," and "they will not lay them down, 'till they punish every thief and mischiefmaker in the nation to fulfil the promises made to you and to carry the laws into effect." Indeed, reports suggested not only that the sticks were distributed widely in the south but that they had an immediate effect. One passed through Coweta, while another was sent to Ooseoochee. Within days, Coweta warriors brought in a handful of stolen horses, demonstrating the power of that coercive symbol.[97]

A relatively peaceful winter hunting season in 1798 and 1799 offered more proof that the sticks and the other laws passed in that year's council were not only being respected but having the desired effect. Community leaders were out watching hunters as they were directed and would report to Hawkins upon their return. Late in 1799 the "special license" to buy horses was in effect, as Hawkins explained to Price's successor as U.S. factor at Coleraine, explaining that he had lately "given some certificates of property with horses." Several headmen, most of them from the Lower Country, were also being paid to bring in both stolen horses and slaves, which was slowly but steadily happening.[98] More importantly, "several horse thieves have been severely whipped, and horses and property to a considerable amount restored for their owners," as Hawkins reported to federal agent Constant Freeman. Even Governor James Jackson was forced to admit that "a disposition friendly to justice is daily increasing and manifested itself by substantial facts." In one particular case that Hawkins recounted several times with pride, a Georgia settler reported losing a valuable horse to thieves from the Lower Country, and headmen there reacted swiftly. They collected a posse of two "principal warriors" and upwards of forty others from across the Lower Country and pursued the trail for over a month, almost to Pensacola. When they finally came up with the thief they demanded property in return for the horse, which they succeeded in returning to Hawkins.[99] If Creeks were forced into an administrative state to provide good neighborhood, at least they were succeeding. The frontiers of Georgia "enjoy more tranquility now than they have done at any period since the treaty of New York," Hawkins was pleased to announce to Georgia governor George Walton late in the summer of 1798. The outlook was positive, which was a sentiment he reiterated months later, at the height of the hunting season. It had been a month "without a single complaint against the Creeks from any quarter." In fact, a group of chiefs from twelve towns along the Chattahoochee River visited him and they all assured him "that the winter shall pass away as it has commenced and that we shall meet in the Spring and congratulate each other on this wonderful change."[100]

With the National Council assuming authority over all Creeks, with control over hunters increasing in their day-to-day activities, and with the established enforcement of coercive punishments on the wayward, there were plenty of examples to suggest that what Creeks were creating was having a strong calming effect on the region. The Mad Dog went so far as to reveal how the laws on horse theft in particular were starting to challenge kin networks, another important measure of their success. Not even the eminent Galphin family was immune. Speaking to Hawkins on the matter the Mad Dog recounted how John Galphin had been accused of abetting horse theft and was being charged in Tuckabatchee for his actions. Jack Kinnard and the Cusseta King, however, prevented his being found guilty—and beaten, if not killed—probably invoking his close personal and perhaps even familial ties. This, however, rubbed the Mad Dog the wrong way. If "ever he trespasses again, he should not be forgiven." The Cusseta Warrior and "all the other chiefs," he declared, "must have him well whipped for stealing" the horses. "I shall not forgive him he best have the law," he concluded, "it is the law of the nation and must not be violated with impunity."[101]

Unfortunately headmen had much more trouble atoning for the thefts and killings that had already taken place, meaning there was still plenty to irritate Georgia authorities and Hawkins. Claims for stolen or destroyed property by the end of the year were still significant, and without any other option Hawkins decided to deduct a sizable portion of the value of the property from the Creek stipend that was provided by the Treaty of Coleraine.[102] In fact, despite the positive atmosphere of the previous National Council and the passing of a peaceful hunting season, Hawkins complained that he was having to work far too hard to push chiefs to act aggressively when the situation called for decisive action. To Secretary of War James McHenry he admitted that "the chiefs of this nation cannot carry their national decrees into effect, one or two towns have acted well and punished theft, but the great body is slow to act."[103] Hawkins's surprisingly harsh criticisms, which would seem to portray the National Council as a letdown, seem strange. Perhaps they did not reveal a failing Creek state project as they much as they revealed the different goals sought by the Creek people and their American neighbors. Hawkins's complaints did not refer to any recent crimes, the lack of which he actually found very promising. In that view, the Creek National Council's gains could not be denied. Yet he was irritated, on the other hand, that Creek headmen promised Seagrove they would execute men, years earlier at Tuckabatchee, and they promised him at Coleraine that they would return property that had been taken in raids both before and after the Treaty of New York. Those were promises Creeks were failing to deliver on. For all the successful political changes Creeks were making that were affecting their everyday lives, it turns out they had trouble turning back time.

Realistically, Hawkins's criticisms were complicated and not entirely honest. The trade in lives that took place with Seagrove at Tuckabatchee was seen as largely symbolic. Creeks probably would not execute the perpetrators of the attack at Trader's Hill, just as Georgians were probably not going to execute David Cornells's murderers. Seagrove understood the intricacies and symbolism of the accord, but Hawkins clearly did not. And then there was Coleraine. Claims for everything that took place before the Treaty of Coleraine in 1796—including the Cumberland raids, the Trader's Hill killings, the Yuchi executions, and countless thefts—had supposedly been extinguished by the treaty, at least as Creeks saw it. Headmen promised to the American commissioners that they would do what they could to turn over stolen goods and execute murderers, but nothing in the treaty text was binding. Similarly, the American commissioners promised that they would do what they could to find justice for stolen Creek horses and killed Creek hunters—particularly the dozen killed by Harrison—but again those were only promises. Nothing would probably get done by either party, making Coleraine the place to wipe the slate clean and create a situation more conducive to future peace. Both the American and Creek delegations understood it that way, by all contemporary accounts. Yet in the wake of the treaty, which Georgia authorities made clear they did not appreciate, state lawmakers still pressed to have all of those claims satisfied. And even though Hawkins was also at the treaty, for some reason he agreed with them.[104] The state's claims were dubious at best, and it is strange to see Hawkins, who was generally a strong ally of Creeks, advocate for them. Nevertheless, state authorities continued to lobby aggressively for property lost more than a half decade earlier, and Hawkins pursued their claims for them. He would surely get little from his Creek counterparts as far as those claims were concerned, but they might explain why in his letters to McHenry he sounded frustrated at times.

That position certainly generated a steady source of tension between Creeks and Hawkins, as well as with the state of Georgia, yet they did not weaken the positive steps Creeks were taking to stabilize the region. It was clear instead that by the turn of the century the Creek-Georgia frontier was a much more stable place than it had been in a long time. The engine of that change was the National Council—a political creation that blended generations of Creek governing traditions with newer, more institutionalized and coercive ones, modeled after contemporary American and European legal conceptualizations of statehood. Laws passed by the council to oversee hunters and punish thieves were in place and they were significantly reducing the instances of crime along the border with Georgia. If Americans wanted good neighborhood, by the turn of the nineteenth century Creeks were in a better position than ever before to provide it to them.

FIGURE 7. Eagle Dance. This is a Removal-era depiction of a ceremonial Choctaw eagle dance. Creeks performed the same dance for Patrick Tonyn and John Stuart on the St. Johns River in 1775, and also for Benjamin Hawkins and James Wilkinson at the 1802 Treaty of Fort Wilkinson. Souvenir of the N. American Indians, as they were in the middle of the nineteenth century. 1850. Pencil drawing. Rare Books Division, New York Public Library, Astor, Lenox and Tilden Foundations.

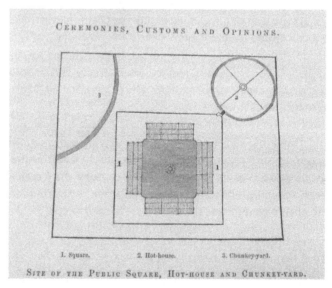

FIGURE 8. Square Ground. This illustration, made in 1791, depicts a standard Creek square ground, with four thatched huts surrounding the square and positioned between the hothouse and the ball field. From Caleb Swann, "Position and State of Manners and Arts in the Creek or Muscogee Nation in 1791."

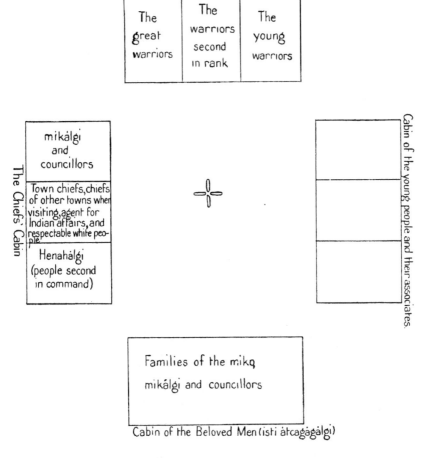

FIGURE 9. Cusseta Square Ground. This is a detailed illustration of a Cusseta square ground, around the time it would have been used by the National Council. Note the location of chiefs, warriors, and other headmen and advisors. John R. Swanton, Social Organization and Social Usages of the Indians of the Creek Confederacy (New York: Johnson Reprint Corp., 1970).

8 /   A Legitimate Creek Nation

We are pretty high toned and mean to keep so, we can shoot and whip,
and we mean to continue the practice until we get our affairs right and can
keep them so.
    —Benjamin Hawkins, August 19, 1802

The National Council was a promising development in a process of Creek political modernization that generated a greater sense of regional stability than either Creeks or their Georgia neighbors had experienced in a long time. It reflected the development of nationalism in Creek Country and a step taken in the direction of an administrative Creek state. Still, its early successes were minor, and even though it continued to pacify Creek hunters and keep the region relatively safe, the National Council faced much larger challenges after the turn of the century that would decide how legitimate, or how contrived, it really was. William Augustus Bowles reemerged in Florida while Georgia state authorities continued to demand remuneration for past raids—demands that American authorities seemed to agree with.

Bowles advocated rejection of the Council while American officials insisted on the sale of Creek lands as the solution to a Creek debt problem that Georgia legislators very skillfully manufactured practically out of thin air, both of which would impact only Lower Country Creeks. The National Council would need to impose its decisions in several circumstances, in short, on communities that were certain to oppose them. Although there was evidence that an evolving Creek leadership group was indeed mitigating interactions with Georgians in ways that had caused trouble in the past, they were claiming relatively limited powers, and those powers were going to have to be expanded greatly. The National Council would face several sources of resistance, both internal and external, that very easily could push the region backward toward an unstable one of community control and chaos. How the Creek leadership—now organized under the Creek National Council—responded would determine how effective Creek political modernization truly was.

At the turn of the eighteenth century members of the National Council—a mix of micos, tustunnuggees, emautlaus, and others—were playing assertive and nontraditional roles in regional Creek politics. Some familiar headmen, like the Fat King of Cusseta and the White Lieutenant of Oakfuskee, faded from the regional scene.[1] Others who had been a part of the emerging Creek leadership remained as steadying voices, like the Hallowing King and the Mad Dog, while the Tallassee King continued to grow more unstable. Still others emerged. Those included Hopoie Haujo of Ocheubofau, or the Hickory Ground, the Singer of Oakfuskee, the Cusseta Mico, and Tuskenhau Chapco of Coweta. The Singer of Oakfuskee, for instance, was regarded in 1804 as one of the most influential headmen in the whole region. By that time, so was Kinnard.[2] Hawkins, for his part, was not so sure about the Cusseta Mico. According to the agent he was "not a firm character," but he was "friendly to peace"; he was the "Great medal Chief" of Cusseta, and his role would continue to expand, particularly considering how important a stable Lower Country remained to regional peace.[3] As the emergence of these men proved the National Council evolved over time, but it remained a place where community headmen became regional leaders. Warriors continued to play important roles as the coercive arm of the Creek administrative state, which meant their involvement in regional politics would only grow as well. They included men like the Big Warrior of Tuckabatchee; the Dog Warrior, Big Warrior, and the Big Feared of Cusseta; and the Little Prince of Broken Arrow.

It was clear by the turn of the century even to Benjamin Hawkins that the National Council was having a positive impact on the region. Hawkins was pleased that "the special license" to buy horses in 1801 was doing its part on the Creek side of the boundary—theft was down considerably.[4] Years of hunts had gone by, in fact, with few significant breaches of the peace. By 1802 the Big Warrior of Tuckabatchee returned from a hunt on the Cumberland River to report to Hawkins that he had "heard of no complaints on that quarter," which was remarkable indeed. When he did run across a horse thief from Eufalahatchee, a Creek community high up in the Upper Country, he immediately seized the horses and made arrangements to have them returned to their owners directly.[5] Such a bloodless hunting season in the Cumberland area had not existed perhaps since the Cumberland settlements existed, continuing to provide evidence to Georgians, to Hawkins, and to Creeks that the decisions of the National Council were workable. Hawkins's only lament, in fact, was that state legislators were not being very reciprocal. In Georgia authorities were loath to prosecute even the worst trade offenders, even though there were several intercourse acts on the books that were designed to make it easy to do so. Their unwillingness to enforce the laws of the United States encouraged questionable trading figures to remain along the border and cause trouble, clouding some of the successes Creeks were having further to the west. They were not Creek disappointments, but state ones, that first confounded the Creek state.

When William Augustus Bowles reemerged in Florida at the turn of the century, on the other hand, all of that stood to change. His actions had the potential to rapidly undo much of what Creeks had only recently accomplished, testing whatever degree of a nation-state had been generated by that time.[6] Having decided that Spanish captivity in the Philippines was no longer to his suiting, Bowles decided to leave and soon was back at the Gulf Coast of Florida. He got off to a rough start, wrecking his ship in the Gulf of Mexico around the mouth of the Apalachicola River. Luckily he ran across an American surveying crew that fed him and probably saved him. He was quick to move north through the Florida panhandle and into the southernmost reaches of Creek Country. There he arranged a modest council at Wekiva, a Lower Creek community on the Chattahoochee River just above the Spanish boundary, and picked up where he had left off seven years earlier.[7] James Durouzeaux, writing from Coweta, summed up the threat Bowles posed in a strongly worded letter to Governor Vincente Folch in Pensacola. If Bowles ever got further into the region, "he will be hard to remove," as he was "a very enterprising man and will tell a thousand lies, and they are fools enough to believe him." He was again making extravagant promises of British support, as he had done in the past, and "except something very speedily sayed or done with this nation of Indians," Durouzeaux worriedly penned, "I am afraid his Majesty will lose all influences with the Creek nation of Indians." American officials, including the commanding officer of Fort Wilkinson, were worried that his effect on the Georgia frontier could be equally disastrous.[8] His success with groups of Seminoles and Mikasukis quickly generated a regional crisis for Spaniards, who already struggled to exert influence in those communities. More importantly, however, the threat was sure to expand into Creek Country, which was a cause for concern both for American and Creek leaders.

Bowles had done tremendous damage only a few years earlier, whipping headmen into an anti-American frenzy in the Lower Country that split communities apart and ultimately sparked violence. The stakes were now possibly even higher. American and Spanish surveyors were in the region running a new international boundary line in response to Pinckney's Treaty, meaning that Bowles had the potential not only to stir up regional chaos but generate some international intrigue as well. All of this would be blamed ultimately on Creeks, forcing headmen in both the Upper and Lower countries to take an aggressive stance against him and against the communities in the southernmost part of Creek Country that were susceptible to his talks. Hawkins took no time warning headmen to do exactly that, reminding them that if any violence spread from Creek Country into Georgia as a result of Bowles's presence, the consequences would be grave. "This will be a serious time for the chiefs," he warned Cornells, and if they did not do everything in their power, "we shall see ruin in our land."[9] Settlers in Georgia were already fearful; they were making defensive preparations of their own that did not bode well for regional peace.[10] Secretary of War James McHenry took time to assure Governor James Jackson that both he and Hawkins had full confidence in the Creek leadership.[11] Nevertheless, headmen needed to demonstrate the power and stability of the Creek state and do it decisively if they wanted to keep the region from descending, once again, into chaos.

Soon Creek headmen convened in the Lower Country and even with Spaniards to do just that. Dozens of chiefs and warriors from the Upper Country, including Holiwahli, Tuckabatchee, Fushatchee, Cooloome, and Wewocao, met with three dozen Cowetas and Cussetas to deliberate on how to approach Bowles.[12] With Seminoles stirring up discontent in the fall of 1799 a decisive show of force was necessary, and the headmen planned their first serious intervention. The talks that resulted from that first council were not lacking in aggressiveness and projected both stern warnings and a strong sense of collectivity. The Mad Dog, who played a leading role in the talks, penned a letter meant to be sent by warriors from the Lower Country into Florida and read aloud there, explaining that all his men, women, and children were to "live in peace and not to be interrupted by the bad conduct of one or two mischief making fellows" and that all the "good chiefs" would help "[put] a stop to their bad talks." The Mad Dog invoked the responsibility of all Creeks, and the usage of leading warriors reflected the new authority of the Creek state. Soon a group of Cussetas, led by the Cusseta King, were moving south with the talks in hand. Meanwhile, according to Spanish and American accounts, upwards of six hundred Creeks, representing twelve towns across Creek Country, met the Spanish commissioners who were busy surveying the boundary line. Again the Mad Dog took the lead. There they consented to send two chiefs "of the first rank" and twenty warriors to the Spaniards "to protect us against the Siminoles, none of whome were present, and who declare they will not suffer us to tread on their land." Soon fifty warriors, a collection from a number of communities, were on their way south to demonstrate the solidarity of the National Council and compel Seminoles to remain peaceful.[13] Their presence had an immediate and positive impact on the American and Spanish crews. The warriors escorted the surveyors personally and disbanded the several skulking gangs of Seminole and Mikasuki warriors that had by that point forced the surveying work to a standstill. When the commissioners' horses were stolen, the Creek warriors hunted them down and had them returned. And when they were harassed again on the way to the St. Mary's River, more Cusseta and Coweta warriors were quick to arrive.[14] Their protection left a positive influence not only on the surveyors and Spanish authorities but on nearby Georgians as well, providing the National Council with another successful demonstration of its increasing authority.

When those actions did not dissuade Bowles from continuing to disrupt Spanish interests along the Gulf Coast, or spread his talks further north, the National Council extended more coercive authority into the region.[15] A signal demonstration was made when they dealt with the uncontrollably wayward Tallassee King and his gang. The aged Tallassee King appeared to have aligned himself with Bowles, and even though Tustunnuggee Haujo, or the Mad Warrior, probably of Cusseta, had already had some of his gang beaten in 1798, it did little to temper his anti-American vitriol. Late in the summer of 1799 a group of young men from the southernmost part of the Lower Country went on a raiding spree after hearing one of his talks, pushing the National Council into a more decisive position. His actions were "much against the wish of the chiefs up this way," James Durouzeaux reported to Barnard from Coweta. He had no doubt that "most part of the towns would have come down" to show "what horse stealing deserved," but the spring harvest prevented them. If it happened again, however, that would not be the case.[16]

That indeed was the case. Soon the Big Feared of Cusseta, along with the Little Prince of Broken Arrow and the Cusseta King, issued a blistering response to the raiding and a strong warning to all those in the

Lower Country who were listening to Bowles's talks. The Big Feared, also known as Tuskegee Tustunnuggee, and the Little Prince, known as Tustunnuggee Hopoie, were leading warriors in the Lower Country; the Big Feared, for instance, was described by Hawkins as the "great warrior of the five great towns" on the Chattahoochee. Together the two, along with the Cusseta King, called for an example to be made of the Tallassee King. There were thirty-eight "great towns in the nation," they declared, and twenty "rogues and mischiefmakers" would not spoil their talks. "Are these 20 to give law to this land? NO. They must not, they shall not." The warriors then invoked the coercive power of the sticks. "Let us try the sticks, that is the law of the Creek people." If a good beating was the solution, then so be it. If it was not, they declared, the Tallassee King and his gang would have to be killed.[17]

Urged on by Hawkins, the National Council set into motion what he referred to as the "new experiment." Having determined that "every one of the leaders should be punished" and that "all their property destroyed and houses burnt," Alexander Cornells and the Mad Warrior took decisive action. They rallied a group of over seventy warriors at Tuckabatchee and together they "marched to put their determination into effect."[18] Soon the Tallassee and Half-Way House banditti had been "punished in an exemplary manner." The group singled out one man in particular, referred to as the Mankiller, who was made example of in a way that must have given pause to everyone in the region. His house was burned, his cooking pots and furniture destroyed, and his livestock killed. He was "beaten for dead" and disfigured, with "one ear cut off with a part of the cheek." According to at least one account, he was also sodomized. Two others nearby were brutally beaten as well and the rest fled, "pursued by some warriors towards the Cherokees." The correction was "a national affair," Hawkins declared, clearly pleased with the action. Warriors from Tuckabatchee, Eufala, Kialijee, and Holiwahli in the Upper Country participated, while chiefs in the Lower Country were reported to "highly approve."[19] The beatings were a decisive stroke and were applauded along the Creek-Georgia frontier as a signal victory for the National Council and the idea of the administrative Creek state.

After assaulting the Mankiller and the rest of the banditti the Mad Warrior made a point to have the associated sticks delivered all the way to the Seminole and Mikasuki towns, and then "as low as a warrior can be found." Such an action was no doubt designed to intimidate the wayward in that neighborhood. It was a frightening demonstration of the National Council's determination to keep the peace by naked violence if necessary, and at the very lengths of Creek Country. Perhaps most telling, the Mad Warrior also posed several questions about the brutal nature of the recent punishment to Hawkins, clearly reflecting on the viciousness of what he had just done and worrying that the sticks' usage directly conflicted with more traditional Creek notions of justice. What would the warriors do about "those who die under the punishment we inflict," he asked; would the one who inflicted the punishment be liable for kin retribution by executing the orders of the National Council? It was the first time he or any other Creek leaders had implemented such a system of corporal punishment in such a manner, and he was unsure of its consequences.

Hawkins's reply was straightforward and supportive. The National Council's jurisdiction and its control over violence was now the law of the land—the only law of the land. If someone did die, it was the law and "the nation who killed him." It was no one else's fault, and if the kin of the accused demanded satisfaction, the Mad Warrior was to tell them that they were not entitled to it, and if they sought it out illegally, they too would pay. "The law says such people must have the sticks, and that is their pay, and if they are killed by the sticks that is their pay. It is the pay of the Nation." Cornells likewise feared violence for his part in the attack and requested Hawkins "take care of his family if he falls in the execution of his duty."[20] Yet neither did he shirk from his responsibilities, as he demonstrated in the Tallassee King affair. New roles for headmen like the Mad Warrior and Cornells were certainly controversial and they were scary, but they were nonetheless clear, and by accepting them the Creek people were beginning to recognize the authority of Creek state power.

Another conference was soon mulling over what to do about Bowles, and headmen there produced more strong talks. Among them was the Mad Dog, who reiterated that Creeks were not interested at all in giving him either aid or land, and according to a Spanish report he referred to the returned adventurer repeatedly as "thief and a vagabond." Hawkins found the continued Creek solidarity very encouraging. "I am certain of one thing," he was pleased to announce to Andrew Ellicott, the American surveyor working with the Spanish, "whatever his views may have been, that in counting on the hearty support of his nation he has been disappointed."[21] The sizable contingency of resolute headmen in Cusseta and Coweta was a particularly valuable counterpoint, keeping Bowles's talks from spreading too rapidly through the Lower Country, where they had the potential to do the most serious damage. One Cusseta warrior "and his whole town," for instance, "were inimical to Mr. Bowles," and when he ventured into their neighborhood the headman publically disgraced him, calling him what was later translated as the "Lying Captain," or the "Prince of Liars," an ignominious title that "he now bears throughout the nation."[22]

When Bowles again made menacing movements toward William Panton's trading store at St. Marks, headmen in the Lower Country remained vigilant, and because of their actions very little of Florida's disruption trickled north. Bowles tried repeatedly to rally Creek communities to his cause, but very few took his invitation. Instead, "our affairs in this quarter are in as good a train as we could expect them," Hawkins penned to merchant Joseph Clay in Savannah, "assisted as they are by mischief-makers."[23] Perhaps in response to the success of the "new experiment," Hawkins called another meeting of the National Council late in November. There headmen continued to develop warriors' new roles by authorizing the creation of special groups of them that could be employed to execute the orders of the National Council at a moment's notice.[24] Using warriors as the legitimate coercive arm of the Creek state was a legal institution that was clearly working, so headmen took little issue with enlarging the system. According to the new program, towns in a general area were grouped together and assigned a set of ten or so warriors, each of which was led by a head warrior of particular trustworthiness and distinction. Nine classes were commissioned in total and stretched the length of Creek Country. When called into action, each of the warriors would be paid daily and furnished with ammunition, providing the Creek National Council with a steady and reliable policing authority that could be raised at a moment's notice and sustained for long periods of time if needed.[25]

The classing of warrior groups was an ambitious extension of the laws laid out in the first few National Councils. By creating a much more encompassing police power that continued to operate independent of traditional community authority, and answerable only to the National Council, larger state institutions were being created that clearly reflected a commitment to extending national jurisdiction over all Creeks. "If a few examples of a general tendency were made" by the warriors, Hawkins suggested, "the impression would be productive of general good."[26] It also signaled the National Council's commitment to maintain order through the use of force. It was "the first time that the nation ever could be brought to provide the means, for executing their engagements." Where in the past there had only been "promises and talks," which were "refractory" and "ineffectual," now with the authority of the Council and the power of the warrior groups "the most abandoned will unquestionably meet the punishment due to their crimes."[27]

These warrior groups, it turned out, were not mere abstractions. They were invoked in several instances, and their actions made a difference on the frontiers. Hawkins quickly sent one of them north to the Cumberland, for example, to crack down on horse theft there. Meanwhile headmen in the Lower Country also decided to test one or more of their classes as a peacekeeping force in Bowles's neighborhood. Not long after, a collection of headmen from along the Chattahoochee met at Coweta Tallahassee—also known as Broken Arrow—to appoint the class that would represent their region. They were then directed to travel south into Seminole country "in the name of the nation" and pressure the wayward chiefs to remain peaceful, and by late December they were on their way.[28] The warriors took with them more evidence of a strong sense of Creek collectivity and of a National Council that was confident in the coercive means at its disposal. Seminoles "must take the talks of the nation to be at peace with their neighbors, to quit stealing property from white people and restore what they have taken without delay."[29]

Backing their efforts, of course, was Hawkins, who wrote strong warnings to Bowles of his own and declared that if the adventurer caused too much trouble, regardless of where he was, the United States military would assist the Creek National Council in having him neutralized.[30] To this was added most of the Lower Country's significant communities, including Coweta, Cusseta, Yuchi, and Ooseoochee, all of whom responded positively to the various acts of the National Council.[31] Most impressive, perhaps, Spaniards were confident enough in the National Council's abilities to ask for its help. By November Durouzeaux, because of his position as Spanish translator, felt sufficiently threatened by Bowles to consider moving away from Coweta. Vincente Folch, then the governor of Pensacola, was planning a raid to seize Bowles; still impressed with what the warriors had done previously to secure Spanish surveyors and commissioners, the governor asked Hawkins for more of them. "If you choose to send a part of 50 or 60 warriors that were as determinate as those that chastised the Chiefs of the part that robbed the commissioners," he said, it would prove tremendously helpful.[32]

Despite warnings that emanated from every corner of the region, Bowles proved as elusive and stubborn an adversary during his second tenure in Florida as he had during his first. The relative calm the National Council was able to project in 1799 was shattered, for instance, when word arrived that not only had Bowles again sacked Panton's trading store but he had forced the surrender of the nearby Fort San Marcos de Apalache (previously referred to by the English as St. Marks) as well.[33] The attacks took place outside of the National Council's primary area of influence, of course, and in sovereign Spanish territory, which was outside Hawkins's or Gaither's jurisdiction as well. Yet Bowles's success at St. Marks nevertheless reverberated through Creek Country. While the Creek National Council had succeeded in stemming his influence to that point, the sacking of a Spanish fort proved simply too enticing an invitation for several communities in the Lower Country to ignore. Perhaps, a few of them began to murmur, he was back for good, and so might be the British. Bowles was still "making efforts to enduce some of them to take part with him" against the Spaniards, Hawkins penned one of his colleagues to the north, "and I believe some will join him." Indeed, many of them had taken his talks and his exciting news "with extravagant joy," he lamented, contemplating "British times and British presents," and a number of young men from five lower towns, most likely Broken Arrows, Chehaws, Hitchitis, Ooseoochees, and perhaps Yuchis, had "flocked down for that purpose." The Tallassee King was allied to Bowles as well, creating a potentially dangerous bridge to communities in the Upper Country. In May 1800 he even managed to distribute a few of Bowles's talks at the Hickory Ground. Although the talks were not particularly well-received, the fact that they were even read aloud in the heart of the Upper Country was still an alarming development indeed.[34]

As was the case at the Hickory Ground, most Creeks were stunned at the San Marcos de Apalache proceedings, and headmen "received the news with much concern, as they see the ruin eventually of their country will likely result for it." Accounts of raiding by other Creeks soon began to circulate, and although most of them were unfounded they offered proof that Bowles's resurgence was beginning to spread the destabilization many had feared. If not dealt with decisively he threatened to undo whatever sense of nationalism that had been knitting Creek Country together for years and reverse the regional stability generated by the National Council. Even recently appointed secretary of war Henry Dearborn was concerned. Of course Hawkins was to have Bowles seized himself, Dearborn declared, if the adventurer ever made the mistake of stepping foot onto American soil. But that seemed unlikely, and the secretary pressed his agent to remain vigilant, "to persevere in endeavoring to fortify the minds of the Indians against his artful schemes."[35] Headmen, it seemed, were up to the task. At a meeting of the National Council that convened shortly after, its members resolved to send another deputation from the Upper Country into Florida. The Singer of Oakfuskee, who had been at the Hickory Ground to hear the Tallassee King speak in 1800, led the deputation. If that peace mission failed, some were unsure how they would respond, but more than a few headmen were mulling over a much stronger show of force, which Hawkins was contemplating as well.[36] Unsure of what actions to take, in July a deputation of chiefs and warriors that represented the Creek Nation, including men from the Hickory Ground and Oakfuskee, the Big Feared and another warrior from Cusseta, the Mad Warrior and the Hallowing King of Coweta, and the Little Prince of Broken Arrow, moved south through Broken Arrow and down to San Marcos de Apalache to assess the situation.[37]

The National Council was never forced into the more confrontational position many were unsure of because little more developed along the Gulf Coast. Spaniards, infuriated by Bowles's successes and embarrassed by the loss of an entire fort, retook Fort San Marcos de Apalache quickly and forced Bowles to retreat to Mikasuki, instantly defusing what had been for them a rapidly deteriorating situation. Cusseta and Chehaw spies were present for the Spanish attack and reported the proceedings back to Hawkins.[38] That did not, however, end the National Council's intervention in Florida. Mico Thlucco, or the Big King of Cusseta, met Spaniards at Apalache with a message from the Creek leadership. They were determined to ensure peace in the region and were sending stern talks all the way to Mikasuki and Seminole communities to make that point clear.[39] His strong talks, which on the one hand the Spaniards found comforting, also hinted at apprehensions among the Creek leadership that, without swift action, control over the Lower Country might slip from their grasp. The Big King's mission, many hoped, would prevent more talks from leaving Spanish Florida and arriving in southern Creek Country.

Bowles's resurgence was one of the first regional conflicts to draw into question the legitimacy of the National Council. Up to that point it had functioned relatively smoothly and with little opposition—most Creeks had abided by its dictates, and security in the region had improved markedly. A leadership group was talking for all Creeks, warriors were acting for all Creeks, under their direction a lot of horse thieves had been beaten and a few had even been killed. None of that had produced any real dissent, which in a way legitimized the National Council and the larger trends of Creek collectivity that supported it. The disruption caused by Bowles's sacking of Apalache provided the first evidence to the contrary—voices of Creek dissent did in fact exist. In particular the Big King's mission perhaps reflected a larger worry that not everyone in Creek Country was being swept up in Creek nationalism, let alone was in agreement with the National Council. At the same time several reports confirmed that the most recent hunting seasons were the most peaceful and uneventful Creeks had ever seen, it was becoming clearer that at least a few headmen were growing disillusioned with the previous few years.[40] In 1801 and 1802 a growing number of community leaders—albeit still a small number—began to question Hawkins, the new direction of Creek political culture, and even the idea of Creek nationalism.

Those reservations did not create voices of militarism, as they had in the past, but a growing number of headmen in the Lower Country, including the Little Prince and the Hallowing King, seemed to be looking backward with a fondness that was becoming unhealthy. It was a look away from Creek nationalism and toward a previous period of autonomy and community leadership that threatened to undermine all that had been established. At the 1801 National Council, for instance, members sat in debate for over a week. Yet, as Hawkins later explained, it ended without dealing with "the ferment which agitates the nation or taking effectual measures for the future." The "ferment" seemed to be a growing unease about the future of Creek Country. Although the council upheld and improved much of their previous legislation, headmen "appeared more uneasy about the mischiefmakers in their lands and the division among the old Chiefs than I have ever known them to be." As the Mad Dog reported a handful of headmen, including some of the more established ones—although unfortunately he did not name names—began making wild suggestions. They considered the possibility of expelling Hawkins, disbanding the National Council, and ending the federal government's involvement in Creek politics generally. With the Spanish, the British, and maybe even the Americans fighting again with each other, perhaps Creeks could once again revive the older play-off system. Many started to "talk of old former times when game was plenty and the British agents used to court, caress and accommodate all the idlers in the nation," according to an exasperated Hawkins. In the post-Coleraine era of Creek-American relations, that was dangerous talk.[41]

It appeared Bowles had again managed, with at least a degree of success, to revive memories of a happier British time, and those memories were causing a number of headmen to start questioning Creek modernization just as it really began to take effect.[42] The reservations also proved surprisingly infectious; they spread within months to head-men who otherwise had been firm supporters of the National Council. Even the Mad Dog, for instance, complained of Georgia expansionists while he reminisced about the old times, which prompted strong replies from Hawkins.[43] It was after the Mad Dog starting talking about Brit-ish superintendent John Stuart that Hawkins apparently decided he had heard enough. Game was gone and hunting would no longer provide for Creeks' wants, he aggressively countered. Americans were there to "help all who will help themselves," not tolerate beggars.[44] By looking back-ward, Hawkins scolded the aging chief, Creeks were not only deceiving themselves, they were poisoning their prospects for long-term stabil-ity. While it appeared those strong talks brought the Mad Dog back to his senses, there were still others in the region who were not swayed by Hawkins's rejoinder. Later, when he requested a council early in 1802 to talk over the journeys he had recently made in Choctaw, Chickasaw, and Cherokee Country, several headmen refused to hear him talk. While Hawkins was a driving force for many headmen there were at least a few, particularly in the Lower Country, who were losing faith not only in Hawkins but in the Creek Nation.[45]

With Bowles still in the region and more headmen questioning the direction of Creek politics, the turn of the century emerged as a crossroads both for the National Council and for the larger Creek modernization project. Creek solidarity was as important as ever, and as it was turning out that was not something Hawkins could control. Only Creeks could fortify the idea of Creek nationalism, and quickly several headmen stepped forward to do so. Late in the summer and early in the fall of 1802 several of them flexed the power of the Creek state renewed, providing more strong actions in the hopes of silencing dissent in the face of increasing factionalism. After the council in 1802 Hawkins called on the warriors to "lift the sticks" and assert the violent power of the Creek Nation over the wayward, which they did. They "whipped severely" a man for stealing Cumberland horses, and Hawkins was confident he would soon hear more of the same.[46] While a deputation including the Hallowing King, the Little Prince, and John Kinnard failed to kill one condemned man who was hidden around the neighborhood of Kinnard's home in the Lower Country, they succeeded elsewhere. Around the same time Hawkins directed three warriors to kill a man who "scalped and otherwise maltreated" a Mrs. Smith, who apparently died from her wounds. It had been years since they had driven the man out of the region but he had returned, and Hawkins pressed them to make an example out of him. Secretary of War Dearborn in June relayed President Jefferson's personal gratitude about "the prompt and honorable manner" in which justice had been "executed on the murderer of Mrs. Smith." Jefferson considered it "the strongest proof of the sincerity and friendship of the creek Nation" and evidence of their "disposition to be good neighbors with our citizens."[47] Such an execution, which hitherto had been almost impossible to achieve, was the strongest evidence yet that Creek state actors meant business.

Creek pro-state figures continued to ascend through the summer of 1802. Hawkins was pleased to report that another condemned Creek killer who had evaded justice for so long had finally been shot. Another Creek man had been whipped for horse theft and a white man also whipped "for encouraging and taking the part of the Creek who was a horse thief." Yet another Creek from an unknown town was also being held in irons to be tried "for repeated thefts." By that point Hawkins's sense of optimism was much healthier than it had been months before, suggesting that the renewed efforts by the Creek leadership to gain legitimacy by performing signal acts of justice was having the desired effect. "We are pretty high toned and mean to keep so," he wrote to newly arrived U.S. factor William Halstead. "We can shoot and whip, and we mean to continue the practice until we get our affairs right and can keep them so." Months later affairs were "daily getting better and better," and the "whole budget of complaints" against Creeks by Georgians was now less than the number of claims by Creeks against Georgians.[48] These were the highest praises Hawkins had ever directed into Creek Country. The Creek National Council seemed to be winning the struggle over the Bowles faction, the "mischiefmakers," and the disbelieving in the region. In the meantime, the Creek-Georgia frontier was as stable as it had ever been.

It was during this period of resurgent Creek nationalism and state power that Georgians and Americans intensified their requests for land, which meant that local political and economic interests would also continue to test the authority of the National Council. Coleraine successfully upheld the sizable cession of land Americans had already gained at New York, but neither of those treaties had been as friendly to Georgians as they would have liked. State authorities doggedly claimed larger concessions from Creeks to their own treaties, made during the Articles of Confederation years, and New York was seen as a bitter disappointment. That was particularly the case with the so-called Tallassee County, a strip of land that stretched south from the Altamaha River to the

Spanish boundary on the St. Mary's River. Georgians gained that land in the Treaty of Galphinton but then lost it at the Treaty of New York, a loss that was upheld at Coleraine. By the turn of the nineteenth century that tragic turn of events still haunted state authorities.[49]

As was the case during the treaties of New York and Coleraine, communities from various parts of the region approached land very differently. The Tallassee County was not an extensive piece of land and Americans and even McGillivray had long claimed that the land around it, at least to the west, was part of the sprawling Okefenokee Swamp, and as such was pretty much useless to Creeks. With the land stripped of any marketable wildlife, Georgians should be allowed to have it if they wanted it, if the price was right of course.[50] Headmen in the Upper Country, who composed a sizable portion of the National Council, could probably be persuaded, sooner or later, to sell for the right price. Clearly communities in the Lower Country felt differently, and the more state authorities pushed for the land the greater the potential to renew a sectional rift in Creek Country. Even Cowetas, who were more invested in the National Council than were other communities in the Lower Country, were torn. The Hallowing King was no fan of Coleraine, particularly after Hawkins's insistence on an American, and not a Creek, interpretation of the new boundary. Communities in the area were still bitter and Hawkins reported that Cowetas generally were "unwilling to understand the treaty."[51] Having the Tallassee County added to Georgia would be a difficult pill to swallow, even for the friendliest communities in the Lower Country. Further to the south things were more volatile still. Along with Coweta and Cusseta, communities like Ooseoochee, Chehaw, Hitchiti, Okmulgee, and Lower Eufala hunted along the edges of the Okefenokee Swamp and then east into the proposed Tallassee County. Their acquiescence to the National Council was critical to its legitimacy. They had not opposed the Council when it came to horse theft but had only somewhat been kept orderly during the Bowles resurgence; to bring up an additional cession of land that they hunted on directly was sure to face stiff opposition. Years earlier the sale of the Oconee lands drove several of the same communities away from McGillivray and Americans and into the open arms of extremists like Carondelet and Bowles. Ceding away the Tallassee County had the potential to create the same kind of repulsion, pitting the National Council with a regional agenda against a few communities that still very much had the potential to think locally.

Despite that opposition, as long as settlers continued squatting on the land, and as long as Georgians parroted claims to stolen horses that American authorities accepted, such a deal seemed inevitable. To Creeks, Georgia's claims were no more legitimate than they had ever been. Most of that property had been taken in raiding that was legal to Creeks; regardless, the treaties of New York and Coleraine were written it would seem to financially cover whatever property Creek communities could not reasonably return. Yet Georgians, with their list of Creek debts, began pressuring headmen for recompense almost as soon as Coleraine concluded. Increasingly, they lobbied Hawkins and even his superiors as well. State authorities were relentless, and they proved remarkably resourceful when it came to using their claims to apply pressure on the National Council.[52] Keenly aware of how many slaves, livestock, homes, outbuildings, and so on they had lost to Creek raiders, going back decades now and regardless of the context in which they were taken, they cataloged everything. Each of those things had a price, and state authorities recognized that there was no other way for Creeks to compensate for those losses except with land. As one settler from Greenesborough explained, "Not one tenth part of the property that has been carried that could be produced were the whole Nation enclined." It had either already been disposed of or was destroyed, so "for my part I dont no what grounds the Government can take to obtain the land to the Oakmulge that had been contemplated on so long, but this, that is to demand the property the Indians have robbed us of." Because headmen had also promised in the treaty negotiations to do their best to surrender up everything they had stolen and clearly were not holding up their end of the bargain, as far as Georgians were concerned there was still legitimate claim to that property, regardless of whatever else had been agreed upon at Coleraine. Not only would they continue to claim horses, slaves, and anything else of monetary value, the Greenesborough man argued, how else were Creeks "to pay, only by a session of land, if they mean to comply with the treaty, which the union are bound to se done."[53]

However spurious, that legal concept certainly was embraced by state authorities, who declared and catalogued their citizens' lost property with a truly bureaucratic dedication, building a strong case for the day when they could finally demand satisfaction.[54] By the turn of the century that day had arrived. The state's attempts to claim stolen property directly, according to the Treaty of Coleraine, were going nowhere.[55] Hawkins warned Creeks of this constantly, yet while Creeks had made strides in halting thefts, securing lost property from more than a decade earlier, when Creek communities were at war with the state of Georgia, was a different matter. That meant that Creek communities, even though their past debts were supposed to have been extinguished at Coleraine, were actually impossibly indebted.

Federal commissioners had guaranteed Creeks the remainder of their land, in perpetuity, in the treaties of New York and Coleraine. Only years later, however, authorities in the Adams administration began openly suggesting that Hawkins secure from the Creek people another land cession as the means to clear their mounting obligations to the state of Georgia.[56] With orders to broach the subject direct from then secretary of war James McHenry, and with state pressure that only increased with time, Hawkins began floating the idea of another land cession as early as 1797, during meetings in both the Upper and Lower countries. Not only was a cession of land Creeks' best way to settle their mounting debts, he urged them, but if they conducted it correctly such a sale would leave the National Council with plenty of cash left over to settle future thefts or raids, or to make bounties available to encourage the return of property, thereby preventing further confrontations. Hawkins not only focused on the Tallassee County but brought up the land between the Oconee and Okmulgee rivers as well, which he was sure would generate more than enough income to keep Creek Country financially secure for generations. Those earliest attempts, however, were soundly defeated. Not only did the majority of Creek headmen decline his advances, it required "that a man should be high in the confidence of the Indians to be able to mention the subject in the public square without being insulted." Even in 1797, however, Hawkins understood that the time would soon come when headmen would have little choice. Moving beyond the debts in claims and in blood that Creeks already owed, he also understood that the deerskin trade continued to decline, and more and more warriors were falling behind on their trading debts, both to private trading outfits like the Panton and Leslie firm and to the operations run by the federal government. As deer became scarcer it was land, he knew, that would be Creeks' only hope for a stable future. If the sale provided the capital and the motivation Creek families would need to begin a transition from hunting to planting and ranching, Creeks would be able to make that latest cession their last. Agents of the Panton and Leslie trading firm knew similarly. They recognized the potential in such a deal to satisfy their accounts and added to the growing chorus in 1798 that either requested or suggested a sale of land.[57]

It took years of constant pressure and ever-increasing debts to wear the Creek leadership down. For two more years, in fact, Hawkins broached the subject only to be aggressively rebuffed. In 1799 land continued to elicit a strong response: "the bare mention excites very disagreeable emotions."[58] It was ill-advised a year later even to bring it up in council because of Bowles's presence. Yet requests continued, including from Henry Dearborn, the new secretary of war, and so Hawkins continued to exert pressure.[59] At the 1801 National Council his withering approach seemed finally to be having an effect. While the atmosphere grew tense as soon as he brought the subject up, and was most likely one of the reasons more headmen began to talk longingly of the past, there was little denying his argument. Whitetail deer were practically extinct, communities lacked trade goods, and hunters had no way to resolve their past debts, let alone buy anything else on credit. And then of course there were the anxious Georgia state authorities waiting in the wings, continually demanding outrageous sums of money for lost and stolen properties. There was less and less future to be found in Bowles's promises, many headmen were also realizing. By that point he was more or less in hiding at Mikasuki, which left Creeks "alarmed at the situation of their affairs." Hawkins was quick to take advantage of the situation; to him, the choice was clear. On the one hand Creeks owed "a debt of blood to the united states." On the other, land was plenty in Creek Country, and a lot of it was no longer useful to communities in any sort of practical way. Creeks only needed a fraction of it to ranch or plant like Americans, Georgians wanted the remainder, and they would pay handsomely for it. Few alternatives remained: "to sell, to steal, or starve."[60] A year later enough of the National Council finally relented. They agreed to meet with American commissioners at the newly constructed Fort Wilkinson, on the Creek side of the Oconee River, to discuss a sale.[61] Members of the National Council, declaring themselves an adequate representation of the Creek Nation, would negotiate.

The Treaty of Fort Wilkinson represented another crossroads moment for the National Council. The differences between the proposed treaty in 1802 and previous treaty attempts, at Coleraine or Rock Landing, would be clear. The previous treaties, like the ones that preceded them into the colonial era, involved scores of headmen, including micos, tustunnuggees, and other community leaders. The importance of an overwhelming representation of communities from all corners of Creek Country was critical to the success of the treaty, which was also demonstrated in examples of failed ones, like the three Georgia attempts in the wake of the Revolution, or even the Treaty of New York. Those treaties did not conform to the traditions of plurality that Emistisiguo once spoke of and were consequently rejected by the majority of Creek people as illegitimate. Even the most recent treaty, at Coleraine in 1796, reflected the continued relevancy of that diplomatic tradition. Dozens of headmen made their mark on the treaty documents, and even though there was some pushback from particular communities, the conference was widely seen as legitimate. New treaties, beginning with the proposed one at Fort Wilkinson, would no longer have so many Creek signatures on them. Diplomatic plurality, long the bane of British, state, and then American officials, was a tradition that the National Council began to challenge as it assumed more control over Creek Country. Creek state control, which at first only extended to maintaining the peace, now began to extend to the maintenance of territorial boundaries. The control of Creek territory and the natural resources held within would now be the business of the National Council, marking another political Creek step consistent with state formation.

The National Council's decision to negotiate such a sweeping land deal was an impressive show of faith in the new consolidated Creek leadership. There was no doubt, however, that it would be contested. While Cusseta and Coweta headmen were present at Fort Wilkinson, for example, others from Ooseoochee and Chehaw were not.[62] Those communities were still receptive to Bowles's competing vision of the Southeast, and although he was in hiding in Mikasuki he was still struggling mightily to disrupt the conference. He was quick to reach out to the Tallassee King, the Little Prince, and even the White Bird-Tail King of Cusseta, asking them all to come south and not to restrain their young men from raiding the frontiers south toward Pensacola.[63] By several accounts, at least a few Creeks from the Lower Country were of the same mind.[64] With the treaty conference at Fort Wilkinson moving forward and with only members of the National Council planning to attend, Creek Country seemed poised to suffer from disruptive but familiar undercurrents of community interest and factionalism.

The Mad Dog, still at the head of the National Council, led the negotiations, claiming that he represented "my young kings, warriors, and my nation." But very quickly he made clear that neither he nor any other member of the council came to Fort Wilkinson in a mood to bargain. The opening of the conference was cordial and full of ceremony, including the Eagle Tail dance, but the discussions quickly grew heated.[65] For days both the American and Creek groups laid out their claims. The council resisted the idea of selling lands but faced relentless pressure from both the Georgians and Hawkins, who turned to pages upon pages of claims for property and blood. At first the headmen were firm and responded by listing their own dead, which included claims from Cusseta and Coweta headmen. The Cusseta Mico lost two men, "and at Coleraine asked for, and think I was promised, satisfaction," which he had not received. And then there was the Mad Dog, who rehashed the death of young David Cornells, which had happened years earlier. Even though American authorities promised several times to see justice served, nothing had ever been done.[66] Why were state authorities demanding satisfaction for promises made to them before Coleraine, when they were unwilling to make good on their own promises, many of which were more recent? Plenty of Creeks, from Cussetas to Yuchis, had died at the hand of state settlers. Why were they expected to pay, the Creek delegation pressed, when their American counterparts were not?

Hawkins countered that argument forcefully with lists of his own, detailing killings by Cowetas and Yuchis, raids on the Cumberland settlements by warriors from the Upper Country, and so on. Creeks would find themselves on the losing side of that sort of challenge, he charged. But it was not just killings; "the keeping of negroes and prisoners, after the peace, was and is a great source of uneasiness." Next was horse stealing and then Bowles. The inability of the National Council to deal adequately with their Seminole neighbors to the south was also a problem, and Hawkins dwelt upon that subject for some time, turning to a familiar approach. The Creek Nation "may be compared to a piece of spunk," he declared, "that fire is struck in it, on the side of the Seminoles, and it is likely to burn up the whole nation, if not timely extinguished." Creeks stood on the precipice, he assured the National Council, yet the American government had provided commissioners to make things work. Those commissioners included himself, one of the Creek peoples' closest friends, and the National Council's most potent allies. "The red people should sell some of these lands to pay their debts, and provide for their future wants," which was what he and the others were there to see done.[67]

After days of tense exchanges, the Mad Dog finally addressed the issue on behalf of the National Council. First were renewed promises and warnings, both of which reflected Creek state power. "We consider that, after this treaty," he declared, "when we go home, we shall try to put in force our warriors; there are a good many towns here present, who speak upon it; there is no other way to fulfil the promise of the old treaty."[68] The council then directed strong words of caution further to the south, strengthening its stance against Bowles in ways that invoked the same collectivity. "You must no longer persist in the conduct you have hitherto pursued," the Mad Dog and Muclassee Hopoie penned to the Seminole communities. "You must drop it; stop where you are, and adopt another course of conduct; you must listen to the voice of the chiefs of the nation." The Mad Dog represented thirty-two towns in all, "while I am speaking, from the whole Creek nation," and it "is they who talk to you."[69]

The National Council's continued projection of Creek solidarity was now a half decade old, but headmen still struggled to project a common voice over the looming and contentious issue of land. Sooner or later, however, the two groups had to find some sort of resolution. Americans pushed for the two separate cessions: the Tallassee County, and then the entire fork of the Oconee and Okmulgee rivers. Together not only would they serve as a payment for whatever Georgians still claimed, but they would fund an annuity that would pay for Creeks' needs for the foreseeable future. At first Hawkins and other American commissioners suspected that they might be able to gain both cessions in their entirety. Surprisingly, the Creek delegation dealt first with the chunk between the Oconee and Okmulgee rivers, and although in the end Americans gained only a portion of what they requested, they did gain quite a bit. Instead of all the land between the rivers Creeks relinquished only an eastern portion it, to be marked out by a physical boundary that ran north along a natural ridge. In debates that demonstrated anew how some communities claimed more control over particular stretches of land than others, that cession was approved relatively easily by headmen reflecting interests in the north. Far away from the Lower Country and close to Cumberland settlements, evidently it was an easy trade. All council representatives present, including the Mad Dog and the Big Warrior of Tuckabatchee, Hopoie Mico of the Hickory Ground, Tuskenehau Chapco of Coweta, and Tussekiah Mico and Cusseta Mico of Cusseta, agreed to the cession after only one round of debate. The lands below the Altamaha, however, were another story.[70]

Because of the Tallassee County's proximity to several Lower Country communities, debates over this tract of land proved much more divisive. Very quickly "such difficulties and divisions ensued in their councils as prevented their coming to any conclusion." It was clear those lands "belonged to certain disaffected tribes" along the Flint and Chattahoochee rivers, including Ooseoochees, Chehaws, Hitchitis, Yuchis, and Broken Arrows, and they were simply not interested in parting with them, regardless of the price. Groups from those communities had purposely boycotted the council at Fort Wilkinson to prove it and instead were probably down with Bowles. If the sale of those lands took place anyway, without them, it was not known just how negatively they would react. Perhaps they would flock to Bowles or even attack the Georgia frontier outright. If that happened, the headmen feared, the consequences would be disastrous.[71] Such strong dissension made dealing for the Tallassee County imprudent, the Creek delegation concluded, and they pressed the commissioners to move on. Hawkins was candid in his later accounts to Secretary of War Henry Dearborn, explaining that there was "apprehension serious and alarming to the old chiefs, that if they ceded any part of their country, their young warriors might resist it," and if they joined in with Bowles, it would "divide the nation, wrest the government from those who at present administer it and by some hasty and imprudent act involve their country in ruin." The Tallassee County had the potential, both he and fellow commissioner James Wilkinson feared, to create too intense a challenge for the Creek state to control, and perhaps even end the Creek National Council.[72] The Tallassee lands were emerging as the biggest test yet to the Creek state-making project.

Those later sentiments were not anything like what either Hawkins or Wilkinson projected in the moment, however. Instead, in multiple speeches they lectured the chiefs aggressively, even condescendingly, over their unwillingness to challenge a few headmen of the Lower Country in the name of the Creek Nation. Who were these dissenting headmen? Where were they? Why did they not respect the council, their Creek representatives, or the American commissioners? Instead, they had "taken the talk of an impostor," Bowles, who was "a pirate, and a common liar."[73] The two were positively ruthless, pressing the National Council to exercise the voice it claimed on behalf of all Creeks and rely on the coercive power of the Creek state to enforce its will. However aggressive or confrontational their approach seemed, it worked. The two wore down the Cusseta and Coweta chiefs in particular. Because they too were presumed to have sway over the claimed lands, they were the key to the deal. Eventually they came around to giving up the lands, meaning the agreement technically had enough authority to move forward. For those two communities to be the most reticent is understandable, for beyond the still somewhat abstract notion of ceding lands on behalf of all Creeks, they would be the ones to answer to their neighbors. As Hawkins and Wilkinson unhappily prepared to leave, however, the Coweta and Cusseta representatives approached them and declared that the Creek Nation was willing to add the Tallassee County. If the price was right they would agree and accept responsibility for their neighbors' objections.[74]

The addition of the Tallassee lands, although hotly debated, represented the Creek Nation's most significant decision to date. It seemed finally to satisfy Georgians' complaints, cleared hunters' outstanding debts, and guaranteed Creek communities a sizable annuity that was guaranteed for at least a decade. Surprisingly, it made Georgians fairly happy as well. While the smaller-than-expected Oconee cession was a bit of a disappointment, the state regained the highly coveted Tallassee County, making Fort Wilkinson an unqualified success.[75] Although the outcome of the treaty was bittersweet, the Creek leadership must have been relieved as well. Over the previous few years they had taken increasingly decisive steps, moving beyond the rhetoric of a Creek Nation and making it a reality. Fort Wilkinson represented the largest, most significant step in that process. Forty or so headmen, a collection spanning Creek Country, made their mark on the treaty, almost a third fewer than did so eight years earlier at Coleraine. Yet they did not complain about that modest showing, as they had in the past. They were, the delegates declared, authorized to speak for all of Creek Country. And the position of the signatures demonstrated the cosmopolitan makeup of the council. The Mad Dog was first to sign. He was followed by Tustunnuggee Thlucco of Cusseta, making a leading warrior the second signature overall. Hopoie Mico was next, followed then by several headmen of note, including the Tallassee King, which was surprising; then the Tussekiah Mico and the White Bird-Tail King of Cusseta; and then Tuskenehau Chapco of Coweta. The Hallowing King's signature was the only conspicuous absence.[76] That was problematic, considering Cowetas and Cussetas provided the most important promises during the treaty negotiations. With or without his input, however, the promises made at Fort Wilkinson still represented the most decisive stand the National Council, which contained a strong Coweta voice, had made yet.[77]

At the end of the conference the aging Mad Dog abdicated his Speaker position to Hopoie Mico of the Hickory Ground. There was no clear mechanism—there certainly was not a written one—to guide such a transition. Cultural dictates and political exigencies were the driving forces behind the National Council, and members appeared to be making the rules as they went along. The seat of the National Council would continue in the Speaker's home square ground, however, and so for the first time that shifted as well, from Tuckabatchee to the Hickory Ground. Hopoie Mico was a well-known supporter of Creek centralization and the idea of the Creek state, and "desirious to introduce a regular & efficient government among his people," according to Hawkins, who saw the transition as a positive one.[78] Americans would need a strong leader during such a critical period; Hopoie Mico's National Council would immediately face pushback, as would the Cusseta and Coweta headmen in particular, about the Tallassee County cession. Resistance was to be expected, of course, but now the National Council would be responsible for physically suppressing dissent in the Lower Country, seeing that the boundary was run, and making good on its future promises to Americans.

Spanish accounts were the first one to describe the fallout. When James Durouzeaux heard rumors of a deal circulating through the Coweta neighborhood he penned Vincente Folch in Pensacola, and he described a lot of confusion and at least some disappointment: There were plenty who seemed "somewhat dissattisfied at their having given so laerg a boedey of land," and "The Indians down in the Lower Towns apaer to be a letle reconciled." Later, his outlook was even more hesitant. "From what I can learn," he penned again from Coweta, "the business is not finally settled as yet," and he actually doubted the treaty would stand because "a great many of the Indians don't approve of it." Further to the south the situation was even worse. Everyone "about Jack Kanards is against it," and, as was suspected, rather than attend the conference many of them had indeed gone south to assist Bowles in his latest unsuccessful attempt to retake Fort San Marcos de Apalache. When they returned home, both Kinnard and Hopoie Haujo of Ooseoochee worried, they would "do some mischief at that place." Durouzeaux hoped the Coweta and Cusseta headmen would be able to put a stop to the business for the sake of planters in Spanish East Florida but warned Folch that they needed to be on their guard.[79]

Although the dissent coming from the Lower Country was not nearly as radical or violent as it had been a decade earlier, it was still alarming. The response from the National Council would heavily influence how, or even if, the most important terms of Fort Wilkinson would be satisfied. Boundary lines, in the past at least, had a nasty habit of not ever being completed. To make sure these new ones did, headmen met in Little Tallassee in October 1802. Although it was not the usual time for a meeting of the National Council it certainly was needed, and there headmen declared their intention to snuff out the loudest voices of dissent. First headmen addressed Bowles, passing "some regulations and laws to drive out of the Nation all stragaelers or mischief makers or any person of a light character and such who had been connected" with him. They ordered "such to leave the Nation" or suffer severe punishment.

They also clamped down further on unauthorized traders and on horse purchases. The declarations were intended to keep peace "with all white people" and "for all Indian Nations to be at peace with each other and to be of one mind and of one Government." This was clearly an attempt to project Creek solidarity, sending a stern warning to the communities in the south not to challenge the treaty or the National Council. Those decisions were spread south, and members of the council sent for Mikasuki headmen in particular, in whose company Bowles still stayed, so that they could bring them around to "the same way of thinking as the whole nation is, and to be of one talk."[80]

The bulk of those talks were directed at Bowles, which hinted at a growing determination among the Creek leadership that his continued residence in the region was simply no longer acceptable. While he had been confined to Mikasuki and in hiding more or less for three years, that did not stop him from putting pen to paper, and what he produced in 1802 and 1803 was very unhelpful to regional stability. Those letters were for the most part localized in the Florida panhandle, stirring up Mikasukis and Seminoles and spreading disruption throughout East and West Florida, yet they always threatened to creep further north. Perhaps his words would have the same disastrous effect after the Treaty of Fort Wilkinson as they had had a decade earlier. Soon he was distributing powder and ammunition at Lower Eufala, a settlement in the Florida panhandle, hoping the Creeks and Seminoles in the area might help him in another attempt to retake San Marcos and then from there raid into East Florida. Those developments were decidedly unwelcomed by Cowetas and Cussetas, who "all seemed very mutch concerned" about his actions.[81] Early in 1803 Bowles was considering moving north directly into Creek Country, through Coweta and even to Tuckabatchee or the Hickory Ground. Evidently he had allies among "the chiefs in opposition" to the National Council there, who seemed interested in listening to him and even having him speak at the council. He was carrying "bad talks," Georgia governor John Milledge warned, he was personally threatening Hawkins, and if people were not careful "it is possible, if not probable," that he could even influence a number of Creeks to raid into Georgia.[82]

The conditions were more than right, in other words, for the Treaty of Fort Wilkinson to cause real trouble for the National Council. What is most impressive about the months after the treaty, then, was how unfounded many of these fears turned out to be. Quite a bit had changed in the previous decade. Bowles's anti-treaty, anti-American talks were lauded after the Treaty of New York, for example. After Fort Wilkinson his talks were largely the same, pushing for a rejection of the treaty and promising British support of Creek hunting lands. But those talks found a much more tepid response from the same communities Bowles was once living among. Indeed, although he pressed forward with his plans to give talks in Creek Country, even at the National Council, there were many more people conspiring against him than were supporting him. Both the Americans and Spaniards were also actively making plans for his capture, but Hawkins feared the legality of seizing Bowles in Creek Country on behalf of the American government and hoped instead that "he be laid hold of by the voluntary exertions of the chiefs, who it seems are inclined to do so if he comes to the ensuing meeting." He also sensed that Spaniards would want him as well, which was indeed the case. A Spanish emissary arrived at Tuckabatchee just before the scheduled National Council to make claims on behalf of the Spanish government and the Panton and Leslie firm, and Hawkins quickly relayed to the headmen that Governor Folch sincerely hoped "that if Bowles or any of his gang should come to the meeting, the chiefs would never allow them to go back."[83]

The chiefs responded to both the Spanish and American requests with resolution. The Singer of Oakfuskee, who had heard Bowles's talks before in the Upper Country and was no fan of his, took a leading role in the plan to seize him. He "saw plainly an end must be put to their disturbances," he declared in a talk to other headmen, "and we should see it." As a voice of Creek solidarity and the developing state structure, the Singer was as clear as he was determined. Creeks would persevere in "organizing a government for his Nation, in making good laws, and causing them to be obeyed," and Bowles had no place in that future.[84] And when Bowles did show, the Singer made good on those promises. With headmen mostly from the Upper Country, including William Weatherford, Sam Moniac, and the Mad Dog, and according to one account "at the head of fifteen hundred Indian warriors," the Singer marched boldly into Bowles's camp, overwhelmed his Seminole and Mikasuki associates, and clapped him in tailor-made handcuffs. Soon he was off, under heavy guard, for Spanish reimprisonment.[85]

The controversial Treaty of Fort Wilkinson and then the subsequent seizure of Bowles were remarkable accomplishments for the National Council—both moved forward with a frankly surprising degree of success. In the wake of Bowles's arrest it was only "a general murmur for the day only" that "ran through the chiefs in opposition." By the evening, "with the prudent conduct of the council of the Nation the whole subsided, and they were brought to take the United States and Spain by the hand of friendship."[86] Bowles, it turned out, went out with little more than a whimper. In his place, Hawkins was quick to laud the chiefs' decisive action. Their years-long response to his presence was perhaps now the National Council's greatest single victory—greater even than the Treaty of Fort Wilkinson. In reflecting on his seizure to James Madison, in fact, Hawkins gave a glowing appraisal, not only of the Council but of its success in the region. Bowles "must have seen a material change in the manners of the Indians," Hawkins was sure. Since his re-arrival in Florida two Indians and three slaves had been shot, almost two dozen Indians had been whipped along with one white man, and other slaves wounded by direct action of the National Council. Perhaps Bowles thought he could change all that, "until he was apprehended in the midst of his guards and adherents and at the eve of imagination of being a king of the four nations, and quits the stage in irons."[87] Even more meaningful was the silence of the "chiefs in opposition." There had been no violent opposition to Fort Wilkinson so far, and not a tear shed over Bowles, who would never be seen again. Creek communities—even the most volatile ones—might not have appreciated the evolving Creek leadership, but they were not showing it. By not rising up at a time when it seemed all but inevitable that they would, even the most hesitant Creeks seemed to be legitimizing the National Council.

The council's work, however, was not done. As the boundary for the Treaty of Fort Wilkinson began to move forward, voices of dissent steadily grew louder. No one was threatening direct opposition, but several communities were signaling they were not ready to watch a surveying crew march through their neighborhoods just yet. "I have been for two months among the upper and lower Creeks," Hawkins wrote in early in 1804, "endeavouring among other things to bring the opposition to aid or at least not to oppose the completion of the line from Alatamaha to St. Marys." More action was necessary to keep the boundary line from again becoming an issue, as it had after the Treaty of New York. As the time grew near the National Council appointed several representatives to do that, and assist both Hawkins and the surveying party. Not surprisingly, the participation of Coweta and Cusseta headmen was significant. Tuskenehau Thlucco of Coweta and the Dog Warrior and Cusseta Warrior of Cusseta assisted personally. Each of them strong tustunnuggees and leaders, the three were making good on the promises they had made during the treaty negotiations.[88]

The surveyors would need that strong show of force. As they began to descend on the Lower Country to mark out the new boundary a handful of local headmen emerged to declare they would not go along quietly. Their plan of resistance, of course, reflected how localized their anger was. The Chehaw, Hitchiti, and Ooseoochee headmen could only disrupt the surveyors when they were scheduled to complete the southernmost extent of the new boundary line, around the St. Mary's River. Nevertheless, they were determined to do that. Earlier they had agreed to send representatives to assist the surveyors and escort them through the region, which was already volatile because of the presence of Mikasukis and Seminoles. In the spring of 1804 the surveying team, led by American army major Constant Freeman, was approaching the section where the Hitchiti and Chehaw headmen were supposed to meet and guide them. When he arrived, however, the headmen were not there, ushering in the sort of confrontation that the National Council feared at Fort Wilkinson. Soon Freeman complained that the headmen had met locally, prior to his arrival, and that their absence was deliberate. A runner brought similar news to Hawkins, that "there was no Indians intended to start from that quarter to attend."[89] Freeman, a long-time actor along the Creek-Georgia frontier, was no stranger to the violence he likely faced without their acquiescence. The surveying party was "without guides to conduct us throu the Country. The Indians are dissatisfied and no doubt would intercept our progress by stealing our horses, and every other means in their power." He rightly understood that without the assistance of the headmen he was in jeopardy as equally as the boundary line. He suggested having warriors from the Upper Country come south to assist them, enlist soldiers from a local federal garrison to escort them, or perhaps even both. To continue otherwise would be inviting violent confrontation.[90]

The intransigent Tallassee King, it turned out, was again at the bottom of the disruption. For years he had translated Bowles's messages and sent other disturbing talks to the Lower Country, and this was no different. By 1802 the National Council was seriously considering the possibility of having him killed, and they considered executing the Little Prince of Broken Arrow as well. Evidently the latter man too was listening to Bowles's talks and was now a part of the more reticent headmen who had caused so much disruption in the 1801 and 1802 National Councils. It never came to that with the Little Prince, however. It is not clear what exactly changed his mind, but he "turned against Bowles" quickly and retained his position of authority in the Lower Country, urging headmen not to do any more damage. The Tallassee King, on the other hand, made no such reversal. He was present for the Treaty of Fort Wilkinson and signed it, yet soon he was back to his old game. He was spouting anti-American rhetoric, claiming to local headmen that the French were "returning to their former places" and by doing so had "put a stop to the people being as good as thir word." Ooseoochee communities were soon all "against running the line," while Chehaws were threatening to raid into southern Georgia.[91] Dissent over the Fort Wilkinson treaty still simmered in the southernmost part of the Lower Country, it was now clear, and without strong action, it would not be going away. The dissent was particularly localized, and not very popular, which must have given the National Council hope. Still, that sort of dissent still had the ability to derail the implementation of Fort Wilkinson, and it had to be addressed.

The council moved quickly to interject, and both Hawkins and Timothy Barnard matched its efforts. Barnard suggested sending Cusseta and Coweta headmen supporters down to Kinnard's, "to push them on."[92] Several headmen soon made independent, coercive visits. The Little Prince traveled south from Broken Arrow to confront Ooseoochee headman Hopoie Haujo "himself to hear from him the reason of this disappointment."[93] Further to the north Alexander Cornells moved to put pressure directly on the Tallassee King, "the head of the opposition, to know from him what he meant." Around the same time several other headmen, led by Speaker Hopoie Mico and Muclassee Hopoie, spent a good deal of the National Council meeting in the spring of 1804 suggesting solutions.[94] It was during that conference that Hawkins pressured the headmen, particularly Hopoie Mico, to take a more decisive stand. "Here the nation are assembled," he declared, and as the great chief, he "must be obeyed as such. Every man, red, white or black, must look here and to you and pay attention to the orders of this assembly delivered by you as the law of the land."[95] Hopoie Mico, like the Mad Dog before him, faced a defining moment. Either Creek state actors would overpower and subdue the dissenters in the Lower Country, or it would fail, undermining the legitimacy of the National Council and drawing into question Creek solidarity.

The 1804 National Council meeting was revealing. Anger over Wilkinson was not particularly widespread, but currents of resentment clearly ran through the Lower Country, and the council's response was less than decisive. Several headmen, led by the now extremely elderly Mad Dog, suggested a delegation move through the opposing towns and work to find a peaceful solution, "and they were certain it would open their ears." Hawkins advocated for a more forceful approach, pushing the chiefs to build upon the assertiveness they had already shown. He took that moment to remind them of the particularly disgraceful actions of the Ooseoochee headmen. Apparently several council headmen had recently confronted them and the Ooseoochees made a scene, spewing contempt for the Mad Dog and Hopoie Mico, Hawkins, and even the president of the United States. Instead, they declared, "they would adhere to old times, they preferred the old bow and arrow to the gun." It had been an insulting and embarrassing confrontation by any standard, and there was no reason to assume members of the National Council would gain anything by attempting to further conciliate such characters. No, this was a time for resolve. "It was not our business to be running after thieves and mischiefmakers and to be influenced in our conduct by that of a people who act like spoilt children." If the opposition would not attend to the orders of their chiefs, "we must make them, our warriors must make them," and if it was necessary, the federal government would make them.[96] Soon Hopoie Mico sent headmen down to Ooseoochee to feel out the situation while he made arrangements to meet afterward in council at Coweta.[97]

Despite Hawkins's encouragement, state and federal authorities offered little help. They never gave up hope for gaining the rest of the Oconee and Okmulgee fork and were quick to begin hoping out loud. That is, of course, far from surprising, considering how little of the land was ceded at Fort Wilkinson. The fork of the Oconee was, to Georgians and even federal authorities, unfinished business. Almost immediately after Fort Wilkinson pressure began to build again, with Secretary of War Dearborn and even President Jefferson advocating for further negotiations.[98] Only with all of the Oconee-Okmulgee lands, even Hawkins was convinced, would Georgians be satisfied and the Creek Nation secure. "If we succeed in bringing the Indians around to accommodate Georgia on Ocmulgee," Hawkins penned Jefferson, "we shall have gained much as that boundary will satisfy Georgia for the present and may remain for ten or twenty years." Meanwhile settlers made their own plans. Upset by the little land they had received in 1802, they were soon moving onto the lands illegally. As early as the spring of 1803 there were reports that plenty had, "and that Several other Famalies were Expected to follow them In a Few Days for the Same purpose." That was sure to enrage Creeks, of course, and so on at least one occasion a Georgia militia commander was forced to take action against the squatters.[99] Even though state authorities in this instance actually made an attempt to control their citizens, which was quite remarkable, they would not do so for long.[100]

Word that Americans were already interested in more land provided little comfort to a National Council that was still struggling to quell resistance created by the last deal. Headmen from Ooseoochee, Chehaw, Hitchiti, and other communities deep in the Lower Country who were already unhappy with the Treaty of Fort Wilkinson would certainly not react well to the idea of selling more, wherever it was. Hopoie Mico decided to travel south personally, in the name of the National Council, and confront the leaders of the resistance directly. Although he was determined, opposition would be strong, and he asked for Hawkins's advice. He got more than he probably bargained for. The Ooseoochee voice alone would be fierce, and the dissenters from that corner would oppose everything, Hawkins warned. Yet the stakes were as high as they had ever been, and as Speaker of the National Council Hopoie Mico had to lead the Creek Nation past them. The solution had to be strong, decisive talk, backed by violence, if necessary. Make an example out of the Ooseoochees, and the rest of the communities would fall in place. Creeks, like Americans, could "set examples and we can compel some to follow and some we know are well disposed and will gladly follow."[101]

Hopoie Mico faced two separate issues at Ooseoochee. First was the failure of Creek headmen in the south to assist in the running of the Fort Wilkinson boundary line; the second was their almost guaranteed refusal to part with the rest of the Okmulgee lands. Both had to be resolved. "I must repeat again you will be opposed, and strongly opposed," Hawkins warned the headman; "you will be threatened." That was indeed the case. When Hopoie Mico and his entourage arrived at Ooseoochee, the conference proved to be just as bad as Hawkins warned—"it was such a one as made the speaker ashamed." The anti-cession, traditionalist stance being asserted by Ooseoochees and others was even more aggressive than he had feared. Not only would they not consent to another land cession, they declared they were backing out of the Treaty of Fort Wilkinson. They then demanded that Hawkins leave the Lower Country altogether. Whether he moved into Georgia or into the Upper Country they did not care, but they did not want anything else to do either with him or with any other white person of authority in the region.[102]

The way the Ooseoochee headmen approached the National Council and American interference was very much reminiscent of an earlier time, one where they clearly did not consider themselves beholden to a larger regional voice or even the voices of those around them. The legitimacy of the National Council hung now on how quickly and completely Hopoie Mico could snuff out this challenge. The Speaker stood his ground at Ooseoochee in what became an impressive show of grit. First came an important and rather impressive assertion. It was he, not Hawkins, who led the Creek people, Hopoie Mico charged. Hawkins was a constant supportive voice of the Creek state, at times pushing the leadership on in their obligations, but he was not at this meeting, now, and he was not someone the dissenters needed to complain about. Hopoie Mico was the Speaker of the Creek Nation and therefore of all Creeks, he countered defiantly, and it was he who had made the trip to Ooseoochee on behalf of its governing body, the National Council. He was quick to continue. The Fort Wilkinson line would go forward. Not only that, but settlers wanted more land, and the Creek Nation was not opposed to a sale if it was made on the right terms. The Okmulgee lands would provide incredible financial stability, he argued, and would gain a much firmer, natural boundary between Georgians than what existed now. The treaty would also continue to develop a strong alliance with the American government, which by that point had already built strings of forts along the boundary lines to protect Creek interests. In short, not only was the Treaty of Fort Wilkinson the best way forward for Creeks, a future land cession was as well. A few straggling dissenters with sad visions of the past would not upset their hopes for a better, more stable Creek future, Hopoie Mico ultimately declared.[103] This was the will of the Creek National Council, and its members would act accordingly.

The evolving boundary dispute and its undercurrents of traditionalism and community interest were reminders that the Creek National Council was by no means in total control of Creek Country. Not all Creeks were swept up in Creek nationalism, which clearly was producing voices of fission as well as fusion, and not everyone recognized the authority of the National Council. But the line Hopoie Mico drew in Ooseoochee was a strong one. Reports circulated, for instance, that it was only a single headman or two from Ooseoochee who constituted the bulk of the opposition, not even the entire community. Of Coweta, Cusseta, Broken Arrow, Yuchi, Ooseoochee, and Oconee communities, only Ooseoochee was wayward, Hawkins confirmed, and the rest needed to unite "with us and let us do what your judgement dictates."[104] The National Council was meeting in ten days. Hawkins and other commissioners would be there to discuss the land deal with members of the Creek National Council, and Hopoie Mico would see to it that the meeting would be productive. "I will see them, talk with them, and do what I think is for the best," he declared to the Ooseoochees. "If you come it is well, if you do not, I know what to do."[105] He and the other headmen present would debate and decide on a cession, with or without the dissenters' input.

In ten days' time that was precisely the case. Soon Hopoie Mico and other representatives of the National Council met Hawkins, James Wilkinson, and another commissioner at Tuckabatchee, where they began discussing a suitable price for the remaining lands east of the Okmulgee River.[106] Several of the dissenting communities from the Lower Country appeared as well, which not only represented a tremendous victory for the Speaker and for the National Council but must have come as a surprise. Ooseoochees were at least willing to hear the offers and voice their disagreements, which for the second time seemed to be an acknowledgment by hesitant Creek communities that the National Council was a legitimate political entity that needed to be considered. Hawkins was proud that the National Council had "agreed that a deputation vested with competent authority shall go to the seat of government this fall to complete the business," and other Creeks seemed to agree.[107] And the deputation punctuated a powerful trend. At Rock Landing there were hundreds of headmen, and scores signed the treaty at Coleraine. At Fort Wilkinson there were far fewer, and at this latest land cession there was perhaps the smallest number of headmen yet—fewer attended now than had even been at the highly contentious Treaty of New York.[108]

Although they made the decision to come, the opposition group, still led by Ooseoochees, Chehaws, and Hitchitis, came strongly opposed to any deal. Even though the land under question was far to the north, they still held firm. The "opposition commenced, and continued to oppose, with all the arguments and rudeness in their power," according to Hawkins, and did so for several days. He worried shortly before the council began that confidence among the National Council members was not particularly high, and the prospects for attaining the land were not necessarily good.[109] Nevertheless, when the commissioners arrived and the council convened Hopoie Mico from the Hickory Ground was there, along with the Big Warrior and the Mad Dog of Tuckabatchee, and the Cusseta Mico and Tussekiah Mico of Cusseta. Another, Hillis Haujo, would later declare that their talks were "the talk of all the nation."[110]

Despite having exerted tremendous pressure on dissenting chiefs to attend the council, Hopoie Mico also proved to be no lackey of the American commissioners. Although prepared to cede Creek lands he was determined to make Americans reach deep into their pockets. He, with several other headmen, knew the quality of the lands, "as well as the obligation they were under to the United States." When it came to grazing, farming, and even timbering—values Americans knew well—Creek land was worth a lot, and he was determined to get every penny, even though what he wanted was far more than Hawkins knew the government was willing to give. He insisted that each town have upwards of $500 in debt forgiven annually in addition to an annuity, which would amount to a much larger yearly arrangement than Creek communities received from Coleraine—a payment they were also guaranteed to receive. And there would be no further land deals, no matter the terms or the price. This made for tense exchanges between the delegation and Hawkins, who insisted that the total sum of such an arrangement was not only unheard of but was a sizable portion of the entire federal government's operating budget. Yet the stakes were high, as the Speaker elaborated. He had won over the dissenting towns with those figures—"the opposition would join, and sign with us," he was told, "if I would give for it what he asked." When Hawkins countered with a third of what he was demanding, Hopoie Mico and the other headmen made it clear they were willing to walk away. "They persisted to the moment of departure, which I offered the sum mentioned in the treaty, and told them expressly, that it was not unlikely it would not be ratified, and we should have the whole subject before us again." Nevertheless it was Hopoie Mico's numbers, amounting to almost twenty thousand dollars in cash, annuities, and debt forgiveness, that were written into the treaty and sent to Congress for ratification.[111]

Hawkins was correct in fearing that the cession was too pricey, and despite Thomas Jefferson's suggestions, Congress did not ratify the treaty. In September, however, Alexander Cornells, the Big Warrior of Tuckabatchee, Tuskenehau Chapco, William McIntosh, and a few other headmen were on their way to Washington to negotiate a settlement with the Jefferson administration directly.[112] A year later the treaty was ratified with slight changes in dollar amounts.[113] The Treaty of Washington, as it was then called, became law. Not only was it a success for Hopoie Mico as Speaker, but this latest treaty punctuated a critical, and successful, few years. Bowles was gone and two separate treaties had negotiated land cessions in both the Upper and Lower countries. These actions were met with opposition but not violence or even widespread dissent. Anger was localized in a few communities to the south, but in the end that was not enough to undo anything. Hopoie Mico, projecting the voice of the National Council, was able to overcome a dangerous resistance, making decisions and declaring them the will of all

Creeks. Headmen in Ooseoochee or Chehaw might not have thought highly of the Mad Dog, or of Hopoie Mico, but ultimately they listened to them. The Creek state system was far from perfect, and certainly was not unanimously accepted, but even the most hesitant Creeks were acting as if it existed.

PART 3

The Fate of the Creek Nation

9 / The National Council Splinters

When the President sees my talk, he will know I have answered in full. I have examined it myself, my chiefs and warriors have examined it they tell you I must not allow it and must say no.
—The Tallassee King, May 15, 1811

Only years after a handful of representatives of the National Council returned from Washington, having concluded a sweeping treaty with the American government, the council's legitimacy was being thrown into question. Political unity in Creek Country began to splinter—more headmen were opposing each other angrily, and more Creek communities were questioning the authority of the National Council. But these new waves of dissent were different. Their sources were all external, associated with either American governmental failures or the pressure of American expansionism, neither of which the Council proved capable of addressing. Federal authorities failed to keep the promises they made in Washington, and they did little to stop continued trespasses on Creek territory by locals afterward. Those, of course, represented long-standing grievances to many Creeks—settlers had always been trespassing on Creek rights, and American authorities had never provided much redress. Yet in the era of the National Council those failures now reflected poorly on a Creek leadership group that had made agreements with the United States using a broad and relatively new authority, had used violence to restrain communities from dissenting, and had done so claiming it was what was best for all Creeks. Every time American officials failed the Creek people, in short, so did the National Council.

Both state and federal legislators introduced new sources of expansionism that not only undermined the authority of the council but chipped away at the sovereignty of the Creek Nation. Tennesseans insisted on river access down the Coosa, Tallapoosa, and Alabama watersheds, for instance, and authorities at both the state and federal levels demanded road access along several routes that traversed Creek Country. All of these requests threatened to grind Creek territorial sovereignty away to nothing, and the National Council fought many of them vigorously. While authorities in the Jefferson and Madison administrations were willing to compensate the Creek leadership to get what they wanted, when the Council turned down their offers they also demonstrated a willingness to simply ignore Creek sovereignty and move forward with their plans unilaterally. They either disregarded or usurped Creek territorial sovereignty when it was more convenient to do so than to accept the decisions of the National Council, delegitimizing and embarrassing the Creek state system they helped create.

Much of that impacted Creek communities unevenly; the pressure of American expansionism fell disproportionately on communities in the Upper Country. Federal legislators, by demonstrating to Creeks that the many changes they had made were essentially meaningless, had sown the seeds of the internal discord that slowly began to emerge within the National Council. And they did so in the region, ironically, that had produced the first real steps in the direction of a Creek nation-state to begin with. Headmen along the Alabama, Coosa, and Tallapoosa watersheds stood to lose much more than did their neighbors to the south, which was also the case when it came to the several post and wagon roads that began to course through their neighborhoods. It was not entirely unhappiness with Americans, then, that began to disrupt the National Council. Territorial concerns that were growing more regional and narrower were creating headmen unsympathetic to the needs of their neighbors, meaning that American expansionism was not only chipping away at Creek territorial sovereignty, it was also chipping away at Creek political nationalism.

The turn of the nineteenth century was a tremendous period of American expansionism. A milestone certainly was Pinckney's Treaty in 1795. It was a treaty that did not involve Creek representatives, of course, even though it would have great bearing on the future of regional politics in the Southeast. In Madrid the governments of the United States and Spain renegotiated access to the Mississippi River, as well as the northern bounds of Spanish West Florida. By resigning its legal claim to most of the land north of the modern-day border of Florida, Spain in effect removed itself from Creek politics, consigning them instead to Americans, which would have devastating long-term implications as far as Creek communities were concerned. The Baron de Carondelet was gone by 1797, replaced by Gayoso. Very soon after the new boundary was drawn, Spanish authorities surrendered their position and fort at St. Stephens, in the Tombigbee District, and it was resettled as Washington County in the Mississippi Territory. Throngs of settlers were not far behind, and soon the U.S. Army constructed Fort Stoddert nearby to solidify possession of the region.[1]

Federal installations like Stoddert represented a dilemma to many Creeks. They were, on the one hand, a sign of stability. In the recent past federal officers had provided dedicated service to Creeks by honoring the American government's treaty agreements with them when their neighbors in Georgia made it perfectly clear they would not. Still, by the dawn of the nineteenth century Stoddert represented one of many forts, outposts, and settlements that marked the shrinking, and now encircled, limits of Creek Country. With federal troops at Forts Hawkins and Lawrence actually in Creek Country and many more on the Georgia border, with the new state of Tennessee to the north, and now with troops at Stoddert and the Mississippi Territory to the west, by the time representatives of the National Council concluded the 1805 Treaty of Washington, Creek Country was pretty well hemmed in.

The Creek leadership group that faced this expanding American presence was also in flux. As had been the case in the past, some headmen faded from Creek politics while others emerged. In the Upper Country the Mad Dog continued to remove himself from politics as he grew elderly, dying in 1812.[2] Little was heard from Charles Weatherford either. Yet Alexander Cornells remained. Although he never gained a position at the head of the National Council, Cornells not only continued to function as Hawkins's assistant and official interpreter for the Upper Country but was, "in fact, the second chief of the nation."[3] Also of importance was Tustunnuggee Thlucco, or the Big Warrior, as well as his son, Tuskenhau.[4] Both men resided in Tuckabatchee, guaranteeing that it would remain central to the operation of the Creek Nation. More surprising was the ascendancy of several headmen from the Lower Country. The Cusseta Mico, already active in the council, continued to grow in importance. Meanwhile the Big Feared of Cusseta, also known as Tuskegee Tustunnuggee, rose in authority as well, as did Tustunnuggee Hopoie, or the Little Prince of Broken Arrow, and the Wolf Warrior of Hitchiti. By that point, according to a contemporary, the Little Prince was "too old for active service" but was in a leadership position in the National Council. And the Wolf Warrior was "the most reputed of our lower chiefs," according to Hawkins.[5]

Having Broken Arrow and Hitchiti headmen rise to positions of regional power was a testament to the stabilizing influence of the National Council along the frontier with Georgia. Hunting lands coveted by communities in the Lower Country, like Hitchiti, were at the root of unhappiness with almost every one of the treaties Creeks negotiated with the state of Georgia as well as with federal authorities, including at Washington. Headmen in the neighborhood had also embraced the anti-American talks of Spaniards and Bowles, even violently at times, with the Little Prince not excepted. He had been so unruly around the turn of the century that the National Council considered having him killed. Yet by 1806 the Little Prince was evidently a reformed man—evidence not only that the National Council was working but also of Hawkins's "civilization" efforts, working as he was his model plantation along the Flint River. The emergence of a leadership group not from Coweta or Cusseta but from communities even further south was the strongest evidence yet that the National Council was being taken seriously by most of the Creek people. Even though it might be disputed, almost everyone now in Creek Country considered it a legitimate voice of the Creek people.

Creeks of mixed ancestry also grew in authority. Timpoochee Barnard was among them. The third son of Timothy Barnard and a Yuchi woman, Timpoochee would gain notoriety as a warrior, "as lion-hearted as Gen. Zachary Taylor," who commanded tremendous respect among the Yuchis in particular.[6] A man of even more consequence was William McIntosh of Coweta. He was the son of John McIntosh, John Stuart's agent to the Lower Creeks during the Revolutionary War, and a woman of the Wind clan. That made William, like McGillivray, a man with a foot firmly in both Creek and Euro-American worlds. But like others in his position, while his unmistakable Americanness and his shrewd politics quickly made him popular in Georgia, he was also a dedicated and active leader in Creek governance. Possibly the most multicultural man in the region since McGillivray, there was also no doubt that McIntosh was a man of more than words. Unlike McGillivray, he rose to prominence not only because of his mixed Creek and Euro-American heritage but because he was a skilled and respected war leader. His Creek title, Tustunnuggee Hutkee, or white warrior, reflected that strong traditional claim to authority. He was a leader in Creek politics when he signed his name to the Treaty of Washington in 1805, he was a member of the National Council not long after, and he directed the "law menders," as the council's classed warriors came to be called.[7]

The evolving leadership group in Creek Country that coalesced under the auspices of the National Council, known also in the period as the "Executive Council," continued to include men of different regions, backgrounds, and ethnicities, as it always had. It also continued to be a contested body. Two Cussetas assassinated Hopoie Mico in 1806, for instance, generating a political crisis only a year after the controversial Treaty of Washington. His death "has perplexed everything here," Hawkins reported to John Forbes of the Panton, Leslie and Company trading firm; headmen were having a hard time finding a suitable successor, suggesting that the National Council still did not represent an entirely unified Creek people. The position was offered to Cornells, who for some reason turned it down, "and they could unite in no other."[8] After another meeting of the council, later in 1806, little had changed. "Our Chiefs are yet divided, proud and jealous, full of intrigue and cannot unite in a speaker." Anger with the Treaty of Washington was apparently still raw, and it was influencing the choosing of a successor. For his part in the treaty Cornells was being threatened, which might explain why he turned down the Speaker position.[9] Although the National Council was never dysfunctional because it lacked a Speaker it was still clearly a controversial state institution, which represented many communities that were grappling with the needs of their American neighbors.

That sort of confusion and jealousy came at a delicate time. As former Indian agent and now trader James Seagrove alluded to in 1807, the previous decade had been a decent one in his neighborhood, around Coleraine. "For near ten years last past," he wrote the governor of Georgia, "we have not had a murder committed by the Indians in our County. And although the red people were almost constantly among our settlers, nothing worse than stealing a few horse or killing a beef noe and then, have we experienced."[10] Still, confronting an effective but wobbly Creek nation-state was an American government that either struggled to uphold or simply ignored the treaty obligations it had so recently guaranteed. Only months, it seems, after Creek authorities ceded a tremendous amount of land to the state of Georgia, settlers were already crossing over the Okmulgee River looking for more. Cattle were roaming on Creek lands and salt licks were everywhere. Settlers were illegally logging, fishing, and even settling on Creek lands only a year after American authorities promised Georgia would never need to ask for more. In 1806 Georgians "were no sooner on their borders of Ocmulgee than they began to trespass on Indian rights," headmen were complaining.[11] This was the clearest, most obviously illegal kind of settler expansion and something that had always irritated Creek community leaders, whether they complained to British, Georgia, or American officials. What differentiated those previous periods of irritation from this newest, most recent one was the claimed authority of the National Council.

Settler trespasses came at a time now when the National Council spoke for Creeks and defended Creek territorial sovereignty, rather than when individual headmen spoke and fought for themselves. That did not bode well for the council, however, because it was becoming clear that it might be able to do only half of what it said—selling land was not difficult, but defending what land remained was turning out to be impossible. Having a strong natural boundary like the Okmulgee was one of the reasons the council gave up the rest of the fork—the same reason they gave up the Oconee River at Coleraine. But again, as they had in the past, settlers and their cattle proved to be excellent swimmers. While Georgia locals might not have cared much for the new boundary, Creek hunters did. And for Creeks not yet reconciled to the Treaty of Washington, seeing settlers already grasping for more must have made the decision of the National Council to cede away their hunting lands even more questionable than it already was. "Their young men had been greatly irritated by the sale of the Ocmulgee fork," and headmen were "much embarrassed to keep them within bounds." Two years after the sale, community leaders admitted they were just beginning to convince their young men to accept the loss of the lands, but now hunters were out for the season and found their territory "occupied by white hunters and the stock of their neighbors," and it was feared "their irritation would revive and produce ill consequences."[12] It was Americans, now, who were not being neighborly, and in the new era of Creek solidarity it was the National Council that would absorb the disappointment of these neighborly failures. It bore responsibility not only for the Treaty of Washington but for Americans' inability to control their settlers afterward, which had members of the council worrying that they would not be able to continue selling the treaty to their own people if Americans appeared unsatisfied with it so soon after it was concluded.

With several versions of the Trade and Intercourse Acts in effect long before the Treaty of Washington, this should not have been the case. Everything the settlers were doing was clearly illegal, but seldom did Creeks see justice achieved for even the most flagrant violations of federal and state laws. In 1805 a horse thief was actually executed in St. Mary's while another one was forced to flee into Spanish Florida.[13] Those legal actions would have been excellent news to Creeks had they not been so far and away exceptional. By 1808 Hawkins was traveling to meet with Georgia governor Jared Irwin directly "to communicate fully with him on the situation of our affairs in my department, as well as on the conduct of some of the citizens altho' on the Indian boundary, and who are intruders on their rights." A year later, complaints were so loud that Secretary of War Dearborn was forced to address them directly, admitting that Creeks had been "robbed and abused," and suggesting that "strong remonstrances should be made to the Executive of Georgia on the subject."[14] For years, in fact, Hawkins pressed Georgia authorities, military commanders, and even the War Department to have complaints addressed, but little was ever accomplished.[15] He also regularly complained, like Seagrove before him, that the Americans he encountered in the neighborhood of Creek Country were, in general, pretty terrible people. They were "loose, worthless characters," they lied and cheated constantly, and every one of them was probably a fugitive from the law.[16] Nevertheless, complaining and arresting people were two different actions. Hawkins and countless other civil and military authorities could do both, yet they complained far more often than they acted. The law was straightforward, but neither Hawkins nor any state authority did much to enforce it. Inaction might not have affected Hawkins too severely, but it reflected poorly on a National Council that promised its own people that the federal government would respect their territorial rights.

Hawkins never reported that the National Council lost faith in him, but the Creek leadership, under pressure from their people, certainly did begin to complain around him. They began to write to state authorities directly, and even to the newly appointed secretary of war, William Eustis, evidence perhaps that they considered Hawkins inattentive to their complaints. Hawkins wrote to Eustis in 1809 that he would be forced to call out federal troops to evict illegal settlers if a petition that came directly from headmen in the Lower Country to Georgia governor Jared Irwin did not compel his own state government to act. Irwin did not completely ignore the request, issuing a proclamation that threatened fines and imprisonment to anyone caught hunting, ranging cattle, or timbering on Creek lands. As expected, however, it did little.[17] Irwin's proclamation "for a short time withdrew some of the abuses but they soon began to accumulate," and within a year it was like it had never been published at all.[18]

Recently calmed and evidently returned to the American fold, the Tallassee King then complained directly to Eustis, forcing him to confront the issue almost as soon as he accepted his position in 1809. At first the new secretary seemed receptive. He assured the Tallassee King that the federal government understood and respected the problems the Creek people faced. The president's "ear is always open to you. He is your friend. He holds out his hand to you." The military should be used to evict illegal settlements, Eustis then reiterated to Hawkins, and the Trade and Intercourse Acts should be relied on to arrest and charge other trespassers.[19] In other words, Eustis offered absolutely nothing new, either to the Tallassee King or to Hawkins. The federal government's unenthusiastic approach to enforcement had been disappointing for the better part of a decade, and in 1809 nothing was poised to change. American officials were directed to rely on the same clearly worded pieces of legislation that state officials and local settlers had been ignoring for years. In 1811 headmen applied again directly to state authorities, this time to Georgia governor David B. Mitchell. Yet past experiences would suggest that state authorities were less than eager to move against their own settlements, and that was indeed the case; Creeks would get little from Governor Mitchell. Two years later two Hitchiti men were killed by Georgia settlers near Hartford, and there were also complaints that "some of their people" had also been robbed. Of course nothing was done then either, including for murder.[20]

Unfortunately the National Council never attached much of a monetary value to many of the settlers' violations, which might have made American authorities more responsive to Creek complaints. In 1812 the Council protested anew "of intrusions on their rights, by building fish traps, driving stock to range on their lands, hunting with dogs and firehunting, cuting cedar and other timber and cultivating fields" on the Creek side of the Okmulgee. When members of the Council complained that these intrusions were in many instances the causes of violence, Hawkins quickly countered that their claims were for "somewhat less than 100 dollars," while claims for losses by whites against Creeks were more to the tune of one thousand dollars, which he then declared would be taken from the Creek stipend—a payment that, ironically, was already late.[21] But how accurate was that one-hundred-dollar valuation? Hopoie Mico, for instance, probably would have considered Hawkins's number a ridiculous lowball figure. When he spoke for the delegation of the National Council that ceded the Okmulgee fork, Hopoie Mico was quick to describe the worth of Creek Country in terms Americans were familiar with. The natural resources in Creek Country, like timber, were among the reasons he insisted Americans pay so dearly for the land they wanted. He was asking upwards of two dollars per acre, which he heard was what Natives further north had gotten out of the government. Hawkins countered that what Creeks were demanding was much more than the government had ever paid for land before, and indeed, the Senate rejected the treaty because it was too pricey.[22] Even after the money figure was adjusted a bit lower in Washington, however, the payout for Creeks was still enormous, and it set an important precedent. Creeks knew the worth of their land and if they negotiated smartly for a legitimate payment, they could get it.

The headmen who succeeded Hopoie Mico tried to understand similarly. William McIntosh, speaking to Thomas Jefferson in 1805, had a clear comprehension of such a monetary value and was also involved in the Treaty of Washington.[23] Years later, faced with continued trespasses in 1809, headmen proposed a plan that would have essentially charged rent for the otherwise illegal use of Creek lands, including for cattle and horses. It was an idea that Hawkins seemed to support, but in hindsight it seems unlikely that such a plan would have worked. Why would settlers and their state representatives agree to do legally and expensively what they were already getting away with doing illegally and freely?[24] Yet while charging rent might not have worked, putting more accurate monetary values on both past and present trespasses certainly could have provided Creeks with the opportunity to give American officials a dose of their own medicine. It would have been particularly ironic to Georgia authorities to be charged in such a way, of course, because the approach had been utilized so well by the state in the past. Compensation owed Creeks for damages would have been in the thousands of dollars, not the hundreds, and Hawkins would have had much less to say toward his Creek charges. Not having countered in such a way, headmen could only enumerate to Hawkins and his superiors another instance in a long history of instances of the American government's failure to uphold its treaty obligations, confirmed by the Senate now several times. When the National Council had taken the government's assurances of territorial security with faith and explained them to hesitant communities, such letdowns were dangerous. The assurances allowed the National Council to secure the Treaty of Washington in their own communities; years later, however, they had almost nothing to show for their promises. Every cow lick and fish trap that turned up in Creek Country offered more evidence to doubtful communities that the Council was failing to deliver to its people on the decisions it insisted were best for them.

Another promise that the National Council used to justify the most recent land cessions was financial independence. Even something as straightforward as annuity payments, however, eventually became another source of disappointment for headmen. Annuity payments of varying amounts—large amounts, however—were guaranteed in several of the treaties Americans concluded with Creeks. Those payments were usually made in a mix of cash and goods, like spinning or weaving tools, farm equipment, clothing, or iron.[25] For years the annuity arrived promptly, with goods arriving directly to Hawkins and certificates for cash sent to banks in Savannah. At the very moment Creeks were complaining anew of American failures to police their borders in 1811 and 1812, however, such regularity was no longer guaranteed. In February 1812, the annuity for 1811 had still not arrived, surprising even Hawkins. "As I know of no cause why the payment of their annuity should be suspended I have none to assign to the Chiefs."[26] The same was the case the next year. "We have heard nothing of the stipend for the last year," Hawkins complained in January 1813.[27] Inconsistent annuity payments of course were not the fault of the National Council; Creeks were not paying themselves tons of iron or thousands of dollars in cash. Nevertheless it still reflected poorly on the council. At a time when the annuities were not only expected but increasingly depended upon—split up, used to supplement the deerskin trade and pay trade debts, and so on—a stoppage that seemed inconsequential in Washington would have been very serious in Creek Country. What, exactly, had those communities given up all of the Oconee and Okmulgee lands for, they must have thought, when that money did not arrive? The National Council relinquished Creek lands for financial stability and was failing, through no fault of its own, to provide it.

Both financial and territorial problems brought the familiar pains of American expansion to Creeks, implicating the National Council in the American government's failures. As early as 1807, however, expansion also had a newer, more dangerous face. Both state and federal authorities began insisting on their free movement between the American settlements that now surrounded Creek Country, which meant of course they wanted free movement through Creek Country.[28] To Creek communities, that was a frightening prospect indeed. That Americans could believe they were legally entitled to travel freely through a sovereign territory seems surprising, but at the time authorities at all levels were clearly convinced. Even though Creek Country was technically a politically and territorially sovereign place, which in theory existed outside of the United States, in reality it very much was not.

Several separate requests for territorial access soon came from both settlers and the federal government. From east of Creek Country, enthusiastic settlers in states that were quickly becoming overcrowded were eyeing land in the newly acquired, rich, and booming Mississippi Territory, and the easiest way there was directly through the heart of Creek Country. Further to the north, settlers in the state of Tennessee insisted on river access down the Alabama watershed to Mobile. That route was the most convenient one for them to bring their goods to market, despite that almost every mile of it lay solely in Creek territory. And then of course the federal government needed a reliable way to get information between all of those groups of people, as well as support its own military forces, creeping ever closer to the Gulf Coast. Each of those requests deeply troubled Creek headmen, who only saw in those avenues of communication or movement innumerable new sources of confrontation. They saw more illegal hunting, fishing, and ranching operations, and even settlements from whites, and they saw more horse theft and robberies from their own, none of which boded well for the peace and prosperity of what was, after all, an independent Creek Country.

At the heart of the matter was the supposed sovereignty of Creek territory. That was a tricky issue that American authorities had been grappling with, but generally accepting of, as far back as Henry Knox in the Washington administration. Federal authorities in the nineteenth century, beginning in the Jefferson administration, were no longer convinced of that diplomatic principle. They began to chip away at Creek territorial sovereignty first by insisting that travel through Creek Country along federal roads, the construction of which was guaranteed in the Treaty of Washington, was actually a sort of natural human right to free movement that everyone on the continent—whether Creek or American, whether located in Creek Country or not—possessed. Within a year several horse paths were being cleared or widened, with the most significant one to run from Athens, Georgia, by Tuckabatchee, and on to Fort Stoddert. The commissioners made sure Creeks understood at the treaty that such paths would be necessary and that Americans would have to be allowed to travel on them safely.[29] To ensure Creek acquiescence, they made strong promises. They reassured members of the council that Creeks would be the ones in control of almost every aspect of the paths. Creeks would be the ones operating whatever river crossings, stables, or layovers were needed on them and would get to make money from them. And no whites would be allowed to settle or even operate businesses along those trails, without the Creeks' approval.

Headmen continued to emphasize that they remembered those promises in the years after the Treaty of Washington even as American authorities' own recollections grew hazy. Almost as soon as the treaty had been concluded, Hawkins was talking about "licencing sober men of good character acquainted with the Indians" to keep houses of "entertainment" and accommodation along the paths, as well as authorize them to trade.[30] Creeks were quick to protest; trustworthy and sober white men were still white men and certainly were not the same as Creeks. Nevertheless, in 1806 Secretary of War Dearborn was authorizing whites to operate the resting and "refreshment" layovers and pushing Hawkins to "explain the business to the Chiefs, as to prevent any opposition on the part of the Creeks to the necessary establishments." Headmen were not interested in those appointments, which irritated Hawkins. "The Chiefs seem determined to admit of no white settlers on the road," but Americans needed "suitable characters" soon, "and I must have one or the other," Hawkins warned.[31] He might not have cared for the distinction, but Creeks certainly did.

Within months a contractor chosen to complete one of the roads was positioning whites along it himself, making arrangements on the Okmulgee River and near Coweta without input from anyone. While those actions surprised and angered Hawkins, they infuriated many headmen, who insisted again that they were the ones supposed to be in control of such matters. Indeed, "the possession of the stages was a principle inducement on the part of the Chiefs to permit the free use of a path thro' their country."[32] This difference of opinion was particularly important, however; it was the first instance of a road dispute that also produced divisions in the National Council. Headmen turned again to Alexander Cornells, who had led negotiations at Washington. He was already on thin ice for his part in the land portion of the treaty and was now taking heat for his perceived complicity in this developing controversy. Headmen "gave so much alarm" that Cornells "actually disavowed any knowledge of his part of the treaty." He was in a tricky situation. Cornells, like William McIntosh and several other headmen, was a savvy and enterprising man. He certainly intended to play a role in the operation of the entertainment houses or ferries for his own financial gain. He certainly did know about that part of the treaty and would have lobbied the council to approve the postal paths if only for his own benefit, but he also certainly would not have wanted unauthorized whites stealing that business from under his nose. But then Cornells was also a Creek headman and a member of the council, which had made promises on behalf of Creek communities that were in danger of being broken. He had several reasons, in other words, to oppose any plan to have outsiders operating anything on the postal roads. Nevertheless, now he was being singled out and even threatened by neighboring headmen, the first evidence yet that American expansionist pressure, represented by a single path, was beginning to chip away at Creek solidarity.

Unfortunately for Creeks, that first postal road was only the beginning. When the council met at Tuckabatchee later that year another one was evidently already in the works, sparking more frustration. Members of the council promised to see the original postal path completed, but as for this new proposal, they were clear. It might make "a good path in all respects comfortable to the treaty," but Creeks were not ready to move forward on it. All plans for further expansion, in fact, were on hold. Communities would not consent to have any more refreshment, entertainment, or other "establishments of accommodation of the post horses or travellers other than such as they now found." The moratorium also came with worrisome news. Some headmen were openly talking "that there was a deliberate plan in operation on the part of the United States to get possession of their country," Hawkins reported, and they could see that the paths were "cutting them in two."[33] At least a few headmen, although they went unnamed, not only were beginning to disagree with each other in response to the road but seemed to be questioning their American friends as well.

Federal authorities only added to the distrust and confusion. The resistance Hawkins encountered late in 1807 was stiff, but it gave the Jefferson administration little pause. By 1808 Dearborn had unilaterally authorized the new trail anyway, to originate in eastern Tennessee and move southwest into Washington County. Rather than ask the council for its acquiescence, Dearborn directed Hawkins simply to break the news gently. He authorized trade gifts as bribes—but not too many, he made clear. It was "presumed that moderate presents to some of the most influential characters, will be deemed sufficient for so trifling a favor." Hawkins relayed his request to the headmen, returning to explain to Dearborn later that it was not the amount of gifts they received but "the apprehension arising from the improper conduct of their young men."[34] Were Creeks in the Upper Country either unable or unwilling to keep angry hunters from assaulting riders on the path? The development of this new road was troubling for several reasons. For the first time federal authorities had flat out ignored the decision of the National Council, unilaterally authorizing the path after receiving a clear refusal from Tuckabatchee and in the face of increasing resistance. This was indeed a troubling precedent to set. Was the United States bound to honor the decisions of the National Council only when the answer to their proposals was yes? To what extent was Creek Country even sovereign at all if American authorities felt entitled to overrule the decisions of the council and impose themselves territorially in such a way? Although Dearborn considered this second route a relatively minor issue, his willingness to move around the National Council to secure it reveals how dismissively Americans were beginning to regard the Creek Nation.

The new road also continued to demonstrate the regional nature of the emerging Creek unrest—a path from Tennessee to the Mississippi Territory would clearly burden communities in the Upper Country more so than those further south. Unlike the first road, which passed through Coweta as well as Tuckabatchee, this second path did not concern the Lower Country much at all. It is not overly speculative to suggest that the voices that had grown so stern recently at Tuckabatchee were probably from that neighborhood, and not from Coweta or Ooseoochee. Hawkins insinuated as much in the following months. "I have never known the nation generally better disposed towards us than they are now," he was pleased to report in December 1808. While he heaped praise on communities in the Lower Country, however, he said nothing about their neighbors on the Alabama watershed. No praise was heaped on them.[35] Such was the case after another meeting, prompting Hawkins to express again a hedged sense of optimism. "I believe the Chiefs will as they can carry their treaty stipulations with us into effect relative to the post path, but it will require yet a little time for them to do as they wish." There was opposition, Hawkins was forced to admit, but then again that mattered little. "We will not look back to the improper conduct of others but proceed to do the best we can for the Government."[36] Hawkins's confidence was deceptive. Unhappiness over postal paths had generated distrust between regional councils and the Upper and Lower countries, there was no general speaker for the Creek Nation, and now headmen were questioning the motives of the American government. Opposition was significant, but American authorities were determined to press forward.

Not only did road construction continue despite Creek opposition, but with each new development it appeared to headmen that the Americans had negotiated with them at best dishonestly, and at worst in bad faith. By 1808, roads obviously built for wagon travel were far larger than the horse paths agreed to in the Treaty of Washington. The road from the American garrison on the Okmulgee River to Hawkins's agency on the Flint River was one such example.[37] Headmen complained continuously through 1809 and into 1810, citing such examples. Speaking in 1809 they complained that the paths they agreed to were supposed to be small, "with logs over the creeks." Yet just recently a contractor had appeared "with his waggon and commenced building bridges." At another council meeting, in February of the next year, the same issue dominated discussion. The contractor "had entered with his waggon and team and commenced and built bridges, whereas the only promise to the President was that he should have a path through their land rendered convenient by boat over the rivers and logs over the creeks." When headmen confronted the contractor angrily it surprised Hawkins. He was a "sober, quiet man, attentive to Indians and to every trust enjoined on him here." How he had "some how given offence to the Chiefs or some of them" confused the agent, particularly since the headmen's reasons were "not explained in their talk," and he chalked up the tense situation simply to misunderstanding.[38]

Angry community leaders, led now by the Tallassee King, did not see the controversy as innocently as had Hawkins. They had explained themselves perfectly well, and to them the road issue sounded more like trickery than confusion. There were more roads than there should be, they were much larger than they should be, and there were innumerable stables, lodges, or other waypoints along them, which no one had agreed to allow. Unwanted white settlers were multiplying along the roads, living in places they were not supposed to and running enterprises they legally could not, and the federal government was doing nothing to remove them.[39] Americans' insistence on access to Creek territory through the construction of roads and their willingness to deal underhandedly to get that access, and even to work around the National Council altogether if need be, was putting tremendous pressure on Creek Country. Government actions were worrying local headmen, who in turn were exerting pressure on the National Council in ways that were disrupting Creek unity.

The result was no better when the disputes concerned river traffic. As the state of Tennessee expanded, its citizens increasingly insisted on enjoying the full and free usage of the Coosa-Tallapoosa-Alabama waterways, which were the only practical means of bringing their goods to market on the Gulf Coast.[40] Yet the confluence of the Coosa and Tallapoosa rivers, where the Alabama River begins, was practically the heartland of the Upper Country; communities lined the shores up and down that confluence for miles. Headmen there were not at all interested in seeing their neighborhoods flooded with flatboats, loaded down with all manner of questionable cargo, liquor of course being at the top of the list. Such was the case in 1809, when headmen seized a flat boat moving down the Coosa. The boat had been built in Cherokee Country to the north, it was loaded down with liquor, gunpowder, and lead shot, and enterprising smugglers were attempting to pass it through Creek Country using fake documents, including a forgery of Hawkins's signature. Such illicit traffic was "alarming, in a high degree," several headmen in the Upper Country would later insist. The liquor alone would "bring ruin on their nation."[41] Nothing good would come from that sort of traffic, and headmen in the neighborhood of the rivers were determined to prohibit it. Because the waterways lay squarely in sovereign Creek territory, refusal was an option, and it was the option Creeks chose; to the dismay of local and federal authorities alike, Creek communities in the Upper Country repeatedly and steadfastly refused their requests to open river traffic to American commerce. Both Timothy Barnard and the interpreter Christian Limbaugh "found it impracticable" in 1810, for instance, "to obtain permission to navigate the Coosa River." They had brought the subject up multiple times in 1810, at councils in both the Upper and Lower countries, but got nothing from the Creek leadership, which continued rejecting their requests out of hand.[42]

Even more frustrating was the American determination to collect trade duties on all the goods that traveled through American territory, into Creek territory, along those same waterways. After the Spanish relinquished control of the Tombigbee District and the American government established Fort Stoddert, federal authorities claimed the right to control the flow of goods along the narrow stretch of the Tombigbee and Mobile rivers that lay within the territory they now owned, and therefore control access to the Alabama, Coosa, and Tallapoosa watersheds as well. Even though the land to the south was still Spanish and the land to the north was recognized more or less as sovereign Creek territory, the land around Stoddert was now American, and federal authorities insisted that goods traveling through it were subject to American taxes. Groups of Alabamas were first to complain about this new development, declaring that they "never paid any thing till the Americans came to Fort Stoddert, and not till they had been there for some time, and they know not why they should pay for what was always their right." Well-respected Coosada headman Captain Isaacs went a step further, "threatening war in case duties should be demanded of them at Fort Stoddert, insulting and plundering some travelers and attempting to injure the post rider."[43] By threatening violence and then actually using it, Captain Isaacs displayed the depth of anger many Creeks living in the neighborhood felt when Americans began to control the use of their own waterways in such a way.

The federal decision to insist on enforcing import duties was fascinating. First, it was simply illegal. It disrupted the free trade Creeks enjoyed at Mobile, which was sovereign Spanish territory, and the free intercourse between Creeks and the Spanish port there was guaranteed, in writing, by the Treaty of Washington. Denying the Mobile trade, in other words, would constitute a clear treaty violation. Not long after Americans established Stoddert, however, they refused to see things that way. And even when authorities hedged on their position in the face of Creek resistance, it seemed only temporary. Americans would not permit trade goods to travel through American territory, which would eventually be exchanged commercially in Creek Country, without paying the applicable duties, regardless of where they came from. "There will be no objection on the part of the government to the free passage of the Indians with their own goods, but it cannot be allowed them to smuggle for foreign or other traders." That presumably would include the Spanish government and the Panton and Leslie Company, which constituted basically all of the Creek trade.[44] This new tax policy evidently trumped federal treaty, but that did not concern the Jefferson administration, and Hawkins was of a like mind. With a meeting of the National Council to convene in August he remarked in June that he would probably "have some difficulty in making the Indians comprehend our right to tax their little traffic passing on the waters of Alabama, and to prevent them on retaliating on the travelers." Yet "when the Chiefs convene I will see what can be done."[45]

Not only were American authorities again violating their own treaties, they were coming to embrace a very interesting definition of Creek sovereignty. As far as the Jefferson administration was concerned, Creeks were not a people sovereign enough to control their own territory, but they were sovereign enough to pay taxes on goods that traveled through American territory to them. The argument being made there bordered on the bizarre, but perhaps Dearborn, Hawkins, and Secretary of Treasury Albert Gallatin legitimately thought they were legally entitled to free access to the Alabama River south through Creek territory for the movement of their commercial goods, while simultaneously insisting that Creeks were not entitled to the same free trade traveling north on the same river because it passed through American territory first. Once again, it would have been interesting to see how the Creek leadership would have responded had a Hopoie Mico or an Alexander McGillivray been around. What if Creeks took the old French trade outpost Fort Toulouse, which lay abandoned at the confluence of the Coosa and Tallapoosa rivers, and reestablished it as an entrepôt in the name of the Creek Nation? What if they then declared the Coosa River open to Tennesseans, but only after they paid the appropriate trade duties required to pass through sovereign Creek Country? One wonders how Jefferson and Gallatin would have responded to that reversal—probably not well. While they never tried something so politically calculated, headmen in the Upper Country were not ignorant about their rights. Captain Isaacs, a son-in-law to Alexander McGillivray, was a shrewd man. So was Cornells—Hawkins's closest ally in Creek Country. When Hawkins spelled out both his and Dearborn's interpretation of the matter, Cornells made it clear that he was with McGillivray at New York in 1790, when Creeks first began negotiating with Americans. There McGillivray understood that Americans "had no right to tax them as in the event of obstructions their commerce was to pass our ports free of duty," and nothing had changed.[46]

By first demanding free travel on roads and rivers inside Creek Country, and then insisting that Creeks pay trade duties on goods arriving from outside of Creek Country, Americans were developing a definition of sovereignty that insisted at some times Creeks were the masters of their territory while other times they were not. By doing that, they were beginning to usurp Creek authority as early as a few years after the National Council consolidated the Creek voice, and had done so with some success. Hawkins might have pontificated about the importance of Creek sovereignty when he pushed for the creation of the council in 1796, but neither he nor his superiors necessarily cared for Creek sovereignty, or even respected it, when it was no longer in their best interest to do so. To insist that Creeks develop a state structure like Americans had, and then begin to undercut its authority almost immediately, was setting a disastrous precedent, particularly for the thousands of Creeks looking on. What use was a centralized administrative structure, designed to make Creeks good neighbors, if their neighbors did not abide by its dictates?

More important, once again the burden of Americans' problematic approach to Creek sovereignty did not fall equally on all Creeks. Postal roads passed near communities like Tuckabatchee more often than Hitchiti. The bridges that would be built, the taverns and overnight layovers that operated, and the illegal settlements that would surely appear had more of an impact in the Upper Country than in the Lower. And when American authorities determined that Creeks could be taxed for goods purchased at Mobile, headmen in the south generally took little exception to it. The decision was "interpreted to the Lower Chiefs, and has given much satisfaction," for instance, and only then did it travel north, where it generated a very different response.[47] Communities like Coweta and Cusseta did not depend on Mobile; neither their connection to the Spanish at Pensacola or St. Augustine nor their duty-free trade in those places was under any threat. In another example of American expansion that abrogated the promises made in Washington, river access and trade duties also singled out communities in the Upper Country as the losers. Not only were communities in the Creek Nation faring differently, it seemed more and more like they were being treated differently. The National Council was evolving into a body where headmen in the Lower Country did not necessarily care about the problems faced by their neighbors to the north. American actions were not only challenging the legitimacy of the National Council or eroding away Creek sovereignty but also undermining the foundation of Creek nationalism.

Unity in the National Council was suffering as early as the summer of 1807. In the years after the Treaty of Washington the council continued to meet regularly, and many times more than once a year, sometimes in the late summer or early fall in addition to the spring. It met in May 1806, and then again in September, for instance. A year later, in September 1807, headmen convened "day and night" for over ten days.[48] Soon regional meetings were convening as often as national ones, however, and headmen from the Upper and Lower countries were meeting separately in Tuckabatchee and Coweta with a regularity that seemed to suggest that there were by that point two separate seats of the council, complete at times with two Speakers. And as regional meetings grew more common, the National Council grew more contested. In one 1807 meeting at Tuckabatchee the council continued "a little perplexed for want of a head," headmen were distrustful of each other, and there was clearly a schism opening between those from the Upper and Lower countries. Headmen from the Upper Country had recently attempted an ouster of McIntosh, "for being too much attached to and in the interest of the white people." Hawkins dismissed the allegations but defended McIntosh as "the Chief for the affairs of the Lower Creeks."[49] Not only was American expansionism causing divisiveness to creep into the National Council, as the contentious atmosphere at Tuckabatchee illustrated, but headmen were accusing each other of colluding with a more suspicious

American government. Months later, in April 1808, headmen from the Lower Country were scheduled shortly to meet at Coweta "on their own affairs and on their own appointment."[50] The Creek National Council still functioned, but it was also splintering under the weight of American pressure.

The 1807 Tuckabatchee conference was also noteworthy for how alienated headmen from the Upper Country evidently considered themselves from their own political process. A Cherokee, Chickasaw, and Choctaw delegation was present, and everyone heard distressed Cherokees speak about supposedly dishonest dealings with Americans and the American agent Return Meigs. Everyone also aired conflicting claims to hunting lands in Tennessee, which sparked anger from the Upper Creek headmen. They "said time out of mind they had claims to the hunting grounds, north of the Tennessee," and that "their old camps were to be seen there long before a white man crossed the mountains." Now they were being "deprived of their mountains" by scheming American speculators, backed it seemed by the American government. Those pleas fell on deaf ears, though, even among neighbors. "The Lower Creeks expressed no opinion" when it came to such charges.[51] A Speaker from the Upper Country proceeded to give an "inflamitory speech" so intense that Hawkins walked out of the conference. Disagreements grew even more heated later, at a meeting at Coweta, which was convened shortly after in an attempt to sort things out. Leaders like Cornells and another from Tuckabatchee continued to side with Americans on several issues, including on postal roads, even though most in their neighborhood disagreed. McIntosh and the Long Lieutenant were even stronger in their support and "recollected the whole stipulation as mentioned in the treaty," which Barnard and James Durouzeaux also believed was the case. In the end there was calm at the meeting, but not for long. For defending the Americans both McIntosh and the Long Lieutenant were ousted from their positions in the National Council. The Little Prince of Broken Arrow and Tuskegee Tustunnuggee of Cusseta assumed their duties but only for a short time. Coweta headmen would not see the two removed, and when they refused to allow it, it appears the coup fell apart.[52]

The growing political impasse continued to reflect poorly on Hawkins, who was failing to grasp the depth of discontent growing in the Upper Country over issues like roads, rivers, and hunting lands. As the loudening voice of an American people was determined to have those things at any cost, maybe he, as their representative, had no choice but to take the positions he did. Regardless, by ignoring the anger that was clearly resulting from such insistent and increasingly intrusive requests, he was not doing himself any favors, and he was contributing to what appeared to be the collapse of the National Council. He could not "account for the change in the Chiefs" at Coweta and was surprised "at the insolence of several of the Chiefs," at Tuckabatchee, in fabricating lies that implicated officers of the United States. He fell back on tired explanations, blaming food scarcities, unruly young people, and continued anger over the loss of hunting lands, even though he turned around to admit that, "with few exceptions," most Creeks were "beginning to be reconciled" to the loss of the lands. He heaped blame on the headmen themselves, whom he charged with inattentiveness and even with fraud and embezzlement. Only then, "they mingle their discontent in the mass of insolent discontent which pervades the rude and ungovernable." Anger was not widespread or deep-seated, Hawkins had convinced himself. Speaking with a man contracted to build one of the postal roads through Coweta—that the headmen had expressly forbidden at Tuckabatchee—he pushed the contractor to continue his work. "This wrong headed course cannot last long in the nation," he insisted. By the time the ferries and flats were operating, the stables and lodging houses were built, he would "find Indians ready to cooperate with you."[53]

Hawkins also continued to downplay the resentment that was growing in the north by focusing on successes in the south and speaking of them as if they reflected all of Creek Country. In general, as he explained to Dearborn, headmen in the Lower Country "conduct themselves well," while his assessment of the Upper Country was decidedly more reserved. Meanwhile, almost at that exact moment, Upper Creek headmen were complaining anew about issues that largely affected only them. Americans had killed one of theirs in Tennessee, which state authorities of course were ignoring. Settlers were also moving onto Upper Creek hunting lands in Tennessee, as well as more territory they claimed in the Tombigbee area, which also was claimed by Choctaws.[54] At the same time Americans were applying constant pressure for roads and rivers, these new state-level sources of expansion were generating new voices of anger. To Hawkins, that all was unrelated.

Not only were these new Creek claims loud, they were clear enough. A Creek had been murdered by settlers and absolutely nothing was being done about it. The second two complaints both concerned ownership of hunting lands and were consistent with claims made by headmen like Emistisiguo more than a generation earlier. Traditional control of those lands, as headmen from Tallassee, Hickory Ground, and Oakfuskee saw it, was basically timeless. It is no surprise, then, that headmen were upset that the loss of those lands to Tennesseans, Mississippians, or even Choctaws was being downplayed by Americans. In Emistisiguo's day, illegal settlers would have been beaten off of those lands, and conflicting claims to the Ceded Lands led to years of violence in 1773. Now, however, American settlers were pouring onto them, American officials neither believed Creeks were entitled to those claims nor cared, and headmen in the south, it appeared, did not care either. Those lands, in other words, were lost, but they were not lost equally to all Creeks.

Not only did Hawkins deny that such issues were widespread sources of regional anger, he did not consider them legitimate, declaring as much to his superiors.[55] Indeed, in a letter addressed to the headmen at the Coweta meeting, he fell back on the same tired threats. Never mind about murdered Creeks, he charged, and focus on your own shortcomings, like theft. It was "growing upon us, and if we do not set seriously to putting an end to it, will ruin our land." Hookchoies and Wewocaos from the Upper Country had "spilt blood on the north side of Tennessee," and their actions had to be dealt with as well. Not only were Creeks not to gain justice for their dead, more was asked of them. "You must exert yourselves, you must pay the debt of blood you owe, by the punishment of the guilty." Old threats, not new promises, were the talk of the day. "You must restrain your young men within the bounds of good neighborhood," he implored. "We must do justice to all, and then with a good free will we can claim it from all."[56]

Hawkins's appeal for justice and good neighborhood was reminiscent of the oldest and sternest talks Americans had ever issued Creeks, either from Hawkins or from Seagrove. They appealed strongly to Creek nationalism, involving all Creeks in the actions of individual towns, and they called upon the power of the Creek administrative state to ensure regional stability. This newest talk was addressed and delivered only to headmen in Coweta, however, where regional political power in Creek Country was represented only unevenly. Hawkins was not even in attendance, and by the Tuskegee Tustunnuggee's own admission only half of the Creek Nation was. Meanwhile, "Creeks from two or three of the upper towns" had been hunting in the vicinity of the Cumberland River, which was square in the territory debated with Tennesseans. They "had murdered some white people" there, and "some of them were killed."[57] Haranguing Coweta headmen about restraint and justice in Tennessee would not serve Hawkins well while the council was failing to secure the interests of half of Creek Country and while he continued aggressively countering legitimate Creek claims with more dubious American ones.

By October 1808 the situation in the Upper Country continued to deteriorate. For the first time headmen from the area no longer considered the recently opened road from Tennessee to St. Stephens, in the Mississippi Territory, safe for riders and requested that Hawkins have it suspended. Hawkins disparaged the news, but again he misplaced the source of the issues. "I find our chiefs unable to unite in any thing," he charged, describing the source of their dysfunction as a failed attempt by headmen from the Upper Country to unite Choctaws, Chickasaws, and Cherokees behind them in a sprawling confederacy. Such a confederacy seems unrealistic, but it is worth noting that if headmen from the Upper Country were serious about creating such an alliance, by that point it was probably in an effort to counter American expansionism. That certainly was not a development conducive to friendly American relations and regional peace, yet it did seem to be the case. To them, according to Hawkins, Tennessean expansion was creating the impression that "their white neighbours are seeking for and will find a cause for war against them" and that headmen "have been tricky among themselves and suspect us of a design to undermine and ruin them as a nation."[58] Not since the 1780s had Creeks spoken of Americans in such ways. Georgia, for the first time in over a generation, did not constitute Creeks' primary threat. By 1808 there were multiple threats.

With a real possibility that headmen from the Upper Country were reaching out to build outside alliances with other Native peoples, the loss of political unity in Creek Country by late 1808 was not only weakening the National Council but undermining the foundation of Creek cultural and political nationalism. Hawkins, as if on cue, used the critical period to make more demands, pressing for the completion of the road waypoints that headmen had recently halted. To no surprise, he got little from the National Council. After "consultation of two days their answer was they could not unite on a Speaker, and would for the present say nothing more on the subject or do more than had been done." His recent demands on Creeks to exercise the coercive power of the state were received almost as unenthusiastically. Several attacks by Creeks—mostly from the Upper Country—were prompting strong demands for satisfaction, but Hawkins was disappointed in his efforts. For the murders of Americans on the St. Mary's River in Georgia, the Duck River in Tennessee, and one in Chickasaw Country, the council had done nothing, and would continue to do nothing. "I could bring them to nothing more than the appointment of myself to represent their situation to the President, and their inability in the present case to give the satisfaction demanded."[59] Far from a period a decade or so earlier, when headmen made extravagant promises of satisfaction that they were not even sure they could keep, their counterparts in 1808 were unwilling to promise anything, which they had no problem admitting to Hawkins.

Benjamin Hawkins's response to conflicting claims made over the Tennessee and Tombigbee lands further reflected an American government growing irritated with the National Council, as well as with Creeks' territorial claims. Both tracts of land were allegedly ceded by Choctaws to Americans, but Upper Creeks continued to claim them as well. The Big Warrior of Tuckabatchee made this clear when he sent a letter to a Choctaw delegation, accusing them of giving away lands that did not belong to them. Hawkins, however, did not agree. Many times, he explained to Dearborn, he alerted Creeks to the Choctaw claim, yet Creek leaders did nothing. The claims "were detailed by me to the Creeks in 1796 as well as 1801, when the Choctaws requested me to settle their boundary with the Creeks." Over and over again he alerted them to an impending deal between Americans and Choctaws to cede lands for debt forgiveness. He continued to alert them to the existence of the treaty for years after one was concluded, "and it was not to be expected that now after waiting so long, ratifying the treaty and paying for their land, that the President could attend to their claims." That ship had sailed, Hawkins declared.

Hawkins took that opportunity to go much further. Not only did he dismiss the land claims, he dismissed the political traditions that were the basis of the Creek claims, privileging American legal precedent over its Native counterpart with a surprising degree of ethnocentric condescension. He ridiculed Creeks' unwritten laws and did so by targeting the wampum tradition. "The doing of business with beads might, if understood, do among Indians," he charged, but not "in their transactions with white people." An agreement made and remembered using beads could be forgotten, he declared, "but an agreement written by a faithful agent would never be forgotten, as it would remain with the records of government."[60] Looking backward for generations, in fact, both Creeks and their American and European predecessors would have found Hawkins's new position statement hard to believe. Native political traditions that included presenting bead belts and using them to orally recall past events had been the basis of diplomacy in early America for generations—much longer than the United States of America, or even the colony of Georgia, had existed in any case. Euro-American diplomats understood those traditions and engaged in them because they were necessary to ensure the legitimacy of the deals they were brokering with their Native counterparts. Hawkins surely understood that legacy; he had been party to more than a few, as far back as the Confederation period. Yet the situation in 1808 was different. No longer did that sort of accommodation appear necessary to American officials, even if it remained necessary to Creeks. Such political traditions were crude and uncivilized, and ultimately temporary, Hawkins apparently believed, and he was less willing than ever to respect them because he was no longer convinced he had to. As much as Hawkins had championed Creek sovereignty and respected Creek traditions in the past, that era seemed to be coming to a close.

A troubling pattern of American demands that now included cultural insults perhaps explains why the Tallassee King, of all people, assumed the speakership position of a seemingly reunified National Council in 1809.[61] That ascendancy only added another chapter to the fascinating political life of a headman who had once been a Revolutionary American partisan; then one of Georgia's strongest political allies; and then a Shawnee and Bowles partisan and an inveterate American foe who once tried to assassinate James Seagrove. Early in the nineteenth century he was a renewed Bowles disciple and an outspoken critic of the National Council who was almost executed by it, and now he was the Speaker of the same council. Hawkins, who a decade earlier tried to get the National Council to kill him, now had to deal with him; he later referred to him as "the oldest and most distinguished micco in the land."[62] Ostensibly the Tallassee King's ascendancy united the council, but it also deepened divisions in the Upper Country, where it was obvious many did not agree with his leadership. As of June 1810, Lower Creeks "unanimously" acknowledged him alone "as King and speaker for the nation," but only "some of the upper towns" agreed. At another meeting at Tuckabatchee it was clear that a power struggle was developing among headmen in the Upper Country that was intense enough to generate an open disagreement between them and headmen from further south. It began as a disagreement most likely between a faction of headmen led by the Big Warrior of Tuckabatchee and another, led almost certainly by the Tallassee King, about the direction the Upper Country should be taking. Arguments about outside alliances, land, and other issues between the two groups "brought about a separation of the Lower from the Upper Creeks, and the Lower Creeks have determined to separate their interest and funds from those of the Upper Creeks." Hawkins acknowledged the split, but he explained it simply: headmen from the south were leaving their northern neighbors to fight among themselves. Nevertheless, "the lower towns are greatly distressed about the conduct of the upper towns," he admitted to the Tallassee King.[63]

There were real problems in the neighborhood of Tuckabatchee, as Hawkins freely admitted: "The Upper Creeks are retarded by the Demon of politiks." Yet in an effort to explain their disagreements, he fell back yet again on oversimplifications that did little to explain the root of the anger in the region. "The great men among them are contending for office and to embezzle their stipend and they leave the people to shift for themselves after misleading them by falsehoods."[64] Hawkins's explanation for all conflict gripping the National Council was simple—it was graft. That the stipend was simply being embezzled seems unlikely; that headmen in the north might have been fighting over how best to use it, on the other hand, seems entirely plausible. Whether to plant or buy implements of husbandry, for instance, or whether to secure lands or rectify debts were all pressing issues. The voice best suited to respond to American expansionism, it turned out, was difficult to find. However remarkable or contested it might have been, on the other hand, the Tallassee King's ascendancy was fitting. A general feeling was spreading among many in his neighborhood that the National Council, if it was to remain relevant, needed to start moving in a different direction. That appeared to be precisely what the Tallassee King and other headmen were attempting. It was during this period too that Creek headmen would be confronted with the clearest examples yet of an American expansionism that just would not relent and of American authorities who were willing finally to ignore the voice of the Creek Nation altogether.

Americans soon seized a portion of West Florida from Spanish authorities, providing the first glimpses of such willingness. When filibustering American settlers first suggested rising up to take possession of the territory, they feared resistance from nearby Choctaw communities, who were friendly with Spanish authorities in the area. The filibusterers hoped to rally Creeks to their support, so naturally they approached Hawkins. In his reply, Hawkins made it clear Creeks "would not be suffered to violate our treaty stipulations with Spain," he replied, "or to intermeddle at all in the affair, unless it was authorized by Government."[65] Creeks never got involved in the seizure of West Florida, but Hawkins's insistence that they were not actually free to do so was a revealing position to take. Not only was Creek Country not territorially sovereign, it was not politically sovereign either. Were Creeks not allowed to pursue their own political course, either to attack or assist sovereign Spanish authorities or to attack a sovereign Choctaw people, unless approved by Washington? After all, Creeks had treaty relations with Spain, dating back to the 1784 Treaty of Pensacola, which predated their relationship with the government of the United States. In fact, by the terms of that treaty Creek warriors might actually have been obliged to support Spain militarily against American-backed filibusterers, just as Spain had supported Creeks against Georgia expansionists in the past. Evidently, at least in the moment, Hawkins had forgotten that treaty. Instead, in his understanding, Creeks were not free to act accordingly without American approval. Based on his insistence that the American government had the right to manage Creek politics, Creek sovereignty was becoming more of a fiction every day.

Attacks on Creek territorial sovereignty, long proven to irritate Creek headmen, only became more barefaced. The commanding officer at Fort Stoddert received orders directly from William Eustis to send survey parties north along the Alabama watershed in 1810, for example. The orders were not discussed with the National Council first, of course, and were only related to Alexander Cornells by Hawkins afterward. It was an aggressive decision that surprised even Hawkins. Two detachments of surveying parties, led by officers from the garrison, were soon taking different routes north along the waterways into Cherokee Country, ostensibly to provide the government with "a more correct knowledge of the rivers and country than they have hitherto had." Even as Hawkins questioned Eustis's approach, however, he took the opportunity to further explain to Creeks what Creek territorial sovereignty actually meant. Americans, he explained, considered all Native lands east of the Mississippi "as a part of themselves born on the same lands with them and entitled to the same rights with them." If Creeks wanted to use "the roads and paths and water courses of the white people," they were free to do so, and if "the white people want to use the roads, paths, and waters within the Indian country they will do so."[66] Creeks, in other words, did not actually control their own territory at all, which must have come as a surprise to the Tallassee King. Creeks did not control Creek Country—Americans did.

We don't know how Cornells worded news of the surveying expeditions to his neighbors, but it is likely he did a better job than Hawkins did in giving him the news. Nevertheless, reports of the parties soon made their way through the region, and they produced an immediate response. According to one account, "the whole of the upper towns are alarmed," guaranteeing a halt the work. Indeed, by the time Cornells had the opportunity to spread news of the expeditions local headmen were already confronting Hawkins about what he knew and why he had not been in contact with them. Facing a response that appeared to be intense, Hawkins backpedaled. He did not know, he responded. Perhaps it was to ascertain a sum of money to be given in the event those waterways might be used, he suggested, although few Creeks would have found such an explanation satisfactory. Creeks could "rest assured no encroachments were contemplated against their territorial rights," he promised.[67] That was a difficult guarantee to defend—how could Creek territorial rights possibly have been encroached upon worse, and in a more deliberate fashion, than with such unannounced and unauthorized surveying parties.

If the immediate response by headmen in the Upper Country was any indication, the surveying parties would not get far. John R. Luckett, leading the first party, made it 127 miles before headmen ordered him to halt until they convened at the National Council in October. Luckett was present for the council; there he witnessed "the conduct and determination of the Chiefs of the Creek nation," none of which was conducive to the success of his mission. Hawkins agreed. He wrote directly afterward to warn Luckett that it was not safe for him to continue and added that nothing was likely to change until the council met again in the spring. Soon Luckett was back at Fort Stoddert. Edmund Pendleton Gaines, the officer tasked with the second surveying expedition, was dealt with similarly. He and his party were actually taken into custody and escorted to the Hickory Ground. The National Council ordered him out of Creek Country, and he too was soon back at Stoddert.[68]

Resistance to this newest assault on Creek sovereignty was strong enough to cause Hawkins to admit that the sentiment among many of the council headmen "for the present is much against the accomplishment of the views of the Government." Yet even then he was sure the resistance was nothing that could not easily be overcome. He thought the same would be the case with river traffic. "The Coosa is necessary to our interior country," he argued, and the Alabama was "the best boatable river in the U.S."[69] It was only a matter of time before Americans would gain the free usage of the entire watershed, he was confident. So, even in the face of strong Creek condemnation, Hawkins intensified the government's argument to a group of thirty-seven headmen, representing seven towns at the northernmost part of Creek Country, including Coosa and Natchez. "The President looks on all people of the United States, white or red, as possessing equal rights relative to roads and rivers. They are free to both." That was the right and honorable way, he urged them, "as I believe we are and should be people of one house as we are people of one land."[70] Two decades earlier American authorities were forced to plead with their Spanish counterparts for access to the Mississippi River. The tone with their Creek neighbors in 1810 was decidedly different. Although delivered in a more paternal, even reserved tone, Hawkins's message was the same as before. Creeks, for insisting that their territory was actually theirs, were in the wrong, and it was only a matter of time before their position would have to change.

This renewed pressure only opened new fissures in the National Council. In May it was assembling, most likely at Tuckabatchee, and headmen were as usual "much divided among themselves on their own affairs." The leadership in the Upper Country was "dissatisfied with their government" and wanted to see change, while headmen from the south stood back. Hawkins, for his part, pressed hard to have the council remain unified. If they could "settle their internal affairs and unite their councils," there might still be hope that the most pressing issues could be solved. Or, as Hawkins wrote in a more candid fashion to Eustis, Americans would "have hoped of obtaining what we want from them. If they cannot we shall meet with delays and difficulties."[71] Although Hawkins hoped that the National Council would remain unified so that he could better manipulate it, the results of that meeting were mixed. The council did coalesce, which was good news indeed. Nine headmen represented the Upper Country, while the Little Prince, Tuskegee Tustunnuggee and Tuskenehau of Cusseta, and Eneah Mico of Coweta represented the Lower Country. In one way the National Council was functioning in a way consistent with its earliest days. But now the Big Warrior of Tuckabatchee was Speaker. The Tallassee King, evidently, had been ousted. It was a development that did not thrill Hawkins, who considered the Big Warrior problematic. The council was now filled with "all good men," the Big Warrior "himself excluded. He is avaricious, ambitious, and intriguing." Thomas Woodward, recalling the era much later in his life, would have agreed. The Big Warrior was "a man of great cunning, and there is but little sincerity in his pretended friendship for the whites."[72]

Hawkins had little reason to be optimistic about the newly reunified council; he gained little from it. Of the several issues up for debate, few were concluded in a way that was acceptable to the American government. When Hawkins approached the council over the relatively minor issue of establishments along the postal roads that already existed, headmen "made no reply except for the town of Cusseta." And that was only a warm-up. Hawkins moved on to a talk directly from President James Madison, which pressed Creeks hard to accept several more American requests that, to that point, they had stubbornly refused. Americans needed the usage of the Alabama watershed, which Hawkins again argued "belonged equally to the red and white man and was a right from nature to be violated by either." Rebuffed again, he could only forward on to Eustis another refusal.[73] The council, speaking again it seemed with one voice, was not saying what Americans wanted to hear. There was, however, an even larger request in Madison's talk. Americans would need to convert one of the postal paths into a much larger wagon road. Such a road had long been a military necessity, according to Secretary of War Eustis as well as his predecessor, Henry Dearborn. It was necessary to move soldiers and supplies to Fort Stoddert and Mobile as quickly as possible. By 1811, with armed confrontation with the British growing more likely, the security of the Gulf Coast became a more pressing issue to the Madison administration, which Hawkins made sure to impress upon headmen at the May council that year.

He made the appeal with urgency, but the idea of a permanent wagon road through the heart of the Upper Country emerged as a line in the sand for many Creeks, and certainly for the Tallassee King. Though he was no longer in control of the council that did not stop him from penning a response directly to Madison, which demonstrated how contested Creek government had become. The proposed wagon road was not the same as a horse path, which Creeks understood well enough; it would be wider, more intrusive, and more permanent. Headmen in the Upper Country made clear they were simply not interested in such a road. "You ask for a path and I say no," the Tallassee King declared; "when the President sees my talk, he will know I have answered in full. I have examined it myself, my chiefs and warriors have examined it they tell you I must not allow it and must say no."[74] The Tallassee King's talk indeed made it all the way back to Washington, but Eustis's rejoinder was every bit as clear. The secretary of war was done with negotiation and seemed willing finally to directly and completely disregard the National Council, something authorities had only tiptoed around in previous confrontations. "You will be pleased to represent to them," Eustis wrote Hawkins, "in such a manner as in *your judgment*, may be most conducive to the attainment of the object, that the proposal was founded in reason and justice, embracing the natural rights and interests of the red, as well as white, people. The answer of the Creeks, appears to be unreasonable, and is by no means satisfactory." Eustis's response reflected much more than debate over one road. The population of Americans encircling Creeks was growing "rapidly," and the time was approaching when they "must have roads, & the use of the water courses to the bay of Mobile." Creek sovereignty would not stop them from having it.

A bit of Eustis's response was the familiar old paternalism. It was better that government direct settler travel, he argued, than let Americans just wander through Creek Country alone. Obviously those were the only two options—settlers with a government road or settlers without one was the only decision the National Council had to debate, and Eustis also ended his response with a vaguely worded threat of force that underscored the government's evolving interpretation of Creek sovereignty: "For the present case, it remains for the Creeks to reconsider whether it will not be to their interest to meet the good will which exists towards them: and to give their consent, rather than compel the Government to the use of means, which it is desirous to avoid."[75] Ultimately the Madison administration did not even give the Tallassee King—or any other Creek voice—time to respond. Eustis wrote Hawkins again less than a month later, informing him that the president had gone ahead and determined that two roads, in fact, were necessary, and he had already authorized them both. One would travel from the Tennessee River southwest to Fort Stoddert and the other from Hawkins's agency on the Flint River to Fort Stoddert. The roads were an absolute necessity, Eustis concluded, and ordered Hawkins to explain "to the Creeks, in such manner as you may judge proper," that such was the case, and the president's actions were consistent "with a friendly disposition towards them, and with a proper respect for their rights."[76]

Hawkins approached headmen with the news at a meeting of the Upper Country at Tuckabatchee. There was, obviously, no negotiation. "The President has given full time to the Indian Chiefs to understand these truths, and to explain them to their young people, that their whole nation may understand them."[77] James Madison had already decided what was best for both Creeks and Americans, and it was already being done. If "the people of the red fire choose to travel thro' the lands of the white first either by land or water they have a right to do it, and if the people of the seventeen white fires choose to travel by land or water thro' the country of the red fire, they have a right to do it." The threat posed to Creek communities if they did not consent was more veiled in Hawkins's address than it was in Eustis's letter, but it was still there. The annuity, for instance, could be withheld to ensure the roads remained safe.[78] More importantly, though, the president was at the head "of the military force of the United States" and had positioned troops all over the place in the south "to secure the rights of the red fires and the white fires."[79] The force of the United States remained along the frontier, but no longer were those forces protecting Creek and American sovereignty evenly.

The Madison administration's declaration was a watershed moment in Creek-American relations. After Tuckabatchee, Hawkins claimed to have won over headmen in the north at the not inconsiderable price of over four thousand dollars' worth of cotton-spinning equipment and iron. Still, he was pleased, writing Madison about how "happily we have succeeded in the road business and for a mere tith, considering the extent of territory thro which they are to pass and the wildness of our people."[80] The administration had in reality achieved much more—it had just rendered the National Council more or less irrelevant and revealed Creek sovereignty to be basically meaningless. As a more-paternalistic-than-ever Hawkins saw things, Americans and Creeks were not politically autonomous people but rather friends who simply shared the lands east of the Mississippi; as far as territorial access was concerned, "they both red and white are people of one fire." As for everything else, of course, "the red people are under their own Laws, and the white people are under theirs."[81] In other words, although Creeks supposedly controlled their own lands, they only did so when American authorities agreed. By simply ignoring the Tallassee King and making a mockery of the Creek National Council in such a way, Americans undermined the legitimacy of the Creek nation-state just years after they praised it as Creeks' best hope for safety and stability.

Hawkins did not see things in such a negative light. Having surmounted stubborn opposition from the Upper Country over the issue of territorial access, he found the years of 1811 and 1812 encouraging. "It is with pleasure I assure you the conduct of our southern Indians is daily more and more friendly towards us," he reported to Eustis.[82] Several postal and wagon roads were either finished or were progressing well, and generally speaking, nothing too terrible was happening on them.[83] When a group Shawnee outsiders led by a man named Tecumseh brought alarming talks of unity and war to Tuckabatchee in 1811, "the Chiefs here unanimously refused to smoke the pipe on its presentation and of course refused to join the war." Tecumseh might have been surprised at such a refusal; Hawkins was present at the same conference, shamelessly pressing Creek headmen to accept yet another American advance.[84] Indeed, despite functioning as little more than a puppet government of the

United States, the National Council actually continued to meet regularly in 1811 and 1812, and acted decisively when required. In 1811, "the chiefs of the whole nation" were slated to meet in council in the spring, much the same as they had done for over a decade.[85] A year later, headmen deliberated "eight days on their public affairs." The only communities not represented were Hitchiti ones, but not because they were opposed to anything, according to Hawkins, but because they were sick.[86] Only months after the controversial road decisions, by all outside accounts the National Council appeared to be doing just fine.

Although the National Council had proven by the tumultuous years of the Madison administration to be entirely incapable of countering American expansionism, it continued to function well as the voice of the Creek administrative state and was more than capable of enforcing the few jurisdictional powers it still retained using violence. Indeed, for more than a half decade earlier, the National Council's warriors had been busy. In 1806 the council began trying perpetrators in front of headmen in a way similar to the proceedings in an American court, something that must have pleased Hawkins greatly. They tried and executed a black man for assaulting a Creek woman in an attack that ultimately killed her. They also tried two white men for theft and saw them whipped, and there was also an outstanding death sentence on two Creek men, judged guilty for murder. American legal precedents continued to penetrate the Creek justice system, it was clear from these proceedings, and impact Creek traditions. The slave man was only executed "after a fair trial and the first one known in this land." Yet his execution was still also distinctly Creek. There were no gallows involved, and the kin of the deceased still played a central role in seeing justice done. Warriors took the condemned to a nearby riverbank, where the brother of the deceased knocked him to the ground with a wooden stake, stabbed him to death with it, and then threw his body into the river.[87] Furthermore, horse theft occurred far less often than it had a decade earlier—a testament to the stability provided by the Creek administrative state. Yet when one did occur late in 1809, headmen "promised to exert themselves to find out and apprehend the thief and send back pay for the horse," if it was indeed a Creek who was guilty of the crime.[88]

As more roads were built in several parts of Creek Country, headmen also struggled, and seemed to succeed, in tempering their young men in ways suggestive of past years. In early 1809 and then again a few months later, headmen continued "to improve their manners" and were "exerting themselves increasingly to protect the traveller in their country and to preserve good neighborhood."[89] When a group of "abandoned characters" were caught plundering in the neighborhood of Pensacola and were fired on by Spanish soldiers, the National Council, which had just met, sent a deputation to "go and see to measures to settle the present misunderstanding and to prevent a repetition of it." They kept headmen in the region until the deputation arrived "to remain there and in the neighborhood to have an eye on the conduct" of the nearby Creeks.[90] The administrative Creek state that was first erected in the late eighteenth century, all of these actions proved, continued to function just fine, even if Americans only feigned their respect of it.

Far away from the Alabama confluence, which was growing more contested by the day, headmen in the Lower Country presided over remarkably peaceful times. Headmen "conduct themselves well," and "those among them who commit petty thefts are punished," Hawkins reported.[91] When the so-called patriot revolution in East Florida began to fall apart, and with war with Great Britain seeming more probable, that remained the case. At a regional meeting in Coweta in May 1812, headmen promised to "not interfere in the wars of the white people and should prepare the minds of their young people to be neighbourly and friendly."[92] When Seminoles began actively fighting the American filibusterers in Florida and were reportedly seeking out possible alliances with the English, headmen provided a stronger response. They dispatched "a deputation of their body," including the "Second Chief of the Lower Creeks," Tuskegee Tustunnuggee, to proceed south and "prepare the Seminoles mind to be friendly and neutral," and even to make a visit to the Spanish position at San Marcos de Apalache.[93] With Seminoles rallying effectively to the Spanish defense of Florida and with the patriot cause floundering, headmen from the Lower Country, led by Cussetas, remained neutral; they were "unanimously determined to preserve the friendship of the United States." Seminoles from Alachua had recently applied to them for assistance, "and they had answered they should send them none, they had brought on themselves a war with the white people, and they might end it."[94] With Tuskegee Tustunnuggee was the Wolf Warrior, who also intervened in Seminole affairs. "You sent me a talk to carry to the Seminoles," he wrote Hawkins. "I did my duty. Part of them would not take the talk so I gave them up to the sword, if the white people choose to give it to them."[95]

Decisive action by headmen in the neighborhood of Coweta ensured that 1812 was a period of relative calm in the Lower Country. That was not necessarily the case further west, where reports implicated communities from the Upper Country in steadily intensifying acts of violence. At first the issues seemed minor. There were a "few thieving, idle Indians" in the area of Fort Stoddert, whose "conduct is improper," and headmen were "taking measures to restrain them."[96] Instead, alarming news arrived from American settlers on the Alabama and Tombigbee rivers, alleging that warriors from the Upper Country, instigated by talks from a so-called Prophet, probably Tecumseh, were threatening them with violence. The report was not entirely false, headmen from the neighborhood admitted to Hawkins, "but as soon as their talks began to circulate the Chiefs of the nation put a stop to it." Although there were a few "bad men" among them, Hawkins was assured, they were "restrained from acting by their Chiefs."[97] As acts of violence continued to spread, however, those assurances turned out to be false. Less than a week after the warning by the Mississippi Territory residents, an American settler family traveling on one of the roads was attacked, leaving one dead. The Big Warrior "and some of the Executive Council" from the Upper Country assured Hawkins they would meet soon "and cause justice to be done without delay."[98] Two months later, however, another man was killed near his home "by four Indians, without the least provocation," information that clearly irritated Hawkins. Again headmen declared they would "see what can be done," but Hawkins's hopes were not high. In the meantime, reports that two families had been attacked in Tennessee had come in, leading Hawkins to doubt that anything short of a show of military force would get the headmen to act.[99]

The deaths concerned "every man, woman and child in this nation," he charged, invoking the culpability of all Creeks as both he and his predecessor had done many times. There were dead settlers everywhere. The list contained old charges, some of which did not specify where the killers were from. A white man was dead at St. Mary's; two travelers were killed by Hitchitis; and a post rider had been shot in the Upper Country. Georgians had recently killed Hitchiti hunters and state authorities had ignored the whole affair, making those retaliatory killings all but inevitable. Yet that, of course, did not stop Hawkins from demanding satisfaction. Other killings on the list seemed more random and involved communities primarily in the north. The traveler to the Mississippi Territory was among them, and his whole party had been assaulted so badly that another had surely died. The death of the Georgia man, Arthur Lott, had also gone unpunished. Then there were the unconfirmed deaths of more settlers to the north, attributed also to warriors from the Upper Country, "and a son of Youholau Chapco, that good old interpreter, brought as I am informed the scalp of one of them to his town." Hawkins's demand was as clear as it had been in similar instances in the past. The killers must be punished, and quickly, and all of Creek Country was responsible for seeing justice achieved swiftly: "Murder you cannot hide. The God of Heaven says it must be punished. I say it must be punished; and the safety and happiness of our nation requires it should be punished."[100]

The Big Warrior stepped forward and promised that justice would be had, and the council's warriors did not disappoint. Within a month the "leader of the banditti who murdered Lott," Hillaubee Haujo, had been tracked to the Hickory Ground. Although Hawkins incorrectly described the Hickory Ground as the home of the Tallassee King, he correctly understood that it was a peaceful white town and therefore was supposedly off limits to the very public act of justice that the Big Warrior had planned. There, in the center of town, Hillaubee Haujo sought refuge. Nevertheless, William McIntosh and the Creek war party hunting him found him. McIntosh shot him right where he sat, and before long his body was floating down the Coosa River. Soon word arrived from Tuckabatchee that warriors "in public service" had killed three more.[101] Creek justice, as usual, was swift and brutal.

The toll in violence continued to rise through the summer and fall of 1812, making the council's actions the most decisive that they had ever been. Early in August six people had been put to death, "adjudged guilty of murdering certain white persons," and five others had been "cropped," or mutilated, for crimes like theft. Those were "favorable accounts" to Americans, demonstrating that Creeks appeared "determined to preserve a good understanding with the United States."[102] The number of thieves punished had further risen, and twenty-five warriors were on their way north to hunt down the perpetrators of the murders in Tennessee.[103] By September eight were dead, and seven "cropped and whipped." The council's actions had been impressive, and there was no doubt the violence meted out was done on behalf of all Creeks, "under the sentence of the chiefs of that nation," marking what was perhaps the single largest campaign of state-sponsored violence that Creeks had ever undertaken.[104] Although the Creek National Council could do nothing to temper its American neighbors' territorial ambitions, its administrative structure was functioning just fine.

With Lower Country communities emerging as a bulwark of the Creek nation-state and with the National Council dealing decisively with regional violence, Creek Country early in 1813 hardly seemed in crisis. Several mail routes and now wagon roads were passing by Tucka-batchee two years after Tecumseh had given his war talks there. Work on roads and bridges, although unpopular in neighboring Creek communi-ties, was moving forward, "and the mails regular." Although marred by the occasional robbery, travel on those routes was deemed generally safe. Even from the most contested regions in Creek Country, travelers "com-ing daily from the westward bear testimony to the friendly disposition of the Indians."[105]

Despite those optimistic reports, many in Creek Country had struggled mightily over the previous few years to stop much of that from happening. The postal paths were at best troublesome, and the military wagon roads were being built against the strongest, clearest "no" that Creek headmen had issued since the Ceded Lands crisis. Not only was the state of Tennessee expanding into Creek hunting lands, state settlers were demanding the use of Creek waterways. All of those controversies originated with American legislators, who made increasing demands for access to Creek Country in ways that directly usurped the authority and territorial sovereignty of the Creek Nation. Not only did American authorities agree with these avenues of expansion, they did not seem to care about keeping the promises they had made either for annuity payments or to keep state settlers off Creek lands. Some of those issues constituted clear treaty violations on the part of American authorities, while others revealed a federal government that simply did not respect Creek sovereignty. But all of those actions also had another common thread: they all constituted failures by the National Council to guarantee for Creek people the promises they made on behalf of them.

10 / The Red Stick War and the Future of the National Council

Sir if there is a flag to be had send it to us for it we fight we will defend it to the last, and it will give great joy to these people to see it flying over their hot house.

—Nimrod Doyle, October 4, 1813

Early in 1813 the National Council was forced to deal with another crisis. Hard-line talks by Natives battling Americans in the "northwest" of modern-day Ohio and Indiana led a visiting Creek delegation from the Upper Country to kill several settler families on its return home. The National Council responded aggressively, systematically executing the perpetrators in a brutal and pitiless fashion. While Americans responded approvingly, the killings set into motion an uprising that soon enveloped the region. The Red Stick War, which began in the spring of 1813, was only put down a year later when American armies marched into the Upper Country and devastated the militant communities. A little more than a year after the fighting began, though, Creek Country was in shambles. Close to a thousand warriors were dead and more were on the run, half of Creek Country was a wasteland, and American authorities walked away with much of what remained.

The Red Stick War has been attributed to several external and internal factors, including American expansionism, economic inequality, a pan-Indian message spread by Tecumseh, religious revelations, and even natural phenomena. Once seen largely as a territorial struggle, with clear regional lines, scholars have more recently added important religious, "friendly," and "progressive" versus "nativist" dimensions as well. They have also correctly noted the clear negative impact of the American civilization plan and the inequality it generated.[1] Yet the war was also clearly a political struggle, pitting two opposing parties against each other over the future of Creek Country. Red Stick goals were relatively simple—kill the members of the National Council and strip Creek Country of all of the foreign, illegitimate, American legal and political principles that formed the council's foundation. They were goals that resonated with many by the spring of 1813. The majority of Upper Country communities had suffered tremendously at the hands of American expansionists. They found the National Council not only unequal to the task of halting that expansionism but implicated in its procession, and for those reasons many became convinced that the destruction of the council was now their best way forward. But although the resulting insurgency fought to tear down the Creek state, its vision to reshape Creek Country was not simply a retreat to a previous, pre-Revolutionary period of local thinking. Red Stick insurgents were rejecting the council and the Euro-American state structure that it represented but not necessarily the sense of Creek nationalism that headmen had begun to envision, from their very neighborhoods, only a generation earlier. Indeed, the calls that surged through the Upper Country still advocated for a unified Creek people. Theirs was a future, however, that did not involve the Creek state as it existed. It did not include Americans, either. For many Creek communities along the Alabama watershed, that was a better alternative to the future they faced.

For many more communities, on the other hand, the future did not look so bleak. To thousands of Creeks, mostly in the Lower Country, the National Council was still the legitimate voice of the Creek Nation. It was not doing such a bad job, and it would endure. Their goals were similarly straightforward. They would crush the insurgency and reassert council control over all of the Upper Country. With the help of American forces, they were ultimately able to do that. Unfortunately for them, however, the Red Stick uprising was much more than the fanaticism of an isolated group of communities, as many in the beginning of the struggle had hoped. Even though warriors representing the National Council eventually declared victory, there was little of Creek Country left for them to reclaim.

In March 1813 a rash of new killings far to the north of Creek Country generated a fresh crisis the National Council was forced to confront. "This year commences with the murder of seven families of our white friends and war talks from the northern nations," Hawkins disparaged. Not only were families killed in Ohio and Tennessee, but they were "most cruelly mangled, shewing all the savage barbarity that could be invented." Because the location of the killings was so removed, in fact, Creeks at first escaped the blame. But a group of Creeks were returning through the area from a visit with Tecumseh and his brother Tenskwatawa. There they had borne witness to the Prophet's talks, which were complete with beads and scalps, and had been directed "to take up the hatchet against the United States."[2] Apparently the talks worked.

Having Shawnee talks spark Creek violence was not an altogether new crisis for Americans. Nearly the same thing had happened almost exactly twenty years earlier, in 1793. Both times Shawnee talks pressed for unity, both times they advocated for violence, and both times they resulted in bloodshed. In this newest instance two headmen from the Upper Country, the Tustunnuggee Ooche of Wewocao, called the Little Warrior, and Oostanaulah Kecoh Tustkey, of Tuskegee, also known as the Tuskegee Warrior, were identified as the perpetrators. The Tuskegee Warrior went so far as to admit to the killings during a meeting of the National Council, which convened soon after he returned. He arrived with talks designed "to engage this tribe in a war with the whites," to which the council did not react well. They reprimanded him "severely" and ordered him "to leave the council house, as a man unworthy to have a seat in it."[3] Although the National Council was reacting sternly to the first accounts of the killings, plenty of damage had already been done.

It was clear from firsthand accounts, and probably from the Little Warrior's own admission, that the killings were not only real but designed to send a message. A pregnant woman was murdered, her unborn child pulled from her womb and impaled on a stake. Such brutality, according to Americans, was almost without precedent: "Of all the murderous acts committed by savages against the people of the United States this is the most outrageous." And the killings were not random; they were not committed by "thoughtless, wild young men," Hawkins charged. They were deliberately perpetrated by two trusted headmen, no less. There was "no instance, in the recollection of the oldest men among us," he wrote to newly arrived secretary of war John Armstrong, "of chiefs, sent on a public pacific mission, ever having acted in so outrageous a manner."[4] Because the headmen accused of the killings had been in the area representing the Creek Nation, in fact, it made the killings "an act of the nation; and the nation must clear themselves of the guilt, by delivering up the culprits to the laws of the United States." Hawkins pushed Cornells, "one of the great chiefs of this nation, and an officer of the United States," to do everything he could to make this point as clear as possible to everyone around him. "You must exert yourself on the present trying occasion" and "cause justice to be done as it is demanded," and as soon as possible. In an open letter to the Upper Country, Hawkins's demands were as strong as any his predecessor, James Seagrove, had ever penned. "You must get together, one and all; turn out your warriors; apprehend the two chiefs and their associates," and deliver them up for justice. "The guilty must suffer for their crimes, or your nation will be involved in their guilt."[5]

Not even two weeks later a man was killed on a postal road and another wounded, deepening what was already quickly becoming a crisis. The National Council, which usually met in the spring, was soon to convene, and the members declared they would be up to the challenge. They were "determined to be friends with the white people" and would "exert themselves with all their strength to this end." If that was not enough, Hawkins wrote Armstrong, he would get the American military involved.[6] Secretary Armstrong went further, making it clear not only that the army was available but that it would be wielded against Creeks if the situation was not handled both swiftly and correctly. "The arms of the United States" would be brought "immediately against the Creek Nation of Indians," he warned, "unless reparations be promptly and satisfactorily made for the recent murders committed by them on citizens of the United States." Armstrong, echoing Hawkins's early ultimatums, also demanded that Creek justice alone would be unacceptable. "Nothing short of taking & delivering over the murderers to the custody of the Governor of the state in which the offences were committed (to be there dealt with according to law) will satisfy the united demands of policy and justice." Warriors were only to seize the perpetrators "and deliver them to me, or some officer of the United States commanding on the frontiers," Hawkins likewise declared, "to be punished according to the Laws of the United States." Creeks were bound by the Treaty of New York to do so, he insisted, and the Creek annuity would also be suspended until those conditions were met.[7]

To say this new ultimatum was simply another case of Americans usurping Creek authority would be an oversimplification. It was rejecting a Creek justice system that had not only been legally established through treaty for almost a generation but been applauded by Americans in the past for its swiftness. A decade earlier, for instance, President Jefferson personally thanked the council for hunting down the perpetrator of a murder and killing him where he stood. Later, in 1806, Hawkins oversaw several whippings and executions ordered by the council that he then rationalized to his superiors. What he was implicated in, after all, was nowhere near established American jurisprudence. As Creeks were an independent people, however, "I shall do in to dispense justice among white and black people according to the authority vested in me by them as heretofore declared," at least until otherwise directed by American authorities.[8] Although Creek techniques were different than American ones, and certainly unrefined by his standards, Hawkins believed that the Creek National Council was the legitimate source of justice within its sovereign territory, and therefore he supported its decisions.

The council had acted similarly in 1812, and its actions were again lauded. Indeed, over the years warriors acting on the orders of the National Council had shot, whipped, mutilated, and even sodomized countless Creeks convicted of crimes against Americans, and they did so without offering the accused anything their American counterparts would have considered close to a recognizable legal proceeding. Americans had no problem with the Creek process, however, because it generated stability. There was also little they could do legally, even if they did disagree. The Treaty of New York, to which Hawkins referred, was contradictory when it came to jurisdiction—it set forth conditions where Creeks were to turn over Creeks to American authorities in some situations but also allowed Creeks to deal with American citizens and fellow Creeks as they wished in others. What had developed out of that was by 1813 pretty well understood. Americans accused of committing crimes against Creeks were to face American justice, and Creeks accused of committing crimes against Americans were to face Creek justice. That was a pillar of Creek territorial sovereignty, the federal government's treaty system, and the foundation for the Trade and Intercourse Acts as well. Although several institutions in Creek Country were consistent with a contemporary Euro-American state, Creeks were supposed to be free to define their own legal traditions, which seemed to be the case. Justice in Creek Country, although it now contained several recognizable aspects to American authorities, was still also very much Creek.

In the wake of the 1813 killings, however, neither Hawkins nor Armstrong considered such understood legal principles valid. At first the American demands seem surprising, but Hawkins had slowly been moving in that direction for some time. He had sided with American expansionist interests more openly now for years and had belittled Creek diplomatic and political traditions in the recent past. Now the secretary of war was of a similar mind. Was a Creek justice system now no longer legal in Creek Country? Even the most effective aspect of the Creek Nation and the one Americans pushed for so insistently—its administrative state structure—was now being thrown into question. Armstrong's unwillingness to allow Creeks to administer justice provided more proof yet that the American government was no longer interested in living with a neighboring Creek state.

Justice would not have to be coerced in such a way—most Creeks, it seemed, shared in the horror of the recent killings. A group of hunters, meeting with a Georgia official, learned of the attacks and expressed their disappointment, "lest the misconduct of a few among them should involve them in a war contrary to the wish of the mass of the nation who they represented as desirious of preserving peace."[9] Headmen in the Upper Country, facing pressure from Hawkins, from state authorities, and even from their counterparts in the Lower Country, were "more alarmed than I have ever known them to be." The "mischiefmakers" among them were "determined to try their strength," suggesting that an insurgency was already building. That did not prevent headmen from the neighborhood, however, from taking swift action. They sat "in council on the subject of the late outrages" in April, "and it is expected that the offenders will be brought to justice."[10] Hawkins, who was present for much of the deliberation, reasserted his demands that the perpetrators be captured, not killed, but several headmen made it clear that probably would not happen. Warriors would try to capture the Little Warrior, but he would surely "endeavor to do all the mischief he possibly can as he is now outlawed in his own Country." Chances of bringing him in alive were slim. Nevertheless, they were out "in all directions to take or kill him." If Americans were to capture him, they were free to "have him taken and treated as your law directs," but it was unclear if the warrior groups out to get him would be so careful as to take him alive.[11]

After seventeen days in deliberation, and less than a month after the killings on the Ohio, groups of warriors organized and led by William McIntosh and the Little Prince were on the trail of the perpetrators. Under the leadership of the two noted warriors—Tustunnuggee Hutkee and Tustunnuggee Hopoie, respectively—the classed warrior tradition that had now been a stabilizing and respected function of the Creek administrative state for years was again being invoked. Nimrod Doyle, one of Hawkins's assistant agents, traveled with the war party, which he reported was over 150 warriors strong.[12] After the party split up one posse, led by the two headmen, tracked a group to a house in the Hickory Ground and surrounded it. "The murderers having discovered them" made it clear they would not be taken alive. After exchanging gunfire for some time the house was set ablaze as a way to force the perpetrators out. The Tuskegee Warrior, who was wounded, burned to death in it but only after he made it clear he had no intention of being taken alive anyway.

He "had killed and eaten white people," and he had been the one to slay and mutilate the pregnant woman on the Ohio, he proudly declared. Two of the other perpetrators, brothers of the Tuskegee Warrior, were dragged out of the burning house and promptly dispatched. Two more, both described as young Tuckabatchees, managed to escape, although one was overtaken and killed. At the same time a second posse, also led by Coweta and Tuckabatchee warriors, tracked another ringleader, the Little Warrior of Wewocao. They overtook him in Holiwahli town, and after a standoff they killed him and two others.[13]

Of course Americans would have preferred these perpetrators be taken alive, the leaders of the posses admitted, but it simply could not be done. "This is the case with all of them: for they all fight till they drop."[14] Hawkins seemed convinced that such was the case—both parties of perpetrators "made battle and fought desperately." He admitted his pleasure directly to the Big Warrior, Cornells, and McIntosh. They had taken the "right way," he wrote, "by punishing immediately every man who violates your Laws, by murdering and plundering your white neighbors." Both warrior parties incurred injuries, even losses, giving their words credit. In one of the confrontations a nephew of William McIntosh was wounded badly; in the other, the council lost three killed and one, with the nephew of the Big Warrior of Tuckabatchee wounded as well.[15] The condemned did not go easily, certainly, but to insist that none of them could be taken alive still seemed only partially to be the case. Several of the accused were clearly executed after they had been captured. If Americans wanted the lives of the perpetrators they would have them, but justice would be had on Creek terms.

While that aspect of the council's justice could not be bent, even by American demands, recognizable aspects of American justice still informed the warriors' approach. After one of the posses killed the Little Warrior they moved to kill another of the perpetrators, who was being protected by his brother. The brother was killed in the firefight while the suspected murderer escaped. A headman from the town, asserting a traditional mico's role in mediation, insisted that the death of the kin of the accused was enough and that "the debt was satisfied." Yet the escaped man was the one implicated in the murders, not his brother. Assistant Agent Doyle read to the warriors Hawkins's charge that it was "not an equal number the white people want, it is the guilty; and they want no innocent person to suffer." The warriors, reflecting on that pillar of American justice, which was now Creek justice, "determined on his execution" and dispatched a new set of warriors from Tuckabatchee to have him either apprehended or executed. After shooting at his pursuers and barely missing one, the wanted man "then drew his knife and tomahawk" to defend himself, clearly with no intention of being taken alive. Three musket balls to the chest later, he was dead.[16]

By late April the justice of the National Council had been distributed and a number of wanted Creeks lay dead. It was a number similar to the number of Americans killed, "and that is all of the party that they could lay their hands on." The murder of the man on the postal road was dealt with similarly. When the council learned who was responsible—two men from Oakfuskee—"we sent out our warriors, and had them put to death." They also executed a woman for a killing on the Duck River in Tennessee, bringing the number of dead to upwards of eleven.[17] Although American authorities demanded that the killers be turned over to their custody—to be tried in American courts and then of course executed—most, like Hawkins, were pleased with the council's swift response. The executions represented a continuation of Creek state violence that was, by 1812, as common as it was welcomed. In the wake of the almost dozen Creeks killed in 1813, American authorities embraced a Creek justice system that had delivered to their citizens something they could appreciate.

Word of the eleven deaths also came with strong reassurances from the Creek leadership. When fears spread that the kin were considering attacks to avenge the executed, one visitor heard from several Creeks that "if there was among a few in the uper towns a disposition to hostility, it is completely suppres'd and that the chiefs have such an overwhelming majority of the nation in their favor, that if there are a few who meditate mischief they will not dare to perpetrate it."[18] In the wake of such threats, in fact, the leadership resolved to "make our law stronger concerning the murderers." Although Tecumseh had been through the Upper Country and had "danced in our square, around our fire," there was nothing to fear from the Creek people, which was a point the council took pains to project. Those who had stood against the National Council—the true voice of the Creek people—had suffered, and they would continue to suffer as long as they acted in such a fashion. "You need not be jealous that we shall take up arms against the United states: we mean to kill all of our red people that spill the blood of our white friends." A new generation of headmen was invested in the Creek Nation in this time of crisis, as an older generation had been during past times of trial. "The young warriors is a making of laws, the more mischief is done the more force to punish."[19]

Furthermore, the council's actions had the same effect they had had for almost a decade—they generated a sense of stability that was comforting to Americans. Indeed, although Americans only partially respected the administrative Creek state in 1813, it was difficult to deny even for Georgia state officials that it was getting quite good. Almost universally, Hawkins was pleased to report, "from the present disposition of the Creeks there is nothing hostile to be apprehended from them."[20] Likewise, Georgia militia commander Thomas Flournoy passed within a few miles of Tuckabatchee on his way to Fort Stoddert and was soon similarly confident. Not only had all of the recent murderers "been put to death, by order of the council," but the council declared to him personally that they would have nothing to do with the British war and would "put to death any man" who challenged their authority. Flournoy was impressed. "What more can we ask of this people? Whilst they pursue this line of conduct, they should meet with the support, countenance & protection of the people of Georgia." The council's response to the killing on the postal road brought even clearer praise. A contractor for the mail service reported that not one rider "had any fears on account of the murder . . . any more than if it had happened in the white people's country." The swift action by the council did Creeks great justice, he continued, and "we think it will have the effect of deterring others from the commission of similar crimes."[21]

Despite the decisive actions taken by the National Council and the sense of stability it generated across the frontier, there were troubling indications that the executions would not bring the closure many hoped they would. None of the murderers died repentantly, for instance, and a few of them made some fortuitous dying threats. After being mortally wounded, for instance, one of the accused uttered that "the nation would be ruined for killing him, and not taking the Prophet's talk." Then there was an alleged invitation from Spanish and even British authorities to come to Pensacola and collect arms and ammunition to use against Americans, which made its way to Big Tallassee. Although the offer turned out "to be a bubble," that did not stop many from heading south anyway.[22] A decent turnout at Pensacola hinted at the turbulent undercurrents of anger toward the council that were beginning to surface, particularly from the Upper Country.

Why the Upper Country generated the majority of the unhappiness that would eventually birth the Red Stick insurgency seems rather straightforward, lending to the ensuing war a fairly clear-cut regional dynamic. Almost all of the previous American expansionist developments, as well as several future plans, impacted communities in the north far more than those in the southeast, generating anti-state forces in the very region Creek nationalism had, ironically, first developed. When it came to territorial access alone, years of expansionism had drawn serious differences between the needs of communities in the Upper and Lower countries—differences that the National Council had demonstrated an inability to reconcile. While headmen in the north fought the construction of several roads through their communities bitterly, in ways that caused rifts to open up in the National Council and even in their own regional ones, proposed roads from Georgia through Hawkins's Agency on the Flint River were practically celebrated in the Lower Country, where headmen promised "to do everything which depends on them to render traveling on the roads safe and that the people traveling on them shall be received and treated friendly as they pass and protected in their persons and property."[23] The reality was that while headmen like the Little Prince of Broken Arrow, along with Cussetas and Cowetas, actually appeared to be warming up to their state counterparts to the east, their neighbors to the northwest, in places like Oakfuskee, Tallassee, and Autossee, faced crisis. When it came to those roads the differences could not be clearer: "the Lower Creeks begin to understand it so, but the Upper Creeks uniformly oppose it."[24]

Reopening debate over the Coosa River only deepened the contrast. It was "alarming, in a high degree," to many Creeks, but Americans insisted. "It must be got over some way, as very soon Tennessee must be gratified on this point."[25] Headmen on the Apalachicola waterway, of course, did not face the same pressure. Waterway access, like road construction, was a regional issue that created controversy in the Upper Country while it bothered few in the south. While the Red Stick War is commonly described in ways that transcended geography, this aspect of the political struggle draws geographic lines that were well-defined. The authority of the National Council was being systematically usurped when it came to the needs of those along the Coosa, Tallapoosa, and Alabama rivers. The council could do nothing to stop the construction of roads, keep Americans off the rivers, or stop either the illicit trade or the illegal settlements that were destroying Creek sovereignty. Even their strongest objections did nothing to halt American expansionists in the federal government, who overruled them without consequence, and more frequently, their own neighbors seemed to agree. Underrepresented in a council that was growing more alienated from their concerns and more closely tied to American interests, the world in which many Upper

Creek communities lived was growing smaller and more contested with each passing day. As the National Council became more unresponsive to the needs of half of Creeks, an uprising against it, and from the Upper Country, seemed increasingly inevitable.

Taken alone, however, the inability of the council to counter American expansionism was not enough to foment the kind of rebellion that members of the National Council began to see in the summer of 1813. While the Creek Nation's governing body could do little to protect the territory or interests of those along the Alabama, Coosa, and Tallapoosa watersheds, it showed little hesitation beating, mutilating, and executing its young men in ways that were still uncomfortable to many. Although Americans reacted with enthusiastic support to the National Council's embrace of state violence, to those in the Upper Country its swift and brutal response to the killings in Ohio and Tennessee seemed to be the final straw. Its actions in 1813 turned out to be the moment when many communities realized that the shortcomings of the National Council far outstripped the stability it provided. It had only absorbed and could only guarantee the worst, most politically, economically, and culturally objectionable parts of American culture. It was after news of the executions rippled through the Upper Country, in the summer of 1813, that the Red Stick insurgency began to spiral out of control.

Representatives of the council in the Upper Country, led by Cornells and the Big Warrior, responded conservatively at first to reports that discontent was turning into rebellion. They heaped scorn on Alabamas, for instance, whom they blamed for the attacks and insisted were outsiders—not even true Creeks. Hawkins believed those early reports and he, like the members of the council, largely dismissed the calls for violence that radiated from the neighborhood of the Alabama communities. Although surrounding neighborhoods were receptive to violent talks, they were not acting on them. "Their people are dancing their dances, but no man has moved to assist them." The Big Warrior, speaking for the council, then penned an invitation to the emerging numbers of so-called prophets, inquiring into their plans as well as their visions: "Now, we want to see and hear what you have seen and heard." There was nothing to fear, he was confident. The perpetrators of the late murders had "suffered for their crimes, and there is an end of it." But as the weeks passed, the killings were not the end of it. The insurgency did of course spread, finding enthusiastic recruits in headmen like Peter McQueen, not to mention stalwart anti-American and former Speaker the Tallassee King.[26] A community or two did not represent the sole purveyors of the extremist Red Stick vision, it turned out—they were not deluded but isolated radicals. Tuckabatchee, a seat of the National Council, was soon surrounded by them. The man who carried the Big Warrior's invitation, for instance, was known to have taken part in the recent executions, and when he arrived with the council's papers he was dealt with accordingly. The insurgents "instantly put him to death, and scalped him," and sent his scalp up to the forks of the Coosa and Tallapoosa, where a growing core of prophets was now popular. Next they raided and burned the house of Captain Isaacs, "one of the Chiefs who led the warriors against the murderers of the white families on Ohio." At first it was reported that Isaacs was killed, along with his nephew "and three more of his party." Isaacs was not lost but was saved at the last minute by warriors friendly to the council; two of his compatriots, however, were not so fortunate.[27]

Although Isaacs's life was saved, his assailants made sure to burn everything he owned. Purging Creek Country of the physical evidence of Americans' negative influence was a popular objective of the insurgency. Warriors routinely struck out at the symbols of the American civilization plan, for example, which had proved so culturally divisive. They burned the houses, fences, and property of headmen in Kialijee, Autossee, Oakfuskee, and wherever they found them in the hinterlands. Cattle, hogs, fowl, and other domesticated livestock were targeted, and cow tails emerged as prizes not unlike enemy scalps. Insurgents even targeted more intimate, household vestiges of American civilization. In Hillaubee, for instance, Red Stick warriors assaulted a Mrs. Grayson, stripping her of her European-style clothing and destroying her spinning and weaving equipment. Creeks of mixed ancestry were even targeted in some instances simply because their existence was further proof of Euro-American interference in Creek culture.[28]

As much pleasure as the attackers took in watching Captain Isaacs's property burn, they would have felt far more accomplished watching him die. For that reason the destruction of Isaacs's house was a success of only secondary importance. The failed attempt on his life represented an opening salvo in what was as much a political struggle as a cultural one, pitting members and supporters of the National Council against an anti-state faction that no longer shared its vision for the future.[29] Red Stick insurgents were doing more than targeting unwanted outsiders or destroying symbols of an unwanted economic culture—Captain Isaacs was no outsider. What he was, however, was an agent of the Creek National Council, making this earliest reported Red Stick attack an assault on the political Creek state. There were evidently plenty of Creeks who felt similarly, and there were plenty of headmen the growing ranks of the unhappy blamed for the position their communities were in. The Big Warrior, Alexander Cornells, Captain Isaacs, William McIntosh, the Mad Dog's son, the Little Prince, and Spoko Haujo of Tallassee were all targets. According to that hit list, provided by a Creek man of mixed ancestry who was himself targeted, political motives were very much at the heart of the insurgency. Every one of those men had colluded with Americans in creating the current Creek state structure—they were the National Council. They had all "taken the talk of the whites," meaning they all had accepted the American political traditions that were at the foundation of the National Council, and now they needed to die.[30]

"The declaration of the prophets is to destroy every thing received from the Americans," as well as "all the Chiefs and their adherents who are friendly to the customs and ways of the white people," one charge went. None of the "customs and ways" of the unwanted Creek state was clearer than the willingness to use violence, demonstrated in the most recent executions. "It is not improbable," Hawkins admitted to Secretary Armstrong, "but the opposition will be strengthened by the friends of those executed" in 1812, as well as the more recent killings in 1813, "as their attack has commenced on the chiefs and warriors who executed the orders of the Executive council," like Isaacs.[31] Other accounts brought similar charges. By giving satisfaction "for the murders on the post road," a Creek informant elaborated, "which it was the duty of their nation to do," such leaders were "placed in a war attitude by their opponents." Doing justice "to the white people" in such an American fashion was the crime, and all of those men were now targeted for death. Distressed headmen, watching the violence intensify into the summer, need look only to Oakfuskee, where insurgents were "killing such men that takes the talks" from Americans "and wishes to do good for the nation." Even the Big Warrior knew the stakes, explaining later that the action of the National Council "was the cause that our young people put all the old Chiefs to death, and to make laws themselves. That made them crazy."[32]

By killing the current generation of Creek leadership, Red Sticks were looking to dissolve the National Council and purge Creek Country of Americans' political traditions in the process. They were not doing so, however, in an attempt to hearken back to a now long ago period of individual Creek community interests but rather to replace the current Creek state with something more responsive to their needs, reinforcing the centrality of both politics and nationhood in the struggle. While the Red Stick War certainly was a rebellion pitting civilization and modernity against nativism, traditionalism, prophets, and religious fanatics, the earliest attempts to kill members of the National Council suggests that the insurgency was a calculated political, anti-state decision as well. Not all Red Sticks rejected all Euro-American cultural influences—things like metal tools, firearms, and cotton clothing, for instance—which they either needed or simply liked having. But all of them were looking to kill the Big Warrior, along with all other members and supporters of the National Council, and then Hawkins, demonstrating the political importance of the anti-state revolution they were undertaking.[33]

There was no doubt that many Red Stick "fanatics," who had embraced either Tecumseh's or Seakaboo's messages or those of more local "prophets," were clearly driven by spirituality. Take, for example, Hillis Haujo, also known as Josiah Francis. Francis was from Auttogee, an Alabama community that, according to early reports, was where the insurgency originated. Even though he was a man of mixed Creek-European ancestry who spoke English fluently, Francis was soon a prophet of immense authority. Only after repeated battlefield losses, and when Red Sticks were refugees in Florida, did his influence finally begin to wane. His name, which meant something like "crazy-brave medicine," hinted that his traditional claim to Creek spirituality was strong, as his leadership in battle appeared to be as well.[34] Plenty of other Red Sticks were more questionable prophets, however, and still others did not claim to channel much spiritual power at all. Consider William Weatherford. Also known by his Creek name, Lamochattee, or Red Eagle, Weatherford was born in Coosada, like fellow Red Stick and "principle War Chief" Jim Boy, also known as High-Headed Jim or Cusseta Haujo. Weatherford was the son of once respected and then exiled trader Charles Weatherford, making him a member of the influential Wind clan and kin to Alexander McGillivray. He was the epitome of a Creek man of mixed ancestry who was, indeed, the son of a man of mixed ancestry. He was then a Red Stick leader who would gain an almost legendary infamy after organizing the Fort Mims attack. But he would not die a Red Stick, making his attachment to the insurgency particularly weak. He personally surrendered to Andrew Jackson near the end of the war and would live the rest of his life either hunting down remaining Red Sticks in Georgia and Florida or living as a well-off and generally well-respected southern planter.[35]

Peter McQueen was just as complicated, and the Tallassee King even more so. The future Red Stick McQueen caught Hawkins's eye while the agent was taking stock of the Upper Country in 1799. Although he was the son of noted Scottish trader James McQueen and a Tallassee woman, the younger McQueen had also attained the title tustunnuggee and was described as the chief warrior of Tallassee. That meant that he, too, was a man of mixed ancestry who appeared to have a foot planted firmly in both Creek and Euro-American worlds. And evidently he was doing quite well by Hawkins. He was "a snug trader, has a valuable property in negros and stock and begins to know their value."[36] A traditional tustunnuggee who was also a plantation owner, with slaves? A man of mixed ancestry indeed. It must have come as a tremendous surprise to Hawkins, then, when more than a decade later McQueen emerged as a leading Red Stick "prophet." There was little prophet to him, it seemed, but there were other reasons why the once respectable McQueen would go rogue. He did not turn out to be such a "snug" trader, for instance, as Hawkins had once suggested. He was deeply indebted to the Forbes and Company trading firm—the successor to the Panton, Leslie and Company operation—which surely informed his decision to join a resistance movement that targeted such symbols of oppression and economic dependence. His anger at John Innerarity, a trader associated with the firm, demonstrated as much. McQueen traveled to Pensacola with other Red Stick leaders looking for arms and ammunition, and when Innerarity turned him down, McQueen proceeded to threaten the trader and berate his employers so viciously that Spanish officers, fearing for Innerarity's life, had to drag McQueen away at bayonet point and parade the entire garrison in front of him in order to calm him down.[37]

Then there was the Tallassee King, who did not express much of a prophetic undertaking at all when he embraced the Red Stick insurgency. As a community mico from a traditionally white town, he would have little claim to such spiritual authority. And as a former Speaker of the National Council, he certainly had not always been an enemy of the Creek state. What he did have, however, was an abiding hatred of American authorities, which went back to the days of James Seagrove, almost twenty years earlier. He no doubt took the opportunity of the rebellion to strike back at a National Council that he had once tried to use, unsuccessfully, and that was now populated by Creek leaders who were doing little more than the bidding of the American government. Then, finally, there was a man like Captain Isaacs, an actual shaman from the Upper Country who did not become a prophet or even a Red Stick but instead ended up supporting the council. Isaacs was a conjurer and a shaman with exceptionally strong ties to the natural world before the uprising—perhaps the most powerful one in all of Creek Country. According to at least one report, Isaacs was with the Little Warrior when the latter man killed the settlers on the Ohio, and it was only "from his tricks and management," and the fact that his wife was the daughter of Alexander McGillivray, that he "was let out of the scrape." He provided information on the killings when he arrived back in Creek Country and took part in the council's executions in 1813, and the unsuccessful attempt on his life months later is considered by some as the beginning of the uprising.[38]

There was certainly a traditionalist, even prophetic strain to the Red Stick insurgency, but that was not all it was, as demonstrated by those who both embraced and resisted it. Anger at the National Council, it turned out, was quite a unifier. Alabama, Coosada, and Koasati communities were among the first to produce prophets and were also among the ones imposed upon most heavily by territorial issues like roads and river access, issues the National Council either could not or would not address. Communities like Holiwahli and Oakfuskee were quick to join the rebellion and had also lost kin to the National Council in 1812 and 1813.[39] Those were no coincidences. What all those communities and Red Stick leaders had in common was a deeply unfavorable view of the National Council and of Americans for both propping it up and then ignoring it. Religious fanaticism or rejection of Euro-American economic and cultural values could be spotty among Red Sticks, but the rejection of the National Council was not.

Neither were Red Stick insurgents demonstrating the contrived reality of Creek nationhood by challenging the current state structure built atop it. According to some accounts, in fact, a hopeful sense of continued Creek unity was actually a driving cause of much of the violence, which only targeted a specific leadership group and those who agreed with its flawed political vision. According to one of the prophets, High Head Jim, "the war was to be against the whites & not between the Indians themselves." Then there was William Weatherford's decision to join the insurgency. He was "as much opposed" to the fighting "as any one living: but when it became necessary to take sides, he went with his countrymen." To join the Americans, he explained, "was a thing he did not think right," and if he stayed with "his people," he might "prevent his misguided countrymen from committing many depredations that they might otherwise do." He apparently told a group of insurgents led by Josiah Francis that he "disapprobated their cause, and that it would be their ruin," but "they were his people—he was raised with them, and he would share their fate."[40] Weatherford, no eminent Red Stick prophet, was not referring to himself by community identity or linguistic group. He was Creek. He was a strong supporter of Creek nationalism, even if he was also a leading Red Stick warrior. As it were, the "revolution-ists" had no "original quarrel" even with the Creeks of mixed ancestry, another account agreed. "If they fall into the new order of things" it would "be well. They will remain unmolested." It would be "by those means," though, that Red Sticks would in the end actually unite the nation "against their white neighbors." Intelligence from the neighbor-hood of Pensacola was similar. It told of Red Stick insurgents whose aim was to kill many "of their own chiefs," which would "effect a complete revolution in the government, and the patriots will obtain an uncon-trollable sway."[41] Unfortunately, no Red Stick went into any great detail about what the "new order of things" would mean for Creek Country. What was relatively clear was that while the vision at Pensacola did not necessarily involve something like Tecumseh's pan-Indian alliance, it did involve Creek leadership—just a different one. The Red Stick upris-ing would wipe Creek Country of the failed, illegitimate, American-style state structure and build upon its ruins something better.

It is worth returning once more to Cherokee Country, to a period of only a few years later, to demonstrate in another fashion how the forces of nation and state formation produced voices and actions of exclusion and resistance, rather than inclusion and harmony. At the same time many Cherokees were conceiving of political collectivity as their best means of survival in the face of American expansionism, they were pass-ing laws that threatened Cherokees who were contemplating emigrating west anyway. Groups of Cherokees who left Cherokee Country for the Arkansas River would no longer be considered members of the Cherokee Nation, according to laws passed in 1817. The Cherokee leadership had specific reasons for passing such extreme and seemingly counterproduc-tive laws. Facing mounting pressure for wholesale removal west, unity was critical. More importantly, American proponents of emigration were making an argument that for each emigrant who went west, the Cherokee people forfeited a proportion of their southeastern homeland. That threatened a piecemeal, but still very deliberate, dispossession of Cherokee Country. And that gave the federal government's agent, Return Meigs, reason to discourage Cherokee assertions of nationalism or sov-ereignty. The Cherokee National Council was attempting to prevent the loss of Cherokee lands by defining nationhood and citizenship and then stripping it from those willingly emigrating away from the homeland to the obvious detriment of others. That decision, however, reveals the destructive possibilities of nation and state formation. Clearly not all

Cherokees believed in the National Council or even the assumption of sovereignty that formed its foundation.[42]

In Cherokee Country, however, those who did not agree with the Cherokee National Council were simply trying to leave. They were not trying to destroy the council and murder all of its members. Unfortunately, in Creek Country, that was precisely the case, and there was no shortage of support for a new vision of Creek governance in the Upper Country that included violent uprising. The Tallassee King was one such supporter. He tried to lead the National Council in a different direction in 1811, assuming the Speaker position in a surprising ascendancy only to be ousted soon after by the Big Warrior, a Speaker much friendlier to American interests. As of the summer of 1813 the Tallassee King had begun a new chapter in the story of his incredible political career—he was now a Red Stick leader, evidence of the power of a new vision of governance that rejected both the Big Warrior and his American overlords. Tuskenehau of Cusseta and Atchau Haujo of Coweta confronted the Tallassee King about his rumored involvement in the insurgency. When they requested he have "the war sticks and projects thrown aside," he dismissed them, declaring instead "his determination to persevere until he destroyed all who aided and assisted to put the murderers to death." Tuckabatchee would burn, he declared, then Coweta. The two communities that most clearly represented the Creek nation-state, if he had his way, would be wiped from Creek Country.[43] The Tallassee King, once Speaker of the National Council, now advocated openly for its destruction.

Before the quick succession of attacks and threats in the summer of 1813, members of the council underestimated the extent of the insurgency's support. When Yaholo Chapco emerged as a voice of resistance after his son was executed by order of the council, for instance, Alexander Cornells dismissed him, along with the rest of the so-called prophets, as "a sort of madness and amusement for idle people." Soon after the failed attack on Isaacs, however, when Red Stick warriors attacked several more like-minded headmen, Cornells's tone was much different. At the exact moment when the National Council had "exhibited the strength and ability of the nation to punish," the prophets' talks were "secretly gaining strength and converts, and where least expected, bursted forth in acts of murder, confident of its strength."[44] Much less confident themselves, nearby members of the council were clearly alarmed. "We are of opinion, if the prophets cannot be crushed, they will bring ruin on us," not to mention war with Americans. The National Council's confusion and inaction in these first months were critical in allowing the insurgency to spread. Soon Autossees, "lately converted" to the Red Stick cause, had driven off many of their headmen. Fooshaujo, one Autossee headman, disappeared. With blood visible on his house, though, there was little hope he was alive.[45] Nearby two Tuckabatchee warriors—including the son of the late Mad Dog—seized an Alabama and were taking him back to Tuckabatchee to be interrogated when they were fired on by a "party of fanatics." Red Sticks secured the escape of the Alabama prisoner, killing one of the young Tuckabatchee warriors in the process. In all, a worried runner from Tuckabatchee reported to Hawkins, insurgents in the neighborhood had killed nine people.[46]

Council-friendly headmen reached out from Tuckabatchee for local support but were alarmed to find the surrounding neighborhoods far from sympathetic. According to the Big Warrior, "seven of the nearest refused to oppose the prophets," prompting him and other friendly headmen to dispatch Cornells to Hawkins immediately, with an escort, to report the troubling news. There the reports alarmed the Little Prince, nearby in Broken Arrow, who immediately gathered fifty warriors at Cusseta for a proposed expedition north. Not even he believed, however, that the situation was as bad as Cornells was making it seem. "Instead of aiding to suppress the prophets," it almost sounded like he was apologizing for them. Messengers sent by the Tallassee King to Cusseta did not help. He insisted that the prophets had not killed anyone. The magic they were producing might have, however, which was an explanation that both the Little Prince and the Cusseta King seemed willing for a time to accept. Not long after, however, insurgents had killed two more.[47]

The path forward from that moment would be a difficult one to deduce. A decisive act by the National Council might have put an end to the insurgency at such a critical juncture. It might at least have kept it from spreading as quickly as it did. Judging from its immediate popularity, on the other hand, such a show of violence might have done neither of those things and might have made the insurgency spiral out of control even faster. Nevertheless, rather than attempt to put a swift end to the Red Sticks, council-friendly headmen sought assistance while the crisis deepened. Cornells was quick to request aid from Hawkins, for instance, after word spread of the attack on Isaacs. That continued to be the case when news of more attacks arrived. Rather than mount an offensive, headmen continued to solicit Hawkins's help; the Big Warrior also wrote General Wilkinson "requesting assistance from him," and Alexander Cornells even traveled to Milledgeville, the capital of Georgia, seeking state assistance.[48] It was a testament certainly to the success of the Creek administrative state that Cornells would think it a good idea—or even safe enough—to travel personally to the state capital of Georgia to request arms, ammunition, and even soldiers to help Creeks mount an attack on their own towns. With the number of unfriendly communities growing around Tuckabatchee, however, the forces of the National Council certainly would need plenty of assistance, at least in powder and ammunition, to effectively quell the uprising.[49] That made it seem like a particularly inopportune time for Americans to again withhold annuity payments. Americans were most likely withholding the payments intentionally because of the uprising, which Secretary of War Armstrong had threatened to do before. If that was the case, it did not have the pacifying effect Americans hoped it would. Instead, warriors friendly to the council complained that they could not pursue the Red Sticks without much-needed supplies. How were they supposed to fight, many complained, when they had no arms, no ammunition, and no money?

Hawkins was unconvinced by these charges, complaining instead that headmen were simply not "equal in their present state of alarm and confusion to such enterprise." Many of them were "astonished exceedingly, alarmed, and timid," caught off guard by "the sudden explosion of this fanaticism." Instead of striking out at the insurgents they began fortifying Tuckabatchee.[50] Headmen certainly considered the insurgency much more alarming than did Hawkins. He, thinking he could put an end to it unilaterally, penned demanding letters to the Red Stick leadership directly, which the Cusseta King, McIntosh, Timpoochee Barnard, and a few other headmen were soon carrying north. With them were warriors from Coweta, Cusseta, Broken Arrow, Ooseoochee, Yuchi, Hitchiti, and Eufala, representing almost every community from the Lower Country.[51] Such a powerful delegation was also certainly supposed to project solidarity, which would be needed; their destination in the neighborhood of Tuckabatchee was a mess by July 1813. Six friendly warriors from Tuckabatchee had recently gotten into a skirmish with a group of Autossees that they caught pillaging local farms. The Tuckabatchees killed three of them, but Autossees retaliated the next night by laying siege to a now "entrenched camp" of Tuckabatchee. The next day they attacked a group of Tuckabatchee men caught outside the town butchering cattle and killed four of them.[52] Battle lines were being drawn and communities were now actually fighting each other, making peace harder to achieve with each passing day.

By the dead of summer in 1813 the regional, political aspect of the Red Stick insurgency was well-defined. The "whole of the upper towns have taken the war club but two," Tuckabatchee was "in great distress," Alexander Cornells's houses and property had been burned, and there were even rumors circulating that the Big Warrior had been assassinated. The latter turned out not to be the case, but Tuckabatchee was definitely in serious trouble. According to one account warriors were abandoning the Big Warrior in droves "and joining the war party and had left him all but sicty men."[53] A group of upwards of two hundred warriors began working their way northwest from Cusseta and Coweta, under the Cusseta King's orders, to come to Tuckabatchee's aid. They "had orders to fight their way" to the Big Warrior, and it was clear they probably would have to.[54] The National Council might be losing the Upper Country, but as the Cusseta King was demonstrating, communities in the Lower Country were developing into a bulwark against the insurgency. That was the case even from its southernmost reaches, as the Wolf Warrior and Kinnard demonstrated. The Tallassee King, for instance, was circulating a call to arms along the Apalachicola watershed and into Seminole Country. More than a decade earlier, in the wake of the Treaties of Coleraine and Fort Wilkinson, he had been a man of tremendous influence in those same neighborhoods. His talks pressed community leaders to reject the authority of the National Council and deny American and Spanish survey parties the ability to do anything in the area, which for a time they did. Now, however, his words found little support. Both Kinnard and the Wolf Warrior made sure of that, traveling south immediately to ensure the Tallassee King's talks would be ignored. With Seminoles busy resisting American filibusterers outside of St. Augustine, Kinnard and the Wolf Warrior had "done all they can to get their people good," and soon they were on their way north, also to support the Big Warrior.[55]

The show of unity from the Lower Country only better defined the regional nature of the struggle. Having several headmen travel north did little to temper the growing insurgency besieging Tuckabatchee, however, which was growing bolder by the day. Red Sticks continued either assassinating headmen friendly to the council or forcing them from the region. By the end of July, several other "friendly chiefs" had been killed, and threats against the council were growing stronger. When the Cusseta messengers delivered Hawkins's demanding letters to the Red Stick leadership outside of Tuckabatchee, Yaulfco Emautla Haujo, of Autossee, dismissed them out of hand. "I will not receive it or any other talk from Colonel Hawkins, or the white people. I am done with him and his talks." Soon the besiegers mounted a massive, weeklong assault against Tuckabatchee, which warriors friendly to the council only successfully repulsed because of the over two hundred recently arrived Cusseta and Coweta warriors. Soon, however, those same warriors were urging the Big Warrior and the others to abandon the town, "as, in the present rage of frenzy, they could not be safe."[56] It was not long before residents of Tuckabatchee and other friendly communities, under a Cusseta and Coweta guard, were retreating to Coweta. Five headmen from Oakfuskee had been executed by their own townspeople, prompting another to make his escape. Along with him were Upper Eufala, Kialijee, and Big Tallassee headmen, who were now also along the Chattahoochee River. There they would at least be able to make a stand, should the Red Stick insurgency continue to intensify.[57] But that left Tuckabatchee, for years the center of the National Council and for almost two decades a bulwark of American support, to be occupied by Red Sticks and physically devastated. "I never expected a civil war among us," a despondent Big Warrior reported to Hawkins, writing as he was from Coweta. The council house of the nation, appointed "to preserve peace and friendship among us, and our white friends," was destroyed.[58]

The loss of Tuckabatchee was a demoralizing blow to the National Council and provided plenty of unsettling evidence that the anti-state insurgency radiating from the Upper Country was no isolated uprising. By no means though had the region been totally conquered. A rash of killings along the Coosa River, for instance, demonstrated how divisive the Red Stick message remained even in the heart of the insurgency. Late in July, an eighteen-year-old Aubecoochee man, reportedly raised in an Alabama town, emerged as a prophet. He invited various headmen from along the Coosa River to witness a demonstration of his prophetic powers. Several went, "accompanied by a crowd of both sexes." After positioning several of the visiting headmen in a line on the riverbank, he and his adherents danced "the dance of the Indians of the lakes before them," before abruptly attacking their guests, killing three and wounding a fourth badly. The surviving visitors escaped across the river, only to return with war parties of their own to retaliate. They "sent after the murderers" and moved to confront the Aubecoochee prophet, only to have another of their own knocked down with a war club and executed "with bows and arrows." Having had enough of the prophet and his adherents, the remaining warriors immediately fell on the dancing insurgents, killed them all, and scalped the Aubecoochee prophet. Then they departed for nearby Oakfuskee, where adherents to the prophet had just recently killed five council-friendly headmen. "They had taken the Prophet's talks, and were dancing their dance," and so the warriors killed several of them as well and "cut the whole off."[59]

It is unclear from what communities the warriors who attacked and ultimately killed the insurgents originated. According to one account it was actually a separate set of Aubecoochee warriors, who "behaved with consummate bravery" to put an end to the prophet and his adherents. Hawkins, trying to rally the National Council to fight more aggressively, lauded the attack at the same time he disparaged the Big Warrior for his inaction. "I am sorry you did not fight first, as Aubecoochee did." Do likewise, he promised, and the National Council would "find friends." Action, he insisted, needed to be swift or more would suffer. Hillaubee warriors were already counting the broken days in preparation for an attack, and it was clear who they were coming for. "You must look out, it is for you," Hawkins warned the Big Warrior.[60]

Even though the majority of the communities in the Upper Country were reported as insurgent in August, divisions like the ones in the neighborhood of Aubecoochee were also widespread.[61] The National Council was not dead there just yet. When insurgent leaders Peter McQueen and the Tallassee King sent out an invitation to thirteen surrounding communities, hoping to raise an army and attack the frontiers, the response was mixed. At least some headmen from the Fish Ponds, Wewocao, Kialijee, and Hookchoie answered that they would not take part. "They had one thousand one hundred warriors, but were not going to fight against the Americans. The prophets were liars." Furthermore, at least a few communities that had previously adhered to the prophets, according to the Cusseta King, "have since thrown it away." Kialijee was among them, and "to a child, has come to the Big Warrior," while friendly Cherokees to the north were reportedly tempering Hillaubee communities and others in the neighborhood.[62] But those communities were also the exception, and at least some felt threatened enough to abandon their homes altogether. By mid-August Aubecoochee, along with Coosa, Natchez, and "some other villages of the upper towns," had fled to Little Turkey's town, in Cherokee Country, and were waiting there until outside assistance arrived.[63] That was in addition to the Oakfuskee, Tallassee, Kialijee, and Eufala headmen who had already fled south. Furthermore, the fratricidal violence seen in Aubecoochee was also relatively common. By the fall of 1813 Wewocao was in turmoil and two headmen were dead. It was also reported that "two of the villages of

Hillaubee have had a battle in which 12 were killed," and the remainder had fled into Cherokee Country. In nearby Kialijee, "more than thirty have been killed on both sides," and ultimately, the "peaceful friendly town" was in ruins.[64]

Despite those areas of contest, in a crisis pitting the National Council against an insurgency that was calling for its violent destruction, the council was losing the Upper Country. According to several estimates, more than two-thirds of the region was unfriendly to the council—2,500 of the 3,000 warriors in the region would fight the forces of the National Council before fighting Red Sticks.[65] The homes of National Council leaders were destroyed, Tuckabatchee had fallen, raiding in the region was ongoing, and pro-council forces were holed up far away, at Coweta. Many in the few communities friendly to the council in the Upper Country, ones like Kialijee, were also refugees, hiding out either in Cherokee Country or along the Chattahoochee.[66] The hinterlands were suffering as well. Raiding in the Mississippi Territory was widespread, the frontier between the Upper and Lower countries was filled with skulking war parties, and by August there were reports that fighting had reached the outskirts of Coweta.[67] By the fall of 1813, indeed, the National Council could no longer claim over half its territory, or half its people.

With refugees and friendly warriors spread along the Flint and Chattahoochee rivers, on the other hand, few in the Lower Country cared for Red Sticks. Now based out of Coweta and Cusseta, what remained of the National Council remained optimistic. If Red Sticks wanted a fight, the Cusseta King declared, they would have it. "If they don't make peace, they will fight until all of it is gone, and one part or the other will be conquered."[68] There was no doubt to leaders like the Cusseta King that the struggle was now a fight to the death. Hawkins pressed the National Council to act as such, at the same time criticizing the Big Warrior harshly for not already having pursued the insurgents and seeing the uprising crushed.[69] The Big Warrior did not see things that way. He and others continued to complain that the council's warriors were hobbled by a lack of arms and ammunition, supplies that would obviously be needed to undertake the sort of offensive Hawkins was demanding. How were they to obtain those things? With the annuity for 1813 still missing, and probably not to be paid at all while the uprising was ongoing, headmen were forced to continue begging for aid from Hawkins and Georgia authorities at the same time those authorities pressed him and his men to act aggressively.[70] "You have promised me great assistance you have promised that before," the Big Warrior complained to Mitchell, "but it is not arivd yet." The Big Warrior's tone was desperate. Send hundreds of men, he pressed; "if you delay you may not find us alive."[71] When warriors finally received the arms and ammunition they required in August and September, their tone changed. "We have made the broken days to go on an expedition against the hostile Indians," the Big Warrior and Tustun-nuggee Hopoie notified Hawkins. In twelve days they would march. In all over five hundred warriors were at Coweta; they were prepared either to defend or to drive north, but according to interpreter Christian Lim-baugh, they were "very desirous to be ordered out against the murderers of their Chiefs."[72] Hawkins certainly was supportive of such action. An assault using all five hundred warriors at the same time would be best, but he also suggested sending them out "in strong parties," under war leaders to take the battle to the insurgents as soon as possible, "by taking provisions, cattle, horses and attacking a town at a time."[73]

Almost to the day, warriors began to move north. Itchhoo Haujo, also known as the Mad Beaver and a man "well known on the frontiers of Georgia," soon returned from one such attack. He, with a party of twenty-three warriors, assaulted a group of four insurgents near New Yaucau, also known as New York, where they "killed and scalped three and wounded the fourth badly." He brought the scalps back to "the public square" at Coweta, gave the war cry, and then issued a call to arms. "You who are afraid look to yourselves, you who are warriors, turn out."[74] Late in August two additional war parties were also out in search of insurgents. McIntosh led one of the parties, which was described as having upwards of 375 warriors. He personally took the fight to the Tallassee King and Peter McQueen, forcing them to flee their communities and retreat to Autossee, leaving his warriors to have their way with what was left. They "took everything, set the place on fire, burnt all their works and their houses and destroyed all their corn."[75] Other war parties were penetrating as far as Hillaubee, and Hawkins described "several detachments of them" hovering in the vicinity of insurgent camps and "patrolling north, as far as the Tallapoosa river."[76] With ammunition now in hand, warriors "determined to give battle" and began to do so; leaders of the National Council were not only attacking hostile villages and stripping the insurgency of food and materiel, they were undermining the legitimacy of the Red Stick cause. The uprising would not overthrow the council, they declared, and would not impose a new Creek order.[77]

Just as those raids were beginning to roll the insurgency back, how-ever, Red Sticks gained a tremendous boost by successfully attacking and burning Fort Mims, a small stockaded outpost in the Mississippi Territory. The attack on Mims had been set in motion weeks earlier, when a group of Red Sticks traveled to Pensacola hoping to receive arms and supplies from the Spanish. On their return north the group of a hundred warriors or so was intercepted by a party of territorial militia, resulting in the battle of Burnt Corn Creek. The battle, although it was inconclusive, still cost the Red Stick warriors the few supplies they had received at Pensacola, and it was infuriating. Rather than attack the National Council at Coweta, which had been the plan, the attack at Burnt Corn Creek had many insurgents looking west instead, into the Mississippi Territory, for vengeance. The retaliation Red Stick warriors got at Fort Mims was more than they ever could have hoped for. The defenders of the fort, caught off guard and unprepared, were overwhelmed. Upwards of 250 settlers were killed and few were spared, the fort was burned, and the Mississippi Territory was immediately thrown into chaos.[78]

The attack on Mims, even though it was a signal victory for the insurgency, did not entirely unify the Upper Country. While it certainly was a success, the attack cost many more lives than the prophets assured their warriors, leading many to question their promises and their leadership. That suspicion led in several cases to violence. One hundred Red Sticks under Prophet Josiah Francis entered a stockade in a town at the fork of the Alabama, for instance, when they "were fired upon, had five killed, and retreated."[79] While those small pockets of resistance remained in the Upper Country, the attack on Mims was an alarming reminder that the National Council had by 1814 lost any semblance of authority there. Warriors from thirteen towns, including Holiwahli, Fooshatchee, or the Fish Ponds, Cooloome, Muclassee, Alabama, Hookchoie, the Hickory Ground, and Wewocao, were all implicated. Warriors from three other towns, Oakfuskee, Tallassee, and Autossee, had been observing Coweta in preparation for an attack at the same time. Only three towns, including Upper Eufala and Kialijee, declared their neutrality, even though little remained of Kialijee by that point.[80] Not only did Fort Mims reenergize the Red Stick cause, the insurgency gained much-needed supplies in the aftermath of the attack, even as friendly council warriors were raiding deeper into the Upper Country. While settlers in the territory panicked and fled, Red Stick war parties were "very active," a worried Hawkins reported. They raided widely between the Alabama and Tombigbee rivers, looting or destroying thousands of head of livestock and adding to their stores of supplies from plantations before burning them.[81] And as some warriors stripped the countryside, others began to replan their attack on the remaining seat of the National Council. According to a worried report from Coweta, the insurgents "meant to come to Coweta, after the friendly Indians, as soon as their wounded were better."[82]

Red Sticks had grown so confident, in fact, that renewed calls for unification were reappearing along the Chattahoochee River. Insurgency goals stressed collectivity, not division, underscoring the strange sort of Red Stick cultural nationalism that appealed for harmony at the same time it sought to destroy the council: "If the red people would unite, nothing could withstand them." But those "who would not join, were to be put to death, and this was the last warning they were to have." And clearly the National Council was still the target. Coweta would be destroyed, then what was left of Tuckabatchee, "in terrorem," then Hawkins, then the state of Georgia.[83] By October, Red Sticks were threatening Ooseoochee and Cusseta as well, and soon headmen were fortifying their communities on the Chattahoochee, "believing they have to contend for their existence."[84] The renewed calls for violence had a sobering influence even on Hawkins. For months now he had looked upon the uprising as a terrible, albeit a localized and ultimately doomed, conflict. His report to the commanding officer at Fort Hawkins in October 1813, after Mims, had a much different tone to it. "I wish to be prepared for events, as well as we can." If Coweta was either routed or its defenders forced to surrender, he feared, the insurgents would "certainly be on us, and attempt to verify their threats against the frontiers of Georgia."[85] "The boasted power of the Prophet to take American forts with bows and arrows, to know the secrets of the enemies, and their determination to put to death every red man who does not join them, has given to many much terror," and nothing would reverse it, Hawkins now admitted, except American forces.[86]

Unfortunately for the National Council and the fate of Creek Country, much of the Red Stick ideology had always threatened Americans. Removing outside political influence was critical to the success of the "revolution" Red Sticks envisioned; the American political and legal traditions that the National Council enforced coercively as the Creek state were as much targets of Red Stick wrath as the Creek leadership itself. The insurgent groups had "for some time evidenced a disposition hostile to the American government" and were succeeding in "killing or driving from their land every chief in the American interest."[87] The American concepts they hoped to remove were clear enough. Ideas of guilt and innocence; the coercive power of the state and its jurisdiction over crimes; and the removal of community leaders and kin members from the process of punishment—these were all foundational aspects of the Creek nation-state that were not traditionally Creek. They were foreign traditions that had been imposed on Creek Country by meddling Americans, according to the insurgents. They were dangerous and they were no longer welcome, and no longer were Americans either.

Even in the earliest months of the uprising, in fact, several Red Stick leaders made it clear that Americans would be targeted as aggressively as the existing Creek leadership. According to Prophet Peter McQueen, Red Sticks "did not want to fight the red people, it was the white people they were fixing for." As soon as the most culpable Creek headmen were dead, insurgent warriors would be after the Americans who had propped them up—men like Hawkins. Nearby, the Tallassee King was of the same mind. The white people would suffer, and he "would not stop till he marches to Ogeechee. There he would pause and rest, then put off for the sea coast."[88] "You think the white people strong and numerous," Autossees later warned. "We shall soon try their strength."[89] After Burnt Corn Creek, "the destruction of every American is the song of the day."[90] Eventually Hawkins, too, recognized the threat. If the insurgency could be confined to an internal struggle, he suggested in June 1813, "it might be policy in us to look on" and let Creeks settle it among themselves. "But as there seems to be an other object coupled with it, and that of hostility to us eventually, we must be ready to apply a military corrective in due time."[91] Georgia officials were raising troops to respond to such threats as early as July, even when Hawkins still hoped the National Council would be equal to the task. But then there was Fort Mims, which was an absolute catastrophe, and Red Sticks followed it with more bold talk. "We have had a successful enterprise westward" at Mims, one Red Stick warrior charged. "We now point our course East after red and white people." They would destroy Ooseoochee and Cusseta, then Tuckabatchee and Coweta; "their destruction is certain and will detain us but a short while. We then take the post road, enter Georgia, ravage all before us," then return.[92]

Americans could not dismiss such threats. The Red Stick insurgency was no longer something best left to Creeks—the safety of the entire region was at stake.[93] Even threats of a widespread slave uprising were warranted.[94] And after Mims, Americans everywhere were outraged. They blamed a sloppy defense at Fort Mims and they blamed regional authorities, but the greatest scorn they heaped on Hawkins, who had been deluded for so long by Creeks who insisted they were friendly. His inattentiveness, they charged, had cost lives.[95] Shortly afterward, and using Mims as a rallying cry, Americans leaped into action. Authorized and supported by the Madison administration, the governments of several states and the Mississippi Territory began to raise armies and were soon directing them into the heart of Creek Country. Major General John Floyd, commanding Georgia's militia forces, moved west with 1,500 men. General Ferdinand L. Claiborne moved north from Fort Stoddert with upwards of 1,200 troops, a mix of territorial militia and regular soldiers from the U.S. Third Regiment. Another large state force, led by Andrew Jackson, was soon pushing south from Tennessee. Each of these armies, beset as they were at times by their own logistical or political issues, was ultimately successful in ending the Red Stick insurgency by overwhelming their forces in several places, killing hundreds of warriors, and destroying their towns. Floyd's Georgia army constructed several forts along the westward journey through the Lower Country, completing Fort Mitchell in unfriendly territory late in 1813. Soon his forces routed a large insurgency group at Autossee, then engaged the largest group at Red Stick warriors to assemble in one battle, at Calebee Creek. Claiborne's Mississippi force, moving north along the Alabama River, sacked and burned the Holy Ground, a prophetic town constructed by Peter McQueen and described by him as invulnerable to American attack. The Tennessee prong of the American offensive, entering the Upper Country from the north, did the most damage, burning Tallusahatchee, Talladega, and Hillaubee.[96] Jackson, his ragtag army freshly augmented with regular soldiers from the 39th Regiment, then crushed the insurgency overwhelmingly at Tohopeka, also known as the battle of Horseshoe Bend, which ended the uprising decisively.[97]

Horseshoe Bend punctuated a trend in American Indian policy. When the federal government faced a devastating invasion of Georgia by Creek forces in the 1780s, it could do almost nothing. In 1793 the Washington administration did not have the money, the manpower, or the desire to go to war with Creeks when outside forces pushed several communities to bloodshed. In 1813, however, much had changed. The federal government was no longer poor, and the military forces of the United States were more than adequate to deal with three thousand Indian insurgents. Federal legislators, beginning during the Jefferson administration, were also much more supportive of state- and territorial-level expansionists than had been their Federalist predecessors. Georgians continued to eye lands in the west and even south, into Spanish Florida. Tennesseans looked to the southwest and Mississippians to the northeast. Each group felt threatened by Red Sticks, certainly, but each also used the opportunity of the war to realize their own territorial ambitions. The U.S. government, more receptive to state desires and with territorial and security desires of its own, fully supported the conquest of Creek Country.[98]

Surprisingly, what was left of the National Council did not see federal or even state motivations the same way. They did not see even the state forces as armies of conquest, and they welcomed the intervention. Floyd's army from Georgia was one of the first to move and would approach the insurgency through the Lower Country. To prepare for his approach, Hawkins ordered "the Indians to take sides, all who are not for the Chiefs are hostile and will be treated accordingly. There is to be no neutrals. The evidence necessary was to go to war." He hoped to have "a corps of 500 to cooperate with our troops" as soon as the army was in the neighborhood.[99] Headmen including the Big Warrior, McIntosh, the Little Prince, and Cornells, however, needed no such ultimatum. As they saw it they had been asking for state assistance for months, and with Red Sticks closing in on the Chattahoochee in the fall of 1813, they were all pleading with Floyd to march his men faster. "Now my friend come and relieve us," the headmen wrote; "come night and day. If you dont come soon we will be in a starving condition." By the time Floyd's army was approaching the Chattahoochee River, in fact, there were plenty of headmen anxious to meet him, "to have an understanding with him relative to their cooperation with him and to explain fully the situation of their country and affairs."[100]

In the meantime, groups of warriors continued to pour into Coweta and Cusseta in anticipation of the invasion. They had no intention of watching the fall of the Red Stick insurgency from a distance. Once-volatile headmen along the Chattahoochee and Flint rivers, at Ooseoochee, Chehaw, and Hitchiti, reported themselves "unanimously friendly to the white people."[101] When there was word that Red Sticks were again planning to assault the Chattahoochee, warriors welcomed the challenge. Nimrod Doyle, one of Hawkins's assistant agents, requested an American flag. "Sir if there is a flag to be had send it to us for it we fight we will defend it to the last, and it will give great joy to these people to see it flying over their hot house." If those "devils should attack us," he declared, "we shall give them hot times." Eufalas, deep in the southern part of the Lower Country, "gave notice to Coweta they should be with them and their warriors and those of Ooseooche, Aupalau, Chooelo, Sauwoogolo, and Hitchiti" and if they could get some ammunition "would make common cause with them and their white brethren."[102] Timothy Barnard reported from the Flint River that communities in his neighborhood—Hitchitis,

Yuchis, and Chehaws, most likely—had gone to Ooseoochee to wait for Georgia state troops to arrive in Coweta, "wich time were to goe on and join the friendly Red people and the white troops to subdue the enemy red people."[103]

Yuchi warriors, along with some Seminoles, were practically the only volatile groups, and their hesitancy prompted strong local action.[104] A group of seventeen Yuchis with a headman left "to the join the prophets" around the time Georgia troops were on the march in September. Along with Tuttallosee Creeks from along the Florida boundary and Mikasukis from inside Spanish Florida, they "were on the way to join the Prophet's party, for a combined attack on Coweta, and then the white people." Five separate Lower Country towns dispatched warriors to cut them off almost immediately. "It is probably they met yesterday; and if their object is as stated, they will be attacked."[105] Even then, that small group of renegades did not represent the majority of Yuchis. Sixty more Yuchi warriors "offered their service to the agent," and more than 175 were prepared to "obey the orders of their Chiefs." A new generation of Barnards was beginning to make its mark on those communities. Three of Timothy Barnard's sons, Timpoochee, Michee, and Coseene, offered to command the Yuchi warriors, and they were to "go immediately and join the Chiefs at Coweta."[106]

When more Yuchis attempted to get down to Pensacola for arms and supplies, Ooseoochees cut them off again, robbed them of their horses, and warned them that "if any of them dared go there for supplies, they should be put to death."[107] That was the case in October, when a group of the "friendly Indians," reported to be upwards of 600 strong, attacked the Yuchis again, killing three this time and destroying their "houses and provisions." A group of Seminoles, who were planning on moving with them north to join the insurgency, promptly retreated.[108] The Yuchis had been cowed into the Prophet's faction "through terror," and they were paying for it. "The friendly chiefs have sent a party who destroyed their towns, and removed every living eatable thing belonging to them."[109] The Lower Country would remain a bulwark of the National Council, and headmen there remained committed to exerting their regional authority using violence.

The pro-council faction would do much more than subdue dissent in the Lower Country. As several armies closed in on the heart of the insurgency, headmen hoping to reassert council authority were already intensifying their own attacks in the region. As Floyd began to fortify positions in Creek Country, Hawkins reported that scouts were out and had "frequent skirmishes with the hostile Indians," which had killed fourteen on both sides.[110] When the Georgia army did arrive, Creek warriors were quick to augment it. At Autossee, for instance, upwards of four hundred Creeks fought alongside almost one thousand state troops. Split into four companies at the time of the assault, the warriors were "placed under the command of leaders of their own selection." Groups of Cowetas, under McIntosh, along with Tuckabatchees, under the Mad Dog's son, "fell in our flanks, and fought with an intrepidity worthy of any troops." It was suspected that groups of insurgents from eight towns in the area were at Autossee for the attack, and several were killed, including, according to the American report, Autossee and Tallassee headmen. According to at least one report, the elderly Tallassee King was killed in the battle. Several of "the friendly Indians" were killed or wounded as well, although the exact number is unknown.[111] Later, when Georgia troops approached New Yaucau, another group of Creeks, used as guides, were with them as well. "The friendly warriors were conspicuously brave at the battle of Auttossee, and Nuo Yaucua," one report went.[112] And a month later, in January, a "very large body of hostile Indians made a desperate attack" on General Floyd's army, camped fifty or so miles west of the Chattahoochee. Timpoochee Barnard, leading a group of Yuchi warriors, "distinguished himself," while other unnamed groups of "friendly Indians" were inactive, "with the exception of a few who joined our ranks."[113]

The arrival of the other American armies seemed to embolden the Creek warriors further. By 1814 it was reported that potentially thousands of warriors "of the friendly Creeks" were at Coweta, "to act as directed."[114] While Creek warriors did not seem particularly active in Claiborne's Mississippi army, there were hundreds that joined with Jackson's Tennessee forces. When his army approached Talladega in January and engaged groups of Red Sticks shortly afterward, he reported upwards of 230 friendly Creeks fighting with him.[115] Hillaubee and Chinaubee communities assisted him as well, even when he was engaging hostile warriors in their neighborhood.[116] In two engagements in the neighborhood of Hillaubee, groups of "friendly Creeks" were praised for their actions.[117] Months later, at Jackson's routing of Red Stick forces at Tohopeka, Creek forces led by William McIntosh played a strong supporting role in the attack, preventing Red Sticks from fleeing across the Tallapoosa River when Jackson began his assault. McIntosh, "who joined my army with part of his tribe," Jackson reported, "greatly distinguished himself."[118]

By early in 1814 American victories over Red Sticks were decisive. The bloodshed, however, made it unclear how much of the Upper Country would remain for the National Council to reassert its control. The death toll was tremendous. Half of the Creek warriors had to be killed "in order to prevent their killing the other half," according to one onlooker, "who are friendly to the United States." Yet "the work of death" was "progressing regularly and certainly."[119] Mississippians killed only thirty-three insurgents at the Holy Ground—a relatively low number compared to the Georgia assault on Autossee, which left at least two hundred dead. Jackson's string of attacks was far more devastating. Tallusahatchee claimed two hundred, in addition to eighty prisoners. Talladega killed three hundred, and the attack on Hillaubee, which was described more as a massacre, killed sixty and resulted in another two hundred prisoners. As Gregory Evans Dowd has calculated, out of a total possible force of perhaps 4,000 Red Stick warriors, 750 had been killed to that point, which, "at a low estimate," meant 20 percent of Red Stick men were dead.[120] And that was before Tohopeka. Scores of Red Sticks from virtually every insurgent community in the Upper Country were collecting there when Jackson's army arrived, and few escaped. Of the Red Stick contingency from Oakfuskee, for instance, less than ten men remained. None of the warriors from the Fish Ponds and only three from New Yaucau remained.[121] In all, anywhere from 557 to over 850 more insurgents perished there, bringing the total death toll upwards of 1,800. By the summer of 1814, in other words, almost half of all Red Stick men were dead.[122]

Compounding the staggering death toll was the physical destruction the war brought to the Upper Country. More than fifty communities had been burned or abandoned, a number that included insurgent towns as well as the friendly towns that resisted, like Kialijee. Even those that were not destroyed were stripped of provisions either by Red Sticks or by invading American forces, leaving their residents with nothing.[123] Tuckabatchee, for instance, was devastated; "their town, cattle, hogs, provisions, and every thing but what they brought off on their backs being destroyed." With their warriors away constantly, the town's seven hundred residents were being fed by American authorities.[124] The Upper Country, less than a generation since forming a bastion of American support, and then the administrative hub of the Creek nation, was in ruins. Much of its population was homeless and facing destitution. If the Red Stick War was a political struggle in which the National Council was challenged to reassert its authority over an insurgency, then its effort was both a success and a spectacular failure. The Red Stick rebellion had been quelled, but the Creek Country that remained was almost unrecognizable.

Nevertheless, what was left of the Red Stick movement collapsed after Tohopeka. Many once insurgent communities were turning on the prophets who remained: "the conquered towns have either killed their Chiefs themselves, or had most of them killed in battle."[125] Such was the case in New Yaucau; there warriors "had determined to take the four principle men of that party, one of which they intended to kill, and to deliver the other three to Col. Hawkins."[126] Other groups surrendered directly to various American forces.[127] By July, for instance, "the whole force of the Alabama" had surrendered to the approaching North Carolina militia, as did the remaining Oakfuskee insurgents.[128] With their communities and their crops destroyed, hunger and destitution continued to take Red Stick lives. "Famine has tamed or destroyed many of them," and they were "making their peace as fast as they can and receiving food from us."[129] As early as May families from the Hickory Ground and large numbers of families from Hookchoie, Holiwahli, Wewocao, and other communities were appearing on ration lists, receiving food from American military forces at the recently constructed Fort Jackson. Wewocao in particular caught Hawkins's eye. It was "one of the most brave and determined of our opponents, always the foremost in battle, and some of them in every battle. Her list shows her distress."[130]

Council-friendly headmen were not so generous. Intent on reassuming control of the region they quickened the pace of their own purge and took a firm stance against those insurgents who remained, whether they planned to give themselves up or not. Headmen "had no confidence in any promises they might make until a great part of them were destroyed." In the Lower Country in particular warriors itched to "destroy their enemy, and their fanaticism." In June 1814 Autossee Emautla and his son were killed, "as prophets or instigators" of war.[131] As soon as there was positive word that a Red Stick exodus was underway to West Florida, "our warriors at Coweta as soon as the facts are ascertained" were determined to hunt them down without American assistance and "destroy them and their hopes." Despite the fact that the American government was now housing and feeding hundreds of former Red Sticks and potentially thousands of their kin, Hawkins had mixed feelings about the council's aggressiveness. On the one hand he was interested in getting past the violence, pushing headmen to moderation. Enough blood had been spilled, and peace could be had if surrender was genuine. If peace terms were not accepted, however, "the war, of course, would continue." That was the case when he called on the Big Warrior, the Little Prince, and others to seize the Red Stick leaders who still remained. "Those you take, you will try, and if guilty, punish your way."[132] Hawkins would find little argument from headmen there.

Both Hawkins and the council were hesitant to declare the struggle won because rather than accept surrender, and despite destitute conditions, many Red Sticks vowed to fight on. "The remains of the eight towns on the Tallapoosa," many of whom had not suffered tremendously during the struggle, showed no intention of giving up. With hundreds more warriors and potentially thousands of Upper Creek residents taking flight south, in search of aid in Florida, the Upper Country continued to collapse, drawing into question whether the region even existed at all anymore.[133] With half of Creek Country physically in ruins and half its population either dead or on the run, national leadership was now really only regional leadership. "You have done right in keeping to Coweta," Hawkins declared to the Big Warrior, the Little Prince, and others, as the headquarters of the nation; "it is so; and all public business must be done there," at least until a reconstituted council could meet and decide on someplace better.[134] Perhaps that might be at a rebuilt Tuckabatchee, but it probably would not be anywhere else along the Alabama, Coosa, or Tallapoosa River.

While headmen took stock of what was left of the Creek Nation, Americans began to position themselves as the victors. Writing to General Pinckney, who assumed command of the military forces in the area, Secretary of War John Armstrong noted that the treaty "should take a form altogether military, and be in the nature of a capitulation." All Creeks were going to come out the loser in these negotiations, it was obvious. Benjamin Hawkins would not even play a direct role in them, as he had in the past, but, "as agent, may be usefully employed."[135] Members of the National Council, who were at Fort Jackson to meet with Andrew Jackson, had no idea what was in store for them. When Jackson assumed control of the negotiations from Pinckney, headmen did not approach him as a conqueror but as a friend and an ally. "We are a poor distressed people, involved in ruin, which we have brought on ourselves," the Big Warrior began. The late struggle was not caused by any foreign power "but of our own color, of our own land, and who speak our tongue."[136] The council heaped gratitude on the Americans for their assistance, offering Jackson, Hawkins, and others individual parcels of land as tokens of their thanks, "to convey their intentions." Creeks, who were "masters of the land," had been uniformly "friendly to the United States, and faithful to their engagements in peace and war."[137]

The American delegation led by Jackson, however, wanted much more land—"as much of the conquered territory as may appear to the government to be a just indemnity for the expences of war, and as a retribution for the injuries sustained by its citizens and the friendly Creeks."[138] But it was not just the insurgent Creeks who lost land, and when new maps were being drawn they were not what the Big Warrior or other members of the council expected. Not even he, a man from the Upper Country, took issue with the loss of lands along the Coosa and Tallapoosa rivers. A loss of that magnitude a decade earlier would have been unconscionable. But in 1814, not much remained in the Upper Country. Much of the population was now huddled in American forts, in Cherokee Country, or along the Flint and Chattahoochee rivers. The rest were traitors to the Creek Nation, on the run and being hunted like animals. Indeed, it was not that headmen did everything they could to retain the Alabama, Coosa, and Tallapoosa watersheds and failed; with the residents of the communities there dead or gone, not many headmen who now constituted the National Council probably cared. Remaining members of the council were shocked, however, to find that the treaty took almost an equal amount of land from the friendly Creek communities in the Lower Country—Cusseta, Coweta, and Ooseoochee—as it did from the offending towns. Americans claimed lands "actually our property," the headmen complained, in almost the same proportion they left "to the conquered Indians between Coosa and Tallapoosa," which was clearly not an equivalent.[139]

Americans had their own reasons for stripping what remained of the National Council of much of the territory that it still controlled, which at the same time stripped it of whatever territorial sovereignty it could still claim as well. The lower portion of the treaty boundary, Jackson explained, which cut across the length of the Florida boundary, was necessary to cut off Creek interaction with the Spanish "in order to prevent further connexions, injurious to our tranquility."[140] No longer would Creeks have free access to Spaniards anywhere, according to this new treaty, which of course was the point. Creek sovereignty was officially dead. It had been a fiction to American authorities for years, and the Red Stick War provided Jackson and other officials the opportunity to do away with it altogether. But then again, many of the headmen present at Fort Jackson probably recognized, as much as Jackson did, what the Creek Nation meant in the post–Red Stick era. Tuckabatchee, Coweta,

Cusseta, and Ooseoochee were the about the only sizable communities that remained of a once sprawling Creek Country.[141] The Creek nation-state would endure, but it was only a shadow of what it had been, and was recognized as such.

FIGURE 10. The Battle of Autossee, 1813. The 1813 Battle of Autossee, depicted here with the Georgia state militia advancing into Autossee against strong Red Stick resistance, is an excellent example of Creek-American cooperation during the Red Stick War. Although not pictured, upwards of four hundred pro-Council Creek warriors coordinated with General Floyd's Georgia militia in the assault on Autossee, and together the forces devastated the Red Stick stronghold. Courtesy of the Hargrett Library, University of Georgia.

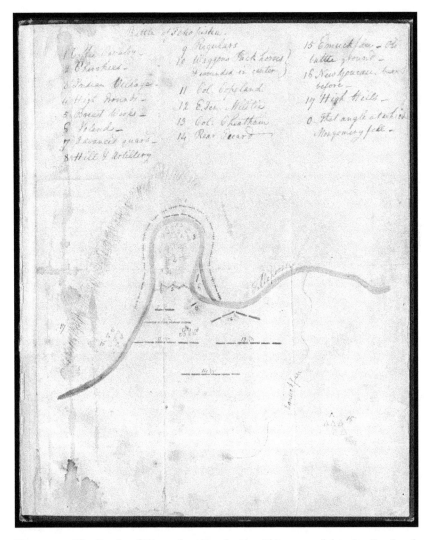

FIGURE 11. The Battle of Horseshoe Bend, 1814. This map of the 1814 Battle of Tohopeka, or Horseshoe Bend, does an excellent job of depicting the position of pro-Council Creek troops, led by William McIntosh, who were positioned on the opposite side of the Tallapoosa River. There, along with Cherokee troops, they played an important role in preventing the escape of hundreds of Red Stick warriors. It is labeled on the map as "1. Coffee Cavalry." Courtesy of the Tennessee Historical Society.

TIMPOOCHEE BARNARD

AN UCHEE WARRIOR.

PUBLISHED BY F. W. GREENOUGH, PHILAD.

FIGURE 12. Timpoochee Barnard. Timpoochee Barnard, one of Timothy Barnard's sons, represented the latest generation of pro-Council Creeks in the nineteenth century. Barnard commanded groups of pro-Council Yuchi warriors during the Red Stick War and participated in several battles. He was also active in the years that followed. He directed Yuchis into Florida in the years after Horseshoe Bend in pursuit of Red Sticks and runaway slaves, and also participated in the First Seminole War. Courtesy of the Library of Congress.

Epilogue: The Creek Nation in the Removal Era

*The treaty with Washington is good with us. The treaty at Ft. Jackson is
not straight. That is all I think of.*
        —The Big Warrior, September 19, 1815

The Creek Nation was in tatters late in 1814, but it was not altogether
destroyed, and it would rebuild. The first year of the victory was a bitter
one, however, for the Creek leadership; it was clear that Creek Country
would not be the same place it had been for generations.[1] Surviving Red
Stick insurgents were fleeing south in the wake of Tohopeka, emptying
Creek Country of upwards of two thousand more Creeks, the majority of
whom would never return.[2] Most would eventually resettle in north and
central Florida, representing a wave of immigration central to the ethnogenesis of Seminoles as a people.[3] From information taken by the Wolf
Warrior and Fallaussau Haujo of Lower Eufala, it appears large numbers
were already in Florida by June 1814 and were being fed by the British
who, at war with the United States of America, had recently arrived in
the Gulf of Mexico.[4]

There were a few Hitchiti communities at the southernmost part of the
Lower Country, like Fowltown and Oketeyoconne, which took part in
the exodus.[5] For the most part, however, what remained of Creek Country quickly began to regroup around the National Council, which reasserted its authority over both the Upper and Lower countries. Although
a great deal of Creek Country was lost to the National Council, quite a bit
remained; towns had to be rebuilt and surrendered Red Sticks had to be
integrated back into them. To project the necessary authority, regional
headmen began meeting again as early as July 1814, a month before the
conclusion of the Treaty of Fort Jackson.[6] The Big Warrior retained a
Speaker position for what remained of the Upper Country. The Little

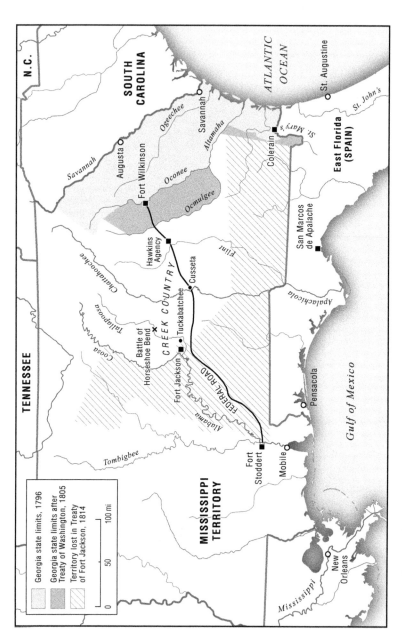

MAP 3. The Creek-Georgia Frontier to 1815. Map by Erin Greb Cartography.

Prince of Broken Arrow was elevated to the speakership for the Lower Creeks.[7]

The National Council needed strong leadership during such a pivotal time, particularly from the Little Prince. Hundreds of Red Sticks lurked just to the south of his neighborhood, where they threatened to drag the region back into chaos.[8] That was the case when a sizable group of insurgents was reported "on their march for the agency and all the forts on this line," planning to divide and attack three newly constructed forts simultaneously. Chehaw and Aumucullee headmen, however, were quick to cut them off. They confronted the group and told them they were "all going to run mad and quit their dances and jine the wite people and they could git something to eat."[9] Local headmen from the neighborhood also used the occasion to assure Hawkins that they would "hold the Americans there friends by the hand" and "join the Cowetas there friends the red people."[10] Many of those same communities also continued to grow friendlier to the state of Georgia. Headmen like McIntosh and the Little Prince had been quick to solicit state aid during the crisis and continued to work with state forces afterward. When a Georgia cavalry party passed through the region on patrol they encountered and were impressed by Chehaws, while warriors from Tullehauna escorted them to the town square. There headmen told them there was a scheduled meeting of several surrounding towns in a few days at Perryman's, in the neighborhood of Hitchiti, "in order to agree with each other," and there headmen promised not to interfere with the ongoing struggle with the British "but to let the two brothers fight their own battles."[11]

Perhaps more surprising, the communities that stretched further south into the Florida panhandle remained relatively calm, at least at first.[12] Even groups of Mikasukis—Hitchiti-speaking Seminoles—were playing it cool, opting to meet with other Seminoles at Lower Eufala and wait for talks from Coweta and Cusseta rather than accept British guns and ammunition. "Those two towns are always sending good talks down this river," Mikasuki headman Kenhajee made it clear; "I shall always abide what the Cussetau and Cowetau do."[13] A similar report had the British soliciting help from Eufalas in order to help fortify their position on the Apalachicola. The Eufalas, however, rebuffed them, and "all the lower towns had already done."[14]

With strong support from the Lower Country and even with Seminoles staying clear, council headmen like the Wolf Warrior and William McIntosh began reasserting the coercive power of the National Council. Even as they scattered and fled, "hostile Indians in small parties continue their plundering and murdering," which necessitated a response. Head-men, having met on the subject, "ordered out since parties to put an end to it by putting to death the guilty." Hawkins solicited Georgia authori-ties to have state troops assist the warriors.[15] The National Council would need to project such authority, particularly into Florida. The arrival of the British military on the Gulf Coast was a dangerous development, threatening late in 1814 to destabilize the region just when calm was beginning to return. Naval forces, seen intermittently off the Gulf Coast, soon entered the Bay of Pensacola. They more or less seized the Spanish garrison there and soon were saying inviting things to the thousands of Seminoles, starving Red Stick Creeks, and even runaway slaves who were lurking in West Florida. The supplies they were handing out were for hunting and survival purposes, the British of course maintained, but they still included arms and ammunition, which offered little comfort to the Wolf Warrior, Fullaupau Haujo of Eufala, or American authorities. "It is not for war they say but it looks very suspicious in my eye," one report went.[16] The threat only expanded when forces appeared off of the mouth of the Apalachicola River. As early as June 1814 British agents had ascended it, seizing and fortifying a John Forbes and Company trading warehouse.[17] According to accounts they were arming Seminoles as well as known Red Stick leaders out of the small but geographically impor-tant position, were making extravagant promises or retaliation against Americans, and were even inviting runaway slaves to seek shelter there.[18]

These advances along the Gulf Coast were part of the larger British strategy in the War of 1812—a plan that called for the destabilization and even invasion of the American south.[19] By the fall of 1814 that plan was already generating regional chaos. Native groups were raiding into Georgia and runaway slaves were fleeing south in alarming numbers.[20] By November Seminoles were "making their War food," had received orders from the British "to make ready and to strike our side without delay," and were actually beginning to march out "against our posts on the road, the frontiers of Georgia or the friendly Indians."[21] Joining Seminoles were growing parties of Red Sticks, and even a handful of Hitchitis from Fowl-town and Oketeyoconne communities along the Georgia-Florida border.[22] Months later, early in 1815, upwards of one hundred Natives, a mixture of Seminoles and Red Sticks, were in the neighborhood of Pensacola. Only days later the Spanish presidio was teeming with hundreds more—a mix of Red Sticks, Seminoles, and runaway slaves.[23]

By late 1814 and into the first months of 1815, these mixed Creek and Seminole groups were routinely harassing settlers in southern Georgia, hovering along the border with East and West Florida, and generating plenty of regional instability.[24] In many ways the National Council dealt with these threats on its own, or at least with Hawkins's prodding. As soon as word spread that Seminoles were beginning to militarize in the fall of 1814, and that Red Sticks were among them, for instance, Hawkins pressed for strong action. "Let us put an end to this mischief making," he soon charged. Creeks who were not agreeing to the American peace terms and raiding in Georgia were to be hunted down and shot. "I do not wish to see you shed the blood of each other," Hawkins explained, but it had to be done. Warriors were also to "attack and take or destroy all the white and black people you find in arms," a sign of the increasing British influence on the region.[25] The council appeared up to the task. William McIntosh reported in December 1814 that upwards of fifteen to sixteen hundred mounted men, including Creeks, Choctaws, and Chickasaws, and American forces, were converging on West Florida to do those things, "in pursuit of the Red Sticks and their allies," and small parties of warriors were regularly dispatched to hunt them down.[26] When a group of raiders from Fowltown entered Georgia from East Florida only to flee back "from our side of the limits," for instance, a party was dispatched after them, according to Hawkins, "and I have ordered out several parties to punish all who continue hostile to us," parties that came from both the Upper and Lower countries.[27] Tallassees hunted one group down, while Chehaws trailed another group that had recently attacked Georgia state forces. "Some detachments of our Indians are out with orders to put them to death," Hawkins reported to Jackson, "and probably will execute their orders in part."[28]

McIntosh and Timpoochee Barnard led larger efforts. Timpoochee Barnard's Yuchi and Aumucullee party was traveling down the forks of the Flint and Chattahoochee rivers late in 1814 and into Florida "to reconnoiter the movement of the enemy." Through November they did so, hunting, they reported, groups of Autossees, Holiwahlis, and Hitchitis. Soon groups of Cussetas were enrolling as well, and the whole group was working with Georgia forces to stabilize the region.[29] McIntosh wielded an even larger group, which he also took south. Anywhere from two to four hundred warriors accompanied him, depending on the report.[30] He passed through Lower Eufala to arrive at Perryman's at Hitchiti, which was reported as a hub of anti-American activity. There he met groups of Seminoles who "seemed surprised at his appearance in arms among them." They assured him "of their pacific disposition and wish to remain in peace and quietness with every body."[31] Whether that was true or not time would tell, but the stability McIntosh was able to project was good news for the National Council.

Creeks also responded favorably when asked to integrate with American forces, providing further proof that the National Council's vision of Creek-American relations was still relevant. Creeks were asked to help the federal government prepare for a mixed Seminole-British assault but also as American forces fanned out to occupy the recently acquired Creek lands. Jackson, worried that regular forces would not be available to do both of those things, began authorizing the raising of Creek troops, which Hawkins was quick to organize.[32] Yuchis and Aumucullees, directed by Timpoochee Barnard, played a role protecting the army outposts, like Fort Lawrence, even while they were also hunting insurgents further south.[33] By November there were thirty at Fort Mitchell as well, and Hawkins was pressing his assistant, Christian Limbaugh, to "enroll all the warriors he can" and to "apply to every town."[34] Both Jackson and Hawkins also had plans to use Creek war parties to assist American forces in defeating the larger British threat that loomed along the Gulf Coast.[35] Upwards of one thousand warriors answered Hawkins's calls to enroll in a Creek force, either actually enrolling and waiting at the ready or declaring their support.[36] Ultimately, they were not used in any significant engagement. Jackson moved south to Pensacola and dealt with the mixed Spanish-British threat there on his own. He then gained his tremendous victory in the defense of New Orleans.[37] While groups of Creeks did not participate in Jackson's larger movements, the enrollment of so many Creek warriors was an impressive show of support by the Creek Nation.

Hawkins, on the other hand, did utilize the Creek force. He marched his "regiment" of hundreds of warriors south, early in 1815, to root out the Seminole and Red Stick camps along the Flint and Apalachicola rivers.[38] Hawkins recorded the composition and origin of regiment, which was surprisingly cosmopolitan. Several communities in the Lower Country contributed dozens and even hundreds of warriors to the force, many of whom actually marched with him. Coweta, Ooseoochee, and Yuchi communities led the list. More surprising, however, was the incorporation of many communities in the Upper Country. Warriors from Tuckabatchee, Kialijee, Upper Eufala, Coosada, and Hookchoie provided hundreds of warriors, representing communities that stayed loyal to the National Council or at least neutral during the war but who had suffered tremendously as a result. Others, like Ocheubofau, Oakfuskee, Tallassee, and Tuskegee, had provided their fair share of warriors to the Red Stick insurgency. They were now providing scores of warriors to Hawkins's regiment—warriors that would be involved in hunting down and possibly killing former neighbors.[39]

Hundreds of Creek warriors marched south representing the power of a seemingly reunified Creek people, and they encountered little resistance as they neared the Florida boundary. As Hawkins later reported, that was not surprising—destitute and starving, there was little fight left in many of the insurgents he found. One thousand, a mix of Red Sticks and Seminoles, surrendered to him promptly, he explained, "and beged for bread." He obliged, demanding they lay down their weapons and return to their homes, which many of them evidently did. Hawkins made it all the way down to the seized warehouse fort on Prospect Bluff, on the Apalachicola, where he reported 750 combatants. He could have attacked, as he felt himself "a match for them with 750," and probably would have, had he not received word of the Treaty of Ghent. With the end of the War of 1812 at hand Hawkins naturally assumed the British forces there would abandon the fort, so he paid them a visit and things went pleasantly enough. He conversed with the two British lieutenants in command and spent a night with them, paraded his Creek army in front of them for a formal military review, fired a "fue de joie" with them, and then left. He disbanded his Creek regiment shortly afterward, directing headmen to spread the word of peace and stability through the region on their way home, ending what appeared to be a powerful and successful show of Creek national power.[40]

Militarily, the Creek Nation appeared up to the task of hunting down the remaining Red Stick insurgents, assisting American authorities, and otherwise bringing stability back to the region. Culturally, they were turning out to be reliable southerners as well. By the late nineteenth century a growing number of Creeks, following Alexander McGillivray's earlier example and perhaps fulfilling his earlier prophecies, were absorbing Euro-American cultural and economic values as equally as political and legal ones. Among those was growing support of the institution of slavery. By the early nineteenth century there were plenty of Creeks who had embraced chattel slavery and many more who at least did not object too heavily to it, or the racial ideology that supported it. The same could not be said about Seminoles or Red Stick refugees, who did not embrace racial slavery so easily.[41] Hawkins had long supported paying Creeks to return runaway slaves, but the need for Creeks as slavers took on a new importance as the Apalachicola Prospect Bluff debacle continued to degenerate into a regional "Negro Fort" nightmare. Unfortunately for

American authorities, British resistance radiating from Prospect Bluff did not stop after the Treaty of Ghent. And while the call to resistance turned out not to resonate terribly deeply with Red Sticks, it resonated much more deeply with hundreds of slaves.[42] Even though the British eventually abandoned their plans to mobilize Natives and slaves against the American South, they did Americans no favors on their way out of the region, leaving the fortified warehouse at Prospect Bluff impressively stocked with weapons, ammunition, and even artillery and leaving the door wide open.[43] By 1816 slaves fleeing Spanish Floridians, Americans in Georgia and the Mississippi Territory, and even Creeks were arriving en masse.[44] Those numbers, when added to the scores of Red Stick and Seminoles who were also there, created a real regional problem that would have to be addressed.

Creeks were called upon to both hunt down and return the hundreds of runaway slaves congregating around the fort, as well as assist in destroying the fort itself. Creek slavers would earn fifty dollars for each runaway they found and returned to the owner, Hawkins promised the Little Prince and the Big Warrior, while "the negros you take who have no white masters will be your property."[45] That turned out to be an enticing offer. On his march south in 1815 McIntosh made it clear that slaves were a priority, gaining assurances from groups of Seminoles that they would do what they could "to hunt up and send all runaway negros in their country to their owners."[46] Later, in 1816, another group led by Timpoochee Barnard was heading south to Seminole Country for the same purpose.[47] The National Council convened later that year on the subject, and Hawkins offered more bounties. The Little Prince was soon at the head of yet another war party, heading south in "an effort of themselves to aid the Seminole Chiefs in destroying the negro establishments in that country" and capturing and returning runaways.[48] Not only was the Creek leadership continuing to reassert control over its remaining territory, it was supporting the larger idea of the South in the process.

The Prospect Bluff "Negro Fort" situation was also important for an intriguing conversation it produced about the continued evolution of Creek politics. Hawkins began a correspondence with Edward Nicolls, the British officer suspected of being behind the developing Prospect Bluff crisis, and the correspondence quickly grew confrontational. Runaway slaves would be free, Nicolls declared, and according to the Treaty of Ghent, which ended the War of 1812, Creek-American relations would return to the state they existed in at 1811. Nicolls's interpretation of the Treaty of Ghent reversed much of America's success in

Creek Country, most notably by negating the Treaty of Fort Jackson.[49] That, of course, Hawkins found preposterous. Nicolls then claimed to have the Creek leadership behind him. It was a group of three headmen who were, interestingly enough, hiding out in Florida, and the Tallassee King was among them. That is a strange development indeed; Georgia state troops claimed to have killed the Tallassee King at Autossee a year earlier.[50] Whether the Tallassee King was alive or not was almost irrelevant by that point; Nicholls's assertions provided Hawkins the opportunity to give him a lesson on the political history of the Creek Nation, as he saw it at least. "The Government of the Creeks is not an ephemeral one," Hawkins charged. It had been around for a while, and in the way it existed at that moment it was over a decade in operation, and "it was the work and choice of the nation." By that he almost certainly meant the National Council, which, as he implied, was still functioning and still relevant. He went on. Warrior groups were "classed and held in readiness to execute the orders" of the council, headed by two Speakers—the Little Prince and the Big Warrior—who operated from two seats of government. The seats alternated between Coweta and Tuckabatchee, "as the occasion required," and there "national affairs alone could be transacted." As for the three random headmen claiming to be "the Sovereigns of this nation," Hawkins claimed "we know nothing of them as such." Two were unheard of and one was the Tallassee King, "a hostile Indian" and by several accounts no longer a living one. It was all nonsense.[51]

Hawkins's exchanges with Nicolls did not amount to much diplomatically. Nicolls evacuated the region in 1816 and left the Prospect Bluff situation to deteriorate on its own. The exchanges were, nevertheless, remarkable. Late in the eighteenth century Hawkins emerged as a critical outside force driving the development of the Creek nation-state. Only years later he was every bit as instrumental in tearing it back down. Now he was lecturing a British officer on its successes. It would seem strange that Hawkins would speak so positively about the Creek nation-state only years after it was almost consumed in a civil war he and other representatives of the federal government more or less generated by ignoring it. Hawkins lauded the council, but by that point his actions reflected the paternalistic approach federal authorities were beginning to take with Creeks, and with all Natives in the Southeast for that matter. It was not simply that federal authorities, including Hawkins, no longer considered Creeks a threat. They were no longer an independent, let alone a sovereign, people.

The years after the Red Stick uprising suggest that American authorities, once only somewhat willing to ignore the Creek nation-state, now considered it more of a novelty than a legitimate regional political power they had to contend with. Not since 1812, for instance, had annuity payments been made to the Creek people. Such a lapse, by 1815, was an obvious violation of no less than three treaties made between the federal government and the Creek people—a stark reminder that even though Americans had pressed Creeks to uphold their treaty obligations, compliance was not a two-way street. Even as the National Council was rallying around American efforts to control the Southeast and battle the British, a year after the end of the Red Stick war, "those friendly to us, or who have been neutral, are naked, in real distress and have rec'd no part of their annuity for three years."[52] Speaking at "a public council of the Creeks," both the Little Prince and the Big Warrior complained anew in May 1815, but their pleas accomplished little.[53] A month later provisions were so short that people had "actually died with hunger," and without immediate assistance, more would. Only in August 1815 did seventeen thousand dollars arrive. That cash payment to Hawkins was not specifically earmarked for the annuity, however, and even if it was, it was in no way equal to the four years of missed payments owed to the Creek people. Hawkins calculated that number to be more than fifty thousand dollars by the end of 1815. Only in the spring of 1816 did more cash arrive, but it was still not enough to satisfy all of the outstanding payments.[54] Long before that point, however, many more Creeks had died of starvation.[55]

Annuity payments of course had been a source of friction in the years before the Red Stick uprising and may have played a role in why Red Sticks decided to give up on the National Council in the first place. Worse, perhaps, if headmen friendly to the council had received the money owed them during the uprising, they could have bought the arms and ammunition they needed to actually put it down. They might even have been able to stop the Red Stick message from leading to the Treaty of Fort Jackson and the subsequent dispossession of Creek Country. But annuity money did not come before the uprising, during it, or for years afterward. Skeptical about shipping money to Creek communities consumed in a civil war seems a clear enough excuse, but denying those payments for a year before the war and then for more than a year afterward raises more serious questions. One possible answer seems clear enough: Why would the American government see paying the annuities necessary when it only made Creeks more dependent on Americans, when

Creeks could do nothing but complain about it, and particularly with a much more important and costly struggle with the British ongoing? Timely or even faithful adherence to Creek treaties simply was no longer a priority for federal authorities who recognized that the National Council could do nothing to compel Americans to be prompt with their obligations, or even honor them at all. If that was the case then federal authorities were right—the Creek people could produce nothing by way of protest, protests that included dying by starvation.

Several other developments suggest the same. Territorial access was clearly no longer an issue. Although communities in the Upper Country like Tuckabatchee were being rebuilt, they were not in a position to contest American travel down the Coosa, Tallapoosa, or Alabama watershed, bringing that once contentious issue to a swift close. Furthermore, military roads constructed in Creek Country during the American invasion—even in the parts that remained Creek afterward—were occupied by state and federal troops without so much as notifying Creek headmen, let alone asking for permission from the National Council. Larger military forces were moving through Creek Country and there was no attempt made to gain Creek acquiescence. Two separate regiments, for example, were "approaching the newly acquired territory" in April 1816, while in May three companies from the 8th U.S. infantry marched over the Okmulgee to reinforce several such positions.[56] And when Americans were having trouble surveying the new boundary line because of Nicolls and the Negro Fort, American troops, rather than Creeks, were charged with protecting the commissioners.[57] While the loss of millions of acres of Creek land in the Treaty of Fort Jackson was a tragedy, so was the loss of Creek control over the land it still claimed.

The new subordinate position of the Creek people was clarified at Tuckabatchee when headmen from across the Southeast met there to confer on a number of issues. Cherokees, Chickasaws, and Choctaws joined members of the National Council, with the Big Warrior representing the Creek Nation.[58] Hawkins was there, as usual, along with Return Meigs, who was the federal government's agent for the Cherokee people. The most important goal of the conference, however, was getting the National Council to ratify the Treaty of Fort Jackson. The U.S. Congress had already done so, but the Big Warrior and the other headmen struggled to understand the hastily made treaty, and it is no exaggeration to say they were horrified by what confronted them. Many of the headmen present were not at Fort Jackson and did not know what the treaty actually stipulated; "it was in the woods, and not in the town house," according to the Big Warrior.[59] The treaty was read at Tuckabatchee, however, and plenty of headmen were there. As the seat of the National Council, that only made sense. "A talk which is made unless done here, is not of much force."[60] How Americans like Hawkins expected the National Council to willfully ratify such a destructive capitulatory document, forced upon the Creek people in a military setting, was nonetheless fascinating. Ratification by the council was still necessary, though, at least technically—Creeks still, supposedly, remained a foreign nation. Yet the Treaty of Fort Jackson was no ordinary treaty, and Creek acquiescence was clearly not really necessary. The treaty devastated the Creek people, it was being forced on them by an American power much stronger than they were, and there was nothing the council could do about it.

American authorities made that perfectly clear as the convention moved forward. Why Jackson took so much land from friendly Creeks was something neither the Big Warrior nor any other headman could understand, no matter how it was explained. Although friendly Creeks in the Upper Country were allowed to keep their homes, and make claims to reparation money set aside, the hunting and grazing lands in the Upper Country were almost totally lost. The loss of so much land to the south, where communities had been the friendliest, was even more outrageous.[61] As the convention wore on, indeed, the Big Warrior subjected Hawkins to a withering jeremiad, making some of the angriest, most resentful charges ever leveled on Americans. The Creek people had leaned on Americans for support as friends and allies, and now they were being destroyed for it. To begin with, the original treaty was forced upon the Creek people before they even understood what was happening. "Before I was settled in my mind what to tell the General, he had made out a treaty, & laid it before me." The Big Warrior loved his land, had called on Americans to help him save his land, and now Jackson was "taking all my land" and "was going to leave us to suffer." The boundary line, he continued, "had divided who had assisted each other." Ratification of such a disgraceful document, the Big Warrior charged, would not be possible. "We had not jointly agreed upon this and you have taken away our land." From his accounts, General Jackson was little help. When the Big Warrior confronted Jackson, complaining that "he was leaving me but a small bit of land," Jackson responded that if Creeks did not like the deal, they could "go down to Pensacola and join your friends, Red Sticks and British." Jackson, once respected as a friend and even as a savior, was being seen very differently now. "After talking to the General

I found out I was in distress. I found the General had great power to distress me."[62]

The Big Warrior's complaints went much further, protesting the American government's unwillingness to follow the political and legal traditions they had espoused for so long—the same ones that had influenced the Creek leadership. Harkening back a generation, the Speaker invoked President Washington, probably citing the Treaty of New York. Creeks and Americans promised to "hold each other fast." Murderers would be dealt with according to law, he asserted, and they had been, representing a pillar of both American and Creek justice that had cost the Creek people so much in the recent struggle: "All the satisfaction demanded near here I gave." The killers were executed, which showed, according to the Big Warrior, that he "had not forgot the law." But when that did not solve the crisis, he continued, Creeks were not afraid to ask for help. "I know the whites always told me, if there was anything I could not do myself my friends would assist me." When they responded that they would help, "they never told me they would take away my land." In short, the Big Warrior concluded, "The treaty with Washington is good with us. The treaty at Ft. Jackson is not straight. That is all I think of."[63]

The American government did not treat the Red Stick crisis fairly, the military response was heavy-handed, Jackson deceived them, the Treaty of Fort Jackson was not made in good faith, and so on. The Big Warrior addressed all of that in a plea that was long and resentful, but it was a plea that did little to affect the outcome of the Tuckabatchee convention. Hawkins, for his part, dismissed most of the complaints out of hand. "It certainly could never be expected," he replied, "by the Creeks that their white friends were to fight for them, furnish them ammunition, compel their enemies to fly their country and then to feed the Creeks for nothing." American intervention came with a price, according to Hawkins, and that price was Creek territory. Confronted by an unfair treaty and getting nothing from Americans, the Big Warrior, and indeed the Creek Nation in general, was left disconsolate. "It is well known we are a small nation. It appears you would shove us off, and take what little we have got. It appears this is the way you are to treat us. It is not the way to treat friends."[64]

Ultimately the National Council refused to ratify the treaty. The Tuckabatchee convention ended and the Native representatives left "without affecting any object for which they convened." The situation was the same months later, and headmen, led by the Big Warrior, made it clear they were doing everything they could to either disclaim the treaty or simply ignore it.[65] The National Council even delegated eight head-men, led by McIntosh, to visit Washington and speak with the Madison administration directly, at least with Secretary of War William Craw-ford. The deputation was to "settle amicably if they could all their affairs with us," and that certainly included refuting the Treaty of Fort Jackson. "They hoped the President would restore back a part of all their lands, retained" by the treaty.[66] Unfortunately for the National Council, how-ever, Americans did not seem too bothered by the opposition. The Treaty of Fort Jackson was supported by Congress, there was no chance either President Madison or Monroe would grant what the National Council was asking, and the Creek people could offer almost nothing by way of resistance. The Big Warrior was a dejected leader, whose faith in Ameri-cans, and even in Hawkins, was gone. "The white people suspected him, General Jackson threatened him and his own people were geting wrath-ful against him." Hawkins attempted to comfort him, asserting that a delay of justice was not a denial of it, but that did little good. The Big Warrior "paused, sighed, and said it would come too late for him."[67]

The reassertion of the National Council's authority, juxtaposed with the massive loss of Creek territory, frames a powerful few years in the Creek Nation. As Hawkins asserted, the Creek government was not an ephemeral one—the National Council survived the Red Stick insurgency and would continue to function for the next two decades in the Southeast much as it had for almost a generation already. Yet as both Jackson's and Hawkins's approaches to Creek sovereignty also suggest, the bargain to have Americans assist in the Red Stick uprising proved disastrous. Forced to accept the Treaty of Fort Jackson, it was now clear the Creek Nation was far outsized by the United States of America and outmatched by it militarily, and was now being treated as such—relegated to a position of dependency by its neighbor to the east. For the small victories won by the Creek people in the post–Red Stick years, they were losing the larger struggle with the Americans. It was the Red Stick insurgency, in short, that dragged the Creek people into the Removal era.

The next decade of Creek politics reveals more of the same. The Creek people managed to do fairly well for themselves during the period, and the Creek nation-state, even though it remained contested, endured.[68] The American civilization plan continued to transform many Creeks from hunters to farmers, and even plantation owners, making peri-ods of famine and destitution like the ones Creeks faced earlier in the nineteenth century less common. And as the American South devel-oped around them, Creek warriors were more invested in its stability.

When the Negro Fort continued to lure slaves away from the Southeast, including from Creek owners, Creek warriors actively participated in its destruction. William McIntosh, Captain Isaacs, and the Mad Tiger of Coweta were marching south with 150 warriors to do that on their own when they encountered and joined an American force approaching for the same purpose. After American gunboats blew the fort up with a spectacular cannon shot, McIntosh's forces were quick to swarm it, dispatching survivors, executing two Red Sticks fingered as the leadership, and then looting what remained. They then proceeded to raid and burn the surrounding settlements.[69]

A much larger Creek force was involved in the First Seminole War in 1817. Raiding by Seminoles and Red Sticks from Spanish Florida continued into Georgia, which again threatened to destabilize the region. The Monroe administration, hesitant at first to authorize a punitive strike because it would involve an invasion of Spanish Florida, eventually relented, directing Andrew Jackson to lead the expedition late in 1817. But of the 3,500 in Jackson's force, upwards of 2,000 were Creeks.[70] Interested in finding more runaway slaves as well as crushing remaining Red Sticks, William McIntosh led the Creek force; John Kinnard and Timpoochee Barnard led groups of Hitchitis and Yuchis, respectively, as well. They seized Red Sticks, Seminoles, and slaves along the Apalachicola, then took part in the assaults of Mikasuki and Suwannee, deeper into Florida.[71] Years later, in 1821, McIntosh would lead another Creek contingent into Florida, this time against the runaway communities south of Tampa Bay.[72] Whether by hunting down and executing remaining Red Sticks, recovering fugitive slaves, or projecting authority into Seminole Country, the National Council was very active in stabilizing the Southeast, for the benefit of Creek Nation as well as the United States of America.

Creeks also continued to further define how their society would be ordered. In 1818 the council developed a written and standardized code of justice, putting their laws to paper for the first time in their history. Euro-Americans, including Hawkins, had long disparaged Creeks for their lack of such clear, familiar structures of government.[73] To refute that criticism and the aggressive behavior it tended to generate from neighboring states, Creeks created such a document, which represented yet another step toward the kind of good government and respectable neighborhood that the Creek people were used to making. Many of the written codes were based on Euro-American legal traditions that had already made their impact on Creek legal traditions, like personal theft, murder, and accidental death. Classed Creek warrior groups acting as

the sole coercive authority of the National Council were further institutionalized. Retaliation against them was proscribed by law, reinforcing the rule of law over the authority of the clan system. Other codes
reflected the more unique Creek avenues of justice, such as cropping or
whipping those guilty of theft. And still other codes were more reflective of the times in which the Creek Nation now existed. Execution was
the penalty for an African American convicted of killing a Creek, for
instance, while a Creek convicted of killing an African American would
be liable for the value of that person, exposing the extent to which racial
slavery had penetrated Creek culture. Similarly, codifying a patrilineal
inheritance of goods upon death represented a much quicker and more
intense infusion of Euro-American culture into Creek law, challenging
the matrilineal traditions that Creeks had observed for generations.[74]

The National Council also continued to pass regulations designed
to better safeguard what the Creek people still controlled, becoming a
stronger and clearer governing body around the same time its Cherokee
counterpart began to emerge as well. It did this by forbidding the sale of
any remaining national property under penalty of death. When William
McIntosh structured the Treaty of Indian Springs in 1821 to free Creeks
of debts by ceding a small strip of land between the Okmulgee and Flint
rivers, the council allowed it but only by strict exemption, and the law was
quickly reapplied. Only years later, in 1824, Georgia state commissioners
backed by the Monroe administration began asking the National Council what it would take to have all Creeks trade their remaining lands in
Georgia and Alabama for something west of the Mississippi. The council,
meeting in Tuckabatchee and led by the Big Warrior, the Little Prince,
and Hopoie Haujo, unanimously rejected the idea in the strongest, most
unified tone to resonate from Creek Country in decades. They followed
that vote up with a written refusal, signed by seventeen headmen. They
then repulsed waves of bribes, demands, and threats hurled at them by
Georgia commissioners when they requested a convention on the subject anyway, which was held at Broken Arrow in the summer of 1824.
That affair represented the closest thing to Shoulderbone Creeks had
seen in decades, and the National Council exhibited spectacular unity.
Afterward, again at Broken Arrow, the National Council reaffirmed the
death penalty for any unauthorized dealing with Americans.[75] Facing
the most dangerous challenge ever leveled against Creeks—removal—
the National Council responded with amazing resolve.

Georgia commissioners turned to William McIntosh, whose likeness
to Alexander McGillivray was becoming closer by the day. McIntosh

slowly grew in power after the Red Stick War, assisted by friends and even kin both in the Georgia and federal governments.[76] Now attempting to placate both his Creek and American friends, McIntosh fell into a trap almost identical to the one that had destroyed McGillivray a generation earlier. The same Georgia commissioners who had failed miserably with the National Council moved almost immediately to court him privately. By speaking with them—which he did constantly, in secret and at his tavern outside of Creek Country—he was doing what he thought was best for many Creeks. He also was doing what was best for his Georgia friends. Lastly, he was clearly doing what he thought was best for him. Like McGillivray he also viewed acquiescence with Americans as a foregone conclusion and attempted to gain the best deal he could while it was available. Commissioners bribed and cajoled him into agreeing to a new Treaty of Indian Springs, which he propped up using the signatures of an entirely illegitimate representation of the National Council that consisted of people he personally picked. When this new treaty was presented again to the actual council, the response was overwhelming. Random Creeks from a handful of communities—neighbors of McIntosh and not actually members of the National Council—had signed the treaty, while others from both the Upper Country and from McIntosh's neighborhood, like Cusseta, Sauwoogelo, Broken Arrow, Ooseoochee, Yuchi, and Eufala, dismissed it, refused to sign it, and warned McIntosh that if he did, he was a dead man. When McIntosh went forward with the agreement anyway he was condemned to death, hunted down, and executed.[77]

The National Council struggled mightily to reverse the damage done by William McIntosh and it succeeded, at least for a time. Congress did, eventually, annul the treaty—the first time a treaty so ratified and signed by the president had ever been reversed. The annulment was forced, in large part, by the unity and resolve of the Creek people, which was too strong for Georgia state authorities to overcome. Those two events—the council's execution of McIntosh and its success in forcing the annulment of the second Treaty of Indian Springs—demonstrated a Creek nation-state that had rebuilt itself and matured tremendously over the previous decade. Indeed, the Creek state was not an ephemeral one, as Hawkins had once charged. It endured a difficult first salvo in the Removal era and continued to order Creeks' everyday lives. As noted Creek scholar Michael Green has concluded, "The execution of William McIntosh for the treason of the Treaty of Indian Springs was the pivotal moment in the history of the Creek Council government."[78]

Those victories, however, were achieved amid the slow but steady evolution in American politics that would, eventually, nullify it all. Within another year the council had signed the Treaty of Fort Mitchell, which relinquished all remaining Creek lands in the state of Georgia. Within a few more years, removal west was becoming a reality.[79] It was a continuation of the development Creeks witnessed directly, first at Fort Jackson and then shortly afterward at Tuckabatchee. The Creek Nation was fighting an impossible uphill battle not only against state-level expansionists but now against expansionists in the federal government that were much stronger. While the Indian Springs treaty fiasco became a national embarrassment that ultimately forced the John Quincy Adams administration to back away from it, such victories were increasingly rare. More receptive to their state-level counterparts than ever, an increasing number of federal authorities began to doubt the necessity to treat with Natives or even to recognize their status as sovereign people at all, drawing into question the long-time and foundational legal approaches that kept the National Council relevant.

Native sovereignty was already under attack as the John Quincy Adams administration was dealing with fallout of the second Treaty of Indian Springs. Andrew Jackson, of course, was a leading architect of the idea. As William McLoughlin has noted in his study of Cherokee political history, the end of the War of 1812, the rise of the Cotton Kingdom in the South, rapid industrialization, and racist nationalism "combined with historical precedents and expediency to inaugurate a major revision of American Indian policy. In this sense, Jackson was the right man in the right place."[80] Treating with Native peoples such as the Creeks had been a product of the government's weaknesses at the time, and not by any acknowledged rights held by those Natives. Jackson, arguing that idea to President Monroe in 1817, was clearly thinking it three years earlier when he drafted the Treaty of Fort Jackson and then shoved it down Creeks' throats. He knew Creeks were in no position to contest it, and he was right. While Henry Knox probably would have disagreed with his approach as well as the legal theory and even the morality underpinning it, Jackson's contentions reflected the new geopolitical reality. The power relationship between Americans and Native Americans had changed so drastically in the nineteenth century that the treaty system was simply no longer necessary. It was an idea embraced by several in Washington, including Secretary of War John C. Calhoun. "Helplessness has succeeded independence," he asserted in his 1818 report to the House of Representatives, which was actually a talk on Indian trade generally. Those "neighboring tribes" were "becoming daily less warlike, and more helpless and dependent on us, through their numerous wants; and they are rendered still more pacific by their fear of forfeiting their land and annuities." In short, there was little to fear from them; they had "ceased to be an object of terror, and have become that of commiseration." Accordingly, Calhoun argued, the time had come "when our policy towards them should undergo an important change. They neither are, in fact, nor ought to be, considered as independent nations. Our views of their interest, and not their own, ought to govern them." Although it would take a few more years, that idea would eventually become policy, helping produce the Jackson presidency and ultimately the Removal Act of 1830.[81] Americans would no longer treat with Native groups as equals because they no longer were equals.

No Native group illustrated that line of reasoning more than the Creek people. Creeks, driven to crisis in the post-Revolution years by political and cultural systems that could not respond to American expansionism, initiated a truly remarkable process of nation and state building, one modeled in many ways after that of their American neighbors. The Creek people altered cultural traditions of peoplehood and kinship, as well as of governance and law, making changes that in some instances were minor but in others were revolutionary. They did so in an effort to become good enough neighbors to Americans so as to gain for themselves lasting peace and permanence in their ancestral homeland. Yet less than a generation later, the Creek people faced removal. At one time an immensely powerful people, both feared and respected, the Creek Nation after 1815 was a shadow of its former self, and American authorities treated it accordingly. Like Cherokees to the north, no matter how good a neighbor Creeks could prove themselves or how successfully they could reinvent themselves as lawmakers, ranchers, or plantation owners, American expansionism still brought their time in the Southeast to an end. The Creek Nation, it turned out, could not save the Creek people.

ABBREVIATIONS

ASPFR   *American State Papers: Foreign Relations.* 6 vols. Washington DC: Gales and Seaton, 1832–61.

ASPIA   *American State Papers: Indian Affairs.* 2 vols. Washington DC: Gales and Seaton, 1832–61.

BHC   Benjamin Hawkins Collection, MS 943. Hargrett Rare Book & Manuscript Library, University of Georgia, Athens.

CFR   Records of the Bureau of Indian Affairs, Office of Indian Trade, Creek Factory Records, 1795–1821. National Archives and Records Administration. Microcopy M1334.

CGHS   *Collections of the Georgia Historical Society.*

CIL   Creek Indian Letters: Letters Talks and Treaties, 1705–1839, in Four Parts. 4 vols. Unpublished typescript, edited by Louise F. Hayes, 1939. Georgia Department of Archives and History, Morrow.

CMT   Mildred Thompson Collection. MS 606. Hargrett Rare Book & Manuscript Library, University of Georgia, Athens.

CO 5/   Public Record Office, Colonial Office Records, Class 5. Vols. 555–58, 560, 568. University Archives and West Florida History Center, John C. Pace Library, University of West Florida, Pensacola.

CROC   Confidential Reports and Other Communications from the Secretary of War. 3rd Congress, 1st Session, 1793. Vol. IIA. Reel 14, in Transcribed Reports and Communications Transmitted by the Executive Branch to the House of

Representatives, 1789–1819. Record Group 233. Microcopy M-1268. National Archives.

DAR   K. G. Davies, ed. *Documents of the American Revolution, 1770–1783*. 21 vols. Shannon: Irish University Press, 1972–81.

EFP   East Florida Papers. Film 55-A. P. K. Yonge Library of Florida History, University of Florida, Gainesville.

EHW   Elizabeth Howard West Papers. MS 111. P. K. Yonge Library of Florida History, University of Florida, Gainesville.

FHP   Felix Hargrett Papers. MS 2311. Hargrett Rare Book & Manuscript Library, University of Georgia, Athens.

FT   Force Transcripts: Georgia Records Council Correspondence, 1782–1789. Unpublished typescript, edited by Louise F. Hayes, 1938. Georgia Department of Archives and History, Morrow.

GLB   Governor's Letter Book, October 20, 1786–May 31, 1789. Unpublished typescript, edited by Louise F. Hayes, 1940. Georgia Department of Archives and History, Morrow.

ID   Indian Depredations, 1787–1825. 4 vols. Unpublished typescript, edited by Louise F. Hayes, 1938–39. Georgia Department of Archives and History, Morrow.

IT   Indian Treaties Cessions of Land in Georgia, 1705–1837. Unpublished typescript, edited by Louise F. Hayes, 1941. Georgia Department of Archives and History, Morrow.

JMP   James McHenry Papers, 1775–1862. MSS 32177. Library of Congress.

JVB   Joseph Valence Bevan Papers. MS 71. Georgia Historical Society, Savannah.

KRC   Keith Read Collection. MS921. Hargrett Rare Book & Manuscript Library, University of Georgia, Athens.

LBH   Letters of Benjamin Hawkins, 1797–1815. Unpublished typescript, edited by Louise F. Hayes, 1939. Georgia Department of Archives and History, Morrow.

LC   Joseph Byrne Lockey Documents Related to the History of Florida. MS 174. P. K. Yonge Library of Florida History, University of Florida, Gainesville.

LJW   C. L. Grant, ed. *Letters, Journals, and Writings of Benjamin Hawkins*. 2 vols. Savannah GA: Beehive Press, 1980.

LTB   Letters of Timothy Barnard. Unpublished typescript, edited by Louise F. Hayes, 1939. Georgia Department of Archives and History, Morrow.

MC John Walton Caughney, ed. *McGillivray of the Creeks.* Norman: University of Oklahoma Press, 1938.

MPASD Mississippi Department of Archives and History. *Mississippi Provincial Archives, Spanish Dominion,* 1759–1804. 9 vols. Cleveland: Bell & Howell, 1969.

PCC Papers of the Continental Congress, 1774–1789. Washington DC: National Archives and Records Service, General Services Administration, 1971. Microcopy M247.

PdE Papeles de Estado. University Archives and West Florida History Center, John C. Pace Library, University of West Florida, Pensacola.

PHL Philip M. Harmer, ed. *The Papers of Henry Laurens.* 16 vols. Columbia: Published for the South Carolina Historical Society by the University of South Carolina Press, 1968–.

PPdC Papeles Procendentes de Cuba. Microfilm copies in Film 12–24. P. K. Yonge Library of Florida History, University of Florida, Gainesville.

PPL Panton, Leslie and Company. *The Papers of Panton, Leslie & Co.* Woodbridge CT: Research Publications, 1986.

SWLR Letters Received by the Office of the Secretary of War Relating to Indian Affairs, 1800–1823. Record Group 75, Microcopy M271.

SWLS Letters Sent by the Secretary of War Relating to Indian Affairs, 1800–1824. Record Group 75, Microcopy M15.

TCC Telamon Cuyler Collection. MS 1170. Hargrett Rare Book & Manuscript Library, University of Georgia, Athens.

Notes

Prologue

1. Wright to Earl of Dartmouth, January 31, 1774, DAR, 8:30–32; Stuart to Haldimand, February 3, 1774, DAR, 8:34–37; Stuart to Haldimand, February 10, 1774, Thomas Gage Papers, vol. 119; Stuart to Earl of Dartmouth, February 13, 1774, DAR, 8:48–49; Stuart to Gage, May 12, 1774, Thomas Gage Papers, vol. 119; Bartram and Harper, "Travels in Georgia, and Florida," 144; Corkran, *The Creek Frontier*, 281–83.

2. Stuart to Gage, May 12, 1774, Thomas Gage Papers, vol. 119.

3. Several book chapters deal with the complexity of the Ceded Lands debacle in depth. They include those in Cashin, *William Bartram*, 38–75; and Snapp, *John Stuart*, 116–46; see also Braund, "'Like a Stone Wall Never to Be Broke,'" 53–79.

4. Stuart to Chester, August 30, 1771, DAR, 3:174–75; Memorial of Governor James Wright to Hillsborough, December 12, 1771, DAR, 3:269–75.

5. Augusta Traders to Habersham, April 16, 1772, DAR, 5:72–73; Cameron to Stuart, March 19, 1771, DAR, 3:72–73.

6. Memorial of Governor James Wright to Hillsborough, December 12, 1771, DAR, 3:269–75.

7. Augusta Traders to Habersham, April 16, 1772, DAR, 5:72–73; Memorial of Traders to Creek and Cherokee Nations to Wright, June 1771, DAR, 3:125–27. The traders later acknowledged that headmen in the Lower Country were volatile. If Stuart could have a meeting in Augusta, "especially those of the Lower Towns, they would readily join in the cession of those valuable lands which are of the greatest importance to this colony although of very little if any to them." See Habersham to Earl of Hillsborough, April 24, 1772, DAR, 5:75–76.

8. Philemon Kemp to Governor of Georgia with Talks from Emistisiguo and Gun Merchant, June 9, 1771, DAR, 3:118–21; Proceedings of Congress with Upper Creeks, October 29–November 2, 1771, DAR, 3:217–21; Emistisiguo to Stuart, April 19, 1772, DAR, 5:74–75; Corkran, *The Creek Frontier*, 278–79.

9. Proceedings of Congress with Upper Creeks, October 29–November 2, 1771, *DAR*, 3:217–21; Corkran, *The Creek Frontier*, 278–79.

10. Chester to Hillsborough, December 28, 1771, *DAR*, 3:280–81; Philemon Kemp to Governor of Georgia with Talks from Emistisiguo and Gun Merchant, June 9, 1771, *DAR*, 3:118–21.

11. For the text of the Pensacola treaty, see Rowland, *Mississippi Provincial Archives*, 1:211–14. For accounts of the Picolata treaty, see Hoffman, *Florida's Frontiers*, 213.

12. Philemon Kemp to Governor of Georgia with Talks from Emistisiguo and Gun Merchant, June 9, 1771, *DAR*, 3:118–21.

13. Mereness, "Journal of David Taitt's Travels," 507–8, 513–15.

14. Hillsborough to Stuart, July 3, 1771, *DAR*, 3:133. The deliberations had been "transacted without my knowledge and concurrence," he complained to Chester, were "irregular and contrary to the King's proclamation, and will of course be disapproved by Government." See Stuart to Chester, August 30, 1771, *DAR*, 3:174–75. The traders' actions were "not only irregular but very culpable, being in opposition to every provision of government as well as the royal proclamation of 1763, that the grant obtained would therefore be of no use," and he pressured them to immediately desist. See Stuart to Earl of Hillsborough, June 12, 1772, *DAR*, 5:113–18. He wrote a particularly long report on the idea later in 1772. See Stuart to Gage, November 24, 1771, Thomas Gage Papers, vol. 115.

15. Stuart to Chester, August 30, 1771, *DAR*, 3:174–75; Stuart to Gage, November 24, 1771, Thomas Gage Papers, vol. 115.

16. Stuart to Earl of Hillsborough, June 12, 1772, *DAR*, 5:113–18; Stuart to Gage, November 24, 1771, Thomas Gage Papers, vol. 115. In Pensacola, Peter Chester felt similarly, worried that the traders' actions were upsetting his hopes of gaining the Mobile land cession. See Chester to Hillsborough, August 13, 1772, *DAR*, 5:164–65.

17. For changing opinions of the cession among regional legislators, and in London, see Hillsborough to Stuart, January 11, 1772, *DAR*, 5:24; Memorial of the Merchants Trading to Georgia to the Board of Trade, March 25, 1772, in Candler et al., eds., *Colonial Records*, vol. 28, part 2, 381–82; Hillsborough to Habersham, August 7, 1772, *DAR*, 5:162–63; Earl of Dartmouth to Stuart, December 9, 1772, *DAR*, 5:242–43; Earl of Dartmouth to Wright, December 12, 1772, *DAR*, 5:243–44; Earl of Dartmouth to Stuart, March 3, 1773, *DAR*, 6:95–96; At a Council in His Honors House . . . , October 23, 1772, in Candler et al., eds., *Colonial Records*, 12:333–34.

18. Stuart to Gage, November 24, 1771, Thomas Gage Papers, vol. 115; Corkran, *The Creek Frontier*, 259, 281.

19. Stuart to Gage, February 15, 1773, Thomas Gage Papers, vol. 117; Stuart to Gage, April 22, 1773, Thomas Gage Papers, vol. 118; Gage to Stuart, June 3, 1773, Thomas Gage Papers, vol. 118.

20. Van Doren, *Travels*, 53–54; Harper, *Travels*, 307–8; Bartram and Harper, "Travels in Georgia, and Florida," 138; Cashin, *William Bartram*, 53–56.

21. Wright to Earl of Dartmouth, June 17, 1773, *DAR*, 6:156–15; Stuart to Earl of Dartmouth, June 21, 1773, *DAR*, 6:158–59; Bartram and Harper, "Travels in Georgia, and Florida," 140, 142–43.

22. Wright to Earl of Dartmouth, June 17, 1773, *DAR*, 6:156–15; Wright to Earl of Dartmouth, December 27, 1773, *DAR*, 6:266–67. Bartram was also impressed. "This new ceded country promises plenty & felicity. The Lands on the river are generally

Rich, & those of its almost innumerable branches agreeable & healthy situations, espe-cially for small farms," and suitable for everything from corn to vineyards, olives, indigo, and even water-powered mills. See Bartram and Harper, "Travels in Georgia, and Florida," 144.

23. Stuart to Earl of Dartmouth, June 21, 1773, DAR, 6:158–59.

24. Affidavit of Joseph Dawes, August 4, 1772, DAR, 5:161–62.

25. Even then they promptly applied to David Taitt, one of Stuart's deputies, to "consult with him about the matter." See Wright to Earl of Dartmouth, January 31, 1774, DAR, 8:30–32.

26. Wright to Earl of Dartmouth, January 31, 1774, DAR, 8:30–32; Stuart to Hal-dimand, February 3, 1774, DAR, 8:34–37; Moultrie to Earl of Dartmouth, February 21, 1774, DAR, 8:54–55; Haldimand to Earl of Dartmouth, March 2, 1774, DAR, 8:58–60.

27. Wright to Earl of Dartmouth, January 31, 1774, DAR, 8:30–32; Stuart to Hal-dimand, February 3, 1774, DAR, 8:34–37; Cameron to Stuart, March 1, 1774, DAR, 8:56–57; Bartram and Harper, "Travels in Georgia, and Florida," 150; Corkran, The Creek Frontier, 282–83. "Things seem to have worn a pacific look in the Upper Creek nation," Taitt had written Stuart. See Stuart to Haldimand, February 3, 1774, DAR, 8:34–37.

28. Corkran, The Creek Frontier, 282–83.

29. As historian Michael D. Green explained, "The security that clan membership provided ranged far beyond the comforting realization that clan relatives in other towns, even those an individual might never have met, could be relied on to provide support and protection. Except in those towns where one's clan did not exist, any Creek knew he was never far from relatives anywhere in the Nation." See Green, Poli-tics of Indian Removal, 6; Ethridge, Creek Country, 110.

30. Wright to Earl of Dartmouth, January 31, 1774, DAR, 8:30–32; Stuart to Hal-dimand, February 3, 1774, DAR, 8:34–37.

31. The pitiful representation illustrated chiefs' fear of British retribution, a legacy the governor of South Carolina had left after his seizure of Cherokee emissaries years earlier under similar circumstances. See Conference between Governor Sir James Wright and Upper Creek Chiefs, April 14, 1774, DAR, 8:90–95; Wright to Earl of Dart-mouth, April 18, 1774, DAR, 8:98–99.

32. Conference between Governor Sir James Wright and Upper Creek Chiefs, April 14, 1774, DAR, 8:90–95. Wright made plans to have proclamations written and deliv-ered throughout the region "putting a total stop to all trade and intercourse whatever to both Upper and Lower Creek Towns." See Wright to Earl of Dartmouth, April 18, 1774, DAR, 8:98–99. Gage agreed with the approach. See Gage to Stuart, May 14, 1774, Thomas Gage Papers, vol. 119.

33. Conference between Governor Sir James Wright and Upper Creek Chiefs, April 14, 1774, DAR, 8:90–95; Stuart to Gage, April 23, 1774, Thomas Gage Papers, vol. 119; Gage to Stuart, May 14, 1774, Thomas Gage Papers, vol. 119; Corkran, The Creek Fron-tier, 283–84.

34. Conference between Governor Sir James Wright and Upper Creek Chiefs, April 14, 1774, DAR, 8:90–95; Bartram and Harper, "Travels in Georgia, and Florida," 157–58.

35. Conference between Governor Sir James Wright and Upper Creek Chiefs, April 14, 1774, DAR, 8:90–95; Corkran, The Creek Frontier, 283–84.

36. Stuart to Earl of Dartmouth, May 6, 1774, DAR, 8:109–10; Chester to Haldimand, May 12, 1774, Thomas Gage Papers, vol. 120.

37. Stuart to Earl of Dartmouth, August 2, 1774, *DAR*, 8:156–57; Corkran, *The Creek Frontier*, 284–85.

38. Wright to Earl of Dartmouth, May 24, 1774, *DAR*, 8:116–17; Ogilvy to Haldimand, June 13, 1774, Thomas Gage Papers, vol. 120; Stuart to Earl of Dartmouth, August 2, 1774, *DAR*, 8:156–57; Bartram and Harper, "Travels in Georgia, and Florida," 150.

39. Wright to Stuart, June 13, 1774, Thomas Gage Papers, vol. 121; Stuart to Haldimand, June 25, 1774, Thomas Gage Papers, vol. 120; Stuart to Gage, July 3, 1774, Thomas Gage Papers, vol. 120; Stuart to Haldimand, July 5, 1774, Thomas Gage Papers, vol. 121; Taitt to Stuart, July 7, 1774, Thomas Gage Papers, vol. 121; Corkran, *The Creek Frontier*, 284–85.

40. Wright to Stuart, June 13, 1774, Thomas Gage Papers, vol. 121; Stuart to Gage, July 3, 1774, Thomas Gage Papers, vol. 120; Stuart to Haldimand, July 5, 1774, Thomas Gage Papers, vol. 121; Stuart to Earl of Dartmouth, August 2, 1774, *DAR*, 8:156–57.

41. A Talk from the Pumpkin King . . . , June 23, 1774, Thomas Gage Papers, vol. 122; Taitt to Stuart, July 7, 1774, Thomas Gage Papers, vol. 121; July 18, 1774, Thomas Gage Papers, vol. 122; At a Council in His Excellency . . . , August 30, 1774, in Candler et al., eds., *Colonial Records*, 12:409–10; Stuart to Earl of Dartmouth, December 15, 1774, *DAR*, 8:244–45.

42. At a Council in His Excellency . . . , August 30, 1774, in Candler et al., eds., *Colonial Records*, 12:407. From the same report it appeared that Lower Creeks were actually getting goods illegally from several traders who were willing to take the chance and that "the Indians were flocking from all Quarters to Purcase the above goods." See At a Council in His Excellency . . . , August 30, 1774, in Candler et al., eds., *Colonial Records*, 12:407–9.

43. Debo, *Road to Disappearance*, 35–36; Corkran, *The Creek Frontier*, 273–87; Braund, *Deerskins & Duffels*, 164. For an example of his policy change, see A Proclamation, October 24, 1774, in Force, ed., *American Archives*, series 4, 1:890–91; A Proclamation, October 24, 1774, in Force, ed., *American Archives*, series 4, 1:1137–38.

44. At a Council in His Excellency . . . , August 30, 1774, in Candler et al., eds., *Colonial Records*, 12:409–10; Stuart to Earl of Dartmouth, December 15, 1774, *DAR*, 8:244–45; Tonyn to Dartmouth, December 14, 1774, CO 5/555.

1. Introduction

1. Durouzeaux to Folch, October 20, 1802, PPdC, legajo 2372.

2. Chester to Hillsborough, December 28, 1771, *DAR*, 3:280–81.

3. Conference between Governor Sir James Wright and Upper Creek Chiefs, April 14, 1774, *DAR*, 4:90–95; Corkran, *The Creek Frontier*, 283–84.

4. Oatis, *A Colonial Complex*; Ramsey, *The Yamasee War*; Jennings, *New Worlds of Violence*; Ethridge and Shuck-Hall, *Mapping the Mississippian Shatter Zone*; Ethridge, *From Chicaza to Chickasaw*; Gallay, *The Indian Slave Trade*.

5. For that approach, which has been explained as the doctrine of neutrality, see Hahn, *Invention of the Creek Nation*, 244–58; Corkran, *The Creek Frontier*, 61; Green, *Politics of Indian Removal*, 21. In principle, Creeks sought benefits from the French, Spanish, and British alike "and as far as possible to avoid hostilities with any of them." By doing so, Creek chiefs would use each colonial power's fear of the other "to extract concessions, and to protect their independent position." While it was not always

adhered to in all circumstances, "it was to develop the sanctity of tradition, and to be a potent force in any councils seeking partisan commitment, and was always available to be thrown as a cloak over any double dealing." Corkran, *The Creek Frontier*, 61; Green, *Politics of Indian Removal*, 21. Englishman James Adair spoke of this in 1775. Creek headmen, "being long informed by the opposite parties, of the different views, and intrigues of those European powers, who paid them annual tribute under the vague appellation of presents, were becoming surprisingly crafty in every turn of low politics. They held it as an invariable maxim, that their security and welfare required a perpetual friendly intercourse with both us and the French." See Adair, *History of the American Indians*, 277.

6. Corkran, *The Creek Frontier*; Snapp, *John Stuart*.

7. The best study of that transition is still by far Saunt, *A New Order of Things*, although it is also touched upon in Ethridge, *Creek Country*; Hudson, *Creek Paths and Federal Roads*; Martin, *Sacred Revolt*; Braund, *Deerskins & Duffels*; Wright, *Creeks & Seminoles*; and Green, *Politics of Indian Removal*.

8. See, for instance, Hahn, *Invention of the Creek Nation*, 7.

9. For the importance of clans, see Green, *Politics of Indian Removal*, 4–5; Hudson, *The Southeastern Indians*, 193; Ethridge, *Creek Country*, 109–11; Hahn, *Invention of the Creek Nation*, 233, 238–44. Scholars have questioned the extent to which kinship identity dictated the day-to-day lives of the Southeast Native peoples. See Piker, *Okfuskee*, 3–4, 7–10; Boulware, *Deconstructing the Cherokee Nation*, 3–5, 10–31; and Sider, *Lumbee Indian Histories*, 228–33.

10. Swanton, *Social Organization*, 276–80, 338–45; Hudson, *The Southeastern Indians*, 223–26, 229–32; Ethridge, *Creek Country*, 102–3; Saunt, *A New Order of Things*, 19–21, 24–27.

11. Bendix, *Nation-Building and Citizenship*, 19.

12. This general definition pulls from several classic studies of nationalism. Those include Anderson, *Imagined Communities*, 1–7; Jusdanis, *The Necessary Nation*, 3–28; James, *Nation Formation*; Hobsbawm, *Nations and Nationalism since 1780*, 1–13; Breuilly, *Nationalism and the State*, 1–16; Kohn, *The Idea of Nationalism*, 1–20; Greenfeld, *Nationalism*, 1–26; Gellner, *Nations and Nationalism*, 3–7; Greenfeld, "Is Modernity Possible without Nationalism?"; and Kamenka, "Political Nationalism," 3–20; and Plamenatz, "Two Types of Nationalism."

13. Champagne, *Social Order*, 6–9; Gellner, *Nations and Nationalism*, 3–7; Giddens, *Nation-State and Violence*, 116–21; Poggi, *The Development of the Modern State*, 1.

14. Skocpol, "Bringing the State Back In," 8.

15. Hahn, *Invention of the Creek Nation*, 231–34; Wright, *Creeks & Seminoles*, 1–4.

16. Sami Lakomäki offers an excellent appraisal of this shift. See Lakomäki, *Gathering Together*, 1–12, particularly 8n12. See also Witgen, *An Infinity of Nations*, 69–107. One of the preeminent scholars of nationalism, Hans Kohn, seemed to agree with the universality of the forces of nationhood: "There is a natural tendency in man—and by 'natural tendency' we mean a tendency which, having been produced by social circumstances from time practically immemorial, appears to us as natural—to love his birthplace or the place of his childhood sojourn, its surroundings, its climate, the contours of hills and valleys, of rivers and trees." Everyone appreciates the familiarity of their own language, their own customs, and their own foods. "Small wonder that he will take pride in his Native characteristics, and that he will easily believe in their

superiority. As they are the only ones in which a civilized people like himself can apparently feel at home, are they not the only ones fit for human beings?" See Kohn, *The Idea of Nationalism*, 4–5.

17. Richter, *Ordeal of the Longhouse*, 39–42, 136–38; Wallace, *Death and Rebirth of the Seneca*, 39–43; White, *The Middle Ground*, 433–68.

18. Witgen, *An Infinity of Nations*, 69–107; White, *The Middle Ground*, 413–68, esp. pp. 416–17; Salisbury, *Manitou and Providence*, 48–49.

19. Richter, *Ordeal of the Longhouse*, 40.

20. Hamalainen, *Comanche Empire*.

21. Cherokee political development has been dealt with most recently in McLoughlin, *Cherokee Renascence*, especially chs. 15–16.

22. See Hatley, *The Dividing Paths*; McLoughlin, *Cherokee Renascence*, 18–21; and Calloway, *American Revolution in Indian Country*, 182–212.

23. O'Brien, *Choctaws in a Revolutionary Age*.

24. Saunt, *A New Order of Things*; Braund, *Deerskins & Duffels*; Ethridge, *Creek Country*.

25. Snyder, *Slavery in Indian Country*. See also Miles, *Ties That Bind*; Yarbrough, *Race and the Cherokee Nation*; Mulroy, *Freedom on the Border*; Saunt, *A New Order of Things*; Littlefield, *Africans and Creeks*; and Littlefield, *Africans and Seminoles*.

26. For this general idea, see Onuf, *Jefferson's Empire*; Prucha, *The Great Father*; Wallace, *Jefferson and the Indians*; Viola, *Thomas L. McKenney*; and Sheehan, *Seeds of Extinction*.

27. For an idea of that approach, see Axtell, "Ethnohistory: An Historian's Viewpoint," 5. Several studies have done an excellent job examining Creek culture and the dynamics of Creek communities. They include, for instance, Ethridge, *Creek Country*; Saunt, *A New Order of Things*; Wright, *Creeks & Seminoles*; Piker, *Okfuskee*; Frank, *Creeks and Southerners*; and Martin, *Sacred Revolt*. A strong counterpoint to those studies can be found in White, *The Roots of Dependency*, which suggests that the development of dependency had a powerful and destructive impact on Native culture.

28. For the stadial idea, see Griffin, *American Leviathan*. See also Blanton and Fargher, *Collective Action in the Formation of Pre-Modern States*, 165–66.

29. Kohn, *The Idea of Nationalism*; Higginbotham, "War and State Formation in Revolutionary America"; Elding, *Revolution in Favor of Government*; Hendrickson, *Peace Pact*; Gould, *Among the Powers of the Earth*. For insightful studies of the Confederation period, see Griffin, *American Leviathan*; Sadosky, *Revolutionary Negotiations*; Ferling, *A Leap in the Dark*; Elkins and McKitrick, *The Age of Federalism*; and Wood, *The Creation of the American Republic*.

30. To see this idea elsewhere, see Lakomäki, *Gathering Together*, 10.

31. With regard to the formative qualities of violence, this study is reflective of Ned Blackhawk's work on colonialism. Blackhawk suggested that through endless attacks or atrocities, violence becomes more than "an intriguing or distressing subject." It becomes a process in itself, "an interpretive concept as well as a method for understanding" Indian-white relations. See Blackhawk, *Violence over the Land*, 3–7. For other studies of violence and the development of the Southeast, see Jennings, *New Worlds of Violence*; Ethridge, *From Chicaza to Chickasaw*; Kenton, *Epidemics and Enslavement*; and Gallay, *The Indian Slave Trade*. For the impact of violence on American settlers, or along the trans-Appalachian West, see Nichols, *Red Gentlemen*

& White Savages; Silver, *Our Savage Neighbors*; Griffin, *American Leviathan*; Knouff, *The Soldier's Revolution*; Pencak and Richter, *Friends and Enemies in Penn's Woods*; Merritt, *At the Crossroads*; and Hinderaker, *Elusive Empires*.

32. Euro-American violence as the means to shape Native identity has been studied far less than the consequences of Native violence on Euro-American settlers. Studies that do look at this aspect of frontier conflict include Merritt, *At the Crossroads*; Dowd, *War under Heaven*; Dowd, *A Spirited Resistance*; and Richter, *Facing East*.

33. This is based on what Pekka Hamalainen called "alternative frontier history." The frontier was a "violent and traumatic place where Natives and newcomers saw one another more as strangers and adversaries than as co-creators of a common world." More often than not, the two groups knew each other all too well, "and generally they did not like what they saw." See Hamalainen, *Comanche Empire*, 7–9.

34. See, for instance, Foreman, *Indian Removal*.

35. Hoboheithlee Micco to the President, May 15, 1811, SWLR.

36. Eustis to Hawkins, June 27, 1811, SWLS, vol. C.

37. For examples of these arguments, see Poggi, *The Development of the Modern State*; Evans, Rueschemeyer, and Skocpol, eds., *Bringing the State Back In*, particularly Tilly, "War Making and State Making as Organized Crime"; Tilly, *Coercion, Capital, and European States*; Midlarsky, *The Evolution of Inequality*; and Lachman, *States and Power*, particularly pp. 25–65.

38. Lakamokin, *Gathering Together*, 11. Also important is Wimmer, *Nationalist Exclusion and Ethnic Conflict*. For particular examples of this in the Southeast, see Hahn, *Invention of the Creek Nation*, 234; and McLoughlin, *Cherokee Renascence*, ch. 11.

39. Condon, *Shay's Rebellion*; Richards, *Shay's Rebellion*.

40. Sadosky, *Revolutionary Negotiations*; Barksdale, *The Lost State of Franklin*.

2. Creek Partisans Emerge during the American Revolution

1. McIntosh to Washington, February 16, 1776, in Force, ed., *American Archives*, series 4, 4:1159–60; Extract of a Letter from Georgia . . . , September 7, 1774, in Force, ed., *American Archives*, series 4, 1:774.

2. Mr. Tennent to the Council of Safety in Savannah, September 10, 1775, in Gibbes, ed., *Documentary History*, 1:168–69.

3. Address by the Commissioners of Indian Affairs . . . , November 13, 1775, in Saunders, ed., *Colonial and State Records*, 10:330–31; Stuart to Legge, December 17, 1775, in Saunders, ed., *Colonial and State Records*, 10:348; Report of Bryan, Houstoun, and McIntosh, n.d., PCC, reel 87, frame 160.

4. Braund, *Deerskins & Duffels*, 26–43, 50; Bast, "Creek Indian Affairs," 8.

5. For discussions of the integration and importance of outsiders, see Frank, *Creeks and Southerners*, 26–45; Martin, *Sacred Revolt*, 70–84; Braund, *Deerskins & Duffels*, 26–43, 50, 82–87, 167; and Perdue, "'A Sprightly Lover,'" 168–78.

6. Mereness, "Journal of David Taitt's Travels," 504–5; Stuart to Clinton, March 15, 1776, Henry Clinton Papers, vol. 14; Braund, *Deerskins & Duffels*, 44–46; Martin, *Sacred Revolt*, 65–66, 71–72; Wright, *Creeks & Seminoles*, 44; Cashin, *William Bartram*, 43–45.

7. Corkran, *The Creek Frontier*, 290–91; Wright, *Creeks & Seminoles*, 44.

8. Mereness, "Journal of David Taitt's Travels," 524; Taitt to Stuart, August 1, 1775, DAR, 11:61–62; Stuart to Clinton, March 15, 1776, Henry Clinton Papers, vol. 14; O'Donnell, *Southern Indians*, 20–24, 27–29; Lowndes to Lauren, March 16, 1778, PHL, 13:8–9; Corkran, *The Creek Frontier*, 289–92; Wright, *Creeks & Seminoles*, 108–9; Martin, *Sacred Revolt*, 65–67; Braund, *Deerskins & Duffels*, 46–47, 166–67; Piecuch, *Three Peoples*, 67; Cashin, "'But Brothers, It Is Our Land We Are Talking About,'" 242. For the stores in Oakfuskee and Chehaw, see Mereness, "Journal of David Taitt's Travels," 524, 545–46.

9. Mereness, "Journal of David Taitt's Travels," 502, 516, 519–21, 540.

10. Mereness, "Journal of David Taitt's Travels," 529–30, 533, 535–36, 541–42, 548–50.

11. The traders' names were John Miller, in Yuchi, Benjamin Stedham in Pallachocola, and Edward Harris in Eufala. Mereness, "Journal of David Taitt's Travels," 548, 550–52, 554–55.

12. Braund, *Deerskins & Duffels*, 40–58.

13. Mereness, "Journal of David Taitt's Travels," 504, 505–7, 10, 512, 522, 527. Richard Brown was a prominent trader in Coosada, with a trading house there, and Thomas Greerson operated out of Upper Eufala. See Mereness, "Journal of David Taitt's Travels," 509–10, 522–25, 527. Further to the north, Robert French lived in Oakfuskee as a hireling of the Campbell and Son firm in Charleston. See Mereness, "Journal of David Taitt's Travels," 529. Thomas Mosley traded out of Wetunkey, and Thomas Graham from Oakchai. See Mereness, "Journal of David Taitt's Travels," 536, 542–43.

14. Mereness, "Journal of David Taitt's Travels," 552, 545, 561; Woodward, *Reminiscences*, 109.

15. Mereness, "Journal of David Taitt's Travels," 508–10, 512, 525–27, 541–42, 544–45. Everyone involved in the enterprise, Taitt disparaged, "excepting a very few are composed of Deserters, Horse thieves, half breeds and negroes." See Mereness, "Journal of David Taitt's Travels," 525.

16. Snapp, *John Stuart*, 126–29.

17. Woodward, *Reminiscences*, 116.

18. Piecuch, *Three Peoples*, 30–35; Snapp, *John Stuart*, 116–46; Howard, "Colonial Pensacola," 385.

19. Bast, "Creek Indian Affairs," 6; Dabney and Dargan, *William Henry Drayton*, 80. Upwards of five hundred men were allegedly after him, but East Florida's governor Patrick Tonyn was resolute that Stuart "most certainly shall not be delivered up." See Tonyn to Gage, July 9, 1775, Henry Clinton Papers, vol. 10; Tonyn to Dartmouth, September 20, 1775, CO 5/555; Tonyn to Gage, September 20, 1775, CO 5/555; Tonyn to [Gage?], CO 5/568, frame 64.

20. Habersham to Chiffelle, June 16, 1775, in Gibbes, ed., *Documentary History*, 1:103.

21. Corkran, *The Creek Frontier*, 237; Braund, *Deerskins & Duffels*, 166.

22. More, like Cameron, were common in Cherokee, Choctaw, and Chickasaw towns as well. Council of Safety to Georgia Council of Safety, July 24, 1775, PHL, 10:243–44; Address by Patrick Tonyn to the Creek Nation . . . , December 1775, in Saunders, ed., *Colonial and State Records*, 10:341–45; Braund, *Deerskins & Duffels*, 166; O'Donnell, *Southern Indians*, 17–19; Wright, *Creeks & Seminoles*, 113; O'Donnell, "The South on the Eve of the Revolution," 67–68.

23. Alden, *John Stuart*, 212; Snapp, *John Stuart*, 78, 97–99; Corkran, *The Creek Frontier*, 301.

24. Alden, *John Stuart*, 297; Snapp, *John Stuart*, 78, 122–46.

25. For Taitt's journey, see Mereness, "Journal of David Taitt's Travels," 493–568. For the Natchez visit, see 531–32. For examples of his meeting headmen in town squares, smoking, and drinking black drink, see 506–7, 509, 513, 514, 516, 530–31, 533, 549.

26. Tonyn to Gage, September 14, 1775, in Force, ed., *American Archives*, series 4, 3:703–5; Taitt to Stuart, August 1, 1775, DAR, 11:61–62; copy of a letter from Brown to Tonyn, May 1776, Henry Clinton Papers, vol. 16; Lowndes to Lauren, March 16, 1778, PHL, 13:8–9; Tonyn to Germain, November 10, 1780, CO 5/560; Corkran, *The Creek Frontier*, 289–92; O'Donnell, *Southern Indians*, 20–24, 27–29; Braund, *Deerskins & Duffels*, 166–67; Piecuch, *Three Peoples*, 67; Cashin, "But Brothers, It Is Our Land We Are Talking About," 242; Wright, *Creeks & Seminoles*, 114; Calloway, *American Revolution in Indian Country*, 257.

27. O'Donnell, *Southern Indians*, 21; Bast, "Creek Indian Affairs," 8–9; Tonyn to Dartmouth, December 18, 1775, CO 5/556; Kalique response at the Cowford, St. John's River, December 7, 1775, CO 5/556; Galphin to Council of Safety, October 15, 1775, PHL, 10:468.

28. Wesson, *Households and Hegemony*, 33–40; Kowalewski, "Coalescent Societies," 116–20. One excellent general study on the transitional period is Ethridge, *From Chicaza to Chickasaw*. For those that focus more specifically on Creeks, see Kelton, *Epidemics and Enslavement*; and Worth, "Spanish Missions and the Persistence of Chiefly Power." Excellent works on the very early transformation of the Southeast and particularly of Creeks include Worth, "Spanish Missions and the Persistence of Chiefly Power"; Hahn, *Invention of the Creek Nation*, 13–26; and Frank, *Creeks and Southerners*, 1–25. Migration and creation legends are also helpful. See Swanton, *Social Organization*, 33–76. Choctaws shared a very similar early history, coalescing as a people in much the same way. See Calloway, *Choctaw Genesis*; and Carson, *Searching for the Bright Path*, 8–25.

29. Wright, *Creeks & Seminoles*, 1–13, 112–14; Swanton, *Social Organization*, 248–49.

30. For this idea, see Calloway, *American Revolution in Indian Country*, 9; and Hahn, *Invention of the Creek Nation*, 5.

31. Some of these traditions are investigated here more than others, but excellent explanations of most of them can be found in Ethridge, *Creek Country*; and Green, *Politics of Indian Removal*. James Carson has explained Choctaw culture as being constructed similarly. See Carson, *Searching for the Bright Path*, 27.

32. For excellent studies of Creek politics and diplomacy in the eighteenth century, see Juricek, *Colonial Georgia and the Creeks*; Hahn, *Invention of the Creek Nation*; Sweet, *Negotiating for Georgia*; Corkran, *The Creek Frontier*; and Crane, *Southern Frontier*.

33. Calloway, *American Revolution in Indian Country*, 45. For examples of this, see Answer to His Excellency Sir James Wright's Talk . . . , July 25, 1775, Henry Clinton Papers, vol. 11; A Talk to the Hon'ble John Stuart . . . , August 15, 1775, Henry Clinton Papers, vol. 11; A talk in answer . . . , September 29, 1775, Henry Clinton Papers, vol. 11.

34. Stuart to Gage, September 15, 1775, in Force, ed., *American Archives*, series 4, 3:714–15; Cameron to Stuart, November 9, 1775, Henry Clinton Papers, vol. 12; Stuart to Clinton, March 15, 1776, Henry Clinton Papers, vol. 12; Stuart to Clinton, March 15, 1776, Henry Clinton Papers, vol. 14.

35. Stuart to Dartmouth, July 21, 1775, DAR, 11:53–54; Corkran, *The Creek Frontier*, 288–89; Stuart to Taitt, August 29, 1775, in Gibbes, ed., *Documentary History*, 1:158–59; copy of John Stuart's Talk . . . , August 1775, in Gibbes, ed., *Documentary History*, 1:159–60; copy of a letter from Brown to Tonyn, May 2, 1776, Henry Clinton Papers, vol. 16; copy of a letter from Brown to Tonyn, May 1776, Henry Clinton Papers, vol. 16.

36. Galphin to Council of Safety, October 15, 1775, PHL, 10:467–68.

37. Galphin to Council of Safety, October 15, 1775, PHL, 10:468; Council of Safety to Wilkinson, October 24, 1775, PHL, 10:503; Galphin to Laurens, February 7, 1776, PHL, 11:94–95; Corkran, *The Creek Frontier*, 292–93.

38. Tonyn to . . . , October 25, 1775, CO 5/568, frame 72; Tonyn to . . . , December 18, 1775, CO 5/568, frame 83; Tonyn to Dartmouth, December 18, 1775, CO 5/556; "Welcome Headmen and Warriors . . . ," Conference at Cowford, St. John's River, December 6, 1775, CO 5/556; Talk to Usitchie Mico . . . , at the Cowford, St. John's River, December 8, 1775, CO 5/556; Tonyn to Taitt, April 20, 1776, Henry Clinton Papers, vol. 15; Corkran, *The Creek Frontier*, 294.

39. O'Donnell, *Southern Indians*, 21; Tonyn to Dartmouth, December 18, 1775, CO 5/556; Kalique response at the Cowford, St. John's River, December 7, 1775, CO 5/556; Galphin to Council of Safety, October 15, 1775, PHL, 10:468.

40. Tonyn to Germain, December 7, 1776, CO 5/557.

41. Brown to . . . , May 2, 1776, CO 5/556, frame 322; Address by the Commissioners of Indian Affairs . . . , November 13, 1775, in Saunders, ed., *Colonial and State Records*, 10:330–31; Address by Hamilton to the Creek Nation . . . , n.d., 1776, in Saunders, ed., *Colonial and State Records*, 10:329–30; Corkran, *The Creek Frontier*, 294; Cashin, *The King's Ranger*, 46.

42. Galphin to Jones, October 26, 1776, in Force, *American Archives*, series 5, 3:648–50.

43. Galphin to Laurens, February 7, 1776, PHL, 11:93–97; McIntosh to Lee, July 29, 1776, in Hawes, ed., "Letter Book of Lachlan McIntosh, 1776–1777: Part I," 159. These pleas evidently hit their mark, and Galphin appeared shortly after in the Lower Country with "promises of ammunition, liquor, and other presents," in a redoubled effort to tease headmen away to a larger meeting at Augusta. See Taitt to Tonyn, May 3, 1776, CO 5/556; Taitt to Tonyn, May 8, 1776, CO 5/556; Brown to . . . , May 8, 1776, CO 5/556, frame 324. Another group under American Jonathan Bryan was on its way into Creek Country with similar talks. See Brown to . . . , May 2, 1776, CO 5/556, frame 322; Taitt to Tonyn, May 1776, CO 5/556.

44. Brown to . . . , May 2, 1776, CO 5/556, frame 322; Address by the Commissioners of Indian Affairs . . . , November 13, 1775, in Saunders, ed., *Colonial and State Records*, 10:330–31; Address by Hamilton to the Creek Nation . . . , n.d., 1776, in Saunders, ed., *Colonial and State Records*, 10:329–30; Taitt to Tonyn, May 3, 1776, Henry Clinton Papers, vol. 16; Taitt to Tonyn, May 8, 1776, Henry Clinton Papers, vol. 16; Corkran, *The Creek Frontier*, 294; Cashin, *King's Ranger*, 46.

45. Taitt to Tonyn, May 3, 1776, CO 5/556; Taitt to Tonyn, May 8, 1776, CO 5/556; the group of Yuchis was later recalled. See Brown to . . . , May 8, 1776, CO 5/556, frame 324; Bast, "Creek Indian Affairs," 12–13.

46. Brown to . . . , May 8, 1776, co 5/556, frame 324; Address by Hamilton to the Creek Nation, n.d., 1776, in Saunders, ed., *Colonial and State Records*, 10:329–30; Bast, "Creek Indian Affairs," 12–13.

47. Taitt to Stuart, July 7, 1776, *DAR*, 13:159–62; Address by Hamilton to the Creek Nation, n.d., 1776, in Saunders, ed., *Colonial and State Records*, 10:329–30; Cashin, *King's Ranger*, 47–48.

48. Tonyn to Taitt, March 30, 2776, Henry Clinton Papers, vol. 16; Galphin to Jones, October 26, 1776, in Force, ed., *American Archives*, series 5, 3:648–50.

49. Galphin to Jones, October 26, 1776, in Force, ed., *American Archives*, series 5, 3:648–50.

50. Mereness, "Journal of David Taitt's Travels," 548; Boyd and Navarro Latorre, "Spanish Interest in British Florida," 93–94.

51. Calloway, *American Revolution in Indian Country*, 258, 260.

52. Brown to . . . , May 8, 1776, co 5/556, frame 324.

53. Taitt to Stuart, July 7, 1776, *DAR*, 13:159–62; Address by Hamilton to the Creek Nation, n.d., 1776, in Saunders, ed., *Colonial and State Records*, 10:329–30; Corkran, *The Creek Frontier*, 297–300; Searcy, *Georgia-Florida Contest*, 30.

54. Stuart to Tonyn, July 21, 1777, co 5/557; Tonyn to Stuart, June 16, 1777, co 5/557.

55. Stuart to Germain, August 10, 1778, *DAR*, 15:180–81; Tonyn to Stuart, September 8, 1778, co 5/558; Corkran, *The Creek Frontier*, 297.

56. Perdue, "A Sprightly Lover Is the Most Prevailing Missionary," 176–77.

57. For evidence of sustained Coweta attacks on Georgians, beginning after the affair in 1777, see Taitt to Stuart, May 23, 1777, *DAR*, 14:93–94; McIntosh to Tonyn, May 29, 1777, co 5/557; Taitt to Brown, May 29, 1777, co 5/557; Stuart to Prevost, July 24, 1777, *DAR*, 14:147–50; Tonyn to Germain, December 26, 1777, *DAR*, 14:275–77; Stuart to Germain, March 5, 1778, *DAR*, 15:54–55; Stuart to Germain, March 10, 1777, *DAR*, 14:49–50; Stuart to Germain, April 13, 1778, *DAR*, 15:96; Stuart to Germain, May 2, 1778, *DAR*, 15:113–14; Stuart to Tonyn, July 10, 1778, co 5/558; and Prevost to Germain, April 14, 1779, *DAR*, 17, 101–2.

58. Gage to Hillsborough, January 6, 1770, *DAR*, 2:25; Gage to Hillsborough, July 7, 1770, *DAR*, 2:136–37.

59. Escotchaby to Stuart, April 26, 1770, *DAR*, 2:86–87; Charles Stuart to John Stuart, June 17, 1770, *DAR*, 2:108–9; Philemon Kemp to Governor of Georgia with Talks from Emistisiguo and Gun Merchant, June 9, 1771, *DAR*, 3:118–21.

60. Stuart to Haldimand, February 3, 1774, *DAR*, 8:34–37; Stuart to Earl of Dartmouth, February 13, 1774, *DAR*, 8:48–49.

61. Cameron to Stuart, March 1, 1774, *DAR*, 8:56–57.

62. Galphin went on to explain that there was a plot formed at that time by a certain "Doctor Willis" and a number of people "in the ceded land of no property" and that the plan was "to have seized all the ammunition, and to have fell upon the Indians and killed them, and declared war on them." See Galphin to Jones, October 26, 1776, in Force, ed., *American Archives*, series 5, 3:648–50.

63. Galphin to Jones, October 26, 1776, in Force, ed., *American Archives*, series 5, 3:648–50; Howe to . . . , September 4, 1777, PCC, reel 87.

64. Galphin to Jones, October 26, 1776, in Force, ed., *American Archives*, series 5, 3:648–50; Galphin to Laurens, July 20, 1777, PHL, 11:403; Galphin to Laurens, October 13, 1777, PHL, 11:533; Clay to Laurens, October 16, 1777, PHL, 11:560–61; Clay to

Laurens, October 21, 1777, *PHL*, 11:576–77; Galphin to Laurens, December 22, 1777, *PHL*, 12:176–77; Galphin to Laurens, March 8, 1778, *PHL*, 12:525–26; Piecuch, *Three Peoples*, 112, 114.

65. Talk Sent by Tom Gray to Indians, December 23, 1776, Hawes, ed., "The Papers of Lachlan McIntosh, 1774–1799: Part IV," 61–62.

66. Galphin to Laurens, October 13, 1777, *PHL*, 11:533; Galphin to Laurens, December 22, 1777, *PHL*, 12:176–77.

67. Governor John Houstoun was described as a "worthy gentlemen" whom Laurens and others hoped would keep the surveyors at bay and the Creeks from slaughtering the inhabitants. Houstoun had declared that he would prevent further surveying and had plans to prosecute the surveyor that had been the cause of so much trouble. See Galphin to Laurens, March 8, 1777, *PHL*, 12:526.

68. Stuart to Germain, March 10, 1777, *DAR*, 14:49–50; Corkran, *The Creek Frontier*, 301–2.

69. Stuart to Germain, March 10, 1777, *DAR*, 14:49–50; Corkran, *The Creek Frontier*, 301–2.

70. Stuart to Howe, April 13, 1777, *DAR*, 14:68–69. "By informations of the different tribes," Tonyn agreed. See Tonyn to Stuart, April 15, 1777, CO 5/557.

71. McIntosh to Tonyn, May 29, 1777, CO 5/557; Taitt to Brown, May 29, 1777, CO 5/557.

72. Taitt to Stuart, May 23, 1777, *DAR*, 14:93–94; Taitt to Brown, May 23, 1777, *DAR*, 14:95–96; Tonyn to Stuart, June 16, 1777, CO 5/557; Wells Jr. to Laurens, June 23, 1777, *PHL*, 11:388; Searcy, *Georgia-Florida Contest*, 109–10.

73. McIntosh to Tonyn, May 29, 1777, CO 5/557; Taitt to Brown, May 29, 1777, CO 5/557; McIntosh to Cameron, July 1777, CO 5/557; Galphin to Laurens, July 20, 1777, *PHL*, 11:402–3.

74. Tonyn to Stuart, June 16, 1777, CO 5/557; McIntosh to Cameron, July 1777, CO 5/557; Wright to Germain, October 8, 1777, *CGHS*, 3:245.

75. Tonyn to Stuart, June 16, 1777, CO 5/557; McIntosh to Cameron, July 1777, CO 5/557; Taitt to Stuart, July 12, 1777, CO 5/557; Stuart to Tonyn, July 21, 1777, CO 5/557.

76. To the Handsome Man . . . , August 13, 1777, *KRC*, box 7, folder 42; Galphin to Laurens, December 22, 1777, *PHL*, 12:175–76; Stuart to Clinton, February 4, 1778, Henry Clinton Papers, vol. 31; Corkran, *The Creek Frontier*, 306–7.

77. Taitt to Tonyn, August 15, 1777, CO 5/557; Taitt to Tonyn,, August 24, 1777, CO 5/557; Searcy, *Georgia-Florida Contest*, 114.

78. Rutledge to Laurens, August 8, 1777, *PHL*, 11:434; Laurens to Galphin, September 16, 1777, *PHL*, 11:522; Corkran, *The Creek Frontier*, 307–8; O'Donnell, *Southern Indians*, 65–66; Searcy, *Georgia-Florida Contest*, 114–15.

79. Stuart to Germain, October 6, 1777, *DAR*, 14:192–94; Stuart to Clinton, February 4, 1778, Henry Clinton Papers, vol. 31; Taitt to Germain, August 6, 1779, *DAR*, 17:181; Corkran, *The Creek Frontier*, 307–8; O'Donnell, *Southern Indians*, 65–66; Searcy, *Georgia-Florida Contest*, 115; Howard, "Colonial Pensacola," 389–90.

80. Howe to Washington, November 3, 1777, in Chase, ed., *Papers of George Washington*, 12:103–4; Washington to Howe, January 13, 1778, in Chase, ed., *Papers of George Washington*, 13:221–22.

81. Galphin to Laurens, October 13, 1777, *PHL*, 11:553; Clay to Laurens, October 21, 1777, *PHL*, 11:576–77; Gervais to Laurens, November 3, 1777, *PHL*, 12:16; Galphin to Laurens, March 8, 1778, *PHL*, 12:525–26; Galphin to Laurens, June 25, 1778, *PHL*, 13:513.

82. Tonyn to Germain, December 26, 1777, DAR, 14:275–77; Gervais to Laurens, November 3, 1777, PHL, 12:16; Grimke, "Journal of the Campaign to the Southward," 121.

83. Corkran, *The Creek Frontier*, 303–4.

84. Taitt to Stuart, May 23, 1777, DAR, 14:93–94; McIntosh to Tonyn, May 29, 1777, CO 5/557; Taitt to Brown, May 29, 1777, CO 5/557; Stuart to Clinton, February 4, 1778, Henry Clinton Papers, vol. 31. According to one report, "several parties" of Cowetas were out well into the winter, according to Stuart, and they were being particularly violent. See Stuart to Germain, April 13, 1778, DAR, 15:96; Stuart to Germain, May 2, 1778, DAR, 15:113–14. One group killed dozens of Georgians during one series of attacks, including a number of Continentals, a handful of whom were officers. Taitt to Tonyn, August 15, 1777, CO 5/557; Taitt to Tonyn, August 24, 1777, CO 5/557; Searcy, *Georgia-Florida Contest*, 111–13.

85. Taitt to Stuart, May 23, 1777, DAR, 14:93–94; Stuart to Prevost, July 24, 1777, DAR, 14:147–50; Searcy, *Georgia-Florida Contest*, 111–13.

86. Galphin to Laurens, October 13, 1777, PHL, 11:552–53; Clay to Laurens, October 21, 1777, PHL, 11:576–77; Drayton to Laurens, November 1, 1777, PHL, 12:2; Galphin to Laurens, December 22, 1777, PHL, 12:175; Galphin to Laurens, June 25, 1778, PHL, 13:514.

87. Gervais to Laurens, August 16, 1777, PHL, 11:461.

88. Elbert to . . . , October 17, 1777, CGHS, vol. 5, part 2, 63; Parole-Washington, November 7, 1777, CGHS, vol. 5, part 2:70.

89. Several sources reported late in 1778 that raids were widespread and that Creeks were devastating the northern frontiers of Georgia. Houston to Laurens, August 20, 1778, PHL, 14:192; Clay to . . . , September 7, 1778, CGHS, 8:109–10; Clay to Laurens, September 9, 1778, CGHS, 8:105–6; Gervais to Laurens, September 21, 1778, PHL, 14:334. Early the next year a group of Cowetas attacked and routed a mounted militia unit there, killing a captain and four others and again spreading panic through the northern frontier. See Gervais to Laurens, February 16, 1778, PHL, 12:451; Galphin to Laurens, March 8, 1778, PHL, 12:526; Searcy, *Georgia-Florida Contest*, 132, 248–49. At the same time Creek chiefs were complaining about settlers on the Ceded Lands, they were increasingly taking matters into their own hands.

90. Galphin to Laurens, October 13, 1777, PHL, 11:553.

91. Clay to Laurens, October 16, 1777, PHL, 11:560–61; Clay to Laurens, October 21, 1777, PHL, 11:576–77.

92. Galphin to Laurens, December 22, 1777, PHL, 12:176–77.

93. Stuart to Clinton, February 4, 1778, Henry Clinton Papers, vol. 31. Stuart had used this tactic before. Before the Revolution, during the Ceded Lands crisis, he had cut off trade to force Creeks to turn over murderers in 1773; when he did it again in 1777, he saw the same results. See Braund, *Deerskins & Duffels*, 160–66.

94. Stuart to Clinton, February 4, 1778, Henry Clinton Papers, vol. 31; Corkran, *The Creek Frontier*, 309–10.

95. Tonyn to Germain, December 26, 1777, DAR, 14:275–77.

96. O'Donnell, *Southern Indians*, 75–76.

97. Stuart to Germain, May 19, 1778, DAR, 15:121–22.

98. Corkran, *The Creek Frontier*, 311.

99. Stuart to Germain, March 5, 1778, DAR, 15:54–55.

100. Stuart to Germain, May 2, 1778, DAR, 15:113–14; Corkran, *The Creek Frontier*, 311–13; O'Donnell, *Southern Indians*, 69–70.

101. Stuart to Knox, October 9–November 26, 1778, *DAR*, 15:211–12.

102. Houstoun to Laurens, October 1, 1778, *PHL*, 14:376.

103. Lowndes to Laurens, September 7, 1778, *PHL*, 14:287.

104. Gervais to Laurens, September 21, 1778, *PHL*, 14:334–35; Houstoun to Laurens, October 1, 1778, *PHL*, 14:376.

105. Corkran, *The Creek Frontier*, 313–15; Galphin to Laurens, June 25, 1778, *PHL*, 13:514.

106. Wells to Laurens, August 23, 1778, *PHL*, 14:213.

107. Stuart to Germain, August 10, 1778, *DAR*, 15:180–81.

108. For the vivid descriptions of this reversal, see Piecuch, *Three Peoples*.

109. This was evident in 1778 when a large American flotilla moved down the Mississippi. With Spanish aid and assistance, the expedition "pillaged and burned plantations, stole slaves, and forced the settlers to flee," bringing the war home to West Florida. See Starr, *Tories, Dons, and Rebels*, 78–122, quotation on 89. See also Wright, *Florida in the American Revolution*, 46–52.

110. Starr, *Tories, Dons, and Rebels*, 150–60, 168–74, 177–79, 193–215; Wright, *Florida in the American Revolution*, 76–81, 84–96. See also Rea, "British West Florida," 61–77; and Fabel, "West Florida and British Strategy."

111. Stuart to Tonyn, July 21, 1777, CO 5/557; Stuart to Prevost, July 24, 1777, *DAR*, 14:147–50; Taitt to Germain, August 6, 1779, *DAR*, 17:178–80.

112. Wayne to Greene, February 1, 1782, in Showman, ed., *Papers of Nathanael Greene*, 10:301–2; O'Donnell, *Southern Indians*, 114–16.

113. Corkran, *The Creek Frontier*, 322; O'Donnell, *Southern Indians*, 121–23.

114. Wayne to Greene, May 4, 1782, in Showman, ed., *Papers of Nathanael Greene*, 11:156.

115. Wayne to Greene, June 15, 1782, in Showman, ed., *Papers of Nathanael Greene*, 11:338; Wayne to Greene, June 24, 1782, in Showman, ed., *Papers of Nathanael Greene*, 11:365–67; Brown to Earl of Shelbourne, September 25, 1782, *DAR*, 21:122; Lee, *Memoirs of the War*, 406–11; Corkran, *The Creek Frontier*, 321; O'Donnell, *Southern Indians*, 123.

3. Georgia Treaties and Creek Partisans

1. For other studies that deal with this period, see Coleman, *The American Revolution in Georgia*; and Phillips, *Georgia and State Rights*, 40–42.

2. Friends and Brothers, January 11, 1782, in Martin, "Official Letters of Governor John Martin, 1782–1783," 282–85.

3. Martin to the Tallassee King and Head Men . . . , July 19, 1782, in Martin, "Official Letters of Governor John Martin, 1782–1783," 313–15.

4. "The violent conflicts of the preceding decades," one historian suggested, "indelibly stamped postwar culture." Entire families and communities "had bled for the land at Indian hands, as passive sufferers and as conquerors, and now that land was theirs." Hinderaker, *Elusive Empires*, 226, 233–34. For an idea of this elsewhere, see Sadosky, *Revolutionary Negotiations*, 121; Calloway, *American Revolution in Indian Country*, 281–87; Horsman, *Expansion and American Indian Policy*, 5; Hurt, *The Indian Frontier*, 103–4; and Prucha, *American Indian Policy*, 34.

5. A Talk sent by his honor the Governor and beloved men of Georgia . . . , IT, 112–14.

6. Martin to the Tallassee King and Head Men . . . , July 19, 1782, in Martin, "Official Letters of Governor John Martin, 1782–1783," 313–15.

7. James Rae letter with enclosed Indian Talk, December 28, 1782, TCC, box 77, folder 25; McMurphy to Martin, September 22, 1782, CIL, 1:30–32; Henderson to Martin, September 23, 1782, CIL, 1:33; Rae to Hall, January 29, 1783, CIL, 1:47.

8. James Rae letter with enclosed Indian Talk, December 28, 1782, TCC, box 77, folder 25; Martin to Pickens, May 27, 1782, CIL, 1:25; Calloway, *American Revolution in Indian Country*, 284; Dowd, *A Spirited Resistance*, 96.

9. Jones to Martin, September 29, 1782, CIL, 1:35.

10. Henderson to Martin, December 23, 1782, CIL, 1:42–44; McMurphy to Martin, September 22, 1782, CIL, 1:30–32.

11. Hatley, *The Dividing Paths*, 12–13; Weisman, *Unconquered People*, 9.

12. Several historians and anthropologists have commented on the presence of moieties as well as the vagueness of the system. See, for instance, Wesson, *Households and Hegemony*, 25–26; Hudson, *The Southeastern Indians*, 234–37; Swan, "Position and State," 265; Ethridge, *Creek Country*, 93–94; Saunt, *A New Order of Things*, 22–23; Green, *Politics of Indian Removal*, 7–8; and Braund, *Deerskins & Duffels*, 7–8. Champagne makes the strongest case for the centrality of the red-white division, as well as for its longevity. See Champagne, *Social Order*.

13. Swanton, *Social Organization*, 55.

14. Swanton, *Social Organization*, 248–57. Swanton referred to Tallassees as Tulsas, who could trace their lineage back to the Mississippian Coosa chiefdom. See Swanton, *Early History of the Creek Indians*, 243–46.

15. Even years later, Benjamin Hawkins commended the unflinchingly friendly disposition of Cussetas toward Americans, something that he saw as abiding even to a fault. See Foster, *The Collected Works*, 59s.

16. Calloway, *American Revolution in Indian Country*, 273–77.

17. Rae to Hall, September 22, 1783, CIL, 1:49; Rae to Hall, September 24, 1783, CIL, 1:50.

18. McMurphy to Martin, September 22, 1782, CIL, 1:30–32; Henderson to Martin, September 23, 1782, CIL, 1:33; Henderson to Martin, September 27, 1782, CIL, 1:34; Carr to Martin, December 13, 1782, CIL, 1:40–41.

19. Substance of Talks delivered at a conference . . . , May 15, 1783, CO 5/560; extract of a letter received by Capt. Bissett, May 20, 1783, CO 5/560; Wright, *Florida in the American Revolution*, 133–35.

20. McGillivray to . . . , April 10, 1783, Alexander McGillivray Letters. In September 1783 it was reported that large numbers of headmen were on their way to Augusta for the general meeting. See Rae to Hall, September 22, 1783, CIL, 1:49; Rae to Hall, September 24, 1783, CIL, 1:50.

21. Articles of a convention held at Augusta . . . , November 1, 1783, KRC, box 6, folder 21; Clarke to Hall, November 6, 1783, TCC, box 39, folder Hall 09; House of Assembly, February 23, 1784, TCC, box 77, folder 15.

22. Augusta, June 6, 1783, IT, 115.

23. Articles of a convention held at Augusta . . . , November 1, 1783, KRC, box 6, folder 21; Clarke to Hall, November 6, 1783, TCC, box 39, folder Hall 09; House of Assembly, February 23, 1784, TCC, box 77, folder 15; A Talk sent by his honor the Governor and beloved men of Georgia . . . , IT, 112–14.

24. Clay to Laurens, March 15, 1784, *PHL*, 16:419.

25. Clarke to Hall, November 6, 1783, TCC, box 39, folder Hall 09; Augusta, June 6, 1783, IT, 115; Treaty of Augusta . . . , IT, 129–31.

26. Extract from the minutes . . . , March 23, 1784, TCC, box 37, folder 14; Downes, "Creek-American Relations," 146.

27. A Talk delivered by the Gov . . . , September 24, 1784, IT, 164–68.

28. To the Governor and Council . . . , May 5, 1785, IT, 169–70; Habersham to Houstoun, June 19, 1784, KRC, box 11, folder 18; Petition of the inhabitants of Burke County . . . , May 5, 1785, TCC, box 23, folder 28.

29. Henderson to Martin, December 23, 1782, CIL, 1:42–44; Rae to Hall, January 29, 1783, CIL, 1:47; Rae to Hall, September 24, 1783, CIL, 1:50.

30. McGillivray to . . . , June 30, 1784, TCC, box 80, folder 5; Downes, "Creek-American Relations," 144–45.

31. McGillivray to . . . , June 30, 1784, TCC, box 80, folder 5; McGillivray to O'Neill, March 28, 1786, *MC*, 104–5; House of Assembly, February 23, 1784, TCC, box 77, folder 15; Downes, "Creek-American Relations, " 144–45.

32. To the Creek Traders . . . , 1783, IT, 116; Memo of the Kings Proposals and Complaints . . . , IT, 117–20.

33. Braund, "'Like a Stone Wall Never to Be Broke,'" 58–59; Ethridge, "A Brief Sketch," 19.

34. The Mortar of Hookchoie, for instance, explained in 1765 how "we had formerly good success in hunting but are now obliged to Cross the Cherokee River for Game." See Wednesday, May 2, 1765, in Rowland, ed., *Mississippi Provincial Archives, English Dominion*, 1:204. The Tussekiah Mico, in a regional meeting, warned both Abihkas and other communities in the neighborhood, as well as Chickasaws, not to harass each other on their hunts. See October 28, 1797, *LJW*, 135.

35. As David Taitt revealed in 1772, "The Fighter and Emistisiguo are gone towards Pensacola to hunt and afterwards to war against the Choctaws, there are some Cowetas and most of the Tallipouses and Savannahs are gone down towards Pensacola and Tensa to hunt." See Taitt to Stuart, November 22, 1772, *DAR*, 5:224. Caleb Swan also mentioned the position of those hunting lands years later when talking about the Alabama River: "This long river, and its main branches, form the western line of settlements of villages of the Creek nation, but their hunting-grounds extend 200 miles beyond, to the Tombigbee river, which is the dividing line between their country and that of the Choctaws." See Swan, "Position and State," 257. See also Braund, "'Like a Stone Wall Never to Be Broke,'" 54–55.

36. Cheehaugh Town, June 28, 1786, CIL, 1:124; Braund, *Deerskins & Duffels*, 62; Wright, *Creeks & Seminoles*, 63–64.

37. For the Yuchi hunters, see Gaither to Blackshear, January 7, 1798, CIL, 2:505. For a Chehaw hunting "many years about Okefinacau (quivering water)," see February 18, 1797, *LJW*, 48–49. For Hawkins being at Broken Arrow (Coweta Tallahassee) and hearing about men from that area hunting in the neighborhood of the Cumberland, see January 23, 1797, *LJW*, 37–38. For attacks on Cussetas, see Freeman to Secretary of War, January 1, 1794, ASPIA, 1:472; Hawkins to McHenry, September 20, 1797, *LJW*, 128–29; and Hawkins to Dinsmoor, September 20, 1797, *LJW*, 130–31. For more on land claims from specific Creeks, see Braund, *Deerskins & Duffels*, 62; Wright, *Creeks & Seminoles*, 63–64; and Braund, "'Like a Stone Wall Never to Be Broke,'" 54–55.

38. Wright, *Creeks & Seminoles*, 63–64; Braund, *Deerskins & Duffels*, 62. "The Indians are extremely tenacious of their hunting grounds," Alexander McGillivray penned in 1785, "of which that between Oconee & Ogeechee [form] a principal part & on which they generally take three thousand deer skins yearly." See McGillivray to Clark, April 24, 1785, CIL, 1:89. Later Hawkins remarked on the staggering numbers of hunters that moved east to the Georgia border each hunting season. See Hawkins to Habersham, December 20, 1797, LJW, 169–70; Hawkins to McHenry, January 4, 1798, LJW, 171–72; and Hawkins to Habersham, December 23, 1798, LJW, 228.

39. Journal entry for February 18, CGHS, 9:86; Braund, *Deerskins & Duffels*, 62; Ethridge, *Creek Country*, 136–37.

40. Kathryn E. H. Braund explores in depth Creeks' individual claims to specific pieces of land that they hunted and managed. See Braund, "'Like a Stone Wall Never to Be Broke,'" 54–55. J. Leitch Wright Jr. also gave evidence that, prior to this period, the sale of lands created controversy in Creek Country. See Wright, *Creeks & Seminoles*, 107–8.

41. White to McGillivray, April 4, 1787, ASPIA, 1:21–22.

42. House of Assembly, February 23, 1784, TCC, box 77, folder 15.

43. A Talk delivered by the Fat King, April 5, 1784, IT, 132–33. For further evidence that the chiefs were provided for well at the treaty, see reports of James Rae, Alexander McDonald, and John Wright, CIL, 1:66; and Publick of Georgia to Andrew Whitefield, September 30, 1784, CIL, 1:67.

44. A Talk delivered by the honorable John Habersham, April 9, 1784, IT, 134–36; Copy of Mr. Barnard's Talk . . . , June 2, 1784, IT, 140–42.

45. Barnard to Carr, October 21, 1784, LTB, 36–37; A talk del'd in Council . . . , July 15, 1784, IT, 148–50.

46. A Talk delivered by the second man of the Cussetaws . . . , July 14, 1784, IT, 145–47; Talk delivered by the Gov. . . . , September 24, 1784, IT, 164–68.

47. A Talk delivered by the second man of the Cussetaws . . . , July 14, 1784, IT, 145–47; A Talk delivered by the Tallassie King, September 20, 1784, IT, 159–60; A Talk delivered by the second man of the Cussetaws . . . , July 14, 1784, IT, 145–47.

48. A Talk delivered by the Tallassie King, September 20, 1784, IT, 159–60; A Talk delivered by the second man of the Cussetaws . . . , July 14, 1784, IT, 145–47.

49. Horsman, *Expansion and American Indian Policy*, 27–28.

50. Copy of Mr. Barnard's Talk . . . , June 2, 1784, IT, 140–42; Cussetaws, June 2, 1784, LTB, 33a–33; Downes, "Creek-American Relations," 146–47.

51. McGillivray to . . . , April 10, 1783, Alexander McGillivray Letters; McGillivray to . . . , June 30, 1784, TCC, box 80, folder 5.

52. McGillivray to O'Neill, November 20, 1784, MC, 84; McGillivray to McLatchy, December 25, 1784, MC, 86.

53. To the Kings Headmen and Warriors of the Creeks, June 10, 1785, MC, 96; McGillivray to O'Neill, September 14, 1785, MC, 97. For his part, McGillivray actually thought violence could be avoided if the Georgians continued down such a path. Later, in the spring of 1785, he still hoped the Georgia legislature would "decide on the part of Justice & humanity" and not plunge the region into "all the Horrors of a merciless Indian War." See McGillivray to O'Neill, November 20, 1784, MC, 84; McGillivray to Clark, April 24, 1785, TCC, box 80, folder 5.

54. Dowd, *A Spirited Resistance*, 96–98.

55. Using Native allies as the backbone of their frontier defenses was an approach deeply ingrained in Spanish policy. See Wright, *Creeks & Seminoles*, 122–23; Weber, *The Spanish Frontier*, 282–83; Berry, "The Indian Policy of Spain in the Southwest"; and Whitaker, "Spanish Intrigue in the Old Southwest."

56. O'Neill to Sonora, July 11, 1787, MC, 156–57. Zéspedes shared these views as well. See Zéspedes to McGillivray, June 13, 1785, EFP, reel 43. For an explanation of this policy to the king of Spain, see Valdez to King of Spain, February 1, 1788, PdE, legajo 3887. See also Berry, "The Indian Policy of Spain in the Southwest," 462–63; and Mohr, *Federal Indian Relations*, 143–47.

57. McGillivray to O'Neill, January 1, 1784, MC, 64–66; Zéspedes to O'Neill, June 15, 1785, in Lockey, *East Florida*, 559–60; Zéspedes to Gálvez, June 20, 1785, in Lockey, *East Florida*, 562–64.

58. Wright, *Creeks & Seminoles*, 50–53. For a complete discussion of the trading firm, see Coker and Watson, *Indian Traders of the Southeastern Spanish Borderlands*.

59. From the Creek standpoint, as J. Leitch Wright asserted, "there was more continuity and stability than the abrupt changes in sovereignty suggested." See Wright, *Creeks & Seminoles*, 454.

60. O'Neill to Ezpeleta, October 19, 1783, MC, 62–63; Miró to Gálvez, August 1, 1784, EHW, box 2, folder Legajo 3885; Ynstrucciones a que debara . . . , July 20, 1784, EHW, box 2, folder Legajo 3885; Miró to Gálvez, April 15, 1784, EHW, box 2, folder AHN legajo 3885.

61. Braund, *Deerskins & Duffels*, 173–74; Weber, *The Spanish Frontier*, 283–85.

62. McGillivray to O'Neill, February 8, 1784, MC, 71; McGillivray to Miró, MPASD, 2:58; Watson, "Strivings for Sovereignty," 402–3; Kinnaird, "International Rivalry," 65.

63. McGillivray to Govr of West Florida, January 1, 1784, CIL, 2:52b–c; Watson, "Strivings for Sovereignty," 403–4. Creek Indians to Zéspedes, December 8, 1784, EFP, reel 43. For an excellent examination of McGillivray's line of thinking here, see Stock, "Sovereign or Suzerain."

64. Miró to McGillivray, June 7, 1784, MC, 77; Zéspedes to Gálvez, June 12, 1785, in Lockey, *East Florida*, 556–58; Miró to Gálvez, April 15, 1784, EHW, box 2, folder Legajo 3885; Puntos que deben observer [Navarro to McGillivray], June 1, 1784, EHW, box 2, folder AHN legajo 3885; Ynstrucctiones a que debara . . . , July 20, 1784, EHW, box 2, folder AHN legajo 3885; Weber, *The Spanish Frontier*, 283–85; Kinnaird, "International Rivalry," 65; Holmes, "Spanish Treaties with West Florida Indians," 142.

65. Rae to Hall, September 24, 1783, CIL, 1:50; Creek Indians to Zéspedes, December 8, 1784, EFP, reel 43.

66. Zéspedes to Lower Creeks, December 8, 1784, EFP, reel 43.

67. Miró to Navarro, April 15, 1784, EHW, box 2, folder AHN legajo 3885; Miró to Gálvez, April 15, 1784, EHW, box 2, folder AHN legajo 3885; Bell and Dugless to Robertson, July 10, 1784, TCC, box 77, folder 7; Pensacola, June 1, 1784, PdE, legajo 3885; Miró to Gálvez, August 1, 1784, EHW, box 2, folder AHN legajo 3885; Gálvez to Gálvez, April 10, 1785, PdE, legajo 3898; Gálvez to Gálvez, April 14, 1785, PdE, legajo 3898; Holmes, "Spanish Treaties with West Florida Indians," 140–43; Weber, *The Spanish Frontier*, 282–83.

68. A Talk delivered by the second man of the Cussetaws . . . , July 14, 1784, IT, 145–46. Later, in 1786, chiefs who wore "British Medals" were requested to come south to

"give them up and take Spanish Ones." See Davenport to Sevier, July 28, 1786, TCC, box 77, folder 26; and Pittslaw to Davenport, September 5, 1786, CIL, 1:136.

69. For a general appraisal of this idea, see Holmes, "Juan de la Villebeuvre and Spanish Indian Policy in West Florida"; Kinnaird, Blache, and Blache, "Spanish Treaties with Indian Tribes," 40–41; Holmes, "La Ultima Barrera"; Berry, "The Indian Policy of Spain in the Southwest"; McGillivray to Zéspedes, May 22, 1785, MC, 87–88; and Downes, "Creek-American Relations," 142.

70. McGillivray to Miró, May 16, 1785, PPdC, legajo 198; McGillivray to Zéspedes, May 22, 1784, in Lockey, *East Florida*, 545–47; Zéspedes to McGillivray, June 13, 1785, EFP, reel 43.

71. McGillivray to O'Neill, July 6, 1785, MC, 90; McGillivray to O'Neill, September 14, 1785, MC, 97; McGillivray to O'Neill, September 14, 1785, PPdC, legajo 198.

72. McGillivray for the Chiefs of the Creek, Chickasaw, and Cherokee Nations, July 10, 1785, MC, 90–91; McGillivray to Miró, August 2, 1785, PPdC, legajo 198; Miró to Gálvez, September 5, 1785, MPASD, 1:522–27.

73. Friends and Brothers, Coweitter, August 17, 1785, CIL, 1:83–84.

74. McGillivray to Pickens, September 5, 1785, ASPIA, 1:18.

75. McGillivray to O'Neill, September 14, 1785, MC, 97; Durouzeaux to Elbert, September 21, 1785, CIL, 1:96–98.

76. McGillivray to O'Neill, February 10, 1786, MC, 102–3; McGillivray to Miró, May 1, 1786, MC, 106–7; McGillivray to Zéspedes, August 22, 1785, EFP, reel 43; Downes, "Creek-American Relations," 150–51.

77. McGillivray to Durouzeaux, September 12, 1785, CIL, 1:94–95; Hawkins to McGillivray, January 8, 1786, EHW, box 2, folder AHN legajo 3886; Downes, "Creek-American Relations," 148.

78. McGillivray to O'Neill, February 10, 1786, MC, 102–3; McGillivray to Miró, May 1, 1786, MC, 106–7; Downes, "Creek-American Relations," 149–51.

79. Sundries furnished the Indians, Savannah . . . , June 10 and 17, 1785, TCC, box 1, folder 11.

80. Hawkins to McGillivray, January 8, 1786, MC, 101; Hawkins to McGillivray, January 11, 1786, PPdC, legajo 2360; McGillivray to O'Neill, February 10, 1786, MC, 102–3; McGillivray to Miró, May 1, 1786, MC, 106–7; Downes, "Creek-American Relations," 151–52; Horsman, *Expansion and American Indian Policy*, 28–29.

81. Barnard to Barnett, June 18, 1785, LTB, 48–50.

82. Dorouzeaux to Clark, May 25, 1785, CIL, 1:76–78; Wright, "Creek-American Treaty of 1790," 383–84.

83. Barnard to Barnett, June 18, 1785, LTB, 48–50.

84. Marbury to Gibbons, December 19, 1785, William Gibbons Jr. Papers, in Stampp, ed., *Records of Ante-bellum Southern Plantations*, series 4, part 2, reel 1.

85. McGillivray to Habersham, November 28, 1786, TCC, box 80, folder 5.

86. McGillivray to Zéspedes, April 25, 1786, EFP, reel 43.

87. Hawkins to McGillivray, January 11, 1786, PdE, legajo 3886; McGillivray to Zéspedes, December 10, 1785, EFP, reel 43.

88. McGillivray to O'Neill, March 8, 1786, MC, 103–4; McGillivray to O'Neill, March 28, 1786, MC, 104–5; McGillivray to Miró, May 1, 1786, MC, 106–7.

89. McGillivray to . . . , Little Tallasee, September 2, 1785, CIL, 1:86–88.

90. McGillivray to O'Neill, March 8, 1786, PPdC, legajo 199; O'Neill to Zéspedes, April 19, 1786, EFP, reel 43; McGillivray to Miró, May 1, 1786, MC, 106–7; McGillivray to O'Neill, March 28, 1786, MC, 104–5; Watson, "Strivings for Sovereignty," 405.

91. McGillivray to Zéspedes, April 25, 1786, EFP, reel 43; McGillivray to Miró, May 1, 1786, MC, 106–7.

92. McGillivray to O'Neill, March 28, 1786, MC, 104–5; McGillivray to Hallowing King, April 14, 1786, PPdC, legajo 37; The Information of Abner Hammond, April 20, 1786, TCC, box 77, folder 33; McGillivray to Hallowing King of the Cowetas, April 14, 1786, CIL, 1:101.

93. McGillivray to Hallowing King of the Cowetas, April 14, 1786, CIL, 1:101; Telfair to Cleveland, Walton, and other Gent . . . , May 1, 1786, McGillivray to Hallowing King of the Cowetas, April 14, 1786, CIL, 1:102.

94. McGillivray to O'Neill, May 12, 1786, MPASD, 2:655–59.

95. McGillivray to O'Neill, March 28, 1786, PPdC, legajo 199; O'Neill to Gardoqui, April 19, 1786, PdE, legajo 3893; O'Neill to Zéspedes, April 19, 1786, EFP, reel 43; McGillivray to Zéspedes, August 3, 1786, EFP, reel 43.

96. Talk from the Lower Towns in the Creek Nation, August 11, 1786, TCC, box 77, folder 33.

97. Copy of Cusata King's Talk . . . , April 11, 1786, TCC, box 78, folder 12.

98. The Information of Abner Hammond, April 20, 1786, TCC, box 77, folder 33. For another group of Creeks going down to St. Augustine, see Carr to Telfair, April 26, 1786, TCC, box 1, folder 32; and McMurphy to O'Neill, July 11, 1786, MC, 118–20.

99. Bell and Dugless to Robertson, July 10, 1784, TCC, box 77, folder 7.

100. Copy of Mr. Barnard's Talk . . . , June 2, 1784, IT, 140–42. For the Georgia preparations, see Gálvez to Gálvez, January 26, 1786, PdE, legajo 3898; Carr to Telfair, April 26, 1786, TCC, box 1, folder 32.

101. Stephens to Read, July 28, 1786, FHP, box 3, folder 41; McGillivray to Spanish Officials, July 10, 1785, MC, 90–93; Downes, "Creek-American Relations," 153–55.

102. White to Gorham, October 11, 1786, in Smith et al., eds., *Letters to Delegates of Congress*, 23:595.

103. Clements to Telfair, May 6, 1786, CIL, 1:103; Telfair to Cleveland, Walton, and Cleveland, May 19, 1786, CIL, 1:109.

104. Inman to Telfair, May 23, 1786, CMT, box 1, folder 1; letter to Inman, May 23, 1786, CMT, box 1, folder 2.

105. Cleveland, Walton, and Cleveland to Telfair, May 15, 1786, CIL, 1:107; Thompson to Governor and Executive Council, May 17, 1786, CIL, 1:108.

106. Clements to Telfair, May 6, 1786, CIL, 1:103; Galphin to Clements, May 6, 1786, CIL, 1:104; Fort to Telfair, May 14, 1786, CIL, 1:105.

107. Clements to Telfair, May 14, 1786, CIL, 1:106; letter to Inman, May 23, 1786, CMT, box 1, folder 2; McMurphy to O'Neill, July 11, 1786, MC, 118–20; E. T. to Houstoun and Few, August 20, 1786, FT, 66–67.

108. A Talk from the head men of the Cussetaws . . . , May 2, 1786, LTB, 51–54.

109. A Talk from the headmen . . . , May 17, 1786, LTB, 51–54.

110. Telfair to Cleveland, Walton, and Cleveland, May 19, 1786, CIL, 1:109; Telfair to Durouzeaux, May 30, 1786, CIL, 1:112; Durouzeaux to Barnard, June 13, 1786, CIL, 1:116–17; Weed and Semple to Telfair, June 19, 1786, CIL, 1:120–23.

111. Letter from Cheehaugh Town, translated by John Harvard, June 28, 1786, CIL, 1:124; Telfair to Cleveland, Walton, and Cleveland, May 19, 1786, CIL, 1:109; Clarke

to Telfair, May 23, 1786, CIL, 1:112; Weed and Semple to Telfair, June 19, 1786, CIL, 1:120–21.

112. E. T. to Houstoun and Few, August 20, 1786, FT, 66–67; E. T. to Sevier, August 27, 1786, FT, 68–69.

113. Telfair to Durouzeaux, May 30, 1786, CIL, 1:110–11.

114. McGillivray to . . . , September 16, 1786, TCC, box 80, folder 5; McGillivray to Habersham, September 18, 1786, MC, 13–131.

115. McMurphy to . . . , May 30, 1786, CIL, 1:113; Durouzeaux to Telfair, June 5, 1786, CIL, 1:114–15.

116. A Talk from the headmen . . . , May 17, 1786, LTB, 51–54.

117. McGillivray to O'Neill, August 12, 1786, MC, 127–28; McMurphy to Telfair, July 30, 1786, CIL, 1:129–32; McMurphy to Telfair, July 30, 1786, CIL, 1:129–32.

118. McMurphy to Telfair, July 30, 1786, CIL, 1:129–32.

119. Barnard to . . . , October 17, 1786, LTB, 66–69.

120. McMurphy to . . . , June 29, 1786, CIL, 1:125–26; McMurphy to Telfair, July 30, 1786, CIL, 1:129–32.

121. McMurphy to . . . , June 29, 1786, CIL, 1:125–26.

122. Durouzeaux to Habersham, September 23, 1786, CIL, 1:139.

123. McMurphy to O'Neill, July 11, 1786, MC, 118–20. McMurphy, like most Georgians, understood that all lands and peoples up to the confluence of the Chattahoochee and Flint rivers were under some level of American jurisdiction. This was a view commonly shared even in Philadelphia. Spaniards and Creeks, on the other hand, recognized the American holdings as essentially the same as the 1773 British holdings. This meant that all the lands to the west of the Oconee belonged to regional Natives, who were now also under the protection of the Spanish crown. See McMurphy to O'Neill, July 11, 1786, MC, 118–20; Wednesday, July 18, 1787, in Ford et al., eds., *Journals*, 33:365–68.

124. McMurphy to O'Neill, July 11, 1786, MC, 118–20; Talk of Part of the Creek Indians to the Georgia Legislature, August 3, 1786, MC, 123.

125. McGillivray to Governor of Georgia, August 3, 1786, TCC, box 80, folder 5; Talk of Part of the Creek Indians to the Georgia Legislature, August 3, 1786, MC, 123; McGillivray to O'Neill, August 12, 1786, MC, 127–28; McMurphy to Telfair, July 30, 1786, CIL, 1:129–32.

126. McGillivray to Governor of Georgia, August 3, 1786, TCC, box 80, folder 5.

127. Barnard to Telfair, August 14, 1786, LTB, 59–61; O'Neill to Sonora, February 20, 1787, MC, 144. Naturally, the flow of weapons increased as well. See O'Neill to Miró, March 1, 1787, PdE, legajo, 3887; McGillivray to O'Neill, March 4, 1787, PdE, legajo 3887.

128. Reports from Augusta, Georgia, August 1 and 15, 1786, MC, 121–22.

129. E. T. to Houstoun and Few, August 20, 1786, in "Some Official Letters of Governor Edward Telfair," 147; E. T. to Sevier, August 27, 1786, in "Some Official Letters of Governor Edward Telfair," 148–49.

130. Telfair to Durouzeaux, May 30, 1786, CIL, 1:110–11.

131. A Talk to the Kings, Headmen, and Warriors . . . , October 21, 1786, TCC, box 77, folder 22; E. T. to James, August 27, 1786, FT, 69–70; E. T. to Twiggs, October 11, 1786, FT, 73; E. T. to James, August 27, 1786, in "Some Official Letters of Governor Edward Telfair," 149–50; Downes, "Creek-American Relations," 155–56.

132. A Talk to the Kings, Headmen, and Warriors . . . , October 21, 1786, TCC, box 77, folder 22; McGillivray to White, April 8, 1787, ASPIA, 1:18–19; McGillivray to Pinckney, February 26, 1789, ASPIA, 1:19–20.

133. Board of Commissioners, November 8, 1786, CIL, 1:145–46; A Talk Delivered by the Kings, Headmen, and Warriors, October 22, 1786, TCC, box 77, folder 22; A Talk Delivered to the Kings, Headmen, and Warriors . . . , October 23, 1786, TCC, box 77, folder 22; Galphin to the Honorable Board of Commissioners, October 26, 1786, TCC, box 78, folder 4; Watson, "Strivings for Sovereignty," 405–6.

134. Downes, "Creek-American Relations, 1782–1790," 159.

135. Barnard to . . . , October 17, 1786, LTB, 66–69.

136. A Talk Delivered by the Kings, Headmen, and Warriors, October 22, 1786, TCC, box 77, folder 22; A Talk Delivered to the Kings, Headmen, and Warriors . . . , October 23, 1786, TCC, box 77, folder 22.

137. Telfair to Martin, November 28, 178[?], in Draper and Harper, eds., *Draper Manuscript Collection*, series XX, Tennessee Papers, vols. 1–3, reel 126; Dowd, *A Spirited Resistance*, 97–98.

138. Talk of the Tallassee King, April 11, 1787, LTB, 73–75; Dowd, *A Spirited Resistance*, 98.

139. Galphin to the Honorable Board of Commissioners, October 26, 1786, TCC, box 78, folder 4; McGillivray to O'Neill, October 30, 1786, MC, 135; Davenport to Governor of Georgia, November 1, 1786, TCC, box 40A, folder Telfair 29.

140. Affidavit of Richard Call, October 4, 1789, TCC, box 78, folder 21.

141. McGillivray to O'Neill, November 9, 1786, LC, box 5, folder November 1786; Dowd, *A Spirited Resistance*, 98.

142. A Talk of the head men of the Buzzard roust . . . , May 1, 1787, CIL, 1:155; Dowd, *A Spirited Resistance*, 98. For a similar report, see White to Knox, May 24, 1787, ASPIA, 1:20–21.

143. McGillivray to Governor of Florida, November 15, 1786, MC, 138–39; McGillivray to Zéspedes, January 5, 1787, EFP, reel 43; Dowd, *A Spirited Resistance*, 98. He also later wrote that, after Augusta, the two "regardless of the voice of the Nation, continued to go to Augusta, and other places within the State, continuing to make such promises, to obtain presents, our customs not permitting us to punish them for the crime." See McGillivray to White, April 8, 1787, ASPIA, 1:18–19.

4. Partisan Creeks at War

1. There is not much coverage of this important period in Georgia history. See Griffith, *McIntosh and Weatherford*, 36–41; Coleman, *The American Revolution in Georgia*, 238–49; Green, *Politics of Indian Removal*, 34–45; and Downes, "Creek-American Relations."

2. McGillivray to Favrot, November 8, 1786, MC, 135–36; McGillivray to Zéspedes, November 15, 1786, MC, 138–40.

3. McGillivray to Habersham, November 28, 1786, TCC, box 80, folder 5.

4. McGillivray to O'Neill, December 3, 1786, MC, 140–41; Dowd, *A Spirited Resistance*, 96.

5. Barnard to Telfair, August 22, 1786, LTB, 61–63.

6. For several investigations into McGillivray's background, many of which point out how exceptional his life was in Creek Country, see Zéspedes to Gálvez, June 12, 1785, LC, box 4, folder May 1785; Report from H. Knox, Secretary of War . . . , July 6, 1789, ASPIA, 1:15–16; Saunt, *A New Order of Things*, 67–76; Dowd, *A Spirited Resistance*, 90–91; Braund, *Deerskins & Duffels*, 171; Wright, "Creek-American Treaty of 1790," 385; and Langley, "The Tribal Identity of Alexander McGillivray."

7. For this idea of Creek identity, see Frank, *Creeks and Southerners*.

8. Swanton, *Social Organization*, 303. According to Green, beloved men sat at councils "offering suggestions and clearing away obfuscation" and were widely respected. Because McGillivray was well versed in European and American culture, and could speak English, he certainly was "politically astute enough," and it is not surprising that, although he was young, he achieved such a title. See Green, "Alexander McGillivray," 49.

9. Speck, *The Creek Indians of Taskigi Town*, 114.

10. A Talk from the Head-men and Chiefs . . . , May 23, 1789, ASPIA, 1:34.

11. Harper, ed., *Travels*, 313–14; Bartram and Harper, "Travels in Georgia, and Florida," 139; "A Sketch of the Creek Country," *LJW*, 1:317–18. For micos, see Swanton, *Social Organization*, 276–98; Wesson, *Households and Hegemony*, 26–28; Hudson, *The Southeastern Indians*, 223–24; Ethridge, *Creek Country*, 102–3; Green, "Alexander McGillivray," 49; and Green, *Politics of Indian Removal*, 8–10.

12. Wright, *Creeks & Seminoles*, 29–30; Griffith, *McIntosh and Weatherford*, 26–28.

13. Carondelet to Aranda, June 11, 1792, PdE, legajo 3898; Dowd, *A Spirited Resistance*, 100.

14. See Green, *Politics of Indian Removal*, 7; Green, "Alexander McGillivray," 50–51; Martin, *Sacred Revolt*, 123; and Ethridge, *Creek Country*, 102–3.

15. Wright, "Creek-American Treaty of 1790," 382; Green, "Alexander McGillivray," 43.

16. For the long-standing disagreements between McGillivray and the two headmen, see Green, "Alexander McGillivray," 49–50. McGillivray personally insulted the prestige of the Fat King and Tallassee King on several occasions. See McGillivray to Governor of Georgia, August 3, 1786, TCC, box 80, folder 5; McGillivray to Pinckney, February 26, 1789, ASPIA, 1:19–20; and McGillivray to O'Neill, December 3, 1786, MC, 140–41.

17. McGillivray to Favrot, November 8, 1786, MC, 135–36; McGillivray to Zéspedes, November 15, 1786, MC, 138–40.

18. McGillivray to O'Neill, December 3, 1786, MC, 140–41; McGillivray to Pinckney, February 26, 1789, ASPIA, 1:19–20.

19. Green, *Politics of Indian Removal*, 33–34; Green, "Alexander McGillivray," 49–50.

20. Martin to [Governor of Georgia,] September 7, 1786, CIL, 1:137–38; O'Neill to Zéspedes, December 29, 1786, LC, box 5, folder December 1786; Barnard to Telfair, August 14, 1786, LTB, 59–61.

21. Zéspedes to McGillivray, May 22, 1786, MC, 112–13; Gardoqui to O'Neill, June 30, 1786, PPdC, legajo 104A; Holton, *Unruly Americans*, 246.

22. Downes, "Creek-American Relations," 160.

23. Barnard to Telfair, August 22, 1786, LTB, 61–63.

24. O'Neill to Gálvez, May 30, 1786, MPASD, reel 2, 564–66; McGillivray to Panton, August 3, 1786, MC, 123; McGillivray to Zéspedes, August 3, 1786, MC, 124–25.

25. McGillivray to O'Neill, October 4, 1786, MC, 132; O'Neill to Miró, October 13, 1786, MPASD, reel 2, 791–95; Zéspedes to Sonora, September 29, 1786, PdE, legajo 3887.

26. Barnard to Matthews, May 1, 1787, TCC, box 1, folder 11; Woods to Telfair, January 14, 1787, TCC, box 77, folder 30. O'Neill reasserted his determination to continue arming communities early in the spring of 1787. See O'Neill to Miró, March 8, 1787, PdE, legajo 3887.

27. E. T. to Habersham, September 4, 1786, FT, 72–73; Mathews to Clarke, April 17, 1787, FT, 95; Mathews to Jackson, April 18, 1787, FT, 96; Sevier to Mathews, March 3, 1787, TCC, box 81, folder 21.

28. Mathews to Barnard, August 7, 1787, LTB, 70–71; Clarke to Mathews, April 13, 1787, CIL, 1:148–49; McGillivray to O'Neill, July 10, 1787, MC, 155–56.

29. Habersham to McIntosh, June 30, 1787, FHP, box 2, folder 33; Cocke to Mathews, June 25, 1787, TCC, box 40A, folder Mathews Letters.

30. For examples of this outreach, see Mathews to Sevier, October 10, 1787, in Jensen, ed., *The Documentary History*, 3:222. For other such discussions, see extract of a letter to Telfair . . . , September 30, 1786, TCC, box 5, folder 2; James Habersham to John Habersham, October 22, 1787, in Jensen, ed., *The Documentary History*, 3, 226; Elholm to Walton, October 23, 1787, TCC, box 5, folder 2; Elholm to Mathews, November 1, 1787, TCC, box 83, folder 7; Mathews to Elholm, November 5, 1787, TCC, box 83, folder 7; Mathews to Barnard, August 17, 1787, FT, 103–4; Mathews to Sevier, August 9, 1787, GLB, 71–72; and G. M. to Cocke, November 8, 1787, GLB, 123. For Edward Telfair's efforts a year previous, see E. T. to His Excellency the Governor of Virginia, May 27, 1786, FT, 63; To Mr. Robert Dixon, May 27, 1786, FT, 64; To His Excellency William Moultrie . . . , May 30, 1786, FT, 64; and Martin to Telfair, July 3, 1786, CIL, 1:127.

31. Cobbs to Twiggs, September 3, 1787, FT, 110; Cobbs to Clark and Jackson, September 3, 1787, FT, 110.

32. Mathews to the Speaker of the Hble House of Assembly, October 18, 1787, GLB, 109–12.

33. Mathews to His Excellency the President . . . , November 15, 1787, GLB, 128–30.

34. G. M. to Cocke, November 8, 1787, GLB, 123; Mathews to His Excellency the President . . . , November 15, 1787, GLB, 128–30; Robert Corry Affidavit, September 3, 1821, ID, vol. 1, part 1, 52–53.

35. Jay to Jefferson, November 3, 1787, in Jensen, ed., *The Documentary History*, 3:261; Miller to Ward, February 10, 1788, in Jensen, ed., *The Documentary History*, 16:104; Gilman to Sullivan, November 7, 1787, in Jensen, ed., *The Documentary History*, 3:261–62; Madison to Washington, October 24 and November 1, 1787, in Jensen, ed., *The Documentary History*, 13:452.

36. McGillivray to O'Neill, July 25, 1787, MC, 159; Robertson to Sevier, August 7, 1787, CIL, 1:157; McGillivray to Miró, October 4, 1787, MC, 160–61; McGillivray to Zéspedes, October 6, 1787, MC, 162–63.

37. McMurphy to . . . , June 29, 1786, CIL, 1:125–26.

38. Jacob Jones and John Cimbro Affidavit, July 2, 1787, ID, vol. 1, part 1, 105. The depredation claims referred to here can be found in the five volumes of ID.

39. Crawford to Irwin, March 3, 178[8], CIL, 1:170.

40. John Armor Deposition, May 5, 1802, ID, vol. 1, part 1, 118; James Helveston Deposition, May 5, 1802, ID, vol. 1, part 1, 124–27.

41. Martin Palmer Affidavit, September 1821, ID, vol. 1, part 1, 134.

42. Mathews to Clarke, April 17, 1787, FT, 95. For general descriptions of Georgia losses, see ID, vol. 1, part 2, 407–55, 501–56.

43. McGillivray to O'Neill, April 18, 1787, MC, 149–50; Mathews to Jackson, April 18, 1787, FT, 96; Watson, "Strivings for Sovereignty," 406; Downes, "Creek-American Relations," 165–67.

44. White to Knox, May 24, 1787, ASPIA, 1:20–21.

45. McGillivray to White, April 8, 1787, ASPIA, 1:18–19. McGillivray later explained that "a general convention was appointed, to be held in May," and a few days before it convened, White arrived. See McGillivray to Pinckney, February 26, 1787, ASPIA, 1:19–20.

46. McGillivray to Pinckney, February 26, 1787, ASPIA, 1:19–20; At a meeting of the Lower Creeks . . . , April 10, 1787, ASPIA, 1:22; Proceedings of the meeting of the Lower Creeks . . . , April 10, 178[7], ASPIA, 1:22–23.

47. Proceedings of the meeting of the Lower Creeks, April 10, 178[7], ASPIA, 1:22–23.

48. McLatchy to Leslie, May 14, 1787, MC, 151–52; McGillivray to Pinckney, February 26, 1787, ASPIA, 1:19–20; White to McGillivray, April 4, 1787, ASPIA, 1:21–22.

49. Proceedings of the meeting of the Lower Creeks, April 10, 178[7], ASPIA, 1:22–23; McGillivray to Pinckney, February 26, 1787, ASPIA, 1:19–20.

50. Barnard to Matthews, May 1, 1787, TCC, box 1, folder 11; McGillivray to O'Neill, June 20, 1787, MC, 153–54; Dowd, A Spirited Resistance, 98–99.

51. McGillivray to O'Neill, April 18, 1787, MC, 149–50; White to Knox, May 24, 1787, ASPIA, 1:20–21.

52. Barnard to Mathews, May 1, 1787, TCC, box 1, folder 11; Barnard to Mathews, August 17, 1787, FT, 103–4.

53. Proceedings of the meeting of the Lower Creeks, April 10, 178[7], ASPIA, 1:22–23.

54. White to Knox, May 24, 1787, ASPIA, 1:20–21; Extracts from the minutes . . . , ASPIA, 1:24.

55. Extracts from the minutes . . . , ASPIA, 1:24; White to Knox, May 24, 1787, ASPIA, 1:20–21.

56. Extracts from the minutes . . . , ASPIA, 1:24; Mathews to Jackson, April 26, 1787, FT, 100; Mathews to Twiggs, April 28, 1787, FT, 101; Mathews to Barnard, April 28, 1787, FT, 101; Mathews to Few and Pierce, April 24, 1787, GLB, 54–55; War Office, July 26, 1788, ASPIA, 1:25; Watson, "Strivings for Sovereignty," 406. Georgians were also constantly wary of further Creek designs. Governor Mathews sent a talk to the Tallassee King, employing Barnard both as the bearer of the letter and as a spy, urging him to "find out the real intention of those people" and give him "the earliest information of their designs." See Mathews to Barnard, April 28, 1787, FT, 101.

57. Cobbs to Twiggs, Clarke, and Jackson, June 19, 1787, FT, 102; Mathews to Twiggs, Clarke, and Jackson, June 28, 1787, FT, 102–3.

58. Barnard to Matthews, June 8, 1787, TCC, box 1, folder 11; Irwin to Mathews, June 11, 1787, CIL, 1:156; Mathews to . . . , August 9, 1787, ASPIA, 1:31–32; Barnard to Matthews, August 18, 1787, TCC, box 1, folder 11; Mathews to Sevier, August 9, 1787, GLB, 68–72.

59. McGillivray to Pickens and Mathews, June 4, 1788, MC, 180–82; Barnard to Mathews, June 8, 1787, TCC, box 1, folder 11; Mathews to Sevier, August 9, 1787, FT, 105.

60. Galphin and Douzeazeaux to . . . , June 14, 1787, ASPIA, 1:32; To the head-men and warriors of the Lower Creeks . . . , June 29, 1787, ASPIA, 1:32–33.

61. Talk of the Fat King to Mathews, July 27 through August 1, 1787, TCC, box 80, folder 5.

62. Cussetas wanted the officer who led the attack and enough militiamen killed to satisfy the twelve murdered hunters. The governor did not respond favorably, vowing not only that he would not deliver up a single man but that if Cussetas "should spill a drop of blood" Georgians would "lay their towns in ashes, and sprinkle their land with blood." See To the Fat King and other head-men . . . , August 7, 1787, ASPIA, 1:33; and Mathews to Sevier, August 9, 1787, JVB, folder 10. Mathews forwarded these thoughts along to William Few and William Pierce, Georgia's representatives in Philadelphia. Continuing to deny any wrongdoing on the part of his militia, he instead insisted that it would be "ill become a free people" to give such satisfaction in the face of all the "murders committed on our peaceful inhabitants in violation of the most solemn treaties entered into us." "When I think of this insolent demand," Mathews continued, "I feel my blood run warm in my veins." See Mathews to Few and Pierce, August 9, 1787, FT, 107–8.

63. Barnard to Mathews, June 8, 1787, TCC, box 1, folder 11; Barnard to Mathews, August 18, 1787, TCC, box 1, folder 11; Petition from Inhabitants of Greene County . . . , July 20, 1787, TCC, box 40A, folder Mathews Petitions; Mathews to Sevier, August 9, 1787, JVB, folder 10.

64. Petition from Inhabitants of Greene County . . . , July 20, 1787, TCC, box 40A, folder Mathews Petitions. The attacks on the Cussetas pushed away one of the Georgians' strongest allies, the Tallassee King. According to Caleb Swan, years later, "he remained refractory for a long time, as well as some of the most important of the lower towns, until, finding the Georgians aimed at them indiscriminately, and a Mr. Alexander killed twelve of their real friends (the Cussitahs), they dropped their internal disputes, and united all their efforts" under McGillivray and against the frontiers. See Swan, "Position and State," 281.

65. Wayne to Delany, May 14, 1788, Anthony Wayne Papers, box 3.

66. McGillivray to O'Neill, November 20, 1787, MC, 163–64; McGillivray to Miró, January 10, 1788, MC, 167.

67. . . . , to Governor, 1788, TCC, box 41, folder 1; McGillivray to Zéspedes, January 5, 1788, MC, 165–66; McGillivray to Miró, January 10, 1788, MC, 167.

68. Handley to Sevier, February 19, 1788, GLB, 137–40; Handley to Winn, March 31, 1788, FT, 143–44.

69. Berrien to Jackson, September 30, 1788, CIL, 1:185–86; Jackson to Handley, October 3, 1788, CIL, 1:187–88.

70. Joseph Clay, in Savannah, recognized that the Oconee raids, if they continued, "must be attended with the most ruinous consequences to this state." The increased powers of the new Constitution were dangerous, but perhaps they were Georgians' only hope. "The new plan of government for the Union I think will be adopted with us readily," he thought, because "of two evils we must choose the least. Under such a

government we should have avoided this great evil, an Indian war." See Clay to Pierce, October 17, 1787, in Jensen, ed., *The Documentary History*, 3:232.

71. Miró to O'Neill, March 24, 1787, MC, 145–46; McGillivray to Zéspedes, June 10, 1788, EFP, reel 43; Miró to O'Neill, June 20, 1786, MPASD, 2:710; Berry, "The Indian Policy of Spain in the Southwest," 467–68.

72. McGillivray to O'Neill, May 12, 1786, MPASD, 2:655–59; Gálvez to Miró, May 20, 1786, PdE, legajo 3886.

73. Miró to Gálvez, April 1786, MPASD, 2:701–2; Miró to O'Neill, May 4, 1787, PdE, legajo 3887; Miró to Gálvez, June 28, 1786, PdE, legajo 3886; Miró to Gardoqui, June 28, 1786, PdE, legajo 3886; Miró to Sonora, June 28, 1786, PdE, legajo 3886; Miró to Sonora, November 25, 1786, PdE, legajo 3887.

74. O'Neill to Miró, April 27, 1787, PdE, legajo 3887; Miró to O'Neill, May 4, 1787, PdE, legajo 3887; Miró to O'Neill, June 20, 1786, MPASD, 2:710; MPASD, 2:731–32; O'Neill to Miró, July 21, 1786, PPdC, legajo 37.

75. Gálvez to Floridablanca, August 26, 1786, PdE, leg 3886; Gálvez to Sonora, August 26, 1786, PdE, legajo 3887.

76. McGillivray to Zéspedes, January 5, 1788, MC, 165–66; McGillivray to O'Neill, April 15, 1788, MC, 176–77; O'Neill to McGillivray, April 21, 1788, MC, 177–78; Watson, "Strivings for Sovereignty," 407.

77. McGillivray to Miró, June 12, 1788, MC, 183–84; McGillivray to O'Neill, July 14, 1788, MC, 190; McGillivray to Zéspedes, August 8, 1788, EFP, reel 43.

78. Miró to McGillivray, August 16, 1788, PPdC, legajo 2360; Zéspedes to McGillivray, July 8, 1788, PPL, reel 4. While slowing the shipment of large amounts of arms, Spaniards still officially backed the Creek position. Both Creek and Spanish sovereignty was at stake, and Miró made it clear that the full force of the Spanish still stood behind the Creeks. He pushed McGillivray to meet with the congressional commissioners when they invited him to do so, but he still encouraged him to be firm. Not only would any compromise deal with the state of Georgia undermine Creek sovereignty, it stood to directly violate of the Treaty of Pensacola. While Miró continued urging McGillivray to meet with James White, he also made clear that he was not to give up an inch of ground and that the Spanish still stood behind the Creek people completely. See McGillivray to O'Neill, April 4, 1787, MC, 147–48; McGillivray to Zéspedes, April 10, 1787, MC, 148; McGillivray to O'Neill, April 15, 1788, MC, 176–77; O'Neill to McGillivray, April 21, 1788, MC, 177–78; Miró to McGillivray, July 8, 1788, MC, 187–88; and Miró to O'Neill, July 12, 1788, MC, 188–89. Arms shipments were also available should the Georgians make any rash moves, and indeed, 1788 saw an increase in Spanish aid. See Espeleta to the Court, November 20, 1788, MPASD, 5:302. See also Berry, "The Indian Policy of Spain in the Southwest," 467–68.

79. McGillivray to Pickens, September 5, 1785, ASPIA, 1:17–18; White to Knox, May 24, 1787, ASPIA, 1:20–21; Extracts from the minutes . . . , ASPIA, 1:24.

80. Din, *War on the Gulf Coast*; Narrett, *Adventurism and Empire*; Wright, *William Augustus Bowles*.

81. Miró to Ezpeleta, July 28, 1788, MC, 191; Kinnaird, "International Rivalry," 71–75; McGillivray to O'Neill, August 12, 1788, MC, 192; Watson, "Strivings for Sovereignty," 407–8.

82. Barnard to Hanley, January 18, 1789, LTB, 86–88. Another trader was already pressing McGillivray, late in 1788, to deal with Bowles. See Leslie to McGillivray, December 11, 1788, in Corbitt, "Papers, IV," 282.

83. McGillivray to Miró, August 12, 1788, MC, 194.

84. While Miró may ultimately have come to believe that McGillivray was less trustworthy than he had supposed, his decisions had not led to an immediate crisis, and there was little reason to confront him aggressively over the issue. He still considered McGillivray far too powerful to lose him as an ally. See Miró to Ezpeleta, August 16, 1788, PPdC, legajo 1394; Miró to Ezpeleta, September 16, 1788, PPdC, legajo 1394; Miró to Ezpeleta, October 20, 1788, PPdC, legajo 1394; and Ezpeleta to Miró, October 24, 1788, PdE, legajo 3887. For his part, Zéspedes continued to voice his absolute confidence in McGillivray. See Zéspedes to Sonora, March 30, 1787, PdE, legajo 3901; McGillivray to Leslie, November 20, 1788, MC, 205–8; McGillivray to Zéspedes, December 8, 1788, EFP, reel 43; and Zéspedes to McGillivray, January 14, 1789, PPdC, legajo 1395. Soon Zéspedes was joined by both Miró and Captain General Jose Ezpeleta in Cuba. Ezpeleta, who was the ultimate authority in the Gulf region, made conciliatory efforts to win McGillivray back. McGillivray's steps were rash, but Ezpeleta ultimately made it clear that, from the top down, the Spanish were determined to back Creeks and protect them. If that meant supplying Creek warriors more freely, then so be it. See Miró to McGillivray, December 13, 1788, MC, 209–10; Ezpeleta to Valdes, November 19, 1788, PdE, legajo 3887; and Valdes to Ezpeleta, February 25, 1789, PdE, legajo 3887.

85. McGillivray to Panton, May 20, 1789, in Corbitt, "Papers, IV," 283–88.

86. Winn, Pickens, and Mathews to McGillivray, November 28, 1788, ASPIA, 1:30; Return of depredations committed by the Creek Indians . . . , ASPIA, 1:77, also in ID, 4:1. See also lists in ID, vol. 1, part 2, 407–55, 501–56.

87. Handley to Gov. of S. Carolina, February 19, 1788, FT, 136–37; Handley to Baldwin, March 24, 1788, GLB, 151–53.

88. Handley to O'Neal, November 7, 1787, FT, 135–36; Handley to Sevier, February 19, 1788, GLB, 137–39; Handley to Mathews, April 2, 1788, GLB, 162–63.

89. Pickens and Mathews to McGillivray, March 29, 1788, MC, 174–75; McGillivray to O'Neill, 28 May 1788, MC, 172–74.

90. Executive Department Minutes, January 7, 1788–January 7, 1789 (unpublished typescript, edited by Louise F. Hayes, 1939), 214, 218, 255. Several representatives "anxiously" waited for word on the federal negotiations, which they hoped would "have the happy effect of stopping the farther Effusion of Blood & establishing a lasting peace." See South Carolina Delegates to Pinckney, June 21, 1788, in Smith et al., eds., Letters to Delegates of Congress, 25:128.

91. Winn to Knox, June 25, 1788, ASPIA, 1:26; Winn to Knox, August 8, 1788, ASPIA, 1:28.

92. Galphin to Pickens and Osborn, May 27, 1789, ASPIA, 1:35–36.

93. Instructions to the Commissioners for treating with the Southern Indians . . . , August 29, 1789, ASPIA, 1:65–68; Report from H. Knox, Secretary of War . . . , July 6, 1789, ASPIA, 1:15–16.

94. Winn to Knox, October 14, 1788, ASPIA, 1:28; Winn, Pickens, and Mathews to McGillivray, July 16, 1788, ASPIA, 1:29.

95. Winn, Pickens, and Mathews to McGillivray, and others . . . , July 16, 1788, ASPIA, 1:29; McGillivray to Winn, Pickens, and Mathews, August 12, 1788, ASPIA, 1:29;

McGillivray to Winn, Pickens, and Mathews, September 15, 1788, ASPIA, 1:30; Winn, Pickens, and Mathews to McGillivray, November 28, 1788, ASPIA, 1:30; McGillivray to Galphin, May 18, 1789, ASPIA, 1:35.

96. McGillivray to Galphin, May 18, 1789, ASPIA, 1:35. In fact, in late 1788 Robert Leslie wrote McGillivray, warning him that there was "a design formed in Georgia to assassinate & murder you at the Treaty proposed to be held, between the Indians and Georgians." See Leslie to McGillivray, December 11, 1788, EHW, box 2, folder AHN legajo 1, no. 5.

97. Campbell to Washington, May 10, 1789, in Twoig, ed., *Papers of George Washington*, 2:253–54; Galphin to Osborne, May 23, 1789, ASPIA, 1:36; A talk from the Head-men and Chiefs . . . , May 23, 1789, ASPIA, 1:34.

98. George Galphin to Pickens and Osborn, May 27, 1789, ASPIA, 1:35–36; A Talk from the Head-men and chiefs of the Lower Creek nation . . . , May 23, 1789, ASPIA, 1:34; McGillivray to . . . , June 16, 1789, CIL, 1:209, also in ASPIA, 1:37.

99. George Galphin to Pickens and Osborn, May 27, 1789, ASPIA, 1:35–36.

100. John Galphin to Osborne, May 23, 1789, ASPIA, 1:36; George Galphin to Pickens and Osborn, May 27, 1789, ASPIA, 1:35–36.

101. For accounts and complaints of attacks, see Johnson to Walton, April 20, 1789, CIL, 1:196–97; Lanier to Walton, April 21, 1789, CIL, 1:200; Clark to Walton, April 25, 1789: CIL, 1:201; Maxwell to Walton, May 24, 1789, CIL, 1:203–4; Clarke to Walton, May 29, 1789, CIL, 1:205; Lanier to Governor, June 4, 1789, CIL, 1:207; McGillivray to Galphin, June 16, 1789, ASPIA, 1:37; McGillivray to Miró, June 24, 1789, MC, 238–40; Sullivan to His Honor the Governor, June 24, 1789, CIL, 1:212; To the Head-men, chiefs, and Warriors, of the Creek nation, June 29, 1789, ASPIA, 1:37; Pickens and Osborne to McGillivray, June 30, 1789, ASPIA, 1:37–38; and Galphin to Osborne, August 1, 1789, CIL, 1:217–18.

102. A Talk from the Head-men and chiefs of the Lower Creek nation . . . , May 23, 1789, ASPIA, 1:34; Galphin to Osborne, May 23, 1789, ASPIA, 1:36; Galphin to Pickens and Osborn, May 27, 1789, ASPIA, 1:35–36.

103. McGillivray to Winn, Pickens, and Mathews, August 12, 1788, ASPIA, 1:29; McGillivray to Winn, Pickens, and Mathews, September 15, 1788, ASPIA, 1:30. For an American's hopeful outlook, see Wayne to Delany, July 4, 1789, Anthony Wayne Papers, box 4.

104. Barnard to . . . , May 27, 1789, LTB, 94–97; Humphreys to Washington, September 21, 1789, in Twoig, ed., *Papers of George Washington*, 4:61–62.

105. Humphreys to Washington, September 26, 1789, in Twoig, ed., *Papers of George Washington*, 4:86–89; Treaty proceedings . . . , ASPIA, 1:72, 73; Camp, Oconee River, September 24, 1789, ASPIA, 1:73; Mattern, *Benjamin Lincoln*, 190–93.

106. Humphreys to Washington, September 26, 1789, in Twoig, ed., *Papers of George Washington*, 4:86–89; Treaty proceedings . . . , ASPIA, 1:72; McGillivray to Panton, October 8, 1789, MC, 251; Indian Camp, Oconee River, September 24, 1789, ASPIA, 1:73.

107. McGillivray to Panton, May 20, 1789, in Corbitt, "Papers, IV," 283–88; Panton to McGillivray, June 7, 1789, in Corbitt, "Papers, V," 375–76; Panton to Miró, June 9, 1789, in Corbitt, "Papers, V," 377–78.

108. Lincoln, Griffin, and Humphreys to McGillivray, September 18, 1789, ASPIA, 1:71; entry for September 20, 1789, 11 o'clock, ASPIA, 1:72; entry for September 21, 1789, ASPIA, 1:72.

109. McGillivray to Panton, October 8, 1789, MC, 251. Spaniards were also pleased with McGillivray's approach to the end of the Oconee raids, as well as his first exchanges with federal authorities. See McGillivray to Winn, Pickens, and Mathews, September 15, 1788, ASPIA, 1:30; McGillivray to Miró, September 20, 1788, MC, 199–201. The governors also, however, pushed McGillivray to take Rock Landing seriously, if only to better make known the Georgians' designs. If they tried another land grab by force, and the American commissioners did "not want to form a treaty their injustice will be made manifest, and the nation will be better in position to defend its rights." It would be much easier for the Spanish to be more forthcoming in their aid as well. See Miró to McGillivray, July 22, 1789, MC, 243–44. McGillivray needed little encouragement. If Georgians were to "give us what we ask for justly," he explained, and return the land they had usurped, "the war on our part will cease." See McGillivray to Miró, August 15, 1789, MC, 249–50; and McGillivray to Miró, August 12, 1789, PdE, legajo 3887.

110. Humphreys to Washington, September 6, 1789, in Humphreys, ed., *The Life and Times of David Humphreys*, 2:6; Humphreys to Washington, September 26, 1789, in Twoig, ed., *Papers of George Washington*, 4:86–89; McGillivray to Leslie, October 12, 1789, MC, 255; Mattern, *Benjamin Lincoln*, 190–93.

111. McGillivray to Panton, October 8, 1789, MC, 251; Mattern, *Benjamin Lincoln*, 190–93.

112. McGillivray to the commissioners . . . , ASPIA, 1:74; Lincoln, Friggin, and Humphreys to McGillivray, September 25, 1789, ASPIA, 1:74; Downes, "Creek-American Relations," 178–79; McGillivray to Panton, October 8, 1789, MC, 251; Talk of the White Bird King, ASPIA, 1:75; Answer of the Commissioners, ASPIA, 1:75; Lincoln, Griffin, and Humphreys to McGillivray, September 28, 1789, ASPIA, 1:75–76; Lincoln, Griffin, and Humphreys to Secretary of War, September 28, 1789, ASPIA, 1:76; Lincoln, Griffin, and Humphreys to Governor of Georgia, October 3, 1789, ASPIA, 1:76.

113. Lincoln, Griffin, and Humphreys to McGillivray, ASPIA, 1:74; Lincoln, Griffin, and Humphreys to McGillivray, September 26, 1789, ASPIA, 1:74–75.

114. McGillivray to the Hon. Commissioners . . . , September 27, 1789, ASPIA, 1:75; McGillivray to Panton, October 8, 1789, MC, 251.

115. Talk of the White Bird King, ASPIA, 1:75; Answer of the Commissioners, ASPIA, 1:75; Lincoln, Griffin, and Humphreys to McGillivray, September 28, 1789, ASPIA, 1:75–76; Lincoln, Griffin, and Humphreys to Secretary of War, September 8, 1789, ASPIA, 1:76; Lincoln, Griffin, and Humphreys to Governor of Georgia, October 3, 1789, ASPIA, 1:76; Mattern, *Benjamin Lincoln*, 190–93.

116. Wayne to Knox, May 12, 1790, Anthony Wayne Papers, box 4; Humphreys to Washington, September 26, 1789, in Twoig, ed., *Papers of George Washington*, 4:86–89; Humphreys to Washington, September 27, 1789, in Twoig, ed., *Papers of George Washington*, 4:91–95; Mattern, *Benjamin Lincoln*, 190–93.

117. Pickens to Martin, October 12, 1789, in Draper and Harper, eds., *Draper Manuscript Collection*, series xx, Tennessee Papers, vols. 1–3, reel 126.

118. McGillivray to Panton, October 8, 1789, MC, 251.

119. Downes, "Creek-American Relations," 168–69, 174–77; Wright, "Creek-American Treaty of 1790," 384–88.

120. Secretary of War Henry Knox rightfully suggested that his feelings were "opposed to a war with the United States, and that he would at this time gladly embrace

any rational means that could be offered to avoid that event." See Knox to Washington, February 15, 1790, in Twoig, ed., *Papers of George Washington*, 5:140–42.

121. Wright, "Creek-American Treaty of 1790," 386–88. For Creek headmen growing irritated, see McGillivray to Panton, May 20, 1789, in Corbitt, "Papers, IV," 287. The arms and ammunition soon arrived. See Panton to McGillivray, June 6, 1789, in Corbitt, "Papers, V," 374.

122. Knox to Washington, February 15, 1790, in Twoig, ed., *Papers of George Washington*, 5:140–42; McGillivray to Howard, August 11, 1790, MC, 273. With Knox and Washington personally pressing him to do so, McGillivray must have felt terribly trapped. See McGillivray to Leslie, May 20, 1790, MC, 263; McGillivray to Miró, June 2, 1790, MC, 265–66; McGillivray to Howard, August 11, 1790, MC, 273; Watson, "Strivings for Sovereignty," 410–11.

123. Questions for the Tallassee King, August 6, 1790, in Knox, *Microfilms*, reel 26.

124. Rough Sketch, August 7, 1790, in Knox, *Microfilms*, reel 26; Minutes of Spanish treaty . . . , August 8, 1790, in Knox, *Microfilms*, reel 26; McGillivray to Howard, August 11, 1790, MC, 273; Watson, "Strivings for Sovereignty," 413; Wright, "Creek-American Treaty of 1790," 386.

125. Wright, "Creek-American Treaty of 1790," 380; Green, "Alexander McGillivray," 55–56. Historian J. Leitch Wright has argued that McGillivray signed his name to the deal precisely because of these terms. They were, in his mind, the way to best maintain his ascendancy in the Creek Nation. Unless he controlled this critical linkage, "he would become indistinguishable from scores of other Creeks chiefs." See Wright, "Creek-American Treaty of 1790," 386–88.

126. Knox to Burbeck, August 16, 1790, Henry Knox Papers; Samuel Smith Affidavit, July 21, 1835, ID, vol. 2, part 1, 112–13.

5. Creek Country in Crisis

1. For a similar interpretation of McGillivray's fall during this period, see Dowd, *A Spirited Resistance*, 102.

2. Several historians have recognized the terrible response many Georgians had to the Treaty of New York in Georgia, and particularly from the backcountry. As George R. Lamplugh suggested, for instance, "Because it struck Georgians where they were most vulnerable," their desire for land and "elbow room," the treaty aroused unprecedented hostility among Georgians toward the central government. By 1793, backcountry settlers, "whose existence focused upon land, were firmly aligned against the Washington administration." See Lamplugh, *Politics on the Periphery*, 64–65; Jennison, *Cultivating Race*, 99–101; Phillips, *Georgia and State Rights*, 42–44; Coulter, *Georgia: A Short History*, 170; and Pound, *Benjamin Hawkins*, 81–82.

3. Sundry Outline of Proposed Treaty with the Creeks, August 7, 1790 in Knox, *Microfilms*, reel 26. The man who met the Creek delegation on the road was also introduced to two chiefs, "who were he said of the most considerable rank." Wm Knox to [Knox], July 14, 1790, in Knox, *Microfilms*, reel 26; Kappler, *Indian Affairs*, 2:28–29.

4. Wright, "Creek-American Treaty of 1790," 393.

5. Green, "Alexander McGillivray," 59. For the best discussion of Creeks' changing attitudes about private property, and about the development of a propertied class of Creek leaders, see Saunt, *A New Order of Things*.

6. Swan, "Position and State," 254.

7. Proceedings of the meeting of the Lower Creeks, April 10, 178[7], *ASPIA*, 1:22–23; McGillivray to Pinckney, February 26, 1787, *ASPIA*, 1:19–20.

8. For different perspectives on the struggle for the "old northwest," see Calloway, *A Victory with No Name*; Sword, *President Washington's Indian War*; Griffin, *American Leviathan*; White, *The Middle Ground*; and Dowd, *A Spirited Resistance*. For the federal response, see Sadosky, *Revolutionary Negotiations*; Nichols, *Red Gentlemen & White Savages*; Jones, *License for Empire*, 157–86; and Horsman, *Expansion and American Indian Policy*.

9. Proceedings of the meeting of the Lower Creeks, April 10, 178[7], *ASPIA*, 1:22–23.

10. Wright, "Creek-American Treaty of 1790," 380, 393; Green, "Alexander McGillivray," 55–56; Wright, *Creeks & Seminoles*, 139–40.

11. State House, Augusta, November 22, 1790, TCC, box 77, folder 17.

12. McGillivray to Panton, October 28, 1791, MC, 298–300; Leslie to Panton, January 30, 1792, MC, 305–6.

13. Extracts from a letter from the Secretary of War to Major Richard Call, May 25, 1791, *ASPIA*, 1:125; extracts from a letter to the same officer, July 13, 1791, *ASPIA*, 1:125; Instructions to John Heth, May 31, 1791, *ASPIA*, 1:125–26. Joseph Ellicott was quickly selected as the primary surveyor and was also dispatched. See Instructions to Joseph Ellicott, September 8, 1791, *ASPIA*, 1:128; Secretary of War to Call, September 8, 1791, *ASPIA*, 1:128; and Wayne to Berrien, December 5, 1791, Anthony Wayne Papers, box 5.

14. The United States of America . . . from the 7th of August, 1790, to the 7th of August, 1791, *ASPIA*, 1:126.

15. Instructions to John Heth, May 31, 1791, *ASPIA*, 1:125–26.

16. It was reported that he was forced to give Spaniards a defense of his conduct after several chiefs "laid the blame" on him when questioned about their supposed hand in the treaty. See *Collections of the Massachusetts Historical Society*, series 3, 5:170. Knox also chastised him for his inability to stop warriors from the Lower Country Creeks from committing robberies and horse thefts. See Secretary of War to McGillivray, July 13, 1791, *ASPIA*, 1:127–28.

17. Panton to Miró, October 8, 1791, MC, 295–97; Quesada to McGillivray, August 20, 1791, EFP, reel 44; Quesada to McGillivray, August 20, 1791, EFP, reel 44; Miró to McGillivray, October 15, 1791, MC, 297.

18. McGillivray to Panton, October 28, 1791, MC, 298–300.

19. McGillivray to O'Neill, October 28, 1791, PPdC, legajo 1445; McGillivray to Miró, November 15, 1791, PPdC, legajo 204.

20. War Office, December 2, 1791, *ASPIA*, 1:184. For another interpretation, see Wayne to Berrien, December 5, 1791, Anthony Wayne Papers, box 3. There were even reports that Bowles put a bounty on his head. See Bowles to Carondelet, March 13, 1792, MC, 310–12; Quesada to Floridablanca, March 25, 1792, PdE, legajo 3889; and Bowles to Aranda, June 23, 1792, PPL, reel 7.

21. Panton to Carondelet, February 14, 1792, in Corbitt, "Papers, VI," 73–74; Panton to Carondelet, March 17, 1792, in Corbitt, "Papers, VI," 74–76; Leslie to Panton, March 9, 1792, in Corbitt, "Papers, VII," 184–86. For the Little Prince being from the Broken Arrow, see Pope, *A Tour*, 54. Hawkins also mentioned him when he was at Coweta Tallahassee, which was another name for Broken Arrow. See January 23, 1797, *LJW*, 37–38.

22. McGillivray to Panton, October 28, 1791, *MC*, 298–300.

23. Statement by Middleton, December 21, 1791, *MC*, 300–301.

24. Secretary of War to Seagrove, February 20, 1792, *ASPIA*, 1:249–50.

25. Leslie to Panton, March 9, 1792, in Corbitt, "Papers, VII," 184–86; Leslie to Panton, March 10, 1792, in Corbitt, "Papers, VII," 186–87.

26. Secretary of War to McGillivray, February 17, 1792, *ASPIA*, 1:246–47; Secretary of War to Seagrove, February 20, 1792, *ASPIA*, 1:249–50.

27. Secretary of War to McGillivray, February 17, 1792, *ASPIA*, 1:246–47; Secretary of War to Seagrove, February 20, 1792, *ASPIA*, 1:249–50; Secretary of War to Seagrove, October 31, 1792, *ASPIA*, 1:259–60.

28. Secretary of War to Seagrove, October 31, 1792, *ASPIA*, 1:259–60.

29. Secretary of War to Seagrove, April 29, 1792, *ASPIA*, 1:253–54; Secretary of War to Seagrove, October 27, 1792, *ASPIA*, 1:262–63.

30. Seagrove to [McGillivray], May 21, 1792, *ASPIA*, 1:298; To the kings, chiefs, head men . . . , May 18, 1792, *ASPIA*, 1:299–301; Secretary of War to Seagrove, April 29, 1792, *ASPIA*, 1:253; Secretary of War to Seagrove, October 31, 1792, *ASPIA*, 1:259–60.

31. To the Kings, Chiefs . . . , February 25, 1792, in Corbitt, "Papers, VIII," 287–88; Secretary of War to Seagrove, April 29, 1792, *ASPIA*, 1:253–55; Secretary of War to Governor of Georgia, July 11, 1792, *ASPIA*, 1:256.

32. Seagrove to Secretary of War, June 14, 1792, *ASPIA*, 1:301–2; Secretary of War to Seagrove, October 31, 1792, *ASPIA*, 1:259–60; The Kings and chiefs of the Cussetuhs . . . , October 6, 1792, *ASPIA*, 1:313; Seagrove to Knox, January 3, 1793, *CROC*, 203–4; Secretary of State to Carmichael and Short, June 30, 1793, *ASPFR*, 1:265–66.

33. For evidence of a growing correspondence between Seagrove and several leading headmen, see Talk from the White Lieut . . . , August 15, 1792, *CIL*, 1:254; To the Kings and Chiefs of the Cussetahs and Cowetas . . . , October 6, 179[2], *ASPIA*, 1:313; [Seagrove] to the White Lieutenant, October 7, 1792, *ASPIA*, 1:313–14; Seagrove to Alexander Cornells, February 20, 1793, *ASPIA*, 1:375; and Seagrove to Fine Bones, Chief of the Broken Arrows, February 20, 1793, *ASPIA*, 1:376.

34. McGillivray to . . . , April 8, 1792, *ASPIA*, 1:296; Secretary of War to Seagrove, April 29, 1792, *ASPIA*, 1:253–55.

35. White to McGillivray, March 5, 1792, *MC*, 315–16; Secretary of War to McGillivray, April 29, 1792, *ASPIA*, 1:255; Seagrove to Washington, April 21, 1792, in Twoig, ed., *Papers of George Washington*, 10:306–7.

36. McGillivray to Carondelet, April 10, 1792, *MC*, 318–20.

37. McGillivray to Panton, March 12, 1792, in Corbitt, "Papers, VII," 189–90; The following are extracts . . . , March 25, 1792, *ASPIA*, 1:295; McGillivray to Panton, March 27, 1792, Corbitt, "Papers, VII," 191.

38. Leslie to Panton, March 9, 1792, in Corbitt, "Papers, VII," 184–86; Seagrove to Secretary of War, April 21, 1792, *ASPIA*, 1:295; Seagrove to Washington, April 21, 1792, in Twoig, ed., *Papers of George Washington*, 10:306–7.

39. David Shaw Affidavit, June 2, 1792, *CIL*, 1:247; John Ormsbay Deposition, May 11, 1792, *ASPIA*, 1:297–98.

40. Extract of a letter from Mr. James Seagrove . . . , May 24, 1792, *ASPIA*, 1:296.

41. Durouzeaux to Seagrove, May 28, 1792, *ASPIA*, 1:302; Secretary of War to Governor of Georgia, July 11, 1792, *ASPIA*, 1:256.

42. John Ormsbay Deposition, May 11, 1792, *ASPIA*, 1:297–98.

43. McGillivray to Seagrove, May 18, 179[2], *ASPIA*, 1:302.

44. Secretary of War to Brigadier General Alexander McGillivray, July 11, 1792, *ASPIA*, 1:256–57.

45. The following are extracts . . . , March 25, 1792, *ASPIA*, 1:295.

46. Carondelet to Oliver, March 30, 1792, PdE, legajo 3898; Carondelet to Las Casas, April 29, 1792, PdE, legajo 3898; Oliver to Carondelet, May 2, 1792, PPdC, legajo 1446; Forrester to Quesada, May 21, 1792, EFP, reel 47b; O'Neill to Carondelet, May 21, 1792, PPdC, legajo 1446; O'Neill to Carondelet, May 31, 1792, PPdC, legajo 39.

47. Barnard to Seagrove, May 10, 1792, *ASPIA*, 1:297; John Ormsbay Deposition, May 11, 1792, *ASPIA*, 1:297–98; Seagrove to McGillivray, May 21, 1792, *ASPIA*, 1:298–99; McGillivray to Secretary of War, May 18, 1792, *ASPIA*, 1:315–16. For Seagrove's views, see Seagrove to Knox, May 24, 1792, *ASPIA*, 1:296; Seagrove to the President, July 5, 1792, *ASPIA*, 1:304–5; Seagrove to the President, July 27, 1792, *ASPIA*, 1:305–6; and Seagrove to Secretary of War, October 28, 1792, *ASPIA*, 1:320–21.

48. Cabinet Meeting . . . , in Syrett, ed., *Papers of Alexander Hamilton*, 14:490. For the arrival of Carondelet, see Berry, "The Indian Policy of Spain in the Southwest," 470–77; and Hoffman, *Florida Frontiers*, 247.

49. Carondelet to Panton, March 24, 1792, *MC*, 316–17; Carondelet to Floridablanca, April 4, 1792, *MPASD*, 4:213. For Thomas Jefferson's thoughts on Carondelet and his effect on the Creeks in 1792, see Jefferson to Carmichael and Short, November 3, 1792, *ASPFR*, 1:259. Spanish commissioners, when in conference with Jefferson, firmly supported honoring their treaty obligations with the Creeks in language that deeply offended him. See Jaudenes and Viar to the Secretary of State, June 18, 1793, *ASPFR*, 1:264–65; and Secretary of State to Carmichael and Short, June 30, 1793, *ASPFR*, 1:265–67.

50. Carondelet to Floridablanca, March 22, 1792, PPL, reel 7; Panton to Carondelet, April 16, 1792, EHW, box 2, folder Legajo 1. Panton tried to reconcile Carondelet to McGillivray, explaining that McGillivray had agreed to the Treaty of New York out of necessity and under pressure from Miró, and that even though he did have an American commission, he was abandoning the Spanish. See Panton to Carondelet, April 16, 1792, in Corbitt, "Papers, IX."

51. Carondelet to McGillivray, February 6, 1792, *MC*, 307; Carondelet to Olivier, February 8, 1792, PPdC, legajo 122A; Carondelet to Oliver, March 30, 1792, PdE, legajo 3898; Carondelet to Aranda, June 11, 1792, PdE, legajo 3898; Seagrove to the President, July 5, 1792, *ASPIA*, 1:304–5.

52. Durouzeaux to Seagrove, May 28, 1792, *ASPIA*, 1:302; Oliver to Carondelet, June 30, 1792, PPL, reel 7.

53. Carondelet to Aranda, June 11, 1792, PdE, legajo 3898.

54. Carondelet to McGillivray, July 6, 1792, PdE, legajo 3898. For more on requesting other Spanish agents to reside in the Nation, see O'Neill to Carondelet, July 13, 1792, PPdC, legajo 39; and O'Neill to Carondelet, July 20, 1792, PPdC, legajo 39.

55. McGillivray to Seagrove, May 18, 179[2], *ASPIA*, 1:302.

56. Carondelet to Panton, March 24, 1792, *MC*, 316–17; McGillivray to Seagrove, May 18, 179[2], *ASPIA*, 1:302; Carondelet to O'Neill, March 30, 1792, PdE, legajo 3898.

57. Carondelet to Las Casas, March 22, 1792, *MC*, 313–14; McGillivray to Carondelet, April 10, 1792, *MC*, 318–20; Carondelet to Panton, March 24, 1792, *MC*, 316–17; Wright, "Creek-American Treaty of 1790," 395–96; Carondelet to Oliver, March

30, 1792, PdE, legajo 3898; Carondelet to Las Casas, April 29, 1792, PdE, legajo 3898. Bowles courted the Spanish as well, pressing Carondelet to use him to keep the Americans at bay. See Bowles to Carondelet, March 14, 1792, PPdC, legajo 2371. This policy was accepted up the Spanish chain of command. See Las Casas to Carondelet, July 5, 1792, PPdC, legajo 1446.

58. Carondelet-McGillivray Treaty, July 6, 1792, *MC*, 329–30.

59. Carondelet to McGillivray, July 6, 1792, *MC*, 330; McGillivray to Carondelet, July 22, 1792, *MC*, 332–33; Oliver to Carondelet, May 29, 1792, PdE, legajo 3898; Carondelet to Aranda, July 7, 1792, PdE, legajo 3898; McGillivray to Carondelet, July 22, 1792, PPdC, legajo 2371.

60. Information of James Leonard . . . , July 24, 1792, *ASPIA*, 1:307–8; anonymous letter to the printer of the Savannah Gazette . . . , July 25, 1792, *ASPIA*, 1:309.

61. Seagrove to Secretary of War, October 28, 1792, *ASPIA*, 1:320–21. For headmen who remained loyal to McGillivray, see Seagrove to the President, July 27, 1792, *ASPIA*, 1:305–6; White Lieutenant to Seagrove, August 1, 1792, *ASPIA*, 1:312; and Talk from the White Lieut . . . , August 15, 1792, *CIL*, 1:254.

62. Panton to Carondelet, February 16, 1793, *MC*, 353; Panton to Carondelet, February 20, 1793, *MC*, 354.

63. Secretary of War to Governor of Georgia, July 11, 1792, *ASPIA*, 1:256; Durouzeaux to Seagrove, June 2, 1792, *ASPIA*, 1:303; Call to Telfair, April 29, 1792, *CIL*, 1:246.

64. McGillivray to Secretary of War, May 18, 1792, *ASPIA*, 1:315.

65. Barnard spoke of Chehawuseche, by whom he might have meant with Chehaws or Ooseoochees. He also mentioned Kitaheetas, who might have been Hitchitis. See Barnard to Seagrove, July 13, 1792, *ASPIA*, 1:309–10.

66. Seagrove to the President, July 5, 1792, *ASPIA*, 1:304–5.

67. Mitchell to Hamilton, August 27, 1793, in Syrett, ed., *Papers of Alexander Hamilton*, 15:296.

68. Carondelet to Floridablanca, March 18, 1792, PPdC, legajo 2353; Carondelet-McGillivray Treaty, July 6, 1792, *MC*, 329–30; Oliver to O'Neill, July 23, 1792, PPdC, legajo 40.

69. Gayoso de Lemos to Telfair, August 29, 1792, TCC, box 3, folder 27; Information by Richard Finnelson . . . , *ASPIA*, 1:288–90.

70. Robertson to . . . , March 12, 1793, *ASPIA*, 1:441; Minutes of information given Governor Blount by James Carey . . . , November 1792, *ASPIA*, 1:329.

71. Barnard to Seagrove, May 10, 1792, *ASPIA*, 1:297.

72. Durouzeaux to Seagrove, May 28, 1792, *ASPIA*, 1:302; Seagrove to Governor of East Florida, June 13, 1792, *ASPIA*, 1:303; McGillivray to Secretary of War, May 18, 1792, *ASPIA*, 1:315.

73. Secretary of War to Governor of Georgia, July 11, 1792, *ASPIA*, 1:256; Call to Telfair, April 29, 1792, *CIL*, 1:246.

74. Seagrove to the Secretary of War, July 5, 1792, *ASPIA*, 1:303–4; Secretary of War to the President . . . , December 13, 1793, CROC, 145–46.

75. Seagrove to the Secretary of War, September 13, 1792, *ASPIA*, 1:311; White Lieutenant to Seagrove, August 1, 1792, *ASPIA*, 1:312; A talk from the kings, chiefs, warriors . . . , August 23, 1792, *ASPIA*, 1:312; Kinnard to [Seagrove], August 28, 1792, *ASPIA*, 1:313; [Seagrove] to Kinnard, October 7, 1792, *ASPIA*, 1:314; Durouzeaux to Seagrove, October 15, 1792, *ASPIA*, 1:321.

76. Galphin to Seagrove, October 15, 1792, ASPIA, 1:321; [Seagrove] to Kinnard, October 7, 1792, ASPIA, 1:314; Seagrove to Kinnard, February 24, 1793, ASPIA, 1:378.

77. Seagrove to the Secretary of War, October 17, 1792, ASPIA, 1:311–12; [Seagrove] to the White Lieutenant, October 7, 1792, ASPIA, 1:313–14.

78. Washington also continued to voice his approval of the chief. See Seagrove to the White Lieutenant, February 20, 1793, ASPIA, 1:376–77.

79. Lakomäki, *Gathering Together*, 27–29, 56–60; Swan, "Position and State," 260; Wright, *Creeks & Seminoles*, 9–10.

80. Information of James Leonard to Seagrove, July 24, 1792, ASPIA, 1:307–8.

81. Secretary of War to Brigadier General Alexander McGillivray, February 17, 1792, ASPIA A, 1:246–47; Secretary of War to Seagrove, February 20, 1792, ASPIA, 1:249–50.

82. Seagrove to Alexander Cornells, February 20, 1793, ASPIA, 1:375; Report of David Craig . . . , March 15, 1792, ASPIA, 1:264–65.

83. Seagrove to Alexander Cornells, February 20, 1793, ASPIA, 1:375; Seagrove to Fine Bones, February 20, 1793, ASPIA, 1:376; Seagrove to the White Lieutenant, February 20, 1793, ASPIA, 1:376–77; Seagrove to the Leader of the Cowetas, February 20, 1793, ASPIA, 1:376; Seagrove to Holmes, February 24, 1793, ASPIA, 1:377; Seagrove to Barnard, February 24, 1793, ASPIA, 1:377–78; Seagrove to Kinnard, February 24, 1793, ASPIA, 1:378.

84. Panton to Carondelet, January 27, 1793, in Corbitt, "Papers, XII," 300–301; Seagrove to Barnard, February 24, 1793, ASPIA, 1:377.

85. The following information delivered by oath . . . , July 24, 1792, ASPIA, 1:307–8.

86. Leonard D. Shaw to . . . , August 18, 1792, ASPIA, 1:278; Secretary of War to Blount, October 9, 1792, ASPIA, 1:261; Secretary of War to Governor of Virginia, October 9, 1792, ASPIA, 1:261; Secretary of War to Governor of South Carolina, October 27, 1792, ASPIA, 1:262; Report of David Craig . . . , March 15, 1792, ASPIA, 1:264.

87. Pickens to Governor of South Carolina, September 18, 1792, ASPIA, 1:316–17. Blount also wrote to McGillivray complaining of Creek involvement on the Cumberland. See Blount to McGillivray, May 17, 1792, ASPIA, 1:269–70.

88. Blount to Secretary of War, August 31, 1792, ASPIA, 1:275–76. Another previous report came to the same conclusion. Attacks on the Cumberland settlements by the Cherokee groups was "to be accounted for by their intercourse with the Creeks and Shawanese, since the defeat of General St. Clair, and the arrival of Bowles from England," in addition to local issues in Cherokee Country. See Information received relatively . . . , March 20, 1792, ASPIA, 1:263.

89. P.S., dated May 31, 1792, attached to Blount to McGillivray, May 17, 1792, ASPIA, 1:269–70; Deposition of James Ore, June 16, 1792, ASPIA, 1:274.

90. Blount to Secretary of War, November 8, 1792, ASPIA, 1:325; Minutes of information given . . . , November 3, 1792, ASPIA, 1:327–29.

91. McGillivray to Carondelet, November 15, 1792, PdE, legajo 3898; Minutes of information given Governor Blount by James Carey . . . , November 1792, ASPIA, 1:329.

92. Carondelet to Montrevill, August 3, 1792, in Corbitt, "Papers, XI," 194–95; Montrevill to . . . , March 11, 1793, in Corbitt, "Papers, XI," 196; Information by Richard Finnelson, ASPIA, 1:288–91.

93. Secretary of War to Governor of South Carolina, October 27, 1792, ASPIA, 1:262. As Knox agreed, "It does not appear in evidence, that the conduct of the said Creeks

is influenced by the result of any deliberations of any assembly of chiefs, or even of towns." See Secretary of War to Seagrove, October 27, 1792, *ASPIA*, 1:262–63.

94. Cornells to Seagrove, January 6, 1793, *ASPIA*, 1:375; Seagrove to David Cornells, February 20, 1793, *ASPIA*, 1:375.

95. Carondelet to Montrevill, August 3, 1792, in Corbitt, "Papers, XI," 194–95; Montrevill to . . . , March 11, 1793, in Corbitt, "Papers, XI," 196; Gayoso de Lemos to Telfair, August 29, 1792, TCC, box 3, folder 27; Information by Richard Finnelson, *ASPIA*, 1:288–91.

96. Barnard to Gaither, March 4, 1793, CROC, 436–37.

97. Seagrove to Alexander Cornells, February 20, 1793, *ASPIA*, 1:375; Seagrove to Fine Bones . . . , February 20, 1793, *ASPIA*, 1:376.

98. Seagrove to the White Lieutenant, February 20, 1793, *ASPIA*, 1:376–77; Barnard to Gaither, March 4, 1793, *ASPIA*, 1:418.

99. Seagrove to Chiefs and Head-men . . . , February 20, 1793, *ASPIA*, 1:375; Seagrove to Fine Bones, February 20, 1793, CROC, 216–17; Seagrove to the Leader of the Cowetas, February 20, 1793, CROC, 218–19.

100. Seagrove to Fine Bones . . . , February 20, 1793, *ASPIA*, 1:376.

101. Seagrove to Cowetas, February 20, 1793, *ASPIA*, 1:376; Seagrove to Holmes, February 24, 1793, CROC, 222–24.

102. Seagrove to Chiefs and Head-men . . . , February 20, 1793, *ASPIA*, 1:375; Seagrove to the Leader of the Cowetas, February 20, 1793, CROC, 218–19.

103. Seagrove to Holmes, February 24, 1793, CROC, 222–24; Seagrove to Kinnard, February 24, 1793, CROC, 226–27.

104. Seagrove to Barnard, February 24, 1793, *aspiA*, 1:377–78; Information by James Carey . . . , March 20, 1793, *ASPIA*, 1:437.

105. At a talk held in the Cussetahs, Creek nation . . . , March 22, 1793, *ASPIA*, 1:383; Talk delivered by Mr. Barnard . . . , March 22, 1793, *ASPIA*, 1:382–83.

106. Barnard to Seagrove, March 26, 1793, *ASPIA*, 1:381–82.

107. Clark to Governor, June 13, 1792, CIL, 1:248; Earley to Clark, October 5, 1792, CIL, 1:258; Clark to Governor, October 15, 1792, CIL, 1:261; Carondelet to Aranda, June 10, 1792, PdE, legajo 3898.

108. Telfair to Gaither, March 4, 1793, *ASPIA*, 1:418; Secretary of War to the Governor of Georgia, March 9, 1793, CROC, 152–53; Secretary of War to Telfair, April 29, 1793, CROC, 153–54.

109. Cuthbert Affidavit, ID, vol. 2, part 1, 23–24; Samuel Smith Affidavit, July 21, 1835, ID, vol. 2, part 1, 112–13; Robert Brown Affidavit, March 14, 1793, *ASPIA*, 1:374; Ann Gray Deposition, March 14, 1793, *ASPIA*, 1:374; Forrester to Quesada, March 13, 1793, EFP, reel 47.

110. Cuthbert Affidavit, ID, vol. 2, part 1, 23–24; Extract from a Deposition by eleven Inhabitants of Glynn county, March 11, 1793, *ASPIA*, 1:368; Telfair to Gaither, March 28, 1793, *ASPIA*, 1:418; Elizabeth Green Deposition, March 23, 1793, IT, 21; Forrester to Quesada, March 19, 1793, EFP, reel 48. Telfair later complained that the southern frontier was practically defenseless and that "the inhabitants of the counties of Glynn and Camden, must remove from their settlements, if speedy and sufficient aid be not afforded." See Telfair to Secretary of War, April 3, 1793, *ASPIA*, 1:368.

111. Jackson to Telfair, March 16, 1793, CIL, 1:271; Houstoun to His Excellency the Governor, March 18, 1793, CIL, 1:275; extract of a letter to General Jackson . . . , April 7,

1793, in Indian Letters, 1782–1839 (unpublished typescript, edited by Louise F. Hayes, 1940), 20.

112. Cuthbert Affidavit, ID, vol. 2, part 1, 23–24; Pricella Thomas Affidavit, July 15, 1835, ID, vol. 2, part 1, 91; Wm. McIntosh to General McIntosh, March 18, 1793, CIL, 1:276; Hardy to . . . , April 1, 1793, CIL, 1:277; Barnard to Gaither, April 8, 1793, ASPIA, 1:419; Forrester to Quesada, April 8, 1793, EFP, reel 48.

113. Seagrove to Secretary of War, March 17, 1793, ASPIA, 1:373–74.

114. Telfair to Secretary of War, April 3, 1793, ASPIA, 1:368; Seagrove to the Chiefs, Head Men, and Warriors, of the whole Creek Nation . . . , March 28, 1793, ASPIA, 1:379; April 8, 1793, CIL, 1:279–80; Gaither to the Secretary of War, April 17, 1793, CROC, 437–38; Forrester to Quesada, March 19, 1793, EFP, reel 48.

115. Barnard to Gaither, April 8, 1793, ASPIA, 1:419.

116. Talk from the Head-men of the Chehaws and Telluiana, March 29, 1793, ASPIA, 1:383.

117. Seagrove to Secretary of War, April 19, 1793, ASPIA, 1:378–79; Secretary of War to Seagrove, June 10, 1793, CROC, 168–69.

118. Copy of a letter from Timothy Barnard, April 19, 1793, ASPIA, 1:386–87. Many headmen had evidently agreed to return the property they had taken, at least until they heard Seagrove's demands for lives, when many became more desperate. Others, including the Tallassee King and another headman from a Chehaw town, simply fled with the property they had taken. See James Aiken's Deposition, May 3, 1793, ASPIA, 1:389–90.

119. Barnard to Seagrove, April 9, 1793, ASPIA, 1:390–91; Gaither to the Secretary of War, April 17, 1793, CROC, 437–38; Barnard to Seagrove, April 19, 1793, ASPIA, 1:386–87.

120. Barnard to Seagrove, April 9, 1793, ASPIA, 1:390–91; Barnard to Seagrove, April 19, 1793, ASPIA, 1:386–87.

121. Copy of Alex Cornells Talk, June 14, 1793, CIL, 1:323–24.

122. Barnard to Seagrove, April 9, 1793, ASPIA, 1:390–91; Gaither to Secretary of War, April 19, 1793, ASPIA, 1:419.

123. Bird King and Cussetah King to Gaither, April 13, 1793, ASPIA, 1:420; The following talks received by Seagrove . . . , April 15, 1793, ASPIA, 1:384; Barnard to Seagrove, April 19, 1793, ASPIA, 1:386–87.

124. Copy of a letter from Alexander Cornells . . . , April 15, 1793, ASPIA, 1:384; Barnard to Seagrove, April 19, 1793, ASPIA, 1:386–87.

125. Copy of a letter from James M. Holmes, April 20, 1793, ASPIA, 1:386; Barnard to Seagrove, April 19, 1793, ASPIA, 1:386–87; Holmes to Seagrove, April 20, 1793, ASPIA, 1:386.

126. Barnard to Seagrove, May 12, 1793, ASPIA, 1:391; List of the unfriendly towns in the creek nation . . . , ASPIA, 1:392. Despite Cusseta attempts to do "all they can to stop the mischief," many seemed beyond the point of simply turning over the guilty, which made the outlook bleak. See Talk from Kinnard and other Chiefs, May 16, 1793, ASPIA, 1:388–89.

127. Barnard to Seagrove, April 19, 1793, ASPIA, 1:386–87; Barnard to Gaither, April 20, 1793, ASPIA, 1:420; Barnard to Gaither, ASPIA, 1:421; Holmes to Seagrove, April 20, 1793, ASPIA, 1:386.

128. Seagrove was particularly critical of the Spanish, whom he accused of directly inciting the recent violence, arming the perpetrators, buying stolen goods and horses from

the raiders, and even offering scalp bounties. "Finding matters going favourable between us and the Creeks," he complained to Washington, they "were determined to have bloodshed at all events." Seagrove to Washington, March 17, 1793, in Twoig, ed., *Papers of George Washington*, 12:335–36. Their "perfidious conduct," he continued to Knox, was "so barefaced" that he did not see how the Americans could not retaliate militarily. See Seagrove to Secretary of War, April 19, 1793, ASPIA, 1:378–79. For all of Seagrove's and Barnard's allegations, see Deposition of Barnard, May 2, 1793, ASPIA, 1:402; James Aiken Deposition, May 3, 1793, ASPIA, 1:389–90; and Galphin Deposition, May 24, 1793, ASPIA, 1:389.

129. Seagrove to the chiefs of the Lower Creeks, May 13, 1793, ASPIA, 1:397.

6. A Stronger Nationhood

1. Knox, pleased with Seagrove's efforts, recommended setting up official and permanent agencies in both the Upper and Lower countries, which Seagrove would head. One could be built in the Cusseta area, he suggested, while the other would surely be located at Oakfuskee, in order to befriend the White Lieutenant, "whose character renders his entire friendship of importance." See Secretary of War to Seagrove, October 31, 1792, ASPIA 1:259–60.

2. Seagrove to the Chiefs, Head Men, and Warriors . . . , March 28, 1793, ASPIA, 1:379; Seagrove to the Kings, Chiefs, Head-men . . . , April 14, 1793, ASPIA, 1:381.

3. The Following talks . . . , April 15, 1793, ASPIA, 1:384. See also Bird King and Cussetah King to Gaither, April 13, 1793, ASPIA, 1:420.

4. Seagrove to Secretary of War, April 30, 1793, ASPIA, 1:384.

5. Copy of a letter from Alexander Cornells . . . , April 15, 1793, ASPIA, 1:384; Copy of a Letter from A. Cornells, April 8, 1793, ASPIA, 1:385; The Mad Dog of the Tuckabatchees' Talk . . . , ASPIA, 1:383; Barnard to Seagrove, April 19, 1793, ASPIA, 1:386–87.

6. "A Sketch of the Creek Country," in *LJW*, 285, 326–27; Swanton, *Social Organization*, 55, 65–68, 243–46, 266–67. For more evidence of this, see Grantham, *Creation Myths and Legends*; Gatschet, *A Migration Legend*; and Lankford, *Native American Legends*.

7. Wright, *Creeks & Seminoles*, 1–5.

8. For this idea, see Piker, *Okfuskee*; Boulware, *Deconstructing the Cherokee Nation*; and Sider, *Lumbee Indian Histories*.

9. Hahn, *Invention of the Creek Nation*, 4–8, and 229–70, particularly pp. 231–34, 241–44, 262–63.

10. Kohn, *The Idea of Nationalism*, 4.

11. Hahn, *Invention of the Creek Nation*, 244–58; Juricek, *Colonial Georgia and the Creeks*, 4–5; Champagne, *Social Order*, 64–74.

12. For Cherokee nationalism as the result of the threat of American expansionism, see McLoughlin, *Cherokee Renascence*, 156, 222–25, quotation on 156.

13. The idea that nation and state formation could be tied to security and necessity is particularly relevant in the development of government in Revolutionary and early Republican America. See Higginbotham, "War and State Formation in Revolutionary America"; Elding, *Revolution in Favor of Government*; Hendrickson, *Peace Pact*; and Gould, *Among the Powers of the Earth*.

14. Copy of a letter from Charles Weatherford, March 9, 1793, ASPIA, 1:385; copy of a letter from C. Weatherford, March 22, 1793, ASPIA, 1:386.

15. Meek, *Romantic Passages*, 264–66; Waselkov, *A Conquering Spirit*, 42–43.

16. Griffith, *McIntosh and Weatherford*, 40.

17. O'Neill to Miró, October 28, 1788, MC, 204–5; Griffith, *McIntosh and Weatherford*, 40–41.

18. Seagrove to the President, July 5, 1792, ASPIA, 1:304–5; Griffith, *McIntosh and Weatherford*, 41–43.

19. Declaration of James Dearment, April 18, 1793, MC, 357; Saunt, *A New Order of Things*, 155.

20. "A Sketch of Creek Country," CGHS, vol. 3, part 1:30–31; Saunt, *A New Order of Things*, 99; Green, *Politics of Indian Removal*, 37, 39.

21. Commissioners to Secretary of War, November 20, 1789, ASPIA, 1:78–79.

22. Dowd, *A Spirited Resistance*, 100; Harper, *Travels*, 315; Mereness, "Journal of David Taitt's Travels," 538–39; Ethridge, *Creek Country*, 103, 213.

23. Durouzeaux to Seagrove, May 28, 1792, ASPIA, 1:302; Durouzeaux to Seagrove, June 2, 1792, ASPIA, 1:303. For a later account of the incident, see Tuckabatchee, April 8, 1793, ASPIA, 1:384.

24. Dowd, *A Spirited Resistance*, 100, 112; Swan, "Position and State," 263; McGillivray to Panton, December 19, 1785, MC, 100; McGillivray to Miró, May 1, 1786, MC, 108–9.

25. "A Sketch of Creek Country," CGHS, vol. 3, part 1:30.

26. Swan, "Position and State," 254; Little Turkey to Blount, June 5, 1793, ASPIA, 1:461. He had sent a runner down to Cusseta, which was "much in favor of the states," to affirm that the Upper Towns "were of the same opinion respecting the Americans, as they were, and not to be deluded with the Shawnee talks." See Barnard to Gaither, March 4, 1793, ASPIA, 1:418.

27. For Tuskena Atca, see White Lieutenant to Seagrove, June 23, 1793, ASPIA, 1:401.

28. David Taitt noted in 1773 that James Germany was a trader in Cooloome, with a house. Mereness, "Journal of David Taitt's Travels," 509. In 1774 the White Lieutenant was apparently a trading factor for Robert Rae, who was also a close friend of the Handsome Fellow. See Piker, *Okfuskee*, 140, 154. Later, Timothy Barnard referred to him as "the Big Half Breed, or White Lieutenant." See Barnard to Seagrove, July 2, 1793, ASPIA, 1:400.

29. Commissioners to Secretary of War, November 20, 1789, ASPIA, 1:78–79.

30. Barnard to Seagrove, July 2, 1793, ASPIA, 1:400–401; Swan, "Position and State," 255, 263.

31. Entry for Thursday, the 8th [1796], in CGHS, 9:29–30.

32. White Lieutenant to Seagrove, August 1, 1792, ASPIA, 1:312; Talk from the White Lieutenant . . . , August 15, 1793, CIL, 1:254.

33. [Seagrove] to the White Lieutenant, October 7, 1792, ASPIA, 1:313–14.

34. "A Sketch of Creek Country," CGHS, vol. 3, part 1:60.

35. Entries for February 2–4, 1797, LJW, 41–44.

36. Barnard to Clarke, April 12, 1785, LTB, 38–39; Barnard to Elbert, June 18, 1785, LTB, 48–49. For the Fat King and the role of micos, or chiefs, see Green, "Alexander McGillivray," 49; Green, *Politics of Indian Removal*, 8–10; and Ethridge, *Creek Country*, 102–3.

37. Swan, "Position and State," 263.

38. Caleb Swan outlined at least three hundred in Creek Country, although that number is probably far too low. He also wrote on their presence in detail, commenting that almost every town had a trader, who employed white packhorsemen. Besides those, "there is, in almost every town, one family of whites, and in some two, who do not trade." Swan, "Position and State," 263.

39. Entry for 21st, February, 1797, CGHS, 9:86; extract of a letter to William Faulkner, November 25, 1797, CGHS, vol. 3, part 1:8–9; Ethridge, *Creek Country*, 64; Woodward, *Reminiscences*, 109; Bulloch, *A History and Genealogy of the Habersham Family*, 71.

40. Barnard to Telfair, August 14, 1786, LTB, 59–60; G. M. to Habersham, February 15, 1787, LTB, 72; John Galphin to Osborne, May 23, 1789, ASPIA, 1:36.

41. Hawkins to Barnard, March 7, 1797, CGHS, 9:96–97; Hawkins to Price, March 9, 1797, CGHS, 9:101–2.

42. Barnard to Telfair, August 14, 1786, LTB, 59–60; G. M. to Habersham, February 15, 1787, LTB, 72.

43. Seagrove to Barnard, February 24, 1793, ASPIA, 1:377–78.

44. Bird King and Cussetah King to Gaither, April 13, 1793, ASPIA, 1:420; The following talks received by Seagrove . . . , April 15, 1793, ASPIA, 1:384.

45. Galphin's Deposition, May 24, 1793, ASPIA, 1:389; Seagrove to Secretary of War, May 24, 1793, ASPIA, 1:387–88. In 1797 Seagrove made John Galphin an express rider. See Seagrove to Price, January 6, 1797, CFR, reel 1. For complaints by Barnard of his "meddling work" early in 1797, probably stealing horses, see Barnard to Price, March 27, 1797, CFR, reel 1.

46. Swan, "Position and State," 254, 256.

47. Swan did not have a particularly positive appraisal of Kinnard. Aside from trading with the Indians around him, "who are dupes to his avarice," he was "addicted to excessive drunkenness, and, like all half-breeds, is very proud of being white-blooded. He is a despot, shoots his negroes when he pleases, and has cut off the ears of one of his favorite wives, with his own hands, in a drunken fit of suspicion." See Swan, "Position and State," 254, 256, 260–62; and Saunt, *A New Order of Things*, 56, 100–101.

48. Barnard to Seagrove, May 10, 1792, ASPIA, 1:297; Seagrove to Secretary of War, September 13, 1792, ASPIA, 1:311.

49. Seagrove to Secretary of War, September 8, 1792, ASPIA, 1:310–11.

50. Durousseau to Panton, July 23, 1796, in Corbitt, "Letters, XVI," 265–66. See also John Galphin and James Douzeazeaux to . . . , June 14, 1787, ASPIA, 1:32; and A talk from the Chiefs, Head-men, and Warriors . . . , June 1, 1789, ASPIA, 1:34–35.

51. James Aiken Deposition, May 3, 1793, ASPIA, 1:389–90; Hawkins to Price, March 9, 1797, CGHS, 9:101–2.

52. Seagrove to the Chiefs, Head Men, and Warriors . . . , April 28, 1793, ASPIA, 1:379; Circular, March 28, 1793, ASPIA, 1:380.

53. Barnard to Seagrove, July 13, 1792, ASPIA, 1:309. In another letter, these same men reiterated their support of Seagrove and their determination to work with him. See A Talk from the Kings chief warriors and head men . . . , August 23, 1792, CIL, 1:255–56.

54. Barnard to Seagrove, April 9, 1793, ASPIA A, 1:390–91.

55. Holmes to Seagrove, April 20, 1793, ASPIA, 1:386; Barnard to Gaither, April 2, 1793, CROC, 438–40.

56. Barnard to Seagrove, March 26, 1793, *ASPIA*, 1:381–82; Barnard to Seagrove, April 19, 1793, *ASPIA*, 1:386–87.

57. Barnard to Seagrove, April 9, 1793, *ASPIA*, 1:390–91; Seagrove to Secretary of War, April 19, 1793, *ASPIA*, 1:378–79.

58. Seagrove to Secretary of War, April 19, 1793, *ASPIA*, 1:378–79; Barnard to Gaither, *ASPIA*, 1:421; James Aiken Deposition, May 3, 1793, *ASPIA*, 1:389–90.

59. Copy of a letter from Alexander Cornells, April 15, 1793, *ASPIA*, 1:384; Talk from Kinnard and other Chiefs, May 16, 1793, *ASPIA*, 1:388–89. For another account of unrest, see Copy of a Letter from James M. Holmes, April 20, 1793, *ASPIA*, 1:386.

60. Weatherford to Seagrove, March 22, 1793, CROC, 267–68; Barnard to Seagrove, March 26, 1793, *ASPIA*, 1:381–82; Barnard to Seagrove, April 9, 1793, *ASPIA*, 1:390–91; Copy of a Letter from Timothy Barnard, April 19, 1793, *ASPIA*, 1:388–87.

61. Barnard to Jackson, April 9, 1793, LTB, 141–44; Seagrove to Secretary of War, April 19, 1793, *ASPIA*, 1:378–79; Barnard to Gaither, *ASPIA*, 1:421.

62. Secretary of War to Seagrove, June 10, 1793, CROC, 168–69; Barnard to Seagrove, April 19, 1793, *ASPIA*, 1:386–87.

63. Copy of a letter from James M. Holmes, April 20, 1793, *ASPIA*, 1:386.

64. Copy of a letter from Alexander Cornells . . . , April 15, 1793, *ASPIA*, 1:384; copy of a letter from Timothy Barnard, April 19, 1793, *ASPIA*, 1:388–87.

65. Copy of a letter from Alexander Cornells . . . , April 15, 1793, *ASPIA*, 1:384; copy of a letter from James M. Holmes, April 20, 1793, *ASPIA*, 1:386; The Following talks . . . , April 15, 1793, *ASPIA*, 1:384; Tuckabatchee, April 8, 1793, *ASPIA*, 1:384.

66. Copy of a letter from Timothy Barnard, April 19, 1793, *ASPIA*, 1:386.

67. Copy of a letter from James M. Holmes, April 20, 1793, *ASPIA*, 1:386; copy of a letter from Timothy Barnard, April 19, 1793, *ASPIA*, 1:386–87.

68. Copy of a letter from Timothy Barnard, April 19, 1793, *ASPIA*, 1:386–87.

69. Copy of a talk from the Big Warrior . . . , *ASPIA*, 1:401–2.

70. Barnard to Seagrove, May 12, 1793, *ASPIA*, 1:391.

71. James Aiken Deposition, May 3, 1793, *ASPIA*, 1:389–90; Talk from Kinnard and Other Chiefs, May 16, 1793, *ASPIA*, 1:388–89; Seagrove to Secretary of War, May 24, 1793, *ASPIA*, 1:387–88; Barnard to Seagrove, May 12, 1793, *ASPIA*, 1:391.

72. Talk from Kinnard and Other Chiefs, May 16, 1793, *ASPIA*, 1:388–89; Seagrove to Secretary of War, May 24, 1793, *ASPIA*, 1:387–88.

73. For an example of the raiding, see James Aiken Deposition, May 3, 1793, *ASPIA*, 1:389–90; Talk from Kinnard and Other Chiefs, May 16, 1793, *ASPIA*, 1:388–89; Barnard to Seagrove, May 12, 1793, *ASPIA*, 1:391.

74. James Aiken Deposition, May 3, 1793, *ASPIA*, 1:389–90; Seagrove to the chiefs of the Lower Creeks, May 13, 1793, *ASPIA*, 1:397; Seagrove to the Chiefs of the Creek Nation, May 27, 1793, *ASPIA*, 1:396.

75. Seagrove to Secretary of War, May 24, 1793, *ASPIA*, 1:387–88; Talk from Kinnard and Other Chiefs, May 16, 1793, *ASPIA*, 1:388–89.

76. Barnard to Seagrove, May 12, 1793, *ASPIA*, 1:39; Talk from Kinnard and Other Chiefs, May 16, 1793, *ASPIA*, 1:388–89.

77. Barnard to Seagrove, May 12, 1793, *ASPIA*, 1:391.

78. Telfair to Knox, July 24, 1793, CROC, 187–88.

79. Barnard to Seagrove, May 12, 1793, *ASPIA*, 1:391; Seagrove to the chiefs of the Lower Creeks, May 13, 1793, *ASPIA*, 1:397; Talk from Kinnard and Other Chiefs, May

16, 1793, *ASPIA*, 1:388–89; copy of a talk from the Big Warrior of the Cussetahs . . . , *ASPIA*, 1:401–2.

80. Seagrove to Secretary of War, May 24, 1793, *ASPIA*, 1:387–88; Telfair to the Secretary of War, July 24, 1793, CROC, 187–88.

81. Secretary of War to Seagrove, October 27, 1792, *ASPIA*, 1:262–63.

82. Barnard to Seagrove, March 26, 1793, *ASPIA*, 1:381–82.

83. Knox to Seagrove, April 30, 1793, CROC, 167–68; Knox to Seagrove, June 10, 1793, CROC, 168–69.

84. Barnard to Gaither, June 21, 1793, *ASPIA*, 1:422; The Mad Dog of Tuckabatchee's Talk, March 22, 1793, *ASPIA*, 1:383.

85. White Lieutenant to Seagrove, June 23, 1793, *ASPIA*, 1:401; Barnard to Seagrove, March 26, 1793, *ASPIA*, 1:381–82.

86. Barnard to Seagrove, April 9, 1793, *ASPIA*, 1:390–91. For more requests from headmen and from Knox, see Barnard to Seagrove, June 20, 1793, *ASPIA*, 1:394–95; Barnard to Seagrove, July 2, 1793, *ASPIA*, 1:400–401; Knox to Seagrove, April 30, 1793, CROC, 167–68; and Knox to Seagrove, June 10, 1793, CROC, 168–69.

87. Galphin to Irwin, August 21, 1793, CROC, 193–95. Another onlooker wrote in September that "Mr. Seagrove the Superintendant for the United States, is expected in the nation dailly, if he should not come, I know not what will be the consequence of the ties in our land." Lallisont to Panton, October 2, 1793, in Corbitt, "Letters, XIV," 79.

88. Weatherford to Seagrove, June 11, 1793, *ASPIA*, 1:395; White Lieutenant, Cornells, and others to Seagrove, June 14, 1793, *ASPIA*, 1:396; Barnard to Seagrove, June 20, 1793, *ASPIA*, 1:394–95.

89. Barnard to Seagrove, June 20, 1793, *ASPIA*, 1:394–95.

90. Barnard to Seagrove, June 20, 1793, *ASPIA*, 1:394–95; Barnard to Gaither, June 21, 1793, *ASPIA*, 1:422; White Lieutenant to Seagrove, June 23, 1793, *ASPIA*, 1:401.

91. Barnard to Seagrove, June 20, 1793, *ASPIA*, 1:394–95; Barnard to Seagrove, July 2, 1793, *ASPIA*, 1:400–401; Barnard to Gaither, June 21, 1793, *ASPIA*, 1:422.

92. Barnard to Seagrove, June 20, 1793, *ASPIA*, 1:395.

93. Barnard to Seagrove, June 20, 1793, *ASPIA*, 1:395; Barnard to Seagrove, June 20, 1793, LTB, 182.

94. For the killing and the development of the crisis around it, see Randolph to Seagrove, June 30, 1793, *ASPIA*, 1:397; Seagrove to Barnard, July 5, 1793, *ASPIA*, 1:398; Barnard to Gaither, July 7, 1793, *ASPIA*, 1:423; Townshend to Jackson . . . , LTB, 200–201; Barnard to Telfair, July 7, 1793, LTB, 202–4; Barnard to Twiggs, July 9, 1793, TCC, box 1, folder 11; and Savannah, July 21, 1793, LTB, 205.

95. Seagrove to Cornells, July 5, 1793, *ASPIA*, 1:398. Seagrove spoke similarly with the White Lieutenant. See Seagrove to the White Lieutenant, July 29, 1793, *ASPIA*, 1:402–3.

96. Seagrove to the White Lieutenant, July 29, 1793, *ASPIA*, 1:402–3; Seagrove to Cornells, July 29, 1793, *ASPIA*, 1:403; Seagrove to the Mad Dog, July 29, 1793, *ASPIA*, 1:403–4; Seagrove to Weatherford, July 29, 1793, *ASPIA*, 1:404–5; Seagrove to the Kings and Chiefs of the Cussetahs . . . , July 29, 1793, *ASPIA*, 1:404.

97. Seagrove to Cornells, July 29, 1793, *ASPIA*, 1:403.

98. Alexander Cornells was pushing Seagrove aggressively to see justice done speedily, informing him that, "without some example is made of those who had a hand

in the death of David, it will be impossible for peace to last long." Cornells to Seagrove, *ASPIA*, 1:407; Seagrove to Secretary of War, August 13, 1793, *ASPIA*, 1:406.

99. Seagrove to Secretary of War, August 13, 1793, *ASPIA*, 1:406.

100. Barnard to Seagrove, October 17, 1793, *ASPIA*, 1:415–16.

101. Barnard to Seagrove, October 18, 1793, *ASPIA*, 1:416; Seagrove to Secretary of War, October 31, 1793, *ASPIA*, 1:468.

102. Seagrove to Secretary of War, November 30, 1793, *ASPIA*, 1:471–72.

103. He also promised to have all of the prisoners taken in the Georgians' latest outrage—the raiding of a friendly Oakfuskee village—returned. Because Georgians had already refused to do that once, Seagrove again applied to Knox directly, explaining that "interference of the General Government may be necessary, ere they are delivered. Should this be the case, I must request that no time be lost." Seagrove to Secretary of War, November 30, 1793, *ASPIA*, 1:471–72; for a Spanish report of Seagrove's arrival and speech in Tuckabatchee, see Milford to Carondelet, March 20, 1794, EHW, box 2, folder AGS legajo 7235. For Oliver's thoughts on it, which were positive, see Oliver to Burgess, November 28, 1793, in Corbitt, "Letters, XIV," 81.

104. Seagrove to Secretary of War, November 30, 1793, *ASPIA*, 1:471–72.

105. Seagrove to Secretary of War, November 30, 1793, *ASPIA*, 1:471–72; "A Sketch of Creek Country," *CGHS*, vol. 3, part 1:27.

106. Seagrove to Telfair, November 30, 1793, *ASPIA*, 1:471; Seagrove to Mathews, June 29, 1795, CIL, 2:440.

107. Freeman to Secretary of War, May 11, 1794, *ASPIA*, 1:485; Seagrove to Secretary of War, May 16, 1794, *ASPIA*, 1:486. For one of Mathews's talks at Augusta and replies from headmen including the White-Bird-Tail King, the Mad Dog, Alexander Cornells, and others, see Corbitt, "Letters, XV," 154–57.

108. A Talk from the Head men of the Cussetas & Cowetas . . . , June 27, 1794, in Corbitt, "Letters, XV," 155–56.

7. The Ascendancy of the National Council

1. Federal successes in the Northwest quelled much of the violence there, allowing President Washington to turn more attention to the Southeast and to the Creek-Georgia frontier. See Prucha, *American Indian Policy*, 49.

2. See Stagg, *Borderlines in Borderlands*, 36–38; Bemis, *Pinckney's Treaty*; and Whitaker, *Spanish-American Frontier*.

3. "The Creeks," June 25, 1795, *ASPIA*, 1:560; Secretary of War to Governor of Georgia, March 20, 1795, *ASPIA*, 1:561; Governor of Georgia to Secretary of War, April 16, 1795, *ASPIA*, 1:560. For the treaty, see Sadosky, *Revolutionary Negotiations*, 165–75; and Pound, *Benjamin Hawkins*, 81–98.

4. Seagrove to Irwin, April 9, 1796, CIL, 2:470–71; Seagrove to Irwin, April 18, 1796, CIL, 2:472–73; A talk from James Seagrove . . . , CIL, 2:474–76.

5. Washington to Senate, January 4, 1797, *ASPIA*, 1:586; Hawkins to Seagrove, *ASPIA* A, 1:587–88; Hawkins to McHenry, May 19, 1796, *ASPIA*, 1:588.

6. Entry for June 9, *ASPIA*, 1:594–95; entry for Sunday, 12th, *ASPIA*, 1:595; Received From the Superintendent . . . , June 14, 1796, *ASPIA*, 1:596; Colerain, 15th June 1796, *ASPIA*, 1:597; entry for June 16, 1796, *ASPIA*, 1:597; entry dated June 22, [1796], *ASPIA*, 1:600.

7. Entry for June 17, 1796, *ASPIA*, 1:597.

8. Kings, Chiefs, and Warriors, of the Creek Nation . . . , *ASPIA*, 1:598; entry titled Mr. Hawkins, *ASPIA*, 1:598.

9. Honorable Commissioners of Georgia . . . , *ASPIA*, 1:603; Commissioners Letter, July 1, 1796, *JMP*, box 2.

10. Commissioners United States, by Mr. Hawkins . . . , *ASPIA*, 1:604-5; entry titled June 25th, *ASPIA*, 1:604. For the Georgian attempt to gain land all the way to the Okmulgee River, see Durousseau to Panton, July 23, 1796, in Corbitt, "Papers, XVI," 265.

11. Kappler, *Indian Affairs*, 2:49-40; June 26, 1796, *ASPIA*, 1:606-7; Horsman, *Expansion and American Indian Policy*, 80-81.

12. This was an important stipulation that Creek chiefs pressed for, demonstrating their continued trust in the federal agents. Garrisons would be positioned on the Creek side of the boundary, and there would "always be a garrison of Federal troops stationed there, to preserve order and good government; they will of course protect you, as you see they do here." See Kings, chiefs, and Warriors, of the whole Creek nation . . . , *ASPIA*, 1:601. See also Commissioners Letter, July 1, 1796, *JMP*, Box 2; and "after June 10, 1796," *JMP*, box 2. For the development of the trading house at Coleraine and then at Fort Wilkinson, see Peake, *A History of the United States Indian Factory System*.

13. Hawkins to McHenry, January 6, 1797, *LJW*, 62-63; Hawkins to Sevier, April 6, 1797, *LJW*, 98-99.

14. Journal entry for February 3, 1797, *LJW*, 42.

15. See Journal entry for December 3, 1796, *LJW*, 8. Hawkins also explained to James McHenry that "the Indians who were at Colerain have spoken highly of the candid, just and friendly conduct of the commissioners . . . and in every town I find some of them, who point me out as one of them." See Hawkins to McHenry, January 6, 1797, *LJW*, 62-63.

16. See Journal entry for December 14, 1796, *LJW*, 17-18; Hawkins to McHenry, January 6, 1797, *LJW*, 62-63; and Hawkins to Gaither, January 1, 1797, *LJW*, 62; Hawkins to McHenry, March 1, 1797, *LJW*, 86. Hawkins still had doubts about some of the Lower Country. Cowetas, for instance, he feared were still too violent, and their chiefs too weak, to depend on them. Still, Cussetas had been friendly for years and remained so. See Hawkins to Cornells, March 6, 1797, *LJW*, 1:92-93. Nevertheless, the situation was much more stable than it had been. "We begin to understand each other," he penned a friend later in 1797, "we have black drink and talks in the day, and dancing at night." Between a short sleep and an early morning "the remainder of the time is claimed by the Indians, and I devote it to them." See Hawkins to Butler, November 9, 1797, *LJW*, 1:148.

17. For an example of this fear, see R. T. to Seagrove, February 19, 1796, *CGHS*, 9:451; Journal entry for December 3, 1796, *LJW*, 1:8.

18. Prucha, *The Great Father*, 1:90; Prucha, *American Indian Policy*, 44-45; Horsman, *Expansion and American Indian Policy*, 62-63.

19. Jones, *License for Empire*, 157-86.

20. Cornells and Mad Dog to Barnard, September 14, 1794, *LTB*, 240; Irwin to Barnard, October 3, 1794, *LTB*, 241.

21. Barnard to Seagrove, December 18, 1794, *LTB*, 242; Barnard to Mathews, January 21, 1795, *LTB*, 243.

22. Secretary of War to Seagrove, January 13, 1795, *ASPIA*, 1:559.

23. Roberts to Secretary of War, May 10, 1794, *ASPIA*, 1:482; Jordan to Gaither, May 5, 1794, *ASPIA*, 1:482–83; Freeman to Secretary of War, May 9, 1794, *ASPIA*, 1:483; Freeman to Governor of Georgia, May 9, 1794, CIL, 2:375–77; Cornells and Mad Dog to Barnard, September 14, 1794, CIL, 2:406.

24. A Message from James Seagrove, September 15, 1796, CIL, 2:489–93. For instance, in July 1797 citizens of Greene County complained that there had been "a considerable number of horses & other property taken from the whites since our commissioners met the Indians at Colerain," and that "Those repeated & aggrevating savage insults on our frontier will inevitably end in the effusion of blood, without the interposition of government." Melton to Irwin, July 27, 1796, CIL, 482.

25. Letter from the Secretary of War to Brigadier General McGillivray, July 13, 1791, *ASPIA*, 1:127–28.

26. St. Marys, December 30, 1795, CFR, reel 1.

27. A Message from James Seagrove, September 15, 1796, CIL, 2:489–93.

28. Journal entry for December 14, 1796, *LJW*, 1:17–18. For examples of whites buying stolen horses, and Hawkins's irritation at it, see Hawkins to Jackson, July 11, 1798, LBH, 31–33; and Hawkins to Milledge, January 3, 1803, LBH, 63–64. For the general practice, see Ethridge, *Creek Country*, 181–85; and Pound, *Benjamin Hawkins*, 170–72.

29. R. T. to Seagrove, February 19, 1796, *CGHS*, 9:451; R. T. to T. B., March 21, 1797, *CGHS*, 9:456.

30. Hawkins to Cornells, March 8, 1797, *LJW*, 1:92–93.

31. Hawkins to McHenry, March 1, 1797, *LJW*, 1:85–87.

32. Barnard to Price, April 20, 1797, CFR, reel 1; Barnard to Price, April 6, 1797, CFR, reel 1.

33. R. T. to [Hawkins], September 19, 1796, *CGHS*, 9:452–53; Barnard to Price, March 27, 1797, CFR, reel 1; Barnard to Price, December 21, 1797, CFR, reel 1; Monday 16th, 1798, *CGHS*, 9:487. For the Little Prince, see Voucher N. 1, November 14, 1799, CFR, reel 2.

34. A talk from the kings, chiefs, warriors . . . , August 23, 1792, *ASPIA*, 1:312; John Kinnard to . . . , August 28, 1792, *ASPIA*, 1:313.

35. Journal entry for February 9, 1797, *LJW*, 1:45; Hawkins to McHenry, March 1, 1797, *LJW*, 1:86; Hawkins to Cornells, March 8, 1797, *LJW*, 1:92–93; Hawkins to Efau Tustunnuggee, April 3, 1797, *LJW*, 1:97.

36. R. T. to Hawkins, April 24, 1797, *CGHS*, 9:458; R. T. to T. B., May 12, 1797, *CGHS*, 9:462; R. T. to Hawkins, May 12, 1797, *CGHS*, 9:463.

37. As the chiefs apologized, they admitted that they could only try to persuade their young men to desist from raiding, not force them to do so. See Hawkins to McHenry, March 1, 1797, *LJW*, 1:86; Hawkins to Barnard, March 7, 1797, *LJW*, 1:91; Hawkins to Cornells, March 8, 1797, *LJW*, 1:92–93.

38. Hawkins to Efau Tustunnuggee, April 3, 1797, *LJW*, 1:97.

39. Meriwether to Montgomery, June 15, 1797, TCC, box 77, folder 28; To his Excellency, James Jackson, April 13, 1798, CIL, 2:521–22; To his Excellency, James Jackson, July 12, 1798, CIL, 2:527–28.

40. For the killing, see Barnard to [Price], August 29, 1796, CFR, reel 1. For two particularly detailed examples of Hawkins's complaints, see Hawkins to McHenry, January 6, 1797, *LJW*, 1:62–63; and Hawkins to Freeman, January 8, 1797, *LJW*, 1:65.

41. A talk from the kings, chiefs, warriors . . . , August 23, 1792, ASPIA, 1:312.

42. Galphin and Douzeazeaux to . . . , June 14, 1787, ASPIA, 1:32. Other attacks on Cusseta hunters brought similar attempts to keep the peace. See Talk from the White Bird King . . . , November 8, 1791, TCC, box 78, folder. 12.

43. White Lieutenant to Seagrove, June 23, 1793, ASPIA, 1:401.

44. For accounts of the killings, see Daniel Currie Deposition, September 17, 1795, CIL, 2:443; Benjamin Harrison Deposition, September 17, 1795, CIL, 2:443; James Vessells Deposition, September 17, 1795, CIL, 2:444; Culpepper Deposition, October 1, 1795, CIL, 2:444; Irwin to Matthews, October 2, 1795, CIL, 2:445; and Pickering to Mathews, November 12, 1795, CIL, 2:456.

45. In May 1797 a group of chiefs had determined to kill the perpetrator, "who had spilt blood on the Oconee." See R. T. to Hawkins, May 12, 1797, CGHS, 9:463; R. T. to A. C., May 18, 1797, CGHS, 9:463-64; and R. T. to Gaither, June 1, 1797, CGHS, 9:464-65. The leader of the war party pleaded that "he lost his son by Harrison and never received satisfaction, altho' he had waited a long time."

46. R. T. to Hawkins, May 12, 1797, CGHS, 9:463; R. T. to A. C., May 18, 1797, CGHS, 9:463-64; R. T. to Gaither, June 15, 1797, CGHS, 9:466. Even Kinnard, who had been a steadfast ally in the past, clearly sympathized with his Yuchi neighbors, declaring that he would not assist until Harrison was brought to the nearest fort, where he could be publicly executed. See R. T. to Hawkins, September 16, 1797, CGHS, 9:471; and R. T. to Hawkins, August 26, 1797, CGHS, 9:469.

47. Hawkins to Barnard, July 13, 1797, LJW, 1:120; Hawkins to Beloved Creeks, July 13, 1797, LJW, 1:121-22.

48. R. T. to Gaither, June 1, 1797, CGHS, 9:464-65; Journal entry for November 24, 1797, LJW, 1:138-39.

49. Hawkins to Thomas, July 14, 1797, LJW, 1:122, R. T. to A. C., May 18, 1797, CGHS, 9:463-64.

50. Barnard to [Price], August 29, 1796, CFR, reel 1; Hawkins to Thomas, July 14, 1797, LJW, 1:122; R. T. to A. C., May 18, 1797, CGHS, 9:463-64.

51. Hawkins to Beloved Creeks, July 13, 1797, LJW, 1:121. There is another very similar talk dated a year later. See Beloved Creeks, July 13, 1798, LBH, 34-36.

52. Hawkins to Beloved Creeks, July 13, 1797, LJW, 1:121.

53. Hawkins to Cornells, March 8, 1797, LJW, 1:92-93; Hawkins to McHenry, January 6, 1797, LJW, 1:62-63.

54. Hawkins to Cornells, October 31, 1797, LJW, 1:146-47; Hawkins to Henley, November 9, 1797, LJW, 1:149; Hawkins to Sackfield Maclin, November 9, 1797, LJW, 1:150.

55. Hawkins to Price, October 23, 1797, CFR, reel 1; Hawkins to Henley, Maclin, Winchester, Robertson, and Byers, all dated November 9, 1797, LJW, 1:149-52; Hawkins to McHenry, November 19, 1797, LJW, 1:157-58; Journal entry for May 27, 1798, LJW, 1:185; Hawkins to Howard, June 9, 1798, LJW, 1:202-3.

56. As game grew scarcer, hunting seasons stretched further and further into winter and spring. For the Creek hunting season, see Wright, *Creeks & Seminoles*, 64-65.

57. Hawkins to Habersham, December 20, 1797, LJW, 169-70.

58. This draws on several definitions of the state and the nation-state as described in Poggi, *The State*, 19-33; and to a lesser extent Poggi, *The Development of the Modern State*, 1; Gellner, *Nations and Nationalism*, 3-5; and Champagne, *Social Order*, 6. For

the concept of legitimacy and nation-building as Americans conceived it, see Gould, *Among the Powers of the Earth*; LaCroix, *The Ideological Origins of American Federalism*; Elding, *Revolution in Favor of Government*; Hendrickson, *Peace Pact*; and Higginbotham, "War and State Formation in Revolutionary America."

59. The White Lieutenant, for instance, spoke candidly to Seagrove on the subject. He continued to blame illegal settlers for Creek troubles, of course; "travelling renegade people," duplicitous traders, and other "bad men" had corrupted young Creek men. Yet, "on account of our not having laws to punish, we, by bad precedents," had become "miserable." White Lieutenant to Seagrove, June 23, 1793, ASPIA, 1:401.

60. The best and most recent examination into Cherokee politics comes from McLoughlin, *Cherokee Renascence*, particularly chs. 2, 7, 10, 11, 13, 14.

61. Hawkins to Price, November 5, 1797, CFR, reel 1; General View, December 8, 1801, ASPIA, 1:646–47; Wright, *Creeks & Seminoles*, 144–47.

62. For the common perception of the National Council, see McLoughlin, *Cherokee Renascence*, 186; Ford, *Settler Sovereignty*, 58–59; Ethridge, *Creek Country*, 228–38; Green, *Politics of Indian Removal*, 12; and Champagne, *Social Order*, 113–19. Champagne saw little change in the Creek polity at all, even up to Removal. See Champagne, *Social Order*, 171–75.

63. Poggi, *The State*, 19–33.

64. Milfort, *Memoir*, 93–97; Swan, "Position and State," 264–65; Wesson, *Households and Hegemony*, 51–53; Foster, *Archaeology*, 102–7; Green, *Politics of Indian Removal*, 8–10, 12–13; Ethridge, *Creek Country*, 95–97, 105.

65. For the layouts of several square grounds and for their similarities, see Swanton, *Social Organization*, 205–97. Hawkins explained the position of buildings in the public square in 1798–99. See "A Sketch of the Creek Country," LJW, 1:318–20. The town square in Oakfuskee was remarkably similar in the mid-eighteenth century. Piker, *Okfuskee*, 112–13. When Bartram traveled through Florida he met with Cowkeeper at Cuscowilla, a Seminole village near modern-day Gainesville. There were forty houses in the village, "sorounding a large open square, in the center of which stands their Council House." Upon his arrival there he "repaired to the public square or council-house, where the chiefs and senators were already convened; the warriors and young men assembled soon after, the business being transacted in public. As it was no more than a ratification of the late treaty of St. Augustine, with some particular commercial stipulations, with respect to the citizens of Alachua, the negotiations soon terminated to the satisfaction of both parties." Another conference was held in a separate Seminole square with traders, which he also witnessed. Bartram and Harper, "Travels in Georgia, and Florida," 147, 158; Van Doren, *Travels*, 167–68. When meeting with a chief, according to Bartram, "with all posseble signs of joy & satisfaction, & told us of some bad talks just arrived from the Nation," presumably after the Christmas killings in 1773, "but he assured us of our safety & his protection." Bartram and Harper, "Travels in Georgia, and Florida," 147.

66. Milfort, *Memoir*, 93–97; Swanton, *Social Organization*, 310–13; Mereness, "Journal of David Taitt's Travels," 502–3.

67. Swan, "Position and State," 264–65.

68. Entry for Monday 16th, in Journal of a voyage to the Creek Nation, PPdC, legajo 2372. For years the regional councils were held at the largest and most significant towns, namely Tuckabatchee and Coweta. The creation of the National Council

further altered that tradition because councils were held at the Speaker's home community. See Ethridge, *Creek Country*, 94–95, 102–7.

69. Bossu, *Travels*, 1:277; Hudson, *The Southeastern Indians*, 223–25, 229; Ethridge, *Creek Country*, 102–7; Green, *Politics of Indian Removal*, 8–10, 12–13.

70. Swanton, *Social Organization*, 313–15.

71. R. T. to A. Cornells, March 30, 1797, CGHS, 9:457.

72. Swanton, *Social Organization*, 321–23.

73. R. T. to Barnard, April 12, 1797, CGHS, 9:458; R. T. to Hawkins, April 24, 1797, CGHS, 9:458; Hawkins to McHenry, November 19, 1797, LJW, 156–57; Hawkins to Faulkner, November 25, 1797, LJW, 161–62.

74. Bossu, *Travels*, 1:249–50; Milfort, *Memoir*, 90–92, 96; entries for Sunday 15th and Monday 16th, in Journal of a voyage to the Creek Nation, PPdC, legajo 2372; Ethridge, *Creek Country*, 104–6.

75. Hawkins to McHenry, June 24, 1798, LJW, 207–9; "A Sketch of the Present State . . . ," LJW, 351–52; Hawkins to Dexter, March 18, 1801, LJW, 356–57.

76. Hawkins to McHenry, June 24, 1798, LJW, 207–9; "A Sketch of the Present State . . . ," LJW, 351–52; Hawkins to Dexter, March 18, 1801, LJW, 356–57. In late 1800 Hawkins moved his agency to Tuckabatchee, most likely to be closer to the proceedings. See Hawkins to Henly, November 9, 1800, BHC.

77. Bossu, *Travels*, 1:276–77; journal entries for May 26–May 30, 1798, LJW, 184–90; entry for May 24, 1802, LJW, 430.

78. Journal entries for May 26–May 28, 1798, LJW, 184–88. Traders were also reported present at the 1802 council. See Hawkins to Halstead, October 3, 1802, CFR, reel 2.

79. Hawkins to Price, May 29, 1798, CFR, reel 1.

80. Journal entries for May 26–May 28, 1798, LJW, 184–88; Hawkins to Price, June 8, 1798, CFR, reel 1.

81. Journal entries for May 26–May 30, 1798, LJW, 184–90; Hawkins to Price, May 29, 1798, LJW, 195.

82. Hawkins to Price, May 29, 1798, LJW, 195; Hawkins to Price, June 5, 1798, LJW, 197–98. Horse theft in particular remained an issue. For complaints of horse thefts around the turn of the century, for instance, see Petition of Sundry Inhabitants of Camden, 1798, CIL, 521; Brown to Jackson, April 24, 1798, CIL, 522–24; and Remonstrance from Montgomery to Jackson, July 17, 1798, CIL, 527–28.

83. Hawkins to Jackson, February 25, 1798, LBH, 28–30; Hawkins to McHenry, June 24, 1798, LJW, 207–9; Hawkins to Jackson, August 2, 1798, LJW, 212–14; Hawkins to Habersham, December 23, 1798, LJW, 228; "A Sketch of the Present State . . . ," LJW, 351–52; Hawkins to Tattnall, May 24, 1802, LJW, 445–46.

84. Journal entry for May 28, 1798, LJW, 187; Hawkins to Butler, June 6, 1798, LJW, 198; Hawkins to McHenry, June 24, 1798, LJW, 207–9; Hawkins to Mitchell, June 9, 1798, LJW, 203–5.

85. Poggi, *The State*, 21, 28–29, 33.

86. For an account of this, see Bossu, *Travels*, 1:250–54.

87. Bendix, *Nation-Building and Citizenship*, 108–9.

88. McLoughlin, *Cherokee Renascence*, 45–46, 139–41.

89. Swanton, *Social Organization*, 297–302, 305; Harper, *Travels*, 314–15; Bossu, *Travels*, 1:235–36; "A Sketch of the Creek Country": LJW 1:318–19; Griffith, *McIntosh and Weatherford*, 28–29.

90. Entry for November 24, 1797, *LJW*, 138; Hawkins to McHenry, November 28, 1797, *LJW*, 167. McGillivray had tried to develop on tustunnuggees similarly, a decade or so earlier, when he envisioned using constables to keep regional order. Those attempts were unsuccessful, as were his efforts to create a repayment and punishment system for horse theft. The infliction of punishments, Caleb Swan explained, still depended "on the superior force of the injured clan." See Swan, "Position and State," 281.

91. Entry for January 24, 1793, *LJW*, 39; entry for January 26, 1793, *LJW*, 39–40; Hudson, *The Southeastern Indians*, 225, 229–30. Swanton asserted, for instance, that even in the post-Removal period, when tustunnuggees acted as a local police, that role "was really a continuation of their duties as police officers for the old council of chiefs." See Swanton, *Social Organization*, 298.

92. Bendix, *Nation-Building and Citizenship*, 17.

93. Hawkins to Jackson, July 11, 1798, *LJW*, 211–12; Hawkins to Jackson, August 2, 1798, *LJW*, 212–14.

94. The Cherokee "lighthourse" patrols, consisting of leading warriors and headmen and paid by the Cherokee National Council, provides another example. McLoughlin, *Cherokee Renascence*, 139–40.

95. Entry for May 27, 1798, *LJW*, 186; entry for May 29, 1798, *LJW*, 189.

96. Hawkins to McHenry, June 24, 1798, *LJW*, 207–9; entry for August 6, 1798, *CGHS*, 9:491.

97. Report of Tustunnuggee Haujo and Robert Walton to Hawkins, November 4, 1799, *LBH*, 44–45; Hawkins to Cornell, July 17, 1798, *CGHS*, 9:488–89.

98. For headmen overseeing hunters, see Hawkins to Price, December 31, 1798, *CFR*, reel 1; Hawkins to Wright, December 5, 1799, *CFR*, reel 2; and Hawkins to Wright, December 10, 1799, *CFR*, reel 2. For the special license, see Hawkins to Wright, November 14, 1799, *CFR*, reel 2. For evidence of returning property, see Voucher N. 5, November 16, 1799 *CFR*, reel 2; Voucher N. 6, November 17, 1799, *CFR*, reel 2; Voucher N. 7, November 29, 1799, *CFR*, reel 2; and Voucher N. 34, December 22, 1799, *CFR*, reel 2.

99. Hawkins to Jackson, August 2, 1798, *LJW*, 212–14; Hawkins to Freeman, August 2, 1798, *LJW*, 214–15; Hawkins to Walton, August 25, 1798, *LJW*, 222.

100. Hawkins to Walton, August 25, 1798, *LJW*, 222; Hawkins to Dinsmoor, January 6, 1799, *LJW*, 235; Hawkins to McHenry, January 9, 1799, *LJW*, 238.

101. Hawkins to Gaither, February 27, 1799, *LJW*, 240–41; Efau Haujo to Hawkins, November 9, 1799, *PPdC*, legajo 216A.

102. Hawkins to McHenry, September 4, 1798, *LJW*, 222–23. At one meeting, although it is unclear when exactly this was, Hawkins focused almost entirely on the return of stolen property, and several times his aggressive talks put both him and the headmen in "ill humour." As soon as he arrived at the council, according to one onlooker, "nothing could be said but about plundered Negroes & stolen horses, that no other business could be brought on." He complained that returning stolen property went back to the Treaty of New York and that he had been in the region for ten years "and this is the tenth time I have told you the same talks." After Hawkins listed property from Cumberland settlements, the headmen grumbled and murmured, "But they say they brought it on themselves we must pay we cannot help ourselves for we are in the power of the White people & we must complie." If they did not return the plundered slaves alone, Hawkins warned them later, "your money will be stopt to pay the owners." See Daniel McGillivray to John Forbes, [1790], Daniel McGillivray Papers.

103. Hawkins to Henley, April 15, 1799, *LJW*, 245; Hawkins to McHenry, April 15, 1799, *LJW*, 245–46.

104. For examples of this, see Milledge to Hawkins, October 8, 1810, CIL, 2:737–39; Stewart to Hawkins, October 12, 1810, CIL, 2:740–41; and Hawkins to Stewart, October 13, 1810, CIL, 2:741–43.

8. A Legitimate Creek Nation

1. Hawkins mentions the White Lieutenant in the fall of 1797 as "one of the 3 most influential chiefs of our land and an old acquaintance of mine" when he met the headman on his way to the U.S. Factory, at Coleraine, with five hundred pounds of dressed leather. See Hawkins to Price, October 30, 1797, CFR, reel 1. This coincides with his retiring out of Oakfuskee, in his old age, to a ranch.

2. Simpson to Innerarity, November 16, 1804, PPdC, legajo 59; Kingsbury to Milledge, February 14, 1803, CIL, 2:667. One of the first mentions of the Singer was in 1797, when he was described as "one of the chiefs of the nation." Perhaps he was the White Lieutenant's replacement in the National Council. See Walton to Price, September 9, 1797, CFR, reel 1.

3. Hawkins to Folch, March 20, 1800, *LJW*, 1:332; Hawkins to McHenry, April 14, 1800, *LJW*, 1:332–33.

4. See General View, December 8, 1801, ASPIA, 1:646–47.

5. March 3, 1802, *LJW*, 413; April 14, 1802, *LJW*, 420–21; To the People near Rocklick, April 14, 1802, *LJW*, 439–40.

6. Bowles's escape from Spanish hands and return to Florida is described in Wright, *William Augustus Bowles*, chs. 6–7.

7. Wright, *William Augustus Bowles*, 114–17. Bowles gave a strong talk there, recounting the numerous injustices done toward Creeks and other Natives since the Treaty of Fort Stanwix in 1768. See Given under my hand at Wekiva this the thirty first day of October 1799 . . . , William Augustus Bowles Collection.

8. Durouzeaux to Folch, November 9, 1799, PPdC, legajo 2355; Kingsbury to Milledge, February 14, 1803, CIL, 2:667.

9. Hawkins to Cornells, December 5, 1799, *LJW*, 276–77; Hawkins to Jackson, August 14, 1800, KRC, box 12, folder 32. For more on the Spanish and American efforts to survey the northern boundary of Spanish Florida, see Pound, *Benjamin Hawkins*, 130–36.

10. Sevier to Cocke, Anderson, and Claiborne, February 25, 1800, Governor Sevier Collection, box 1, folder 8; Hawkins to Jackson, August 14, 1800, KRC, box 12, folder 32.

11. McHenry to Jackson, August 13, 1799, TCC, box 6, folder 6.

12. Statement by Benjamin Hawkins, May 8, 1799, *LJW*, 248; Hawkins to Minor, May 2, 1799, *LJW*, 247; Panton to Gayoso de Lemos, May 12, 1799, in Corbitt, "Papers, XIX," 162.

13. Efau Haujo to Hawkins, April 9, 1799, PPdC, legajo 216A; Statement by Benjamin Hawkins, May 8, 1799, *LJW*, 248; Powers to Gayoso, May 11, 1799, PPdC, legajo 216A; Minor to Gayoso, May 30, 1799, PPdC, legajo 2371; Hawkins to Folch, August 22, 1799, PPdC, legajo 216A; Hawkins to William Hawkins, September 21, 1799, *LJW*, 258.

14. The U.S. Surveyor, Andrew Ellicott, worried that he did not have the authorization to repel the Seminoles by force. See Hawkins to McHenry, October 5, 1799, *LJW*,

260; Hawkins to Ellicott, November 3, 1799, *LJW*, 266–67; Wright, *Creeks & Seminoles*, 150–51. The Spanish detachment was particularly impressed by the chiefs, who wrote about the survey and Creek involvement in detail. See Minor to Gayoso, August 5, 1799, PPdC, legajo 2355.

15. Hawkins to McHenry, October 26, 1799, *LJW*, 263–64. For Bowles's talks making their way into the Lower Country, see Hawkins to Schaumburg, November 10, 1799, *LJW*, 270.

16. Durouzeaux to Barnard, August 2, 1799, PPdC, legajo 2355; McLeod to Jackson, October 2, 1799, CIL, 2:582–83. When a group of Georgians stole horses from a friendly Coweta hunting party, the Coweta chiefs presumed it was done because a war party from the Half-Way House towns stole theirs, and they were simply in pursuit. Instead of retaliating, the chiefs promised they would do what they could to get the stolen horses back from the Half-Way House men as a solution to the problem. See R. T. to Gaither, June 1, 1797, CGHS, 9:464–65.

17. Hawkins to Cornells, November 5, 1799, *LJW*, 267–68. For the Big Feared and Little Prince, see Voucher N. 1, November 14, 1799, CFR, reel 2; and Voucher N. 16, January 8, 1800, CFR, reel 2.

18. Report of Tustunnuggee Haujo and Robert Walton to Hawkins, November 4, 1799, LBH, 44–45; Folch to Hawkins, December 8, 1799, PPdC, legajo 2355. For the Mad Warrior possibly being from Chehaw, see February 18, 1797, *LJW*, 48.

19. Hawkins to Panton, October 9, 1799, *LJW*, 261–62; Report of Tustunnuggee Haujo and Robert Walton to Hawkins, November 4, 1799, LBH, 44–45; Hawkins to McHenry, October 26, 1799, *LJW*, 269; Hawkins to Folch, November 17, 1799, *LJW*, 272–74.

20. Report of Tustunnuggee Haujo and Robert Walton to Hawkins, November 4, 1799, LBH, 44–45; Hawkins to McHenry, October 26, 1799, *LJW*, 269.

21. Hawkins to Ellicott, November 3, 1799, *LJW*, 266–67; Someruelos to Urquijo, January 30, 1800, PdE, legajo 3889.

22. Hawkins to McHenry, October 26, 1799, *LJW*, 263–64; Hawkins to Ellicott, November 3, 1799, *LJW*, 266–67; To Choctaw Chiefs, enclosed in Hawkins to McKee, August 26, 1800, *LJW*, 347–48.

23. For a meeting on the Apalachicola where he held out significant offers of powder and ammunition, see Portell to Folch, November 13, 1799, *MPASD*, 6:834–36; Hawkins to Clay, April 4, 1800, KRC, box 12, folder 29. With the southern limits of the region passive, Hawkins described to Colonel David Henley in 1800 that progress in Creek Country was moving along slowly, but as usual. "While some parts mend slowly others relapse a pace." See Hawkins to Henly, November 9, 1800, BHC.

24. Hawkins to Shaunburg, November 29, 1799, *LJW*, 274–75; Hawkins to McHenry, December 4, 1799, *LJW*, 275–76; "A Sketch of the Creek Country," *LJW*, 316–17; Hawkins to Jackson, December 20, 1799, LBH, 48–50.

25. Hawkins to Schaumburg, November 29, 1799, *LJW*, 274. See Hawkins to McHenry, December 4, 1799, *LJW*, 275–76. For the distribution of the classes, see "A Sketch of the Creek Country," *LJW*, 290.

26. Hawkins to McHenry, April 15, 1799, *LJW*, 245–46.

27. Hawkins to Folch, December 8, 1799, *LJW*, 277–78. The mode of having chiefs answerable to the conduct of hunters was also discussed. See Hawkins to Jackson, December 20, 1799, LBH, 48–50.

28. Hawkins to McHenry, November 6, 1799, *LJW*, 269; Hawkins to McHenry, December 4, 1799, *LJW*, 275–76; To various Creek Chiefs . . . , December 10, 1799, *LJW*, 279. Likewise Tuskegee Tustunnuggee and the Cusseta Mico were also traveling south as messengers and spies. See Hawkins to Cornells, December 5, 1799, *LJW*, 276–77; Hawkins to Folch, December 22, 1799, *LJW*, 282–83; Hawkins to Tuskegee Tustunnuggee, March 12, 1800, *LJW*, 331–32; and Hawkins to Folch, March 20, 1799, *LJW*, 332.

29. Hawkins to Various Chiefs, December 10, 1799, *LJW*, 279; Hawkins to McHenry, December 21, 1799, *LJW*, 281–82; Hawkins to Folch, December 22, 1799, *LJW*, 282–83. Chehaw and Cusseta spies were in Spanish Florida when Apalache was taken, as well as when the Spanish took it back. See Hawkins to Jackson, July 18, 1800, *LJW*, 342.

30. As Hawkins wrote, "If we can get them all together, Col. Gaither and Col. Butler would be glad to see them and give some of the physic the white people give to rogues, and those who oppose the Law of the Nation." Hawkins to Cornells, November 5, 1799, *LJW*, 267–68; Hawkins to McHenry, November 6, 1799, *LJW*, 269; Hawkins to Bowles, December 10, 1799, *LJW*, 279.

31. Hawkins to McHenry, December 21, 1799, *LJW*, 281–82.

32. Durouzeaux to Folch, November 9, 1799, PPdC, legajo 2355; Durouzeaux to Folch, November 21, 1799, PPdC, legajo 2355; Folch to Hawkins, December 6, 1799, PPdC, legajo 2355; Thomas to Bowles, December 27, 1799, PPdC, legajo 216A.

33. For Bowles's taking of the fort, and then the Spanish counterattack that forced him to retreat, see Wright, *William Augustus Bowles*, ch. 8.

34. McGillivray to Panton, May 6, 1800, Daniel McGillivray Papers; McGillivray to Panton, May 9, 1800, Daniel McGillivray Papers; Hawkins to Panton, June 11, 1800, *LJW*, 336–37; Hawkins to Dexter, June 11, 1800, *LJW*, 338; Hawkins to Henly, November 9, 1800, BHC; Wright, *William Augustus Bowles*, 128, 139, 152.

35. Hawkins to Panton, June 11, 1800, *LJW*, 336–37; Hawkins to Dexter, June 11, 1800, *LJW*, 338; Hawkins to Henly, November 9, 1800, BHC. Groups of Hitchitis were implicated later in 1801 with the theft of thirty-eight slaves from Francisco Fatio's plantation in East Florida. See Fatio to [Hawkins], September 4, 1801, SWLR, reel 1; Barnard to White, September 27, 1801, SWLR, reel 1; and Durouzeaux to Hawkins, September 26, 1801, SWLR, reel 1. Barnard, however, assured Hawkins that they had played no part in the robbery. See Barnard to Hawkins, October 9, 1801, SWLR, reel 1. For Dearborn's worries, see Dearborn to Hawkins, June 10, 1801, SWLS, reel 1.

36. McGillivray to Panton, May 9, 1800, Daniel McGillivray Papers; Hawkins to Panton, June 11, 1800, *LJW*, 336–37; Hawkins to Dexter, June 11, 1800, *LJW*, 338; Hawkins to Jackson, June 12, 1800, *LJW*, 339. After the attack, Hawkins alluded to having made plans with Gaither to call out federal troops to assist Creek warriors if the chiefs decided on using force. See Hawkins to Dexter, July 28, 1800, *LJW*, 343; and Hawkins to Dexter, August 20, 1800, *LJW*, 345.

37. Hawkins to Panton, July 10, 1800, *LJW*, 339–40.

38. Hawkins to Jackson, July 18, 1800, KRC, box 12, folder 31; Hawkins to Jackson, August 14, 1800, KRC, box 12, folder 32. Evidently Bowles ordered some of the Chehaws who came down to meet with him to fire on the Spanish, "which they refused to do." See Hawkins to Jackson, July 18, 1800, KRC, box 12, folder 31. For Bowles largely confining himself to Mikasuki, see Hawkins to Dearborn, July 18, 1801, SWLR, reel 1.

39. Hawkins to Dexter, August 20, 1800, *LJW*, 344–45. Tuskegee Tustunnuggee and Eufala Tustunnuggee of Cusseta followed up in 1802 with a similar meeting. See entry dated February 25, 1802, *LJW*, 412.

40. Hawkins reported several times in 1801 and 1802 that things were looking as peaceful and stable as he had ever seen them. See Hawkins to Wright, July 7, 1801, CFR, reel 2; entry for March 3, 1802, *LJW*, 413; entry for April 14, 1802, *LJW*, 420–21; entry for April 15, 1802, *LJW*, 421–22; and Hawkins to Dearborn, March 21, 1802, *LJW*, 437–38.

41. Hawkins to Dearborn, June 1, 1801, *LJW*, 359–60; Hawkins to Wright, June 8, 1801, CFR, reel 2; entry dated January 24, 1802, *LJW*, 407.

42. Hawkins to Wright, July 16, 1801, CFR, reel 2; entry for February 25, 1802, *LJW*, 412; Hawkins to Dearborn, March 21, 1802, *LJW*, 437–38.

43. Hawkins to Dearborn, June 1, 1801, *LJW*, 359–60; entry dated January 24, 1802, *LJW*, 408–9; entry dated January 29, 1802, *LJW*, 409.

44. Entry dated February 9, 1802, *LJW*, 410; entry dated March 27, 1802, *LJW*, 417–18; entry dated April 6, 1802, *LJW*, 419.

45. Entry dated March 27, 1802, *LJW*, 417–18; entry dated April 6, 1802, *LJW*, 419. Partisan groups, he warned, would, "as they have done for two years past," endeavor "to divide and distract us by folly of this sort." The authority of the nascent Creek leadership group was still weak, and if the chiefs were not careful it would be destroyed. The Mad Dog, as Speaker of the National Council, had to keep it all together, by force if necessary. See entry dated March 27, 1802, *LJW*, 417–18.

46. Hawkins to Wright, June 8, 1801, CFR, reel 2.

47. Hawkins to Dearborn, May 2, 1802, *LJW*, 440–41; entry dated May 19, 1802, *LJW*, 428–29; Dearborn to Hawkins, June 2, 1802, SWLS, reel 1.

48. Hawkins to Halstead, August 19, 1802, CFR, reel 2; Hawkins to Halstead, November 9, 1802, CFR, reel 2.

49. Jackson to Senators and Representatives in Congress, February 15, 1798, TCC, box 78, folder 12; Jones to Jackson, May 25, 1800, TCC, box 83, folder 10; Clark to Tattnall, May 17, 1802, TCC, box 48, folder 1.

50. For the quality of the land, see Swan, "Position and State," 256.

51. Hawkins to Cornells, October 31, 1797, *LJW*, 146–47.

52. For an example of this approach, see Milledge to Meriwether, February 23, 1803, CIL, 2:657–61; and Milledge to Merriwether, February 27, 1804, CIL, 2:693–94.

53. Foster to Hammond, August 22, 1798, CIL, 2:529–30. See also Hammond to Jackson, August 27, 1798, CIL, 2:531–33; and Hammond to Jackson, November 8, 1798, CIL, 2:535–36.

54. Edward Telfair had, in the past, "ordered all property to be rendered in on oath, that has been taken by the Creek Indians," during the period of the Coleraine treaty. See Melton to Jackson, March 6, 1799, CIL, 2:553–55.

55. From 1798 into 1799 Georgians attempted to regain their lost property by traveling into Creek Country according to rules set out at Coleraine. Predictably, those attempts accomplished little, and even Hawkins did "not appear sanguine in his expectations of recovering property stipulated to be delivered up" by either the Treaty of New York or the Treaty of Coleraine. See Hammond to Jackson, November 8, 1798, CIL, 2:535–36. See also McLeod to Jackson, May 6, 1799, CIL, 2:558–59. Plans for sending commissioners into Creek Country continued into the nineteenth century. See Stewart et al. to Milledge, January 28, 1803, CIL, 2:664.

56. Copies of letters from the Secretary of War to the President, August 29, 1796, JMP, reel 5, series D; McHenry to Hawkins, September 8, 1796, JMP, reel 5, series D.

57. Hawkins to McHenry, November 19, 1797, LJW, 157–60; Hawkins to Jackson, February 25, 1798, LBH, 28–30; McGillivray to Panton, May 7, 1798, Daniel McGillivray Papers.

58. Hawkins to Panton, January 28, 1799, LJW, 240. Even though headmen were still forcefully rejecting calls for another lend cession, Georgia officials were growing more clamorous for one. See Jones to Jackson, April 17, 1800, TCC, folder 44, box 8; and Jones to Jackson, May 25, 1800, TCC, box 83, folder 10.

59. "I believe until Bowles is effectually removed," Hawkins wrote to Jackson, "and the ferment he has occasioned, has subsided, it would be ill judged to press it." See Hawkins to Jackson, August 14, 1800, KRC, box 12, folder 32; Dearborn to Hawkins, December 9, 1800, SWLS, reel 1.

60. Hawkins to Dearborn, June 1, 1801, LJW, 359–60; Hawkins to Dearborn, March 21, 1802, LJW, 437–38.

61. Entry dated January 24, 1802, LJW, 408–9; Hawkins to Clay, March 21, 1802, BHC. There were reports that Bowles was attempting to disrupt the meeting but was ineffectual. See entry dated May 8, 1802, LJW, 426; entry dated May 11, 1802, LJW, 427; and To James Wilkinson, Benjamin Hawkins, and Andrew Pickens, July 17, 1801, ASPIA, 1:651.

62. Hawkins and Andrew Pickens lauded the Creek delegation, describing it as "more full and respectable than we have ever known one to be." See Hawkins and Pickens to the Governor of Georgia, May 17, 1802, ASPIA, 1:671. James Durouzeaux, writing as a Spanish agent, agreed. "A very great number of Indians are gone to the Treittey at the Oconey. What the result of it will be is out of my power to form any [?] . . . their will be great debaitt, as the Georgians will be asking of land for damages suffered and the Indians are determined not to give any land." Durouzeaux to Folch, May 26, 1802, PPdC, legajo 2372; for the same, see Durouzeaux to Capt. Dureveil, June 5, 1802, PPdC, legajo 2372.

63. Durouzeaux to Folch, May 2, 1802, PPdC, legajo 2372; Durouzeaux to Folch, May 8, 1802, PPdC, legajo 2372.

64. Hawkins to Dearborn, July 18, 1801, LJW, 361–62; Hawkins to Dearborn, March 21, 1802, LJW, 437–38; Hawkins to Dearborn, May 2, 1802, LJW, 441; Hawkins to Dearborn, May 8, 1802, LJW, 442; Hawkins to Dearborn, May 16, 1802, LJW, 444.

65. Entry for May 24, 1802, ASPIA, 1:672. Also in LJW, 430–31; Hawkins to Dearborn, May 30, 1802, LJW, 446–47. For a detailed account of the conference, including the dances and ceremonies that opened it, talks from the Mad Dog, the Coweta Mico, and General Wilkinson, see entries for May 23 through June 30, 1802, ASPIA, 1:672–81. For the headmen's complaints about Georgians, see Hawkins to Dearborn, February 1, 1802, LJW, 433; and Wilkinson and Hawkins to Dearborn, July 15, 1802, ASPIA, 1:669–70. The Mad Dog was particularly bitter, disparaging the movement of whites onto Indian lands and the inability of the federal government to do anything in response. Soon Hopoie Mico, Tuskenehau Chapco of Coweta, and Cusseta Mico added complaints and claims against Georgians of their own. See entry for June 9, 1802, ASPIA, 1:674–75.

66. Tuskenehau Chapco complained that they were charged with killing a black slave but that "we lost a man by the Americans, in our hunting ground, and this negro was taken for it." See entry for June 9, 1802, ASPIA, 1:675.

67. Entry for June 9, 1802, ASPIA, 1:675; entry for June 12, 1802, ASPIA, 1:676–77.

68. Entry for June 9, 1802, *ASPIA*, 1:676. Unfulfilled claims for murders, attacks, and thefts were lengthy. See entry for June 12, 1802, *ASPIA*, 1:676–77.

69. Efau Haujo to the Seminoles, June 30, 1802, *ASPIA*, 1:680.

70. Dearborn to Wilkinson, April 12, 1802, *ASPIA*, 1:693; Wilkinson, Hawkins, and Pickens to Dearborn, May 30, 1802, *ASPIA*, 1:673; Hawkins to Dearborn, May 30, 1802, *LJW*, 446–47; entry for June 8, 1802, *ASPIA*, 1:673–74; entry for June 9, 1802, *ASPIA*, 1:675–76; Hammond to Tattnall, June 11, 1802, *CIL*, 2:607–8; entry for Thursday, 12th, in Journal of a voyage to the Creek Nation, *PPdC*, legajo 2372.

71. Hawkins to Dearborn, July 15, 1802, *LJW*, 448–49.

72. Hawkins to Dearborn, June 17, 1802, *LJW*, 447–48; Wilkinson and Hawkins to Dearborn, July 15, 1802, *ASPIA*, 1:669–70.

73. Entry for June 9, 1802, *ASPIA*, 1:675–76.

74. Entry for June 13, 1802, *ASPIA*, 1:679; Wilkinson to Tattnall, June 15, 1802, *CIL*, 2:649; Wilkinson, Hawkins, and Pickens to Dearborn, June 17, 1802, *ASPIA*, 1:680.

75. For a copy of the Treaty of Fort Wilkinson, see Thomas Jefferson, President of the United States . . . , June 16, 1802, *ASPIA*, 1:669.

76. Kappler, *Indian Affairs*, 2:59; Thomas Jefferson President . . . , June 11, 1803, *CIL*, 2:657–61. In 1805 the Hallowing King was dead, although the date of his death is not certain. See Hawkins to Dearborn, April 1, 1805, *LJW*, 490–91.

77. Dearborn to Hawkins, May 5, 1803, *SWLS*, reel 1; Thomas Jefferson President . . . , June 11, 1803, *CIL*, 2:657–61.

78. Hawkins to Dearborn, July 15, 1802, *LJW*, 448–49. Hopoie Mico was also referred to as the Fushatchee Mico, the King of the Hickory Ground, by Hawkins. See Hawkins to Wright, October 31, 1799, *CFR*, reel 2.

79. Durouzeaux to Folch, July 14, 1802, *PPdC*, legajo 2372; Durouzeaux to [Folch], July 29, 1802, *PPdC*, legajo 2355.

80. Durouzeaux to Folch, October 20, 1802, *PPdC*, legajo 2372; Durouzeaux to Dueberil, November 9, 1802, *PPdC*, legajo 2372.

81. Durouzeaux to Folch, May 8, 1802, *PPdC*, legajo 2372; Miller to Folch, June 20, 1802, *PPdC*, legajo 2372; Durouzeaux to Folch, July 14, 1802, *PPdC*, legajo 2372.

82. Milledge to Kingsberry, February 14, 1803, *CIL*, 2:667; Hawkins to Halstead, March 24, 1803, *CFR*, reel 2; Hawkins to Halstead, April 12, 1803, *CFR*, reel 2; Hawkins to Milledge, May 30, 1803, *LBH*, 66.

83. Entries for Thursday 12th, and Tuesday 17th, in Journal of a voyage to the Creek Nation, *PPdC*, legajo 2372. Dearborn had made it clear to Hawkins in the past that if Bowles was ever in the United States, "no exertion should be wanting on your part for securing him." See Dearborn to Hawkins, April 6, 1802, *SWLS*, reel 1. Dearborn reiterated that command a year later but also suggested that if the chiefs wanted to seize him and turn him over to the Spaniards for the reward they were offering, that would be fine as well. See Dearborn to Hawkins, May 24, 1803, *SWLS*, reel 1.

84. Durouzeaux to Duebruil, June 2, 1803, *PPdC*, legajo 2372; Durouzeaux to Duebruil, June 29, 1803, *PPdC*, legajo 2372.

85. Journal entries from Sunday 22nd through Tuesday 31st in Journal of a voyage to the Creek Nation, *PPdC*, legajo 2372; Woodward, *Reminiscences*, 49–50, 89; Wright, *William Augustus Bowles*, 162–68; Griffith, *McIntosh and Weatherford*, 51–52.

86. Hawkins to Milledge, June 8, 1803, *LJW*, 454.

87. Hawkins to Madison, July 11, 1803, *LJW*, 458.

88. Hawkins to Milledge, April 16, 1804, TCC, box 76, folder 25; Adams to Milledge, April 18, 1804, TCC, box 45, folder 3; Journal of the Commissioners . . . , January 20, 1804, TCC, box 77, folder 12.

89. Dearborn to Hawkins, October 6, 1803, SWLS, reel 1; Dearborn to Milledge, October 6, 1803, SWLS, reel 1; Barnard to Hawkins, May 17, 1804, in Journal of the Commissioners . . . , January 20, 1804, TCC, box 77, folder 12; Freeman to Hawkins, May 17, 1804, TCC, box 78, folder 12. See also Adams to Milledge, May 17, 1804, TCC, box 45, folder 3.

90. Hawkins to Milledge, March 14, 1804, LBH, 75–76; Freeman to Hawkins, May 17, 1804, TCC, box 78, folder 12.

91. Entry for Thursday 12th, in Journal of a voyage to the Creek Nation, PPdC, legajo 2372; Durouzeaux to Folch, July 14, 1802, PPdC, legajo 2372. "It seems the Rascally Tame King sent to the lower towns to inform the Indians that that meeting is put off, that *he* is to be the Head of the assembly, that *he* will send forth the broken days and that the English are arrived in Augustine and Tampa, and that the Indians would see the red coats in a very short time." See entry for Saturday 21st, in Journal of a voyage to the Creek Nation, PPdC, legajo 2372. Durouzeaux also listed several chiefs and their place in the debate, including Hopoie Haujo, Muclassee Hopoi, and Hopoie Mico. See Durouzeaux to Hawkins, May 28, 1804, TCC, box 78, folder 12; and Wright, *Creeks & Seminoles*, 149–51.

92. Barnard to Hawkins, May 17, 1804, TCC, box 1, folder 11.

93. Durouzeaux to Hawkins, May 28, 1804, TCC, box 78, folder 12.

94. Journal entry dated June 26, 1804, LJW, 468–69; Hill to Milledge, June 7, 1804, in Journal of the Commissioners . . . , January 20, 1804, TCC, box 77, folder 12; journal entry dated June 26, 1804, LJW, 468–69; journal entry dated June 28, 1804, LJW, 469. For Muclassee Hopoie acting as Speaker and for the National Council being held again at Tuckabatchee, see Durouzeaux to Folch, April 14, 1804, PPdC, legajo 2372; and Durouzeaux to Folch, April 16, 1804, PPdC, legajo 2372.

95. Journal entry dated June 30, 1804, LJW, 472.

96. Journal entry dated June 30, 1804, LJW, 472–73.

97. Journal entry dated July 1, 1804, LJW, 474; Hawkins to Barnard, May 30, 1804, LBH, 80–82.

98. For Dearborn's incessant requests, see Dearborn to Hawkins, February 19, 1803; Dearborn to Hawkins, May 5, 1803; Dearborn to Anderson, May 5, 1803; Dearborn to Hawkins, May 24, 1803; Dearborn to Hawkins, July 13, 1803; and Dearborn to Hawkins, April 2, 1804, all in SWLS, reel 1. For Jefferson, see Jefferson to Jackson, July 16, 1803, CIL, 2:668.

99. Hawkins to Jefferson, July 11, 1803, LJW, 456; Dickson to Milledge, April 6, 1803, TCC, box 45, folder 4; Hawkins to Milledge, September 6, 1803, LJW, 459–60; Reid to Milledge, April 24, 1804, TCC, box 45, folder 5.

100. Dearborn to Wilkinson, April 12, 1802, ASPIA, 1:692; Jefferson to Jackson, February 18, 1803, CIL, 2:668; Dearborn to Milledge, June 1, 1803, CIL, 2:674; Hawkins to Milledge, September 6, 1803, LBH, 69–70; Hawkins to Milledge, May 8, 1804, LJW, 465; Adams to Milledge, May 17, 1804, TCC, box 45, folder 3.

101. Journal entry dated July 15, 1804, LJW, 476–79.

102. Journal entries dated July 15 and 30, 1804, LJW, 476–80.

103. Journal entry dated July 30, 1804, LJW, 479–80.

104. Journal entry dated June 30, 1804, *LJW*, 472–74.

105. Journal entry dated July 30, 1804, *LJW*, 479–80.

106. Milledge to Clark, McCall, and Adams, June 7, 1804, LBH, 83–84.

107. Hawkins to Milledge, August 15, 1804, *LJW*, 481; Hawkins to Dearborn, November 3, 1804, *LJW*, 482–84.

108. Dearborn to Hawkins, May 5, 1803, SWLS, reel 1.

109. Hawkins to Dearborn, November 3, 1804, *LJW*, 482–84.

110. Interpreted by Alexander Cornells . . . , LBH, 96. For some of the proceedings of the council, see LBH, 86–98.

111. Hawkins to Dearborn, November 3, 1804, *LJW*, 482–84; Hawkins to Milledge, November 9 1804, *LJW*, 484.

112. Clark to Milledge, September 28, 1804, LBH, 98–99; Hawkins to Dearborn, March 5, 1805, *LJW*, 489; Hawkins to Dearborn, June 14, 1805, *LJW*, 493; Griffith, *McIntosh and Weatherford*, 54–63.

113. For the negotiation and ratification of the treaty, see Kappler, *Indian Affairs*, 2:85–86; Treaty concluded between the United States . . . , November 3, 1804, ASPIA, 1:691; Jefferson to the Senate, December 13, 1804, ASPIA, 1:690–91; Hawkins to Milledge, November 17, 1805, *LJW*, 499; Baldwin to . . . , December 23, 1805, TCC, box 1, folder 10; Wailes to Milledge, July 15, 1806, TCC, box 45, folder 7; Early to Milledge, April 19, 1806, TCC, box 45, folder 3; and Pound, *Benjamin Hawkins*, 184–87.

9. The National Council Splinters

1. McKee to McHenry, October 26, 1797, JMP, box 2; Waselkov, *A Conquering Spirit*, 56–71; Dowd, *Sacred Revolt*, 155; Hoffman, *Florida's Frontiers*, 251–52.

2. Estimate of the stipend to the Creeks . . . , April 24, 1813, ASPIA, 1:841.

3. Hawkins to Armstrong, April 26, 1813, ASPIA, 1:841.

4. Woodward, *Reminiscences*, 94.

5. Hawkins to Secretary of War, November 9, 1812, in November 28, 1812 edition, *Niles Weekly Register*, 3:205; Woodward, *Reminiscences*, 35.

6. Woodward, *Reminiscences*, 109.

7. Frank, *Creeks and Southerners*, 100–106; Green, *Politics of Indian Removal*, 37–38, 54; Griffith, *McIntosh and Weatherford*, 54.

8. Hawkins to Forbes, May 29, 1806, *LJW*, 505; Hawkins to Milledge, June 9, 1806, *LJW*, 505.

9. Hawkins to Jefferson, September 13, 1806, *LJW*, 507–9.

10. Seagrove to Irwin, June 3, 1807, CIL, 716–18.

11. Hawkins to Milledge, June 9, 1806, *LJW*, 505–6; Hawkins to Dearborn, October 15, 1807, *LJW*, 529.

12. Hawkins to Dearborn, October 15, 1807, *LJW*, 529.

13. Hawkins to Dearborn, November 28, 1805, *LJW*, 502; Hawkins to Dearborn, December 27 1805, *LJW*, 503.

14. Hawkins to Dearborn, January 22, 1808, *LJW*, 531; Dearborn to Hawkins, January 2, 1809, SWLS, vol. B.

15. Hawkins talked about specific cases of illegal settlers several times. He pursued one particular illegal settler, a certain Roderick Easly, relentlessly, having him removed several times by military force and then finally tried in court. See Hawkins to

Eustis, January 1810, *LJW*, 560; Hawkins to Eustis, June 21, 1810, *LJW*, 563–64; Hawkins to Eustis, June 30, 1810, *LJW*, 564; Hawkins to Bulloch, October 19, 1809, *LJW*, 574; Hawkins to Eustis, December 24, 1810, *LJW*, 578.

16. Hawkins to Eustis, June 9, 1812, *LJW*, 609; Hawkins to Armstrong, March 1, 1813, *LJW*, 629.

17. Hawkins to Eustis, June 18, 1809, *LJW*, 555.

18. Hawkins to Eustis, October 10, 1809, *LJW*, 556–57; Hawkins to Irwin, October 15, 1809, *LJW*, 557–58.

19. Eustis to Hawkins, November 9, 1809, SWLS, vol. C.

20. Hawkins to Mitchell, July 1, 1811, *LJW*, 589; Hawkins to Mitchell, July 16, 1811, *LJW*, 589; Hawkins to Mitchell, January 20, 1813, *LJW*, 628.

21. Hawkins to Eustis, May 11, 1812, *LJW*, 608.

22. Hawkins to Dearborn, November 3, 1804, *LJW*, 482–83. Also in ASPIA, 1:691–92.

23. Griffith, *McIntosh and Weatherford*, 60–61.

24. Hawkins to Eustis, October 10, 1809, *LJW*, 556–57; Hawkins to Irwin, October 15, 1809, *LJW*, 557–58.

25. See, for instance, Hawkins to Dearborn, November 24, 1805, *LJW*, 2, 500–501; Hawkins to Dearborn, February 24, 1807, *LJW*, 513–14; Hawkins to Dearborn, January 1, 1809, *LJW*, 546–48; and Hawkins to Eustis, January 6, 1811, *LJW*, 581–82.

26. Hawkins to Eustis, February 26, 1812, *LJW*, 602. For problems with the 1811 annuity payment, see Hawkins to Eustis, November 25, 1811, *LJW*, 598; Hawkins to Eustis, December 24, 1811, *LJW*, 599–600; Hawkins to Eustis, February 3, 1812, *LJW*, 601; and Hawkins to Eustis, March 9, 1812, *LJW*, 602. For the problem continuing again in 1813, see Hawkins to Eustis, November 2, 1812, *LJW*, 620–21; and Hawkins to Monroe, January 11, 1813, *LJW*, 627.

27. Hawkins to Mitchell, January 20, 1813, *LJW*, 628.

28. For issues of territorial access and their impact on Creek politics, see Griffith, *McIntosh and Weatherford*, 64–68.

29. Hawkins to Jefferson, September 13, 1806, *LJW*, 507–9; Hawkins to Meriwether, April 18, 1807, *LJW*, 516; Dearborn to Hawkins, June 28, 1805, SWLS, vol. B.

30. Hawkins to Dearborn, December 7, 1805, *LJW*, 502–3.

31. Dearborn to Hawkins, September 10, 1806, SWLS, vol. B; Hawkins to Jefferson, September 13, 1806, *LJW*, 507–9.

32. Hawkins to Dearborn, January 22, 1807, *LJW*, 510–11; Hawkins to Meriwether, April 18, 1807, *LJW*, 516–17.

33. Hawkins to Dearborn, September 16, 1807, *LJW*, 525.

34. Dearborn to Hawkins, December 8, 1808, SWLS, vol. B; Hawkins to Dearborn, January 7, 1809, *LJW*, 548.

35. Dearborn to Hawkins, December 8, 1808, SWLS, vol. B; Hawkins to Dearborn, January 7, 1809, *LJW*, 548.

36. Hawkins to Chandler, January 19, 1809, *LJW*, 549.

37. Hawkins to Reichel, July 8, 1807, *LJW*, 519.

38. Hawkins to Eustis, December 28, 1809, *LJW*, 559; Hawkins to Eustis, February 14, 1810, *LJW*, 561.

39. Hudson, *Creek Paths and Federal Roads*, 67–80.

40. Eustis to Meigs, Hawkins, and Dinsmoor, March 6, 1810, SWLS, vol. C.

41. Hawkins to Smith, April 23, 1809, *LJW*, 550; Hawkins to Armstrong, April 26, 1813, ASPIA, 1:841. See also Hawkins to Tustunnuggee Thlucco, Cornells, and

McIntosh, April 24, 1813, *ASPIA*, 1:842; and Big Warrior and Alexander Cornells to Hawkins, April 26, 1813, *ASPIA*, 1:843. For similar interpretations, see Collins, "A Packet from Canada," 55.

42. Hawkins to Eustis, June 21, 1810, *LJW*, 563.

43. Hawkins to Dearborn, June 28, 1807, *LJW*, 518–19.

44. Dearborn to Hawkins, August 18, 1807, *SWLS*, vol. B. See also Dearborn to Hawkins, May 1, 1806, *SWLS*, vol. B.

45. Hawkins to Dearborn, June 28, 1807, *LJW*, 518–19.

46. Hawkins to Dearborn, June 28, 1807, *LJW*, 518–19. Hawkins did consider this hypothetical years later. See Hawkins to Eustis, May 22, 1811, *LJW*, 88.

47. Hawkins to Meriwether, October 1, 1807, *LJW*, 526; Hawkins to Dearborn, October 8, 1807, *LJW*, 527.

48. Hawkins to Forbes, May 29, 1806, *LJW*, 505; Hawkins to Milledge, June 9, 1806, *LJW*, 505; Hawkins to Jefferson, September 13, 1806, *LJW*, 507–9; Hawkins to Dearborn, September 16, 1807, *LJW*, 524.

49. Hawkins to Meriwether, April 18, 1807, *LJW*, 516; Hawkins to Dearborn, July 23, 1807, *LJW*, 522–23.

50. Hawkins to Dearborn, April 17, 1808, *LJW*, 532.

51. Hawkins to Dearborn, September 16, 1807, *LJW*, 525.

52. Hawkins to Meriwether, October 1, 1807, *LJW*, 526–27; Hawkins to Dearborn, October 8, 1807, *LJW*, 527–29.

53. Hawkins to Meriwether, October 1, 1807, *LJW*, 526–27; Hawkins to Dearborn, January 22, 1807, *LJW*, 531.

54. Hawkins to Dearborn, June 16, 1808, *LJW*, 533–34. Hawkins talked about the same claims in a letter to Dearborn, October 22, 1808, *LJW*, 541.

55. Hawkins to Dearborn, June 16, 1808, *LJW*, 533–34.

56. To the Creeks of the 12 Towns of the Lower Creeks . . . , April 24, 1808, *LJW*, 534–35.

57. Hawkins to Dearborn, June 27, 1808, *LJW*, 536; Hawkins to Dearborn, June 30, 1808, *LJW*, 537.

58. Hawkins to Dearborn, October 16, 1807, *LJW*, 540.

59. Hawkins to Dearborn, October 16, 1807, *LJW*, 540.

60. Hawkins to Dearborn, October 22, 1807, *LJW*, 541–42.

61. Hawkins to Eustis, October 19, 1809, *LJW*, 556–57.

62. Hawkins to Eustis, April 8, 1810, *LJW*, 562.

63. Hawkins to Eustis, July 21, 1810, *LJW*, 564–65; Hawkins to Hopoithle Mico, July 18, 1810, *LJW*, 566.

64. Hawkins to Reverend Christian Benzien, October 7, 1810, *LJW*, 569.

65. Hawkins to Eustis, August 21, 1810, *LJW*, 566–67.

66. Hawkins to Cornells, September 25, 1810, *LJW*, 568; Hawkins to Eustis, October 8, 1810, *LJW*, 570.

67. Hawkins to Eustis, October 8, 1810, *LJW*, 570.

68. Hawkins to Luckett, October 24, 1810, *LJW*, 574; Hawkins to Gaines, October 25, 1810, *LJW*, 575.

69. Hawkins to Eustis, November 5, 1810, *LJW*, 575–76.

70. Hawkins to Eustis, February 24, 1811, *LJW*, 585.

71. Hawkins to Eustis, May 12, 1811, *LJW*, 587.

72. Hawkins to Eustis, May 22, 1811, *LJW*, 588; Hawkins to Mitchell, July 1, 1811, *LJW*, 589; Woodward, *Reminiscences*, 116.

73. Hawkins to Eustis, May 22, 1811, *LJW*, 588.

74. Hoboheithlee Mico to the President, May 15, 1811, SWLR.

75. Eustis to Hawkins, June 27, 1811, SWLS, vol. C.

76. Eustis to Hawkins, July 20, 1811, SWLS, vol. C.

77. To the Chiefs of the Convention, enclosed in Hawkins to Eustis, October 3, 1811, *LJW*, 593–94.

78. Hawkins to Hampton, August 26, 1811, *LJW*, 590–91.

79. Hawkins to Eustis, October 3, 1811, *LJW*, 593; To the Chiefs of the Convention, enclosed in Hawkins to Eustis, October 3, 1811, *LJW*, 593.

80. Hawkins to Madison, October 3, 1811, *LJW*, 595.

81. To the Chiefs of the Convention, enclosed in Hawkins to Eustis, October 3, 1811, *LJW*, 593.

82. Hawkins to Eustis, November 11, 1811, *LJW*, 597–98.

83. Hawkins to Eustis, November 4, 1811, *LJW*, 597; Hawkins to Eustis, November 18, 1811, *LJW*, 598.

84. Hawkins to Eustis, September 21, 1811, *LJW*, 591.

85. Hawkins to Eustis, December 31, 1810, SWLR, 1811.

86. Hawkins to Eustis, November 9, 1812, *LJW*, 621; also in November 28, 1812 edition, *Niles Weekly Register*, 3:205.

87. Hawkins to Jefferson, September 13, 1806, *LJW*, 507–9.

88. Hawkins to Eustis, December 28, 1809, *LJW*, 558–59.

89. Hawkins to Dearborn, January 27, 1809, *LJW*, 548–49; Hawkins to Eustis, May 21, 1809, *LJW*, 551.

90. Hawkins to Eustis, October 10, 1809, *LJW*, 556–57.

91. Hawkins to Dearborn, June 16, 1808, *LJW*, 533–34.

92. Hawkins to Eustis, May 11, 1812, *LJW*, 608.

93. Hawkins to Eustis, August 8, 1812, *LJW*, 613; Hawkins to Eustis, September 20, 1812, *LJW*, 618.

94. Hawkins to Eustis, October 12, 1812, *LJW*, 619–20; Hawkins to Mitchell, October 30, 1812, *LJW*, 620.

95. Hawkins to Eustis, November 9, 1812, *LJW*, 621; also in November 28, 1812 edition, *Niles Weekly Register*, 3:205.

96. Hawkins to Eustis, March 9, 1812, *LJW*, 603.

97. Hawkins to Eustis, March 30, 1812, *LJW*, 604.

98. Hawkins to Eustis, April 6, 1812, *LJW*, 605; Hawkins to Mitchell, April 6, 1812, *LJW*, 605–6; Woodward, *Reminiscences*, 35–36.

99. Hawkins to Eustis, May 25, 1812, *LJW*, 609; Hawkins to Eustis, June 9, 1812, *LJW*, 609.

100. To the whole Chiefs of the Nation, enclosed in Hawkins to Eustis, June 22, 1812, *LJW*, 610–11; Griffith, *McIntosh and Weatherford*, 80–83.

101. Hawkins to Eustis, July 13, 1812, *LJW*, 612–13; Hawkins to Mitchell, August 31, 1812, *LJW*, 616; Griffith, *McIntosh and Weatherford*, 82–83.

102. Hawkins to Eustis, August 3, 1812, *LJW*, 613; The Chronicle, in September 5, 1812, edition, *Niles Weekly Register*, 3:16. Two of the beaten and cropped were from the Lower Country. See Hawkins to Eustis, June 9, 1812, *LJW*, 609.

103. Hawkins to Eustis, August 24, 1812, *LJW*, 615–16.

104. Indian Retaliation, Savannah, October 29, in December 5, 1812 edition, *Niles Weekly Register*, 3:223; Hawkins to Mitchell, September 7, 1812, *LJW*, 617.

105. Hawkins to Secretary of War, January 11, 1813, *ASPIA*, 1:838; Hawkins to Mitchell, December 1, 1812, *LJW*, 622. For a steady series of reports that practically guaranteed safe travel, see Hawkins to Eustis, November 2, 1812, *LJW*, 620–21; Hawkins to Eustis, November 9, 1812, *LJW*, 621; Hawkins to Eustis, November 2, 1812, *LJW*, 620–21; Hawkins to Eustis, December 7, 1812, *LJW*, 623; Hawkins to Monroe, January 18, 1813, *ASPIA*, 1:838; and Hawkins to Armstrong, March 1, 1813, *ASPIA*, 1:838–39.

10. The Red Stick War and the Future of the National Council

1. For an excellent appraisal of these shifts, see Thrower, "Casualties and Consequences." For examples of older studies that stressed territorial issues, see Halbert and Ball, *The Creek War of 1813 and 1814*; Southerland and Brown, *The Federal Road*; and, more recently, Hudson, *Creek Paths and Federal Roads*. For studies that downplay geographic distinctions and territorial issues in favor of culture and wealth, and even spiritual revivalism, see Ellisor, *Second Creek War*, 9–12; Dowd, *A Spirited Resistance*; Dowd, "'Thinking outside the Circle'"; Martin, "The Creek Prophetic Movement"; Martin, *Sacred Revolt*; and Saunt, *A New Order of Things*.

2. Hawkins to Cornells, March 25, 1813, *LJW*, 630–31, also in *ASPIA*, 1:839; Hawkins to Upper Creek Chiefs, March 25, 1813, *LJW*, 631–32, also in Hawkins to Tustunnuggee Thlucco, Oche Haujo, and every Chief of the Upper Creeks, March 25, 1813, *ASPIA*, 1:839; extract from Executive Minutes, April 9, 1813, *CIL*, 3:773.

3. Hawkins to Upper Creek Chiefs, March 25, 1813, *LJW*, 631–32; Hawkins to Armstrong, March 29, 1813, *LJW*, 631–32, also in *ASPIA*, 1:840.

4. Hawkins to Upper Creek Chiefs, March 25, 1813, *LJW*, 631–32; Hawkins to Armstrong, March 25, 1813, *ASPIA*, 1:840.

5. Hawkins to Cornells, March 25, 1813, *LJW*, 630–31; Hawkins to Upper Creek Chiefs, March 25, 1813, *LJW*, 631–32.

6. Hawkins to Armstrong, April 6, 1813, *LJW*, 633, also in *ASPIA*, 1:840

7. Pinckney to Hawkins, January 4, 1813, *CIL*, 3:765; Armstrong to Hawkins, May 1, 1813, *SWLS*, vol. C; Armstrong to Mason, April 23, 1811, *SWLS*, vol. C.

8. Hawkins to Jefferson, September 13, 1806, *LJW*, 507–9.

9. Report of J. C. Warren to his Excellency D. B. Mitchell, May 13, 1813, *CIL*, 3:775–77.

10. Hawkins to Armstrong, April 6, 1813, *LJW*, 633; Flournoy to Mitchell, April 15, 1813, *Niles Weekly Register*, 4:160.

11. Talk of Big Warrior and Alex Cornells, April 18, 1813, James Caller Papers, folder 10.

12. Hawkins to Mitchell, April 26, 1813, *LJW*, 633–34; Report of J. C. Warren to his Excellency D. B. Mitchell, May 13, 1813, *CIL*, 3:775–77; Flournoy to Mitchell, April 15, 1813, *CIL*, 3:780.

13. We, chiefs, now in council, of the Upper Creeks, to Hawkins, April 26, 1813, *ASPIA*, 1:841; Big Warrior and Alexander Cornells to Hawkins, April 26, 1813, *ASPIA*, 1:843; Report of Nimrod Doyell, May 3, 1813, *ASPIA*, 1:843–44; Hawkins to Mitchell, April 26, 1813, *LJW*, 633–34; Report of J. C. Warren, May 13, 1813, *CIL*, 3:775–77.

14. We, chiefs, now in council, of the Upper Creeks, to Hawkins, April 26, 1813, *ASPIA*, 1:841; Big Warrior and Alexander Cornells to Hawkins, April 26, 1813, *ASPIA*, 1:843.

15. Hawkins to Mitchell, April 26, 1813, *LJW*, 633–34; Hawkins to Armstrong, April 26, 1813, *LJW*, 635–36; Hawkins to Tustunnuggee Thlucco, Alexander Cornells, and William McIntosh, April 24, 1813, *LJW*, 636–37.

16. Report of Nimrod Doyell, May 3, 1813, *ASPIA*, 1:843–44.

17. We, chiefs, now in council, of the Upper Creeks, to Hawkins, April 26, 1813, *ASPIA*, 1:841; Big Warrior and Alexander Cornells to Hawkins, April 26, 1813, *ASPIA*, 1:843. See also Hawkins to Cornells, March 25, 1813, *ASPIA*, 1:839.

18. Report of J. C. Warren to his Excellency D. B. Mitchell, May 13, 1813, *CIL*, 3:775–77.

19. We, chiefs, now in council, of the Upper Creeks, to Hawkins, April 26, 1813, *ASPIA*, 1:841. See also the talk in Big Warrior and Alexander Cornells to Hawkins, April 26, 1813, *ASPIA*, 1:843.

20. Hawkins to Armstrong, June 7, 1813, *LJW*, 640.

21. Flournoy to Mitchell, April 26, 1813, *TCC*, box 77, folder 30. For a similar report, see Report of J. C. Warren to his Excellency D. B. Mitchell, May 13, 1813, *CIL*, 3:775–77; and Hawkins to Armstrong, May 10, 1813, *LJW*, 639, also in *ASPIA*, 1:844.

22. Report of Nimrod Doyell, May 3, 1813, *ASPIA*, 1:843–44; Hawkins to Armstrong, May 3, 1813, *LJW*, 637–38; Hawkins to Armstrong, May 17, 1813, *LJW*, 639.

23. Hawkins to Eustis, September 30, 1811, *LJW*, 592.

24. Hawkins to Hampton, August 26, 1811, *LJW*, 590; Hawkins to Mitchell, October 21, 1811, *LJW*, 597.

25. Hawkins to Armstrong, April 26, 1813, *LJW*, 635–36; Hawkins to Armstrong, May 3, 1813, *LJW*, 637–38.

26. Report of Cornells to Hawkins, June 22, 1814, *ASPIA*, 1:845–46; Hawkins to Armstrong, June 28, 1813, *ASPIA*, 1:847; Hawkins to Armstrong, June 22, 1813, *LJW*, 641; and entry for June 23, 1814, *ASPIA*, 1:846.

27. Report of Cornells to Hawkins, June 22, 1814, *ASPIA*, 1:845–46; Hawkins to Armstrong, June 22, 1813, *LJW*, 641, also in *ASPIA*, 1:847; Saunt, *A New Order of Things*, 254; Dowd, *A Spirited Resistance*, 170.

28. Saunt, *A New Order of Things*, 254–69; Dowd, *A Spirited Resistance*, 169–70, 186–87; Martin, *Sacred Revolt*, 142–43.

29. Saunt, *A New Order of Things*, 254–55.

30. Sam Manac [Moniac] deposition, August 2, 1813.

31. Hawkins to Armstrong, July 28, 1813, *LJW*, 651–52; Toulmin to Claiborne, July 23, 1813, Harry Toulmin Papers, folder 2; Hawkins to Armstrong, June 22, 1813, *LJW*, 641.

32. Talosee Fixico to Hawkins, July 5, 1813, *ASPIA*, 1:847; [Big Warrior] to Walton, July 24, 1813, *CIL*, 3:786–87; entry dated September 19, in Journal of Occurrences at the Convention . . . , September 9, 1815, *LJW*, 756–57.

33. The Red Stick War as primarily a religious uprising has been argued best in Waselkov, *A Conquering Spirit*, 72–95, 114–49; and Nunez, "Creek Nativism and the Creek War of 1813–1814." For the argument that Red Sticks selectively struck at physical symbols of Euro-American culture, see Dowd, *A Spirited Resistance*, 169–70; and Saunt, *A New Order of Things*, 254–56.

34. Waselkov, *A Conquering Spirit*, 92–93, 125–27; Griffith, *McIntosh and Weatherford*, 79–80.

35. Frank, *Creeks and Southerners*, 121–23; Waselkov, *A Conquering Spirit*, 34–47, 91–95. For Jim Boy, see Woodward, *Reminiscences*, 86; and O'Brien, *In Bitterness and in Tears*, 157–58.

36. A description of the towns on Coosa and Tallapoosa . . . , *LJW*, 1:290; Woodward, *Reminiscences*, 110–11; Waselkov, *A Conquering Spirit*, 215n38; Covington, *The Seminoles of Florida*, 33–34.

37. Martin, *Sacred Revolt*, 134–35; John Innerarity to James Innerarity, July 27, 1813, CIL, 3:795–802.

38. Woodward, *Reminiscences*, 36–37, 95–96; Waselkov, *A Conquering Spirit*, 83; Martin, *Sacred Revolt*, 124–25; Dowd, *A Spirited Resistance*, 170. Even the Big Warrior was, at one time, on the fence. When Tecumseh made his appearance at Tuckabatchee, in 1811, the Big Warrior "was inclined to take the talk, and at heart, was as hostile as any, if he had not been a coward." See Woodward, *Reminiscences*, 37, 95–96.

39. Green, *Politics of Indian Removal*, 40; Martin, *Sacred Revolt*, 134–35.

40. Woodward, *Reminiscences*, 37, 96; Sam Manac [Moniac] deposition.

41. Hawkins to Armstrong, July 28, 1813, *LJW*, 651–52; Toulmin to Claiborne, July 23, 1813, Harry Toulmin Papers, folder 2.

42. See McLoughlin, *Cherokee Renascence*, ch. 11.

43. Report of Cornells to Hawkins, June 22, 1814, ASPIA, 1:845–46.

44. Report of Cornells to Hawkins, June 22, 1814, ASPIA, 1:845–46; Saunt, *A New Order of Things*, 252.

45. Entry for June 23, 1814, ASPIA, 1:846; Talosee Fixico to Hawkins, July 5, 1813, ASPIA, 1:847; Hawkins to Armstrong, June 28, 1813, ASPIA, 1:847; [Big Warrior] to Walton, July 24, 1813, CIL, 3:786–87.

46. Hawkins to Armstrong, June 28, 1813, ASPIA, 1:847; Talosee Fixico to Hawkins, July 5, 1813, ASPIA, 1:847.

47. Report of Cornells to Hawkins, June 22, 1814, ASPIA, 1:845–46.

48. Entry for June 23, 1814 [1813], ASPIA, 1:846. See also Hawkins to Armstrong, June 22, 1813, ASPIA, 1:847; Hawkins to Armstrong, June 27, 1813, *LJW*, 642–43, also in ASPIA, 1:847; Talosee Fixico to Hawkins, July 5, 1813, ASPIA, 1:847; and [Big Warrior] to Walton, July 24, 1813, CIL, 3:786–87.

49. Mitchell agreed to loan McIntosh and the council weapons and powder on credit, against their annuity. See Hawkins to Pinckney, July 9, 1813, *LJW*, 644–45, also in ASPIA, 1:848.

50. Hawkins to Armstrong, July 6, 1813, *LJW*, 643–44, also in ASPIA, 1:848; Hawkins to Mitchell, July 7, 1813, *LJW*, 644. Hawkins confronted the Big Warrior about his unwillingness to attack the prophets early. The Big Warrior was "slow to hear, and as slow to act," he charged. Hawkins to Tustunnuggee Thlucco, July 26, 1813, *LJW*, 649.

51. Woodward, *Reminiscences*, 38; A demand of the fanatical chiefs, July 6, 1813, ASPIA, 1:848.

52. Hawkins to Mitchell, July 11, 1813, *LJW*, 645–46.

53. Cusseta Mico to Hawkins, July 10, 1813, ASPIA, 1:849; affidavit of James Moore, July 13, 1813, TCC, box 77, folder 1.

54. Extract, July 12, 1813, *ASPIA*, 1:849; Cusseta Mico to Hawkins, July 10, 1813, *ASPIA*, 1:849; Hawkins to Mitchell, July 11, 1813, *LJW*, 645–46; Hawkins to Armstrong, July 20, 1813, *LJW*, 647–48, also in *ASPIA*, 1:849.

55. Cusseta Mico to Hawkins, July 10, 1813, *ASPIA*, 1:849; Hawkins to Armstrong, July 13, 1813, *LJW*, 646, also in *ASPIA*, 1:848; Hawkins to Mitchell, July 13, 1813, *LJW*, 646.

56. Hawkins to Armstrong, July 20, 1813, *LJW*, 647–48; Hawkins to Armstrong, July 28, 1813, *LJW*, 651–52, also in *ASPIA*, 1:849–50; Hawkins to Mitchell, July 22, 1813, *LJW*, 648; Tustunnuggee Thlucco to Hawkins, July 26, 1813, CIL, 3:790–91.

57. Hawkins to Armstrong, July 20, 1813, *LJW*, 647–48; Durouzeaux to McIntosh, July 14, 1813, TCC, box 78, folder 5; [Big Warrior, Little Prince, Tustunnuggee Opoi] to Walton, July 24, 1813, CIL, 3:786–87; Walton to Mitchell, July 26, 1813, CIL, 3:788–89; Tustunnuggee Thlucco to Hawkins, July 26, 1813, CIL, 3:790–92.

58. Hawkins to Armstrong, July 26, 1813, *LJW*, 648–49, also in *ASPIA*, 1:849; Hawkins to the Secretary of War, July 28, 1813, *LJW*, 651–52; Hawkins to Armstrong, June 7, 1814, *ASPIA*, 1:858; Tustunnuggee Thlucco to Hawkins, July 26, 1813, CIL, 3:790–91.

59. Hawkins to Armstrong, July 28, 1813, *LJW*, 651–52; extract of a letter, dated Creek Agency, 27th of July, 1813, in September 25, 1813 edition of *Niles Weekly Register*, 5:56.

60. Extract of a letter, dated Creek Agency, 27th of July, 1813, in September 25, 1813 edition of *Niles Weekly Register*, 5:56; Hawkins to Tustunnuggee Thlucco, July 26, 1813, *LJW*, 649–50.

61. Hawkins to Armstrong, August 10, 1813, *ASPIA*, 1:851; Big Warrior and all of the friendly chiefs to Hawkins, October 4, 1813, CIL, 3:825–26.

62. Hawkins to Armstrong, September 13, 1813, *ASPIA*, 1, 852; Cusseta Mico to Hawkins, July 10, 1813, *ASPIA*, 1:849; Big Warrior and all of the friendly chiefs to Hawkins, October 4, 1813, CIL, 3:825–26.

63. Hawkins to Mitchell, August 17, 1813, *LJW*, 654–55.

64. Extract of a letter, dated Creek Agency, 27th of July, 1813, in September 25, 1813 edition of *Niles Weekly Register*, 5:56; Hawkins to the Secretary of War, July 28, 1813, *ASPIA*, 1:849–50; Hawkins to Mitchell, August 9, 1813, *LJW*, 653; Hawkins to Armstrong, September 13, 1813, *LJW*, 660; Floyd to Mitchell, September 15, 1813, CIL, 3:818; Hawkins to the Secretary of War, October 11, 1813, *ASPIA*, 1:852.

65. Hawkins to the Secretary of War, July 28, 1813, *ASPIA*, 1:849–50; Big Warrior and all the friendly chiefs to Hawkins, October 4, 1813, CIL, 3:825–26; Saunt, *A New Order of Things*, 256.

66. Hawkins to Armstrong, August 10, 1813, *ASPIA*, 1:851; Floyd to Mitchell, September 15, 1813, CIL, 3:818; Big Warrior and all the friendly chiefs to Hawkins, October 4, 1813, CIL, 3:825–26.

67. Hawkins to Mitchell, July 27, 1813, *LJW*, 650–51; Hawkins to Armstrong, July 28, 1813, *LJW*, 651–52; August 2, 5 p.m., in Hawkins to Armstrong, July 28, 1813, *LJW*, 652; Claiborne to the Governor, State of Georgia, August 14, 1813, CIL, 3:810813.

68. Cusseta Mico to Hawkins, July 10, 1813, *ASPIA*, 849.

69. See, for instance, Hawkins to Mitchell, August 17, 1813, *LJW*, 657; Hawkins to Armstrong, August 23, 1813, *LJW*, 658–59, also in *ASPIA*, 1:851–52; Hawkins to Armstrong, September 6, 1813, *ASPIA*, 1:852; and Hawkins to Armstrong, September 13, 1813, *ASPIA*, 1, 852.

70. For evidence of these requests, see Hawkins to Armstrong, July 26, 1813, *ASPIA*, 1:849; Hawkins to the Secretary of War, July 28, 1813, *ASPIA*, 1:849–50; Big Warrior and

Tustunnuggee Hopoie to Hawkins, August 4, 1813, *ASPIA*, 1:851; Hawkins to Mitchell, August 19, 1813, *LJW*, 657–58; and Hawkins to the Secretary of War, August 23, 1813, *ASPIA*, 1:851–52.

71. Big Warrior to Mitchell, August 2, 1813, CIL, 3:803. The Big Warrior sent an even more dire warning in October. See Big Warrior and Little Prince to Hawkins, October 7, 1813, CIL, 3:829.

72. Big Warrior and Tustunnuggee Hopoie to Hawkins, August 4, 1813, *ASPIA*, 1:851; Big Warrior to Hawkins, August 1, 1813, *ASPIA*, 1:851; Hawkins to Mitchell, August 9, 1813, *LJW*, 653.

73. Hawkins to Mitchell, August 17, 1813, *LJW*, 655.

74. Hawkins to Mitchell, August 17, 1813, *LJW*, 656; Hawkins to Armstrong, August 23, 1813, *LJW*, 658–59.

75. Hawkins to Armstrong, September 6, 1813, *ASPIA*, 1:852; Hawkins to Mitchell, August 17, 1813, *LJW*, 657; Hawkins to Mitchell, August 28, 1813, *LJW*, 659.

76. Hawkins to Floyd, October 4, 1813, *ASPIA*, 1:855; Hawkins to the Secretary of War, October 25, 1813, *ASPIA*, 1:857; Hawkins to Cook, October 3, 1813, *LJW*, 669.

77. Fort Hawkins, September 21, 1813, *ASPIA*, 1:853; Big Warrior and Little Prince to Hawkins, September 24, 1813, CIL, 3:820.

78. Wright, *Creeks & Seminoles*, 173–74; Saunt, *A New Order of Things*, 262–64; Waselkov, *A Conquering Spirit*, 98–138; Dowd, *A Spirited Resistance*, 185–86; Dowd, *Sacred Revolt*, 150–51, 156–57; Griffith, *McIntosh and Weatherford*, 95–111.

79. Fort Hawkins, September 21, 1813, *ASPIA*, 1:853; Griffith, *McIntosh and Weatherford*, 110.

80. Hawkins to Floyd, September 30, 1813, *ASPIA*, 1:854.

81. Hawkins to Cook, October 3, 1813, *LJW*, 669, also in *ASPIA*, 1:854; Fannin to Mitchell, September 25, 1813, CIL, 3:819; Waselkov, *A Conquering Spirit*, 140–42.

82. Hawkins to the Secretary of War, October 11, 1813, *ASPIA*, 852; extract of a communication from the chiefs at Coweta to Colonel Hawkins, September 18, 1813, *ASPIA*, 1:853; Hawkins to Cook, October 3, 1813, *ASPIA*, 1:854.

83. Hawkins to the Secretary of War, September 26, 1813, *ASPIA*, 1:854; Hawkins to Floyd, September 30, 1813, *ASPIA*, 1:854.

84. Hawkins to Floyd, October 4, 1813, *ASPIA*, 1:855; Hawkins to Cook, October 3, 1813, *LJW*, 669.

85. Hawkins to Cook, October 3, 1813, *ASPIA*, 1:854. For similar letters, see Hawkins to Floyd, September 30, 1813, *ASPIA*, 1:854; Hawkins to Floyd, October 4, 1813, *ASPIA* A, 1:855; and Hawkins to Armstrong, October 4, 1813, *ASPIA*, 1:855.

86. Hawkins to Floyd, September 30, 1813, *ASPIA*, 1:854.

87. Carson to Claiborne, July 30, 1813, Joseph Carson letter.

88. Hawkins to Mitchell, August 28, 1813, *LJW*, 659; Talosee Fixico to Hawkins, July 5, 1813, *ASPIA*, 1:847.

89. Hawkins to Armstrong, June 28, 1813, *LJW*, 643, also in *ASPIA*, 1:847. See also Hawkins to the Big Warrior, Little Prince, and other chiefs . . . , June 16, 1814, *ASPIA*, 1:845.

90. Hawkins to Mitchell, August 17, 1813, *LJW*, 656.

91. Hawkins to Armstrong, June 27, 1813, *ASPIA*, 1:847.

92. Hawkins to Mitchell, July 27, 1813, *LJW*, 650–51; Hawkins to Floyd, October 4, 1813, *LJW*, 670.

93. Extract of a letter, dated Creek Agency, 27th of July, 1813, in September 25, 1813 edition of *Niles Weekly Register*, 5:56; Hawkins to Cook, October 3, 1813, LJW, 669–70; Hawkins to Armstrong, October 4, 1813, LJW, 670; Waselkov, *A Conquering Spirit*, 147–49. Indeed, according to a report from Sam Moniac, a Creek of mixed ancestry and a man of considerable property in the region, original attack plans were complex. As of August, communities on the Coosa and Tallapoosa would attack the Tensaw and surrounding settlements; communities at the northernmost part of Creek Country would attack Tennessee; and finally, Seminoles and Lower Creeks "were to attack the Georgians." The attack would be "made at the same time in all places" as soon as ammunition was distributed. See Sam Manac [Moniac] deposition.

94. Extract of a letter, dated Creek Agency, 27th of July, 1813, in September 25, 1813 edition of *Niles Weekly Register*, 5:56; Hawkins to Cook, October 3, 1813, LJW, 669–70; Hawkins to Armstrong, October 4, 1813, LJW, 670; Waselkov, *A Conquering Spirit*, 147–49.

95. Waselkov, *A Conquering Spirit*, 153–58; Dowd, *A Spirited Resistance*, 157–58.

96. Kanon, "Before Horseshoe"; Dowd, *A Spirited Resistance*, 186–87; Waselkov, *A Conquering Spirit*, 163–71; Martin, *Sacred Revolt*, 158–61; Griffith, *McIntosh and Weatherford*, 112–38; O'Brien, *In Bitterness and in Tears*, 63–139.

97. Dowd, *A Spirited Resistance*, 187; Martin, *Sacred Revolt*, 161–63; Waselkov, *A Conquering Spirit*, 170–71; O'Brien, *In Bitterness and in Tears*, 141–52; Griffith, *McIntosh and Weatherford*, 138–50.

98. Dowd, *A Spirited Resistance*, 152–55.

99. Hawkins to Armstrong, September 21, 1813, LJW, 664; Hawkins to Armstrong, October 18, 1813, LJW, 673.

100. Hawkins to Armstrong, October 25, 1813, LJW, 674; Big Warrior, McIntosh, Little Prince, and Cornells to Floyd, November 18, 1813, CIL, 3:839.

101. Hawkins to Mitchell, September 6, 1813, LJW, 660; Hawkins to Armstrong, September 13, 1813, ASPIA, 1:852; Hawkins to the Secretary of War, October 11, 1813, ASPIA, 1:852.

102. Hawkins to Floyd, September 26, 1813, LJW, 667; Hawkins to Armstrong, September 26, 1813, LJW, 666; Doyell to Hawkins, October 4, 1813, CIL, 3:826–27.

103. Barnard to Mitchell, August 28, 1813, TCC, box 46, folder 14.

104. Big Warrior and all of the friendly chiefs to Hawkins, October 4, 1813, CIL, 3:826; Big Warrior and Little Prince to Hawkins, October 7, 1813, CIL, 3:829.

105. Hawkins to Armstrong, September 13, 1813, ASPIA, 1:852; Hawkins to Armstrong, October 11, 1813, LJW, 672, also in ASPIA, 852.

106. Hawkins to Mitchell, August 17, 1813, LJW, 654–55.

107. Hawkins to the Secretary of War, September 21, 1813, ASPIA, 1:853–54.

108. Hawkins to Armstrong, October 18, 1813, LJW, 673; Hawkins to Floyd, October 12, 1813, CIL, 3:833. When there were further reports of troubles early in 1814, Hawkins again suspected Yuchis and directed headmen to send another group of warriors from Auputtanee, a Cusseta village, to "trace up the thieves and punish them." Hawkins to Lewis, February 16, 1814, LJW, 678.

109. Hawkins to Cook, October 3, 1813, ASPIA, 1:854; O'Brien, *In Bitterness and in Tears*, 93.

110. Hawkins to Parker, November 8, 1813, LJW, 674.

111. Floyd to Pinckney, December 4, 1813, in December 25, 1813 edition of *Niles Weekly Register*, 5:283–84; Floyd to Early, December 12, 1813, CIL, 3:846; O'Brien, *In Bitterness and in Tears*, 95–96.

112. Hawkins to Early, December 15, 1813, *LJW*, 676; Hawkins to Armstrong, July 13, 1814, *ASPIA*, 1:860.

113. Floyd to Pinckney, January 27, 1814, in February 19, 1814 edition of *Niles Weekly Register*, 5:411; Woodward, *Reminiscences*, 40.

114. The Creeks, January 15, 1814, edition of *Niles Weekly Register*, 5:331.

115. Jackson to Pinckney, January 29, 1814, in February 26, 1814 edition of *Niles Weekly Register*, 5:427–29.

116. Morgan to Meigs, February 4, 1814, Gideon Morgan Papers, box 10.

117. Cocke to Early, January 28, 1814, TCC, box 77, folder 30.

118. Jackson to Pinckney, March 28, 1814, in April 23, 1814, edition of *Niles Weekly Register*, 6:130; Griffith, *McIntosh and Weatherford*, 145–47.

119. February 5, 1814 edition of *Niles Weekly Register*, 5:384.

120. Dowd, *A Spirited Resistance*, 186–87; Martin, *Sacred Revolt*, 158–61; O'Brien, *In Bitterness and in Tears*, 79.

121. James and James to Adams, May 20, 1814, TCC, box 77, folder 1; Adams to Early, May 20, 1814, TCC, box 47, folder 3.

122. Dowd, *A Spirited Resistance*, 187; Martin, *Sacred Revolt*, 162–64.

123. Dowd, *Sacred Revolt*, 163–64.

124. Hawkins to Armstrong, June 7, 1814, *LJW*, 682–83.

125. Hawkins to Armstrong, July 19, 1814, *LJW*, 689–90.

126. James and James to Adams, May 20, 1814, TCC, box 77, folder 1; Hawkins to Armstrong, July 13, 1814, *ASPIA*, 1:860; Hawkins to Armstrong, August 16, 1814, *ASPIA*, 1:860.

127. Hawkins to Early, June 15, 1814, TCC, box 76, folder 25.

128. Hawkins to Graham, July 5, 1814, *LJW*, 688–89.

129. Hawkins to Armstrong, June 21, 1814, *LJW*, 685; Hawkins to Armstrong, July 3, 1814, *LJW*, 688.

130. Hawkins to Pinckney, May 17, 1814, *LJW*, 680–81; Waselkov, "Fort Jackson and the Aftermath," 165.

131. Hawkins to Pinckney, April 25, 1814, *LJW*, 679, also in *ASPIA*, 1:858; Hawkins to the Big Warrior, Little Prince, and other chiefs . . . , June 16, 1814, *ASPIA*, 1:845.

132. Hawkins to Pinckney, May 17, 1814, *LJW*, 680–81; Hawkins to Pinckney, April 25, 1814, *LJW*, 679, also in *ASPIA*, 1:858; Hawkins to the Big Warrior, Little Prince, and other chiefs . . . , June 16, 1814, *ASPIA*, 1:845.

133. For these reports, see Hawkins to Early, May 25, 1814, TCC, box 76, folder 25; Hawkins to Pinckney, May 17, 1814, *LJW*, 680–81; Hawkins to Armstrong, July 3, 1814, *LJW*, 688; Hawkins to Graham, July 5, 1814, *LJW*, 688–89; and Hawkins to Armstrong, July 19, 1814, *LJW*, 689–90.

134. Hawkins to Big Warrior, Little Prince, and other Creek Chiefs, June 16, 1814, *LJW*, 687–88.

135. Armstrong to Pinckney, March 20, 1814, *ASPIA*, 1:837; Hawkins to Armstrong, April 25, 1814, *LJW*, 679.

136. Report of Charles Cassedy, August 8, 1814, *ASPIA*, 1:837.

137. Benjamin Hawkins, Eight P.M., *ASPIA*, 1:837; Statement signed by Tustunnuggee Thlucco . . . , August 9, 1814, *ASPIA*, 1:837–38.

138. Hawkins to William Hawkins, April 16, 1814, *LJW*, 680.

139. Benjamin Hawkins, Eight P.M., *ASPIA*, 1:837; Statement signed by Tustunnuggee Thlucco . . . , August 9, 1814, *ASPIA*, 1:837–38. For Hawkins's later thoughts on the treaty, see Hawkins to Graham, August 1, 1815, *LJW* 2:743–45.

140. Jackson to the Secretary of War, August 10, 1814, *ASPIA*, 1:838; Sadosky, *Revolutionary Negotiations*, 199.

141. Hawkins to Jackson, August 6, 1814, *LJW*, 692.

Epilogue

1. For an excellent appraisal of this period, see Waselkov, "Fort Jackson and the Aftermath."

2. Hawkins to William Hawkins, April 26, 1814, *LJW*, 2:680–81; Hawkins to Graham, July 5, 1814, *LJW*, 2:688; Hawkins to Armstrong, July 13, 1814, *ASPIA*, 1:860; Hawkins to Armstrong, August 16, 1814, *ASPIA*, 1:860. For other accounts of this exodus, see Saunt, *A New Order of Things*, 276–78.

3. Waselkov, "Fort Jackson and the Aftermath," 158; Ellisor, *Second Creek War*, 12–13; Mahon, *History of the Second Seminole War*, 6–7; Covington, *The Seminoles of Florida*, 33–34, 36–37; Weisman, *Unconquered People*, 5–27, 43–49.

4. Report of supplies to the Indians by the British and Spanish . . . , June 14, 1814, TCC, box 76, folder 25.

5. Report of Supplies to the Indians by the British . . . , June 14, 1814, *LJW*, 2:683–84.

6. Hawkins to Armstrong, July 3, 1814, *LJW*, 2:688; Report of Fallaupau Haujo and Noocoosa Haujo, enclosed in Hawkins to Jackson, August 6, 1814, *LJW*, 2:690–91.

7. Hawkins to Tustunnuggee Hopoie and Tustunnuggee Thlucco, enclosed in Hawkins to Jackson, August 30, 1814; *LJW*, 2:694.

8. Report of supplies to the Indians by the British and Spanish . . . , June 14, 1814, TCC, box 76, folder 25.

9. Hawkins to Jackson, November 4, 1814, *LJW*, 2:701; Wigginton to Hawkins, December 2, 1814, TCC, box 76, folder 24.

10. Barnard to Hawkins, November 3, 1814, TCC, box 1, folder 11.

11. Tooke to Early, November 21, 1814, TCC, box 47, folder 04; Thomas to Early, September 26, 1814, TCC, box 77, folder 31.

12. Tooke to Early, November 21, 1814, TCC, box 47, folder 04; Pinckney to Early, November 22, 1814, TCC, box 47, folder 04.

13. Tustunnuggee Thlucco and Tustunnuggee Hopoie to Hawkins, June 13, 1814, TCC, box 77, folder 33.

14. Milledgeville, June 1, in June 18, 1814 edition of *Niles Weekly Register*, 6:264.

15. Hawkins to Early, April 21, 1815, TCC, box 76, folder 25; Waselkov, "Fort Jackson and the Aftermath," 160–62.

16. Report of Supplies to the Indians by the British . . . , June 14, 1814, *LJW*, 2:683–84; Saunt, *New Order of Things*, 276–78.

17. Report of Supplies to the Indians by the British . . . , June 14, 1814, *LJW*, 2:683–84; Hawkins to Armstrong, June 21, 1814, *LJW*, 2:685; Hawkins to Graham, July 5, 1814, *LJW*, 2:688–89.

18. Hawkins to Armstrong, July 13, 1814, *LJW*, 2:689.

19. Waselkov, "Fort Jackson and the Aftermath"; Owsley, *Struggle for the Gulf Borderlands*; Remini, *Andrew Jackson*.

20. Hawkins to Armstrong, August 16, 1814, *LJW*, 2:693–94; Hawkins to Jackson, August 30, 1814, *LJW*, 2:694; Hawkins to Monroe, October 26, 1814, *LJW*, 2:698; Hawkins to Early, November 5, 1814, *LJW*, 2:702–3.

21. Hawkins to Early, October 30, 1814, *LJW*, 2:698; Hawkins to Little Prince and Big Warrior, November 3, 1814, *LJW*, 2:700; Cook to Early, November 16, 1813, CIL, 3:864.

22. Hawkins to John Houston McIntosh, November 26, 1814, *LJW*, 2:706–8.

23. Hawkins to Early, February 15, 1815, *LJW*, 2:717; Hawkins to Early, February 20, 1815, *LJW*, 2:718; Saunt, *A New Order of Things*, 278–79.

24. Hawkins to Earl, April 21, 1815, *LJW*, 2:724–25.

25. Hawkins to Jackson, August 30, 1814, *LJW*, 2:694; Hawkins to Tustunnuggee Hopoie and Tustunnuggee Thlucco, enclosed in Hawkins to Jackson, August 30, 1814, *LJW*, 2:694; Hawkins to the Little Prince and Big Warrior, November 3, 1814, *LJW*, 2:700.

26. McIntosh to Early, December 12, 1814, TCC, box 47, folder 4.

27. Hawkins to Dallas, May 5, 1815, *LJW*, 2:725.

28. Hawkins to Jackson, May 5, 1815, *LJW*, 2:725–26; Hawkins to Pinckney, May 12, 1815, *LJW*, 2:726.

29. Hawkins to Early, November 3, 1814, TCC, box 76, folder 25; Hawkins to Lagueux, November 5, 1814, TCC, box 76, folder 25; Hawkins to Early, November 29, 1814, TCC, box, 76, folder 25; Hawkins to Early, November 15, 1814, *LJW*, 2:706; Hawkins to Jackson, including enclosure, November 11, 1814, *LJW*, 2:704–5.

30. Jackson to Hawkins, September 19, 1814, ASPIA, 1:861; Hawkins to Monroe, October 5, 1814, *LJW*, 2:696, also in ASPIA, 1:861.

31. Hawkins to Early, October 12, 1814, TCC, box 76, folder 25; Hawkins to Monroe, October 12, 1814, *LJW*, 2:696–97; Griffith, *McIntosh and Weatherford*, 164.

32. Hawkins to Armstrong, August 16, 1814, *LJW*, 2:693–94; Hawkins to Early, November 1, 1814, *LJW*, 2:699.

33. Hawkins to the Little Prince and Big Warrior, November 3, 1814, *LJW*, 2:700; Hawkins to Early, November 3, 1814, *LJW*, 2:700–701; Hawkins to Jackson, November 4, 1814, *LJW*, 2:701; Wigginton to Hawkins, December 2, 1814, TCC, box 76, folder 24.

34. Hawkins to Early, October 30, 1814, *LJW*, 2:698–99.

35. Hawkins to Early, December 1814, TCC, box 76, folder 25; O'Brien, *In Bitterness and in Tears*, 175–76.

36. For Hawkins's raising that force and for the growing size of it, see Hawkins to Early, November 3, 1814, TCC, box 76, folder 25; Hawkins to Lagueux, November 5, 1814, TCC, box 76, folder 25; Hawkins to Early, November 29, 1814, TCC, box, 76, folder 25; Hawkins to Early, November 15, 1814, *LJW*, 2:706; Hawkins to John Houston McIntosh, November 26, 1814, *LJW*, 2:706–8; and Hawkins to Jackson, December 27, 1814, *LJW*, 2:711.

37. O'Brien, *In Bitterness and in Tears*, 175–86.

38. Hawkins to Blackshear, January 11, 1815, *LJW*, 2:714; Hawkins to Early, January 22, 1815, *LJW*, 2:715; Hawkins to Monroe, January 23, 1815, *LJW*, 2:715–16; Hawkins to Early, February 20, 1813, CIL, 3:871.

39. The warriors enrolled in the service of the U. States . . . , in Hawkins to Monroe, January 23, 1815, *LJW*, 2:715–17.

40. Hawkins to Jackson, February 27, 1815, *LJW*, 2:721–22; Hawkins to Monroe, March 6, 1815, *LJW*, 2:722–23; Hawkins to Dallas, May 5, 1815, *LJW*, 2:725; Hawkins to Gaines, June 14, 1815, *LJW*, 2:735–36.

41. Changing Creek ideas about race, and the eventual embrace by many of chattel slavery, has been examined most recently in Snyder, *Slavery in Indian Country*, particularly pages 182–212. It is also addressed in Saunt, *A New Order of Things*, 111–35; and Wright, *Creeks & Seminoles*, 73–99. For the more complicated approach to race, slavery, and runaway slaves in Seminole Country, see Snyder, *Slavery in Indian Country*, 312–243; Saunt, *A New Order of Things*, 236–48; and Mulroy, *Freedom on the Border*, 6–34.

42. The growth and destruction of the "Negro Fort" at Prospect Bluff has been studied extensively. The most recent study comes from Millett, *The Maroons of Prospect Bluff*. It is also addressed in Saunt, *A New Order of Things*, 273–88.

43. Hawkins to Nicolls, March 19, 1815, *LJW*, 2:723; Hawkins to Dallas, May 19, 1815, *LJW*, 2:727–28.

44. Hawkins to Jackson, March 24, 1815, *LJW*, 2:723–24; Hawkins to Early, April 21, 1815, *LJW*, 2:724.

45. Hawkins to Tustunnuggee Hopoie and Tustunnuggee Thlucco, enclosed in Hawkins to Jackson, August 30, 1814, *LJW*, 2:694–95; Hawkins to Early, November 15, 1814, *LJW*, 2:706.

46. Hawkins to Monroe, October 12, 1814, *LJW*, 2:696–97.

47. Hawkins to Jackson, March 21, 1816, *LJW*, 2:778.

48. Hawkins to Crawford, April 2, 1816, *LJW*, 2:779; Hawkins to Crawford, April 21, 1816, 781–82.

49. Nicolls to Hawkins, April 28, 1815, *LJW*, 2:729–30; Hawkins to Cornells, June 24, 1815, *LJW*, 2:736–37.

50. Floyd to Early, December 13, 1813, *CIL*, 3:846; O'Brien, *In Bitterness and in Tears*, 99.

51. Nicolls to Hawkins, April 28, 1815, *LJW*, 2:729–30; Hawkins to Nicolls, May 28, 1815, *LJW*, 2:732–33.

52. Hawkins to Monroe, October 5, 1814, *LJW*, 2:696; Hawkins to Monroe, October 12, 1814, *LJW*, 2:696–97; Hawkins to Early, February 15, 1815, *LJW*, 2:717–18.

53. Hawkins to Dallas, May 26, 1815, *LJW*, 2:731.

54. Hawkins to Iverson, June 2, 1815, *LJW*, 2:735; Hawkins to Dallas, June 27, 1815, *LJW*, 2:738; Hawkins to Jackson, August 4, 1815, *LJW*, 2:746–47; Hawkins to Crawford, September 9, 1815, *LJW*, 2:751; Hawkins to Crawford, February 22, 1816, *LJW*, 2:774–75. For the arrival of some of those payments, see Hawkins to Crawford, April 1, 1816, *LJW*, 2:778–79.

55. Hawkins to Jackson, August 12, 1815, *LJW*, 2:748.

56. Hawkins to Crawford, April 2, 1816, *LJW*, 2:779–81; Hawkins to Graham, April 23, 1816, *LJW*, 2:782–83; Hawkins to Early, May 30, 1815, *LJW*, 2:734–35.

57. Hawkins to Sevier and Barnett, August 19, 1815, *LJW*, 2:748–49; Hawkins to Graham, August 28, 1815, *LJW*, 2:749.

58. Hawkins to Dallas, July 21, 1815, *LJW*, 2:742–43.

59. Entries dated September 16 through September 18, in Journal of Occurrences at the Convention . . . , September 9, 1815, *LJW*, 2:753–55.

60. Entries dated September 16 through September 18, in Journal of Occurrences at the Convention . . . , September 9, 1815, *LJW*, 2:753–55.

61. Wright, *Creeks & Seminoles*, 186–87.

62. Entry dated September 18, in Journal of Occurrences at the Convention . . . , September 9, 1815, *LJW*, 2:755–56.

63. Entry dated September 19, in Journal of Occurrences at the Convention . . . , September 9, 1815, *LJW*, 2:756–57.

64. Entry dated September 20, in Journal of Occurrences at the Convention . . . , September 9, 1815, *LJW*, 2:758–60.

65. Hawkins to Graham, September 22, 1815, *LJW*, 2:763; Hawkins to Crawford, April 1, 1816, *LJW*, 2:778–79.

66. Hawkins to Jackson, March 21, 1816, *LJW*, 2:778; Hawkins to Crawford, April 2, 1816, 779–81.

67. Hawkins to Graham, April 23, 1816, *LJW*, 2:782–83.

68. For two studies of the post–Red Stick years, see Ellisor, *Second Creek War*; and Green, *Politics of Indian Removal*.

69. Saunt, *A New Order of Things*, 287–88; Wright, *Creeks & Seminoles*, 198–99; Griffith, *McIntosh and Weatherford*, 172–78; O'Brien, *In Bitterness and in Tears*, 192–96.

70. Mahon, *History of the Second Seminole War*, 24–28, with Creek participation particularly on p. 25; Covington, *The Seminoles of Florida*, 28–49; Griffith, *McIntosh and Weatherford*, 178–94; O'Brien, *In Bitterness and in Tears*, 196–220.

71. Wright, *Creeks & Seminoles*, 204–8. For one account of an attack McIntosh led in Florida, along with Hitchitis under Kinnard and Yuchis under Barnard, see Woodward, *Reminiscences*, 50–51, 54–55.

72. Wright, *Creeks & Seminoles*, 210–11.

73. Green, *Politics of Indian Removal*, 70–71.

74. Green, *Politics of Indian Removal*, 69–71.

75. Green, *Politics of Indian Removal*, 73–74.

76. Frank, *Creeks and Southerners*, 107–13.

77. The many events surrounding the 1825 Treaty of Indian Springs can be seen in Green, *Politics of Indian Removal*, 69–97; and Frank, *Creeks and Southerners*, 97–98.

78. Green, *Politics of Indian Removal*, 97, 98–125. See also Cotterill, *The Southern Indians*, 211–22.

79. Green, *Politics of Indian Removal*, chs. 6–8.

80. McLoughlin, *Cherokee Renascence*, 209. See also Sadosky, *Revolutionary Negotiations*, 189–205.

81. Jackson to Monroe, March 4, 1817, quoted in Green, *Politics of Indian Removal*, 48; Calhoun to the House of Representatives, December 5, 1818, *ASPIA*, 2:181–83. For a general outline of the transition to the Removal era, particularly in Creek Country, see Sadosky, *Revolutionary Negotiations*, 189–205; Green, *Politics of Indian Removal*, chs. 6–8; O'Brien, *In Bitterness and in Tears*; Hurt, *Indian Frontier*, especially ch. 6; Foreman, *Indian Removal*, 107–77; Remini, *Andrew Jackson and His Indian Wars*; Wallace, *Jefferson and the Indians*; Wallace, *The Long, Bitter Trail*; and Debo, *The Road to Disappearance*.

Bibliography

Archival/Manuscript Sources

Alabama Department of Archives and History, Montgomery, Alabama

James Caller Papers, SPR554
Joseph Carson letter, SPR42
Henry Knox Papers, SPR716
Sam Manac [Moniac] deposition, SPR26
Alexander McGillivray Letters, SPR248
Daniel McGillivray Papers, SPR745
Harry Toulmin Papers, SPR234

Georgia Department of Archives and History, Morrow

Creek Indian Letters: Letters Talks and Treaties, 1705–1839, in Four Parts. 4 vols. Unpublished typescript, edited by Louise F. Hayes, 1939.
Executive Department Minutes, January 7, 1788–January 7, 1789. Unpublished typescript, edited by Louise F. Hayes, 1939.
Executive Department Minutes, May 15, 1792–August 4, 1793. Unpublished typescript, edited by Louise F. Hayes, 1939.
Force Transcripts: Georgia Records Council Correspondence, 1782–1789. Unpublished typescript, edited by Louise F. Hayes, 1938.
Governor's Letter Book, October 20, 1786–May 31, 1789. Unpublished typescript, edited by Louise F. Hayes, 1940.
Indian Depredations, 1787–1825. 4 vols. Unpublished typescript, edited by Louise F. Hayes, 1938–39.
Indian Letters, 1782–1839. Unpublished typescript, edited by Louise F. Hayes, 1940.

Indian Treaties Cessions of Land in Georgia, 1705–1837. Unpublished typescript, edited by Louise F. Hayes, 1941.

Letters of Benjamin Hawkins, 1797–1815. Unpublished typescript, edited by Louise F. Hayes, 1939.

Letters of Timothy Barnard. Unpublished typescript, edited by Louise F. Hayes, 1939.

Georgia Historical Society, Savannah

Joseph Valence Bevan Papers, MS 71

Hargrett Rare Book & Manuscript Library, University of Georgia, Athens

Telamon Cuyler Collection, MS 1170
Felix Hargrett Papers, MS 2311
Benjamin Hawkins Collection, MS 943
Keith Read Collection, MS 921
C. Mildred Thompson Collection, MS 606

Library of Congress

James McHenry Papers, 1775–1862, MSS 32177

National Archives, Washington, DC

Confidential Reports and Other Communications from the Secretary of War. 3rd Congress, 1st Session, 1793. Vol. IIA. Reel 14, in Transcribed Reports and Communications Transmitted by the Executive Branch to the House of Representatives, 1789–1819. Record Group 233, Microcopy M-1268.

Letters Received by the Office of the Secretary of War Relating to Indian Affairs, 1800–1823. Record Group 75, Microcopy M271.

Letters Sent by the Secretary of War Relating to Indian Affairs, 1800–1824. Record Group 75, Microcopy M15.

Papers of the Continental Congress, 1774–1789. General Services Administration, 1971. Microcopy M247.

Records of the Bureau of Indian Affairs, Office of Indian Trade. Creek Factory Records, 1795–1821. Microcopy M1334.

P. K. Yonge Library of Florida History, University of Florida, Gainesville

East Florida Papers, Film 55-A. Originals located in Archivo General de Indias, Seville, Spain.

Elizabeth Howard West Papers, MS 111

Joseph Byrne Lockey Documents Related to the History of Florida, MS 174

Papeles Procendentes de Cuba, microfilm copies in Film 12–24. Originals located in Archivo General de Indias, Seville, Spain.

Tennessee State Library and Archives, Nashville

Gideon Morgan Papers
Governor Sevier Collection

University Archives and West Florida History Center, John C. Pace Library, University of West Florida, Pensacola.

William Augustus Bowles Collection, Accession M1968–11/24
Panton and Leslie Collection, M1986–10
Papeles de Estado, microfilm copies in the Panton and Leslie Collection. Originals in the Archivo Historical Nacional, Madrid, Spain.
Public Record Office, Colonial Office Records, Class 5, Vols. 555–58, 560, 568. Microfilm copies in the Panton and Leslie Collection. Originals in the Public Records Office, Kew, United Kingdom.

William L. Clements Library, University of Michigan, Ann Arbor.

Henry Clinton Papers, 1736–1850, M-42
Thomas Gage Papers, 1754–1807, M-341
James McHenry Papers, 1777–1832, M-844
Anthony Wayne Family Papers, 1681–1913, M-398

Published Sources

Adair, James, and Samuel Cole, eds. *Adair's History of the American Indians.* Johnson City TN: Watauga Press, 1930.
Adelman, Jeremy, and Stephen Aron. "From Borderlands to Borders: Empires, Nation-States, and the Peoples in Between in North American History." *American Historical Review* 104, no. 3 (June 1999): 814–41.
Alden, John Richard. *John Stuart and the Southern Colonial Frontier: A Study of Indian Relations, War, Trade, and Land Problems in the Southern Wilderness.* Ann Arbor: University of Michigan Press, 1944.
American State Papers: Foreign Relations. 6 vols. Washington DC: Gales and Seaton, 1832–61.
American State Papers: Indian Affairs. 2 vols. Washington DC: Gales and Seaton, 1832–61.
Anderson, Benedict. *Imagined Communities: Reflections on the Origin and Spread of Nationalism.* New York: Verso, 2006.
Anderson, Fred. *The Crucible of War: The Seven Years' War and the Fate of Empire in British North America, 1754–1766.* New York: A. A. Knopf, 2000.
Axtell, James. "Ethnohistory: An Historian's Viewpoint." *Ethnohistory* 26, no. 1 (Winter 1979): 1–13.
———. *The European and the Indian: Essays in the Ethnohistory of Colonial North America.* New York: Oxford University Press, 1981.

Barksdale, Kevin D. *The Lost State of Franklin: America's First Secession.* Lexington: University of Kentucky Press, 2009.

Bartram, William, and Francis Harper. "Travels in Georgia, and Florida, 1773–1774: A Report to Dr. John Fothergill." *Transactions of the American Philosophical Society* 33, no. 2 (November 1943): 121–242.

Bast, Homer. "Creek Indian Affairs, 1775–1778." *Georgia Historical Quarterly* 33, no. 1 (March 1949): 1–25.

Bemis, Samuel Flagg. *Pinckney's Treaty: America's Advantage from Europe's Distress, 1783–1800.* New Haven CT: Yale University Press, 1960.

Bendix, Reinhard. *Nation-Building and Citizenship: Studies of Our Changing Social Order.* Berkeley: University of California Press, 1977

Berry, Jane M. "The Indian Policy of Spain in the Southwest, 1783–1795." *Mississippi Valley Historical Review* 3, no. 4 (March 1917): 462–77.

Blackhawk, Ned. *Violence over the Land: Indians and Empires in the Early American West.* Cambridge MA: Harvard University Press, 2006.

Blanton, Richard, and Lane Fargher. *Collective Action in the Formation of Pre-Modern States.* New York: Springer, 2008.

Bossu, M. *Travels through That Part of North America Formerly Called Louisiana . . .* 2 vols. London: Printed for T. Davies, 1771.

Boulware, Tyler. *Deconstructing the Cherokee Nation: Town, Region, and Nation among Eighteenth-Century Cherokees.* Gainesville: University Press of Florida, 2011.

Bouton, Terry. *Taming Democracy: "The People," the Founders, and the Troubled Ending of the American Revolution.* New York: Oxford University Press, 2007.

Boyd, Mark F., and José Navarro Latorre. "Spanish Interest in British Florida, and in the Progress of the American Revolution: (I) Relations with the Spanish Faction of the Creek Indians." *Florida Historical Quarterly* 32, no. 2 (October 1953): 92–130.

Bradburn, Douglas. *The Citizenship Revolution: Politics and the Creation of the American Union, 1774–1804.* Charlottesville: University of Virginia Press, 2009.

Brannon, Peter A. "The Pensacola Indian Trade." *Florida Historical Quarterly* 31, no. 1 (July 1952): 1–15.

Braund, Katherine E. Holland. *Deerskins & Duffels: The Creek Indian Trade with Anglo-America, 1685–1815.* Lincoln: University of Nebraska Press, 1993.

———. "'Like a Stone Wall Never to Be Broke': The British-Indian Boundary Line with the Creek Indians, 1763." In *Britain and the American South: From Colonialism to Rock and Roll,* edited by Joseph P. Ward, 53–80. Jackson: University Press of Mississippi, 2003.

Breuilly, John. *Nationalism and the State.* Chicago: University of Chicago Press, 1994.

Bulloch, Joseph Gaston Baillie. *A History and Genealogy of the Habersham Family*. Columbia SC: R. L. Bryan Company, 1901.

Bunn, Mike, and Clay Williams. *Battle for the Southern Frontier: The Creek War and the War of 1812*. Charleston SC: The History Press, 2008.

Calloway, Colin G. *The American Revolution in Indian Country: Crisis and Diversity in Native American Communities*. New York: Cambridge University Press, 1995.

———. *A Victory with No Name: The Native American Defeat of the First American Army*. Oxford: Oxford University Press, 2014.

Calloway, Patricia. *Choctaw Genesis, 1500–1700*. Lincoln: University of Nebraska Press, 1995.

Candler, A. D., et al., eds. *The Colonial Records of the State of Georgia*. 32 vols. Athens: University Press of Georgia, 1904–.

Carson, James Taylor. *Searching for the Bright Path: The Mississippi Choctaws from Prehistory to Removal*. Lincoln: University of Nebraska Press, 1999.

Carter, Clarence, and John Porter Bloom, comps. *Territorial Papers of the United States*. 28 vols. Washington DC: U.S. GPO, 1934–.

Cashin, Edward J. "'But Brothers, It Is Our Land We Are Talking About': Winners and Losers in the Georgia Backcountry." In *An Uncivil War: The Southern Backcountry during the Revolution*, edited by Ronald Hoffman, Thad W. Tate, and Peter J. Albert, 240–75. Charlottesville: Published for the U.S. Capital Historical Society by the University Press of Virginia, 1985.

———. *The King's Ranger: Thomas Brown and the American Revolution on the Southern Frontier*. Athens: University of Georgia Press, 1989.

———. *William Bartram and the American Revolution on the Southern Frontier*. Columbia: University of South Carolina Press, 2000.

Caughey, John Walton. *McGillivray of the Creeks*. Norman: University of Oklahoma Press, 1938.

Champagne, Duane. *Social Order and Political Change: Constitutional Governments among the Cherokee, the Choctaw, the Chickasaw, and the Creek*. Stanford CA: Stanford University Press, 1992.

Chase, Philander D., ed. *The Papers of George Washington*. Revolutionary War Series. 14 vols. Charlottesville: University Press of Virginia, 1985–91.

Coker, William S., and Thomas D. Watson. *Indian Traders of the Southeastern Spanish Borderlands: Panton, Leslie & Company and John Forbes & Company, 1783–1847*. Gainesville: University Press of Florida, 1986.

Coleman, Kenneth. *The American Revolution in Georgia, 1763–1789*. Athens: University of Georgia Press, 1958.

———. "Restored Colonial Georgia, 1779–1782." *Georgia Historical Quarterly* 40, no. 1 (March 1956): 1–20.*Collections of the Georgia Historical Society, Volume III, Part 1*. Savannah GA: Printed for the Society, 1848.

Collections of the Georgia Historical Society, Volume V, Part 1. Savannah GA: Braid & Hutton, Printers and Binders, 1901.

Collections of the Georgia Historical Society, Volume V, Part 2. Savannah GA: Morning News Print, 1902.

Collections of the Georgia Historical Society, Volume VIII. Savannah GA: Morning News Printers and Binders, 1913.

Collections of the Georgia Historical Society, Volume IX. Savannah GA: Morning News, 1916.

Collections of the Massachusetts Historical Society. 71 vols. Boston: The Society, 1792–.

Condon, Sean. *Shay's Rebellion: Authority and Distress in Post-Revolutionary America.* Baltimore: Johns Hopkins University Press, 2015.

Corbitt, D. C. "Papers Relating to the Georgia-Florida Frontier, 1784–1800. IV." *Georgia Historical Quarterly* 21, no. 3 (September 1937): 274–93.

———. "Papers Relating to the Georgia-Florida Frontier, 1784–1800. V." *Georgia Historical Quarterly* 21, no. 4 (December 1937): 373–81.

———. "Papers Relating to the Georgia-Florida Frontier, 1784–1800. VI." *Georgia Historical Quarterly* 22, no. 1 (March 1938): 72–76.

———. "Papers Relating to the Georgia-Florida Frontier, 1784–1800. VII." *Georgia Historical Quarterly* 22, no. 2 (June 1938): 184–91.

———. "Papers Relating to the Georgia-Florida Frontier, 1784–1800. VIII." *Georgia Historical Quarterly* 22, no. 3 (September 1938): 286–91.

———. "Papers Relating to the Georgia-Florida Frontier, 1784–1800. IX." *Georgia Historical Quarterly* 22, no. 4 (December 1938): 391–94.

———. "Papers Relating to the Georgia-Florida Frontier, 1784–1800. XI." *Georgia Historical Quarterly* 23, no. 2 (June 1939): 189–202.

———. "Papers Relating to the Georgia-Florida Frontier, 1784–1800. XII." *Georgia Historical Quarterly* 23, no. 3 (September 1939): 300–303.

———. "Papers Relating to the Georgia-Florida Frontier, 1784–1800. XIV." *Georgia Historical Quarterly* 24, no. 1 (March 1940): 77–83.

———. "Papers Relating to the Georgia-Florida Frontier, 1784–1800. XV." *Georgia Historical Quarterly* 24, no. 2 (June 1940): 150–57.

———. "Papers Relating to the Georgia-Florida Frontier, 1784–1800. XVI." *Georgia Historical Quarterly* 24, no. 3 (September 1940): 257–71.

———. "Papers Relating to the Georgia-Florida Frontier, 1784–1800. XIX." *Georgia Historical Quarterly* 25, no. 2 (June 1941): 159–71.

Corkran, David H. *The Creek Frontier, 1540–1783.* Norman: University of Oklahoma Press, 1967.

Cotterill, R. S. *The Southern Indians: The Story of the Civilized Tribes before Removal.* Norman: University of Oklahoma Press, 1954

Coulter, E. Merton. *Georgia: A Short History.* Chapel Hill: University of North Carolina Press, 1960.

Covington, James W. *The Seminoles of Florida.* Gainesville: University Press of Florida, 1993.

Crane, Verner. *The Southern Frontier, 1670–1732*. Tuscaloosa: University of Alabama Press, 2004.

Dabney, William M., and Marion Dargan. *William Henry Drayton & the American Revolution*. Albuquerque: University of New Mexico Press, 1962.

Davies, K. G., ed. *Documents of the American Revolution, 1770–1783*. 21 vols. Shannon: Irish University Press, 1972–81.

Debo, Angie. *The Road to Disappearance: A History of the Creek Indians*. Norman: University of Oklahoma Press, 1941.

Din, Gilbert C. *War on the Gulf Coast: The Spanish Fight against William Augustus Bowles*. Gainesville: University Press of Florida, 2012.

Dowd, Gregory Evans. *A Spirited Resistance: The North American Indian Struggle for Unity, 1745–1815*. Baltimore: Johns Hopkins University Press, 1992.

———. "'Thinking outside the Circle': A Tecumseh's 1811 Mission." In *Tohopeka: Rethinking the Creek War and the War of 1812*, edited by Kathryn E. Holland Braund, 30–52. Tuscaloosa: University of Alabama Press, 2015.

———. *War under Heaven: Pontiac, the Indian Nations, & the British Empire*. Baltimore: Johns Hopkins University Press, 2002.

Downes, Randolph C. "Creek-American Relations, 1782–1790." *Georgia Historical Quarterly* 21, no. 2 (June 1937): 142–84.

Draper, Lyman Copeland, Josephine L. Harper, and the State History Society of Wisconsin, eds. *The Draper Manuscript Collection*. 491 vols. Chicago: University of Chicago Press, 1980.

Edmunds, R. David, ed. *American Indian Leaders: Studies in Diversity*. Lincoln: University of Nebraska Press, 1980.

Elding, Max M. *A Revolution in Favor of Government: Origins of the U.S. Constitution and the Making of the American State*. New York: Oxford University Press, 2003.

Elkins, Stanley, and Eric McKitrick. *The Age of Federalism: The Early American Republic, 1788–1800*. New York: Oxford University Press, 1993.

Ellisor, John T. *The Second Creek War: Interethnic Conflict and Collusion on a Collapsing Frontier*. Lincoln: University of Nebraska Press, 2010.

Ethridge, Robbie. "A Brief Sketch of Creek Country in the Early Nineteenth Century." In *Red Eagle's Children: Weatherford vs. Weatherford et al.*, edited by J. Anthony Paredes and Judith Knight, 19–35. Tuscaloosa: University of Alabama Press, 2012.

———. *Creek Country: The Creek Indians and Their World*. Chapel Hill: University of North Carolina Press, 2003.

———. *From Chicaza to Chickasaw: The European Invasion and the Transformation of the Mississippian World, 1540–1715*. Chapel Hill: University of North Carolina Press, 2010.

Ethridge, Robbie, and Sheri M. Shuck-Hall, eds. *Mapping the Mississippian*

Shatter Zone: The Colonial Slave Trade and Regional Instability in the American South. Lincoln: University of Nebraska Press, 2009.

Evans, Peter B., Dietrich Rueschemeyer, and Theda Skocpol, eds. *Bringing the State Back In.* New York: Cambridge University Press, 1985.

Fabel, Robin F. A. "West Florida and British Strategy in the American Revolution." In *Eighteenth-Century Florida and the Revolutionary South*, edited by Samuel Proctor, 49–67. Gainesville: University Press of Florida, 1978.

Ferling, John E. *A Leap in the Dark: The Struggle to Create the American Republic.* New York: Oxford University Press, 2003.

Force, Peter, ed. *American Archives.* 9 vols. Washington DC, 1837–53.

Ford, Lisa. *Settler Sovereignty: Jurisdiction and Indigenous People in America and Australia, 1788–1836.* Cambridge MA: Harvard University Press, 2010.

Ford, Worthington C., et al., eds. *Journals of the Continental Congress, 1774–1789.* 34 vols. Washington DC, 1904–37.

Foreman, Carolyn Thomas. "Alexander McGillivray, Emperor of the Creeks." *Chronicles of Oklahoma* 7, no. 1 (March 1929): 106–20.

Foreman, Grant. *Indian Removal: The Emigration of the Five Civilized Tribes of Indians.* Norman: University of Oklahoma Press, 1953.

Foster, Thomas H., II. *Archaeology of the Lower Muskogee Creek Indians, 1715–1836.* Tuscaloosa: University of Alabama Press, 2007.

———, ed. *The Collected Works of Benjamin Hawkins, 1796–1810.* Tuscaloosa: University of Alabama Press, 2003.

Frank, Andrew K. *Creeks and Southerners: Biculturalism on the Early American Frontier.* Lincoln: University of Nebraska Press, 2005.

Gallay, Alan. *The Formation of a Planter Elite: Jonathan Bryan and the Southern Colonial Frontier.* Athens: University of Georgia Press, 1989.

———. *The Indian Slave Trade: The Rise of the English Empire in the American South.* New Haven: Yale University Press, 2002.

Garden, Alexander. *Anecdotes of the Revolutionary War in America.* Charleston: Printed for the Author, by A. E. Miller, 1822.

Gatschet, Albert S. *A Migration Legend of the Creek Indians.* New York: AMS Press, 1969.

Gellner, Ernest. *Nations and Nationalism.* Oxford: Blackwell, 2006.

Gibbes, R. W., ed. *Documentary History of the American Revolution, Consisting of Letters and Papers . . .* 3 vols. New York: D. Appleton & Co., 1855–57.

Giddens, Anthony. *The Nation-State and Violence.* Berkeley: University of California Press, 1985.

Gould, Eliga H. *Among the Powers of the Earth: The American Revolution and the Making of a New World Empire.* Cambridge MA: Harvard University Press, 2012.

Gould, Eliga H., and Peter S. Onuf, eds. *Empire and Nation: The American Revolution in the Atlantic World.* Baltimore: Johns Hopkins University Press, 2005.

Grant, C. L., ed. *Letters, Journals, and Writings of Benjamin Hawkins.* 2 vols. Savannah GA: Beehive Press, 1980.

Grantham, Bill. *Creation Myths and Legends of the Creek Indians.* Gainesville: University Press of Florida, 2002.

Green, Michael D. "Alexander McGillivray." In *American Indian Leaders: Studies in Diversity,* edited by R. David Edmunds, 41–63. Lincoln: University of Nebraska Press, 1980.

———. *The Politics of Indian Removal: Creek Government and Society in Crisis.* Lincoln: University of Nebraska Press, 1982.

Greenfeld, Liah. "Is Modernity Possible without Nationalism?" In *The Fate of the Nation State,* edited by Michel Seymour, 38–50. Montreal: McGill-Queen's University Press, 2004.

———. *Nationalism: Five Roads to Modernity.* Cambridge MA: Harvard University Press, 1992.

Grenier, John. *The First Way of War: American War Making on the Frontier, 1607–1814.* New York: Cambridge University Press, 2005.

Griffin, Patrick. *American Leviathan: Empire, Nation, and Revolutionary Frontier.* New York: Hill and Wang, 2007.

Griffith, Benjamin W., Jr. *McIntosh and Weatherford, Creek Indian Leaders.* Tuscaloosa: University of Alabama Press, 1988.

Grimke, John Fauchereau. "Journal of the Campaign to the Southward: May 9th to July 14th, 1778." *South Carolina Historical and Genealogical Magazine* 12, no. 2 (April 1911): 118–34.

Hahn, Steven C. *The Invention of the Creek Nation, 1670–1763.* Lincoln: University of Nebraska Press, 2004.

Halbert, H. S., and T. H. Ball. *The Creek War of 1813 and 1814.* Tuscaloosa: University of Alabama Press, 1995.

Hall, Leslie. *Land and Allegiance in Revolutionary Georgia.* Athens: University of Georgia Press, 2001.

Hamalainen, Pekka. *The Comanche Empire.* New Haven: Yale University Press, 2008.

Harmer, Philip M., ed. *The Papers of Henry Laurens.* 16 vols. Columbia: Published for the South Carolina Historical Society by the University of South Carolina Press, 1968–.

Harper, Francis, ed. "Travels in Georgia and Florida, 1773–74: A Report to Dr. John Fothergill." *Transactions of the American Philosophical Society* 33, no. 2 (November 1943): 121–242.

———. *Travels of William Bartram, Naturalist Edition.* Athens: University of Georgia Press, 1998.

Hatley, Tom. *The Dividing Paths: Cherokees and South Carolinians through the Era of Revolution.* New York: Oxford University Press, 1993.

Hawes, Lilla M., ed. *Collections of the Georgia Historical Society, Volume X.* Savannah GA: Georgia Historical Society, 1952.

———. *Collections of the Georgia Historical Society, Volume XI.* Savannah GA: Georgia Historical Society, 1955.

———. *Collections of the Georgia Historical Society, Volume XII.* Savannah GA: Georgia Historical Society, 1957.

———. "Letter Book of Lachlan McIntosh, 1776–1777, Part I." *Georgia Historical Quarterly* 38, no. 2 (June 1954): 148–69.

———. "The Papers of Lachlan McIntosh, 1774–1799, Part II." *Georgia Historical Quarterly* 38, no. 3 (September 1954): 253–67.

———. "The Papers of Lachlan McIntosh, 1774–1799, Part III: The Letter Book of Lachlan McIntosh, 1776–1777." *Georgia Historical Quarterly* 38, no. 4 (December 1954): 356–68.

———. "The Papers of Lachlan McIntosh, 1774–1799, Part IV." *Georgia Historical Quarterly* 39, no. 1 (March 1955): 52–68.

Hawes, Lilla Mills, and Karen Elizabeth Osvald, eds. *Collections of the Georgia Historical Society, Volume XIX.* Savannah GA: The Society, 1976.

Hendrickson, David C. *Peace Pact: The Lost World of the American Founding.* Lawrence: University Press of Kansas, 2003.

Henri, Florette. *The Southern Indians and Benjamin Hawkins, 1796–1816.* Norman: University of Nebraska Press, 1986.

Higginbotham, Don. "War and State Formation in Revolutionary America." In *Empire and Nation: The American Revolution in the Atlantic World*, edited by Eliga H. Gould and Peter S. Onuf, 54–71. Baltimore: Johns Hopkins University Press, 2005.

Hinderaker, Eric. *Elusive Empires: Constructing Colonialism in the Ohio Valley, 1673–1800.* New York: Cambridge University Press, 1997.

Hobsbawm, E. J. *Nations and Nationalism since 1780: Programme, Myth, Reality.* New York: Cambridge University Press, 2012.

Hoffman, Paul E. *Florida's Frontiers.* Bloomington: Indiana University Press, 2001.

Hoffman, Ronald, Thad W. Tate, and Peter J. Albert, eds. *An Uncivil War: The Southern Backcountry during the American Revolution.* Charlottesville: Published for the U.S. Capitol Historical Society by the University Press of Virginia, 1985.

Holmes, Jack D. L. "Juan de la Villebeuvre and Spanish Indian Policy in West Florida, 1784–1797." *Florida Historical Quarterly* 58, no. 4 (April 1980): 387–99.

———. "Spanish Treaties with West Florida Indians, 1784–1802." *Florida Historical Quarterly* 48, no. 2 (October 1969): 140–54.

———. "La Ultima Barrera: La Luisiana y la Nueva Espana." *Historia Mexicana* 10, no. 4 (April–June 1961): 637–49.

Holton, Woody. *Unruly Americans and the Origins of the Constitution.* New York: Hill and Wang, 2007.

Horsman, Reginald. *Expansion and American Indian Policy, 1783–1812.* Norman: University of Oklahoma Press, 1967.

———. *The Frontier in the Formative Years, 1783–1815.* New York: Holt, Rinehart and Winston, 1970.

———. *The New Republic: The United States of America, 1789–1815.* New York: Longman, 2000.

———. *Race and Manifest Destiny: The Origins of American Racial Anglo-Saxonism.* Cambridge MA: Harvard University Press, 1981.

Howard, Clinton L. "Colonial Pensacola: The British Period Part III: The Administration of Governor Chester, 1770–1781." *Florida Historical Quarterly* 19, no. 4 (April 1941): 368–401.

Hoxie, Frederick E., Ronald Hoffman, and Peter J. Albert, eds. *Native Americans and the Early Republic.* Charlottesville: Published for the U.S. Capitol Historical Society by the University Press of Virginia, 1999.

Hudson, Angela Pulley. *Creek Paths and Federal Roads: Indians, Settlers, and Slaves and the Making of the American South.* Chapel Hill: University of North Carolina Press, 2010.

Hudson, Charles. *The Southeastern Indians.* Knoxville: University of Tennessee Press, 1976.

Humphreys, Frank Landon, ed. *The Life and Times of David Humphreys: Soldier—Statesman—Poet.* 2 vols. New York: G. P. Putnam's Sons, 1917.

Hurt, R. Douglas. *The Indian Frontier, 1763–1846.* Albuquerque: University of New Mexico Press, 2002.

James, Paul. *Nation Formation: Towards a Theory of Abstract Community.* London: Sage, 1996.

Jennings, Matthew. *New Worlds of Violence: Cultures and Conquests in the Early American Southeast.* Knoxville: University of Tennessee Press, 2011.

Jennison, Watson W. *Cultivating Race: The Expansion of Slavery in Georgia, 1750–1860.* Lexington: University of Kentucky Press, 2012.

Jensen, Merrill, ed. *The Documentary History of the Ratification of the Constitution.* 24 vols. Madison: State Historical Society of Wisconsin, 1976–.

Jones, Dorothy V. *License for Empire: Colonialism by Treaty in Early America.* Chicago: University of Chicago Press, 1982.

Juricek, John T. *Colonial Georgia and the Creeks: Anglo-Indian Diplomacy on the Southern Frontier, 1733–1763.* Gainesville: University Press of Florida, 2010.

Jusdanis, Gregory. *The Necessary Nation.* Princeton NJ: Princeton University Press, 2001.

Kamenka, Eugene. "Political Nationalism: The Evolution of an Idea." In *Nationalism: The Nature and Evolution of an Idea,* edited by Eugene Kamenka, 3–20. New York: St. Martin's Press, 1976.

Kanon, Tom. "Before Horseshoe: Andrew Jackson's Campaigns in the Creek War Prior to Horseshoe Bend." In *Tohopeka: Rethinking the Creek War and the War of 1812*, edited by Kathryn E. Holland Braund, 105–21. Tuscaloosa: University of Alabama Press, 2015

Kappler, Charles, comp. *Indian Affairs: Laws and Treaties.* 7 vols. Washington DC: GPO, 1904–79.

Kelton, Paul. *Epidemics and Enslavement: Biological Catastrophe in the Native Southeast, 1492–1715.* Lincoln: University of Nebraska Press, 2007.

Kinnaird, Lawrence. "International Rivalry in the Creek Country: Part I. The Ascendency of Alexander McGillivray, 1783–1789." *Florida Historical Society Quarterly* 10, no. 2 (October 1931): 59–85.

Kinnaird, Lawrence, Francisco Blache, and Navarro Blache. "Spanish Treaties with Indian Tribes." *Western Historical Quarterly* 10, no. 1 (January 1979): 39–48.

Knouff, Gregory T. *The Soldier's Revolution: Pennsylvanians in Arms and the Forging of Early American Identity.* University Park: Pennsylvania State University Press, 2004.

Knox, Henry. *Microfilms of the Henry Knox Papers Owned by the New England Historic Genealogical Society and Deposited in the Massachusetts Historical Society.* Boston: Massachusetts Historical Society, 1960.

Kohn, Hans. *The Idea of Nationalism: A Study in Its Origins and Background.* New York: Macmillan, 1944.

Kowalewski, Stephen A. "Coalescent Societies." In *Light on the Path: The Anthropology and History of the Southeastern Indians,* edited by Thomas J. Pluckhahn and Robbie Ethridge, 94–122. Tuscaloosa: University of Alabama Press, 2006.

Lachman, Richard. *States and Power.* Cambridge: Polity Press, 2010.

LaCroix, Alison. *The Ideological Origins of American Federalism.* Cambridge MA: Harvard University Press, 2010.

Lakomäki, Sami. *Gathering Together: The Shawnee People through Diaspora and Nationhood, 1600–1870.* New Haven: Yale University Press, 2014.

Lamplugh, George R. *Politics on the Periphery: Factions and Parties in Georgia, 1783–1806.* Newark: University of Delaware Press, 1986.

Langley, Linda. "The Tribal Identity of Alexander McGillivray: A Review of the Historical and Ethnographic Data." *Louisiana History: The Journal of the Louisiana Historical Association* 46, no. 2 (Spring 2005): 231–39.

Lankford, George E., ed. *Native American Legends: Southeastern Legends— Tales from the Natchez, Caddo, Biloxi, Chickasaw, and Other Nations.* Little Rock AR: August House, 1987.

Lee, Henry. *Memoirs of the War in the Southern Department of the United States.* 2 vols. Philadelphia: Bradford and Inskeep, 1812.

Littlefield, Daniel F., Jr. *Africans and Creeks: From the Colonial Period to the Civil War.* Westport CT: Greenwood Press, 1979.

———. *Africans and Seminoles: From Removal to Emancipation.* Westport CT: Greenwood Press, 1977.

Lockey, Joseph Byrne, ed. *East Florida, 1783–1785; A File of Documents Assembled and Many of Them Translated by Joseph Byrne Lockey.* Berkeley: University of California Press, 1949.

Mahon, John K. *History of the Second Seminole War, 1835–1842.* Gainesville: University Press of Florida, 1991.

Martin, Joel. "The Creek Prophetic Movement." *Alabama Heritage* 23 (Winter 1992): 4–13.

———. *Sacred Revolt: The Muskogees' Struggle for a New World.* Boston: Beacon Press, 1991.

Martin, John. "Official Letters of Governor John Martin, 1782–1783." *Georgia Historical Quarterly* 1, no. 4 (December 1917): 281–335.

Mattern, David B. *Benjamin Lincoln and the American Revolution.* Columbia: University of South Carolina Press, 1995.

McLoughlin, William. *Cherokee Renascence in the New Republic.* Princeton NJ: Princeton University Press, 1986.

Meek, Alexander B. *Romantic Passages in Southwestern History.* New York: S. H. Goetzel & Co., 1857.

Mereness, Newton, ed. "Journal of David Taitt's Travels from Pensacola, West Florida, to and through the Country of the Upper and the Lower Creeks, 1772." In *Travels in the American Colonies*, edited by Newton Mereness, 493–568. New York: Macmillan, 1916.

Merritt, Jane T. *At the Crossroads: Indians and Empires on a Mid-Atlantic Frontier, 1700–1763.* Chapel Hill: University of North Carolina Press, 2003.

Midlarsky, Manus I. *The Evolution of Inequality: War, State Survival, and Democracy in Comparative Perspective.* Stanford CA: Stanford University Press, 1999.

Miles, Tiya. *Ties That Bind: The Story of an Afro-Cherokee Family in Slavery and Freedom.* Oakland: University of California Press, 2018

Milfort, Louis LeClerc de, and John Francis McDermott. *Memoir, or, A Cursory Glance at My Different Travels & My Sojourn in the Creek Nation.* Chicago: R. R. Donnelley & Sons Company, 1956.

Millett, Nathaniel. *The Maroons of Prospect Bluff and Their Quest for Freedom in the Atlantic World.* Gainesville: University Press of Florida, 2003.

"Minutes of the Executive Council, May 7 through October 14, 1777: Part III." *Georgia Historical Quarterly* 34, no. 2 (June 1950): 106–25.

Mississippi Department of Archives and History. *Mississippi Provincial Archives, Spanish Dominion, 1759–1804.* 9 vols. Cleveland: Bell & Howell, 1969.

Mohr, Walter Harrison. *Federal Indian Relations, 1774–1788.* Philadelphia: University of Pennsylvania Press, 1933.

Mulroy, Kevin. *Freedom on the Border: The Seminole Maroons in Florida, the Indian Territory, Coahuila, and Texas.* Lubbock: Texas Tech University Press, 1993.

Narrett, David. *Adventurism and Empire: The Struggle for Mastery in the Louisiana-Florida Borderlands, 1762–1803*. Chapel Hill: University of North Carolina Press, 2014.

Nichols, David Andrew. *Red Gentlemen & White Savages: Indians, Federalists, and the Search for Order on the American Frontier*. Charlottesville: University of Virginia Press, 2008.

Nunez, Jr., Theron A. "Creek Nativism and the Creek War of 1813–1814." *Ethnohistory* 5, no. 1 (Winter 1958): 1–47.

Oatis, Steven J. *A Colonial Complex: South Carolina's Frontiers in the Era of the Yemasee War, 1680–1730*. Lincoln: University of Nebraska Press, 2004.

O'Brien, Greg. *Choctaws in a Revolutionary Age, 1750–1830*. Lincoln: University of Nebraska Press, 2005.

O'Brien, Sean Michael. *In Bitterness and in Tears: Andrew Jackson's Destruction of the Creeks and Seminoles*. Westport CT: Praeger, 2003.

O'Donnell, James III. "Alexander McGillivray: Training for Leadership, 1777–1783." *Georgia Historical Quarterly* 49, no. 2 (June 1965): 172–86.

———. "The South on the Eve of the Revolution: Native Americans." In *The Revolutionary War in the South: Power, Conflict, and Leadership: Essays in Honor of John Richard Allen*, edited by Robert W. Higgins, 64–78. Durham: Duke University Press, 1979.

———. *Southern Indians in the American Revolution*. Knoxville: University of Tennessee Press, 1973.

Onuf, Peter S. *Jefferson's Empire: The Language of American Nationhood*. Charlottesville: University Press of Virginia, 2000.

Owsley, Frank Lawrence Jr. *Struggle for the Gulf Borderlands: The Creek War and the Battle of New Orleans, 1812–1815*. Gainesville: University Press of Florida, 1981.

Panton, Leslie & Company. *The Papers of Panton, Leslie & Co.* Woodbridge CT: Research Publications, 1986.

Peake, Ora Brooks. *A History of the United States Indian Factory System, 1795–1822*. Denver: Sage Books, 1954.

Pencak, William, and Daniel Richter, eds. *Friends and Enemies in Penn's Woods: Indians, Colonists, and the Racial Construction of Pennsylvania*. University Park: Pennsylvania State University Press, 2004.

Perdue, Theda. "'A Sprightly Lover Is the Most Prevailing Missionary': Intermarriage between Europeans and Indians in the Eighteenth-Century South." In *Light on the Path: The Anthropology and History of the Southeastern Indians*, edited by Thomas J. Pluckhahn and Robbie Ethridge, 165–78. Tuscaloosa: University of Alabama Press, 2006.

Peters, Richard, ed. *Public Statutes at Large of the United States of America . . .* 18 vols. Boston: Charles C. Little and James Brown, 1845–.

Phillips, Ulrich Bonnell. *Georgia and State Rights*. Macon GA: Mercer University Press, 1984.

Piecuch, Jim. *Three Peoples, One King: Loyalists, Indians, and Slaves in the Revolutionary South, 1775–1782.* Columbia: University of South Carolina Press, 2008.

Piker, Joshua. *Okfuskee: A Creek Indian Town in Colonial America.* Cambridge MA: Harvard University Press, 2004.

Plamenatz, John. "Two Types of Nationalism." In *Nationalism: The Nature and Evolution of an Idea,* edited by Eugene Kamenka, 22–36. New York: St. Martin's Press, 1976.

Poggi, Gianfranco. *The Development of the Modern State: A Sociological Introduction.* Stanford CA: Stanford University Press, 1978.

———. *The State: Its Nature, Development and Prospects.* Stanford CA: Stanford University Press, 1990.

Pope, John A. *A Tour through the Southern and Western Territories of the United States of North America . . .* New York: Charles L. Woodward, 1888.

Pound, Merritt B. *Benjamin Hawkins, Indian Agent.* Athens: University of Georgia Press, 1951.

Proctor, Samuel, ed. *Eighteenth-Century Florida and Its Borderlands.* Gainesville: University Press of Florida, 1975.

———. *Eighteenth-Century Florida and the Revolutionary South.* Gainesville: University Press of Florida, 1978.

Prucha, Francis Paul. *American Indian Policy in the Formative Years: The Indian Trade and Intercourse Acts, 1780–1834.* Cambridge, MA: Harvard University Press, 1962.

———. *The Great Father: The United States Government and the American Indians.* 2 vols. Lincoln: University of Nebraska Press, 1984.

Ramsey, William L. *The Yamasee War: A Study of Culture, Economy, and Conflict in the Colonial South.* Lincoln: University of Nebraska Press, 2008.

Rea, Robert R. "British West Florida: Stepchild of Diplomacy." In *Eighteenth-Century Florida and Its Borderlands,* edited by Samuel Proctor, 61–77. Gainesville: University Press of Florida, 1975.

Remini, Robert. *Andrew Jackson.* Baltimore: Johns Hopkins University Press, 1998.

———. *Andrew Jackson and His Indian Wars.* New York: Viking, 2001.

Richards, Leonard. *Shay's Rebellion: The American Revolution's Final Battle.* Philadelphia: University of Pennsylvania Press, 2002.

Richter, Daniel K. *Facing East from Indian Country: A Native History of Early America.* Cambridge MA: Harvard University Press, 2003.

———. *Ordeal of the Longhouse.* Chapel Hill: Published for the Institute of Early American History and Culture, Williamsburg, Virginia, by the University of North Carolina Press, 1992.

Rowland, Dunbar, ed., and the Mississippi Department of Archives and History. *Mississippi Provincial Archives, English Dominion.* 9 vols. Nashville TN: Press of Brandon Printing Company, 1911.

Sadosky, Leonard J. *Revolutionary Negotiations: Indians, Empires, and Diplomats in the Founding of America*. Charlottesville: University of Virginia Press, 2009.

Salisbury, Neal. *Manitou and Providence: Indians, Europeans, and the Making of New England, 1500–1643*. New York: Oxford University Press, 1982.

Saunders, William, ed. *Colonial and State Records of North Carolina*. 28 vols. Wilmington NC: Broadfoot Publishing, 1993. Accessed in *Documenting the American South*, http://docsouth.unc.edu/csr/.

Saunt, Claudio. *A New Order of Things: Property, Power, and the Transformation of the Creek Indians, 1733–1816*. New York: Cambridge University Press, 1999.

———. "Taking Account of Property: Social Stratification among the Creek Indians in the Early Nineteenth Century." *William and Mary Quarterly* 57, no. 4 (October 2000): 733–60.

Searcy, Martha Condray. *The Georgia-Florida Contest in the American Revolution, 1776–1778*. University: University of Alabama Press, 1985.

Sheehan, Bernard W. *Seeds of Extinction: Jeffersonian Philanthropy and the American Indian*. Chapel Hill: Published for the Institute of Early American History and Culture at Williamsburg, Virginia, by the University of North Carolina Press, 1973.

Showman, Richard K., ed. *The Papers of Nathanael Greene*. 13 vols. Chapel Hill: Published for the Rhode Island Historical Society by the University of North Carolina Press, 1976–.

Sider, Gerald M. *Lumbee Indian Histories: Race, Ethnicity, and Indian Identity in the Southern United States*. New York: Cambridge University Press, 1993.

Silver, Peter. *Our Savage Neighbors: How Indian War Transformed Early America*. New York: W. W. Norton, 2008.

Simpson, John Eddins, ed. *Collections of the Georgia Historical Society, Volume xvii*. Savannah GA: The Society, 1976.

Skocpol, Theda. "Bringing the State Back In: Strategies of Analysis in Current Research." In *Bringing the State Back In*, edited by Peter B. Evans, Dietrich Rueschemeyer, and Theda Skocpol, 3–38. New York: Cambridge University Press, 1985.

Smith, Paul H., et al., eds. *Letters of Delegates to Congress, 1774–1789*. 25 vols. Washington DC: Library of Congress, 1976–2000.

Snapp, J. Russell. *John Stuart and the Struggle for Empire on the Southern Frontier*. Baton Rouge: Louisiana State University Press, 1996.

Snyder, Christina. *Slavery in Indian Country: The Changing Face of Captivity in Early America*. Cambridge MA: Harvard University Press, 2010.

"Some Official Letters of Governor Edward Telfair." *Georgia Historical Quarterly* 1, no. 2 (June 1917): 141–54.

Southerland, Henry deLeon Jr., and Jerry Elijah Brown. *The Federal Road through Georgia, the Creek Nation, and Alabama, 1806–1836*. Tuscaloosa: University of Alabama Press, 1989.

Speck, Frank. *The Creek Indians of Taskigi Town*. Millwood NY: Kraus Reprint, 1974.

Spero, Patrick. "Matters of Perspective: Interpreting the Revolutionary Frontier." *Pennsylvania Magazine and Biography* 132, no. 3 (July 2008): 261–70.

Stagg, J. C. A. *Borderlines in Borderlands: James Madison and the Spanish-American Frontier, 1776–1821*. New Haven CT: Yale University Press, 2009.

Stampp, Kenneth M., ed. *Records of Ante-bellum Southern Plantations: From the Revolution through the Civil War*. Frederick MD: University Publications of America, 1985–.

Starr, Joseph Barton. *Tories, Dons, and Rebels: The American Revolution in British West Florida*. Gainesville: University Press of Florida, 1976.

Stock, Melissa A. "Sovereign or Suzerain: Alexander McGillivray's Argument for Creek Independence after the Treaty of Paris of 1783." *Georgia Historical Quarterly* 92, no. 2 (Summer 2008): 149–76.

Swan, Caleb. "Position and State of Manners and Arts in the Creek or Muscogee Nation in 1791." In *Information Respecting . . . the Indian Tribes of the United States*, vol. 5, edited by Henry R. Schoolcraft, 251–83. Philadelphia: Lippincott, 1855.

Swanton, John R. *Early History of the Creek Indians and Their Neighbors*. Gainesville: University Press of Florida, 1998.

——. *The Indians of the Southeastern United States*. Washington DC: GPO, 1946.

——. *Social Organization and Social Usages of the Indians of the Creek Confederacy*. New York: Johnson Reprint Corp., 1970.

Sweet, Julie Anne. *Negotiating for Georgia: British-Creek Relations in the Trustee Era, 1733–1752*. Athens: University of Georgia Press, 2005.

Sword, Wiley. *President Washington's Indian War: The Struggle for the Old Northwest, 1790–1795*. Norman: University of Oklahoma Press, 1985.

Syrett, Harold C., ed. *The Papers of Alexander Hamilton*. 27 vols. New York: Columbia University Press, 1961–.

Thrower, Robert G. "Casualties and Consequences of the Creek War." In *Tohopeka: Rethinking the Creek War and the War of 1812*, edited by Katherine E. Holland Braund. Tuscaloosa: University of Alabama Press, 2012.

Tilly, Charles. *Coercion, Capital, and European States, AD 990–1990*. Cambridge MA: Blackwell, 1990.

——. "War Making and State Making as Organized Crime." In *Bringing the State Back In*, edited by Peter B. Evans, Dietrich Rueschemeyer, and Theda Skocpol, 169–91. New York: Cambridge University Press, 1985.

Twoig, Dorothy, ed. *The Papers of George Washington: Presidential Series*. 14 vols. Charlottesville: University of Virginia Press, 1987–2011.

Van Doren, Mark, ed. *Travels of William Bartram*. New York: Dover, 1928.

Viola, Herman. *Thomas L. McKenney: Architect of America's Early Indian Policy, 1816–1830*. Chicago: Sage Books, 1974.

Wallace, Anthony F. C. *Death and Rebirth of the Seneca*. New York: Knopf, 1970.
———. *Jefferson and the Indians: The Tragic Fate of the First Americans*. Cambridge MA: Belknap Press of Harvard University Press, 1999.
———. *The Long, Bitter Trail: Andrew Jackson and the Indians*. New York: Hill and Wang, 1993.
Ward, Matthew C. *Breaking the Backcountry: The Seven Years' War in Virginia and Pennsylvania, 1754–1765*. Pittsburgh: University of Pittsburgh Press, 2003.
Waselkov, Gregory A. *A Conquering Spirit: Fort Mims and the Redstick War of 1813–1814*. Tuscaloosa: University of Alabama Press, 2006.
———. "Formation of the Tensaw Community." In *Red Eagle's Children: Weatherford vs. Weatherford et al.*, edited by J. Anthony Paredes and Judith Knight, 36–45. Tuscaloosa: University of Alabama Press, 2012.
———. "Fort Jackson and the Aftermath." In *Tohopeka: Rethinking the Creek War and the War of 1812*, edited by Kathryn E. Holland Braund, 158–69. Tuscaloosa: University of Alabama Press, 2015.
Watson, Thomas D. "Strivings for Sovereignty: Alexander McGillivray, Creek Warfare, and Diplomacy, 1783–1790." *Florida Historical Quarterly* 58, no. 4 (April 1980): 400–414.
Weber, David J. *The Spanish Frontier in North America*. New Haven CT: Yale University Press, 1992.
Weisman, Brent Richards. *Unconquered People: Florida's Seminole and Miccosukee Indians*. Gainesville: University Press of Florida, 1999.
Wesson, Cameron B. *Households and Hegemony: Early Creek Prestige Goods, Symbolic Capital, and Social Power*. Lincoln: University of Nebraska Press, 2008.
Whitaker, Arthur P. "Alexander McGillivray, 1783–1789." *North Carolina Historical Review* 5, no. 2 (April 1928): 181–203.
———. "Alexander McGillivray, 1789–1793." *North Carolina Historical Review* 5, no. 3 (July 1928): 289–309.
———. "Spanish Intrigue in the Old Southwest: An Episode, 1788–1789." *Mississippi Valley Historical Review* 12, no. 2 (September 1925): 155–76.
———. *The Spanish-American Frontier, 1783–1795: The Westward Movement and the Spanish Retreat in the Mississippi Valley*. Boston: Houghton Mifflin, 1927.
White, Richard. *The Middle Ground: Indians, Empires, and Republics in the Great Lakes Region, 1650–1815*. New York: Cambridge University Press, 1991.
———. *The Roots of Dependency: Subsistence, Environment, and Social Change among the Choctaws, Pawnees, and Navajos*. Lincoln: University of Nebraska Press, 1983.
Wimmer, Andreas. *Nationalist Exclusion and Ethnic Conflict: Shadows of Modernity*. New York: Cambridge University Press, 2002

Witgen, Michael. *An Infinity of Nations: How the Native New World Shaped Early North America*. Philadelphia: University of Pennsylvania Press, 2012.

Wood, Gordon S. *The Creation of the American Republic, 1776–1787*. Chapel Hill: Published for the Institute of Early American History and Culture at Williamsburg, Virginia, by the University of North Carolina Press, 1969.

Woodward, Thomas S. *Woodward's Reminiscences of the Creek, or Muscogee Indians . . .* Montgomery AL: Barrett & Wimbish, 1859.

Worth, John E. "Spanish Missions and the Persistence of Chiefly Power." In *The Transformation of the Southeastern Indians, 1540–1760*, edited by Robbie Ethridge and Charles Hudson, 39–64. Jackson: University Press of Mississippi, 2002.

Wright, J. Leitch Jr. "Creek-American Treaty of 1790: Alexander McGillivray and the Diplomacy of the Old Southwest." *Georgia Historical Quarterly* 51, no. 4 (December 1967): 379–400.

———. *Creeks and Seminoles: The Destruction and Regeneration of the Muscogulge People*. Lincoln: University of Nebraska Press, 1986.

———. *Florida in the American Revolution*. Gainesville: University Press of Florida, 1975.

———. *William Augustus Bowles, Director General of the Creek Nation*. Athens: University of Georgia Press, 1967.

Yarbrough, Fay A. *Race and the Cherokee Nation: Sovereignty in the Nineteenth Century*. Philadelphia: University of Pennsylvania Press, 2008.

Index

To order or obtain more information on these or other University of Nebraska Press titles, visit nebraskapress.unl.edu.

CPSIA information can be obtained
at www.ICGtesting.com
Printed in the USA
LVHW111218221218
601087LV00009BB/108/P